D0874132

RELIGION OF REASON
OUT OF THE SOURCES OF JUDAISM

"Blessed are ye, O Israel,
who purifies you,
and before whom do you purify yourself?
It is your Father in Heaven."
                    (R. Akiba in Yoma 85ᵇ)

HERMANN COHEN

Drawing by Max Lieberman

Courtesy of Gerhart M. Riegner

RELIGION OF REASON

OUT OF THE SOURCES OF JUDAISM

Hermann Cohen

Translated, with an Introduction, by
Simon Kaplan

Introductory Essay by
Leo Strauss

FREDERICK UNGAR PUBLISHING CO.
New York

Translated from the original German, second revised edition,
Religion der Vernunft aus den Quellen des Judentums
by arrangement with Joseph Melzer Verlag, Darmstart

Copyright © 1972 by Frederick Ungar Publishing Co., Inc.
Printed in the United States of America
Library of Congress Catalog Card Number 79-125962
ISBN 0-8044-5229-6

Translator's Preface

This volume is the first translation of any of Hermann Cohen's major works into the English language. The difficulties inherent in any translation are well known. To put it in Hermann Cohen's own words: "One can only translate words and hardly the texture of a sentence, but only in the sentence does the word receive its inner life. And without the soul of a word, the spirit of a word also remains lifeless in a different language. The general difficulties of translation increase when the content is a religious one."

Although the text is in German, Cohen's religious thought is based on the original Hebrew. Thus both the German meaning and the underlying Hebrew conceptions had to be taken into consideration when rendering the text into English. Furthermore, the peculiarities of Cohen's style did not make the task of translation easier. There were, in addition, textual problems, owing to the fact that Cohen died before completing the final editing and that the work was published posthumously (see the editor's remarks to the second German edition).

For quotations from the Bible and the Prayer Book I have used the Jewish Publication Society Bible (1955) and the Standard Prayer Book (1957). When the standard German translation differed from these English versions, I have retained the reading which I considered closest to Cohen's intentions. In some cases Cohen translated the original Hebrew on his own. In such cases I have adapted the English version to Cohen's German version. Sometimes Cohen italicizes words in a biblical quotation and in a few cases interpolates. Those additions are indicated by parentheses.

That part of the original text which Cohen revised himself (up to p. 311) abounds in the use of italics. I left them unchanged, contrary to English usage. The few words I added in the text, as well as some references to biblical and other quotations, are in brackets.

I take pleasure in acknowledging my indebtedness to all those who gave me advice and counsel and to those who assisted the project financially.

In the first place, I express my gratitude to my old friend Dr. Aaron Steinberg for his unceasing encouragement and his valuable suggestions about the translation; in his capacity of cultural director of the World Jewish Congress, he made it possible to bring this translation to its completion. I am also obliged to Dr. Gerhart M. Riegner, secretary general of the World Jewish Congress, for his interest in the project and his assistance in its final realization. I am grateful to Dr. Leo Strauss, who from the very beginning of the translation always showed warm interest and contributed needed advice. I am indebted to Professor Werner J. Dannhauser for the many valuable corrections he made in the early stage of the manuscript. I extend special gratitude to Professor David R. Lachterman, who made very valuable suggestions about terminology and who read the manuscript and suggested corrections. I am thankful to Dr. Laurence Berns for the helpful assistance he rendered in proofreading and to Cantor Henry Hammer for locating and checking the biblical and rabbinic quotations. Finally, I owe deep gratitude to my wife, who encouraged me to undertake the translation and played an active part in bringing it to its completion.

I would like to acknowledge the grants I received for the translation from both the Cultural Funds of the Conference on Material Claims Against Germany, Inc., and the Leo Baeck Institute, New York, N.Y. I also thank the World Jewish Congress and Mr. Emanuel de Kadt, Fellow of the University of Sussex, England, for the financial contribution toward publication of the book.

Acknowledgment is due to the publisher, Mr. Frederick Ungar, for his willingness to finance and publish this difficult book and to his staff for their cooperation in this complicated work through all the stages of production.

S.K.

St. John's College
Annapolis, Maryland
August, 1971

Contents

TRANSLATOR'S INTRODUCTION[*]

The mature work of Hermann Cohen (1842-1918) was done in the final period of the Reform movement in Germany, at the end of the nineteenth and the beginning of the twentieth centuries. Reform Judaism and its antithesis, Neo-Orthodoxy, were by then well established. Just as Mendelssohn, inspired by the ideas of the Enlightenment, reinterpreted traditional Judaism, so it was Cohen, one of the leading German philosophers of his time, who approached the traditional sources of Judaism with his system of Neo-Kantian philosophy. The vigor of his thinking, together with his reverence for the sources of Judaism, made Cohen the greatest exponent of Jewish philosophical thought since the Enlightenment of which he is, perhaps, the culminating point.

In 1880, when Cohen was thirty-eight, he published an article entitled *Ein Bekenntniss zur Judenfrage* [A Profession of Faith on the Jewish Question]. Years later Cohen himself designated 1880 as the year of his "return." For although he had received a good traditional upbringing and education (in his childhood and youth) from his father, and later in the Rabbinical Seminary in Breslau, he had hitherto devoted himself almost entirely to philosophy. Two of his basic works on Kant had already appeared before the publication of this article: *Kants Theorie der Erfahrung* [Kant's Theory of Experience] and *Kants Begründung der Ethik* [Kant's Foundation of Ethics]. It was the former which perhaps more than any other contemporary work brought about the rediscovery and reinterpretation of Kant. The ideas developed in it became later the foundation of Cohen's system of idealism.

After his appointment to the University of Marburg (1873), Cohen's teaching led to the foundation of the "Marburg School of

[*] This introduction is based on my article "Hermann Cohen's Philosophy of Judaism" published in *Judaism*, Vol. I, No. 2.

Philosophy," whose head he was until his retirement (1912). It was during this time that he published his major work: the three volumes of his *System der Philosophie* [System of Philosophy], consisting of Logic, Ethics, and Aesthetics. It was also at this time that he completed his third volume on Kant: *Kants Begründung der Aesthetic* [Kant's Foundation of Aesthetics].

The older Cohen grew, the more fervently he devoted himself to Jewish religious problems, on which he wrote extensively. Part of these writings were collected posthumously (1924) in the three volumes of the *Jüdische Schriften* [Jewish Writings]. Two interrelated ideas dominate Cohen's thinking: the ethical idea of the one God and the resulting idea of an ethical mankind. Jewish monotheism is for Cohen the original source of these ideas, and the moral improvement of mankind is to him the specific task of the Jewish people. It was also the idea of one God as well as the teachings of the prophets which he incorporated into his *Ethics,* although in such a form as to make religion a mere complement of ethics, into which it was absorbed. "Ethics simply cannot recognize the independence of religion . . . it can recognize religion only as a natural process which in its cultural maturity coincides with ethics," wrote Cohen in 1907 in his *Ethik des reinen Willens* [Ethics of Pure Will]. Yet the problem of individuality, which found no solution within his system of ethics, led Cohen eventually to revise this view.

In his *Begriff der Religion im System der Philosophie* [Concept of Religion in the System of Philosophy], which appeared in 1915, three years before his death, Cohen assigned to religion a "special" task within the framework of ethics. This special task of religion, as distinguished from ethics, is to supply a foundation for individuality. Ethics knows only the general law of duty. In the presence of the individual, with his imperfections and frailties, it stands silent and helpless. Man, in the consciousness of his frailty, realizes that he himself cannot be the source of forgiveness for his own transgression. In his helplessness, he finds and recognizes God as the sole source of forgiveness. To cognize God, however, means, in monotheistic religion, to *re*cognize, to acknowledge God; it means to love him. And thus the ethical knowledge of man's guilt is transformed into the religious love of God. But the love of God, according to the biblical commandment, involves the whole man: he must love God with all his heart, with all his soul, with all his strength. Religious love embraces every aspect of the human consciousness. "The love of God," says Cohen, "must unite all things and all problems of the world."

Along with the love of God, religion reveals God's love of man, for God is the forgiver. In religion thus arises the reciprocal relation—the "correlation," as Cohen puts it—of God to man and man to God. This correlation is the special content that distinguishes religion from ethics; it corresponds to the biblical concept of the "covenant" with God, as Franz Rosenzweig put it.

It was with this concept of religion that Cohen approached the traditional sources of Judaism. The result was his most mature work, *Die Religion der Vernunft aus den Quellen des Judentums* [Religion of Reason out of the Sources of Judaism], which appeared posthumously (1919). According to the subtitle originally intended by the author, it is a "Jewish philosophy of religion and a Jewish ethics."

The "uniqueness" of God is the concept from which Cohen develops the doctrine of monotheism. He distinguishes between "uniqueness" and "oneness." The latter expresses merely a negation of the manyness of the polytheistic gods. The statement, God is "one," as in the *Shema*, is not merely a negation of God's manyness but carries also the positive meaning of God's exclusive uniqueness. Uniqueness, as expressed in the rabbinical term *jihud*, signifies the exclusive otherness and incommensurability of God's being in relation to other modes of being. Positively expressed, God's uniqueness means that his divine being transcends all human or natural existence. Therefore, pantheism, which teaches the identity of God and nature, is incompatible with monotheism. This essential "otherness" or "yonderness" of God excludes the possibility of an intermediary, whether between God and nature, as in the Logos of Philo, or between God and man, as in the person of the Christian savior. Similarly, the uniqueness of God excludes the "incorporation" of God in the Trinity, for the Trinity compromises the exclusive uniqueness of God.

Divine being, which is the only true being, and in relation to which all other being is "only appearance" or mere "existence," does not imply that God stands outside all relation to the world and to man. A relation to the world and to man, a relation compatible with his uniqueness, is inherent in God's being: the unique God is Creator and Revealer.

For Cohen, however, creation does not have the literal-"mythological" sense of the biblical narrative. Nor does it have the meaning ascribed to it by the theory of emanation, according to which the genesis of the world is contained in God's being. If that were true, says Cohen, "God and nature would be the same thing," and then God could not be the Creator. On the other hand, Cohen also discards the traditional concept of creation as a single event in time, a "work in the beginning." This he replaces with the later concept of "renewal of the world." In accordance with his logic, he interprets the latter as a continuous preservation and renewal of the world, thus deviating from the traditional teaching of the unique act of "creation out of nothing."

The biblical narrative of the creation distinguishes the creation of nature and of animals, who were created "after their kind," from the creation of man, who was created in God's "image." Man, created in God's image, is conceived of not only as a particular species of animal but as a creature endowed with knowledge, above all the knowledge of good and evil. By virtue of the creation of man's reason, man transcends the world of animals and enters into the realm proper and peculiar to himself, the realm of correlation to God. This correlation to God, which constitutes the content of religion, is the "characteristic difference that distinguishes man from animals." Thus, the creation of man's reason determines his being, a being separated from all living creatures for the sake of his relation to God. Cohen finds this separation formulated in the words of the *Neilah* prayer: "Thou hast distinguished man from the very beginning and hast acknowledged him worthy to stand before Thee."

Even though man's reason is derived from God, man is free to choose between "life and Good and death and Evil" (Deut. 30:15). Cohen invokes the talmudic saying: "Everything is in the hand of God, except the fear of God," which in this context means that man should "stand" before God only in freedom.

As the traditional term of "standing" before God indicates, the relation of man to God is not a contemplative one. Since God is "unique," God cannot, as medieval thought believed, become an object of knowledge, not even "analogically." God's relation to man in revelation is no "unveiling" (*revelatio*) of God's being. The traditional term for revelation is "the giving of the Torah." In the "laws and ordinances," as in the Torah in general, God reveals not his being but his will, and he does not reveal his will in respect to his being, but in respect to man. Even in speaking to Moses "face to face," God says nothing more of his being than "I am that I am." He reveals to Moses not his being but only his "back," that is to say, the "wake" or effects of God's actions, which the Jewish tradition interprets as God's works in distinction to his being. The "works" are not God's qualities but rather his "actions" with regard to man; they should be understood as "normative" for the actions of man. Basing himself on Maimonides, Cohen interprets the "thirteen qualities" that God reveals to Moses (Exod. 34:6,7) not as qualities of God but

as "attributes of God's action," that is, as norms for the road of man's
ascent to ethical perfection.

Cohen sums up the "thirteen qualities" in two concepts: love and
justice. These are not revealed in order that man should know God
through them, but in order that man should worship God through
love and justice in his own actions. To have knowledge of God is
to acknowledge him as the Father of mankind, to love him. But the
love of God as the Father of mankind implies for man God's forgiveness. In his worship of God, man's love of his fellowmen corresponds
to God's love of man: for only because God is the common "Father"
do "other men" become "fellowmen," or brothers.

Cohen finds the mutual relation of God and man expressed in the
biblical passage: "Ye shall be holy, for I the Lord your God am
Holy" (Lev. 19:2). Thus holiness becomes common to God and man,
with the distinction that God *is* holy, while man should *become* holy.
To Cohen, this means that God as the ethical prototype prescribes
man's ethical ideal. Hence, God's holiness means for man the "infinite task" of man's ethical perfection. The chasm between God and
man remains unbridgeable, and there is no end to man's striving to
achieve the ethical ideal of holiness.

It now becomes clear that for Cohen the revelation of the Torah
does not have the traditional sense of definite "laws and ordinances."
In the Torah, the eternal law, the eternal "source" of ethical reason,
is revealed as a "foundation" for historically changing "laws and
ordinances." For Cohen, this justifies the reform of certain laws in
the light of historical development, though the reform must harmonize
with the eternal "source" of ethical reason. Nor is revelation to be
understood as an isolated historical event occurring on Mount Sinai.
Cohen interprets the rabbinical tradition, according to which the
whole Torah, including the oral tradition, was given "to Moses on
Mount Sinai," as implying that the revelation is a "living and re-
newable continuity." The words from Deuteronomy, "The Lord made
not this covenant with our fathers, but with us, even us, who are all
of us here alive this day" (Deut. 5:3), are taken to mean that the
living continuity of revelation extends to the Jew of every present
and future, and is not limited to the single historical event on Mount
Sinai.

Revelation did not begin on Mount Sinai, for through Noah God
concluded a covenant with the whole human race. The "seven commandments of the sons of Noah," which God revealed to Noah, constitute an "ethical foundation" for the entire human race. Upon this

"ethical foundation" will arise "the pious men of the nations of the world," who like the Israelites have a share in the "world-to-come." For Cohen this equality, this participation of all the pious—Jew and non-Jews alike—in eternal life, is the ethical consequence of the idea of the one God, which alone can shape the idea of one mankind.

In the development of monotheism, the idea of one mankind culminated in prophetic messianism. The prophets, as Cohen interprets them, transfer the revelation from the various ordinances given on Mount Sinai to the "heart of man," which is equated with the ethical. God reveals "what is good" (Mic. 8:6), that is, the ethical. The prophets therefore warn, on the one hand, against social-political sin and on the other, against individual sin. The widow, the orphan, the stranger, they are the symbols of social sin in general, the sin against one's fellow man. Interpreting the prophetic teaching Cohen stresses emphatically that poverty, unrestricted property, and wars are the social sins which hinder the realization of the unity of mankind as envisaged by the prophets in the Messianic Age. The Sabbath, with its idea of universal rest and peace, accompanies the Jew throughout his life and is at the same time the living symbol of that age to come, the age of the Kingdom of God. Cohen interprets the Messianic Age not as the end of time but as the dawn of a new era, the ethical age, in which the nations of the earth will find reconciliation and peace. The messianic peace is not merely negative: it means not merely that war, this specifically human struggle, will cease; it also carries the positive significance of inner peace for the human soul and a united mankind. It is in this sense, Cohen believes, that the Messiah is proclaimed the "prince of peace."

With the messianic ideal, the prophets introduce a new concept of history unknown to the Greeks. For the Greeks, history was the "knowledge of the past"; for the prophets, history is "the province of the seer," the vision of the ideal future. The Greeks oriented their concept of history "in space"; for them, the world was divided into their own society and the barbarian world outside its borders; there was no concept of one mankind. The vision of the prophets orients history not in space but in time, and this time is the future. In this future, despite all present and past experience, the ethical ideal of a united mankind will be realized. Thus, history is not "eternal recurrence," as Plato conceived it, but a development toward the ideal future of mankind.

God's covenant with Noah guarantees the realization of this future. His covenant with the earth guarantees the preservation of nature for the realization of the ethical ideal. His "providence for the human race" creates in the messianic age "new heavens and a new earth" (Isa. 65:17), that is, a "new historical reality." Only then will true history, the history of a united mankind, dawn and the "victory of the good" be realized. It is in this sense that Cohen affirms: "Monotheism is the true consolation of history."

The unique God is not only mankind's "God of history." He is in equal measure the consolation of the individual person, of erring, frail man, in his "specifically human" quality of sinfulness. In consonance with the Jewish tradition, Cohen rejects the doctrine of Original Sin; man does not sin because Adam transmitted to his descendants a vitiated nature. Man does not sin in consequence of Adam's sin, but because of his own transgression. But man's guilt is not man's tragic end: it shall not be his ruin, for God has no "pleasure at all that the wicked should die. . . ." God's pleasure is rather "that he should return from his ways and live" (Ezek. 18:23).

The traditional way of "return" from sin is *teshubah*. This word means both conversion and turning back and is usually translated as "repentance," which does not exactly render the concept. While repentance primarily expresses the recognition of guilt and an attitude of regret, *teshubah* implies the act of "turning away" from God, which is sin, and *teshubah* enables man to "return" to God, to become free from sin and achieve forgiveness.

The pre-exilic concept of *teshubah* led to the ritual of sacrifice. The blood of the sacrificial animal replaces the blood, that is, the life, of the sinner. In the blood of the animal, the sinner sacrifices himself. He lays his life in God's hand, and only God can give back to him his life cleansed of sin. Because of this cleansing through *teshubah*, the prophet Ezekiel attached especial importance to sacrifice. Cohen, however, although invoking Ezekiel, believes that the instrument of *teshubah* required by Ezekiel—sacrifice—was merely historically determined. The mediation of priest and sacrifice distorted the "immediate" relation of the sinful man to God. Cohen cites the psalm, "The sacrifices of God are a broken spirit, a broken and a contrite heart" (Ps. 51:17), which he takes to mean that man himself, without the mediation of sacrifice or priest, must stand "immediately" before God.

In *teshubah*, man recognizes himself, and himself alone, as the author of his sinful deed. Sin, as the knowledge that one has "turned away" from God's will, thus becomes a "turning into" oneself, an avowal of the sin, and this is self-condemnation. Out of the depths of despair in himself as sinner, man recognizes his own isolation from

God and men. He recognizes his guilt and the suffering that he has brought on himself and which no other man can forgive or take away. From this isolation in suffering, man recognizes that only God can forgive his sin. Thus, the knowledge of sin leads man to the knowledge of God or, rather, to the avowal of his sin before God. Between the "turning away" from God and the "turning back" to God, there occurs a transformation in which the human self, cleansed of sin, is born. In *teshubah* God gives to man "a new heart . . . and a new spirit" (Ezek. 36:26). Man, "conceived in sin" (Ps. 51:5), attains his true self, his purified "humanity," only when he is "reborn" in *teshubah*, which is when the truly human individual is born.

Does man—erring and sinful man—ever reach the moment in which he is freed from sin and forgiven by God? Man knows only the commandment to cast off his sin; he knows only the labor of self-purification, the endless task of achieving holiness, the goal of which is the holiness of God. But the sure knowledge of achievement and forgiveness is denied him. Man's hope is his firm "trust" (*emunah*) in God, the merciful and forgiving.

This "reliance" or "trust" or "fidelity," as the word *emunah* should be translated, must be distinguished from "faith." Faith aims at the knowledge of, or participation in, the very *essence* of God, as, for example, faith in the passion and resurrection of Christ. Faith in the sacrament whereby bread and wine are transformed into the body and blood of Christ, even when this is conceived symbolically, implies an act which imitates or participates in the essence of God. Jewish "trust," however, never refers to the essence of God's being but to his will and actions *with regard to man* exclusively.

The expression of God's will toward man is the law, which is therefore the object of "fidelity" and the connecting link between man and God. But the law never prescribes an action intended to imitate or to participate in the essence of God, for its aim is not to know but to obey God. The law does, it is true, provide for symbols, such as circumcision, phylacteries, fringes, and so forth; but their only meaning is to bring one to "remember all the commandments of the Lord, and do them" (Num. 15:39).

"Trust" in God is thus at the same time "fidelity" to the "lawful," that is, the ethical act. And the meaning of "trust" is precisely this: from his "trust" in God's forgiveness, the erring and sinful man gathers the strength for the ethical act of self-purification. Or, in the words of the Midrash that Cohen cites, "only after the action" that man performs "does the holy spirit rest upon him."

While in Christian teaching forgiveness of sin rests essentially on faith and the grace of God, in the Jewish meaning of trust, according to Cohen, the act of self-purification incumbent upon man is strictly separate from the grace of God. No one can relieve man of his task of self-purification from sin; man himself must perform it. And only God can forgive sin; "no son of God shall purify you, but your Father alone." Cohen finds this relation of man to God and God to man expressed in the words of Rabbi Akiba: "Happy are you, Israel: who purifies you and before whom do you purify yourself? It is your Father in Heaven."

Cohen sees penance *(teshubah)* as the climax and epitome of all purification; and the words of the Mishnah, "Do penance a day before your death," are to be taken as an injunction to do penance every day of our lives. Penance should not, however, be performed in the mystical isolation of the individual; it should take place in public, in the community of the "participants in guilt and fellow-worshipers." On the Day of Atonement the sin of the entire community of Israel is forgiven.

In the rhythm of the Jewish year, the Day of Atonement is the climax toward which man strives. After man has taken on himself all the pain and suffering of self-purification, God makes him pure and guiltless on the Day of Atonement. This is the moment for which man has been waiting in all his self purification. This is the moment when eternity penetrates time, when man's penance is transformed into reconciliation with God, and when man is reborn in innocence. But it is "only for a moment" that man is freed from his guilt and suffering; the "road to life" is again opened to him. Afterwards he may "strive and err" again, for, as Ecclesiastes says, "there is not a just man on earth that doeth good, and sinneth not" (Eccl. 7:20). But the words of Ezekiel still remain in force: sin shall not be man's ruin but shall lead to repentance. Repentance elevates man to the heights of reconciliation with God, so that, according to the Talmud, "In the place where the repentant man stands, the perfectly righteous may not stand."

Just as the individual stands before God in repentance and hopes for forgiveness, so the whole people of Israel, apart from other peoples, stands before God and hopes for forgiveness and redemption. In Balaam's words, Israel is a people that "shall dwell alone and shall not be reckoned among the nations" (Num. 23:9). The real history of Israel, Cohen believes, confirms this statement of the heathen prophet, for Israel lacks the common characteristics of a nation: soil, language, state. The soil of Israel is hallowed soil; the language, the holy language; and the state, the future Kingdom of God. Israel's history begins with the call to Abraham: "Get thee out of thy country and from thy kindred and from thy father's house" (Gen. 12:1). Israel's history begins with the exile. Even the gathering of Israel into a state was only a transitory phenomenon; in reality it was a "gathering for exile." It is a "miracle" that the Jewish people has been preserved in dispersion, for the "peoples of the world" disappear with the loss of state.

Among the Jews, the state was replaced by the community of the congregation, the sword by the law, for, in the words of Saadia, quoted by Cohen: "Our people is a people only by virtue of its Torah." The community became the congregation of those who studied the Torah and were faithful to the law; it became "people and religion" at once. This community has "isolated" itself from the "peoples of the world" through the idea of the unique God and his law. Cohen regards the entire law as an instrument of this separation. In obedience to the commandments, this separation becomes a living relation to God.

God's commandment—the *mitzvah*—has the double meaning of commandment and duty. The commandment comes from God, but duty comes from man. It is the function of the *mitzvah* to integrate the entire life of the Jew and all his acts through the eternal law. Thus the difference between profane and sacred falls away, for every act stands in the service of the "ideal of holiness." All earthly activity is embraced and illumined by the divine law: "God gives the Torah as He gives everything, life and bread, and death too." With the *mitzvah*, the Jew takes upon himself the "yoke of the Kingdom of God," and all his acts serve the "sanctification of God's Name."

Their election for the "sanctification of the Name" is the "greatest happiness" of the community of Israel, just as the commandment "to lay down their life for the holiness of the divine Name" has become the "greatest martyrdom" in history. All other peoples, to be sure, have also suffered in history, but their suffering was contingent on shifts in political power. With the disappearance of their political power, the peoples disappeared too. The history of Israel has taken a different course: only with the loss of its state, with the emergence of the "world-mission" of realizing the messianic ideal, did the true historical existence of the people of Israel begin. The "uniqueness" of the history of Israel rests precisely on the fact that its historical mission in the world began only with the loss of all earthly power and treasure, with "political defenselessness." Political defenselessness, suffering, and martyrdom become the true "historical characteristics" of the history of Israel: "It passes through history like a Job."

Non-Jewish peoples, with a "self-righteousness dangerous for their own morality," interpret this suffering as God's punishment for the sins of Israel. It is true that the sufferings of Israel have the significance as punishment too; or rather, Israel is "chosen" by God for punishment: "You only have I known of all the families of the earth: therefore I will punish you for all your iniquities" (Amos 3:2). But this election for punishment does not exhaust the meaning of the suffering of Israel. Israel's suffering has another, quite independent meaning.

Job is the prophet who reveals this meaning through his own suffering. Job's suffering is not brought about by his sins, as his friends in blind "self-righteousness" assume; no, Job suffers innocently. Thus Job reveals the truth that there is a suffering that is not punishment, not the consequence of sin. He does not suffer for his sins, but "for others," for his friends, for the world, which does not understand the meaning of this suffering. Job reveals the truth that the sufferings of men belong to the "divine plan of salvation." Suffering is no "defect" in human history; it is "integrated with the divine organization of the world" as the source of purification for redemption. The true "saving forces" of history are not the state, not power and earthly happiness, but the purifying suffering that binds man to the true goal of history, redemption. Israel knows and freely professes this revelation of suffering, and if Israel has throughout its history been "a people of suffering," suffering has also become "its vital force," from which it has gathered purification for redemption.

Traditional Jewish exegesis, to which Cohen adheres, sees the people of Israel in the suffering "servant of God" (Isa. 52,53), in the Messiah. "But thou, Israel, art my servant . . . whom I have chosen . . . and said unto thee: Thou art my servant" (Isa. 41:8,9). Israel is the messianic people; it suffers "for the peoples who do not accept the unique God." This suffering should indeed be the punishment visited upon the other peoples, who are unwilling to accept the unique God. But because Israel has been chosen to recognize the unique God, it sees the guilt and the sins of other peoples and takes their suffering voluntarily upon itself. "By his knowledge shall my righteous servant justify many, for he shall bear their iniquities" (Isa. 53:11). Thus Israel has been chosen to be the "servant" of many peoples, to "suffer in their place." "He was wounded for our transgressions, he was bruised for our iniquities: the chastisement of our peace was upon him" (Isa. 53:5). The peoples of the world do not "consider" the sacrificial sufferings of Israel. They do not realize that Israel's suffering is the "suffering of love" for the sake of their redemption, that Israel suffers "the martyrdom of monotheism."

God loves Israel because he loves those who suffer. Israel is therefore God's vessel on earth, his "treasure," through which God's will on earth will be fulfilled. "God loves in Israel nothing but the human race," says Cohen, for Israel takes upon itself a yoke of suffering for the redemption of all mankind, which will also be the redemption of Israel. In its suffering, Israel longs for the messianic age, when "the Lord will be one and His name one" (Zech. 14:9) for the entire human race.

Religion of Reason out of the Sources of Judaism follows on the one hand Cohen's philosophic methodology according to which "true religion . . . is based on the truth of systematic philosophy."* On the other hand, the book breathes traditional piety and love for the people who suffer the "martyrdom of monotheism." This inner dialogue between Cohen's philosophy and his religion, between reason and piety, seems to remain an uncompleted dialogue through all of Cohen's Jewish writings.

---

*Hermann Cohen, *Begriff der Religion im System der Philosophy,* pp. 137-38.

INTRODUCTORY ESSAY—*by Leo Strauss*

I doubt whether I am the best mediator between Hermann Cohen (1842-1918) and the present-day American reader. I grew up in an environment in which Cohen was the center of attraction for philosophically minded Jews who were devoted to Judaism; he was the master whom they revered. But it is more than forty years since I last studied or even read the *Religion of Reason,* and within the last twenty years I have only from time to time read or looked into some of his other writings. I write this Introduction at the request of the publisher and of the translator. I can do no more than to give an account of the thoughts that occurred to me at a renewed reading of *Religion of Reason.* Perhaps they will be helpful to some readers.

Present-day readers can hardly avoid feeling that *Religion of Reason out of the Sources of Judaism* (first published in German in 1919) is a philosophic book and at the same time a Jewish book. It is philosophic since it is devoted to the religion of reason, and it is Jewish since it elucidates, nay, articulates that religion out of the sources of Judaism. This impression, while correct, is not as clear as it appears at first sight.

The Jewish religion might be understood as revealed religion. In that case the philosopher would accept revelation as it was accepted by Jews throughout the ages in an uninterrupted tradition and would bow to it; he would explicate it by the means of philosophy and especially defend it against its deniers or doubters, philosophic and nonphilosophic. But this pursuit would not be philosophic since it rests on an assumption that the philosopher as philosopher cannot make or on an act of which the philosopher as philosopher is not capable. Cohen excludes this manner of understanding the relation between philosophy and Judaism by speaking of the religion of reason. "Revelation is [God's] creation of reason." Revelation is not "an historical act." For Cohen there are no revealed truths or revealed laws in the precise or traditional sense of the terms.

xxiii

Let Judaism then be the religion of reason. Yet this can hardly mean that Judaism and the religion of reason are identical. Is the religion of reason found also, hence accidentally, in Judaism? Or is it the core of Judaism and only of Judaism? Cohen rejects both extremes. In particular he refuses to claim that Judaism is "the absolute religion." (This is not to deny that Cohen sometimes calls Judaism, and only Judaism, "the pure monotheism.") His solution of the difficulty is indicated by the word "source." Judaism is the source, the fountainhead of the religion of reason. The Jews "created the religion of reason." Judaism has taught mankind the religion of reason. The other religions either are altogether inadequate or they are derivative from Judaism. It is true that Judaism was not always in every respect the religion of reason. It needed the aid of Platonic and above all of Kantian philosophy to free itself completely from mythical and other irrelevancies. But this aid merely enabled Judaism to actualize fully what it meant to be from the beginning and what it fundamentally was at all times.

When one says that Cohen's *Religion of Reason* is a philosophic book, one is likely to assume that the religion of reason belongs to philosophy, that it is perhaps the most exalted part of philosophy. Yet Cohen makes a distinction between philosophy as philosophy, i.e., as scientific philosophy, and religion, and accordingly says that "Judaism has no share in philosophy" or that "Israel has no creative share in science." Nevertheless, there is according to him a kind of philosophic speculation whose matrix is religion and especially Judaism. This does not, however, do away with the fact that Cohen's *Religion of Reason* forms no part of his *System of Philosophy (System der Philosophie)*.

The relation between religion and philosophy, between the *Religion of Reason* and the *System of Philosophy,* is complicated by the fact that the central part of the *System,* the *Ethics of the Pure Will (Ethik des reinen Willens,* first published in 1904), contains, and in a way culminates in, doctrines that at first glance seem to belong to the religion of reason: the doctrines of the unique God and the messianic future. Cohen has made these doctrines integral parts of his *Ethics;* he has transplanted them out of the sources of Judaism into his *Ethics.* He solves this difficulty by distinguishing between the God of ethics and the God peculiar to religion. Yet since it is reason that shows why and how ethics must be transcended by religion, religion "enters into the system of philosophy." Accordingly, the *Religion of Reason* would have to be understood as the crowning part of Cohen's *System of Philosophy.*

However, the last part of the title ("out of the Sources of Judaism") suggests that the *Religion of Reason* transcends the boundaries of the *System of Philosophy*, or of any system of philosophy. It suffices, perhaps, to compare the full title of Cohen's work with that of Kant's *Religion within the Limits of Mere Reason*.

The obscurity that remains is ultimately due to the fact that while Cohen had a rare devotion to Judaism, he was hardly less devoted to what he understood by culture (science and secular scholarship, autonomous morality leading to socialist and democratic politics, and art); hence his insistence in particular on the "methodic distinction between ethics and religion." That distinction implies that while religion cannot be reduced to ethics, it remains dependent on "the method of ethics." Man's moral autonomy must not in any way be called in question. Cohen's goal was the same as that of the other Western spokesmen for Judaism who came after Mendelssohn: to establish a harmony between Judaism and culture, between *Torah* and *derekh eretz*. But Cohen pursued this goal with unrivaled speculative power and intransigence.

Cohen's *Ethics* and, in fact, his whole *System of Philosophy* precedes his *Religion of Reason* "methodically." Futhermore, he is compelled now and then, especially in Chapters X and XI, to take issue with the Protestant, especially German, biblical criticism of his time and with the philosophy of history on which it is based. Finally, the order of the argument within the chapters does not always have the lucidity of which it is susceptible. These facts are likely to cause considerable difficulties to the reader of the *Religion of Reason*. They can be overcome by repeated readings. In the following remarks I could not help reproducing or imitating difficulties that Cohen has left unresolved.

The *Religion of Reason* presupposes, fundamentally, the *System of Philosophy*, but it does not force the Jewish data into that system as into a Procrustean bed. Cohen follows the intrinsic articulation of that Judaism which was authoritative for him as a liberal Jew who abhorred mysticism. He interprets Jewish thought by "idealizing" or "spiritualizing" it, i.e., by thinking it through and by understanding it in the light of its highest possibilities. In so doing he claims not merely to follow the only sound rule of interpreting any worthwhile text but to continue the process that had been going on in Judaism starting with the Bible itself.

Cohen follows the intrinsic articulation of the Bible by devoting the first chapter to the uniqueness of God. For the account of creation with which the Bible opens presupposes that one knows somehow what is meant by God. The decisive elucidation of what the Bible understands by God is given in the words that "the Eternal is one" and that His name is "I am": He is the one, the only one who or what is; compared to Him, nothing else is. "There is not only no other God but altogether no being except this unique being." Nature, the world, man included, is nothing. Only God's uniqueness thus strictly understood can justify the demand that man should love God with his whole heart, with his whole soul, and with his whole might.

It would not have been in accordance with the Bible or with Cohen's *System of Philosophy* if he had opened his work with a demonstration of the existence of God. God's uniqueness excludes His having existence, existence being essentially related to sense perception. According to Cohen, the idea of God, God as an idea and not a person, is required in the first place in order to establish the indispensable harmony between nature and morality: the ethically required eternity of ethical progress, the ethically required prospect of an infinite future of ethical progress is not possible without the future eternity of the human race and therefore of nature as a whole; God "secures the ideal." It is incorrect but not altogether misleading to say that, according to Cohen, God is postulated by ethical reason.

The uniqueness of God demands or implies the rejection of the worship of "other gods." Cohen is himself animated by the prophets' "holy zeal against the false gods" when he says in his own name that "the service of other gods or of idols must be altogether exterminated." That holy zeal must overcome all hesitations stemming from the charm exerted by Greek plastics and even from compassion for the worshippers of false gods. At this point more than at any other Cohen reveals how radically he had come to question "culture" as he and his contemporaries understood it. The worship of the other gods is, according to him, necessarily worship of images. In agreement with the Decalogue, but not with Deuteronomy 4:15-19, he denies that there can be worship of sun, moon, and stars as such.

It follows furthermore from God's uniqueness that all things or beings other than God (except human artifacts) are His work. They do not come into being out of God, through emanation, for this would mean that Becoming is part of the true Being, whereas there is only and indeed "an immanent relation" of Being, the unique Being, to Becoming, of God to the world; Becoming is implied in the concept of God, in the definition of God as the unique being. It is in this way that Cohen is able to speak of creation. Creation is "the logical consequence" of the uniqueness of the divine being, nay, it is simply identical with it. Creation is therefore necessary. Cohen does not speak of creation as a free act. Nor is creation according to him a single act in or before time. Creation is continuous creation, continuous renewal. The sources of Judaism that Cohen uses for elucidating creation are almost all post-biblical. He derives his main support from Maimonides. Maimonides' doctrine of creation as set forth in the *Guide of the Perplexed* is, however, not easily recognizable in Cohen's interpretation.

Creation is above all the creation of man. But whereas creation as such is the immanent relation of God as the unique Being to Becoming, and Becoming is coeval with God, surely man, the human race, is not coeval with God. Cohen begins to treat the creation of man in the chapter on revelation. In revelation, he says, God enters into relation with man; he had not said that in creation God enters into relation with the world. Revelation is the continuation of creation since man as the rational and the moral being comes into being, i.e., is constituted, by revelation. Revelation is as little miraculous as creation. That is to say, it is not a unique event or a number of unique events in the remote past. Cohen follows closely the first and classic document of this idealization, Moses' extensive speech in Deuteronomy in which revelation is presented as not in heaven or, as Cohen almost contends, stemming from heaven but as originating in the heart and reason of man, which are indeed God-given. "Man" here means the children of Israel. Hence, while revelation is not a unique event, it is primarily addressed to a unique people. Monotheism is to have its foundation in a national consciousness, or, more precisely, monotheism is to be the foundation of the consciousness of a nation: Israel, and Israel alone, came into being by virtue of dedication to the only God. Monotheism is not to have its foundation in the consciousness of select individuals. The outstanding individuals, in the first place Moses himself, are only the instruments of the spiritual liberation of the nation, representatives of the Jewish people, teachers of Israel, but by no means mediators between God and Israel.

Cohen had no doubt that in teaching the identity of Reason and Revelation he was in full agreement with "all," or "almost all," Jewish philosophers of the Middle Ages. He mentions in this respect with high praise, apart from Maimonides himself, Ibn Daud, who had assigned a very low status to "the prescriptions of obedience" as distinguished from "the rational principles" and had inferred from the weakness of their rank the weakness of their causes. Cohen abstracts from the fact that Ibn Daud says also—and this he says at the very end of his *Emunah Ramah*—that "the prescriptions of obedience" are superior to the rational ones since they call for absolute obedience and submission to the divine will or for faith. The perfect emblem of "the prescriptions of obedience" is God's command to Abraham that he sacrifice his only child Isaac—a command that flagrantly contradicted His previous promise and therefore transcended reason. One need not be concerned here with whether and how Ibn Daud resolved the contradiction between the thought of which Cohen approves and the thought that Cohen dismisses, but one cannot help being impressed by his attempt to find the highest or deepest ground of "the prescriptions of obedience" in Abraham's willingness to sacrifice Isaac. The religion of reason leaves no place for absolute obedience or for what traditional Judaism considered the core of faith. The reader will have no difficulty in grasping the connection between the disappearance of obedience proper and the idealization or spiritualization of creation and revelation.

Owing to its peculiar function, which was to articulate the meaning of revelation especially from Moses' speech in Deuteronomy, the chapter on revelation had left obscure the relation of revelation and hence of God to man as distinguished from Israel. This relation becomes the theme in the next chapter. Cohen takes his bearings by the second account of the creation of man (Genesis 2), which he regards as freer from myth than the first (Genesis 1). The tree of knowledge indicates that it is knowledge that distinguishes man from all other creatures and that it is knowledge, especially the knowledge of good and evil, that characterizes his relation to God. That relation is correlation. Although God is not thinkable except as creator of the world and the world is not thinkable except as God's creature, the relation of God and the world is not yet correlation. God's relation to the world points to, or is absorbed by, His relation to man. In Cohen's deliberately exaggerated expression, God's being becomes actual in and through His correlation with man. "God is conditioned by the correlation with man. And man is conditioned by the correlation with God." God cannot be thought properly as being beyond His relation to man, and it is equally necessary to understand man, the creature constituted by reason or spirit, as essentially related to the unique God Who is spirit. Reason is the link between God and man. Reason is common to God and man. But it would contradict reason if man were only the passive partner in his correlation with God. Correlation means therefore also and especially that God and man are equally, if in different ways, active toward one another. (The reader must keep in mind the question of whether Cohen has always done justice to divine activity in the correlation.) Since these insights concern man as such, the "original

universalism of the spirit in Israel" leads to the final universalism of
the spirit in all men without any difference of rank whatever.

The full meaning of the correlation between God and man begins
to come to sight only when human action is taken into consideration.
Human action must be understood in the light of divine action and
vice versa. The divine attributes of action (Exodus 34:6-7), as
Cohen, following Maimonides, calls them and which he reduces to
love and justice, are not meant to reveal the essence of God; yet
they are adequate as the norm and model for man's actions. Love
and justice together are holiness. "You shall be holy, for I, the Lord
your God, am holy." (Leviticus 19:2). Here the correlation is ap-
propriately expressed, "and with the correlation mythology and
polytheism cease. Holiness becomes morality." For with the progress
of biblical thought Might recedes into the background and Holiness
comes to the fore. As the quoted verse from Leviticus makes clear,
holiness is for man a task, a never-ending, infinite task or an ideal,
while it characterizes God's being; it is the ground of God's being, of
His uniqueness. But God is only in regard to man: God is the Holy
One for the sake of the holiness of man, which consists in man's
sanctifying himself. Accordingly, the holy spirit is the spirit of man
as well as of God, as Cohen tries to show by interpreting Psalm 51,
"the classical passage" on the holy spirit, or rather on the spirit of
holiness. To understand the holy spirit in isolation, as a person of its
own, is tantamount to destroying the correlation: the holy spirit is
the correlation between God and man. The competence of the holy
spirit is limited to human morality—"the holy spirit is the human
spirit"—but human morality is the only morality and therefore includes God's morality: there is no other standard of goodness and
justice for God than for man. Cohen's notion of holiness does not
seem to have much in common with "the so-called Holiness code"
(Leviticus 17ff.), but—and this is of no mean significance—according to him morality, human, rational morality demands the un-
qualified abstention from incest.

Human action is, to begin with, action directed toward other men
whom we know or believe to know from experience. The others, the
men who live at our side, become inevitably those against whom we
live; they are therefore not yet our fellowmen. Our fellowmen we do
not know through experience pure and simple but only by virtue of
the command that we love them. Only on the basis of this intrahuman
correlation can the correlation of God and man become actual: in
man's behavior toward men, not in his behavior toward God, the
distinction between good and evil arises. It is in the light of "the

social love" of our fellowmen that we must understand the love that proceeds from God and the love that is directed toward him. Cohen discusses the intrahuman relation first on the political and legal level. He takes his bearings by the talmudic concept of the sons of Noah and the seven commandments given to them. The sons of Noah do not have to adhere to the religion of Israel, i.e., they do not have to acknowledge the only God although they are forbidden to blaspheme and to worship other gods; they are not believers and yet they may be citizens of the Jewish state. In this way Judaism laid the foundation for freedom of conscience and for toleration. Cohen does not claim to have proved that Judaism has laid the foundation for the freedom of conscience of all Jews.

Cohen then goes on to discuss "the discovery of man as the fellow-man" on the plane of "the social question" or, as he also says, of "the economic problem," i.e., of "the social distinction of the poor and the rich." For the prophets and the psalms it is poverty and not death and pain that constitutes the great suffering of man or the true enigma of human life. Our compassion for the poor, our love of the poor makes us understand or divine that God loves the poor and therefore in particular Israel (cf. Isaiah 41:14 and Amos 7:5), but Israel is only the symbol of mankind. God's love of the poor animates the whole social legislation of the Bible and above all the institution of the Sabbath, which prescribes rest also and in particular for servants and maids. Poverty becomes the prime object of compassion, of the affect that is a factor, nay, the factor of the moral law. In his *Ethics* Cohen had characterized the affect in general as a motor of the moral law. In his *Religion of Reason* he goes much beyond this by almost identifying the affect that fulfills that function with compassion. Here more than in the preceding chapters Cohen's heart speaks, and the fear that the Jewish heritage might be eroded vanishes. In his *Ethics* he had denied that love is the affective basis of virtue as such, and he replaced compassion by the virtue of humanity to which he devoted the last and crowning chapter. But the last and crowning chapter of the *Religion of Reason* is devoted to peace in the full Jewish meaning of *shalom*. This does not mean that he abandons the teaching of his *Ethics*; he keeps it intact as the ethical teaching; he merely supplements it by the religious teaching; but in so doing he profoundly transforms it. Humanity is among other things the virtue of art; peace is the virtue of eternity. The chapter on peace, and hence the *Religion of Reason*, concludes with an articulation of the Jewish posture toward death and the grave.

The chapter entitled "The Problem of Religious Love" is the only chapter that carries "problem" in its heading. One cannot say that this is intentional: Cohen does not write like Maimonides. But intentional or not, it is surely remarkable. Cohen speaks of the problem of religious love because he finds that religious love is taken too much for granted. Particularly striking is what he says about man's love of God. The love of God is love of an idea. To the objection that one cannot love an idea but only a person Cohen replies that "one can love only ideas; even in sensual love one loves only the idealized person." Pure love is directed only toward models of action, and no human being can be such a model in the precise sense. Pure love is love of the moral ideal. It is longing, not for union with God, but for nearness to God, that is to say, for never-ceasing, infinite sanctification of man: God alone is holy.

"The discovery of man as the fellowman," while articulated out of the sources of Judaism, belongs in itself, as one can say with some exaggeration, to the competence of ethics; the discovery of "the individual as the I" surely goes beyond that competence and is peculiar to religion. The discovery of man as the fellowman was achieved by "the social prophets"; the discovery of the individual as the I was the great progress due to Ezekiel, who seems to be unduly concerned with sacrifices and the temple and therefore to be regressive. It could seem that the discovery of the fellowman, the Thou, implies the discovery of the individual as the I. According to Cohen this is not the case, if one understands "individual" in the strict sense, "the absolute individual," "the isolated individual," whose concern transcends state and society—which are ultimately "only dark blind masses"—and therefore transcends ethics. The correlation between God and man is above all the correlation between God and the individual; the absolute individual, "the seeing individual," is man standing before God.

Regardless of whether one accepts Cohen's religion of reason, one must ponder carefully his confrontation of the seeing individual with the dark blind masses of state and society. Only in the I can the individual be discovered; only on the basis of this discovery can the fellowman be seen as an individual and thus truly become a fellowman. The reason is this: I have no right to set myself up as a moral judge of other human beings, be they poor or rich; even the judge who condemns the criminal is not meant to pass a moral judgment. But I must pass moral judgment on myself. The individual is discovered by his realization that he is morally guilty and by what that realization leads to. He cannot acquit himself, and yet he needs liberation from his feeling of guilt, i.e., purification from his guilt, his sin. Only God can liberate the individual from his sin and thus transform the individual into an I. The I liberated from sin, the redeemed I, the I redeemed before God, the I reconciled with God is the ultimate goal toward which man must strive.

For the reconciliation with God can only be the consummation of the reconciliation of man with himself. This reconciliation consists in man's "repentance," in his return from his evil ways or, more tellingly, in his making himself a new heart and a new spirit. The first step in this return is man's confession of his sin, his self-punishment, in and before the stateless congregation, i.e., together with all other members of the congregation as his fellow sinners. The return is the return to God Who alone redeems from sin. This redemptive aspect of God is what is meant by His goodness or grace as distinguished from His holiness. "It is the essence of God to forgive man's sin . . . for His essence consists in His correlation with man." When Cohen speaks, deeply moved, of God's help in reconciling man to Him, he is never oblivious of man's autonomy, which is indeed inseparable from his finiteness or frailty; he is not even oblivious of it when he interprets the verses in the prophets and the psalms in which God is compared to the shepherd and men or the souls to His lambs. But it should be noted that in speaking of God's goodness Cohen calls His good action "person-like."

Cohen confirms and deepens his doctrine of reconciliation in his discussion of the Day of Atonement, which in German is called the Day of Reconciliation, and of its primacy over all other festivals in the Jewish year. In this context he makes clear how he understands the relation of sin and punishment: the punishment is the suffering that is inseparable from human life and that leads to man's redemption provided he recognizes it as divine dispensation, as necessary for the development of his self.

The justification of suffering, and hence in particular of Israel's suffering, and not the prospect of the messianic age as the ideal goal of political and social progress, leads Cohen in his *Religion of Reason* to the discussion of "the idea of the Messiah and mankind." According to him, the idea of mankind, of all men without distinctions like those between Greeks and barbarians or between the wise and the vulgar, has at least its historical origin in religion, in monotheism; the unique God is the God of all men, of all nations. "For the Greek, man was only the Greek," despite the fact that the Stoa at any rate was "cosmopolitan," for the Stoa thought only of the individuals, not of the nations. The universalism of the prophets, which comprehends in one thought and hope all nations, is "a thought of the boldest and world-political courage"; the prophets thus became "the originators of the concept of world history," nay, of "the concept of history as the being of the future," for they placed the ideal, which is opposed to all present and past reality, not beyond time but in the future. Mankind as one, because unified in its highest aspiration, never was or is, but will be; its development never comes to an end; that development is progress. By turning toward the future the prophets completed the break with myth that had been achieved by monotheism, the message of the unique God as the God of morality. Israel, the eternal people, is the symbol of mankind. Israel had to survive the destruction of the Jewish state; it has to survive for all times because it is the creator of the Bible, and creation is in this case, too, a never-ending renewal. The Jewish state as one state among many would not point as unmistakably to the unity of mankind as the one stateless people dedicated uniquely to the service of the unique God, the Lord of the whole earth.

This is the meaning of Israel's election: to be an eternal witness to pure monotheism, to be *the* martyr, to be the suffering servant of the Lord. The misery of Jewish history is grounded in messianism, which demands humble submission to suffering and hence the rejection of the state as the protector against suffering. Israel has the vocation not only to preserve the true worship of God but also to propagate it among the nations: through its suffering Israel acquires the right to convert them; the freely accepted suffering makes manifest the historic worthiness of the sufferer. For the prophets and by the prophets Israel became the rest or remainder of Israel, the ideal Israel, the Israel of the future, that is to say, the future of mankind. The patriotism of the prophets is at bottom nothing but universalism.

In this spirit Cohen discusses the messianic passages in the prophetic books. In his idealizing interpretation there is no place for the hope that Israel will return to its own country, to say nothing of the restoration of the temple. He justifies this interpretation in particular by the fact that Jeremiah foretold the return from captivity of Israel's bad neighbors who had also been deported, but this does not do away with the fact that he brought the same good message to Israel. Nor does Ezekiel's prophecy that after Israel's "merely political restoration" it will extirpate the abominations, do away with the fact that he prophesied also and in the first place Israel's "merely political restoration." It is perhaps more important to note that according to Cohen's interpretation of Isaiah 9:6-7 the day of the Lord can no longer seriously be thought to be imminent, for the new time is meant to be a new eternity: could not eternity, even a new eternity,

be imminent? Cohen himself admits that the prophets did not explicitly place the end of the days in a wholly remote future; he
traces that fact to the preponderance of their concern with a political
future of their own nation and of mankind. He, however, regards as
the essence of messianism the "supra-sensuousness"—the eternal futurity—of the earthly future of mankind within its natural development, which is a progressive movement.

The concern with the earthly and natural (nonmiraculous) future
seems to be weakened by the beliefs in the immortality of the soul
and in the resurrection of the body. These beliefs are unacceptable
to Cohen in their traditional, "dogmatic" form. He is therefore compelled to examine the sources of Judaism on these subjects and to
idealize what they say as much as possible. Belief in the survival of
the souls is in an early stage connected with the worship of ancestors.
In this stage the grave is of utmost importance, as it still is in the
biblical stories of Abraham and Joseph. Dying is understood in the
Bible as going to one's fathers: the individual soul goes or enters into
the soul of the people, and the people does not die. Immortality
means, therefore, the historical survival of the fathers, i.e., of the
individual in the historical continuity of his people. Cohen uses this
apparently redundant expression in order to exclude any thought of
the survival of the souls in the literal sense. On the basis of messianism, immortality comes to mean the survival of the soul in the historical process of the human race. Even more than immortality can
the "image" of resurrection convey the thought of the eternal sequence of generations of men in the historical unity of the peoples
in general, and of the messianic people in particular. This does not
mean that the individual is only a link in a chain, for through the
discovery of the individual in the light of holiness, i.e., morality,
resurrection takes on the purely moral meaning of rebirth, of self-
renewal; the link gives life to the chain of the generations.

It is characteristic of monotheism, as distinguished from myth, that
it seeks a meaning of death only for the sake of the morally concerned individual. Accordingly, Koheleth says that when man dies
the soul returns to God Who has given it—and not to the nether
world of myth. Only in this way can one reconcile death with the
infinite task of morality or self-purification. This infinite endeavor
must be understood in the spirit of messianism: the other life is the
historical future, the future in the unending history of the human
race. Under "Persian influence" the beliefs in immortality and resurrection combined, became active in the Jewish mind, and were identified with the belief in the messianic age throughout rabbinical

antiquity; hence the historical character of the messianic future became endangered: the messianic future, which is to come by virtue of man's actions, was in danger of being understood as the shadowy kingdom of heaven in the Beyond for whose coming one can only wait and pray. This danger was averted in Judaism, however, because of the persistent awareness of the difference between the messianic age, on the one hand, and immortality and resurrection, on the other; that awareness was most clearly expressed by Maimonides in his *Code.*

Cohen especially loathed the notion of hell; concern with eternal punishment, as more obviously the concern with reward, stems from man's natural eudemonism and is therefore incompatible with ethics proper. It is true that justice, and hence also punitive justice, is thought to be an attribute of God; but, as Cohen says, tacitly but all the more remarkably deviating from Maimonides (*Guide of the Perplexed* I 54), His justice, as distinguished from His love, cannot be the model of human action; His punitive justice remains entirely His mystery and cannot be the concern of morally concerned men. For an understanding of this assertion one must consider that, according to Cohen, Maimonides asserts for the messianic time "in precise clarity the principle of socialism"; he probably means by this the disappearance of all obstacles to the knowledge of God. He is, of course, silent about the "Laws concerning Kings and Their Wars" with which Maimonides so impressively concludes his *Code.* It is therefore all the more praiseworthy that Cohen accepts the notion, so deeply rooted in Jewish piety, of "the merit of the fathers": "the patriarchs alone have every merit that their descendants can acquire." Here enthusiasm for the future gives way to gratitude for the past; it would be better to say that enthusiasm for the future reveals its being rooted in a past to which veneration and gratitude are due. These apparently contradictory tendencies are reconciled by an idealizing interpretation or by the fact that the religion of reason is the religion of reason out of the sources of Judaism. Under no circumstances must the merit of the fathers be permitted to cast the slightest doubt or veil on the autonomy of the individual.

The most obvious difficulty to which Judaism is exposed in modern times is caused by its being Law, an all-comprehensive, sacred law. Cohen was assisted in overcoming these difficulties by his failure to take into consideration the extreme questioning of law as such as it was known to him from Plato's *Statesman.* He has the courage to say that Revelation and Law are identical. According to him, the Law is either the moral law or is meant to contribute to man's moral education. More precisely, all particular commandments concern means; their suitability is therefore subject to examination. In the last analysis the Law is symbol. The only danger entailed in the universal supremacy of the Law, the subservience of everything a man does to the ideal of holiness, is that it leaves no room for man's theoretical and esthetic interests, for "culture" in one sense of the term; but these interests lack the firm center that only the unique God of Jewish monotheism can supply. Besides, this danger can be reduced, and partly has been reduced, by correctives that do not render questionable the Law as a whole.

Cohen admits that, indirectly through Moses Mendelssohn and directly through the Reform movement through which the Jews gained access to the culture of the nations in whose midst they live, the power of the Law has been weakened, but he insists that it has not been destroyed. The survival of Judaism still calls for a certain self-isolation of the Jews within the world of culture and therefore for the Law, however much its scope and its details may have to be modified; it calls for such an isolation "as long as the Jewish religion stands in opposition to other forms of monotheism" or the other forms of monotheism stand in opposition to the Jewish religion, in other words, as long as the messianic age has not yet come.

Yet isolation is not the sole purpose of the Law; its main purpose is the idealization or sanctification of the whole of human life through the living correlation with God. In the chapter on the Law, Cohen engages in a critique of Zionism about which it is not necessary to say anything since it is easily intelligible to every reader. As the reader can hardly fail to notice, in the same context Cohen seems almost to face the possibility actualized not long after his death by national socialism. But his "optimism" was too strong.

The soul and inwardness of the Law is prayer. Prayer gives life to all actions prescribed by the Law, so much so that one may doubt whether prayer is commanded in any of the 613 particular commandments of which the Law is traditionally held to consist. Prayer is the language of the correlation of man with God. As such it must be a dialogue while being a monologue. It is this because it expresses man's love of God as an actual experience of the soul, for the soul is given by God and hence is not exclusively the human soul; therefore it can speak to God and with God. Love of God is the highest form of human love; it is longing for God, for nearness to Him. This must not make one forget that man's longing for God is longing for his redemption, for his moral salvation—a longing that originates in anguish. But man is not merely his soul; all human cares and sorrows become legitimate themes of prayer. Above all, the dangers to intellectual probity are impenetrable for man; if all other purposes of prayer could be questioned, its necessity for veracity, for purity of the soul cannot: God alone can create in man a pure heart. Cohen speaks with emphasis of the danger to veracity that comes from one's fear of being despised by flesh and blood for confessing and professing the religious truth. The Jewish notion of prayer is characterized by the fact that the synagogue is not called a house of prayer but a house of learning or study, for that house is built not for the individual who prays in solitude but for the congregation that lives in anticipation of the messianic kingdom of God; for its coming "in your lives and in your days and in the life of the whole house of Israel" Jews pray in the Kaddish. Yet the congregation cannot be preserved without the Law and therefore without the study of the Law.

The headings of the last five chapters are the only ones that are identical or almost identical with chapter headings in the *Ethics*. The chapter entitled "The Virtues" takes the place of the chapters of the *Ethics* that are entitled "The Concept of Virtue," "Truthfulness," and "Modesty." The reason for this change is the following. In the *Ethics* Cohen had said that, according to the prophets, God is truth, and they meant by this that "the true God is the ground of morality." But he had continued: "But this is the difference, this is the gulf between religion and ethics, that in ethics no extraneous foundation can be laid; even God must not be for ethics the methodic ground of moral knowledge." Accordingly, in the *Religion of Reason* the true God becomes the ground of morality or more specifically of the virtues; the discussion of the virtues in general and of truth and truthfulness in particular cannot even externally be separated from one another. This is not to deny that even in the *Religion of Reason*, while insisting that "religion must be truth," he still says: "what would truth be without scientific knowledge as its foundation?" It is possible, though, that he means here by "scientific knowledge" rational knowledge and in particular ethical knowledge. Since God is the truth, He cannot in any way be or become a symbol. Truthfulness or intellectual probity animates Judaism in general and Jewish medieval philosophy, which always recognized the authority of reason, in particular. But truthfulness requires knowledge, and our knowledge is imperfect. Therefore truthfulness must be accompanied by modesty, which is the virtue of skepticism. In his *Religion of Reason* Cohen makes no distinction between modesty and humility except to say that he who is humble before God is modest toward men. In his *Ethics* he had said that modesty keeps unimpaired the feeling of one's own worth whereas humility makes the assumption of one's own worthlessness.

In the chapter on fidelity in the *Ethics* Cohen had said that religion must transform itself or be transformed into ethics: religion is a state of nature while the state of maturity is ethics. The transformation must be prepared by the idealization of religion. But this presupposes in the first place fidelity to religion, fidelity to one's religion. In the same chapter he comes to speak of the apparent conflict between fidelity to one's "lost nationality" and fidelity to the state: did he have in mind the Jews in particular? He speaks of gratitude only to the state. In the much shorter chapter on fidelity in the *Religion of Reason* he speaks much more fully of the connection between fidelity and gratitude; he quotes there "If I forget thee, let my right hand forget me." A peculiarly Jewish act of fidelity is the study of the Torah. "Fidelity in the study of the Torah did not permit that the noble character of the folk soul perish amidst the oppression of millennia." He does not speak of the moral obligation not to desert one's people especially when they are in need—and when are Jews not in need?—because for him this went without saying. Almost his whole work, his whole life bears testimony to this fidelity and his gratitude to the Jewish heritage—a fidelity limited only by his intellectual probity, by a virtue that he traced to that very heritage.

Cohen was a faithful warner and comforter to many Jews. At the very least he showed them most effectively how Jews can live with dignity as Jews in a non-Jewish, even hostile, world while participating in that world. In showing this he assumed indeed that the state is liberal or moving toward liberalism. Yet what he said about Jewish martyrdom provided, without his being aware of it, for the experience that the Jews subject to Hitler were soon to undergo. He did not provide what no human being could have provided, a way of dealing with a situation like that of the Jews in Soviet Russia, who are killed spiritually by being cut off from the sources of Judaism. It is a blessing for us that Hermann Cohen lived and wrote.

RELIGION OF REASON
OUT OF THE SOURCES OF JUDAISM

To the memory of my father

*May his soul be bound
in the bond of life.*

EDITOR'S REMARKS
TO THE SECOND GERMAN EDITION

The new edition of Cohen's *Religion of Reason*, which has become necessary after ten years, could not be simply a reproduction of the first edition. Nor could it confine itself to the correction of the many obvious misprints that were noticed and censured by the attentive reader. That the text lagged behind the precision and neatness usually characteristic of Cohen's publications is due to unfortunate conditions during the first printing. Although Cohen himself proofread more than the first half of the book and, as was his habit, supplied elaborate changes and improvements, particularly of a stylistic character, this was done with already feeble strength as regards externals. Hence, some distorting mistakes, some misplaced lines were left in that part of the proof supervised by Cohen himself. The editor of this new edition had at his disposal, through the courtesy of the author's widow, Martha Cohen, not only the author's typed manuscript but also Cohen's very penetrating galley proofs. Further, the remarks which Franz Rosenzweig entered in the author's copy were made available, for which the editor is thankful; and, finally, the editor used his own notes, which originated during the repeated readings. The editor therefore hopes that he has succeeded in refining the text, in eliminating obscurity, and in correcting mistakes. He tried to be guided by caution; wherever the text at hand could be retained, even though difficult to interpret, the editor avoided making changes. The peculiar stamp of Cohen's language made this caution necessary.

On page 311 of the present edition—in the middle of the chapter on Immortality and Resurrection—begins that part of the book which Cohen did not correct himself. The task of Cohen's friends who devoted themselves to the editing of the completed manuscript was difficult. Time was pressing; the book had to be completed. The manuscript was typed from dictation and was therefore not free from the well-known mistakes in the stenographer's understanding and in disorders of construction, which characterize this kind of manuscript.

Hence, it is understandable that this second part of the book, although it was inspected by many careful eyes, also appeared with many mistakes. With regard to this part the editor also hopes he was able, with the help of the still available manuscript, to make improvements. Marginal comments by other people, which got into the text, were eliminated, the text was purified of misplaced words and sentences and all kinds of errors. Of course, one should not forget that the author's own finishing touches are missing in the second half of this great work.

In the survey that follows* an exact account is given of the changes of some importance that were made in the second edition. The frame of this survey is extended to include also incidental observations that throw an interesting light upon the origin of the text, although they do not cause any new modification of it. To the new text with the new page and line numbers is added in brackets the previous text with the old page and line numbers. Not shown, however, are corrections of simple misprints and incorrect spellings (for instance of names); the carefully improved punctuation that Cohen still very often handled according to phonetic principles, which often upsets the modern eyes; as well as the numerous changes of incorrect numerical references from the Bible and Talmud. The quotations from the Bible and Talmud were closely checked and wherever necessary corrected. The passages from German poets, which Cohen rendered from memory, were put, not without hesitation, into their original wording. It might be not without significance how a quotation from Goethe presented itself in Cohen's mind. Yet the quotations in question did not seem to have such significance. However, there seems to be no doubt that such a meaning is to be attributed to the sayings of Rabbi Akiba, which Cohen rearranged, and which form the motto of the book and appear in the same translation in the text. This rearrangement has a deep meaning, and to reestablish the original quotation would have meant a wrongly understood historical faithfulness.

On the other hand, it must be emphasized that the title under which the book appeared in the first edition and became known in public has undergone a change. From two letters which Cohen wrote in July and December, 1917, to the Society for the Promotion of the Science of Judaism (Gesellschaft zur Förderung der Wissenschaft des Judentums) it follows with complete certainty that Cohen wanted the book to be named "Religion of Reason out of the Sources of

*In the German edition p. 625ff.

Judaism" and that the intensifying article (*The* Religion) stood on the title page of his work by default. In the new edition Cohen's will now comes into its own. It may also be of interest that at that time the board of the Society decided, at a meeting at which Cohen was not present, to give to the work the name "Jewish Religious Philosophy" since it had to appear in the series of the "Outline of the General Science of Judaism." Cohen assented to this with the modification that the subtitle should read: "Jewish Religious Philosophy and Ethics." Why this addition was omitted could not be made clear from the available correspondence.

Dr. Leo Rosenzweig compiled with renewed care the references from Hebrew sources. The ones given previously were most assiduously scrutinized, and new ones could be added from Cohen's notes.

BRUNO STRAUSS

Elucidation of the Title and Articulation of the Task

1. What a science means and what its contents are can only be shown by unfolding its content. Whence a science takes its material is of no great consequence for the substantive value of its content. It seems to be from an alien point of view that philosophy raises the question about the sources of our consciousness of space: geometry unfolds its teaching independently of this question, let alone the answer to it.

It is otherwise with religion. There is only *one* mathematics, but there are many religions. At least, it seems so. This is so not only with religion but also with all the institutions and spiritual trends of human culture except the sciences. There are many customs, many codes, many states, and therefore the question arises whether all these different cultural phenomena have something in common, which, despite their differences, would make it possible to recognize a unifying concept of all of them.

Among the sciences it is only psychology that can raise the question: out of what sources of consciousness can the content of science be derived? But it is *history* that confronts religion, as well as the kindred cultural concepts, with the question: what development has religion, in particular, and other cultural institutions as well, taken in the course of time and among the various peoples?

Thus, there arises an intellectual desire and soon also a scientific endeavor to trace the historical development of all the phenomena of culture. The problem of history comes, as it were, into direct opposition to the problem of the substantive content of religion. One denies the possibility of knowing what religion is, if its substantive content is not uncovered out of its historical development. But what, then, is this content? The question is not raised in this way, for one assumes that only the historical development leads to its discovery.

However, what then is the element that is supposed to undergo development? Again, the question is not raised in this way. This element is considered to be generally known, whereas, on the contrary, it is the real problem.

2. These obscurities are connected with the concept of *development* as it is used in the humanities *(Geisteswissenschaften)* in distinction from, say, embryology. Instead of starting, as in anatomy, from the descriptively obtained concept of the organism, to reconstruct it in its development, one thinks it possible to start with a vague, entirely indefinite and imprecise notion of religion. This is done not only in order to depict this notion in its historical forms but also in order to determine from them the concept of religion itself. The general procedure of induction is applied here. And here, as everywhere else where induction is meant to be not only a preparatory step but a definitive solution to a problem, this procedure undoubtedly founders.

The manifold appearances of alleged religion in the variety of its contradictory forms would render it impossible to find a common concept of religion, rather than secure for induction the prospect of a general concept of religion as the final goal of inductive sampling. There is no opposition to reason and understanding, no opposition to human morality in the broadest sense, which has not become the point of gravity of some religion. Therefore, one can understand those prejudices against religion that not only deny its intelligibility but also any spiritual value at all, thus denying and destroying the entire problem of religion. The history of religion has no means whatever of securing the legitimacy of religion; according to its own methodological concepts, there is no other legitimation for religion than that represented in the historical fact of religion. History thus surrenders the problem of discovering a concept of religion not only to the uncertainties of a more or less exhaustive compilation but also, in full accord with its own systematic tendency, to the possible results of induction, with all the latter's broadness and ambiguity. The concept of religion as understood by induction is only the result of development, whereas it should be the prototype, the model which traces the way of development.

3. The title written at the head of this book contains the program for the book.

Obviously a number of fundamental concepts are joined together in the title of the book. Are these concepts, however, unified with one another? They obviously limit each other; does this determination, however, lead to a precise definition?

4. Obviously *reason* is meant to make religion independent of the

descriptions supplied by the history of religion. We do not shrink from the argument that reason must rule everywhere in history. However, history in itself does not determine the concept of reason. The concept of reason has to engender the concept of religion. The concept is always a separate problem, which must serve as a presupposition for the problem of development.

5. We find a similar methodological situation in the concept of Judaism, though the conflict with history is in this case less extreme. For the question regarding the concept of Judaism does not entirely hover in the air between the opposite poles of induction and deduction; Judaism has literary sources, and as much as these may differ in their objective value and literary clearness, the historical material is nevertheless narrowed down and limited in these sources, so that in this case induction seems not entirely hopeless. In this case, too, the necessary presupposition we recognized for all spiritual, and therefore also for all literary, development holds true without reservation. It is impossible to develop a unifying concept of Judaism out of the literary sources unless the concept of Judaism itself is anticipated as an ideal project, in a manner methodologically analogous to the study of the organism.

At this point, too, a difficulty is cleared up, which continues to hold against the legitimacy of induction. For in the case of Judaism the sources do not consist of an infinite and still incomplete variety of materials; instead, it is a definite and narrower range of subjects, which is presented as the source material. Furthermore, this material has its history. Therefore, the objection that history in itself is in opposition to the objective value of the concept is removed. This objection is based on a misunderstanding. The concept, like everything spiritual, requires history for its own development. However, history by itself does not determine anything about the essence and peculiarity of the concept, which, in the course of history up to now, may not yet have developed to its final realization.

If, however, we connect the concept of religion with the literary sources, if we relate the concept of Judaism to its literary sources, then we acknowledge that history, literary history, is the factor by virtue of which the actuality of Judaism comes to its realization. However, this factor, to be sure, does not possess the value of a criterion, a value possessed only by the concept, considered both as problem and as method, as task and as presupposition.

6. Even if the difficulty which lies in the predominant understanding of the notion of development is grasped, one is still misled by the question: how is it possible for the ideal concept of the object

in question to be anticipated beforehand? This can be understood in the case of an organism, but how can it be understood in the case of a spiritual organism, insofar as one is even permitted to assume this concept? How is it possible to start with the allegedly finished and complete concept of religion or of Judaism, and from this supposition consider the literary sources as material that can be tested by this concept? Is it not simply an insoluble contradiction that one has to start with the supposition of an ideal concept in order to be able even to begin a correct induction, in order to be able to undertake and carry through the systematic use, the questioning, not to mention the command, of the source material?

This question is the fundamental question of all *knowledge;* it is the magic word that illuminates all the obscurities, all the difficulties, all the innermost depths of the theory of knowledge. Insofar as religion, insofar as Judaism presents a conceptual problem, and insofar as this problem has to be solved, if the literary sources are not forever to remain a book with seven seals, the disclosure and the depiction of these concepts—religion and Judaism—have to be obtained from the understanding of the respective concepts themselves. The worshiper of fire, not only the worshiper of the sun, might perhaps have the same single religion along with the prophets, with Judaism. However, even if I am referred to the literary sources of the prophets for the concept of religion, those sources remain mute and blind if I do not approach them with a concept, which I myself lay out as a foundation in order to be instructed by them and not simply guided by their authority.

Hence there is another source besides the merely literary one which gives me guidance in the use of the literary sources. What is this other source?

A. REASON

1. It is not possible to say that *consciousness (Bewußtsein)** is to be thought of, and sought, as this other source. For consciousness is, properly speaking, only another expression for history. As all culture is developed by history, so also is it developed by consciousness; the only difference is that consciousness actualizes the nar-

*The unity of the different directions of the mind in logic, ethics, aethetics, and religion. See pages 7 and 379. The concept is fully developed in Hermann Cohen's *Logik der reinen Erkenntnis.* [S.K.]

rower history of man. If consciousness, therefore, cannot be thought of as the other source, which besides and over and above history vouches for the legitimacy and value of religion, then the other source can be expressed only through the word "reason" as it appears in the title of our book. *The concept of religion should be discovered through the religion of reason.* The sources of Judaism should be shown and proven to be that material which in its historical self-development must engender and verify the problematic reason, the problematic religion of reason. Thus, history itself again becomes the literary touchstone for the creativity of reason; however, it is not merely life or instinctive production that is able to testify to the legitimacy of reason and its specific character. Reason itself is the problem that exists for every concept, for every possible knowledge of a concept, which consequently has to be presupposed and set up as a foundation for the concept of religion and for the concept of Judaism. Consequently, by placing the problem of religion in a necessary relation to the problem of reason, we introduce the problem of religion into general philosophy.

2. All considerations which might be raised against this have to be withdrawn for the time being. No offense must be taken at the notion of reason as the source of religion. It must not be asked whether it is the only source, or whether there is another placed beside it or ranked above it. All these questions must not mislead us; they would divert us from the systematic path, on the threshold of which we have just stepped. Reason is the source of concepts, and the concept has to be the source; it must never be thought of as an estuary for the inductive tributaries which flow into it. Reason is the rock out of which the concept originates and out of which it has to originate for the sake of systematic examination, if the course the concept takes in the river basin of history is to come to view. The main point now is to define precisely this concept of reason if one has to start with a concept of religion, with a concept of Judaism, in order to use the literary sources correctly.

A straight road leads us from the historical concept of Judaism to the *philosophy of religion.*

Philosophy is the science of reason. And if the concept is the pre-eminent witness for all science, then all science and all possible knowledge have in the concept their entire content and in reason their common source. Reason is the organ of concepts.

What holds true for every science holds no less true for religion. Insofar as religion, too, consists of concepts and is based on concepts, its ultimate source can only be reason. This connection with reason determines and conditions its connection with philosophy, understood as the universal reason of human knowledge. Let us in the first place give a negative account of claims which are to be rejected from religion because of this recourse to reason.

3. The *senses* are in direct opposition to reason; basically they are common to animals and men. If reason is the source of religion, then first of all *instinct* is rejected, as a kind of intelligence common to man and animal. Religion, however, might be the mark that distinguishes man from animal. Therefore, everything that is merely natural instinct cannot be considered an originative force of religion. And the rejection of the natural instinct excludes animal *intelligence* as well as animal *affect*. Instinct unites both of these basic animal powers. Religion is generated neither by the primitive instinct that, as it were, desires to remain forever fettered in the prison of obscurity, nor by a natural impulse that desires to set up an elemental force in order to fight it, as well as to prostrate itself before it, and at least temporarily render itself defenseless. Religion has nothing in common with such instinctive drives; its origin is reason.

4. Along with the instincts, all the other forces propelled by the senses are to be rejected. Anything connected with *pleasure* and *pain* cannot be valid as a positive motive power of religion. Pleasure and pain are blood-witnesses of animal life; reason does not originate in their tracks. Pleasure and pain as basic vital powers do, to be sure, control the whole organism. Therefore one must search out all those hiding places in which the vital powers of pleasure and pain creep into the creativity of reason in order to distort and to make it, and its origin, ambiguous. The religion of reason protests against all the alleged powers of the self, against all those pretended powers of the *I*, which are rooted in pleasure and pain. All animal selfishness and self-love, all eudaemonism, which recognizes only pleasure as a legitimate criterion, all materialism, which honors only debit and credit and considers give and take as the essence of man, are eliminated by reason. The subjective basis of materialism lies in the principle of pleasure. What matter means to the nature of the world, pleasure means to human nature. It is the consciousness of animal sensuality.

5. *Naturalness in its primitive historical form* is also rejected together with sensuality as a source of religion, insofar as its factual reality is, properly speaking, merely contingent. It is reason alone that elevates historical actuality to necessity, the meaning of which is the abolition of contingency. It is contrary to reason that religion should be only a contingent province of *imagination*, or that it should be connected with powers motivated by affects. It is also contrary to

reason that religion should be a contingent province, which could emerge out of the relations and interactions of the *social forces* and the forms in which they manifested themselves. This origin, too, would fail to give religion its own peculiar meaning which would distinguish it from the function of animal secretion. The religion of reason is opposed to the idea that religion is an invention of the people of a certain rank, whether priests or rulers or the privileged classes. The religion of reason is not a deceit of the priests and no sop which the powerful invented for the weak. Just as little is it a substitute for, or a tribute to, the weaknesses and shortcomings of human understanding. Neither is it a precautionary measure against the indignation of those whose general human abilities were inhibited and limited by social fetters. The religion of reason is particularly not a substitute for that privation, which by nature exists for a great many, inasmuch as they do not have an equal share in science and philosophy. Nor is it the case that he who has a share in science and philosophy thereby and therein possesses religion; rather is it religion which has a share in reason, and this means: reason does not exhaust itself in science and philosophy.

6. *The religion of reason turns religion into a general function of human consciousness;* it makes consciousness human. The universal human consciousness unfolds in a manifold variety, represented in the consciousness of different peoples; but in no particular people's consciousness is the religion of reason exhausted. Everything human, as it originates in any people, makes its contribution to reason in general, and thus to the religion of reason also. This is the sound core in the thinking of the *history of religion.* All people, even those in the most primitive conditions of culture, have their share in religion. The interest in tracing all the turns and changes by which the spirit of religion sprouts and grows is not only justified by a general love for mankind; it is also beneficial to, and necessary for, the general knowledge of man. Nevertheless, reason remains the distinctive mark and the systematic criterion.

For insofar as reason is the beginning of all human consciousness, all peoples indeed participate in the religion of reason. However, insofar as a *distinction* must be made between *consciousness* and *reason,* insofar as reason as such is not identical with the human spirit, but only with the specific form of human spirit in *science and philosophy,* the religion of reason only stands for the specific content that actualizes itself in the general spirit of peoples, in their science, in philosophy as well as in religion. Only in this specific content does reason manifest itself as a universal human power. The religion of reason cannot be the religion of a single people, or the bastard offspring of a single age; reason must be uniform in all those men and peoples who have become conversant with science and philosophy. This uniformity gives to religion the original imprint of universal humanity, the only indispensable limiting condition being the degree to which humanity has reached the stage of articulation displayed in scientific culture.

7. This universality, which becomes the fundamental condition for the religion of reason, seems to be contradicted by our intention to derive the latter from the sources of Judaism, as if it were only out of these literary sources that the religion of reason could originate, and as if one could not assume an influx to these sources and, hence, to religion of reason, either before or afterward. If it were so, then, to say the least, the criterion of universality would be endangered; the criterion of reason would lose its precision, and the actuality in which it realizes itself would lapse into an appearance of contingency. What bestows necessity on historical actuality, on its individual phenomena, is exactly the universality, which, in spite of all social obstructions and despite all shortcomings, is able to wrestle its way into the history of the particular people. In this wrestling, reason brings itself to the light of day; it achieves its progress and especially its continuity, upon which the meaning of history is based and in which history becomes the history of reason.

Therefore, it would have been an irreparable mistake in our arrangement if we were to limit and confine the religion of reason to the Jewish religion because of its literary sources. This limitation would be an insoluble contradiction to the signpost of reason. It would be otherwise, however, if in Judaism the concept of a *source* were to have a peculiar significance and a peculiar methodological meaning with regard to the religion of reason. If this is the case, then the source does not shut itself off from other religious monuments, but rather becomes an *original source* for other sources, which latter in turn would still retain our undiminished recognition as sources of the religion of reason. In this case, there would be less reason to fear a confinement to the Jewish people and its religious productions the more the Jewish sources retain their fresh and vital fruitfulness for all other sources that sprang from them. Only insofar as the original source has as such an undeniable spiritual and psychological advantage must this supremacy of reason in the primary origin (Ursprünglichkeit)* of the sources of Judaism remain indisputable.

*The term also suggests primitiveness and originality. [S.K.]

8. The universality of reason implies another consequence for human consciousness, which, if it were considered by the history of religion, would have given to it a more profound point of gravity. One has preferred, however, to follow the tracks of religion among the savages of America, rather than in Plato, Aeschylus, and Pindar. The connections of religion with philosophy are set as a task by the watchword of reason. Moreover, the religion of reason achieves its greatest triumphs and suffers its gravest conflicts, as well, with regard to its most proper and intimate motivations because it is almost indissolvably fused with the problems of philosophy. This connection with philosophy, proclaimed by reason, suffices to relieve us of doubt about the meaning of our appeal to the sources of Judaism. Judaism, to be sure, has no share in philosophy—but does not this introduce the same contradiction that we recognized in the lack of religion in other peoples than the Jews? However, could philosophy mean the universality of reason of every culture, if the religious sources of Judaism had entirely no share in it?

Here, too, the riddle is solved in the distinction between the *primary origin* and derivative actuality. And to this we have to add, without doubt, the characteristic of a *peculiarity* of method, which objectively distinguishes primary origin from all the indefiniteness with which any gradual development is burdened. The Greeks bestowed upon philosophy a peculiar character that distinguishes it from the speculation, however profound, of other peoples. Similarly, the Greeks stamped upon the sciences, which they borrowed from the Oriental peoples, the stamp of the specific method of science. Their philosophy brought forth their science, and, in a certain sense, their science brought forth their philosophy. This science, and especially this philosophy, became the common property of all civilized peoples. Although the Jews resisted Greek science, they could not resist their philosophy. Indeed, they produced the religion of reason, and to the degree that the share of religion in reason brings with it positively the essence of reason, this homogeneity unavoidably demands that religion be connected, if not with science, yet with philosophy. We should not gloss over the fact that the concept of philosophy is changed and distorted if it is not practiced as scientific philosophy; but the universal character of reason, even if science is excluded, connects religion with philosophy.

Therefore it will be our task to investigate in the sources of Judaism the original philosophic motives in which, and by virtue of which, the religion of reason succeeds in making its way. And we shall have to pay attention to the fact that it was not only in the later history of the Jews, when Greek influence had already become an actuality, that this original force of reason began to stir, but that already in the original religious thought itself this connection with philosophical reasoning emerges. These traces have to be considered as reason's oldest monument and are in no way to be suspected, on the basis of any historical schematization, as later interpolations. The religion of reason preserves for the sources of Judaism their original, natural, human connection with philosophic speculation, which therefore is as little an imitation of the Greeks as it is a borrowing from the Greeks. The philosophical element in the biblical sources has to possess the same originality as belongs in general to the share religion has in reason.

9. The connection that reason establishes between religion and philosophy confers an important position upon reason with regard to religion. Reason not only stands in opposition to all sensuality of the spirit and heart; it means positively an intrinsic rule of lawfulness (*Gesetzlichkeit*), the archetype of all lawfulness. Religion certainly cannot be deprived of the originative principle (*Ursprung*)* of its intrinsic rule of lawfulness and its development. If, at first sight, it might appear that through reason the region of religion is limited to human consciousness, to the human mind, we need not be troubled by this objection, because reason does not exclude any other spiritual force, and because no such force can be in opposition to reason. However, we must also consider positively how the force of lawfulness invalidates such an objection.

Reason is the organ of laws. The religion of reason, therefore, comes under the light of lawfulness. All the contingency, all the arbitrariness, all the illusions, which are connected with the idea of a historical occurrence, being merely factual are dissolved like shadows by this light of reason. Primary origin, which we have considered up till now to be merely of historical derivation, appears now to be founded beyond all the limits of history: lawfulness becomes the foundation of primary origin. And there can be no stronger, no more profound foundation than that of lawfulness. Primary originality is no warrant for a final solution to a problem; only lawfulness is.

If any obscurity has remained because we attached religion to the province of the problems of reason, it is now cleared up: wherever lawfulness rules, there the domain of reason is secured. The objections

---

*The term is a basic principle in Hermann Cohen's *Logik der reinen Erkenntnis*, meaning the originative act of reason as distinguished from sensuous or empirical data. [S.K.]

that originate in the distinction between the human and some other kind of reason we leave unconsidered for the time being. Lawfulness is so weighty that against it every objection has to retreat. For what more reliable and certain basis than lawfulness could another reason offer? If, therefore, reason offers lawfulness to human knowledge, then already at this point it becomes clear that a connection between human reason and some other kind of reason can be aspired to and entered into: lawfulness forms the bond between both kinds of reason. Consequently, we shall have to investigate how also the other kind of reason, reason as the archetype of lawfulness, proves true.

B. RELIGION

1. Up till now we have developed a provisional notion of the meaning of reason as it realizes itself in philosophy. We must now look for a similar notion of religion. It is not enough to know that religion presupposes the concept of religion that develops itself not only in the history of religion in general but particularly in the sources of Judaism. We must take up another consideration, namely, how we can find a provisional notion of the content of this concept of religion. This content is also significant for the whole sphere of the concept of religion. We would be unable to examine the sources of religion unless we first determined the sphere of the concept of religion. The sphere of this concept does not come under the domain of induction, but belongs completely to the first principles, which are the presupposition of all induction. Only the sphere of a concept points out its content.

Since religion has been defined as religion of reason, *man* is established as its sphere as well as its content. Whether religion comes from man is not the question at this point, since it has been established that it proceeds from lawfulness. However, that the sphere of religion extends over man, and that all questions of man therefore become questions of religion, is established by the connection between religion and reason. The connection between religion and philosophy can no longer appear questionable if religion, through reason, does indeed have its share in the knowledge of man. Only this question may be raised: What exactly is the share that religion contributes to the content of the concept of man, to the knowledge of man?

It may seem as if all the contributions that are comprised under the scientific knowledge of man have already been exhausted. If we disregard, as is fitting, the bodily side of the organism, and even if we disregard the widely ramified and deep-rooted domain of historical anthropology, we are still confronted with *ethics*, which, as a branch of the system of philosophy, claims to govern all human affairs. Ethics, consequently, must deny a similar share in the knowledge of man to any other kind of knowledge, including religion, insofar as it claims to be knowledge. This objection that ethics makes, however, not only deprives religion of its possible content but also takes away from religion the prerogative of reason, which we acknowledged to give man his legitimate title as man. In that case, the religion of reason could not aspire to its own proper content; at the same time it could have no sphere of its own in a teaching about man, for insofar as this sphere is determined by the concept of man, it would fall to the domain of ethics.

2. This conclusion entails a further one. It consists of an alternative, in which either of two choices seems to be equally fatal for the problem of the religion of reason.

Either it turns out that religion, as a doctrine about man, falls under the domain of ethics; in this case, to be sure, there is no doubt about religion's connection with reason, but its *independence* as the religion of reason is thereby threatened. It is only ethics which in its doctrine about man holds the share of reason that the religion of reason claims for itself. Consequently, this claim seems untenable and intelligible only as a prejudice, which prevails in history particularly when human problems are interwoven with those of mythology. If the voices that were always raised against the independence of religion came into their own, the problem of a religion of reason would be untenable.

Or, contrary to all expectations, it might turn out that ethics, as a branch of systematic philosophy, and until now expounded as such, is not sufficiently able to master the entire content of the concept of man, and that religion on its part is able to fill this gap. Then, however, new and great difficulties would arise. They would not consist in the fact that religion would have to enter the system of philosophy —the considerations against it, even historically, would have little weight—but rather in the fact that the methodological concept of ethics would become ambiguous. Ethics intends to offer *the* doctrine about man: Should it aspire only to a part of it? Should ethics have to share its labor with religion? Is it already beyond doubt that because of the share religion has in reason, its share is methodologically the same as that of ethics? And even if this were beyond doubt, because it had been brought to a positive solution, there would still remain great doubt about the method of ethics. Can it do only half of the job, is it only able to complete its concept of man through that concept of man that religion is able to unveil? Hence, the danger of a methodological conflict within the domain of philosophy would arise. There cannot be two independent methods, side by side, for the solution of the problem of man. Moreover, methodologically one cannot admit the possibilty that ethics might share and equate its autonomy in the knowledge of man with some other kind of knowledge.

For religion itself a grave danger would arise if, as the religion of reason, it were permitted and, indeed, had to maintain an absolute independence of knowledge against ethics. All the dangers that religion faces in the course of history in respect to the theoretical as well as to the practical aspects of culture become understandable from the viewpoint of this problem of method. There cannot be two kinds of reason with regard to the doctrine of man.

3. If, in the beginning, we pay no heed to the doubts that concern method, and concern ourselves with the ethical content of the concept of man, then we become aware of a shortcoming, which appears in the depth of the ethical concept of man.

Ethics, in its systematic opposition to everything sensual and everything empirical in man, arrives at the great consequence that it must first tear away from man the *individuality* of his I, in order to return it to him from a higher pinnacle, and in a form not only higher, but also purified. In ethics *the I of man becomes the I of humanity,* and only in humanity is that true objectivization of man achieved which can secure the ethical concept of the human subject. As long as man is incapable of this self-objectivization, as long as he remains imprisoned in the vagueness of the empirical, he fails to achieve that *purity,* which ethics in accordance with its method has as its goal. In that case man is merely a sensual being, and, as such, not a historical individual. He becomes the latter only when the methodological means of history are accomplished in the concept of man; but all these methodological means of history have as their final goal humanity. Ethics can recognize and give recognition to man only as a member of humanity. As an individual man he can only be a representative carrier of humanity. And as this carrier of humanity, he does not lose his individuality when he thus becomes the symbol of humanity. Humanity bestows upon him true individuality with this symbol.

4. Humanity, however, is not the only symbol for the individuality of man that can rescue him from the ambiguity of empiricism. The

abstraction of humanity actualizes itself in history in the *state*. The state is the transitional organism from individual man to humanity. The state seems to have its point of gravity in the empirical notion of man, for man seems by his nationality to be fused to his state. Thereby arises, simply on the basis of origin, the illusion that the state and nationality, state and people, are identical. In this way, the concept of the state is narrowed down to the natural concept of man.

On the other hand, the state grows beyond natural bounds and the main function of its organism, which forms its *constitutional system,* points ever more emphatically and hopefully to a goal which unites the state with ethics through the concept of humanity. For, in spite of all the sovereignty due to the state, international law from of old holds before it the notion of a *federation of states* and makes it an ideal for the state; it prescribes to the state the great teaching: the state is unable to fulfill its concept unless it is able to elevate and to purify its individuality in a federation of states. Hence, in the state, also, man becomes the carrier of humanity.

All the danger that the method of ethics faced is now eliminated. The individuality of man, which ethics bases on humanity, is now free of any semblance of paradox; the state mediates between the empirical individual and the idea of humanity, whose carrier man becomes. The individuality of the state, in which the empirical man participates with his whole heart and in accordance with whose rhythm man's own pulse beats, actualizes the miracle which seems to lie in the ethical doctrine that humanity is the fulfillment of man. The state, particularly in this age, makes it clear beyond any doubt that man completes his higher metabolism in the organism of his state. The individuality that man puts into the state makes him discover the state out of the abstraction of humanity, the legal form of which is the federation of states.

5. Nevertheless, the fault which lies in the richness and variety of the ethical doctrine of man now becomes in all respects clear. It might perhaps be sufficient for an individual man to become conscious of his own individuality only in and through the state, which mediates between the individual and humanity; yet another mediation is needed besides the one required between the I and humanity. Besides the I, and distinct from the It, there arises the He. Is the He only another example of the I, which is therefore already established by the I? Language alone protects us from this mistake; language sets up the Thou before the He. Is the Thou also only another example of the I, or is a separate discovery of the Thou necessary, even if I have already become aware of my own I? Perhaps the

opposite is the case, that only the Thou, the discovery of the Thou, is able to bring myself to the discovery of I, to the discovery of the ethical knowledge of my I.

However, if this were the case, then this question would arise for ethics: Is it within the competence of the ethical method to bring about the discovery of the Thou? In accordance with its concept of man, as the man of humanity, is ethics able to enter into this classification of individuals? Does ethics have the methodological means for establishing it, if its goal is the *totality (Allheit)** which is realized in humanity? Would not such a division and gradation lie in the general direction of *plurality (Mehrheit)** and thus be an aberration from ethics' unifying goal of totality?

One should not object that insofar as the problem of ethics is man in the history of humanity, ethics necessarily has to take up the problem of the plurality and distinctions of men. For this objection is settled by acknowledging the problem of plurality, although the solution of it comes out of totality and, therefore, only in accordance with totality. Thus, there still remains the question whether the notion of a plurality of men does not raise problems that cannot be solved directly through the fundamental concept of totality, a question that becomes urgent with regard to the problem of the Thou, even if it might have remained veiled by the He.

What difference does it make from the point of view of humanity if I should have to address another example of humanity not merely as He, but expressly and above all as Thou? What significance would this claim in general have for ethics, which has no regard for persons, for which each person represents the same symbol of humanity? Should the question arise, however, as to the specific value and distinction of this address that marks out the Thou and seems to endanger the identity of mankind, then it becomes necessary to investigate the particular contribution that the discovery of the Thou makes to the concept of the human individual. At this point, then, it will be necessary to determine the *share religion wins in reason.*

6. The Thou is a classification within the notion of humanity,

*Categories in Hermann Cohen's *Logik der reinen Erkenntis* and *Ethik des reinen Willens.* In its ethical application *totality* means the final integration of the individual in the ideal unity of mankind, which is considered absolute and is realized through the unity of the state as a step in this integration. The unaccomplished, open unification represented by the notion of plurality retains the reference to diversity and particularity and is therefore a relative unification, such as is represented, for example, by the notion of a people or congregation. See page 404. [S.K.]

which humanity itself is unable to achieve; nevertheless, because of the Thou, all the methodological doubts about the share religion obtains in the tasks of reason which might have arisen disappear. The authority of ethics remains unshaken. However, the new supplement does not contradict the unity of its method, since the method of ethics fails and must fail in regard to the new problem of the Thou, while at the same time the concept of the individual demands the Thou. However, the Thou still belongs to the infinite series of the members of mankind; therefore, the method of treating it is necessarily a new one, but not a foreign one. It supplements the one method of ethics, but a *peculiarity* has to be granted it, since peculiarity cannot be denied to its problem—the Thou, although the Thou as well as the individual member belongs to the unity of mankind. This unity, however, can come about only through the totality of ethics. Hence the supplement to the one method becomes justified. It makes possible, within the totality, the discovery of the new link of the Thou. The Thou introduces a new problem into the concept of man, which, however, still reaches its completion—as individual also—in the concept of humanity. The new problem of the individual, therefore, cannot invalidate the association of religion with ethics; it cannot violate the unifying method, which unites both problems in the one problem of man.

7. Up until now the kind of human peculiarity inherent in the Thou has not been positively determined; apparently, it is the *personality* that is brought to light more through the Thou than through the He. The He is more subject to neutrality, which makes it hardly distinguishable from the It, and it seems that ethics intends such a neutral objectivity also for my I, since it tries to remove all my sensible characteristics. Should it remain at that? Does the organism with its metabolism remain absolutely indifferent to the I? And must this statement be valid without limitation, notwithstanding the indisputable connection between man's moral task and his sensible conditions?

8. There is a historical model for the necessity of supplementing ethics by religion; this is offered by *Stoicism* in its relation to the *suffering* of man. Stoicism proclaims suffering as indifferent (ἀδιάφορον) and therefore excludes it from morality. This conclusion drawn from the dualism of Stoicism, which with regard to all questions wavers between spirituality and materialism, is doubly in error. In the first place, suffering is in no way an indifferent element for the I. Perhaps because of its moral demands, the self-consciousness should not be indifferent to one's own physical suffering. Secondly, the observer should not let himself be indifferent to the other man's

suffering. There arises the question of whether it is not precisely through the observation of the other man's suffering that the other *is changed from the He to the Thou*. The affirmative answer to this question brings to light the specific power of religion, without detriment to its participation in the method of ethics.

9. If the meaning of physical suffering, of physical ill in the human world, has always been a question for theodicy, then one could perhaps state this meaning in a paradox: the suffering, the *passion (Leiden)* is for the sake of *compassion (Mitleid)*.[1] Man is so much in need of the affect of compassion that suffering itself is explained through it, and at this crossroad all ethics clearly and sharply separates itself from metaphysics in all its varieties. The deepest meaning of Christianity, too, becomes intelligible from this point of view. "Ah! to the woe of earth, still we are native here."* The psalm that "makes men not much lower than divinity," lacks this insight. The psalm breathes only optimism because the highest good is secured in the "nearness to God." The prophet, however, does not look down from this height to humankind with indifference. He hopes that in some time to come, God "shall blot out the tear from every face." "My tears gush forth, the Earth takes back her child."† Thus, through the testimony of the tear, Faust describes man in his earthly existence. And what else should be the moral vocation of man but the transfiguration and elevation of his earthly existence?

Up to this point, in opposition to the Stoics, one could still admit compassion into ethics. One could receive it in order to justify through it an anthropological ethics. However, if the question arises what ethics should do, what it can do in order not so much to abolish suffering but rather to satisfy compassion—to this question ethics will be unable to give an answer that will have more than a pedagogical or practical effect. Ethics is unable to answer the question through the establishment of a concept of principle. Ethics then, as one would say today, has indeed to become pragmatic. Compassion has to become a useful illusion through which suffering is shared with others and thereby decreased. Beyond this illusion there is supposedly no help. That is why some varieties of metaphysics reject this affect, because it presupposes only an illusion. I imagine that I suffer together with somebody else, but this other is no other but I myself, who through the illusion of my intellect appear to myself as another. This reverie is taught by Schopenhauer.

---

*Goethe, *Faust*, Part 1. [S.K.]
†*Ibid.*

Spinoza, in turn, also must reject this affect, because he, together with the Stoics, rejects all sensible affects. For him there is only knowledge, namely, knowledge of the one substance. Human beings, however, are altogether only modes, only singular things of this one substance. Here one is like the other, no one has a worth of his own; rather, each one is only the expression of the one substance. And whatever is not knowledge belongs equally to evil; compassion is of the same breed as envy. It makes no difference whether I am led by compassion to the other man or I am led back by envy from the other to myself. This doctrine of the soul is the consequence of the fundamental Stoic idea of indifference to suffering. It makes compassion a worthless illusion.

Ethics, however, also must be distinguished from *pessimism* at this crossroads of religion. For the distinction between pessimism and optimism is only concerned with the practical reform of earthly existence. Optimism is in no way "the wicked way of thinking," as Schopenhauer defames it, but its wisdom has a practical significance that always has been confirmed by theodicy, namely, to better the existence in the world in accordance with moral rule and thus to lessen human suffering. If, however, pessimism objects that all these endeavours are futile, are love's labor lost, then although this objection is in contradiction to the still recognizable progress of world history, the thesis of pessimism is not thereby refuted; for this thesis arises out of a metaphysics that claims to be independent of experience. The metaphysical meaning of suffering makes suffering the only reality in human existence proper, and the practical consequence of this metaphysics of pessimism is therefore the realization and verification of this principle in the negation, in the repeal of existence. However, if this wisdom is considered to be metaphysics, in no case can it be considered ethics; for the latter is throughout the affirmation, development, and elevation of human existence. If ethics now sees existence afflicted with suffering, then compassion becomes for it only a signpost for the question: How can suffering be overcome? Subjectively, suffering is pain; does compassion abide on one level with pain, or does it contain in itself a means of dissolving it? Is it perhaps the wound itself, which brings with it its own healing?

10. This is the turning point at which religion, as it were, emerges from ethics. The observation of another man's suffering is not an inert affect to which I surrender myself, particularly not when I observe it not as a natural or empirical phenomenon, but when I make of it a question mark for my whole orientation in the moral world. It is only narrow-mindedness that could make me indifferent to suffering,

and it is only ignorance of the specific worth of man that, guided by erroneous metaphysics, degrades compassion to a reflex action. In suffering, a dazzling light suddenly makes me see the dark spots in the sun of life. Even though insight into the ground of suffering may remain forever hidden to me, it is not a theoretical interest that is aroused in me through this observation. It is the whole meaning of ethics, as the teaching of man and his worth, of which I have to despair, if this, man's worth, is primarily expressed in suffering. The whole meaning of humanity in that case would become untenable to me, to say nothing of whether I could still take any interest at all in my own existence.

This insight into suffering puts before us the most difficult alternative that faces ethics, and therefore also puts compassion on a summit, which opens the vista for its affirmation. However, if interest in suffering and compassion now is recognized as an ethical interest distinct from a theoretical explanation of the world, and therefore distinct also from all alleged metaphysics, then the questions arise: What does ethical practice gain? Of what method can it take possession in order to solve this fundamental riddle of ethics? The concept of man seems to have reached its limit at this point, unless this limit is pushed back and the concept of man is supplied with a new extension. Thus we touch here upon the *borderline at which religion arises*, and at which it illuminates the human horizon with suffering.

11. If now, however, through suffering and compassion, the Thou in man is discovered, then the I may reappear liberated from the shadow of selfishness. Furthermore, even one's own suffering need not now be accepted with plain indifference. To have compassion with one's own suffering does not have to be simply inert and fruitless sentimentality. Corporeality belongs, as matters stand, to the soul of the individual and the soul is neglected when the affliction of the body is neglected. Humanity requires consideration for one's own suffering.

With the suffering of the I, other injuries besides those of the imperfection of the senses also come to light. Moral frailty now needs renewed examination, and it is superficial for, and damaging to, morality, if a correspondence is assumed between wickedness and *ill fortune,* or even between virtue and well-being. If the question of the cause of ill fortune should not be a theoretical question for ethics, much less can the question of the origin of evil become a theoretical problem. For then this theoretical interest would immediately address the question to my fellowman, whom I would have to make into a carrier of evil, and, thus, the barely discovered Thou would at once be lost again. However, this study of evil would unavoidably have to seek out and examine the majority of men.

If, however, I discover my own I through the Thou, I may study this delicate question in terms of myself and spare my fellowman from my possible self-righteousness. If, then, religion has its deepest basis in man's self-knowledge, then Ezekiel stands immediately beside Socrates. As the latter through self-knowledge theorectically established man and, with him, ethics as well, so Ezekiel established religion in man's self-knowledge of his sin.

The discovery of man through *sin* is the source from which every religious development flows. This knowledge is conceived as self-knowledge. *Hence religion separates itself from mythology,* in which man is not yet the originator of his own sin but merely the heir of his ancestors and their guilt. With the statement "the soul sins," the person is founded in this soul who in self-knowledge of his sin lays the foundation for the self-origination of his morality. It is, however, a long road from sin to virtue, and this long road that man must travel lies between religion and ethics. His spiritual guide on this road is *the other concept which, besides that of man, is characteristic of religion.*

12. Is *God* actually characteristic of religion? Did not rather every ethics, modern and ancient, more or less openly make use of God for its foundation? And if even our own *Ethics of Pure Will* elevated the idea of God to its keystone, how is it still possible to think of God as the property of religion?

Let us remain with our own ethics, which, more definitely than any previous one, adopts the idea of God into the content of ethical teachings. Yet the meaning of the idea of God in this ethics wholly corresponds to the concept of man in general. Just as man there signifies humanity, so God permits the completion of the doctrine of humanity only. As man in ethics is merely an example of humanity, so God is only the guarantor of humanity. Humanity is the subject of universal morality. According to ethics, the individual man is able to fulfill the demands of morality only in the image of humanity and, therefore, only within ethics' own competence, namely, in *the autonomous law of its reason.* The latter is not responsible for anything that happens beyond its borders and basically, therefore, is not interested in the outward success or failure of moral duty. Yet here, too, religion objects to this fiction of indifference.

It must not be a matter of indifference whether my morality and all men's morality remains dutiful striving only, sufficient in itself; rather, I have to take an interest in the question of whether the *ideal* has life and actuality. Even though this identity can only be achieved in the approximation to the ideal, the inexorable goal of the approximation is the permeation of actuality with the ideal. However, this proper goal of ethics has to recede in face of the scientific rigor of ethics, because of which it has to maintain the separation of actuality from the ideal, and generally between idea and actuality. This rigor brings about the illusion that ethics deals only with law and rule, but never with human actuality.

13. Religion opposes this kind of "rotten reasoning," and thereby establishes its own worth. The God of whom religion teaches means nothing else but the repeal of this prejudice of ethical rigor. Plato once says in passing, although in the *Theatetus*, that evil can never cease, for it has to remain in opposition to the good. This idea separates Judaism from paganism, even from the paganism in Platonism. If the prophet, in opposition to Parsiism, makes God also the creator of evil, *this evil is rather the ill*, which men usually identify with evil. The prophet, however, intends to teach that God can be the creator only of perfection, which is expressed and signified by *peace*.

Hence, it is understandable that monotheism reaches its summit in Messianism. *Messianism,* however, means the dominion of the good on earth. One daily encounters the opinion that the Messiah could come only when injustice ceases. However, this is exactly the meaning of the Messiah: that injustice will cease. This view, which even Plato did not have, is the new teaching that the one God brings to messianic humanity. Morality will be established in the human world. Against this confidence, no skepticism, no pessimism, no mysticism, no metaphysics, no experience of the world, no knowledge of men, no tragedy, and no comedy can prevail. The distinction between ideal and actuality must not be transferred to the realm of the shadows and receive this kind of eternalization; it will be buried by the Messiah. The virtue of men will still have to tread new ways of unsuspected steepness, but a level of morality will be attained, which will secure the course of human morality.

14. We have depicted the messianic God as the God of ethics, but in the interest of historical clarification we must add that in our *Ethics of Pure Will* this messianic God appears only as the God of ethics. Just as scientific ethics must use all its literary sources correctly, so have we transplanted this God from the religion of monotheism into ethics. And yet this God, derived from religion, is an ethical God merely in virtue of the connection that exists between monotheism and morality; he is not yet the God of religion proper. The apex of monotheism is Messianism, but its center of gravity

lies in the relation between God and the individual. At this point Ezekiel deviates from the mainstream of Messianism, insofar as he ceases to look at the world and turns to an inward look into the individual.

Ezekiel transmitted to religion the God of the individual man. Now the question of the Thou and the I can be raised anew. If it at first appeared dangerous to morality that the Thou be under the sign of sin, then the real image of sin, the mirror as a means of self-knowledge, has now been formed. In myself, I have to study sin, and through sin I must learn to know myself. Whether other men sin has to be of less interest to me than that I learn to realize how I myself in my innermost being am afflicted by sin, and instead of all sentimentality about my suffering, I should rather become sensitive to my moral frailty.

15. *The connection between sin and suffering,* which mythology discovers as its deepest mystery, may now become in some way intelligible to me. Now it does not do any harm when I detect moral deficiency in the tragic suffering of men, in the hero on the stage or in man on the world stage; for now I myself have become the true archetype of human frailty. Now I would not slip into the unfortunate idea, which would dull my compassion irreparably, that the Thou suffers for his sins; now I am permeated by the thought that I do not know any man's wickedness as deeply, as clearly, as my own. And if suffering is a payment for sin, I would wish to test this only in myself.

However, the God of religion is never a theoretical concept only, never a concept which merely should enlarge and enlighten man's knowledge and understanding. Hence, also, the knowledge of one's own sin and, through it, of oneself is for the sake of improvement, of paving the way to God. *God is not a concept of fate;* he does not have to reveal where suffering comes from. And as little has he to reveal where sin comes from. The legend of the Fall originated in Persia. The one God, therefore, cannot be responsible for the relation between life and guilt, let alone for a parity between them as measured by human standards. We shall have to recognize the depth of the monotheistic teaching of God in this high point of its view that all measuring and comparing of the inner *dignity* of man with the outward appearance of his earthly lot is futile and meaningless, shortsighted and deluded. The old question of why it goes badly for the good and well for the bad will receive an answer, of which even the Platonic wisdom had no inkling.

16. The prophets were not philosophers, but they were politicians,

and in politics they were more consistent idealists than Plato himself. In politics, they were, with all their patriotism, messianic world citizens. Their own state was for them merely a stepping-stone to the federation of mankind.

They recognized another problem in the state besides the international one; they recognized that the distinction between poor and rich presented the greatest danger to the equilibrium of the state. *The poor became for them the symbol of human suffering.* If their messianic God is to annul suffering by establishing morality on earth, he has therefore to become lord over poverty, the root of human suffering. Thus, their God becomes the God of the poor.[2] The social insight of the prophets recognizes in the poor the symptomatic sign of the sickness of the state. *Thus, their practical view is diverted from any eschatology of the mysteries.* They do not view death as suffering; death can offer no magic mysticism to them. Their view is concerned with men in the economic stream of the state and with its seemingly deep-rooted poverty, which manifests for the prophets the root of social suffering, the only one that can be redressed and therefore the only one worthy of notice.

17. If, then, it is the case that it is the prophetic religion which, just as it discovered man in the suffering of poverty, also discovered the unique God as the unique advocate of the poor, as the unique helper of all ranks of men, then through this peculiar realization of morality, *religion itself becomes a peculiar branch within the moral teaching.* Furthermore, it will have to be examined whether this peculiarity is due only to historical contingency or whether the concept of religion, the concept of monotheism, attests itself in this discovery, so that it has to be acknowledged as a necessary consequence of the concept of religion. The religion of the unique God had to let this ray of hope rise up for men out of the tribulations of social misery, out of the innermost contradictions of political justice. Ethics remains unchanged in its basic theoretical value, according to which its method has to guide the determination of human worth; but religion has discovered objective insights and derived them from its own principles of the concept of God and the concept of man, which remained closed to the method of ethics. These objective insights establish the peculiarity of religion, which is the more undisputed as the application of these religious concepts adapts itself to the general method of ethics.

C. THE SOURCES OF JUDAISM

1. We have now obtained a preliminary articulation of reason and religion; we turn now to the *sources of Judaism,* out of which the religion of reason should be derived. We ought not to begin with the concept of Judaism, for the latter should be demonstrated as the religion of reason. Through this demonstration, which this book has to give, the concept of Judaism will come to be determined. If we wished to begin with the concept of Judaism, we would still have to anticipate its sources. Rather, we have to start with the general methodological meaning of these sources.

Basically, even in the sources the whole concept of Judaism is anticipated. For from the sources emerges everything that comes to light as Judaism. There is, however, good methodological reason for separating institutions and monuments, on the one hand, from literary sources, on the other. Only the latter bring to light the content of monuments, so that they come to be properly understood only through the written sources.

The literary sources are the immediate manifestation of the spirit, which in other monuments works through more remote means. The literary sources are the true sources for the workings of the spirit, of a national spirit, which strives to produce something of its own and of primary origin. The sources designate the primary origin and the only thing of primary origin is the national spirit, which in turn becomes the prime ground for the individual.

2. The literature of the Jews, as primary in its origin as it is, is a national literature. This characteristic of a primary origin has been and remains the common feature of Jewish literature; to the extent to which the primary origin is preserved, to that extent the national character of Jewish literature is preserved. Its primary origin, however, consists in, and is rooted in, the idea of the unique God. The words "Hear, O Israel" and "the Eternal is Unique" complement each other. The spirit of Israel is determined by the idea of the unique God. Everything that comes forth from the spirit of Israel comes forth just as much from the unique God as it does from the national spirit in its primary origin and peculiarity.

However, the productions of this basic idea are manifold; they traverse a long history. Even the first beginnings do not lack a great and seemingly contradictory variety.

It is characteristic that Deuteronomy refers to the "statutes and ordinances" for the value of its new teaching. Moral forms of legality are spoken of as products of the new religion. Thus, there arises *a con-*

nection between religion and social politics. For the "statutes and ordinances" through which the "wisdom" of this people, as well as God's guidance, are to be proven are forms of legality in which social and individual morality are to be established and strengthened. Deuteronomy assumes a reciprocal action between religious theory and ethical practice. Through this the religious sources extend over the institutions of the state. This connection between theory and practice remains decisive for Judaism and therefore for its literary sources as well.

The entire Pentateuch uniformly has this twofold characteristic. It teaches not only the knowledge of God and man but also the care and encouragement of this knowledge. It is therefore a source both for the productions of the mind, which the national spirit creates, as well as for its practical creations. The "teachings" (תורות) appear in Deuteronomy later than the "statutes and ordinances" (חקים ומשפטים).

3. The scope of the sources, however, is even broader in the whole Old Testament. The national literature begins with the national *history* and with the myths and sagas that surround it. This history gradually changes into *politics.* This process of change is accomplished through the ideas of the prophets, and for this change, also, Deuteronomy is an instructive document. In it Moses, in his speech, traces the early history, in order to expound its application to future politics. Politics seems *to be properly native* to the ideas of the prophets. Solon, too, has been called a prophet, but even he lacks the degree of primary origin that distinguishes prophetic naiveté. Prophecy is the spiritual focus of Jewish creativity. Its root lies buried in history, in national history, with its native ethics, and this root still gives to the stem, the higher it grows, its life-giving sap. What is the distinguishing characteristic of the prophetic idea? It is the notion that religion and politics are inseparable. Politics is for religion a lifeline that has to die when politics ceases. And what becomes of it then?

4. Other powers of a genuine national spirit are also alive in Judaism. The *lyric,* which is the root of poetry, is also a Jewish national source. *Thus, the psalms grow out of prophecy.* Again, another peculiarity of the Jewish spirit is the unity of the spirit of the people with its creation, namely, with religion. The psalms have been compared with the *Babylonian* psalms. The comparison holds true for the external form of the triumphal song and for the hymn to gods and heroes. However, the kinship of the psalms to prophecy is lacking there, and no loftiness of poetic soaring is able to replace the lack

of this unity; otherwise, it would be possible to call the songs of Pindar psalms. It is no accident that parts of the prophetical writings could have wandered over into the psalms, and vice versa.

Though the psalm becomes *epigrammatic* poetry, it does not contract and ossify into prose; Koheleth soars up to the Song of Songs, and the Proverbs deepen into Job. Thus, with the exception of the drama, the whole range of poetic forms is here the literary source, and the reason for the omission of drama now becomes intelligible. Prophecy exhausted and surpassed all tragedy, albeit not its specific form. The practical aspect of prophecy absorbed the form of this art.

Perhaps the greatest riddle in these religious sources is their duality. In all other traditions there is only one origin, only one kind of source. Israel is an exception even in this, and this exception continues without interruption to bring forth new exceptions. The prophets already are independent bearers of the tradition, next to Moses, who lived long before them, in deep obscurity, so that they have to lift the veil of myth from him. And after the prophets, the writers of the Hagiographa become an independent source. How singular, how instructive is this characteristic, which the national literature stamped upon its holy writings. However, the marvel becomes even greater.

5. The Canon had not yet been established, when already new carriers of the old world appeared. Their name, "scribes" (סופרים), is the more peculiar as it carries in it a historical contradiction. For these "scribes" were much rather speakers, as of old only the prophets and the singers were. When the Canon fixed and closed the written teaching, there had long since existed an "oral teaching," which grew out of the national spirit and which was held in no less regard. It was not the caste spirit of those learned in the writings who wished to measure themselves against the authority of the Bible, but it was the original force of the national spirit, which was aware of its own naturalness, which recognized its right even with regard to the original written teaching. It was this national spirit, which intended to, and had to, carry through the homogeneous development of the original teaching. The Torah would have had only temporal value if this continuation had not been recognized as the continuous development of the fundamental national spirit.

Thus, the *Talmud* and the *Midrash* become sources of Judaism as valid as the Bible in its manifold parts. One should not take offense at the manifold content of the Talmud; the "statutes and ordinances" are the original documents of the Torah.

The natural strength that brought forth the Talmud shows itself in the fact that the Talmud originated in Babylon as well as in the motherland. The people were not content with the lively communication that was continuously maintained between the scholars of Babylon and those of Palestine; thus originated the *Babylonian Talmud* and the *Palestinian Talmud,* though the latter was less voluminous. Hence, two great creations grew up as "oral teaching," and even with the loss of the ancestral home the national spirit did not feel itself paralyzed; on foreign soil, too, there bloomed, with the same national strength, the ancient spirit of the "statutes and ordinances," in which the oral teachings were rooted.

6. The duality of this undivided national spirit also presented itself in another way. Already in Deuteronomy it is generally not understood how the prophetic spirit could cling to national customs. Particularly in the case of sacrifice, this ambiguity seems offensive. Although one can usually understand national and political adaptation to local conditions, one is inclined, on the contrary, to demand of the prophets that they be pure angels of their doctrine. Even Jeremiah, radical as he is, is not entirely free from the one-sidedness of patriotism. Ezekiel, however, was a great master of political practice. After the state had been irretrievably lost, Ezekiel wanted to save the people in the *congregation* (קהל), and in order to rally the congregation he needed the sanctuary and therefore also the sacrificial cult. He anticipates the future politics of Ezra and Nehemiah.

Therefore, one should not be surprised that Deuteronomy does not abolish sacrifice, though it urges the inmost purity of intention. One should think that henceforth the main emphasis was firmly placed on the religion of the heart, since through Ezekiel, particularly, repentance became the inward substitute for sacrifice.

7. Just as, however, piety for sacred institutions created no schism in the prophetic teaching, so also were poetry and prose preserved in all the sources and through the whole history of Judaism in harmony with religious fertility. This duality is established by the unity of *Halachah* and *Haggadah* in both Talmuds and in all forms of Midrash.

The Halachah is the "law" as it is called in Deuteronomy. The law originally was civil law and state law. The law, however, included sacrificial law, and the latter in turn included the whole sphere of the ceremonial law, in which the dietary laws are prominent. The Halachah is concerned in the first place with the civil code, as it grew out of the Pentateuch; and, in connection with Roman and Byzantine law, the Talmud established a legal system for the protection of property.

Law is directly connected with logic, and, therefore, it was jurisprudence especially which discovered and developed the *rules* that guide and control the deduction of legal cases from legal principles. Practical application, therefore, also introduced *logical theory* into the sources of Judaism.

However, already in Deuteronomy the statutes and ordinances have a definitely moral character. Just as the prophets begin with the statutes and ordinances, and as poetry arises out of prophetic teaching, so does this fusion continue its development in the oral teaching. The Midrash is not only halachic Midrash but preeminently Haggadah. Moreover, the Talmud does not only discuss Halachah; rather, sermons with an edifying devotion suddenly intrude themselves into the midst of legal discussions. It is characteristic of this duality that it does not put two separated styles side by side, but that these grow as two branches of the same tree. The Halachah is hardly thought of as a special subject next to the Haggadah, and in no way can the Haggadah be considered separate or of less value than the Halachah. The logic which the Halachah employed for jurisprudence became the sole source of legitimation, covering all interpretations of the Haggadah, including the play of wit. In this unity the "oral tradition" had to prove itself. It is spontaneous, as the "fruit of the lips," whereas the written tradition is stamped on brazen tablets.

8. There is another characteristic of the "oral teaching"; it is not an immediately finished product, but an open one, one that always continues to be produced. The book is closed; the mouth, however, remains open; for the sake of the national spirit it may not become silent. The "oral teaching" bears the stamp of lasting national productivity.[3]

Out of this national feeling arose a term that otherwise would seem paradoxical: revelation took place not only in the Torah on Sinai, but also in the Halachah which was revealed to "Moses from Sinai" (הלכה למשה מסיני). This continuation of revelation seems perfectly natural. There is no arrogance in this assertion of the scribes (such an opinion is based on a lack of historical information); it is rather the outflow of a critical self-consciousness with regard to the written law. The original critical feeling of Deuteronomy, that "the Torah is not in heaven but in your heart," remains alive in this thought and in the courage and clearness of this assertion. The national spirit is not dead, and it is not localized in Palestine. The testament of Rabbi Jochanan ben Zaccai became the journeyman's book of the Jewish people: where the Talmud is taught, there the Torah is alive. It should not remain merely the written Torah: it is in your heart, in your mouth; hence it had to become the oral teaching.

This oral teaching had to become as fully valued a source of

Judaism as the Bible, and in all its stylistic forms, the oral teaching had to retain its full value as a source.[4] Both are supported by the *one* logic, by the same methodological deduction.

9. One misunderstands the talmudic exegesis of the Bible if one wishes to understand it merely on the basis of this formal logical deduction. The opposite is the case. First, the thought is thought, whether it occurs in the Haggadah as a moral thought in the imaginative style of poetry or in the Halachah as a law for which, as for all other thoughts, one will subsequently find the sanction in the Bible.

Through this psychological form of thought, the claim of the oral teaching becomes all the more understandable. Otherwise, it would be almost inconceivable that the memory of the talmudic scholar could find in the great treasure of biblical words and its sentence structure the analogy exactly appropriate to the case at hand. The opposite case makes it conceivable. As much as the problem is alive, so is the word. The written teaching itself becomes an oral one. Logic confers seriousness upon the imagination, because the imagination is sustained and supported by the stern objectivity of a problem.

10. However, the sources are in no way exhausted by the two Talmuds and the many collections of the Midrashim. At all points at which Judaism came in contact with other peoples it absorbed influences from them, even in religion itself. It was this way in Persia, it repeated itself in Alexandria, and it occurred with particular fruitfulness in the Arabic Middle Ages. In Alexandria the relation of Judaism to Greek philosophy was already established; the latter was also received by Islam, and thus the relation between the Jewish religion and Greek philosophy was strengthened.

The dialogue with philosophy bore fruit in two directions. First, the Jews participated, by right, in philosophy itself, and books originated that made philosophy most important even in their titles. Besides, philosophy grew into religious inquiry itself. Already the Mishnah, in the "Sayings of the Fathers," and also the Midrash have recognizable traces of this. Now, however, the independent science of the exegesis of the Bible and the Talmud establishes itself. Often the same authors are devoted to independent philosophy and to Bible exegetics. Thus philosophy is unintentionally brought into religious literature, *and the whole wide sphere of Bible exegetics becomes a source of Judaism.*

11. The claim to be a source is now all the more befitting to independent philosophic work, since the latter is the native soil of

exegetics. As in all monotheistic religions, in Jewish thought, also, a vehement conflict is kindled on the border of religion and philosophy, a conflict that can never be entirely extinguished. Maimonides is the focal point of these unceasing agitations. However, his predecessors as well as his successors are no less genuine and productive sources of living Judaism. They produced the popular devotional and educational literature. The title *"Books of Discipline,"* under which these moral teachings are collected, stresses the practical character of these writings and makes their value as sources of religion indubitable.

12. The area of the sources becomes ever greater, and it is not yet exhausted. For a large sphere of religious poetry enlarges the old liturgy with constantly new additions of poetry, which are received by the yearning prayer into its own cycle. These new poetic compositions even became historical sources, for they depict in lamentations the persecutions that marked the Jewish Middle Ages up to modern times. The name which is attached to them, "prayers for forgiveness" (סליחות) , bears witness to their religious character. The history of the Jews grows more and more into the history of Judaism. "Sufferance is the badge of all our tribe." With this sentence Shakespeare uttered a historical judgment.

However, we may also use this sentence for the history of religion. In the liturgical poetry of the Middle Ages, which is a continuation of the psalms, some seed for a new fertilization of religious thoughts and feelings may be contained. Again, the greatest of these poets, Yehudah Halevi, was perhaps an independent philosopher, and perhaps even greater as a religious thinker as well as a philosopher was Solomon Ibn Gabirol, who since the thirteenth century was temporarily veiled as an Arab, under the mutilated name of Avicebron. In this case, also, religious practice merges in a living way with religious and philosophic speculation.

13. Thus, we now come to a more precise comprehension of the concept of *Judaism*, which the title of this book contains. Judaism means religion. Yet, as much as this religion, as messianic religion, from its very outset intends to be the world religion, it has nonetheless been, and remains everywhere, and during the whole time of its development, the uniform expression of the Jewish *national spirit*, and this, in spite of all the influences of which it partook. This religious productivity bears witness to the national spirit. The concept of this national spirit is therefore not based on a racial unity, but, objectively, on the uniformity of this religious literature. The

religious literature is the most significant source of the Jewish national spirit.

Whatever the Jews have accomplished in the course of history in trade and commerce, in all the branches of earning a livelihood, in the sciences and arts, surely the religious spirit has stamped upon all this, upon all their cultural achievements, its characteristic, but this characteristic is not unambiguous. In all these achievements, culture in general has as great a share as the Jewish religion itself. The meaning of Jewish nationality is determined by religious Judaism. The latter is the only Judaism, and the religious sources the only life sources of Judaism.

This idea establishes also the *uniformity* of the history of Judaism. Deep inner struggles, to be sure, mark the history of Jewish religion, making its unity questionable. We have already encountered the conflict between the prophets and the priestly religion. In present-day biblical studies, the opposition between prophetic religion and law is considered unbridgeable. We now disregard the question already touched upon, whether the opposition of principles must also be opposition in the consciousness of the persons. The opposition of the principles of intellectualism and mysticism offers at this point an analogy, which shows that in the most profound representatives of mysticism this opposition came to a most fruitful solution. We would like at this point, however, to profit from the ambiguity, which usually affects a *national* religon, in order to clarify the religion of Judaism with regard to its uniformity.

Among our own contemporaries the problem of a unified Judaism is the main difficulty in respect to practical politics also. The uniformity seems to be almost as much a miracle *(Wunder)* as the continuance of the Jews and their religion. How can this miracle be explained?

14. The magic word, which contains the watchword, also contains the solution of this riddle. What the "Hear, O Israel: the Eternal our God, the Eternal is unique" means for the inner life and continuance of the Jews, this, one may say, is entirely misunderstood outside of Judaism. Biblical studies therefore try to change the translation. Out of "unique" they want to make "only one," in order to explain away the historic-systematic strength of the passage and to deprive it of the weighty character which it indubitably carries in the context of Scripture as an introduction to the idea of the love of God. The emphatic expression "Hear, O Israel" also has the meaning of a historical formula. This formula is the rallying idea, the unifying concept of Judaism. One may believe

as much as one wishes in the letter of the sacrificial and ceremonial law; the unity of God elevates belief to such a speculative height that by comparison all other problems become secondary, even if one treats them as questions of main importance by bestowing upon them objective and historical motives. Moreover, on the other hand, he who takes offense at the many accessories that surround the core of the Jewish religion will find that as soon as the call "Hear, O Israel" comes alive in him, all skepticism is silenced, and the unity of God strengthens the unity of religious consciousness.

Judaism is a unifying concept not only for the unity of the people but also for the unity of religion. This unity proves itself in the same way in the concept of the unique God as in the concept of man who himself is unique among all the beings of nature. Thus, we arrive at another consequence, which is to be derived from the concepts united in the title of this book.

15. Usually a distinction is made between religion and morality, not only between religion and ethics. Ethics originated in Greek philosophy and has been preserved in systematic philosophy. Only by analogy can this concept be used outside philosophy. There-fore, in this book we have already anticipated our method, according to which the religion of reason attains and preserves its own peculiar task, insofar as it acknowledges and verifies for its own method the autonomy of ethics.

With regard to religion the autonomy of ethics consists in the lay-ing down of first principles for its own concepts. These first prin-ciples, however, separate themselves into a system, and have no effect beyond it. Thus, we have recognized humanity and the in-dividual as the limits of ethics, at which point religion establishes its own foundations. In the concept of the individual, the ethical concept of man is incorporated into religion.

If, however, this incorporation of man into the religion of reason is a consequence of the sources of Judaism, then the religion of rea-son cannot recognize a distinction in content between religion and morals, between Jewish religion and Jewish morals, with the excep-tion of the methodological distinction between ethics and religion. The concept of man belongs to the Jewish religion, and for the content of this concept it does not concede any supremacy to ethics, except for recognizing its systematic method.

In the same way, the concept of the unique God belongs to Jewish moral teaching. Jewish sources make it unmistakably clear that it was in teaching about man, not only about man as an in-dividual but also about nations and mankind, that the idea of the unique God came to be discovered. All the particulars in the wide variety of "statutes and ordinances," every moral regulation, every moral precept, every moral institution, all are rooted in the "Hear, O Israel."⁵ *There is no distinction in the Jewish consciousness between religion and morals.* Only where pantheism undermines the modern subconsciousness is skepticism with regard to the so-called existence of God entertained, and one then tries to recover at least moral teachings from an insolvent Judaism. This recovery is not even sufficient for the popular mind; for the latter, also is affected by the pantheistic sickness through monism and the poetry of nature. Only pantheism is responsible for the fact that religion has crept into hiding behind moral teaching.

Religion itself is moral teaching or it is not religion, and moral teaching is autonomous only as philosophical ethics. This autonomy, however, is not impaired by the borrowings from history, which ethics has to make from religion for its concepts of God and man, as it has had to borrow from all other factors of history and science. Only *one* condition is attached to this assimilation of religious insights to ethics: the original communion, which is designated as reason, by virtue of which religion is characterized as the religion of reason.

How could religion be the religion of reason, if at the same time it were not moral teaching? In this identity of religion and morality, the religion of reason also proves itself subjectively to be Judaism, the uniform production of the Jewish people, the people who attest themselves as one people through this uniformity of religious production. From the unique God, the view of Judaism is directed to one mankind, and in the same way to each individual man in his own uniqueness. This point of view determines the originality and peculiarity of the Jewish spirit.

It is claimed that for this Jewish spirit only God exists and not the world. This saying might at most be valid with regard to the indifferent world of nature, but never for man. Only an alien pattern, innocently taken into Judaism from malicious polemics, can erect an opposition between God and man, between religion and morality in Judaism. The well-known saying of the prophet speaks against it: "It has been told thee, O man, what is good" (Micah 6:8). Thus, with regard to the problem of the good, God and man come into a necessary community. God has to proclaim the good and proclaim it to man. Does he have anything else to say at all? And is there any other being to whom he has anything to say? Reason with its principle of the good unites God and man, religion and morality.

16. Thus, the principle of reason has led us to the unity of religion and morality, and if the sources of Judaism unveil the religion of reason, then, in addition, this concept of reason will also grant to the Jewish religion its true unity. All considerations of a material character, however much one tries to transfigure them, remain material, so long as they are tied up with consanguinity. They not only make it difficult to understand spiritual analogies, which are found *among other* blood lineages, but also make them suspect. If, however, reason is the guiding principle, then a safe standard is achieved, which not only delineates the peculiarity of a certain religion but also rallies and secures the community of the spirit at large. In this community the peculiarity of a certain religion does not become a barrier which excludes the possibility of other religions. Insofar as they attest themselves as religions of reason on the basis of their sources, they prove their religious legitimacy. The sovereign concept of reason opens the possibility that many religions may be collected under it.

The *philosophy of religion* has scientific truthfulness only when it strives objectively and impartially to refer to its sources, to excavate them through its own research, and to illuminate them through its own criticism. I know myself to be free from the prejudice of all shades of Christian theology and Christian philosophy of religion, insofar as they proclaim the *absoluteness* of Christianity; I do not assert that Judaism alone is the religion of reason. I try to understand how other monotheistic religions also have their fruitful share in the religion of reason, although in regard to *primary origin* this share cannot be compared with that of Judaism. This primary origin constitutes the priority of Judaism, and this priority also holds for its share in the religion of reason. For the primary origin is the distinctive mark of creative reason, which makes itself independent of all other charms of consciousness, and which produces a pure pattern. Primary origin bears the marks of purity. And *purity* in creativity is the characteristic of reason.

CHAPTER I

God's Uniqueness

1. It is God's uniqueness, rather than his oneness, that we posit as the essential content of monotheism. Oneness signifies only an opposition to the plurality of gods. It is questionable whether this idea was the primary idea of monotheism, whether it by itself was capable of prevailing against polytheism. For in polytheism the point in question is not only the gods and their plurality but also their relation to the cosmos and its vast natural powers, in all of which a god first appeared. Therefore, if monotheism opposed polytheism, it also had to change God's relation to the universe in accordance with its new idea of God. From the point of view of the new notion of God, therefore, one cannot rest satisfied with the distinction between one God and many gods; rather, the oneness of God has also to be extended over nature, which manifests itself in many forces and phenomena.

Thus, from the very outset the concept of God's oneness involves a relation to nature. This oneness immediately acquires a significance that takes it beyond the opposition to plurality and elevates it even beyond mere opposition to the notion of *composition*. The notion of composition contains a relation to nature; therefore, with regard to nature also, the meaning of the oneness of God must ward off the notion of composition.

2. At this gateway to religion the biblical sources pose a methodological difficulty for us. It would seem that the thought of the oneness of God would alone unlock the gateway not to religion but rather to philosophy and metaphysics, especially if that oneness signified uniqueness. What does uniqueness mean in relation to the universe? And the uniqueness of God has to be thought of in relation to the universe, since the oneness of God would suffice with respect to the plurality of gods. The uniqueness of God is therefore in opposition to the universe. What does this opposition mean?

35

The problem of philosophy arises as soon as one begins to think of a relation to the world. Religion is not philosophy. However, the religion of reason, by virtue of its share in reason, has at least some kinship with philosophy. It is therefore not surprising that this share in reason, akin to that of philosophy, begins to stir within religion, starting, it would seem, with its concept of God.

3. All objections against this idea do not originate in historical methodology that has to entertain complicated motivations of reason, even in its most primitive stages, in order to explain the basic concepts of human culture. The monotheistic principle possesses such a depth of culture that it is easily understood that all the problems of the natural world and its analogue, the moral world, were already present in its origins. Where and in what this origin of monotheism lies cannot be summarized into a formula of one concept, both because indeed God and the world always belong together and because the primeval theme of God cannot be determined without the primordial theme of nature.

Do not all spiritual creations contain in themselves the insoluble riddle of their origin? Supposedly one has to search for the conditions that prepare or make possible the historical appearance of these creations. One has to seek out the general historical conditions that further spiritual development. But even if the general historical atmosphere is illuminated, in the last analysis the spiritual impulse with which the spiritual movement in question begins, in such a way that it must recognize its origin in this impulse, will have to remain unexplained.

4. If it is true to say of the individual artist that it is his individuality alone that is the ultimate foundation for the intrinsic order of lawfulness his work exhibits, and if, with certain reservations, the genius at work in the production holds sway in every spiritual creation, then this secret of the spirit grows more mysterious in the case of the *national spirit.* Monotheism is not the thought of one man, but of the whole Jewish national spirit unfolding in the creation and development of this thought which impregnates the entire thinking of the people. One would have to be able to gather into one primeval word the whole history of this people if one were to attempt to formulate the primeval motive out of which monotheism originated.

The historical and political conditions do not offer a basis for sufficient elucidation either; they constitute the spiritual mystery of the people's character. However, the people have to have some relationship with other peoples, just as the one God does to the many gods. This necessary supposition is confirmed by the tradition itself;

tradition does not question the existence of an original polytheism. The further development of polytheism leads to its self-dissolution in monotheism. The historical conditions could be summarized by one many-sided moment of historical experience: the people were originally inhabitants of Canaan, then emigrated to Egypt, and from there wandered back to the motherland.

Monotheism, therefore, comes to be not as a creation out of nothing but has its precondition in polytheism, which in Canaan was Israel's religion also. A further precondition is the emigration to Egypt, where the new seed of monotheism could have been conceived and nourished. And the political strength the people acquired to migrate back to their ancestral mother country could have had its germinating vigor in the new religious motivation of monotheism, so that both elements can be explained, one through the other: the wandering back and the origin of the new God.

These historical elements, however, are no more than preconditions lacking as yet the positive element for the new God, who originated in relation not only to the multiple gods but to nature as well. We must provisionally consider the possibility that the sources in their naiveté perhaps veil this original speculative relationship. We shall therefore have to attempt to give a preliminary orientation regarding the problem of the relation of the sources to their content.

5. It is already striking that Judaism presents its chief sources in *literary* documents, whereas polytheism possesses them above all in monuments of *plastic* art. Plastic art turns itself into an analogy of nature. The form of poetry, the original language of literature, however, can make thought more spiritually inward than plastic art. And Hebrew poetry limits itself to *epics* and *lyrics*. *Rhetoric,* instead of the drama, appears on the border of poetry and makes use particularly of the epic form.

This originally epic form of monotheistic thought explains the *naiveté* in the style of the Bible. This naiveté, moreover, embraces the innermost content of the thoughts expressed as well as the account and the redaction of the origins of national history. This redaction of the ancient sources follows a rule that is intelligible only through the original epic form of the national spirit. The original layers of thought are not covered up or smoothed over, much less eliminated, but another layer is superimposed upon them in such a manner that the lower layer can still be seen through the upper layer.

Owing to this peculiar style, the understanding of the sources of the Bible and its literary criticism become entangled in great difficulties. Against every routine approach the insight must prevail that progress in religious understanding has been accomplished through the revision and reinterpretation of the sources, while these themselves remain preserved in their individual layers and have been at most rearranged or given different emphasis. We shall have to confirm this view of exegetics in tracing the different stages of the development within the monotheistic concept of God.

6. An almost insoluble riddle is already posed by the *plural* form of the name of God: *Elohim*. The routine explanation is that this name of God preserves the traces of an original polytheism, and that again and again polytheism breaks through against the new name *Yahveh*, as if there were a residue of polytheism that was not absorbed by monotheism. Contradictions and residues of duality are the usual aids of routine criticism of this sort, which, however, is unable to do justice to the problem of the style of a *national spirit* in its historical development.

If the preservation of the plural form, Elohim, seems to be a riddle, it is canceled out by an even greater riddle: that the *singular forms* of the adjective, as well as the tenses of the verb, are made to agree with this plural form. This psychological riddle is a logical monster that cannot exist. Therefore, logic here has to assist psychology. If the purport of this grammatical form is nonsensical and utterly absurd, psychology has to be taught by logic that the intention of this word in the plural form could not be plurality, but, as its connection with the singular form proves, singularity.

If this self-transformation of the plural form into a singular should still remain questionable despite the assistance of logic, then this question would be canceled by this insight: the new God was thought of as a unity, with such energy and clarity that the grammatical plural form could not impair this new content of thought. On the contrary, the preservation of the plural form testifies to the vigor of the new thought, which simply took no offense at all at the plural form. A literature that let come to be the "Hear, O Israel" could unhesitatingly let the old name survive after the reinterpretation had been secured, even without adding the new name of God.

We abstain from entering into the discussion of the Elohistic and Yahvistic sources. Yet we may indicate that from the point of view of our method the unity of both sources cannot be considered entirely out of the question. It is in no way the case that only one source is monotheistic; rather, the Elohistic source also has its complete and certain share in the striving toward pure monotheism.

7. Another name of God is also given from of old: *El Shaddai*.

With regard to the explanation of this name, we adhere to the disadvantageous position which holds that it is connected with *shed,* the general name for demons. The literary advantage of this name consists in its opposition to the new name Yahveh: "And I appeared to Abraham, Isaac and Jacob as El Shaddai, but my name Yahveh I did not disclose to them." Thus it is said (Exod. 6:3) at the summoning of Moses. There Yahveh is not only opposed to Elohim and to El but to El Shaddai. A later stage of interpretation, however, turned the Shaddai into the Almighty.

The positive idea of a creator and the negative idea of the destroyer are connected with this word throughout the biblical language, and it is characteristic of Job that he prefers to use this name of God, which designates God's primeval power. Therefore Maimonides' interpretation of this name exhibits a correct feeling for language: he starts out with the root די, which in the word expresses self-sufficiency, and at the same time he proves this self-sufficiency by stating, "that He is sufficient in himself to bring forth the world" (יש לו די להמצאת דברים זולתו).

8. Thus, even the oldest name relates God to the world, namely, as *creator.* Therefore the opinion that holds that the new name Yahveh contains this relation even more definitely is justified. Otherwise one would have to assume that the summoning of Moses and the revelation of God as Yahveh refer back to a name of God that is merely a magic name. If, however, the juxtaposition of both names properly signifies a development of the one name into the other, then this too shows that God's relation to the world is of primary origin and based on the essence of God. Thus every trace of artificial interpretation and unhistorical rationalization disappears when we assume that the share monotheism has in reason extends also to the *problem of being,* and when we try to derive this share of reason from the sources. In any case, the connection of the root of the word Yahveh with the word "being" (היה) is a philological fact. We shall have to observe how the first revelation clarifies this connection of God with being.

9. First, however, some information should be given about the general connection between the three concepts of being, unity, and God, which was also established in Greek philosophy and already realized in the philosophy of the Eleatics. Xenophanes was the first in the Eleatic tradition to establish this connection. He already conceived the cosmos under the concept of being. He was not brought to the idea of the unity of nature by the presupposition of some kind of matter and its transformation, but only through a presenti-

ment of being could the idea of an ordered unity of the cosmos have
originated.

In opposition to sensible appearances, which involve only change
and motion, the being of nature had to be thought of as an object
of thought, as opposed to perception. The distinction between thought
and perception is determined by unity. One can hardly be certain
whether unity or being is the first product of thought. They belong
together, they originate in reciprocity. Without unity the cosmos
could not be thought of as being; without being the cosmos could
not be thought of as unity.

The reciprocity between being and unity is based on the efficacy
of a third concept, the concept of God, which appears, according to
Xenophanes, in unity with the other two. "With an eye on the whole
cosmos," he said, "this unity is God." Be that as it may, the philosophical concept of God also originated in connection with the
concepts of world and unity. But the difference between the philosophical and the religious concept of God soon becomes a power
in the history of the mind. For here the case is not that the cosmos
is thought of as unity, nor that God is thought as unity, but that both
entities are one. Both, however, represent being, and both make it
into *one* being. Thus, on the threshold of Greek philosophy, *pantheism* arises.

10. Within philosophy, therefore, the concept of unity makes
manifest the connection of the concepts of God and the world, viz.,
the unity of the being of the cosmos and its identity with the unity
of God. Here, too, the connection with being brought forth the notion of the one God; for the connection between being and the
cosmos had as its consequence the connection between God and
unity. But here the thought of God did not go beyond the conception of unity. Therefore this unity at once turns into the identity
of God and the world. The unity of God is therefore basically nothing else than the unity of the world, and it is only the means through
which the unity of the world was, if not discovered, at least confirmed.

The share religion acquires in reason should not be limited to this
confirmation. Pantheism is not religion. This fundamental thought
we shall have to clarify step by step. Thus, also, unity cannot be
the deepest meaning of monotheism. Unity is always only the negative expression of monotheism, designating only its distinction from
polytheism. Furthermore, it is the negative expression against pantheism, insofar as unity negatively opposes the idea of *composition*
and therefore also excludes the identity of God with the world.

Composition, however, would have been the characteristic of pantheistic thinking and would have been the characteristic of the cosmos, if God's unity had not brought about the unity of the cosmos. Thus unity, as opposed to the idea of composition, is in fact only a negative attribute. The Arabic philosophers admitted its validity in this capacity alone.

11. Uniqueness has positive meaning. It, too, gathers under its protection the concepts of being and God, but now the strict *identity* of both concepts sets in. Unity becomes identity, an advance in thought achieved by Parmenides in Greek speculation. Only God has being. Only God is being. And there is no unity that would be an identity between God and world, no unity between world and being. The world is appearance. This thought already flashes its light into the future: only God is being. There is only *one* kind of being, only one unique being: God is this unique being. God is the Unique One.

In the "Hear, O Israel" this uniqueness is designated by the word *Ehad.* In the rabbinical writings the more precise Hebrew word *Jihud* appears, as the designation of the uniqueness of God. It designates the Unique One, and through this meaning of the word the uniqueness of God is freed of the ambiguity which is connected with the word "unity." God's essence is also designated in rabbinic and religious-philosophical literature, in connection with this word, as *Jihud* (יחוד).

The word *ahduth* (אחדות), which is connected with the word *Ehad* (אחד), is also used. However, it may not be correct to say that Arabic usage was the decisive motive for its adoption. For *Jihud* does not solely or chiefly mean the subjective act, through which the self achieves unity with God by devotion to him, by acknowledging his unity, but it can also mean God's causative act of bringing about unity. *Ahduth* represents the unity as actuality, as being; *Jihud,* on the contrary, represents the function through which this unity is achieved. What is of importance for us is this thought: throughout the development of religion unity was realized as uniqueness, and this significance of the unity of God as uniqueness brought about the recognition of the uniqueness of God's being, in comparison with which all other being vanishes and becomes nothing. Only God is being.[6]

12. The difference between Jewish religion and Greek speculation, including pantheism, consists in the designation of this being as the *One Who Is Being,* in *the transformation of the neuter into a person.* This, to be sure, makes anthropomorphism unavoidable, and the de-

cline of Jewish thought into myth would have been unavoidable if
the *fight against anthropomorphism* had not proved from the very
beginning of the oral teaching to be the very soul of Jewish religious
education. It is perhaps possible to say that this fight already played
a role in the compilation of the Canon of Scripture. We do not,
therefore, at this stage of our exposition need to take offense at the
transformation of an abstraction into a person, especially since its
connection with *being* already at least diminishes the danger that is
connected with the notion of the person. God is not that which is,
nor is he only the one, but the Unique One that is.

13. Among all the wonders of style in the books of Moses, the greatest is perhaps the account of the *first* origin of monotheism. The first
revelation of this God of being occurs at the Burning Bush. The
mythical miracle of the fire that does not consume the bush merely
constitutes the backdrop for one of the first acts of world history:
the liberation of Israel from Egyptian bondage. Moses, who tended
the sheep of Jethro, his father-in-law, is called upon by God from out
of the bush. And the place where this call occurred is referred to as
holy ground. God calls himself at first "the God of thy Father, the
God of Abraham, the God of Isaac, and the God of Jacob" (Exod.
3:6). "I will send thee unto Pharaoh, that thou mayest bring forth My
people, the Israelites, out of Egypt. . . . And Moses said unto God:
Behold when I come unto the children of Israel and shall say unto
them: the God of your fathers hath sent me unto you, and they shall
say to me: what is His name? What shall I say unto them? And God
said unto Moses: 'I am that I am'" [Exod. 3: 10-14].

The falsity of Kautzsch's translation is fatal: "I am who I am." It
is scarcely intelligible, if not meaningless. The meaning of his error
is disclosed in his annotation: "There is still considerable dispute about
the original meaning of the name. It is only certain that the explanation of the name means . . . an imperfect *qual* form of the verb
hawa (an older form for *haja*) in the sense of 'He is.' In this understanding He is hardly thought of as being the 'true being' in the
philosophical sense of the word, but rather as the perpetual and un-
changing One." The admission that God here reveals himself as the
"perpetual and unchangeable One" is adequate for our "philosophical
sense." In no way do we impose our philosophical explanation upon
the text, but we undertake an explanation in order to throw light
upon the original depth of the biblical word, and in order to make
understandable the historical strength of its source. Moses asks by
what name he should name God to the Israelites, and God answers:
I am the One that is. I am the One, that can be named in no other

way than by "I am." Thereby is expressed the thought that no other being may affirm about itself this connection with *being*.

Let us continue with the text that immediately after this says: "[and God said:] Thus shalt thou say unto the children of Israel; 'I am' hath sent me unto you" [Exod. 3:14]. Thus it is not Yahveh who has sent Moses. But Moses is to name the name of God by this verb form of the first person in answering the question of the Israelites about the name of their God. In such a definite way *being* is named as that element in the name that designates the *person* of God. If this is not yet philosophy, it is certainly reason in the original sense of the word.

If the text then continues, "the Eternal, the God of your fathers, the God of Abraham, the God of Isaac, and the God of Jacob has sent me unto you," then this seems to contradict the objection Moses makes (verse 13): ". . . when I come unto the children of Israel and shall say unto them: the God of your fathers has sent me to you, and they shall ask me," etc. The text, however, says further (verse 15): "this is My name forever and this is My memorial unto all generations." The solemnity of these expressions in instituting God's name for all future times and the invocation of all future generations can only be explained by its relation to the new name of the One that is. The text, however, wants to exclude even a semblance of difference between the new name and the historical one. And the historical name in no way signifies a national God, but only the God of the fathers, who, moreover, was previously designated as "your God." Thus it becomes clear that God, as the One that is, is the God of Israel. He refers therefore to eternity and to all generations. Under this new name Moses has to awaken Israel's trust in the God of their fathers.

This is the content of the manifestation in the Burning Bush and its tremendous symbolism. The bush is not consumed. God is the One that is. The translation of God's name, Yahveh, as the Eternal One, corresponds to this basic source of God's revelation. The Eternal One designates the One that is as God, as God in distinction from the world, as the Unique One in comparison to whom the world is said to have no being. With this limitation of its sense, being here loses its philosophical meaning. However, we cannot rescue the latter by establishing an identity between the unique being that is and the being of the world.

The unique being, which is represented only by the unique God, in the first place negates the being of all other gods. "The gods of the nations are nothing" (אלהי העמים אלילים [Ps. 96:5]). This Hebrew word (אל) originates from a root that plainly means negation. The contempt that monotheism has for all kinds of polytheism is nourished by the insight that it is not only an erroneous concept that paganism assumes but a misconception that negates being. Being, however, has to be asserted, has to be understood correctly. This principle of reason guides monotheism. The plurality of gods is in contradiction to being.

In this way the Decalogue also becomes intelligible. "Thou shalt have no other gods before me." One should translate: thou shalt not take any other beings for God. The other is opposed to the Unique One. As far as true being is concerned, there is no other beside him and outside of him. Not only is there no other God, but there is no other being, beside this unique being. Isaiah does not merely say, "there is no God beside Me" (ומבלעדי אין אלהים [Isa. 44:6]); he also says, "Nothing is beside Me" (אפס בלעדי [Isa. 45:6]). Nonbeing, as nothing, is opposed to the unique being.

14. Hence the uniqueness of God consists in *incomparability.* "To whom then will you liken Me, that I should be equal?" (ואל מי תדמיוני ואשוה [Isa. 40:25]). "There is none like unto Thee" (אין כמוך [Ps. 86:8]) is not a precise translation. For it must also mean: *nothing* is like unto Thee. The incomparability points as much to nature as to every other concept of God. Therefore the question above must refer to things (אל מה) as well as to persons (אל מי).

15. Uniqueness, therefore, also entails the *distinction between being and existence.* The share of reason in monotheism is strongly confirmed in this distinction. For existence is attested by the senses, through perception. On the other hand it is reason which, against all sense-appearance, bestows actuality upon existence, discovers and elevates the nonsensible to being, and marks it out as true being.

This priority of reason in the original purity of monotheism can be seen negatively in the error that the *ontological* argument of the Middle Ages could not avoid. When this argument unites the *existence with the essence* of being, it in no way grants reason sovereignty, as it may appear, but it confuses thought and sensation, as if it were only through the recognition of sensation in its own peculiarity, in its sovereignty, that reason could achieve perfection; as if it were only sensation that grants reason its right. Thus one can grasp the argument of the *doctrine of attributes* that Islamic and Jewish monotheism raises against Christian ontology.

16. Uniqueness in this sense, therefore, is also distinguished from *simplicity,* since the latter is merely opposed to composition, which is the general characteristic of matter. This simplicity, however, is not sufficient to explain the being of God. The unique being of God is such that it does not admit any mixture, any connection with sensible ex-

istence. Ontology, which is based on this connection of being and existence, contains no safeguard against *pantheism;* indeed, pantheism bases itself on ontology and all its main representatives.

Monotheism can tolerate no such mixture, no such distortion of being by existence. In its eyes pantheism is nothing other than anthropomorphism. Moreover, all these problems disappear before the uniqueness of being. Not only does the thesis *Deus sive natura* contain a contradiction, but the ontological argument does so as well, insofar as it involves existence in essence. The unity of substance may thereby be defined, but its uniqueness is abolished. The position of monotheism leads to the consequence "Nothing is beside Me." Cosmos and nature are negated.

17. Must we not now ask: what could be the final meaning of God if he had no world, which is after all the human world? No offense should be taken at this question; a clear and satisfactory answer is required. God cannot remain without the world, without the human world. However, nature must not be set up in being together with God. Nature is subject to the limitations of space and time. These basic concepts of metaphysics also arise in the reasoning of monotheism. Space, however, cannot be a limitation of God's being. "The fullness," the whole "of the world is His glory." This is perhaps the meaning of the sentence in the vision of Isaiah (מלא כל הארץ כבודו [Isa. 6:3]). Although formerly the earth, the world was nothing; it should now contain in it the fullness, the infinitude of God's glory. The limitations of space have now fallen before the monotheistic view. Thus it becomes understandable that in the religious philosophy of the Middle Ages, as well as in the Talmud, *space* (מקום) becomes a name of God. This tendency is already recognizable in the warding off of anthropomorphism that is characteristic of even the oldest translations of the Bible.

18. There is still another expression for the godhead, which this surpassing of space makes intelligible: the *Shechinah.* The root of the word means "to lie" and "to rest." In this meaning it is generally connected with God. The use of this word as a name of God apparently is intended to describe being through rest. All change, all alteration, must be eliminated from God's being. The philosopher says: God is substance. Monotheistic religion says: God is Shechinah, absolute rest. Rest is the eternal prime cause of motion. This is also what is meant with regard to God. Motion, however, is to be excluded from his essential being. This in no way means that through the being of God motion is made impossible; rather, it is precisely through this being of rest that the being of motion becomes possible.

19. *Time,* like space, is not a limitation to the divine being. "I am the first and I am the last" (אני ראשון ואני אחרון). "I am He; I am the

first, I also am the last" (Isa. 44:6; 48:12). It is not enough to say: "I am the first and I am the last"; it is also not sufficient if one adds "and beside Me there is no other God." One also has to add: "nothing *is* beside Me." Only through this is the *eternity* of God founded on his uniqueness.

20. By being opposed to time, God's being also excludes change. "I, the eternal One, do not change" (אני ה' לא שניתי [Mal. 3:6]). This determination of reason touches upon the boundary of ethics. The unchangeableness of God follows chiefly from the meaning of being as *continuance*. Continuance, however, is also the basis and presupposition of motion. Therefore, in order to distinguish God's being from all temporal *becoming*, the negative attribute of unchangeableness is necessary. "I am that I am." Being is here determined as the being of an I, and not of a substance that becomes the basis for the motion of matter. In this distinction between unchangeableness and continuance, the *ethical* meaning of God, as the Unique One, originates. The ground for this meaning is already prepared by the exclusion from God's being of all the characteristics that constitute *matter*.

21. This general opposition to *materialism* is analogous to monotheism's rejection of the philosophy of *idealism*. Philosophical idealism is based on the idealism of nature, and it is only on this basis, which justifies the natural sciences, that the idealism of ethics is established. Judaism rejects this idealistic basis. All the enthusiasm of thinking is limited to reflection on the unique being of God. Nature is nothing in itself. If through this limitation science is lost, compensation for this loss is to be sought in the depreciation of all earthly things in view of their irrelevance with regard to the knowledge of the *good*.

Opposition to *eudaemonism* is therefore deeply rooted in monotheism. "Vanity of vanities, all is vanity," says Koheleth (Eccles. 1:2). One admires in Psalm 73 the lines: "Why should I care about the heavens? With the covenant with you I have no desire for the earth." Even without the positive completion of the sense that this verse provides, the basic idea of the unique being of God is already the confirmation of this frame of mind, of this fundamentally religious intention. There is no interest in heaven and earth: "They change, you remain." The psalmist and the prophet see in all change the symptom of annihilation, which can only be transitory. Only the One that is, is everlasting, is eternal, He cannot change.

The description of nature in Psalm 104, which Alexander von Humboldt so deeply admired, contains, along with the naiveté of its nature poetry, a primary feeling for a *sublimity that is beyond all the beauty of nature,* and maintains this mood as vigorously as it does the feeling for the sublimity of *nature.*

That this religious people, with the share its religion has in reason, should not have taken part in *science* would not be intelligible if its spirit had not been filled with this world-historical one-sidedness: there is only one unique being, and only this has to be thought through in all its foundations and consequences. Nature, however, is and remains nothing in comparison with the being of God's I. Only in this way could the metaphysics of monotheism be the origin of the unique God of ethics. Only in this way could the causality of nature be the origin of the teleology of morality.

22. Offenses against this rigid uniqueness were unavoidable, and God's unique being had to be defended against them. They were unavoidable at home, even without contact with foreign views. In Persia monotheism had to resist the doctrine of the *two* divine powers, which, to be sure, were related not only physically to *light* and *darkness* but directly to ethics, to *good* and *evil.* Monotheism had to affirm itself against this dualism. We shall see later how this affirmation was substantiated ethically; for the time being it suffices to point out that Isaiah, in opposing God to nothing, adds the following: "I form the light and create darkness; I make peace," etc. (Isa. 45:7). Peace is here coordinated to light, though one would expect it to be coordinated, instead, to the good, for immediately after this God declares himself, even according to the usual translation, to be the creator of evil. Peace, according to the Hebrew root of the word, means *perfection.*

Uniqueness stamps itself with this teleological perfection in order to strike down the thought of the *two* powers. The uniqueness of God's being exempts itself from any comparison not only to all worldliness but also to all imaginary world powers. There can as little be two equivalent kinds of being, as two governments of the world. All apparent existence is transitory, and as such, nil. It cannot have its own God, since it does not have its own true being.

23. Another contradiction arose in monotheism due to the operations of reason, and was even nourished by the Jewish spirit itself. The disdain for nature goes against Greek thought, and all mysticism, which arose there also, was unable to cripple this resistance. When the Jews in Alexandria took up, according to the talmudic image, "the beauty of Japheth into the tent of Shem," when they wanted to blend the Torah with "Greek wisdom," they took offense at the independence of nature for seeming to oppose its own being to God's being. If, however, God was to be responsible for the being of nature and, on the

other hand, the Jews were not to fall into the Persian error of the two powers in the world, they had to find in reason itself a means of putting a similar, though not equal, being of nature alongside God's being. This was the origin of the mediating being of the *Logos*.

Uniqueness excludes any *mediation* between God and natural existence. The Logos, however, must inevitably become a second God, and yet there is no first, but only the one unique God. We will forthwith and also later have to draw out the consequences that the problem of the Logos has for the uniqueness of God; at this point we wish only to emphasize the contradiction which the idea of the Logos, in all its gradations, constitutes. There is no mediating being, not to mention a mediating person, that solves the problem of the origin or of the government of the world.

There is no change in this basic error if one transfers the mediation to reason instead of being in order to explain the being of nature. Reason can acknowledge only one unique kind of being, and therefore only one unique kind of God. The unique God wards off any mediating God, or God beside God. It is even a distortion of Plato, the ethical Plato, if the beyondness of the *good* is bridged by the Logos and connected to this-worldly being. In this manner one may develop at best the *Timaeus* with its Demiurge, but not the *idea* of the *good* in the *Republic*.

24. All other ideas of God originating from the notion of the Logos are also excluded; as expressions of *"partnership"* (שׁיתוּף) they are distinguished from pure monotheism.[7] The distinction between uniqueness and unity is the foundation of the distinction between monotheism and all dualism, as well as the belief in the *trinity*. The latter has its basis, as does dualism, in the recognition of another being beside the being of God. We cannot now judge the legitimacy of this claim, particularly since it does not base itself on science but, even in the most ideal interpretation, on morality alone. However, the correct *preparation* for morality should first be acquired. This preparation depends on one fundamental idea: that nature, that man himself, has no original worth, no worth of its own. If nature and man should be able to attain any worth at all, it could only be derived from the unique worth of God's being.

The *Logos,* with all its consequences, suffers from a basically erroneous idea. It overrates the importance of *existence* with regard to nature and the human spirit. It is characteristic of this idea that Philo, the Jew, establishes by the word for "reason" this other God beside God *(Nebengott).* Moreover, if it is possible to say that the trinity has its best objective and historical basis in the *immortality* of the human soul, then the reason for the falling away from pure monotheism shows itself here also: it is an exaggerated claim that man should possess eternal and therefore true being.

25. The Jewish notion of immortality culminates in this idea: "the spirit returns to God, who gave it." Only in God's being can the being of man be founded , and therefore only when "the dust returns to the earth, from which it has been taken," only when the form of human appearances passes away. Even immortality offers no excuse in monotheism for a comparison between God's being and any spiritual being. From this point of view, too, matter remains transitory dust. All natural poetry is shattered on the rock of the insight that allots sublimity to the unique God exclusively.

An important moment already comes to the fore, which lays down the bridge between the root of monotheism and its peak formed by Messianism: *the distinction between eschatology and Messianism.* The dignity of man is not grounded merely in the individual man but in the idea of humanity. The latter, however, escapes representation in plastic art almost as much as it remains denied to God's uniqueness.

CHAPTER II

Image-Worship

1. We have already begun to consider how the share that reason has in religion led to the *transformation of knowledge into love,* and now the development of our considerations will supplement this basic element. We now proceed to this development. *Knowledge* would have been only a theoretical attitude, whereas reason, understood at this point as moral reason, as practical reason, would have to act. Love is this *self-transformation of reason,* as it were, from its preliminary theoretical precondition to its ethical ripeness and maturity. Therefore, the relation of man to the unique God has to activate and to attest itself in love. Only this surplus of love over knowledge is to be considered here at first. To have knowledge of God means to acknowledge God. And acknowledgment excels knowledge, as the action of the will excels the thinking of the understanding.

If God were only an object of knowledge, then he could not be the unique God, for knowledge also has entirely different objects and problems. The unique God, therefore, must determine a different attitude of the human spirit with regard to himself. Thus *love* becomes the requirement of this attitude toward the Unique One. Hence, the *acknowledgment* of love becomes a new deed of consciousness, an action, a primary act of the moral consciousness, of the will in its specific peculiarity, and in its distinction from the reason that aims at knowledge.

2. *Love* for the unique God, therefore, has first a negative meaning: not merely knowledge but a new power of consciousness must be awakened. If ethics had not discovered the notion of the will, it would have had to come from religion; and who is able to measure the share that religion has in this? If, however, love means *will,* then this meaning explains all the ambiguities in the idea of the love of God. The false directions of the will correspond to the erroneous forms of love considered as a basic power of consciousness.

3. From the knowledge of the erroneous forms of love we gain the knowledge of the right form. *Polytheism* is rooted in the love for the manifoldness of natural appearances and natural powers. It loves this plurality, and in this love and out of it seeks to know it. Although *pantheism* resolves this plurality into unity, it too is originally attracted by the plurality, the riddle of which it tries to solve through the concept of unity. Here love itself seems to be dissolved in knowledge; basically, however, love continues to cling to the *infinite* variety of particular appearances and is only theoretically reabsorbed into knowledge through unity. In all respects this kind of theoretical love remains predominant in the attitude of the will to the plurality of gods, as well as to the unified God.

The contrary is the case in monotheism, which has destroyed the bridge between the plurality of things and the uniqueness of God's being. There love has to stamp itself with the peculiar spiritual form of religion, for which any theoretical attitude is only preparatory. Thus, in monotheism, *devotion to God* becomes the proper form of knowledge of God.

Devotion and love belong together; they are a conceptual unity (ידע). To these another word of the same kind must be added, "service," the basic word for work (עבודה).

4. The original form of *work* is slavery. Slavery means the complete surrender of the human being to the master, who is his owner. The growth of language is everywhere determined by the progress of cultural concepts. Slavery, too, became a humane relation; how could it have happened otherwise under the sovereignty of monotheism? Thus, the word denoting devotion to God remains, since the most distant times, "servitude." Moreover, the highest peak of Messianism is reached in the designation of the *Messiah* as the "Servant of the Eternal." Devotion to God requires the whole man and it acquires the whole man.

5. There are, therefore, two conditions for the love of the unique God: *acknowledgment,* and surrender to the unique God. Acknowledgment means an *action of the will* as distinguished from mere theoretical knowledge. To come to know God, therefore, becomes to love God, becomes active devotion to and acknowledgment of, God. This is one condition, the consequence of which we will only be able to derive later.

6. The other condition is undivided surrender to the unique God. It excludes the profession and acknowledgment of all gods except the Unique One. And it excludes any activity, devotion, and service that recognizes other gods. Only to one Lord can man make himself a ser-

vant. If man is to surrender his entire being to another being, as love, as the willpower requires it, then this being has to be the unique being. There cannot be another God. There cannot be another being beside God's unique being. Therefore, there can be only one unique worship of God, one unique love of God. Monotheism cannot permit any tolerance of polytheism. *Idolatry* has to be destroyed absolutely. This decision is the precondition of true monotheism, the monotheism of love for God, of worship grounded in love.

One has not acquired a true understanding of monotheism, which unites theory and practice, if one has not understood the destruction of idolatry as a relentless necessity, if one believes one is able to detect even a trace of intolerance, of fanaticism and misanthropy in this holy zeal against the false gods. These suspicions merely disclose that one's own heart is not completely filled with the unique God and with the necessity of his unique being, with the double necessity of knowledge and acknowledgment that constitutes man's relation to this unique God. On the other hand, for one who has made the unity of this duality of knowledge and will his own, there is no alternative: the worship of the unique God unavoidably exacts the destruction of false worship. In this respect there can be no pity and no regard for men. The love for God roots out all quietism. The true worship must be established and secured among men. Therefore the worship of false gods has to be annihilated from the earth. There is no alternative in the history of God's spirit. There is no higher spiritual authority that could release men from this fundamental duty. As monotheism and polytheism are absolutely contradictory, so are the worship of God and idol worship.

7. In these considerations there is no higher authority to which we may appeal. Rather, we must try to understand the *world history of the spirit* from its own principles. In this theoretical problem of the history of the spirit, we cannot give any consideration to *tolerance*, the duty of which is to understand and approve every point of view. Tolerance can be of value only for the ethical problem of world history in its practical application to men and peoples, from the viewpoint of the education of mankind. If, however, the *prophets* had creatively to form the history of the spirit, then for them tolerance had to be an alien, a disturbing point of view. Therefore we need not consider the primitive age and the rudeness of its customs in order to understand the hostility of the prophets to idol worship; the opposition in principle between monotheism and polytheism sufficiently explains the historical duty of monotheism in its negative attitude toward polytheism.

To be sure, men had to be sacrificed for this purpose, men from their own people no less than from other peoples. However, the advocates of monotheism did not fail to recognize the humanity of men as such. "Thou should not abhor the Edomite, for he is thy brother" (Deut. 23:8). Only the historical principle, insofar as it is to be victorious, necessarily requires the destruction of idol worship.

8. The opposition between the unique God and the gods is not limited to *number*; it becomes prominent in the distinction between the unseen *idea* and a perceptible *image*. And the immediate share reason has in the concept of the unique God is verified in this opposition to the image. Every image is a likeness of something; but of which archetype, however, is God's image a likeness?

Does there exist an archetype of God in an image at all? The images of gods have to be images of something else, to which the meaning of a god is attributed. At this point again there arises a contradiction between the unique being of God and all imaginary being. The images of gods cannot be images of God. Rather, they can be only images of objects of nature.

Thus, prophetic monotheism is necessarily opposed to, necessarily contradicts *art*. Art is the original activity of the human spirit, in creating first of all images as likenesses of the natural things that fill the universe. But starting with the sensible things, art soon presumes to depict the being of gods. This is the path that art takes among all peoples. Let us first ask how we can understand the anomalous attitude that the monotheistic spirit presents with regard to all human consciousness at this decisive turning point in any culture.

9. This question is concerned not only with the original direction of the monotheistic mind but to no less a degree with its anomalous exemption from the historical influence of art. No people in world history could avoid it, not even the most noble one; how, then, is it to be understood that the prophets withstood all the magic of art in Babylon, as well as in Egypt, and were able to maintain and carry through their resistance against these sublime creations with an attitude of scornful rejection? If art is a universal tendency of the human mind, and if, on the other hand, plastic art and poetry mutually act on each other, how is it to be understood that the monotheistic spirit could become masterful in poetry and yet sustain its power of resistance against plastic art?

At this point we are unable to give an exhaustive answer to this question. This will have to be attempted when we deal with the monotheistic concept of man. At this point it is only a question of the unique God who represents unique being. Therefore no image of him is permissible unless it be an archetype, rather *the* archetype itself.

This would not be an image since an image is only a likeness. Monotheism's opposition to plastic art is therefore based on the concept of being and its uniqueness. And if this seems to be an anomalous attitude with regard to the universal art consciousness of mankind, then one should rather ask the opposite question, whether the universal consciousness of art is not an anomalous attitude with regard to the monotheistic logic of unique being. Thus the argument about the anomalous attitude reverses itself, and monotheism with its *historical partiality* comes into force against all the other world powers of the spirit, which are themselves no less partial. Only one exception is to be conceded here, but this exception, which monotheism in its enmity toward the plastic arts admitted, is not anomalous.

The gods must be destroyed, for they have no being, but are only images. The worship of the gods is image worship. The worship of God, however, is devotion to the true being. The fight against the gods is therefore the fight of being against seeming, the fight of archetypal being against likenesses that have no archetype.

Thus, there is a development in the Decalogue from the prohibition of other gods to the prohibition of likenesses of God. And this prohibition is not limited to the sentence "Thou shalt not bow down unto them, nor serve them"; nor to the following: "Thou shalt have no other gods before Me." The assault on art becomes direct and explicit: "Thou shalt not make unto thee a graven image nor any manner of likeness" (Exod. 20: 3-4). Polytheism is attacked at its root, and the root is not in the *immediate* deification of natural phenomena but in that deification that is brought forth through the human spirit by the human hands. Only through art does that "that is in heaven above and on earth beneath or that is in the water under the earth" turn into a seductive archetype. "Thou shalt not make . . . an image nor any likeness," that is to say, the image has to be a likeness. Of God, however, there can be no likeness; he is absolutely the archetype for the mind, for the love of reason, but not an object for imitation.

The *iconoclastic turmoil* in which Islam and, in the background, the Jews take part is a turning point that is characteristic of the history of Christianity and of the schism of the Church into Eastern and Western. The problem of the person of *Christ* in his meaning as the Son of God is already connected with the question of the image even without the complication of the likeness. And that which is merely a consequence in thought with regard to Christ, is in every plastic image of God a contradiction of monotheism. The prophets grasp this contradiction in its very root: in the making of images.

10. This fight aims no less at *pantheism,* which does not recognize any difference between God and all the objects of nature. In opposition to this, monotheism says: the tree, the rock, the water are not my brethren. Even Goethe himself says that there is something that "alone" distinguishes man "from all beings we know." Perhaps it turns out to be that that which "alone" constitutes this distinction is connected with unique being, so that God may not be identified with "all beings." Pantheism is in accord with an aesthetic idealization of the entirety of nature; therefore the source of art of the spirit must be curbed all the more.

11. The prophets would not have been able to carry on the fight against art in the images of God if they themselves had not been able to lead it as artists, namely, as poet-thinkers in the full power of their poetic imagination. The second Isaiah, who completed the doctrine of Messianism, proves himself in this respect also as completing monotheism. The unity of the monotheistic thinking shows itself again in this, so far as it most intimately unites the one kind of monotheistic thinking, which is the prophetic, with the other, which is represented by the psalms. It happens that this continuous unity is also preserved in the later poetry of the synagogue. Michael Sachs, in a sensitive anticipation of the iconoclastic turmoil, produced the hymn "And All Shall Come" for the services of the New Year and the Day of Atonement.

In this hymn there is one word that makes a corresponding word in the prophets and the psalms more intelligible. And this deeper understanding brings to light the aesthetic consciousness that nourished the fight against the images of the gods. This hymn says: "They will be *ashamed* of their images." The images must be ashamed of themselves because they are merely illusions. But, above all, the image worshipers and, indeed, the image makers must be ashamed of the illusory images they produce in order to worship them.

When image worship begins to produce shame, then idol worship declines. This is not the way a satiric poet would judge; he would not address himself to man's shame; this is the judgment only of humor, which is itself a basic power of aesthetic consciousness, a power that is patient and mild. And Isaiah, with his customary intensity, lets this humor be seen.

To the sentence "I am the first, and I am the last; and beside Me there is no God," Isaiah adds a scourging speech against the idol makers. "They that fashion a graven image are all of them vanity; and their delectable things shall not profit; and their own witnesses see not, nor know; that they may be ashamed" (Isa. 44:9). The usual translation renders "ashamed" as "confounded" or "ruined," but the prophet is much more concerned that the image makers as well as their witnesses, the image worshipers, be ashamed of their work and deed. It is the shame itself, not shame as disgrace in the eyes of others, let alone destruction, that the prophet makes the touchstone of one's self-knowledge. "Who hath fashioned a god, or molten an image that is profitable for nothing? Behold, all the fellows thereof shall be ashamed; and the craftsmen skilled above men; let them all be gathered together, let them stand up; they shall fear, they shall be ashamed together. The smith maketh an axe and worketh in the coals, and fashioneth it with hammers, and worketh it with his strong arm; yea he is hungry, and his strength faileth; he drinketh no water, and is faint. The carpenter stretcheth out a line; he marketh it out with a pencil; he fitteth it with planes and he marketh it out with the compasses, and maketh it after the figure of man, *according to the glory of a man* . . . and he takes . . . the oak, which he strengtheneth for himself one among the trees of the forest; he planteth a bay-tree and the rain doth nourish it. Then a man useth it for fuel; and he taketh thereof, and warmeth himself; yea, he kindles it, and baketh bread; yea, he maketh a god and worshippeth it; he maketh it a graven image, and falleth down thereto. IIe burneth the half thereof in the fire; with the half thereof he eateth flesh; he roasteth roast, and is satisfied; yea, he warmeth himself, and saith, 'Aha, I am warm, I have seen the fire'; *and the residue thereof he maketh a god*, even his graven image; he falleth down unto it, and worshippeth it, and prayeth unto it, and saith 'Deliver me for thou art my god' . . . and none considereth in his heart, neither is there knowledge nor understanding to say 'I have burned part of it in fire; yea, also I have baked bread upon the coals thereof; I have roasted flesh, and eaten it: and shall I make the residue thereof an abomination? shall I fall down to the stock of a tree?' He striveth after ashes, his deceived heart hath turned him aside, that he cannot deliver his soul, nor say, is there not a lie in my right hand?" (Isa. 44:9-20).

The shame of the makers as well as the worshipers of the images is set repeatedly as a goal and a test. And the conclusion is important: that they will recognize "is there not a lie in my right hand?" *To recognize the lie and the self-deception in idol worship* is what matters. And the humor is morally well aimed insofar as it stresses the heterogeneity in the use of the same wood that serves for heating and baking as material for the image. All the implements of art and all its magic are unable to change anything in this material evidence; it is the same wood out of which the God is carved and on which the roast is roasted. Thus the material out of which the image is made condemns the end for which it is formed. And with the image God is made vain, who for consciousness, for worship, is alive in no other way than in the image.

It is futile to object that the image worshiper does not worship the image but the object it represents. This objection only betrays a misconception of true monotheism. For this is exactly what distinguishes it from all idol worship: that the unique God cannot be thought of as the object of an image. No matter that the image worshiper may worship only the object represented by the image, monotheism teaches that God absolutely cannot be an object that can be thought of through the instruction of an image. *And it is the proof of the true God that there can be no image of Him.* He can never be known through a likeness, but simply and solely as archetype, as archetypal thought, as archetypal being.

The prophet's irony about the manufacturer of images comes forth with all the elementary, inchoate force of a *myth*. It is fire, myth's primary element, with which culture begins. It is, therefore, mythical consciousness with which the prophet makes the image maker exclaim: "Aha, I have seen fire." With this the prophet makes him, as it were, a worshiper of fire. And since all culture begins with fire, it is no insult to art if it is led back to this vision of fire.

The psalm makes *shame* the last recourse for the idol worshiper. "Ashamed be all they that serve graven images, that boast of idols" (Ps. 97:7). "They that make them (images) are like unto them; yea, every one that trusteth in them" (Ps. 115:8). The image makers are also affected by the nothingness of the images. No splendor of artistic creativity is of help here; the prophet does not let himself be misled by these magic powers. If art shows such a way, it is, for the prophet, a wrong way. The prophet is careful to see that this verdict does not affect all art, not even all plastic arts. For *architecture* did not fall into the worship of images. It rather may create works for men who worship the unique God, though not for God to dwell in. And besides architecture, a wide area of art opens up for *poetry*.

12. Furthermore the question may be raised whether the plastic arts are permissible at least for the representation of *man?* This question, however, leads us beyond the point we have reached; we have not yet considered the relation that should exist between God and man. However, already at this point the question has to be asked whether the monotheistic concept of man could have originated at all if it had been formed in close connection with the development of the concept

of God in the plastic arts. The concept of man, which monotheism had to develop, required an independence from the plastic concept of man, as well as from the plastic concept of God. Other sources of consciousness had to be opened and made productive if a concept of man befitting the unique God was to be discovered.

Finally the question may be raised whether the peculiar kind of poetry of the Bible could have arisen if the plastic arts had not been checked. This peculiarity consists in the lyric poetry of the psalms, which sing neither of God alone nor of man alone. Plastic art, however, can only present an isolated depiction of both. Thus plastic art would have impeded the lyric style, for which the relation of God and man becomes the problem of its monotheistic aim.

CHAPTER III

Creation

1. We have recognized that God's being is unique and distinct from anything else presumed to have being. The distinction between the oneness and the uniqueness of God has thereby also been clarified. The Eleatics conceived of oneness for the purpose of thinking of the cosmos. That they were already in need of the concept of God in order to explain this oneness, the world unity, proves the connection between the concepts of God and oneness. With the Eleatics, however, the oneness of God is only an auxiliary concept for the unity of the cosmos, and thus this unity of God and the world is of use only to pantheism. As opposed to this, monotheism is in need of oneness only with regard to God, not to the cosmos. Therefore, oneness had to become that uniqueness by virtue of which God's being is distinct from any being of nature.

Yet this absolute distinction cannot be final, for it contradicts as much the meaning of God as that of being. The share of reason in religion cannot be exhaustively determined by the notion that being, this universal concept of reason, is reserved for God only, and is absolutely removed from the world. The concept of being would thereby rather be abolished and with it the concept of reason.

Also, with regard to God, the share of reason in religion cannot consist in the understanding that being should be reserved only for him: what kind of God would it be who had only a negative relation to the world? Pantheism cannot be defeated by denying being to the world in every sense. The uniqueness of God's being attains its positive value only through the determination and the limitation of the being of the world; otherwise the notion of uniqueness would remain only a negative determination. But there is in uniqueness an immanent relation to the world, and the being of the world is distinguished from God's being through his uniqueness.

2. However, what kind can the being of the world be, if it is

not true being? The philosophical concept of being gives an informative answer to this question. Being is conceived of in regard to the problem of *becoming*. Thus, being, properly speaking, is not conceived for its own sake but only for the sake of becoming. If the concept of being originates with the notion of the cosmos, then it originates in the problem of becoming; for the cosmos displays eternal becoming. Before Greek speculation came upon the thought of being, it was stirred from all sides by the problem of becoming and it searched in all the changes of becoming for an orientation with regard to the manifoldness of the cosmos. Thus change and becoming had to precede the conception of unity and being.

3. The fundamental concept of *substance* traverses all phases of philosophy and science. And in conformity with the loftiness and maturity of thought that Leibniz achieved with his *principle of living force*, Kant was able to break away from all scholasticism with regard to the concept of substance, and to make it a *presupposition* for the concepts of relation. The position that Kant gave to substance as a precondition for causality and reciprocity of action tore away, as it were, the absolute independence of substance. It has absoluteness as a category only as a "precondition" of causality. This absoluteness does not rest in the category itself, is not confined to it itself, but realizes itself only insofar as it *makes causality possible*, for the latter could not do its work without the former.

This is the position substance holds within the knowledge of nature. It is being, as the presupposition for becoming, for occurrence in accordance with the principle of causality; it is the being for *motion*. For motion is becoming on the basis of causality. Hence the *being* of substance means that substance is presupposed by the causality of motion.

4. What reason, as philosophy, achieves and clarifies in the realm of science and knowledge must have its analogy in the share of reason in religion. The divine being would not be a determination of reason if the same relation that holds true with regard to the becoming of things did not also hold true for the relation of the divine being to the natural and human world. This immanent relation of being to becoming is not in contradiction to the uniqueness of the divine being, which rather acquires its positive content through this immanency. We now understand the uniqueness all the more, in that we now clearly recognize the immanency of God's relation to becoming as the presupposition, and therefore also as the immanency, of causality. The unique being of God now means to us that he contains in

himself the fundamental condition for causality. We now recognize the uniqueness of the divine being as the unique *causality*.

Abundant problems tower up before us at this point. Out of the misty sea of myth, questions emerge; chaos arises. There also arises an opposition to all metaphysics with its claim to the exclusive ownership of the specific share reason has in religion. Causality may remain the special field of science, but there may be another kind of causality that originates on the border of science. And because it originated on the border we are positively permitted to step beyond the knowledge of nature and natural science in order to discover and fulfill, with its aid, the world of the spirit, the human world of morality. Thus there originate new meanings for the uniqueness of being in God and for God: new meanings for God, because for the world of becoming, for which the unique being is the foundation. Only gradually can all these meanings of the uniqueness of being be developed. To begin with, we remain at the abstraction of being in its relation to the abstraction of becoming.

5. In order to understand the tendency of the ancient biblical sources to struggle to free themselves from original mythical elements, it would be appropriate to begin with that philosophical speculation that consciously tried to develop the share of monotheism in reason out of the logic of principles. In *Islam*, in the problem of the "negative attributes," this share of reason became the fundamental problem. Thereby, a community between religion and philosophy was established. Certainly there are general motives at play in the treatment of this problem, such as, in the first place, *agnosticism*, the peculiarly religious form of skepticism. It is also certain that the rejection of any positive attributes of God was intended to protect monotheism against being weakened and obscured. The plurality of these positive attributes and particularly their interconnection seemed to threaten the unity of God. An attempt to defend monotheism against pantheism is also at work here. A Jewish philosopher expresses this thought in the sentence: "If I were to know Thee, I would be Thee." All these motives are fully effective in the attempt to solve this fundamental problem, yet they do not exhaust its significance.

6. Among Jewish philosophers it is Maimonides especially who gives the problem an entirely different turn, a new point and a new meaning. He corrects the term "negative attributes"; it is characterized by him as a half-truth, as a deficient term. It is not positive determinations that should be negated by the negative attributes; this would not convey sufficient meaning. And it would also be a false beginning. For are there, after all, positive determinations of God? This is, as-

suredly, the prior question. In order to answer this question the problem of negative attribution must be defined more exactly. Since there are indeed no positive determinations yet, they cannot be negated. Rather, what is to be done is precisely to make use of the unique kind of being that is God's against the other, spurious kinds of being. What, however, could be negated, if there could as yet be no positive determinations?

7. In the oldest age of Greek speculation a *concept* and a mode of *judgment* originated that would almost be a riddle if the meaning of this concept, as it unveils itself in scientific usage, had not gradually clarified the solution of this riddle. *Privation* (μή), a concept in between affirmation and negation, seems to be only a play of wit, a hairsplitting distinction used by lawyers for their legal quibbles and by the popular orators of Greece. The term also seems to have served the Sophists as a model and pretext for their wantonness and their adventures in reckless thinking. In the Greek language this particle, which is akin to negation, and even seems entirely to belong to it, was also in general and daily usage.

We are of the opinion that Democritus and especially Plato intended for this particle and for this concept a meaning which is *entirely different from negation*, which even reaches out beyond the meaning of affirmation, insofar as it intends to bestow a foundation to affirmation.

Later the concept of privation together with the corresponding mode of judgment originally founded on this particle was falsely and misleadingly identified with the Latin particle *non*. The identification was made possible by removing from the Latin particle the proper meaning of privation, a negativity that is not the same as negation. Despite the fact that the particle *non* contains almost none of the original negativity and thus obscures the legitimate meaning of the classical differentiation of privation and negation, the providential meaning, as it were, of this *differentiation*, the warding off of mere negation, has not been entirely extinguished and destroyed in it.

8. A favorable circumstance contributed to this, namely, the concept of the *infinite* was joined to these concepts of negation. The differentiation of the infinite from negation did not solve the problem entirely; there still remained the problem that the proper *foundation* of the being of any entity in its particular relations has to be established in the alleged negation or, rather, in the infinite. Thus it is a question not only of warding off negation but of providing a foundation for the positivity, the affirmation of being. Thus privation became the infinite judgment.

Maimonides was the genuine philosopher of monotheism not only in his Jewish universalism but also in the loftiness of his philosophic concern for the problem of creation and in the honesty of his thinking with regard to this problem. He tried to secure the share of reason in his religion by following in the metaphysical tracks of Aristotle.

However, if Aristotle, through the idea of the eternity of the world, kept the claim of reason safe against the problem of creation out of nothing, then Maimonides had to attempt to save the share of reason in the monotheistic concept of creation. Even if he were not to have made the well-known remark—if Aristole had proven the eternity of the world with compelling evidence, the biblical account of creation would have to be reinterpreted accordingly—even then, without this frank declaration, the consistency of his rationalism would have demanded that he overcome the literal meaning of the account of creation. Besides, he is not the first to aspire to, and to accomplish, the rationalization of the biblical teaching on creation; we shall see that the Talmud also pursues this rationalistic tendency, and even transplants it into the daily prayers.

Maimonides becomes a classic of rationalism in the monotheistic tradition most decisively, perhaps, through his interpretation of the crucial problem of negative attributes. He elucidates the traditional problem of negative attributes through the *connection of negation and privation*. It is not the positive attributes that are negated but those of privation. God is not inert. This example points the way; and the clarity of Maimonides' thought shows itself in the fact that he does not consider the privative form of the word only, but rather the meaning of privation in a seemingly positive word. Inertness, for instance, has the privative meaning that makes it possible to dispense with the privative form of the word, which has to use the privative particle.

9. However, Maimonides is not satisfied with this elucidation, but clarifies beyond any doubt the purpose that all this formalism has to serve. If the negative attribute of privation has the meaning that God is not tired [inert], then the deeper meaning of this figure lies not only in the warding off and exclusion of inertness from God but in basing this exclusion on a new and genuine positivity and, hence, entirely rooting out the negation. This new positivity has been discovered and determined in the concept of the *originative principle (Ursprung),** which has been distinguished as a category in my Logic of Pure Knowledge. The share of reason in religion has to discover what the logical meaning of originative principle is for the problem of creation And this was the meaning for the problem of creation that Maimonides

*See note p. 10. [S.K.]

bestowed upon the negative attribute of privation.[8] God is not inert; this means: he is the *originative principle of activity*. In this way Maimonides explains the original name of God, which has been understood from the very beginning as meaning *omnipotence:* "He is sufficient to produce things beside himself" (cf. p. 39).

In these words the omnipotence of God acquires the meaning of a genuine attribute, which negates the negativity contained in a privation. What it means to "negate" in this way is clarified in the meaning of privation. Creation can now no longer be in contradiction to reason. In this logic the religion of creation itself has become reason. God is not inert; this means: God is the prime cause of activity, God is the creator. His being can be determined in no other way than by the immanence of creation in his *uniqueness*. Creation is not a heterogeneous concept in—or in addition—to God's being. Instead, precisely this is the meaning of his being as uniqueness: that becoming is thought of as in him, therefore proceeding from him; it must be derived from his concept.

We find the same meaning that critical philosophy has assigned to *substance as a foundation of motion* again in the share of reason that Maimonides determined with regard to the monotheistic problem of creation. In this respect also, he does not follow Aristotle blindly, but carries through the rationalism of his own doctrine of God.

10. The distinction of monotheism from *pantheism* depends on the exact understanding of the term "creation." Immanency is the condition of *emanation*. Becoming, the presumptive being, has to be explained. From what, however, could the origin of becoming be derived if not from true being? That the latter is the unique being cannot exclude the thought that false being can be explained through the true being. If, however, this explanation is understood in a materialistic sense, so that dependence is thought of as emanation, then one acknowledges material immanence and, along with the latter, pantheism.

Therefore, one must think of dependence in its logical significance in such a way that one excludes a material origination of becoming from being. The process of becoming belongs to becoming itself and may not be shifted to being. In this procedure the uniqueness of being proves itself as the sufficient cause of the origin of becoming. This sufficiency, however, exhausts itself in its *logical* meaning, and it is distorted if the logical meaning is transferred to a material occurrence.

11. The impediments to the problem of creation lie in the mythical point of view; this, however, refutes itself by giving precedence to the notion of *chaos*. It is therefore logical that the account of creation in Genesis does not begin with chaos; but that chaos (*tohu wabohu*)

starts only after the earth has already been created. Moreover, it is characteristic that the first word that designates the act of creation does not imply a material beginning but, according to the usual translation, a beginning in time. The rabbinical tradition, however, explains the *beginning* (ראשית) in such a way that it belongs to God's power, to the essence of God, to create the world.[9] The riddle of creation in time remains, but it remains with God. And now it is important to determine the concept of God in such a manner that the creation does not offer a genuine riddle but, rather, finds its solution in the definition of God. Mythology is thus overcome through the definition of God.

The opposition between *immanence* and becoming, however, becomes a difficulty when we attempt the definition of God. It has already turned out that this alleged contradiction has dropped out of rational thinking and has retreated into mythology. Becoming cannot be explained in terms of being if one says that becoming was previously contained in being and then proceeded out of it, for this understanding does not yield a purely logical dependence. The difference between being and becoming is to be thought of as corresponding to the difference between *affirmation* and *negation*. Negation has to be warded off from God; through this, becoming, insofar as it is false being, is removed from unique being. Nevertheless, becoming has to be explained by being. Consequently, being must appropriate to itself a designation which indeed distinguishes it from negation, but which answers to the thought of negation as it appears within the problems of becoming. The concept of privation originated from these considerations. And thus it was applied to the problem of the divine attributes.

It was not possible merely to substitute privation for negation; nothing would have been gained by this, for privation would have remained obtuse and empty. However, by connecting it with negation, one was able to breathe a new meaning into it, through which that intrinsic meaning first came to light that gave life to this kind of thinking about the nature of God. If God is recognized through the attribute of being not inert, then he becomes recognizable as creator; *thus,* the idea of *creation is taken into the concept of God.* The riddle of creation is thus resolved through the definition of God. For now creation rather means God's being, which is the being of the originative principle. And becoming now has its basis in this being as the originative principle. The error of thinking that becoming might have, or must have, *come forth* from being, in which it was contained, can no longer arise; for in the light of pure logical knowledge, these metaphysical notions are now unmasked as mythological.

Also, chaos is no longer necessary; logically, chaos is merely the un-determined, not the infinite, which is designated by privation. And this infinite is directly related to the finite and its determinability.

12. The concept of the originative principle as used for the con-cept of the divine being also settles the problem of the *nothing*, which is a stumbling block for the thought of creation. The Hebrew word that seems to correspond to *nothing* (אין) in no way means merely nothing; it means, rather, the relative infinity of privation. The latter, however, is not found within becoming, with matter, with the nonexistent primeval substance, but rather within the unique be-ing of God. Creation as a problem of thought finds its complete solu-tion in this concept, in the unity of the concepts of the uniqueness of being and the infinite, privative originative principle. If God is the unique being, then he is the originative principle for becoming and in this originative principle becoming, as a problem of thought, has found its primary basis. The primary basis of *emanation* is not in thought; it is not of logical but of mythological origin, which is no better than chaos and the nothing. God is positively determined in those negative attributes that exclude *privation*, not positivity.

This kind of privation has to be adapted to the problem of the unique being. Thereby one secures the relation of being to the finite, to becoming, and privation is freed from the arbitrariness of the un-determined. This necessary relation of being to the finite, to becom-ing, invests the philosophic defense against negation with the new value contained in the thought of the *originative principle.* The finite is to attain its originative principle in the infinite, in the negation of privation. Logically, the problem of creation is thus solved. And, logically, creation is no longer a riddle. Creation, which could have been found only in the concept of God, here has been solved through the idea of God's uniqueness. *Thus creation is the consequence of God's uniqueness.* And one is thus entitled to say: the uniqueness of God's being is actualized in creation. The negation of privation would have missed its goal if it were not related to the finite, which requires its originative principle, but cannot find it in itself.

The riddle of creation therefore remains, properly speaking, not with God, but rather with nature and its becoming. The latter can have its foundation only in being. This is the watchword that Par-menides proclaimed. However, he did not remain in the position of Xenophanes, who assumed the unity of God and the world. This would have been the unity of being and becoming. And it is this false unity that Parmenides combatted in Heraclitus. Pantheism only re-peats the error that Parmenides illuminated with such great acuteness and with such fruitful results for philosophy and science. Creation is necessary in order that the prejudice that makes being identical with becoming, the prejudice in which pantheism has its logical root, should not persist.

Creation is God's primary attribute; it is not only the consequence of the uniqueness of God's being; creation is simply identical with it. If the unique God were not creator, being and becoming would be the same; nature itself would be God. This, however, would mean: God is not. For nature is the becoming that needs being as its foundation.

Being is a first principle that is not contained in becoming, that rather has to be the foundation for becoming. Philosophy as well as science is opposed to the thought of the unity of being and becoming. Pantheism is therefore a logical contradiction even for the scientific problem of being and becoming. Yet, the solution of this contradiction is only a prelude to the main share of reason in religion, to the main share of reason in a region of thought beyond the problems of science, in the human problem, in the problem of *ethics*.

13. The specific meaning of the monotheistic concept of creation concerns *ethics*. Therefore we shall be able to unfold this meaning only in connection with the creation of *man*, in connection with the creation of reason itself. The stumbling block in the entire problem of creation is that it is understood with regard to all creatures indiscriminately. Metaphysics gives this guidance to natural science and *pantheism* owes its distinguished reputation to the fact that it follows metaphysics. If, however, as we saw from the beginning, reason takes two main roads that diverge at a decisive point, then the question of creation cannot be posed with regard to all creatures indiscriminately but, rather, in accordance with these two main roads. One merely supposes that there is a dualism in this approach. It is rather the unity of the method that, although based on the separation of the problems, seeks to bring about the unity of knowledge on the basis of this separation. The distinction of the methods leads to the unity of methods. However, the separation has to come first. Logic is the logic of science. Ethics can set up its own logic only by analogy to science.

Therefore, before we develop the ethical meaning of creation, we would like to point to the form Jewish monotheism took in regard to this question, taking our bearings from the standard established by Maimonides.

14. Two teachings of the Bible are considered, according to the Talmud, as esoteric: creation and the divine Chariot (מרכבה) in the vision of Ezekiel. And many questions in the Talmud, e.g., those which are concerned with the pure animals, are considered, and for

the most part, dealt with, from this scholarly point of view. "The Act in the Beginning" (מעשה בראשית) is the primary and most frequent expression for creation. However, this term did not remain the only one. How could another term come to be side by side with this one? We have to ask this question, in accordance with the meaning creation has for the unity of God. However, the fact that this term has been assigned its place in physics, and that the latter has been subordinated to a metaphysics, seems suspicious, for metaphysics in its mythology also deals with creation. Thus, the creation proper becomes almost an exoteric, and the Chariot an esoteric problem. Therefore, "creation in the beginning" does not seem to have been considered as the last word on the problem.

In a later time, however, the term "renewal of the world" (חדוש העולם) emerges. One cannot avoid the thought that the concept of renewal had to soften the abruptness of the beginning. Therefore, not "creation in the beginning" but "renewal," which idealizes the beginning and makes creation a matter of *continuity* within which each day is a new beginning, is to be the adequate term for creation. The men of the Great Synagogue have established this thought in the daily prayer: "In His goodness He constantly renews in each day the work of the beginning." Thus the act of the beginning is renewed each day. And the renewal takes place continuously (תמיד). Each day is a new beginning; and the continuity is the true beginning. This renewal replaces creation.

There is no doubt that a replacement takes place here. It may very well be that renewal is not expressly thought of as opposed to the creation in the beginning; nevertheless the necessary question remains: how could this new term arise and be accepted even though it appears to soften the biblical term? Due to what need was the suspicion of this opposition not shunned, and particularly not shunned even in the daily prayer itself? Does one not have to think that the opposition between the Chariot and the "creation in the beginning" had to be diminished so that the latter no less than the former could retain its esoteric character? And it probably corresponds to the actual circumstances that the creation in the beginning hovers and oscillates between the exoteric and esoteric teaching.

15. The real cause for the introduction of the concept of renewal rests with the ethical problem, as is indicated in the prayer by the one word *goodness*. We can already see that in the rabbinical writings there is, as we shall try to prove, a further development of the share of reason in religion, despite all appearances to the contrary. It

is clear, too, that the rabbinical writings take offense at the vagueness and ambiguity of the biblical term for creation and therefore comprehend the continuous renewal of the world as creation.

The importance of our concept of *originative principle* is further corroborated by this. For the originative principle does not only stand for the first beginning—this would be mythological—but has to establish permanence and therefore continuous preservation as well. Thus the originative principle needs permanence, the word for which is contained in תמיד of the prayer. The question is clearly more and more removed from myth, which does not go beyond the marvel of the temporal beginning. The unique being, however, has to be related constantly to becoming, and thus the originative principle has to prove itself in the continuous preservation or, to speak from the point of view of creation, to prove itself in the renewal. Even without the introduction of the ethical point of view, the metaphysical point of view, which is dominated by the problem of being, requires this revision in the terminology, which looks very much like a correction.

This revision becomes the predominant term in the language of medieval Jewish philosophy. The renewal of the world now signifies the creation of the world. The creator now becomes the renewer. And since his act, his creating, is his being and does not enter as a foreign power into his essence, the primary origin in God of the becoming of the world now signifies that becoming, insofar as it is constant, has its originiative principle in God's being, in God's creating.

Is, however, the constant being really a constantly *new* being? Is it not, insofar as it is determined by the divine being, always the same? The term itself gives an answer to this question and through this elucidation the term attains its proper significance.

It is not the case that becoming is always the same. This self-identity is valid only for being. The finite, however, is always new: therefore, since it does not have its creative power in itself, it must always be renewed. Thus it can be seen that the new term was not invented in order to avoid skepticism, which in turn could not escape the problem of creation, but that there is a positive meaning to the term. It is this positive meaning of the term that is able to lead the metaphysical problem of being and becoming into the *ethical* problem. The latter must attempt on its own to establish a connection between the unique being and finite becoming. The steady renewal on each day is the bridge between the infinite and the finite, whereas the temporal beginning lies in the obscurity of myth. Now, however, each day poses the same question: with the question of the beginning enters also that of constancy. The concept of creation in the beginning could not satisfactorily answer these questions; hence, the concept of the renewal of the world had to be introduced. This concept makes the newness in each stage of becoming into a problem and attempts to solve it through God's being.

It is no longer a question of a mythical interest in a unique primeval act. If we disregard all ethics, the interest in the problem of creation becomes, in comparison to the myth, more scientific. One marvels not so much at the beginning, but rather at the constancy in becoming, the permanency in change. It is always something new, but this newness may have its origin in the same old foundation.

The renewal therefore is not the renewal out of chaos or out of nothing—if it were so, one could rest satisfied with the idea of creation. Renewal, rather, emphasizes each point in becoming as a new beginning.

The choice of this term shows more mature thought than is the case in myth. The concept of renewal is scientifically more direct and it surpasses the myth of the beginning, even without considering the relation to ethics that it introduces. The notion of newness in becoming is the scientific idea. But this newness must be continuously renewed. The share of religion in reason proves itself with regard to creation in the concept of the renewal of the world. The concept of beginning is positively surpassed as a religious problem by the concept of renewal.

In monotheism the problem of creation is not exhausted in the creation of the world; in Greek philosophy the question concerns only the origin of the cosmos. Here in monotheism, however, *man* as the carrier of reason and as the rational being of morality occupies a privileged position. Because of this, the problem of creation transfers its meaning from the realm of causality to the realm of teleology. Consequently the share of reason in religion also takes cognizance of the problem of ethics, whereas creation, insofar as it is seen from the point of view of causality, requires only a coming to terms with logic. With regard to the latter, creation appears as a miracle, and reason claims to elevate this anomaly of a miracle into the normality of thought.

This interest in the dissolution of miracle is present also in another concept that, properly speaking, presupposes the creation of man as a rational being. But since this particular creation is preceded by the general creation of the world, we shall, in order to avoid a seeming anomaly in thought, follow the general notion of creation, and first discuss the concept just mentioned, out of which the other, the particular kind of creation, may emerge as a consequence.

CHAPTER IV

Revelation

1. Becoming is dependent on being. This logical determination is no longer disturbed by mythological notions of emanation. However, from the variety of becoming, the special problem of *human reason* arises. The general logical determination must attain its eminent significance in this special determination. God's uniqueness must prove itself true in its relation to this special problem. This is the most general sense of revelation: *that God comes into relation with man.* And this most general sense is at the same time the proper one. For the opinion that God also reveals himself in the world is an incorrect idea that vacillates in the direction of pantheism and that has been corrected through our doctrine of creation: God in no way reveals himself in something, but only to something, in relation to something. And the corresponding member of this relation can only be man.

Revelation therefore differs only in this respect from creation, that the latter is concerned with the general metaphysical problem of being and becoming, which, however, borders on the special problem of morality. This problem is taken up by revelation. It is therefore possible to say that revelation is the continuation of creation insofar as it sets as its problem the creation of man as a rational being. Hence, from the concept of the creation of morality, it already follows that revelation can be related only to man, the bearer of morality.

The exposition of revelation can therefore precede the chapter on man only on the condition that the appearance of a miraculous anomaly is dispelled from the problem of revelation. Just as being is the necessary presupposition for becoming, so is it also, and in an eminent way, for the becoming of a man. It is only by virtue of revelation that the *rational creature*, man, comes to be. This statement is of the same logical power as the one about the uniqueness of being as substance, namely, it has to be the presupposition for becoming. If, however, reason means not only knowledge of nature, which has its special foundations, but rather preeminently the knowledge of morals, then the origin of this moral reason, of this moral becoming, has to be placed in God, who is the unique being and therefore also the precondition for the knowledge of morals.

2. The opposition between the logic of concepts and the sources of religion must become even more explicit here than in the problem of creation. For the danger of materializing God and his relation to man is here more immediate. The *communication* that God issues to man seems inevitably to make him participate in man—and man in God; but this assails the uniqueness of God's being. There seems to be no way to evade this inescapable mythology.

Pantheism slips into this gap of reason. But pantheism can bridge this gap only by denying it and not recognizing it as a gap. According to its teaching, God's communication to man is not communication to another being but to himself. His communication is rather a self-unfolding. But the difficulty of creation is repeated in this: becoming is inserted into being and abolished. According to this view of revelation God becomes identified with man, whereas according to monotheism, God always is only the precondition for all becoming, consequently also for the morality of men, and this in spite of the seeming independence of this problem.

Revelation does not mean the causal origin of the coming-to-be of moral reason; it is only a precondition for this special kind of causality. Therefore, the alleged anomaly may be only an error. The point in question is not the *causality of the communication* of reason from God to man; causality is in no way the point in question; the point is the precondition for causality, even before it puts itself to work elsewhere. This precondition for causality, however, is already contained in being, out of which it is distinguished for the special meaning of creation that is constituted by revelation. This special problem of becoming is the relation of becoming to man's reason. For this peculiar problem, however, being is the necessary precondition, which in the case of this distinctive problem is no longer called creation, but revelation. Revelation too cannot be a miracle; it is not an anomaly. For being has the immanent meaning of revelation as well as of creation. *Revelation is the creation of reason.*

3. If we now proceed to elucidate from biblical sources the share of reason determined by the foregoing in this fundamental problem of religion, we are, more than ever, prepared for a great difficulty. Monotheism grows out of myth, and, with myth, it also grows out of the national *epic*. The Bible is not a didactic poem or instruction in the doctrine of faith. Neither is it a history of literature; it is itself

national literature. Every national literature, however, is guided, in the naiveté of its creation, by the consciousness that the nation itself has created what the written work records. Thus a conflict unavoidably arises between the literary originality of the people's spirit and the mythological meaning of revelation. This is the first form of the conflict between revelation and the national writings.

The books of Moses contain a double form that has always been recognized by the tradition, insofar as it has designated the fifth book a "Repetition of the Torah" (משנה תורה). Through this repetition, it seems, the naiveté is broken; for apparently it has to contain a reflection on that which the preceding books have rendered in a naive exposition. From this higher point of view, the book of Deuteronomy is extremely interesting, so much so that one may point to this as a sign of the especially good fortune of the scriptural teaching.

All the scruples that emerge against the originality of the national production of religion are considered by this reflective repetition. However, the criticism of this reflection penetrates even deeper in that it considers above anything else those doubts in regard to revelation that must be raised from the point of view of God's spirituality. And only out of this deeper criticism do the less important scruples, which arise from the point of view of national originality, become really strong. The most important point in consideration is not the opposition of national originality to divine revelation, but, in general, the problem of revelation as the communication of God to man.

4. Revelation is first of all a singular event in the history of the people: the revelation on Sinai. Is it the unique one? Is not the whole Torah a revelation? And was the Torah in the entire fullness of its content revealed on Sinai? The rabbis did not shrink from the consequence that Mosaic teaching already contained, namely, that the whole content of the Torah was included in the revelation on Sinai. They even went so far as to explain their own expositions as oral Torah, expositions they based on those laws (Halachoth) which they designated as given "to Moses on Sinai." Despite all this, the Decalogue, as the revelation proper on Sinai, retained its special place. Thereby, however, the content of the concept of revelation came to fluctuate.

This revelation on Sinai was bound to offend the reflection of Deuteronomy in many ways. In the first place the danger of a material conception of God was concealed in the theophany itself. It is very instructive to learn how Deuteronomy strives to avert this danger. "Take ye therefore good heed for your souls (the concern is therefore about your soul) for ye saw no manner of form on the day that the Eternal spoke unto you in Horeb out of the midst of the fire. Lest you deal corruptly, and make you a graven image, even the form of any figure, the likeness of male or female" (Deut. 4:15, 16). The verses following this one describe the entire circle of gods of the other peoples.

In no such manner did the unique God reveal himself on Sinai. "And the Eternal spoke unto you out of the midst of the fire; ye heard the voice of words, but ye saw no form; only a voice" (Deut. 4:12). Is not, however, the voice a form, a bodily organ? One is inclined to think that it was the "voice of words" that they heard; thus not the voice but only the words were perceptible. For hearing is as bodily as seeing and therefore had to be guarded against as much as seeing. Therefore hearing must here be understood not only as understanding, as the verse says: "All the Eternal has spoken, we will do and understand"; but "understanding" must be comprehended more exactly in the usual meaning of hearkening, i.e., obeying, so that hearing means only the inner spiritual hearing that has as its consequence the doing. Be that as it may, it is clear from the above precautions that all materiality was to be kept away from revelation.

This consideration extends even to Mount Sinai itself. "And ye came near and stood under the mountain; and the mountain burned with fire unto the heart of heaven, with darkness, cloud, and thick darkness" (Deut. 4:11). Maimonides calls attention to the distinction between the fire in the mountain and the darkness and thick darkness about it. God himself is neither in light nor in darkness: only a subjective barrier separates man from God. Therefore, there is only a subjective dividing wall (מחיצה) between God and man even in revelation. And the proof of this subjective separation is the figure of Moses, who constitutes a peculiar anomaly in the relation between God and man in revelation.

5. Deuteronomy seeks to establish monotheism as the deepest meaning and value of the Jewish *people*. On the basis of this nationalism, polytheism is to be fought, all idol worship is to be destroyed among one's own people, as well as among all the surrounding peoples. For this goal and purpose Deuteronomy constantly proclaims the extermination of all idol-worshiping peoples as well as the destruction of Israel, except for a remnant. The national consciousness is aroused for this world-historical purpose of establishing and strengthening monotheism. For this sole purpose the *early history* of the people is recapitulated. And this *recapitulation* is the main thread of this great speech in the fields of Moab. Monotheism has to be in accord with this main thread of *national consciousness*, and all opposing motives must be exposed as illusory.

The revelation of a unique God to a *unique* people is already such an opposing motive. Nevertheless, this thought should not be shunned if it is necessary to arouse the basic religious and spiritual powers of the nation. Therefore, the review of the encounter of the people with the seven other peoples is presented before the story of revelation begins. The epic quality of the account is not disturbed by the inserted *self-criticism* of naive monotheism. For the motivations which are expressed in "God is jealous," and "a consuming fire," and which incite to political action, are sufficiently amended through the inner monotheistic motivation: "for a merciful God is the Eternal, your God."

The motivations of love and justice also are naively entwined and interpenetrating in the whole speech, whose main purpose is national politics. Although it says, "You shall . . . perish," nonetheless it says, "He will not fail thee, neither destroy thee" [Deut. 4:31]. All forms of autochthony are annulled by the naive original form of revelation.

6. Another form of antinomy is the *double relation* in which Moses stands *to God and to Israel*. No serious objection can be raised against the call to Moses, since through this theophany the people itself should be aroused to national consciousness. For Moses is precisely the tool for this national elevation. The unique God can reveal himself only in the spirit, and he is supposed to have appeared in the spirit only to the entire people. This mediation of the spirit, however, makes the mediation of an individual spirit inevitable. The material theophany was in need of an individual merely as a blind seer; the spiritual theophany cannot dispense with a spiritual mediator. And a virtue was made of necessity: Moses is the national hero, the creator of the people, as it were, who elevated the people to a nation from the furnace of slavery. His uniqueness therefore does not stand in opposition to the entire people in its unity.

Thus the apparent contradiction that is expressed in the sentences "face to face He spoke to Moses" (פנים אל פנים) and "the Eternal spoke with *you* face to face" (Deut. 5:4) is reconciled. To the first passage Ibn Ezra gives the explanation "without mediator." Thus, "face to face" means to him only *immediacy*. Moses himself, however, is not considered as a mediator, which he nevertheless was between God and Israel. He is considered only as a representative of the people, who therefore is not, as a unique member, thought of in opposition to the whole people.

When God for the second time speaks face to face with the people, the verse says, by way of addition, as it were, or even in amendment: "I stood between the Eternal and you . . . to declare unto you the word of the Eternal" [Deut. 5:5]. The theophany is here changed to an apostleship. Moses becomes the herald. Such a one is necessary, for revelation is to be a spiritual communication. And yet it is continually repeated: "For you saw no manner of form on the day that the God spoke unto you in Horeb out of the midst of the fire" (Deut. 4:15).

The reason given by the text at this point for the intervention of Moses is obviously not on that high level of reflection that could secure the spirituality of revelation: "For you were afraid because of the fire and went not up into the mount" [Deut. 5:5]. However, this short-coming is rectified by the sentence: "But as for thee, stand thou here by Me, and I will speak unto thee all the commandment, and the statutes, and the ordinances, which thou shalt teach them" (Deut. 5:28). The herald here becomes a *teacher*. And Moses is competent for this vocation: he is the teacher of monotheism. Revelation must permeate this teaching of a personal spirit, and through this national teacher the national consciousness is brought to maturity.

Consequently, the intervention of Moses does not establish a counterinstance to the thought of the national origin of monotheism. There is even a daring expression that puts the fact of revelation in agreement with this thought: "The Eternal made not this covenant with our fathers, but with us, even us, *who are all of us here* alive this day" (Deut. 5:3). In this sentence the whole historical thread is rejected with the strongest emphasis, and, yet, much less still is it abolished; rather, it is immediately attached to the men of the present. Thereby the spirituality of revelation is detached from the single event in primeval times, and in all clearness established in the living renewal of the national continuity.

7. The intervention of Moses against the immediate relation of God to Israel makes the epic life of Moses a tragic one. He who led Israel out of Egypt is not permitted to lead them into the Promised Land. "But the Eternal was wroth with me for your sakes" (למענכם) [Deut. 3:26]. What does this "for your sakes" mean? Here, too, I assume that monotheistic reflection broke through the naive account. A trespass on Moses' part has to be devised for the sake of the people, in order not to becloud pure monotheism for them by the illusion of a demigod, a superman. Instead of drawing the water from the rock by word, he struck it. "Because you did not sanctify Me," because you, Moses and Aaron, through the use of the rod eliminated the spiritual power of the word, you have impaired the holiness of God, which is based on spirituality.

For the sake of the people, for the sake of its education to monotheism, Moses had to become a sinner, and this sin had to be marked by punishment: "Thou shalt see the land . . . but thou shalt not go

thither" [Deut. 32:52]. Moses must transmit his vocation to a successor; the illusion that he was a mediator between God and man must
be destroyed: someone else takes his place. And yet it says about him:
"Now the *man* Moses was very meek, above all the men that were
upon the face of the earth" (Num. 12:3). Certainly not without
intention is Moses called the man Moses, and distinguished from all
men on earth. And his mark of distinction is not heroism, but humility.
Thus, through the man Moses, the spiritualty of revelation is protected.

8. Also the idea of monotheism, the central theme of the book, is
strengthened as in a tragedy through the *death* of Moses before the
entry of the people into the Promised Land. God alone establishes a
national abode for monotheism. Moses must die before this takes
place: "and no man knoweth of his sepulchre unto this day" (Deut.
34:6). Just as his life is no objection to revelation, so also is his death
the seal to this same idea. The individual dies, even the most favored
one; God, however, lives for the entire people, for which the immediate relation to God is proper. If Moses' sin were not the tragedy of
his life, then according to the pattern of drama, it would be his death,
which constitutes the supreme purification of the human, the highest
catharsis.

9. It would not be too artificial also to consider the account of the
two tables as part of a tendency to idealize the revelation. Out of anger
at the falling away of the people to the golden calf, Moses breaks the
tables written by God. How could this sin be imputed to him, which
moreover was not even attributed to him as a sin? To be sure new
tables must be readied and again be written by God. But the fact remains that the first ones could have been broken, and this serves the
tendency to spiritualize the revelation.

The spirit of revelation does not consist in the fact of writing on
the tables. What the Mishnah (The Sayings of the Fathers 6,2) says
is right: "Do not read 'engraved' (אל תקרא חרות אלא חרות) on the
tables, but read 'freedom.'" Of course, the text is not easily adapted to
this interpretation, but the meaning of this interpretation is correct,
and that is what matters for the purity of monotheism.

10. Another thought runs through this speech and is directed against
the material understanding of revelation: the "statutes and ordinances," the wisdom of which is stressed. In what do they and the testimonies (עדות) that are added to them consist? Why not rest satisfied with the revelation, especially since it is now renewed, as it were,
through the solemn enunciation: "Hear, O Israel, The Eternal our God,
the Eternal is unique" (Deut. 6:4)? It is said: "Our God," which is

significant, for monotheism is to be founded in the national consciousness.[10] And yet things do not remain at this basic idea, but even as a
consequence of this idea, there is reference to the "statutes and ordinances," in which the proof of the truth of monotheism is supposed
to lie. What is the content and character of these "statutes and
ordinances"?

11. As the expression itself indicates, they are not concerned with
prescriptions for divine worship, among which the commandment for
the destruction of idol worship can indeed not be counted, but are
concerned with purely moral prescriptions and *social and political* institutions and requirements, as well as with the entire institution of
law and *courts of justice* in theory and practice. In order not to inter-
rupt the continuity of our exposition, we will not enumerate the whole
content of these statutes and ordinances, but we may maintain that
the moral, the legal, the political, the social foundations of human
culture are put down in these chapters 12 to 28 of Deuteronomy. The
question of the content and character of the statutes and ordinances
is thus answered.

If, however, revelation is ultimately based on these statutes and
ordinances, then, beyond any doubt, the tendency of revelation is to
detach its meaning from the *fact* on Sinai and base it rather on the
content. Although the content is derived from Sinai, where it was
written down, it is completed by the continuity of the national history.

Moses is conscious of being the teacher of Israel in these statutes
and ordinances, "which I teach you" (Deut. 4:1): "Behold I have
taught you statutes and ordinances, even as the Eternal my God commanded me" (Deut. 4:5). And in accordance with this teaching it is
said: "For this is your wisdom and understanding in the sight of the
peoples, that, when they hear all these statutes, shall say: 'Surely this
great nation is a wise and understanding people'" (Deut. 4:6). And
immediately following this it is said: "For what great nation is there,
that hath God so nigh unto them, as the Eternal our God is when-
soever we call upon Him?" [Deut. 4:7].

Thus also this *nearness of God*, which becomes an important religious element, is immediately afterwards based on the statutes: "And
what great nation is there, that hath statutes and ordinances so righteous as this law which I set before you this day" [Deut. 4:8]. Moses
is said to have given these statutes *today;* nevertheless, he can freely
proceed to the continuity of the national history, which only completes its meaning in this "today." Entirely in keeping with this unifying thought, it is further said that God proclaimed the ten words and
wrote them on the tables of stone: "and the Eternal commanded me at

that time to teach you statutes and ordinances" (Deut. 4:14). Even the expression "Hear, O Israel" refers to them (Deut. 5:1). In them revelation proves itself in its wisdom and reason.

12. The *national origin* is also referred to them: "When thy son asketh thee in time to come, saying: 'What mean the testimonies and the statutes, and the ordinances, which the Eternal our God hath commanded you?' Then thou shalt say unto thy son: 'We were Pharaoh's bondmen in Egypt; and the Eternal brought us out of Egypt . . . and the Eternal commanded us to do all these statutes'" (Deut. 6:20-24).

13. Finally, the basic commandment to *love* God, which is joined to the "Hear, O Israel," is connected to them: "Therefore thou shalt love the Eternal thy God, and keep His charge, and His statutes, and His ordinances, and His commandments, always" (Deut. 11:1). Of course, no distinction is made between the political character of these laws and those laws that are directly concerned with the strengthening of monotheism. Such a distinction would be against the style of a speech in which reflection makes itself intentionally archaic. Besides, such a precise and scientific distinction could not be expected even in that more mature time. The fact that the appeal is to the wisdom and reason of these statutes and ordinances and to the wisdom of the people itself is sufficient to show beyond doubt the tendency to idealize the fact of revelation.

Up to now only the fact of revelation itself was in question, namely, the extent to which it is compatible with the spirituality, with the uniqueness of God's being. And the people and Moses are, as it were, only anticipated, since we did not advance yet to the creation of man as a rational being. Like creation, revelation too can come to completion with the revelation to reason, to man's spirit, which is therefore the presupposition for it. Man, not the people, and not Moses: man, as rational being, is the correlate to the God of revelation.[11]

14. First, however, we must consider the account of the theophany, in which Moses is the only active spectator. Only two personal entreaties are reported of Moses. The one, already mentioned, is concerned with Moses' coming to the Promised Land; the other is a theophany. Already in the first entreaty the reason made known for it was the wish: "Show me now Thy ways, that I may know Thee" (Exod. 33:13). Afterward, however, Moses entreats: "Show me, I pray Thee, Thy glory" (Exod. 33:18). In the latter case the danger of God's materialization, which lies in the question itself, seems unavoidable, whereas in the former entreaty only the knowledge of God's way, which meant only God's acts, was intended.

The verses that follow the above contain an instructive example of the way in which the old layers of the tradition are not suppressed, but on the contrary, preserved, and even at the most difficult points. The older version seems to be put forward in verses 20-23: "And He said 'Thou canst not see My face, for man shall not see Me and live.' And the Eternal said: 'Behold, there is a place by Me and thou shalt stand upon the rock. And it shall come to pass, while My glory passeth by, that I will put thee in the cleft of a rock, and will cover thee with My hand until I have passed by. And I will take away My hand, and thou shalt see My back; but My face shall not be seen.' "

If we begin with the first of these verses, its content already shows an unmistakable dependence on the general myth that man cannot remain alive after God has appeared to him. The following verses about the place, the rock, and about the covering with the hand, as well as the taking away of the hand are also entirely mythological. The greatest offense, however, is the passing by of the glory. This material element made it possible to translate the word אחורי as "backside," as if the face meant the frontside and not rather only "the forward." If, however, the word corresponding to "the forward" is the "backward," this latter need not be the back.

The Hebrew word in question occurs, besides this place, only once more, namely in Exodus (26:12), as "the back of the tabernacle." Otherwise, it occurs often in the singular form in the sense of futurity, as in Isaiah 41:23: "Declare the things that are to come hereafter." By taking this as the meaning of the word, Jewish exegetics has always tried to eliminate the offensive meaning of the sentence: according to this interpretation, the sentence would mean that only by his works, only by that which follows from his essence, can God be known, not, however, by this essence itself. Despite all this, the entire answer to this entreaty, already offensive in itself, is fraught with great danger for the spirituality of the monotheistic revelation.

Hence it is understandable that two other verses precede the above-mentioned ones and answer Moses' entreaty from an entirely different point of view: "And He said: 'I will make all My good pass before thee, and will proclaim the name of the Eternal before thee; and I will be gracious to whom I will be gracious, and will show mercy on whom I will show mercy.' " (Exod. 33:19). In the first place let us consider the erroneous translation of Kautzsch: "I will make pass all my beauty, and will proclaim the name Yahveh before thee." The word טוב in no way means beauty, which would be another word for glory, therefore signifying God's essence. The word also does not mean goodness as such, but what proceeds from goodness: the good.

Thus one may also explain the retention of the offensive phrase "I will make pass by," namely, not my essence, but my effects. Thus, also, the opposition to Moses' entreaty for the show of glory, hence of essence, becomes clear and is thereby removed: My effects you shall see, then I shall call, the Eternal is *before* you. These effects are my good, my grace and my mercy. Thus, Jewish exegetes were correct in understanding the word, which occurs in this grammatical form only once, not as a bodily backside, but as the effects of the action of God's essence.

15. We now turn again to Deuteronomy. The speech does not rest satisfied with the warning that protects the spirituality of revelation against bodily perception. It is also not satisfied with the transfer of the historical fact close to present actuality, in order to make the active responsibility of the people all the more urgent. Instead, it almost approaches the threshold of a rational solution of the exceptional fact.

This progress is accomplished by the verses: "For this commandment, which I commanded thee this day, is not too hard for thee, neither is it far off. It is not in heaven that thou shouldst say: 'Who shall go up for us to heaven, and bring it unto us, and make us to hear it, that we may do it?' Neither is it beyond the sea, that thou shouldest say: 'Who shall go over the sea for us, and bring it unto us, and make us to hear it, that we may do it?' But the word is very nigh unto thee, in thy mouth, and in thy heart, that thou mayest do it" (Deut. 30:11-14). Thus the teaching is no longer in heaven, and it has not come from heaven, but apparently its origin is made wholly subjective: in your heart and in your mouth. In the heart of man and in the rational speech of man "the word" is contained, as the commandment is called here. It is not far from the spirit of man, but near to it. Revelation has its foundation in the heart and in the most proper power of man, which is speech.[12] Certainly it was not the intention of these verses to contest the revelation on Sinai, but one cannot fail to see that through these verses interest is turned away from the fact that happened only once. The spiritualization and idealization of the fact is achieved through its internalization into the spirit of man.

This spirit of Deuteronomy lives in the prophets, who, like Jeremiah, prophesy the "new covenant" that God will make with Israel: "Behold, the days come, saith the Eternal, that I will make a new covenant with the house of Israel, and with the house of Judah: not according to the covenant that I made with their fathers . . . But this shall be the covenant that I will make with the house of Israel after those days, says the Eternal, I will put my law in their inward parts, and in their hearts will write it; and I will be their God, and they shall be My people" (Jer. 31:31-33). Inward parts are substituted for the mouth, and the Torah, by being inscribed on the heart, has become a covenant.

16. And what Jeremiah calls the new covenant, Isaiah calls the "new spirit" (רוח חדשה) and Ezekiel the "new heart" (לב חדש).

Deuteronomy is unmistakably here the high point, because it states the opposition to the alleged origin of the monotheistic teaching in heaven. Hence, already at this point, even without basing man's relation to God in regard to creation and revelation in the reason of man, revelation—and creation also—is transfigured to a purely spiritual meaning. Spiritualization was the necessary consequence of God's uniqueness, which as the spirituality of his being must be thought of in opposition to all sensibility.

Other evidence for this tendency, which can be traced in very early documents of monotheism, will be presented gradually as we develop the basic concepts. The share that we generally assumed for reason in the religion of monotheism already makes this tendency necessary, as does even the concept of reason itself, as well as the concept of man as rational being. If man is to be God's creation and if revelation is to be possible with regard to him, it can only be through his reason; consequently, revelation itself can only be thought of as the revelation to reason.

By now the relation between God and man proves itself to be a *correlation*. The uniqueness of God determines his relation to man's reason. And man's reason, as God's creation, determines man's relation to God as a rational relation, and therefore determines also the consummation of this rational relation in revelation, which together with the creation establishes the correlation of man and God.

17. The attempt of the Jewish philosophers of the Middle Ages to establish an accord between reason and revelation and therefore, though more or less definitely, the origin of revelation in reason, may be justifiably considered the legitimate continuation of monotheism. This is already proved by their presupposing that almost all the foundations of principles are those of reason. Although the expression for the principle is changeable — sometimes it is called "root" (שרש), sometimes "foundation" (יסוד), sometimes "principle" (עיקר), and so on—there is throughout a general prevalence of the pregnant expression: "first principles of reason" (מושכלות ראשונת). Hence, certain passages of revelation are not established as principles, but propositions of reason are established as principles for revelation and even for the unity of God and the creation. Thus, reason is made the root of the content of revelation. And no offense should be taken because the correlation of God and man, this correlation of the divine

spirit to the human, has as an unavoidable consequence a kind of identity of logical reason in both.

18. Finally, we may therefore venture to put forth as a characteristic of revelation the general view that every philosophy, every spiritual-moral culture, requires the presupposition of the *eternal* as opposed to the transitoriness of all earthly institutions and human ideas.

The Greeks distinguished the "unwritten laws" from the written ones. The latter are statutes from human hands. It is not important that they should be written, though the highest certitude is inherent in the written and the state law. Even the positive laws require for their more profound verification conformity with the unwritten laws. If the actual ruler, like Creon, proclaims a law, it is not binding for Antigone, and she knows herself free from the wantonness of transgressing the law because, in her love for her brother, she appeals to the unwritten laws. These unwritten laws contained the morality of the Greek national spirit before it was formulated and motivated by the philosophers. Yet philosophic ethics was no safeguard against sophistry, which broke forth out of the ranks of philosophy itself. What in later times has been designated by the term "by nature" (φύσει) in opposition to convention, designated as "statute" (συνθήκη = νόμῳ) is nothing other than that "in itself," that eternal, that unwritten, which precedes any recorded writing, precedes, as it were, any culture, must precede it, because it lays the foundation for every culture.

19. What the Greeks called the unwritten law, the Jews called written teaching. They wanted to disregard in it the connection with reason, asserted elsewhere, because their vision, their interest, was pointed to the future, which they intended to keep connected with the past. Therefore they fix the past as written teaching, in order to strengthen oral teaching as teaching. The Greek from the very outset addresses his criticism to the present, for which he has to lay a foundation in the past. The Jew, however, does not want to deepen the present through criticism, but rather through establishing its connection with the eternal, with written law.

This *eternal*, as the *foundation of reason* in all of its content, the Jew calls *revelation*.

But is the name *revelation* itself customarily or traditionally used? This question is to be answered in the negative. The technical term is "the giving of the Torah" (מתן תורה). This giving does not contain a mystery. In all benedictions on the Torah it says: "He, who hast given us the Torah"; and in the liturgy God is called "the Giver of the Torah." There is nothing said about a mystery, nothing about unveiling (*revelatio*). God gives the Torah as he gives everything, life and bread, and also death. Revelation is the sign of reason, which is not animal sensuality but comes from God and connects with God.

20. What the Greeks in connection with the unwritten laws in later times called the eternal, philosophy, at the time of Plato and Aristotle, called *a priori* and *a posteriori*. These terms contain an ambiguity with regard to time, similar to that contained in the idea of theophany with regard to space. In theophany the front and back were misunderstood in terms of bodily space. If, however, the *a priori* from the very outset is understood as that which is prior to, and the foundation for, any sense perception and experience, then we recognize the spiritual connection that here binds the demands of reason with revelation.

Philosophy restrains every seemingly justified interest in the *development* of concepts and the whole content of consciousness with the reply that that development cannot be entirely carried through, that a foundation, therefore, has to be marked out that firmly withstands, as it must, any analysis. As philosophy requires the eternal, in which all change in human consciousness with all its treasures has its prime ground, so also religion, because of its share in reason, is overpowered by this problem and enlivened by this interest. Not even Moses, as little as Solon or Lycurgus, can have given the law out of his own spirit, nor can it merely have stemmed from the patriarchs, but the law, in opposition to all historical potential, must have come in immediate succession from God, the unique being.

If, as we have seen, this spiritual succession was, in the course of political events, designated as an historical act in order that it might be considered a national one, then, as we have also seen, in the beginning of proper, that is to say literary, history the criticism and correction appeared, which *transferred Sinai into the heart of man*. The eternal, which is removed from all sense experience, therefore also from all historical experience, is the foundation and the warrant of the very spirit of national history. It precedes because it is a foundation. It must precede, because it must be laid as a foundation. Reason does not begin with history, but history has to begin with reason. For the beginning has to be more than a temporal beginning; it has to mean the eternal originative principle.

CHAPTER V

The Creation of Man in Reason

1. The first two chapters of Genesis report the creation of man, the second chapter differently from the first. In the first, after the creation of all other living creatures, it says: "And God said: 'Let us make man in our image, after our likeness; and let them have dominion over the fish of the sea, and over the fowl of the air' . . . And God created man in His own image, in the image of God created He him; male and female created He them" (Gen. 1:26,27). The record apparently has the features of ancient mythology, but this is soon corrected. "Let us make man in our image"; this plural form is annulled by a singular: "and God created man in His own image"; and apparently because of this correction the expression "in the image of God created He him" is repeated. But does there exist an image, a likeness of God, according to which man could have been created?

In the second chapter, after the establishment of the Sabbath at the completion of the creation, it says suddenly: "and there was not a man to till the ground; but there went up a mist from the earth, and watered the whole face of the ground. Then the Eternal God formed man of the dust of the ground, and breathed into his nostrils the breath of life; and man became a living soul" [Gen. 2:5-7]. Now the image of God has disappeared and the earth has become, linguistically, the root of man, as well as the mother-ground for man: dust of the earth. Thus not only God, but the Eternal God has now made man. He breathed the breath of life into him, and thereby made him into a living soul. The soul's breath of life has thus joined the dust. And the matter did not rest at the primitive image of the earth, but now life and soul make up man. So deep was the influence of Yahvism.

2. Immediately after this follows the account of Paradise, in which the mystery of life is transplanted to the Tree of Life, which is joined however, by the Tree of Knowledge of good and evil. Whereas in the first chapter God created man as male and female, the woman is here

not created, but as the correct expression goes, "made" out of the rib of man: "And the rib, which the Eternal God had taken from the man, made He a woman" (Gen. 2:22). And the following admonition, "Therefore shall a man leave his father and his mother, and shall cleave unto his wife, and they shall be one flesh" (Gen. 2:24), makes the meaning of the change unmistakeable.

Therefore it does not say at the beginning God created man, but he formed him (וייצר). And hence he first made the human female from the human male in order that they become through marriage one flesh, although they were merely dust of the earth when they were created as man, male and female. The second chapter therefore places the creation entirely in the center of culture, whereas the first chapter, with its image of God and the likeness of man, very naively intends to give to myth a monotheistic coloring, which then asserts itself in the thought of man as God's *image*.

3. However, this thought itself can only be an image. "What likeness will ye compare Him" (Isa. 40:18). There can be no image of God. Therefore man cannot be an image of God. What the intended improvement of the myth here means by image follows from the meaning that we generally had to grant to creation. Creation is the logical consequence of God's unique being, which would have no meaning if it were not the presupposition of becoming. In all becoming, however, man is the focal point, not, to be sure, insofar as he is a living creature, but insofar as the tree of knowledge blooms for him. The mythical language expresses it thus: knowledge brings death. Or as the serpent interprets it: "And ye shall be as God, knowing good and evil" (Gen. 3:5).

Thus the question of creation, in the case of man, now concerns *knowledge*. And with regard to knowledge the question concerns the relation of man to God. The serpent calls it identity; our philosophical language calls it correlation (*Korrelation*), which is the term for all concepts of reciprocal relation. A reciprocal relation exists between man and God. God's being is the foundation for the being of creation, or rather for the existence of creation. But in the case of man's existence, creation does not suffice; if it did, God's being would be the presupposition only of man as a living creature. In the case of man, God's being must be the presupposition for knowledge. And knowledge is concerned not only with the knowledge of nature, but is also concerned with "the knowledge of good and evil." The essence of man is dependent on the knowledge of morality. Reason is not only theoretical, but also practical, ethical. The creation of man must mean the creation of his reason.

4. The prophet Zechariah has accurately expressed the relation of the *spirit* to creation: "The Eternal who stretcheth forth the heavens and laid the foundation of the earth, and formed the spirit of man within him" (Zech. 12:1). God is not only the creator of heaven and earth, but he formed the spirit of man in his body. The spirit of man is not a reproduction, not a homogeneous development from the creation of man's body within the general creation of heaven and earth; rather, the spirit of man expressly requires God himself as its creator.

Later we will have to draw the monotheistic consequences of this thesis for morality, for the ethical meaning of man; at this point it is important only to establish the correlation of man and God on the basis of the theoretical foundation of the spirit, of reason in general. Job expresses this correlation from God's side: "The Spirit of God hath made me and the breath of the Almighty giveth me life" (Job 33:4). But Job expresses this relation even more specifically: "But it is a spirit in man; and the breath of the Almighty that giveth them understanding" (אכן רוח היא באנוש ונשמת שדי תבינם) [Job 32:8]). Consequently, man's spirit is based on God's spirit, not only as a living creature, or only as an intellectual creature, but his reason, which in an eminent way is moral reason, is also derived from God.

The spirit of God no longer hovers only above the waters: all knowledge and all art come from him; thus Bezalel, thus Joseph and all Judges, the hero Samson and the King Saul, the prophets as well, have all their wisdom from God. Nevertheless the specific ethical spirit is not yet expressed in all these manifestations. Even the Messiah has only "the spirit of counsel and might, the spirit of knowledge and the fear of God" (Isa. 11:2). More explicitly, even the spirit of Messiah is not yet related to God's spirit.

An immediate relationship exists between the spirit of the *people* and the spirit of God: "Would that all the people were prophets, that God would put His spirit upon them" (Num. 11:29). This original universality of the spirit in Israel leads to great consequences. Isaiah says: "For the earth shall be full of the knowledge of the Eternal" (Isa. 11:9). And with Jeremiah even the difference of degrees of knowledge among men is suspended: "for they shall all know Me, from the least of them unto the greatest of them" (Jer. 31:34). And Joel finally pours out the spirit of God "upon all flesh . . . and upon the servants and upon the handmaids" (Joel 3:1,2). And finally Ezekiel changes the new convenant of Jeremiah into the new heart and new spirit: "And I will put my spirit within you" (Ezek. 36:26,27; 39:29). And what Ezekiel in this verse promises for a future time, Zechariah assumes from the very beginning: as God spans the heaven and establishes the earth, so also he formed the spirit of man within him; Ezekiel only says more accurately how this was accomplished: God has put his spirit within man.

Hence in the spirit, in the theoretical and in the moral reason, the correlation between God and man is established and strengthened. For where God creates, there his unique being unfolds as the foundation for becoming, which in virtue of this being attains its foundation and its meaning. And in all becoming the highest problem is man, who is not merely life but also reason. Moreover only through reason, through the ability of knowledge does that man arise who can come into correlation with God. Considered from God's view too, reason is the condition by virtue of which God can come into correlation with man. And this correlation is based on the concept of the unique being, which is the presupposition of becoming. As being is therefore the presupposition of the foundation, so is becoming—and, thus, man—the presupposition for the unfolding of the foundation. Correlation represents this reciprocal dependence. Reason is the concept through which the correlation is accomplished and therefore must be common to God and man.

Creation and revelation take effect only through reason. Both of these concepts turn out to be expressions of the correlation, and therefore both of them are based on the concept of reason that is achieved in the creation of the man of reason and also in the revelation of God to man. Already the creation as the creation of reason does not leave man in passivity, for this would be in contradiction to the concept of correlation. And revelation even more so cannot make man passive. For this would contradict the concept not only of correlation but even more so of reason, which revelation has to reveal.

Reciprocity enters man's knowledge of God in accordance with correlation. It is as if God's being were actual in man's knowledge only, so tremendous is the effect of the correlation. Man is no longer merely God's creature, but his reason, by virtue of his knowledge and also for the sake of it, makes him at least subjectively, as it were, the discoverer of God.

Thus one can understand how the *spirit* becomes the fundamental concept of religion, the mediating concept, the concept that effects the correlation between God and man.

Spirit is usually understood merely in opposition to matter and to life. Spirit is therefore in the first place, soul. As soon, however, as the spirit becomes God, and God becomes spirit only, polytheism is overcome. God, as spirit, is not in fire, not in the wind, nor in the material power of man, but he becomes an infinity that man cannot escape:

"Whither shall I go from Thy spirit?" (Ps. 139:7). All corporeality now vanishes from God, and in this warding off of materiality the uniqueness of God's being proves itself. *God is unique. This now means: God is spirit.*

5. However, the spirit does not have only the negative meaning of an intermediary between the corporeal world and God's uniqueness; rather it has the positive meaning of the spirit that does not need any other mediation than the one that its own concept accomplishes. God is spirit; this sentence, according to the correlation that exists between being and becoming, also means: man is spirit. This equation, however, is not to be misinterpreted as identity; for God's being is unique. But his uniqueness, as spirit, establishes the becoming of man, as spirit. The spirit unites both members of the correlation.

To be sure, the spirit of man cannot be the spirit of God. However, God gives his spirit to man, as the correlation requires. Therefore the spirit of man, though not identical with God's spirit, must yet be comparable to it. The correlation is necessary: creation and revelation make it necessary. It cannot violate the uniqueness of God's spirit. The correlation, however, becomes effective only through the spirit. Therefore, the spirit of man must have been given to him by God.

The spirit of God is inexhaustible, in its power and its kind. His being is indeed unique. Therefore, for the comparison that the correlation makes necessary, nothing else remains but what Job says when he describes the human spirit as "a portion and inheritance" in the Godhead. "For what would be the portion of the Godhead from above? And the heritage of the Almighty from on high?" (Job 31:2). God's full legal ownership of the human spirit is there expressed by the two words that designate hereditary possession (חלק ונחלה), as if Job intended to say, my spirit has a share in God's creation from above, and it is the inheritance, which the Almighty let me have from on high.

The abstract expressions for God, "the Godhead" and "the Almighty," as well as the sensible origin from "above," from "on high," also require our attention. They allow us to recognize the tendency of the thought involved: to derive the essence of man entirely from God and to establish it in God's uniqueness. The derivation from above gives a better foundation than the "portion," which in any case means only a share in a possession. Thus it remains the case that correlation is the decisive concept, and portion and inheritance are only expressive images, which are weaker than the conceptual relationship of correlation.

6. Out of this rationalism, which is based on the spirit as the connecting concept in the correlation of God and man, one can explain the emphasis that Deutoronomy in particular, and with it all the

prophets, puts upon the *knowledge* of God. They make knowledge a
condition for reverence of God and, more particularly, the condition for
the love of God as well. If there could have been a question how knowledge could be thought of as love, then the opposite question may now
arise: how could love be thought of as knowledge? If, however, love
is the inmost expression of the correlation, then knowledge makes this
inmost kind of relation clear: it is the spirit of knowledge that constitutes this bond between God and man:[13] "Know this day, and lay
it to thy heart" (Deut. 4:39). Hence, affection is established throughout in knowledge; the heart, in the spirit.

We could not understand how the prophets could play so unem-
barassedly with the fire of knowledge if monotheism, in full consciousness, did not desire to make the spirit its foundation, if it were not
permeated by the insight that the unique God is rooted in knowledge;
and that without this root and without an active connection with it
no growth of monotheism would be possible.[14] Man is spirit. And the
spirit comes from God, "who gave it," who planted it in man. This spirit
has to prove itself in reciprocal action: through knowledge and in
knowledge God enters into necessary correlation to man.

Prayer also recognizes this relation to knowledge. In the main daily
prayer, the "Eighteen Benedictions," the first of the supplications reads:
"Thou favorest man with knowledge." It is as if it were to say: the first
of God's favors is the endowment of knowledge, and there can be no
other kind of favor but that which is dependent on knowledge. Thus
knowledge plainly becomes the fundamental condition of religion, of
reverence for God.

Monotheism arose in a spiritual culture that was without any creative share in scientific culture. However, the spirituality of monotheism
demands a share in reason, a share in knowledge, especially if monotheism is also to create ethics. Ethics, however, in the Greek sense, in
the scientific sense, is dependent on logic. And the progress of logic
in turn is dependent on the advancement of science. The prophets
have no science, and therefore no scientific, no philosophic logic; therefore also no scientific, no philosophic ethics, and yet prophecy must
gain a share in knowledge. We understand now how the emphasis
that is put upon knowledge tries to compensate for this inner deficiency, and also how, out of this emphasis, the concept of the spirit
as a connecting link between God and man originated. And when one
thinks through the difference that exists between monotheism and all
mysticism, a difference that also grows out of the ground of science
and philosophy, then one will not underestimate the value that is inherent in this persistent stressing of knowledge. The primitive or-

iginality of this value asserts itself in the whole history of Jewish monotheism. It also explains Jewish history from the standpoint of its share
in ancient culture, as well as in its share of the culture of the Middle
Ages and modernity.

7. A very noteworthy document of this share of religion in knowledge is found in the Talmud, and indeed with an unsurpassed application: "In that hour, in which man is led to judgment, it is said to
him: did you execute your business (livelihood) in good faith? Did
you appoint times for the study of the Torah? . . . Did you pursue
your studies with wisdom (method)? Did you make inferences on the
basis of one sentence to another?" (Sabbath 31a).[15] Rashi gives an explanation of the last question: "The inference of one sentence on the
basis of another, that is knowledge." According to this passage one has
to consider how much the Talmud must have esteemed methodical
knowledge if it made it into a question that the highest judge puts to
a man's soul. It is not enough that times were appointed for the study
of the Torah, so that the study should be pursued regularly; it was also
necessary to show that the study had been performed in a methodical
way and with logical method. The method, however, consists in the
deduction of one sentence from another, which is set down as its
foundation.

The analogy that in my pamphlet, *Deutschtum und Judentum*
[The German Nation and Judaism], I tried to establish between
these two national spirits on the basis of their common participation
in the Greek spirit is confirmed in the strictest sense by this talmudic
document. For Plato, the ideal representative of the Greek spirit,
founded knowledge on the giving of an account (λόγον διδόναι), which
consists in deducting one sentence from a preceding one, until the
process is completed in the establishment of the *first principle*. That
the German spirit has renewed this genuine idealism may be left
out of consideration at this point.

However, the agreement between the Jewish and the Greek spirit,
which the above example displays, is certainly surprising. The soul is
asked whether it fulfilled the study in obedience to the method, and
the method itself is made the object of a question. The derivation, the
deduction from a principle, is the giving of an account. And, in the
terminology of the medieval philosophers, the term first principle
(הנחה) is preserved.

8. Not only the idea of a first principle was affirmed in this terminology; as a consequence of this principle of knowledge, the content of
several other principles of reason was distinguished. They are called
"first intelligibles" (מושכלות ראשונות), and this term is more exact than

those of synonymous meaning that were more often used such as "roots" (שרשים) or "foundation-stone" (יסוד) or "principles" (עקרים). All philosophers, with one exception, which needs to be accounted for, agree on this foundation of first principles. Why do they not content themselves with the presupposition of first principles for the doctrine of faith? Why do they contest the legitimacy of such a dogmatic determination of principles? How can they make any distinction at all between the first principles of faith and the first principles of reason?

If, however, these philosophers cannot assume a real opposition between these two sources of the spirit, which is alive in themselves, then the distinction allotted to the first principles is only understandable if they are no less valid as first principles for the doctrine of faith, as the foundation of the articles of faith. And thus the thought of reverence of God through knowledge comes to its pure fruition, in consequence of which the correlation between God and man is accomplished by virtue of the spirit. The first principles that are thus distinguished are not alien to the spirit of the knowledge of God, understood as reverence of God; instead, the principle of the spirit, the principle of knowledge, the principle of methodical knowledge, fulfills the share that reason has in religion, and with this fulfills the correlation between God and man.

The Jewish philosophy of the Middle Ages does not grow so much out of Islam as out of the original monotheism. The more intimate relationship between Judaism and Islam—more intimate than with other monotheistic religions—can be explained by the kinship that exists between the mother and daughter religion. Already in the prophetic writings the intellectual disposition of monotheism is securely established. And the further development of monotheism in the history of Judaism, as in the cultural history of the Jews, is a necessary consequence of this original disposition.

9. And yet, while considering this intellectual disposition with regard to the spirit of God and the spirit of man, we have so far established only the preliminary meaning of reason in monotheism. So far the spirit, in the case of man as well as in the case of God, has had only an intellectual meaning as its methodological foundation. Only when reason becomes moral reason, only when the spirit governs and secures more than the problem of causality, as is the case in creation and revelation; only when the question wherefrom and whereby is supplemented with the question whereto and wherefore; only when the interest in the cause is supplemented by the interest in the *purpose*, only through this supplement does reason cease to be half of reason, only through this supplement does the spirit become one and whole.

The correlation of God and man, as established by creation and revelation, fulfills its meaning only through the addition of moral demands. The latter do not remain fixed to the question of cause. What would be gained if I were able to penetrate the mysteries of creation and revelation? Would I thereby understand the unique being of God better than I have to understand it through correlation?

The correlation elevates and guides me beyond causality to the new interest, which opens the question of purpose. The purpose of man is now in question.

And the new question arises: is the purpose of man contained in God's purpose, as correlation requires it to be, and does God's spirit and his correlation with man's spirit make it possible to accomplish the necessary unification of these purposes? Hence purpose becomes the new guiding concept of knowledge and at the same time a new concept of the content of the spirit. And with the notion of purpose the concept of correlation moves from the realm of theoretical knowledge into the realm of the ethical.

CHAPTER VI

The Attributes of Action

1. The Talmud contains the following report: "In the presence of Rabbi Chanina somebody once prayed the words: O God, great, powerful, fearful, sublime, and so on. Then Rabbi Chanina said to him: have you now exhausted the praise of your Lord?" And he limits the right to invoke the characteristics of God in prayer to the invocation expressed in the scripture (Berachoth 33b). The scripture, however, names in the theophany, which we considered above (see p. 42 ff.), the "thirteen characteristics" the Talmud recounts: "merciful and gracious, long-suffering, and abundant in love and truth (*Treue*); keeping love unto the thousandth generation, forgiving iniquity and transgression and sin; and that will by no means clear the guilty" (Exod. 34:6-7). These thirteen characteristics are actually only two: love and justice.

Unity is not even contained in them, not to mention that there is no reference to omnipotence and omniscience. The characteristics of *being* are therefore entirely omitted, and what is there left in the modifications of love and justice? The characteristics are thought through and ordered in an entirely new relation, namely, as "attributes of action" (תוארי המעשה), as Maimonides designates them. The place of being is taken by action. And the place of causality, therefore, is taken by purpose.

2. What does action mean in the case of God? Is it not fulfilled with the creation? However, creation and revelation both come under the realm of causality; their cause is not purpose, but simply being. From these causalities of God one must distinguish action, which is determined by love and justice. Action therefore does not ensue according to causality, but according to the new kind of causality that is formed by purpose. What, accordingly, does action mean in the case of God?

This question finds its answer through another question: what does

94

purpose mean in the case of God? This question already implies the problem of correlation. For, properly speaking, with regard to being there can be no question of its purpose. The question of the purpose of being transcends being proper and relates itself to correlation. The same is the case with the problem of action, which as love and justice is distinguished from the causality of creation.

Action in the case of God is related to the possibility of action in becoming, namely, in man. And this possibility is related not to causality but comes under the viewpoint of purpose. Hence the attributes of action are not so much characteristics of God, but rather conceptually determined models for the action of man. The unity of the concepts of love and justice in the concept of action, and consequently in purpose, elevates characteristics to norms (י"ג מדות).

And already this term "norm," which is otherwise only logically valid, and which in the Talmud is established for these thirteen characteristics, shows their designation as precepts and models, which are clearly distinguished from the determinations of being. These norms are contained in the essence of God, but it is impossible to imagine that they could exhaust this essence: they could have been conceived for man only, could be valid for the actions of man only.[16]

3. We here come again to the same thought to which we were led while considering the biblical passages concerning Moses' entreaty for God's appearance (cf. p. 79 f.). God wants to reveal only the effects of his essence to Moses, not his essence itself.[17] These effects, which there we recognized as aftereffects of God's essence, were the only knowable characteristics of God. Now these effects become more precisely known as actions. They are now therefore no longer merely aftereffects, which would still be connected with causality, but as norms of action, as love and justice, they originate not in causality but in the purpose of the action, which is determined by love and justice. At this point, again, being steps out of its confines and enters into correlation with becoming in man.

If we now turn from the philosophical designation of these legitimate thirteen characteristics, for which we are particularly indebted to Maimonides, and consider other biblical sources, we find above all two concepts in which these moral characteristics of God are comprised: *holiness* and *goodness*.

There is a question as to which one of these concepts precedes the other in the development of the biblical thinking; or, rather, the question is answered by the relation Deuteronomy has to the so-called laws of holiness, whereas it is only later that the concept of God's goodness, as the unique good one, becomes the leading thought, as it does in the psalms. The thought may have been instrumental in bringing about the lyrical style of the psalms.

4. *Holiness* originally means separation. As the myth generally separates from common usage particular places, houses, vessels, animals and finally also persons, so the sacrificial worship in the sanctuary and with the priest intensified and made distinct this meaning of holiness as separation. Polytheism does not go beyond the holiness of things. If God is also called holy in polytheism, the reference is to his statue in the separated place of his temple.

A great center of gravitation comes into the world with the words: "Ye shall be holy; for I the Eternal your God am holy" (Lev. 19:2). This word "holy" has a twofold meaning: it relates holiness to God and to man. And one is to assume that only through this unified relation to God, as well as to man, can holiness be thought of as possible with regard to God himself; as on the other hand one might say that only through the coming to be of holiness in God does its relation to man simultaneously become possible. The correlation becomes effectual and with it mythology and polytheism cease to be. Holiness becomes *morality*.[18]

5. What is the difference between that which we scientifically call morality and the religious expression of holiness? The difference is to be derived from the difference of the tense of the verb in the sentence in which holiness is used with regard to God and man. With God it is being: "For I am holy." With regard to man, however, it says: "Ye shall be holy." Hence one may translate: "Ye shall become holy." Holiness thus means for man a task, whereas for God it designates being.

This designation of being with regard to God is not concerned with his metaphysical causality but with his purposive acting, which is the model for the purposive action of man. In holiness God becomes for man the *lawgiver* who sets tasks for him. Only as a holy one can he set these tasks; for holiness, already according to its original meaning, separates God from all sensibility. And this elevation above sensibility is the thing that is set as a task for man.

If one were not to shun the paradox, one could think that holiness exists not so much for God as for man. Out of God's being, out of his uniqueness, holiness separates itself and does so only out of consideration for man. It is, however, not a particular characteristic, but rather is the unity of all characteristics of action.

The contrary question, therefore, whether holiness is possible for man, cannot be asked. This is a question of causality, which at this point entirely recedes before the new interest in and the new problem of purpose. Without the purpose of holiness the being of man becomes void. Holiness is his purpose, which sets for him his task, God's task.

6. Modern biblical research damages its own understanding of the ethical meaning of holiness and its connection with the fundamental concepts of monotheism because it cannot refrain from blindly mixing a historical interest in the literary and cultic development of these concepts with the inner connection that permeates them. Therefore its objective understanding is constantly hampered by historical elucidation. Philological research has not yet been enlightened by the understanding that all spiritual progress is accompanied by secondary material factors. These factors, much as they might hinder and limit, work not only as forces of opposition, but very often they give wings to the flight of ideas.

Biblical research, in any case, influenced by dogmatic tendencies, has a predilection for clinging to secondary material, to the state of affairs of the time and to political circumstances; but it neglects to investigate and to illuminate the inner, relentless chain of the motivation of ideas. Holiness, to be sure, originated with sacrifice, and developed with the sacrifice, but as sacrifice is surpassed by morality, so is holiness removed from sacrifice and together with morality brought to a new separation.

7. We shall better understand this development of the concept of holiness if we do not start from the laws of holiness but with the innovation in the name of the unique God that Isaiah brings about by designating him as the "Holy one," the "Holy one of Israel." Isaiah's style makes it evident that he is conscious of the fact that he is introducing a new concept of God, a new knowledge of God. He does not abrogate the four-letter name, which was so solemnly introduced to Moses at the first revelation. But he feels the vocation not only to deepen the knowledge and reverence of the Unique One, of the only unique being, but also to further this knowledge practically through the new knowledge of holiness.

Therefore he begins his career with this vision of holiness, in which, characteristically enough, he imitates Moses' humility. For as the latter shies away from his vocation because of a bodily impediment, so this humility in Isaiah becomes even more moralistic: the uncircumsized lips become the unclean lips. And yet the call comes to him: holy is the Eternal.

Why does Isaiah repeat this call three times? Did he intend to write the text for the musical treatment of the Sanctus? It is obvious that the three times holy, which the angels called one to another, has the meaning of a proclamation of a new content of the divine teaching. The final clause itself, which is also attributed to the angels, confirms this idea: "the whole earth is full of His glory." The separation of heaven and earth ceases; God does not live only in heaven, but the whole earth is full of his glory. This seeming extension of God's location also is rather an intensification of the spirituality that does away with the primitive meaning of holiness. And finally the moral meaning of the new holiness is confirmed by the threat of punishment which Isaiah has to announce to his people.

8. The "Holy One of Israel" is therefore the prevailing name of God in Isaiah and is also preserved in the Deutero-Isaiah. "His name is the Holy One of Israel" (Isa. 47:4). "And the neediest among men shall exult in the Holy One of Israel" (Isa. 29:19). "The High and Lofty One that inhabiteth eternity, whose name is Holy" (Isa. 57:15). Holiness is substituted for the place on high as God's abode: "I dwell in the high and holy" (Isa. 57:15). Also it is identified with God's unity: "There is none holy as the Eternal; for there is none beside Thee" (1 Sam. 2:2). The spiritualization, which the psalm produces by putting the praises of Israel in the place of Zion and Jerusalem, is also joined to holiness: "Thou art holy, that are enthroned upon the praises of Israel" (Ps. 22:4). Thus holiness is connected with spirituality but develops out of the latter into morality.

And what is the essence of morality? It consists of the correlation of God and man. Correlation is therefore based on holiness and therefore is entirely different from separation. Morality branches off into the reciprocal relations of men and therefore also into the correlation with God. Holiness develops into an embodiment of all these branchings out of the correlation. Thus God, the holy one, *is* for the sake of the holiness of man. And holiness also becomes the embodiment of the thirteen characteristics of God: it comprises justice and love; it makes love akin to justice.

9. Isaiah still uses the expression the "mighty One of Israel." It nearly corresponds to the name "Almighty God" (אל שדי), which name was replaced by that of the One that is. But the expression occurs in Isaiah only once, which shows how much might recedes before holiness. And the connection of holiness with human things and institutions, which Deuteronomy maintains, becomes decisive for the prophets. Thus everywhere the idea of Deuteronomy was effective, that the truth of the Torah is to be proven by the "statutes and ordinances."

It would, however, be mechanical, and in truth unhistorical, if one were to demand a strict realization of this connection between God and man in all human endeavors, and if one were to consider each exception as a proof that this connection was not grasped in all its clarity. Who is going to expect clarity in the development of these basic eternal concepts, a clarity which in the naive stage of the development is bound to be lacking? Clarity is a sign of reflection; in its primitive steps the naive course of history falters everywhere. This proves all the more the naiveté of historical development, but it cannot be counted as an argument against the general tendency of the development. Thus holiness, to be sure, also progresses side by side with its primitive meaning, which, however, it outgrows. This connection should not mar the new formation, which is a new flowering on the old stem, a new fruit from the old root. For sacrifice is the root of worship, just as polytheism is undisputably the root of monotheism. But a new sun rises above the old root and brings to light a new growth.

What then is morality? This question has a different meaning when the sociologist rather than the moralist asks it. Therefore, one should not ask of religion in its naive stage of development a definite treatment and realization of this concept. Morality is indeed called holiness there, and with this is expressed the connection of the old with the new. The only symptom of development that can be required is the preponderance of human morality.

CHAPTER VII

The Holy Spirit

1. What is human morality? We do not cease to ask this question. However, with what intention did the prophet isolate morality as a problem? In monotheism every characteristic of man proceeds from God. The problem of morality, therefore, has first to be raised with regard to God. The predominance of divine morality is expressed by holiness, which by virtue of monotheism is distinct from the holiness of polytheism.

Pagan holiness remains sensuous desire, even when it requires abstention from the sensuous; it is always inwardly connected with man's senses. Monotheistic holiness is directed to the *spirit* of man, and not indeed to the intellect alone; it is as morality that the spirit is to engender itself. Holiness effects the development of the spirit of knowledge into the spirit of the will and action; holiness serves as a mediating concept for this development. And as the spirit in general is the mediating concept in the correlation of God and man, so also the spirit serves to mediate holiness in order to bring about this correlation.

2. The origin of the concept of the holy spirit thus seems to be necessary, since it was implied in the problem of morality. We also understand how, with the derailment of *Hellenism* from the track of pure monotheism, there could originate the materialization and personification of the *Logos* as a holy spirit mediating between God and man. The mediation, however, can be thought of as correlation only conceptually. As soon as it is not confined to a strict conceptual abstraction, as soon as it is imagined as a material connection of powers, which afterwards become persons, the connection assumes the form of a community. And with this in mind, it may happen that the tasks of the community are subdivided; it may then also happen that holiness is made into a special task of a particular agency of this community. In pure monotheism, however, only the individual members of the cor-

100

relation, God and man, can have holiness as a task. And when the spirit is called holy, then one means its community with God and with man: one means its realization of the correlation.

Now it is already striking that in Jewish monotheism the holy spirit is not so much related to God as to man, so that it is not thought of as a specific characteristic of God. But even more striking is the fact that in the Old Testament the use of this term is extremely rare. Altogether it occurs only three times: twice in two consecutive verses in Isaiah, and once in the psalms.

3. The first mention seems to be colorless. After the sentence, "In His love and in His pity he redeemed them, and He bore them and carried them all the days of old," it says, in this speech of tremendous beauty: "But they rebelled, and grieved His holy spirit" (Isa. 63:9,10). Suddenly for the first time mention is made of God's holy spirit. Since God's spirit is a common expression for the essence of God, and since holiness is the new expression for the essence of God, the new word formation cannot become striking. Striking, instead, is the fact that it occurs only now and is repeated only once. It also appears striking that the new expression is chosen in this connection. To convey the idea of grieving God, the new creation of the holy spirit was hardly necessary.

Immediately afterward Isaiah tells how the people remembered the days of old: "Where is He that put His holy spirit in the midst of them?" [Isa. 63:11]. Now the appeal to the holy spirit seems to have a better foundation. For if it is the case that the called one is God himself who has put his holy spirit into Moses' heart, or if it is the case, as Rashi[19] in a more monotheistic way understands it, that God is being called upon, God who through Moses put his holy spirit into the *people,* in both cases nothing else is being said about the holy spirit than what is generally valid with regard to the spirit of God in its relation to the spirit of man: He "formed the spirit of man within him" (Zech. 12:1). As God put his spirit into man, so in the same way it says here for the first time that God has put the holy spirit into the midst of the people, into the heart of the people. Apparently the people represent man better than even Moses does, notwithstanding the customary understanding according to which Moses as prophet is more qualified to receive the holy spirit.

However, the prophet as such never and nowhere has a holy spirit, and even the Messiah does not have it; why should Moses suddenly come to have it? God has put the holy spirit into the people, into its heart, as God generally put his spirit into the heart of man.[20]

Since, therefore, the holy spirit does not differ at all from the spirit in general, it remains a literary riddle how it could suddenly appear in this passage, which is not distinguished by a new religious truth, even if the reminiscence is a deeply religious one.

4. By our turning now to the classical passage, in which the holy spirit appears, we cannot avoid an anticipation that has to do with the concept of man in his moral reason, namely, in his *sinfulness*. Only one other time do the words "holy spirit" occur, in Psalm 51. This psalm is a psalm of genuine repentance imbued with the whole power of remorse and hope of forgiveness. Perhaps it was the depth of this prayer of repentance that occasioned the title: "After he had gone in to Bathsheba." This is not contradicted by verse 6: "Against Thee, Thee only, have I sinned." For the strong consciousness that all sins against another person are subordinate to the sin against God speaks out in this sentence.

Nor does the poet at once seek support in his own consciousness: "Behold, I was brought forth in iniquity, and in sin did my mother conceive me" (Ps. 51:7). The poet wants relentlessly to expose only the human sin. There is no thought of original sin. The verse that follows says: "Behold, Thou desirest truth in the inward parts; make me, therefore, to know wisdom in mine inmost heart." And now forgiveness is called upon: "Purge me with hyssop, and I shall be clean; wash me and I shall be whiter than snow . . . hide not Thy face from my sins." Along with sin as a specific human quality, we also anticipate *forgiveness* as a specific attribute of God, which up to now we have neither developed from his uniqueness, nor from creation and revelation, nor from holiness. The holy spirit, however, will lead us upon this road.

The psalm does not stop with the prayer for forgiveness, but the poet turns now to his own heart and spirit, and there the concept of creation reappears. "Create in me a clean heart, O God; and renew a steadfast spirit within me" (Ps. 51:12). Here we are introduced to the correct concept of the *spirit*: *that it is always renewed* and that its foundation is in this continuous renewal. Apparently the power of sin is weakened through this unceasing recreation of the spirit. This is the second great teaching, which is responsible for the appearance of the holy spirit at this point.

5. At this high point of religious knowledge, which we have now only to anticipate, we can begin to understand that the spirit, the spirit of God as well as the spirit of man, is called a holy spirit. And this is the third great teaching these verses reveal: the holy spirit is fully as much the spirit of man as the spirit of God. The holy spirit of man is the bulwark against the predominance of sin, it is the

protection against the illusion that sin could efface the concept of man. The concept of man consists in his spirit, and this spirit is holy. Therefore sin cannot destroy the spirit of man, the concept of man.

The poet continues: "Cast me not away from Thy presence; and take not Thy holy spirit from me" [Ps. 51:13]. I have Thy holy spirit. Sin cannot frustrate it in me. And Thou cannot take away from me Thy holy spirit because of my sin. Kautzsch is incorrect in interpreting the holy spirit as "the spirit of prophecy," and in this error he fails to grasp the distinctiveness of monotheism; for God puts even the spirit as such not only into the people but also into the individual, and indeed into every man, not only into the prophet. And what is valid for the spirit as such must be valid for the holy spirit, which is not a new spirit but the old spirit as such, the spirit of God and the spirit of man.[21]

6. Through the spirit each man is called to holiness: to every man the commandment of holiness is issued, and thus God desires to be hallowed through every man. The correlation has as its consequence this reciprocal effect. The one commandment "Ye shall be holy" [Lev. 19:2] has as its consequence the other: "And ye shall hallow Me" (וקדשתם אותי). This is the analogue of the sentence: "I will be hallowed among the children of Israel" (Lev. 22:32). God accomplishes his holiness in man. The correlation requires this. And men fulfill their striving for holiness in the acceptance of the archetypal holiness of God, in imitation of which they sanctify themselves.

7. The reciprocity of the correlation has as its consequence a new reciprocal effect from God back to man: "*sanctify yourselves . . . and be ye holy*" (Lev. 11:44). Through this double reciprocity the concept of man is intensified to its ideal, and the ideal of holiness in God is fulfilled. The sanctification of oneself, too, corresponds to God's bestowal of holiness; for the latter is not to be thought of as the transference of a part of holiness, but only as a demand, therefore as an elevation to the duty to sanctify oneself. The interpretation of the *Sifra* is therefore based on a generally correct exegesis: "This is the holiness of the commandment."

The correlation becomes ever more clear. The sentence "I sanctify you" corresponds to the sentence "Him shall ye sanctify" (Isa. 8:13). In what else should the holy spirit prove itself than in the sanctification of God through it? The holy spirit has to be firmly established among men. The Mosaic teaching already taught this in a mythical way. No other sin is known of Moses than his failing by hitting the rock. Instead of hitting the rock, Moses should have spoken to it. Moses violated the sanctification due to God. By his act he was, so to speak, denying God as spirit.

8. One is perhaps inclined to say that Psalm [51], mentioned above, represents the idea of the holy spirit more conclusively than the passage, also mentioned above, in Isaiah [63:9,10], with its literary suddenness and uniqueness. The holy spirit accomplishes the correlation between God and man. The spirit is God's creation, but just as we recognized creation as a "renewal on every day," so also is the creation of the holy spirit a continuous new creation. In this renewal we may perhaps recognize the difference between the holy spirit and the spirit in general.

The spirit in general, if I disregard the fact that God has put it in me, could perhaps not effect the renewal continuously. This question would concern experience, which is in many ways contradictory. The holy spirit, however, which so inwardly and in such an eminent way shows the connection of man with God, so that no sin can break that connection, this holy spirit gives to the spirit of man in general its true foundation, as the psalm expresses it. The creation of the spirit, as the holy one, is now understood as a continuously new creation. And since the creation itself is only a kind of correlation, *self-sanctification* becomes a necessary consequence of the creation of the holiness of the spirit. The holy spirit in man must therefore be active in the same way in the continuous new creation as the holy spirit in God, which also is dependent on the correlation.

9. The consequences of this idea of the holy spirit of the correlation of man and God extend over the entire sphere of the monotheistic teaching. We do not now intend to anticipate any further. Only the text of the verse from the psalm requires a correction. Namely, it never speaks either there or in Isaiah of the holy spirit absolutely. It is not, it is true, designated expressly as the spirit of man: David does not call it his spirit, yet he calls it in God "Thy holy spirit." At this point a general correction would be in order.

"Holy spirit" is, generally speaking, an incorrect translation. The correct one should be: the spirit of sanctity or of holiness. Thus the verse in the psalm does not say "Thy holy spirit," but "Thy spirit of holiness," or, even more exactly perhaps, "the spirit of Thy holiness." The spirit is determined by holiness; God is determined by the holiness of the spirit, and, according to the correlation, so also is man.

10. The continuous renewal of the spirit necessitates a release from sin. In order to accomplish this the correlation of God to man actualizes the idea of God's uniqueness by *averting any mediation,* which might creep into this correlation for the purpose of this release. If the

holy spirit were to be isolated in a person of its own, the correlation would be destroyed. The holy spirit can be neither God alone nor man alone, but neither can it be God and man at the same time; it is an attribute of both, or rather the connection of both. The spirit is nothing else but the connecting link of the correlation, and holiness even more is nothing else but the medium that accomplishes the correlation: how could the holy spirit be anything other than that function which signifies the correlation? The function has only one logical meaning, namely, unification. But this unification must only be thought of as a correlation. Only the correlation keeps the unification within the bounds of abstraction. The unification is in no way a connection of the kind objects may have. God and man have to remain separated, insofar as they are to be united.

The supposition of the separation of both elements, which have to be united, is valid for the logical concept of unification in general. Without this condition the unification is thought of materially. God depends on the correlation with man. And man is dependent on the correlation with God. The high point of this correlation is reached in the concept of the holy spirit. But even with regard to it, God has to remain God, and man, man, if the holy spirit is to be common to them; if it is truly to mean the sanctification of man through the spirit of God, and again the sanctification of God through the spirit of man; and if the correlation is to be thought of as a unification in the holy spirit.

11. The holy spirit, as the link that accomplishes the correlation of God and man, makes the uniqueness of God even more evident, for this unification excludes *mediation*. It is historically understandable that as soon as the strict idea of the monotheistic correlation went astray, under the influence of Platonism, the first harm could be done to the idea of the holy spirit. For it appears so rarely in the Bible, and carries with it the semblance, the illusion of mediation, a concept that is lacking in precision and seems to contradict the idea of God's uniqueness.

Judaism is still reproached by Christianity, as well as by pantheism and mysticism, for not allowing any connection between man and God. And this reproach includes the suspicion that Judaism has obstructed culture. Against this, we have in logical strictness to recognize the connection as in fact a *unification* and not as a vague image of *connection*. This mission is accomplished in Jewish monotheism by the holy spirit, and in this mission we come to understand its single and unique occurrences in the Bible.

12. For this unique occurence in the psalm accomplishes the *limita-*

tion of the holy spirit to *morality*. And from this follows the superiority of the monotheistic correlation, which is unification through the holy spirit over any kind of pantheism. For the holy spirit limits that area of the spirit that connects God and man to holiness. And through this limitation and its exclusiveness, holiness becomes morality. The ethics of critical idealism has clarified this determination, because, to begin with, it laid down the distinction between the certainty of scientific knowledge and that of ethics.

Through this distinction, Kant established the veracity of ethical knowledge, whereas Descartes still remains inside the medieval way of thinking, which assumes that reason has the same value for moral *and* logical problems of knowledge. In this, its systematic arrangement, critical idealism completes the historical tendency of the *idea of faith* of the Reformation. Judaism accomplishes through the holy spirit this fundamentally honest tendency, through which it strikes down pantheism, whereas the misuse of the idea of the holy spirit calls it forth.

By ignoring or disputing this basic critical insight, *pantheism* puts itself into irreconcilable opposition not only to ethics but in general to scientific philosophy, which cannot begin at all if it does not start with this distinction. The tension between pantheism and religion is also based upon this deficiency. Pantheism simply uses the holy spirit for all kinds of knowledge; Judaism, on the contrary, limits its meaning to morality.

Judaism in its biblical sources does not philosophize, but the basic logic of monotheism carries through its consequences beyond biblical limits. Through the "statutes and ordinances" the holy spirit actually becomes morality; in the same way the holy spirit in later history always more and more definitely stamps itself onto the moral spirit, onto moral reason. And the priority given to it over any other qualities of the spirit makes it possible to recognize in it the nucleus of the thought that Kant expressed by the "Primacy of the Practical Reason." The holy spirit does not remain "the God of the spirits of all flesh." In this phrase the lack of differentiation of the theoretical and moral spirit is still inherent. The holy spirit determines the spirit through holiness. Thus, to be sure, the holy spirit had finally to appear; but it also becomes understandable that it could be discovered only in connection with the problem of sin and also only in the lyric form of the psalm.

13. This concurrence of lyric poetry in the discovery of the holy spirit again shows the deep-reaching consequence of the principle. Man in his ultimate depth is to be established and founded by the

holy spirit: man in his correlation with God, man in accordance with the uniqueness of God, man himself as unity, as individual.

Here again we cannot avoid an anticipation which points to the content of the problem of the *individual*. Here, too, the chasm that separates monotheism from pantheism widens. Man, as holy spirit, becomes an individual. The spirit does not make man into an individual; only the holy spirit does this. Nor does reason make the individual the neutral reason that aims at the true as well as at the good—this is the way in which, at its best, pantheism thinks. Monotheism, however, following by its own dim impulse the trail of ethics, does not acquiesce to this kind of sameness of reason. Monotheism, although it surmises the peculiar world of human knowledge, does not grant that there are limits to moral knowledge. Man, as holy spirit, has to know what holiness is. And even God's holiness cannot object to man's own competence in holiness.

This humility of recognizing the limits of human knowledge, which at the same time is the greatest human pride, is surmised by the Greek mind in the *Idea of the Good*. But the latter, in the Greek mind, becomes a God, and thus there is no correlative link to the holy spirit of man. Because there is no unification, one has to look for a mediation. And it was the misfortune of monotheism that the Jew Philo, with his *Logos*, followed Plato, whom he thought he was only understanding logically, when at this point he should have maintained the independence of monotheism. But Philo was not the only Jew who more or less expressly was charmed by the magic of pantheism and half-understood Platonism; far into the Middle Ages the most pious Jewish intellects struggled with the ambiguities of pantheism. Characteristically enough they were religious poets, such as Solomon Ibn Gabirol, who for a long time was masked as Avicebron.

14. The novel world-historical form Jewish monotheism bestowed upon the problem of morality was the only one that could check all mysticism. A sentence in the Midrash makes this consequence clear: "I call as witness heaven and earth for that, that be it an Israelite or a pagan, a man or a woman, a slave or a maidservant, only according to the action one does, the holy spirit rests upon him."[22] Action is the testimony, the criterion of the holy spirit. Every distinction of creed, of nationality, of rank, disappears before this criterion of man: only before this criterion, and not before any other. That man has reason and spirit besides this, and with them produces science, does not prove him to be holy spirit; only his action has this power of proof. Only his moral action proves him as holy spirit and thus as man.

This sober and clear moral insight is worlds removed from, and sub-
limely beyond, the desires of *mysticism,* which remains suspended in
the shadowy world of an imaginary theory. We shall come to recognize how Messianism, despite its alleged utopianism, nourished this
moral sobriety. It is the precursor of the Messiah, the prophet Elijah,
to whom the Midrash ascribes the wonderful pronouncement recorded above. Man in the infinity of his moral tasks, in the infinitely
distant view of his horizon, man in his moral absoluteness, detached
from all the relativity of nature and history, this absolute man becomes
the carrier and guarantor of the holy spirit.

But the holy spirit rests upon man, even in opposition to the thought
that only God is determined by it. Rather, the holy spirit only originates in the correlation of God and man. This consequence is the
peak of the monotheistic meaning of the holy spirit.

15. The above-mentioned Midrash is not the only place in which
this insight is found, and there are not merely other single passages,
whether in the Midrash or even in the Talmud, which support it, but
there is another, as it were, systematic feature that is of importance.
The teaching about the virtues, as the Talmud develops it, appears to
be guided by this systematic idea. In the ranks of virtues the holy
spirit also appears, and it is not even in the highest rank. There are
several lists of virtues, which, however, differ according to the sequence in which they list the virtues. Dominant, however, is the
specification: "Holiness leads to the holy spirit."[23] It is not the holy
spirit but the moral activity of man that effects holiness. Holiness in
its basic biblical meaning alone can lead up to the height of the holy
spirit as a quality of the human character.

If in a certain passage *resurrection* is placed above the holy spirit,
we find in the same passage the correction: "But pious deeds of
loving kindness (גמילות חסדים) excel all other virtues." The designation
of the holy spirit as a step on the ladder of the virtues of man goes
through the whole literature of the Talmud and Midrash, and is also
preserved in the religious philosophy of the Middle Ages. It is the
distinctive mark of pure monotheism and at the same time, what
has to be identical, the distinctive mark of genuine, pure morality, de-
void of any mysticism. This morality is sober and stern, and pointed
exclusively to the problem of human action, in order to determine it
exactly, as well as to purify and elevate it in accordance with the
principle of correlation.

16. In the holy spirit, therefore, the highest consequence of the correlation is determined: the equivalence of knowledge of God and knowledge of morality. Knowledge of morality and knowledge of nature do

not coincide, as pantheism, which is rooted in this error, thinks. Therefore, whatever the knowledge of God might have in common with the knowledge of nature, as in the problem of creation, in this the holy spirit has no share. Its competence is limited to the humanly moral. And this humanly moral it makes identical with the divine, by virtue of which no interest in God is appropriate to man other than in the question of what the divine has to mean for the human.

Hence, the holy spirit accomplishes the monotheistic determination of the concept of holiness. Despite the natural and historical conditioning of the new worship by the old, all the previous meanings of holiness are abolished by the new worship. What holiness meant before, theoretically, mythologically, as well as practically in the cult, is from now on pushed back into the unmasked nimbus of pagan worship. Holiness becomes purely human. "Thou shalt be holy." Mysticism, which like pantheism has its basis in the equivalence of theoretical and ethical knowledge, remains even today as in the past and labors under the spell that factual connection between God and man is possible and permissible. It does not recognize that the factual is only the present degree of approximation. Nor does it recognize the difference that distinguishes action from mere knowledge. The holy spirit is the spirit of moral action, and as such the spirit of man. This knowledge of man becomes a means for the knowledge of God. Theoretically also the holy spirit accomplishes the correlation; also theoretically the holy spirit turns out to be the mediating concept of the knowledge of God through the knowledge of man.

Now there is no longer any other problem of the divine but the one the holy spirit discovers in morality, in man. "Thou shalt be holy, for I am holy, the Eternal, your God." The appearance of a paradox has disappeared. Holiness unifies God and man. And this unified holiness unambiguously defines itself as morality. There is no other morality but that of man, which even includes the morality of God. And there is no other holiness of God but that of man, which even includes the holiness of God. Every suggestion of anthropomorphism and every appearance of an enhancement of the human and a degradation of God are now removed. For these objections could only be related to the limits of man's theoretical reasoning, as well as to the inefficacy of his power, whereas the holy spirit unifies God and man only in holiness and through this determines for man holiness as morality.

17. Indeed, morality is a problem only for man among all the natural creatures. Theoretically, morality constitutes the content of ethics, and practically it is the content of man's *self-education*. This self-education appears in the light of religion as the *divine education* of mankind.

Hence morality and religion are conceptually distinguished. If, however, religion has its own share in the spirit of man, in the development of the human consciousness of culture, then the concepts of God and man meet again. Correlation enters the picture, as much in accordance with the concept of God as with that of man. The correlation, however, should not shrink to identity. This results in the disease of pantheism. The divine reaches, theoretically as well as practically, beyond the human. But in the divine it is possible to distinguish the holy.

Holiness should not be indiscriminately extended over all of God's authority, and therefore certainly not over all concerns and powers of man. The value of the holy spirit consists exactly in its unequivocal elucidation of the concept of holiness. Holiness is through and through only morality. And with God also it has only that meaning of morality that requires correlation with man. Whatever else God's holiness might mean literally belongs to the chapter on the negative attributes.

18. You might imagine that God is called the Holy One because he is hidden in the unfathomable obscurity of the human spirit. Against this delusion of mysticism, Isaiah, who made holiness his fundamental theme, coined the sentence: "God the Holy One is sanctified through righteousness" (נקדש בצדקה [Isa. 5:16]). God is not determined as holy through the secrets of his essence. And, generally speaking, not through knowledge does he become the holy God, but only through the act of santcification; his holiness is effected through action, which man has to accomplish.

Isaiah does not tire of emphatically enjoying this connection between the sanctifying action of man and the holiness in God himself, and not only the holiness in man. "I will be hallowed among the children of Israel" (Lev. 22:32). "Ye shall sanctify Me." "Him shall ye sanctify" (Isa. 8:13). The correlation requires that his being as holiness is determined by the sanctification that man is able to fulfill through sanctifying himself. "Sanctify yourselves . . . and be ye holy" (Lev. 11:44). The holy spirit in man becomes alive insofar as man sanctifies himself. And in this self-sanctification he accomplishes the sanctification of God. For what could holiness in God mean if it were not the archetype for the action of man?

19. But you should just as little imagine that you might, you ought, to become saints by penetrating the mystery of divinity and thus factually participate in the divinity. Factual participation would not mean the activity of sanctifying, but a kind of natural and actual share in the divinity, through which you were to become holy. The following passage is directed against this delusion: "I am the Eternal who sanctify you" (Exod. 31:13; Lev. 20:8; 21:8). This passage is directed

against the excess of mysticism and the asceticism of saints. Never can man reach the ideal of holiness with his own self-sanctification alone.

And this highest human ideal becomes a false pretence, a false target, if man, in violation of the correlation, ascribes holiness to himself. Holiness is an elevated state neither of knowledge nor of action, but is only the task and ideal of action. You desire to strive for holiness: prove it by your humble self-restraint to do your purely human action. The latter, however, can never be completed; it can only persist in the elevating of the task. You desire to prove your holiness through a higher insight. You prove with this claim that you did not understand at all the road to which holiness is directed. You desire to prove your holiness through a perfection which you allot to your entire human doings: you prove with this fancy only that you did not understand the entirety of human doings, the problem of human action as an *infinite* task, which is determined through the correlation of God and man.

What else, in the last resort, could be the meaning of this comparison, usually forbidden, but that man in all his endeavors remains linked to holiness, to God? This linking of the human creature to God at the same time means the limitation of his action no less than the limitation of his knowledge. And should the holy spirit have liberated man from this, his fundamental condition, as it is according to the basic teaching of religion? Man should be able to become a saint in the sense that he should surpass human limitation, that he should be allowed actually to draw near to God. At the same time it is to be understood that this drawing near is rather an eternal task, only his eternal aim of carrying out the correlation with God. The holiness of man consists in self-sanctification, which, however, can have no termination, therefore cannot be a permanent rest, but only infinite striving and becoming.

20. Only a misunderstanding of the reciprocal effect that exists between the holy and the spirit brings about the mistake of isolating the holy spirit either in God or in man. As little as God can tolerate the assistance of the holy spirit, so little can man tolerate the isolation of his holiness. This intent is contradicted by the confinement of man's holy spirit to action, to morality. In the same way as false religion in its pretended independence is thwarted by the morality of the holy spirit, in the same way is the false psychology of man as a saint rejected by the ethical determination of the holy spirit. Only in the correlation to God, and only in the infinity of its fulfillment, and only in the confinement of holiness to moral action, therefore only in the ab-

straction of eternal moral becoming, does the holiness of man, as the holy spirit, consist.

The correlation does not remain limited to God and man, but inasmuch as it becomes more profoundly defined as reciprocal effect, it extends over the concepts of holiness as well as of the spirit. These fundamental concepts also enter into the reciprocal effect of the correlation. Holiness determines and actualizes the spirit as moral spirit. And in the same way the spirit determines and actualizes holiness as the action of moral reason.

CHAPTER VIII

The Discovery of Man as Fellowman

1. Up to now we have come to know man only as holy spirit, only as a being of moral reason. In this concept man is only an abstraction of religion based on its share in reason, in morality. Considered as this abstract moral creature, man has as yet no relation to historical experience, let alone to the knowledge of nature, except insofar as historical experience presupposes the relation to morality. But morality itself denotes up to now only a problem that originates in the correlation between God and man, and which is to be solved through holiness. Therefore man himself is only a problem.

2. Experience, natural as well as historical, shows man in new problematic shapes, and these branch off into two main groups. One of these groups is formed by man as *individual;* the other by man as *plurality (Mehrheit).** Plurality, in turn, raises the problem of *totality (Allheit).** In the first instance these groups are distinguished only from the point of view of singularity and plurality.

One cannot stop with singularity, for, properly speaking, it belongs to plurality, in which it forms just one link. But plurality, as a logical class, forms a unity, and as such it needs and is able to form a new class, that of totality; in the same way singularity too poses the problem of unity, by virtue of which it is able to join totality, which it also needs. Whenever abstractions such as classes and ranks are in question, unity becomes a problem.

3. We shall not consider yet the unity of singularity, but first the unity of plurality, and we shall do this without at first taking in consideration how it flows into and joins with totality. The unity, which makes plurality into the concept of a class, extends its power over every individual member of the plurality. Thus, man arises as plurality, which in itself forms the unity of a group. At the same time man

*See note p. 15. [S.K.]

113

as such, as one member of this group, also poses in himself the problem of unity. Thus a concept arises that grasps man, not yet indeed as an individual with the full weight of the concept but as a unit in a series: one man next to other men, just *the next man (Nebenmensch)*. And this experience—for this conception of the next man is taken from experience—poses for ethics and also for religion, in accordance with the latter's share in reason, the problem of the *fellowman (Mitmensch)*.

Popular thinking finds it strange that the fellowman is a problem for ethics as well as for religion. To be sure, the next man is simply perceived, but is he not already a fellowman? The assumption of such an identity of the next man and the fellowman is the prejudice of popular thinking in which ethics, as the teaching about the pure man, cannot exist, from which it cannot arise. And insofar as it could arise, it would have constantly to fight the prejudice that this next man of the natural and historical experience is the whole man and that he represents the whole problem of man. The next man is in no way already the fellowman. Experience itself contests and refutes this identity.

It is therefore necessary that there be a conceptual knowledge that expedites the development of the next man into the fellowman. Only conceptual knowledge, only ethics on the basis of logic can achieve this; and by virtue of the share of religion in reason, this task has also to be alloted to religion. For what value would the share of religion in reason have, if this difference between the next man and the fellowman did not become a problem for religion also? If, however, the correlation between God and man is the fundamental equation of religion, then *man* in this correlation must first of all be thought of as fellowman.

4. The concept of the fellowman conceals a correlation of its own, namely, that of man and man, but in this narrower correlation there is merely an initial unfolding of the meaning and the content of the more universal one. For the correlation of man and God cannot be actualized if the correlation of man and man is not first included. The correlation of man and God is in the first place that of man, as fellowman, to God. And religion proves its own significance first of all in this correlation of the fellowman to God, in which, indeed, man as fellowman becomes a problem, and is engendered through this problem.

The share of religion in reason is the share of religion in morality, and no problem of morality takes precedence over this problem of the fellowman. The possibility of ethics is tied to this problem. If the fellowman is leveled down to the next man, it would still be questionable whether sociology could arise; but there is no question that in that case ethics would be impossible. And since the share of religion in reason consists in its share in morality, if ethics is impossible religion also becomes untenable; for then the correlation disintegrates: man then is no longer fellowman, the link in the correlation with God, and no other concept of man but the moral concept of the fellowman can be established in this correlation. Hence ethics and religion depend, with regard to the concept of man, on the concept of the fellowman.

5. The sources of monotheism flow within the historical and literary experience of the Jewish people and the Jewish community. The antinomies, which we found in the development of monotheism in regard to its determination by a national literature, will recur in the human part of the correlation. The experiences of man as the next man contradict the demands on the fellowman that the correlation of man and God makes.

The national consciousness calls first upon the Israelites. This, however, contains an ambiguity, insofar as the Israelite is a son of Adam and a son of Abraham. We shall see how this opposition is reconciled in an unifying concept.

The concept of the Israelite also contains a further ambiguity, insofar as it signifies not only a difference of religion but also a political distinction. For Israel became a state, and in the concept of a *citizen* of a state an opposition arises between the native and the foreigner. We shall also see that this opposition is reconciled and overcome through a unifying concept, which eradicates not only hostility but also indifference to the foreigner.

6. Finally there is another opposition in man, as fellowman, which emerges from the meaning of plurality. The fellowman is a member of a *people*, in the first place of the people of Israel. But Israel is surrounded by other peoples and it makes wars and concludes peace treaties with them. Opposition with regard to the state is repeated on the level of the people, but it is not the same. For the concept of the people was altered through the national goal of monotheism. Unavoidably, uniqueness is attached to one's own people. This uniqueness is demanded by monotheism, the fulfillment of which is dependent on national opposition to other peoples.

With regard to other peoples, therefore, Israel is not simply a people among a plurality of peoples. Because of its calling to profess the unique God and also to accomplish the historical work of the universal recognition of the unique God, Israel itself is distinguished as a unique people. The other peoples are enemies of the unique God and therefore enemies of the unique people. If this opposition were to exhaust the relationship between the people of Israel and the peoples of the world, the concept of monotheism would fail. At the same time, that member of the correlation that is constituted by fellowman in the plurality of the peoples would drop out of the concept of mono-theism. We shall see how this conflict, upon which the destiny of mono-theism hinges, is resolved through a unifying concept. The signifi-cance of this concept becomes all the more important, as through it the plurality in the concept of fellowman is transformed and elevated into totality.

7. Let us first consider the antinomy between the Israelites and the foreigner (נכרי). It is resolved through the concept of the stranger (גר).

The stranger is not a new concept first discovered by monotheism and put in opposition to the foreigner. The natural communication of men and peoples, even in war, brought it about. Wandering and traveling were always in use among men and peoples; through this the immigrant became both guest and friend, a *guest-friend* (*Gast-freund*).

The humanism of the Greek teaching about the gods is shown by the fact that the highest god, Zeus, is made to be the god of hospi-tality, of guest-friendship (Ζεὺς ξένιος) . And to the guest-friend one must be faithful, in war and in peace. When Diomedes and Glaucus recognize each other as guest-friends in the midst of the fighting, they do not, it is true, cease to fight one another, but a knightly feeling of guest-friendship induces them to exchange their weapons. To be sure, the knightly feeling of guest-friendship does not prevent them from cheating. This paradigm of classical sentimentality un-masks the moral indifference that still afflicts the concept of guest-friendship. The guest-friend is still far from being the stranger in that positive sense of the idea which monotheism develops.

8. The moral powers that are released by the various representa-tions of the concept of the fellowman can only be depicted in col-laboration with their opposing motives and their conciliatory con-cepts. But it is from the point of view of monotheism, and the creation and revelation corresponding to it, and, on the other hand, also from the point of view of man, as the holy spirit, that we must first of all inspect the biblical sources of this opposition. There we at first en-counter Noah, who is no longer Adam but not yet Abraham. Con-ceptually, therefore, the wonderful concept formation of the *Noa-chide, the son of Noah* (בן נח) is, as a conciliatory concept, much

loftier than that of the stranger; but the latter originates in the first beginnings of biblical monotheism, whereas the former is devised only later by rabbinical thought as a significant consequence of monotheism.

The significance of the Noachide for monotheism is already contained in the biblical reinterpretation of the Babylonian Flood saga. Noah becomes the symbol of the human race, whose preservation God sets himself as a task. He makes a covenant with Noah that no flood will recur to destroy all living things. God makes, therefore, a covenant with living creatures in general and in particular with the human soul. And nature becomes, as it were, the witness for this covenant in the form of the rainbow which appears on the vault of heaven. Thus God places himself into an unceasing, a conceptual, correlation with nature and with the human race within nature, with man as fellowman.

The account, to be sure, begins with the verse: "And God said unto Noah: the end of all flesh is come before Me; for the earth is filled with violence through them; and, behold, I will destroy them with the earth" (Gen. 6:13), or as is said later: "And I, behold, I do bring the flood of waters upon the earth, to destroy all flesh, wherein is the breath of life, from under heaven: every thing that is in the earth shall perish" (Gen. 6.17). Nevertheless this verse immediately follows: "But I will establish My covenant with thee; and thou shalt come into the ark, thou, and thy sons, and thy wife, and thy sons' wives with thee." Thus through this exemption of Noah and his family, God's announced intent is immediately thwarted. The revision of the whole saga is initiated and expressed in the self-correction of this intent. Nor is an expressed motivation lacking: "For thee I have seen righteous before Me in this generation" (Gen. 7:1). Thus righteousness has not entirely vanished among men, and it must be preserved in man. The human race, therefore, cannot be destroyed.

9. The expression in which God announces his renunciation of the flood seems to be unique: "And the Eternal said in his heart: 'I will not again curse the ground any more for man's sake; for the imagination of man's heart (imagination *(jezer)* does not mean impulse, but the product of it) is evil from his youth; neither will I again smite anymore everything living'" (Gen. 8:21). And thus God blesses Noah and his children and at the same time prohibits the eating of meat with blood in it, connecting with it the warning: "And surely your blood of your lives will I require; at the hand of every beast will I require it; and at the hand of man, even at the hand of every man's brother, will I require the soul (life) of man. Whoso

sheddeth man's blood, by man shall his blood be shed; for in the image of God made He man" (Gen. 9:5,6). It seems that in order to prevent murder, the eating of meat with blood in it was prohibited. Only man, the image of God, is mentioned here, and one man is called the brother of the other. Consequently, according to the covenant with Noah, every man is already the brother of every other.

10. It is in this connection that the covenant which God establishes with Noah is to be understood: "Neither shall all flesh be cut off any more by the waters of the flood; neither shall there any more be a flood to destroy the earth" (Gen. 9:11). And thus the rainbow is set up as a sign of the covenant between God and the earth, between God and every living soul in all flesh, and, to be sure, as an "everlasting covenant" for "perpetual generations" (Gen. 9:12,16). As a natural consequence of this covenant between God and man, which comes into being through the mediation of Noah, the Talmud creates the wonderful concept of the son of Noah.

In the prehistory of monotheism, Noah is followed by Abraham. God makes an "eternal covenant" with him also, for his descendants and their possession of Canaan. It is already significant that the angels, who announce the son to Sarah, are directed, after having completed their mission, not to hide from Abraham the destruction of Sodom: "Shall I hide from Abraham that which I am doing; seeing that Abraham shall surely become a great and mighty nation, and all the nations of the earth shall be blessed in him" (Gen. 18:18). The reasons for the blessing of the descendants of Abraham are not missing: "They may keep the way of the Eternal, to do righteousness and justice" (Gen. 18:19).

And now comes the episode of Sodom, which is introduced by Abraham's dialogue with God. The angels had already left, when Abraham drew near before God and said: "Wilt Thou indeed sweep away the righteous with the wicked?" (Gen. 18:23). "That be far from Thee to do after this manner, to slay the righteous with the wicked, that so the righteous should be as the wicked; that be far from Thee; shall not the Judge of all earth do justly" (Gen. 18:25). Already here God again comes into relation with the entire earth, and indeed not only as its preserver, as in the case of Noah, but as its *judge*. And as such He will show forbearance for the whole city if there be found fifty, or forty-five, or thirty, or twenty, or finally only ten righteous men in the city.

Thus the blessing that Abraham shall bring "to all the nations of the earth" is based on law and justice. And the promise made to the great people whose father shall be Abraham, is connected to the blessing for "all the families of the earth" (families!). This promise at the very origin of the people of Israel connects this people with the peoples of the world and thus paves the way for the idea of the "fellowman."

11. Therefore the dispute between Rabbi Akiba and Ben Azai about the very verse that introduces the love of one's neighbor is not idle. Akiba says: "Thou shalt love your other *(rea)*, he is as you. This is a great embodiment of the Torah." Ben Azai says: "This is the book of the generations of man (Gen. 5:1). This is a greater embodiment than the other" (Talm. Jerus. Ned. p.9).[24] We should consider the conclusion that follows: "In the day that God created man, in the likeness of God made He him." Which foundation is the superior? Perhaps the first, which stresses the equality between man and man, which makes man into "the other," and therefore into the fellowman? Or the one that makes man, as God's creature, the image of God? Evidently Ben Azai is right.

We can understand how the acknowledgment of the other as the fellow countrymen only arose from a biased misinterpreation. Not to speak of the fact that it is senseless to say, love your fellow countryman as yourself, if the love of man in general has as yet not even been discovered—either the national feeling is already so strong that I feel in my fellow countryman my blood and my image, in which case the commandment is superfluous; or the national feeling still has to be taught, in which case, however, the intensification "as yourself" or even "he is as you" is only intelligible if the notion of the fellow countryman has already been permeated by the concept of man in general. The equality of the fellow countryman is clearly based on the equality of man; otherwise my fellow countryman is my neighbor, with whom I quarrel, or the poor man, who hates the rich who oppress him. The moral concept of the fellow countryman has as its indispensable supposition the general concept of man.

It is this general supposition to which Ben Azai refers. And therefore it makes no sense to think one perceives the fellow countrymen in Rabbi Akiba's sentence. The whole Torah, starting with the creation of man, refutes this vexatious opinion. The love of the neighbor is dependent upon God's creation of man, and not upon the subjective feeling with which I love myself or somebody else. "This is the book of the generation of man . . . in the likeness of God made He him." Upon this principle rests the history of mankind. In monotheism lies the origin of the history of man. And monotheism itself prevents any inner partition between believers in monotheism and all nonbelievers. The Israelite is a son of Noah before he is a son of Abraham.[25] And even as the son of Abraham, his blessing is dependent on the blessing of all the peoples of the earth. But before he is a son of Abraham and a son of Noah, the Israelite is, just as every man is, God's creature and is created in his image.

12. We turn now to the political antinomy between Israel and the *foreigner*. We have already encountered the necessity that the mission of monotheism imposed on humanity, namely, that this mission required the destruction of polytheism, which destruction in turn entailed the destruction of idolatrous peoples. This anomaly can be resolved only on the basis of historical considerations. The share of religion in reason retreats in this case before the logic of facts, a logic that cannot hold its own before pure ethics. Can one, however, ask why God did not arrange it, did not command it, differently? Theodicy becomes absurdity in the case of this question. We therefore have to disregard this anomaly and, despite its contradictory character, attempt a conciliation.

Although the worshipers of idols have to be fought no less in one's own people than in the alien peoples, it nevertheless says: "Thou shalt not abhor an Edomite, for he is thy brother." This is one of the golden sentences in support of neighborly love: the Edomite, this enemy of Israel, is called "brother." Consequently not only is the Israelite a brother, but even the hostile worshiper of idols is called the same. Then it is no wonder that this prohibition is also extended to the Egyptian: "Thou shalt not abhor an Egyptian" (לא תתעב מצרי). And the four hundred years of slavery are not recalled there; rather, there this thought is emphasized: "because thou wast a stranger in his land" (Deut. 23:8). The stranger is not thought of as a slave, but as a guest-friend, who requires the piety of guest-friendship. Humanity is already so rooted in the stranger that the slave, as stranger, can be admonished to the bond of gratitude.

13. Thus the concept of the stranger is extended to include the whole problem of the foreigner *(nokri)*. At this point we shall not go into the exceptions, which can be explained by the state law as well as by the religious ritual. We are concerned only with the formation and distinctiveness of the basic concept of the fellowman. In this respect, however, Solomon's speech at the dedication of his Temple is significant: "Moreover concerning the foreigner *(nokri)* when he shall come out of a far country . . . and prays toward this house, hear Thou in heaven" (1 Kings, 8:41-43). It is not far from this to the sentence in which Messianism reaches its peak: "For mine house shall be called a house of prayer for all peoples" (Isa. 56:7). Thus the foreigner becomes fellowman through the community of prayer,

but this development presupposes the collaboration of Messianism. It would seem, therefore, that monotheism must be fully developed if the foreigner is to be recognized as fellowman.

14. The meaning of monotheism penetrated deeper into the concept of man, so that monotheism could discover this concept even without actualizing its own concept in the messianic concept of man. In this way monotheism was best able to correct its own teaching with respect to the strict commandment to destroy idol worship and idolatrous peoples. Thus, man is also recognized in the *non-Israelite*, and this recognition is also confirmed by a political acknowledgment of him.[26] The blemish of idol worship is thus separated, if not from the concept, at least from the representation of man. Man need not be an Israelite in order not to have to be a worshipper of idols.

Of course, the worship of idols is ineradicably blemished. The worship of idols signifies in ancient Jewish consciousness in no way a religious notion exclusively, but at the same time chiefly a purely moral one. It is a profound saying of the Talmud that the Israelites would not have submitted so constantly to idol worship if sensual pleasure were not connected with it.[27] And the prohibition of idol worship also affects the sexual licentiousness, which was particularly connected with the worship of Astarte. The more striking, therefore, is the purely moral share of reason in monotheism, as seen in the literary fact that monotheism made the foreigner into fellowman, even without his joining the monotheistic religion. And this consideration is the more important as it is actualized in the realm of politics.

15. Out of the foreigner and stranger comes to be a new concept of the *"stranger-sojourner"* (‏גר תושב‎).

The legislation with regard to this member of the state, as which he was received, is first of all characterized by the complete equality under the law that was granted to the *ger* [stranger]: "One Torah shall be to him that is homeborn, and unto the stranger that sojourneth among you" (Exod. 12:49). Thus the distinction from the homeborn is invalidated in favor of the sojourner. The law has to be uniform for all who live in the country and do not merely pass through it. And the sojourner does not need a patron in order to conduct a case in court, as he did in Greece and in Rome, for "the judgment is God's" (Deut. 1:17). Law does not have its origin in human statutes but comes from God. Therefore God gives also to the stranger his share in the law of the land, although he does not profess the one God.

This is a great step, with which humanitarianism begins, namely, in the law and in the state, even though this state is based on the unique God, and even though the sojourner does not recognize him! Thus it is understandable that this first step is consequently followed by others.

16. It is exactly in this steady progress in the development of monotheism in all its human relations that the basic concepts of its later period are uniformly connected with the primitive beginnings. The stranger-sojourner became, in talmudic times, the *son of Noah*. We still need elucidation exactly at what point in the talmudic sources the one concept changes into the other. In the codification of Maimonides, however, which takes into consideration a third concept that is instrumental for the concept of the fellowman, it is perhaps possible to detect, in the difference between the new concept and the other two, the respective difference between the first two.

This third concept denotes "the pious of the peoples of the world" (חסידי אומות העולם). This concept relates to the peoples outside of Israel, and therefore abstracts from Israel's religion and still acknowledges piety in these people.

Hence, this wondrous concept is unequivocally a borderline concept between religion and morality, a concept that delineates, and frees, morality from religion.

Through this concept Maimonides completes the distinction between the "sojourner" and the "Noachide." He is in need of such a distinction because he codifies the entire law, including the law of the state. For the law itself in its own development it is not necessary to make this distinction. The law can consider both concepts as two terms for the same legal idea. The stranger is in the first place a son of Noah, and this is his protection against the deficiency that he is not the son of Abraham. But as a Noachide he is not bound to the law of Moses, but only to the seven precepts, "the seven commandments of the sons of Noah" (שבע מצות בני נח).[28] And these seven precepts have a strictly moral character.

Only *one* religious tie seems to be contained in them, namely, the abstinence from blaspheming God and from worshiping idols. Here, the difference between the ethical concept of the Noachide and that of the political sojourner contains an admonition. If the law already goes so far as to permit nonbelievers in the unique God to settle in the land, then provision must be made that the land should not be desecrated through idol worship and its inhabitants not be induced to it. Otherwise, however, there are only moral precepts to which the Noachide is obligated, and the precept of the "juridical institutes" *Gerichtsverfassung* (דינים), to which the Noachide must submit, deserves particular attention. We recall the "statutes and ordinances" which Deuteronomy emphasized with great vigor as the meaning and value of the Torah. In the acceptance of the law the Noachide acknowledges morality, while the acknowledgment of religion is not imputed to him.

The concept of the Noachide is the foundation for natural law not only as an expression of the objective law but also as a determination of the subject of law. Noah has received no other revelation yet but that of man as a living creature. Man is, to begin with, life and soul. But already upon this foundation he becomes fellowman. The Noachide embodies this thought, and it is important evidence for the inner coherence in the history of monotheism, for the homogeneous continuation of the biblical spirit by tradition, that the Noachide as an institution of state law belongs to the oldest reports of the Mishnah.

The seven obligations of the Noachide consist of six prohibitions and one precept. The prohibitions, except for the blasphemy of God and idol worship, are the following: incest, murder, robbery, eating of a limb of a living creature. And the precept is concerned with the establishment of courts of justice. Consequently, with the exception of the concern for the preservation of monotheism in the land against the seductions of idol worship and blasphemy, the precepts required of the Noachide are moral precepts. The belief in the Jewish God is not required.

One is not permitted to force even a slave to this belief. Further, whoever turns to Judaism together with his children is not permitted to accomplish the conversion for his immature children; until they are able to decide themselves, they remain Noachides (Tr. Kctuboth, 11a).

The Noachide is therefore not a believer, and yet is a citizen of the state, insofar as he becomes stranger-sojourner. The Noachide is *the forerunner of natural law* for the state and also for freedom of conscience.

The Noachide thus is evidence for the true meaning of the theocratic constitution: that it is not built on the unity of state and religion, but on the unity of state and morality. The Noachide, who is not a believer in God, may still join the state, because he is recognized as a moral person by his acceptance of the seven precepts. This consequence also follows from the further development of the notion of the Noachide in the Talmud into the "virtuous or pious among the peoples of the world." And these virtuous people have a share in bliss, in eternal life, which is the religious expression of morality[29] (Tosefta Sanhedrin 13 and the formulation of Maimonides, with his own addition, which undoubtedly follows as a deduction from Sanhedrin 105a).

17. Through the legislation of the Talmud we therefore recognize the decisive equation: Stranger = Noachide = Pious of the [gentile] Peoples of the World. Johann Selden in *De jure naturali et gentium juxta disciplinam Ebraeorum* [Natural Law and the Gentile Peoples

of the World According to the Hebrew Teaching (London, 1640)] already knows this equation. And he explains the title of his book by the fact that the significance of the Hebrews for the law of the world (*pro jure mundi*) is a result of their laws. But Christian writers "nowhere explicated" this (p. 158). Professor Andreas Georg Waehner of Göttingen also expressly recognizes the connection of the Noachides with the "Virtuous of the Peoples of the World" in a book of the year 1743, *Antiquitates Ebraeorum* (I, 601). Hugo Grotius also praises the institution of the Noachide.

The connection of these three concepts is understandable. As for the two latter concepts, they are already explicable from the basic tendency of Deuteronomy: to make understandable to this great people the Torah as a document of reason and "insight." This reason therefore reaches beyond the border of the people itself, and the Torah on Sinai receives its preparation, so to speak, in accordance with the "statutes and ordinances" upon the justice of which the entire Torah is finally based.

The Noachidic obligations therefore form an original Torah of their own, which is the foundation for law and state.[30] The harmony between religion, on the one hand, and law and state, on the other, becomes a principle of *theocracy*. The Noachide, indeed, grew out of the stranger-sojourner.

Monotheism created a spirituality of God and thereby also a spirituality of man's soul. This idea is developed in Deuteronomy. In this way the principle of spirituality could and had to become the principle of morality, and therefore, in connection with the law and politics, mature to the principle of freedom of *conscience*. The Noachide, with his offshoot the "Virtuous of the Peoples of the World," is the first and perhaps the most genuine representative of the freedom of conscience and of tolerance.

18. These developments prove unambiguously the true meaning of the commandment of so-called *neighborly love*. If the neighbor originally had had the basic meaning of fellow countryman, then the concept of the Noachide, not to mention the purely theoretical concept of the "Virtuous of the Peoples of the World," could not have developed out of the stranger. But even the stranger is not the ultimate source of this development, which is to be seen rather in monotheism itself. Out of the unique God, the creator of man, originated also the stranger as fellowman.

In spite of all these connecting thoughts, one has to emphasize mainly the *political* and legislative execution of the basic concept of the stranger. Johann David Michaelis, in his *Mosaic Law,* already recognized the connection between the stranger and the neighbor: "Moses commands, as far as a lawgiver can do it, the love of strangers, and explicitly subsumes them under the name of neighbor, whom one has to love as oneself" (3rd. ed., 1793, part 2, p. 445). It is, alas, understandable that not only denominational bias fails to acknowledge this climax of the Jewish spirit in its prehistory. Does not even the world today still struggle with these conflicting concepts, and this not only in the necessity of war, which moreover, in no way excuses this confusion and brutalization? Only pure monotheism explains and only its strict acknowledgment can solve this riddle.

19. Let us now review the main determinations of this *legislation for strangers.* The principle is: "As for the congregation there shall be *one* statute both for you and for the stranger that sojourneth with you, a statute forever throughout your generations; as ye are, so shall the stranger be before the Eternal" (Num. 15:15,16). "Ye shall have one manner of law, as well for the stranger as for the homeborn; for I am the Eternal your God" (Lev. 24:22). This reasoning is quite instructive: it deduces the law pertaining to the stranger from monotheism. And it is particularly instructive that monotheism is expressed here through an appeal to "your God." Because the Eternal is your God, you must make one law for the stranger as well as for yourselves. This is also applicable to the slave, according to the preceding ordinances, which will be considered later.

The first chapter of Deuteronomy begins with the account: "And I charged your judges at that time, saying: 'Hear the causes between your brethren, and judge righteously between a man and his brother and the stranger that is with him' " (Deut. 1:16). The admonition does not stop with the brethren, but with the stranger, since for each one "the stranger is with him" is added to it. "Thou shalt not pervert the justice due to the stranger, or to the fatherless; nor take the widow's raiment to pledge. But thou shalt remember that thou wast a bondman in Egypt" (Deut. 24:17,18). Here, as everywhere else, the stranger is put together with the orphan and the widow, and in the national memory Egypt is to remain the country in which the Israelites, though they were bondmen or slaves, yet were strangers.

20. Also in the money traffic the equality of law is extended to the stranger, at least in principle: "And if thy brother be waxen poor, and his means fail with thee; then thou shalt uphold him; as a stranger and sojourner shall he live with thee. Take thou no interest of him or increase; but fear thy God; that thy brother may live with thee" (Lev. 25:35ff.). In the following verses there is again a reference to the exodus of the Israelites from Egypt. But here the most remarkable

thing happens: the *stranger-sojourner* too is *called brother;* and it is comanded that his life be preserved. Almost more important than the prohibition of taking interest from the stranger is this recognition of him as brother.

Unfortunately Kautzsch made a senseless and deplorable mistake in his translation of this verse: "And if thy brother waxes poor . . . thou shalt uphold him as a stranger and sojourner, so that he shall have his sustenance next to you." If then the brother becomes poor he is to be made into a stranger and sojourner! So far, indeed, equality under the law did not go as to put the poor Israelite on a par with the stranger. And to "live with thee," means more in the biblical language than to "have sustenance next to you." These errors of translation could hardly find another explanation than in a basic error about the original meaning of monotheism.

In the sentences on Mount Ebal in which the curses are expressed it says: "Cursed be he that perverteth the justice due to the stranger, fatherless, and widow" (Deut. 27:19). Legislation concerning aliens is here put under the protection of the basic principles of public and private morality.

21. A monstrous defamation of the Israelitic law is the slogan *an eye for an eye.* We consider it here only insofar as it concerns the stranger. "And if a man smite the eye of his bondman, or the eye of his bondwoman, and destroy it, he shall let him go free for his eye's sake. And if he smite out his bondman's tooth, or his bondwoman's tooth, he shall let him go free for his tooth's sake" (Exod. 21:26,27). Thus is revealed the meaning of the above legislative abbreviation: that a slave is immediately set free through injury of an eye, or even only of a tooth. How much more must this meaning prove true for the free Israelite. That the law relates also to the stranger follows from the fact that Israelite may be sold to a stranger whom he is indebted (Lev. 25:47). The principle of equality before the law goes even so far as to draw the consequence that the Israelite may become a slave to a stranger.

22. From these concepts of the civil law, we may explain why the *cities of refuge* were also open to the stranger. "For the children of Israel, and for the stranger and for the sojourner among them, shall these six cities be for refuge, that everyone that killeth any person through error may flee thither" (Num. 35:15). Thus, the unintentional sin of killing, the *shegagah,* is to be extended to the stranger also. Hence, it is only a modest consequence that Ezekiel draws that at the division of the inherited land, the stranger should be allotted an equal share with the Israelite (Ezek. 47:22). Hence the equality of Is-

raelite and stranger is carried through down to the basic rights of the soil.

23. To this political equality corresponds the religious equality, which is carried out under the guidance of tolerance. The stranger is not subject to circumcision and just as little to the prohibition of eating dead animals (Deut. 14:21). It is therefore characteristic that the prohibition of eating blood is also extended to the stranger. "For the life of the flesh is in the blood" (Lev. 17:11, ff.). And life is, linguistically, at the same time the soul. And the soul should attain reconciliation. Therefore the blood is only consecrated upon the altar for atonement.

Even without this relation, however, an immediate connection is recognizable between blood and bloodshed, so that the inclusion of this prohibition into the moral code of the stranger is not a liberation for him. On the contrary, it is an amazing superficiality, met with far and wide in exegetical literature, to proclaim that the exception which permits the stranger to eat dead animals constitutes a proof of discriminating legislation for the stranger.

As Solomon in his dedication of the Temple prays also for the stranger, so also is the stranger free to sacrifice (Num. 15:14-16; 1 Kings 8:41-43). Hence, it is a consequence of this that the Talmud ordered sacrifices for the seventy peoples.

24. Finally, out of these basic determinations of the law the general commandment of the love of the stranger becomes intelligible. Verses 17 and 18 in chapter 19 of Leviticus, which reveal the so-called love for the neighbor, are elucidated by verses 33 and 34 of the same chapter, which are as follows: "And if a stranger sojourn with thee in your land, ye shall not do him wrong. The stranger that sojourneth with you shall be unto you as the homeborn among you, and thou shalt love him as thyself; for ye were strangers in the land of Egypt; I am the Eternal your God." Here, too, through the concluding sentence "I am the Eternal your God," one is enjoined to recognize the distinctiveness of this commandment. "And a stranger shalt thou not wrong, neither shalt thou oppress him; for ye were strangers in the land of Egypt" (Exod. 22:20).

Finally this *love* is based on the highest motive: God loves the stranger. In the wonderful speech reported in Deuteronomy it says of God: "He doth execute justice for the fatherless and widow, and loveth the stranger, in giving him food and raiment. Love ye therefore the stranger, for ye were strangers in the land of Egypt" (Deut. 10:18,19). And about this God it is said: "He is thy glory and He is thy God" (Deut. 10:21). Here, too, national history is understood as a support for the love of the stranger, which, psychologically as well as objectively, is the foundation for the love of the fellowman.

25. The proper historical understanding of monotheism must be based on the correct understanding of the Israelitic *theocracy*. Religion develops in connection with the development of the state. This connection can result in unavoidable disadvantages; in the observation of the primitive development of these ancient relationships, however, it is better to begin with the resulting advantages, which in turn diminish the disadvantages. The prophets fight the priests. But if the priests are servants of the state and therefore also rulers of the state, so also are the prophets politicians, and they are unable to develop religion in any other way than by participating in the conflicts within the state and society. If, therefore, their religion must affirm and realize its share of reason in morality, it must be inextricably linked with politics and its view of the social question. Therefore the stranger as such cannot be the exclusive origin of the idea of the fellowman, but the legal and political conditions of the native, the native born, brought about the intervention of the prophets in behalf of the stranger.

The social differentiation between poor and rich poses the most difficult question for the concept of man, for the unity and equality of men. The "next man" (*Nebenmensch*) becomes unavoidably the "opposing man" (*Gegenmensch*), for the social differentiation does not appear to be organized according to rank and order of coexistence, but according to subordination and subjugation. It is in opposition to this that the problem of the fellowman has to arise. Even more than the question of the stranger, the question of rich and poor is asked in one's native land and among one's own people; this human question is asked with regard to every man, with regard to every fellowman.

God, the Unique One, as the unique creator of all men—how can he be responsible for this deep inequality of men? This question certainly originated very early, but the difficulty of the economic problem always pushed it aside. Already in Deuteronomy two sentences stand side by side: one sets up the negative demand, while the other represents the inherited experience against utopianism. The one says: "There shall be no needy among you" (15:4). The other, however: "For the poor shall never cease out of the land," (15:11). The demand in its rigor is not softened by the presumed experience. For if the latter were right, still the admonition that there should be no needy would be correctly stated. This correction of society and its history is the demand of the unique God.

26. How can God allow this gaping difference between men? This question is answered by religious consciousness, and the gradations in

the shades of the answers it provides correspond to the steps of its own development.

The difference between poor and rich is not the only one among men. Neither are the distinctions represented by the mental and aesthetic appearances of man the most conspicious, nor are these the ones that arouse the most shocking doubts about God's justice. For man is as gladly appreciative as he is skeptical. When he sees disadvantages in himself, he rejoices in the advantages of others, whom he is always willing to honor as masters and demigods. A mean between the intellectual and the aesthetic is bodily strength and heroic courage, which men need more immediately than intellectual advantages, and whose aid gives to men's existence a more positive value than the aesthetic gleam emanating from them. The primitive man, being a nomad and hunter, lives in the magic of war; therefore, heroism is his first ideal of man. And hence he surmounts the offense the awakening religious consciousness ought to take at the unequal distribution of the vital powers in man.

This awakening, however, also stirs up the recognition of the other difference in man. Cain kills his brother. The Bible does not fail to supply a reason for Cain: God turned his favor to Abel's sacrifice and not to his. Was it unjustified envy, or did the feeling originate in a justified accusation against God? It is as if the Bible wanted to teach in this, properly speaking, the first sin, that no apparently justified pretext whatever should be an inducement to envy. The pretext aims at God; the envy, however, aims at man, rather upon two men: upon the other as much as upon oneself. And hence in this simple example the paradigm of every moral conflict originates. Questions are raised against providence and God's government from all sides, so that the relation of man to God remains everywhere obscure. But this obscurity can never govern the relation of man to man. Murder does not accord in any way with the preferential treatment that God allows. Indeed, the whole history of mankind is such that God seems to favor some over others. However, men should not govern their relation to other men according to this appearance.

In spite of this, man acts this way even if he does not take God's injustice as a pretext. Disordered relations and wrongdoing do arise among men. The moral difference between good and bad arises. This difference arises out of the primeval moral problems that primitive social relations bring forth, even before religious motives play their part. The violation of legal norms, which are already set up in primitive forms of society, makes moral distinctions necessary: the legal becomes the moral. For already in the archaic forms of society the ideal human relations, such as those of the generations and the family, intertwine with the material-legal relations of tribe and property. Thus the difference of good and bad arises as a purely human distinction.

27. Soon, however, gods enter the horizon of primitive man, and the spheres of man are touched by them. In monotheism it is significant that the first human sin is fratricide; the murdered man is the brother, and the murderer is the brother. The ties of blood are already known, but not acknowledged. All men are brothers, yet murder is transmitted among them. The bond of blood is an unreliable tie among men. Moreover, vengeance, which man is able to exercise, is also afflicted with defectiveness and injustice. Therefore the Bible intercedes for the murderer: "Whosoever slayeth Cain, punishment shall be taken on him sevenfold" (Gen. 4:15). Human justice always remains imperfect. In God alone can justice be found.

28. Thus arises the difference between good and bad in the light of the unique God. In polytheism, therefore, the religious and hence absolute difference between good and bad cannot arise. The gods favor men in accordance with their own discretion, even in accordance with their caprice. Because of this Homer is the Bible of freethinkers. The gods cannot be united in their government, for then they could not be different individuals. Monotheism is based on a uniform comprehension of the distinction of good and bad, and thus on a uniform attitude of God to man, as well as of man to God. The correlation between God and man is defined as that between religion and morality.

Polytheism is deprived of any norm for the correction of religion by morality. If Hippolytus remains chaste toward Phaedra, then he transgresses against the worship of Aphrodite. Every divinity has his own code of morality. Monotheism creates with the one divinity also the one morality as well. The unique God, therefore, also unifies the concept of man, and every breach of this unity of man is a violation of morality. The distinction between good and bad is more and more removed from the obscurity of the divine, and is independently expressed in human relations.

Gradually, however, specifically religious conceptions also unfold, and in monotheism especially they must be interwoven with purely moral ones. There the question may already arise, how can God vindicate the distinction of good and bad in man, how could it come about in his creation? The serpent seduced Eve, and Eve, Adam; God, however, does not sanction this excuse, and he punishes the transgression of his prohibition.

This first *sin* of the human couple was committed only against God, but Cain's sin was the first sin against man. And for this sin Cain is taken under God's protection. This difference in *retribution* already shows the relation that God assumes with regard to man's transgressions: the transgressors against man are punished and at the same time protected, whereas the transgression against God is the origin of culture insofar as its consequence is the establishment of labor. Thus from the very outset God's sovereignty is established with regard to all human sins.

29. Does this sovereignty prevail with regard to *social* differences? Good and bad are under God's grace, as this sovereignty is called later. The primitive religious conscience does not ask about the reason for and the justice of the differences in the bodies and minds of man; for this purpose it is still too much engrossed in mythical beginnings. But the social differences become offensive not only in themselves, but especially since they are felt as a hindrance to the mental, and even perhaps to the moral, development of man. Therefore it must become a religious question how the difference between poor and rich is compatible with the unity of God.

30. The question soon becomes more intense when the simple religious consciousness takes cognizance of social processes. A comparison between social and moral differences emerges, and the question is raised whether there is any correspondence between these differences. On the contrary, the insight is unavoidable that there is no such harmony between them, that instead a strict opposition seems to be the rule. Thus the statement: "The righteous, he fares badly; the bad one, he fares well!"

Language does not yet know how to overcome this dissonance, it does not yet distinguish between good and well-being, between bad and ill. But the question in which "the bad one" is called the villain (רשע) and "the good one" is called the righteous (צדיק) shows that the feeling for the difference is already manifest. The question could not have arisen, except on the basis of this difference.

And how does the religious consciousness find an answer to this primeval question? Should perhaps the answer suffice that in God's knowledge the thing is correct, and that only in our knowledge does it appear incorrect? This answer might perhaps suffice in the case of a villain who is well off, because the more profound consciousness may be able to ignore this well-being, and because his villany itself is, properly speaking, a riddle in every sense, so that the knowledge of it and the judgment about it can be only subjective and illusory. On the other hand, in the case of the righteous one who fares badly, the question cannot be left in suspense. Should one perhaps lose con-

fidence in his righteousness and with this be in danger of losing confidence in God's justice in general? This danger, however, would be
unavoidable; for how could the misfortune of the righteous be reconciled with God's justice?

31. Should one perhaps find a way out of this by declaring that
misfortune is irrelevant? Should the religious consciousness perhaps
adopt the wisdom of *stoicism?* The religious consciousness was protected against this ambiguity by its natural connection with the political and purely moral. Even if the individual were able and were permitted to train himself successfully and with good reason to disregard
his own well-being and woe, he is not permitted to disregard the woe
of the other fellow. He might perhaps even disregard the well-being
of the evil one, but he is not permitted to disregard the woe of the
good one.

Precisely in this lies the sound value of the connection between religious consciousness and morals, and of the grounding of the moral
on the social and political. Thereby, the feeling of *indifference* with
regard to well-being and woe cannot arise and assert itself. For well-
being and woe do not have the vague meaning of a subjective well- or
ill-feeling, although this subjectivity is more or less attached to all
variable and passing states of the body. But when well-being and ill
are actualized objectively in the social differences of poor and rich,
then the indifference toward them becomes insincerity, frivolity,
cruelty. No man may doubt that these differences are not indifferent
to men. From the social point of view, stoicism is either hyprocrisy or
unforgivable ignorance.

32. Monotheism completes its development in the prophetic teaching; from the social-moral point of view, one may even say it develops
toward the prophets. For the *peculiar* characteristic of the prophetic
teaching consists in the connection of the alleged independence of
evil with the alleged independence of morals. The prophet does not
know this isolation. He knows only the correlation of God and man,
of man and God. He is therefore as much interested in *politics* as in
the divine rule of the world. And politics for him certainly includes
foreign, international politics, but is, in the first place, social politics.

The relations between man and man form the lower or rather the
inner correlation within the correlation of God and man. Therefore
the questions of the prophet cannot be isolated either from the distinction of good and bad, or from the meaning of good and bad in the
absolute relationship of man to God; rather, his question about the
distinction of good and bad must objectify itself by turning to the
social differences of poor and rich. The moral excellence of the proph-

ets consists in their refusal to measure and weigh the difference between well-being and ill according to subjective differences, to which
disease and death itself belong. Instead, they measure them according to the objective social contradictions that upset the balance of
society.

The prophet rises above the level of primitive belief, which blindly
assumes a correspondence between goodness and well-being and
between evil and woe. This correspondence would do well if well-
being and woe were only subjectively distinguished. The social differences, however, must be recognized as objective; otherwise, the
concept of the essential moral and cultural tasks of man is in danger of
being destroyed. The concept of man grows in the reciprocal correlation between men, and accordingly the content of the correlation of
God and man also grows.

The social complexity of men grows into this correlation and cannot be isolated from it. This is the meaning of the prophetic teaching.
The prophet does not close his eyes to moral corruption, to the moral
doom that lies in social differences. The prophet's truthfulness does
not allow the slightest trace of a solution in which well-being is considered as the *reward* and ill-fatedness as the punishment for the
moral, for the religious behavior of man. Man's relation to God may
remain a mystery; his conduct to other men is not permitted to be
considered such. With regard to man, one has to judge and to decide.
For the decision about good and bad is connected with this decision.
The distinction between good and bad comes to nothing if it coincides with the distinction of well-being and ill.

If this were the case, then the concept of man with regard to the
creation of the concept of man as fellowman would be defeated. The
concept of the fellowman cannot come to my consciousness if his well-
being and woe are indifferent to me. Even without any consideration
of a more or less intimate knowledge of the man's physical well-being
and woe, this indifference simply blocks the formation of the notion
of man as fellowman. This is even more so if the indifference stands
firm with regard to moral behavior also. This connection of moral
with physical behavior contains implicitly the distinction between the
religious and the moral. The behavior of man to God, which may be a
mystery, can, however, in some way be controlled by the behavior of
man to man. The distinction of good and bad originates in this behavior, not in the behavior of man toward God. The prophetic teaching brings forth the sobriety and clearness, and its originality consists
in the elucidation of these concepts.

It is therefore not any concern for *eudaemonism* that caused the prophets to enter into the question of the correspondence that exists between the moral and the physical—in this respect they truly do not fall short of stoicism—but rather the fact that the fundamental question about God and man, about religion and morality, is at stake in this relationship. So far as I am concerned, my own well-being or woe might remain indifferent to me, but this cannot be the case with regard to the next man. But this need not be especially the case with regard to the complication that arises out of the question whether well-being and woe coincide with good and bad. And with regard to this complication there need be no demand for indifference, perhaps there ought to be none, even with regard to myself.

33. This fundamental point should be considered once more. With regard to well-being and woe the point is that they are not indifferent physical, even bodily goods. Life and health themselves might become indifferent in the face of fate and death. For *death* is a metaphysical evil, and mystics may brood about its cause or possible abolition. This is no theme for moralists, and therefore also not for true religiosity. It is different with *sickness*, for it is a chapter of the social question. And it is the social well-being or woe that comes into relation with moral distinctions. As little as moral distinctions could be indifferent, so little is it permissible that social well-being or ill should simply be indifferent.

The great achievement of the prophetic teaching, and that which also shows its inner connection with true morality, consists in this: prophetic thought does not indulge in speculations about the meaning of life in the presence of the riddle of death; it puts aside the question of death and therefore also of *afterlife*, despite the fact that their moral significance is not hidden from it. Nonetheless prophetic thought puts aside these questions of life and afterlife in the face of the life whose meaning is in question because of the evil which is represented by *poverty*. *Poverty becomes the main representation of human misfortune.* Thereby physical ill in general becomes moral ill; but in that sense that the question of morality is directed to God, and it has to be divorced entirely from the question of man's guilt, if it is not to become ambiguous.

34. Another form of woe also, which is no less ambiguous, namely, *suffering*, is settled and surmounted by social objectivization and by the isolation and precision of the problem. In suffering, physical ill changes into the psychic ill, and with this transition ambiguities are unavoidable. The psychic is as much physical as spiritual, as much material as moral. Which meaning predominates in suffering as the woe of man? And to what extent is this meaning in harmony or dis-

harmony with moral behavior? The metaphysics of suffering, which considers suffering as the fate of mankind, or even more ambiguously, as the fate of all living creatures, does not belong to an earnest religion; its earnestness has nothing to do with the play of poetry and art. Suffering only reaches ethical precision as social suffering. Whoever explains *poverty* as the suffering of mankind, he creates ethics, or, if not philosophical ethics, yet still religion with its share of reason. Only the religion of reason is moral religion, and only moral religion is truthful and true religion.

35: The prophets, as well as the psalms, have the social insight that poverty represents the great suffering of mankind, and they therefore have the religious insight that poverty is the great question mark against divine *providence;* they realize that the true riddle of human life is not death, but poverty, and that it is the true riddle because its solution requires truthfulness and is conceivable only by truthfulness, while death is a riddle only the mystic can solve. The mystic, however, would dispense with truthfulness, even if it contained truth.

For truthfulness can only be brought about in one of two ways: either in the way of scientific method or in the way of religion's analogy to reason. Religion, however, which in accordance with its share in reason, has to strive to be analogous to ethics, must and can undoubtedly prevail in the social conception of man, in the social conception of the relation of man to man. The correlation of God and man is built only upon the basis of this social relationship.

36. Ill, as represented objectively in poverty, led us to consider suffering. And we considered the ambiguity in the psychic meaning of suffering. The depression that the consciousness undergoes in suffering may also be the consequence of physical effects. Exaltation also, which marks the feeling of happiness, is connected with the body. And as with happiness, so every kind of feeling of unhappiness remains undetermined and ambiguous not only morally but even psychospiritually. But we are not interested in the development of this idea for the sake of uncovering the feeling of well-being in the bad man. We are concerned not so much with the denial of this elated feeling but rather with the pressing question, which we have to put to God, of how his idea is compatible with this psychic success, which is not merely physical, that evil has in man.

Likewise the unhappy feeling must also not be leveled down to subjectivity and made psychically illusory. Suffering is an actual feeling, which is not only mirrored in a social reality, namely, poverty, but also has to be conceived and understood as a prevailing reality of consciousness; it fills the entire human consciousness and helps to de-

termine all its other procedings and activities. Therefore its objectivization should not be permitted to be erased; the suffering of poverty
must always remain the problem: the religious problem, but not the
metaphysical one.

37. If we have previously said that in the problem of poverty the
woe of man has to be recognized by the true religion, we can now
say with the same firmness that in poverty the woe becomes the
suffering of the human race, as far as we can trace it in human history up to now. Woe and ill are not only physical concepts; suffering
has elevated them to the psychic and thereby to the whole complexity
of the soul, which comprises the spiritual and the moral.

A new factor of consciousness has thus been revealed: the suffering
of the human soul, of the human spirit. This suffering, as everything
psychic, is not entirely separated from the physical; suffering is also
pain. But the suffering of the spirit is not the pain of the animal; for
the animal is not social. It is questionable whether the physical pain
of another animal, if it is not its own young, arouses its sympathy in
it; in no case can this reaction be caused by a spiritual suffering not
present in the herd. *Only social suffering is spiritual suffering.* All the
complexity of consciousness, including knowledge, is affected by it and
brought to take part in it. This is the profound meaning of social suffering: that the entire consciousness of culture is implicated in it.

Stoic apathy is therefore entirely inadmissible; it excludes ethics
and at the same time includes the renunciation of culture. I cannot
be indifferent to poverty, because it is the sign of the distress of culture, and because it calls into question true morality. Poverty cannot
be compared to physical suffering, because the latter is individual and
subjective, whereas social suffering is not only the suffering of the
majority but also the qualitative evidence of the low level of the
culture.

38. This situation brings about a new tragic motive of its own. However, in tragedy only the hero, only the individual suffers; in social
suffering the entire culture assumes a tragic role. And culture here is
not an abstraction, but the most vivid actuality, the majority of the
human race in every people and in every epoch. Thus the poor man
typifies man in general. Thus the next man becomes fellowman.
For even if I had no heart in my body, my education alone would
have brought me to the insight that the great majority of men cannot
be isolated from me, and that I myself am nothing if I do not make
myself a part of them. In these unavoidable connections between myself and the majority, a relationship arises that means more than

merely coordination or even subordination, but which produces a community. And this community produces the fellowman.

39. The community is *reciprocal action*. In reciprocal action community comes to be and is achieved. How will the reciprocal effect between the suffering that in my consciousness becomes an object of my insight and knowledge, and the other parts and activities of my consciousness manifest itself? Until now the community, the fellowman, remained merely the problem posed by suffering as a social problem, a problem not yet solved, however. The solution depends on the way in which the reaction to suffering is voiced.

40. According to the mythological point of view which everywhere is the original form of religion, the solution is the same as that indicated by tragedy, which itself arises from the myth: the *guilt* of man, of the hero himself, is the ground of his suffering. This ground is probably also the cause, at least the only intelligible subjective ground. Upon this mythical ground tragedy builds its own aesthetic microcosm of man and its world of the spectator. Religion, however, goes its own way, and it cannot rest satisfied with myth. The goal of its way is, however, always God. Through the correlation of man and God it seeks man and finds God; it seeks God and finds man. However, how is this correlation to teach one to find a way out of this great conflict of suffering, a way that brings a solution?

41. The book of guilt must be destroyed; social insight destroys it. For, disregarding the antinomy between individual and society in the question of guilt, the latter cannot be considered in this connection because thereby the discovery of the fellowman would be missed. I am to change the next man into the fellowman. For this purpose the idea that the suffering of the majority of men is an attribute of the majority because of its guilt is of no help. Already in the tragedy the hero cannot be a scamp, for then I would not be able to be morally interested in him. Much less can the idea of guilt be useful for the discovery of the fellowman out of the suffering of the majority.

If suffering is to be taken as the result of the history of the world, how can I reconcile God's justice with it? If I can neither understand the justice and meaning of providence in the world, on the one hand, nor, on the other, consider social suffering as the consequence of guilt, does not the correlation between God and man become disordered?

42. The prophets here take the straight road upon which monotheism methodologically parts from polytheism. The latter everywhere proceeds from the gods. Mythical consciousness takes this as its starting point and stops at that. From the gods the mythical fantasy

turns to the cosmos and only gradually to men, whom, however, it at first knows only as heroes, and this means as demigods. Religion, on the contrary, is concerned more with man than with God. God's justice will somehow be accomplished, but law and order among men are not to remain the great question. This question affects the heart. From the heart must come the reaction, the counteraction which we seek so that the community may be formed, so that the fellowman may arise. The counteraction must become a counter feeling to suffering: it must not remain simply knowledge but must become a powerful feeling.

Therefore suffering, to the exclusion of any other feeling, must fill out the consciousness, if it is to be understood correctly and evoke a correct reaction. Therefore any trace of an interest in a subjective or in an individual ground for suffering has to be eliminated. As much as such an interest may be justified for the individual from another point of view, at this point it would disturb and hinder the insight to be gained. Suffering is a social suffering; therefore, an understanding of it cannot be furthered by any kind of insight that concerns only the individual.

Guilt is and remains the attribute of the individual. And the plurality is also only a plurality of individuals. The plurality itself cannot have any guilt. And about the individual in general I do not want to know at this point. The suffering is not an individual suffering but the social state of distress of the human race. Poverty is an economic concept, not a moral one. Guilt, from the point of view of religion, is written on an entirely different page. If religion intends to discover the fellowman through social suffering, and if this· discovery is tied up with the reaction to the knowledge and feeling of suffering, then religion has to disregard its other interests and obligations and ascertain this reaction exclusively in the psychic nature of man's consciousness. Hence *pity* is disclosed as a psychic factor.

43. Since the time of the *Stoics* pity has been suspect, although in ancient tragedy it was valid as the natural tragic lever; even though it was still connected with fear, it was elevated above this selfish motivation, elevated to a more universal motive and acknowledged as a tragic factor. The Greek word means "to be moved to pity," which shows itself in lamentation (ἔλεος). This natural power of antiquity also withered away in the age of the Stoics, and humanitarian abstraction replaced the immediate naturalness of human feeling. Pathos is replaced by ethos. *Apathy* becomes the goal of morality.

The Stoics, it is true, in no way lack the precision of morals and humanity which respects the slave, extends the law to foreigners and allies; in a word, they are not lacking in the objectification of morality in law and state. But all this objectification bears the stamp of the Roman character; it lacks the free subjectivity of Hellas, which even Hellenism cannot transmit. Tragedy becomes comedy, insofar as it achieves significance at all. The image of divinity becomes a portrait, as the ideal of art. The natural feeling for suffering has slackened long ago and almost died away. In the Saturnalia the Roman finds consolation for his bad conscience about his slave economy.

Men, to be sure, remain men, but when pity moves the stoic, it becomes like a faded tale of moral abstraction; there are many such tales, more or less valid only for utopia. In this atmosphere of dying antiquity the thought of Epicurus is more natural than stoicism, which is only a paradox, as is also their key word about the ideal of apathy, the virtue of the *wise*.

44. To what extent stoic morality is only an abstraction is most clearly seen in the repudiation of pity. This repudiation is motivated by the point of view of the individual, who is represented by the wise. And a slave also may be wise. Therefore the slave does not represent social misery. Man consists of his spirit. Everything else about him is accidental. Therefore only the spirit is connected with him. Man, that is to say the wise man, therefore does not suffer, he has no feeling: how would I with my feeling encounter his? He does not suffer: how could therefore my pity affect him, or even discover him for me?

It is very consistent that in stoicism pity becomes an *affect*, and indeed in the indeterminate way which here surrounds the idea and concept of affect. Pity is nothing other than an *elemental common feeling*, like hunger and ease, like pleasure and aversion and pain, like pride and envy, in short, like *passion* in general. The passions, however, are pinpricks of the lower body, as are the elemental common feelings also; they are the bodily, the nervous lower strata of the psychic. They do not belong to the clear transparent upper regions of the psychic, of the consciousness. Therefore they cannot be the levers, much less the regulators of moral consciousness.

Therefore, also, pity cannot be marked out and distinguished as a social affect. Hence it is considered as an ambiguous factor of consciousness, determinable by no criterion, guided by no spiritual norm. I have pity in the same way as I yawn, too, when somebody else yawns. It is an echo of the reflex movement—then, to be sure, animals too should unmistakably show it. Nevertheless human reflex action might perhaps have a hidden drawer in its reflex mechanism. This ignorance notwithstanding, the fact remains that pity is seemingly unmasked as a mere bodily function. Where the social idea does not become a fundamental problem, there pity is not honored.

45. Spinoza has found much approval with his theory of affects. In it, however, he follows the path of stoicism. Pity, according to him, stems from the same source as envy. This one sentence passes judgment on the validity of his view, and at the same time illuminates the ground of it. Envy, as I think, originates only out of a presumed insight into a surplus by which another exceeds me. If transferred to society, the ground of envy would therefore be only the opinion of a plus on the one side, not of a minus on the opposite side. Envy could therefore originate only with the poor man, who discovers the surplus, the plus of the rich. Envy would thus be the opposite of pity.

Spinoza, however, in no way wants to interpret pity as such an opposite motive. He wants to teach the wisdom that one should not trust pity, because its source is as subjective as the source of envy. Just this, however, shows the abyss in his thinking; he does not see the chasm that exists between pity and envy. This comparison is only possible when one does not think about social suffering. And as the stoic which he ultimately is, Spinoza indeed fails to think about the social suffering of the human race.

According to him, the "many" are, in any case, wholly incapable of real morality, which rests on true knowledge. How could the many, who always reveal only the preliminary stage of human dignity, be worthy of true pity? As there is no social suffering, so there can and need not be social pity. This is the reason for Spinoza's disdain and rejection of pity.

46. And what is the reason behind pity according to Schopenhauer? With him, too, the reason in the first place lies in his metaphysics, in the predominance of knowledge which constitutes his metaphysics, though the latter sets the so-called *will* above the intellect. For this will is anything else but will. Therefore it is understandable that pity also is deprived of its immediate power of feeling and unmasked as a kind of metaphysical clairvoyance. Pity should only reveal to me that the other is rather myself. Therefore if I have pity for him, I have it rather for myself. Pity raises the veil of Maya and unveils the mystery of the individual, the *principium individuationis*: I am always only myself, and as many men as I seem to see, yet they are all always only myself.

Knowledge, of course, would never have brought me to this truth if it had not dawned on me in the thing-in-itself of the will, if pity, the organ of the will, had not put this truth into focus. Thus pity is more than knowledge, which represents merely the phenomena. Pity is the messenger of the will, therefore of the thing-in-itself. And this thing-in-itself means the identity of all that appears as man.

47. Pity, as understood by Schopenhauer, becomes a mediating concept for the metaphysical knowledge of man. But exactly at this point the difference between metaphysics and ethics becomes clear, and no less also the difference between metaphysics and religion. This characterization of pity is also unable to help me to discover the fellowman. For the latter becomes in this view an illusion. For the majority of people knows man not as fellowman but only as the next man, and even he is only an appearance which, according to this metaphysics, is no different from an illusion.

The thing-in-itself, however, as unity, is not even the unity of men, but that of the universe. The will is certainly not differently present in man and in the stone, which falls according to the force of gravity. And Schopenhauer is entirely in agreement with Spinoza, according to whom the stone too would ascribe freedom of the will to itself, if it were to have consciousness. According to Schopenhauer also, the will can mean the world in itself only by being removed from any knowledge and therefore also from the knowledge of morality. Wherever morality does not present a special problem which is to be distinguished from the logical roots of the principle of sufficient reason, there the fellowman cannot become a problem, even within the thing-in-itself of the world. Neither can pity there become a factor of the moral will.

48. And this exactly is what is of importance: pity must be stripped of the passivity of a reaction and must be acknowledged as a whole and full activity in itself. The moral, the pure will,* is determined by the factor of the affect. The affect therefore must be *pure*, it must be freed from the bodily duality and ambiguity. Pure activity is never a reaction, if the latter merely represents a terminating process. But reaction, as a reciprocal effect, aims toward a goal. This goal is the community, in which the fellowman originates. This kind of counter effect, which is a reciprocal effect, is achieved by pity. And pity turns out to be a factor of the pure will, as a lever of moral consciousness. It is the fundamental power of the moral universe, which unlocks the fellowman. Pity constitutes the key to the fellowman.

49. Morality and religion have here a common border. This border is not a limit. The share of reason in religion draws this border, which cannot be a limit for it. Ethics does not despise the affect, which, though not a factor, is yet *a motor* of the pure will. We have deter-

*For the relation of pure will to reason and affect, see p. 324 and p. 404. [S.K.]

mined the distinction in this way in our *Ethics of Pure Will*. And if I am to make the distinction between affect and the appearance of an indifferent agility more exactly recognizable, the affect of pity, as an original power of the pure will, will best serve this purpose.

Every metaphysical and ethical misunderstanding of pity originates in the erroneous view that pity is only reflexive and is only incited in and by myself. We, on the contrary, recognize the connection of pity with the problem of the fellowman. Consequently, pity is so little reflexive from the other man back to the self that, rather, the other man, who supposedly merely drives me back to myself, and who until now counts only as the next man and does not yet exist as the fellowman, is to be created through pity as the fellowman. How could, therefore, pity mean the reflection from him back to myself?

50. It is even a question, as yet not asked, whether I myself already do exist before the fellowman is discovered. Consequently the end point of the reflex motion is not yet given, let alone the starting point. Also from the point of view of the I, it therefore turns out to be a misinterpretation that pity is a mere passive reflex action upon myself. Even from the point of view of this alleged end point of the I, we can now discern that the whole conception is wrong and that the error consists in this: the fellowman is thought of merely as the next man and not as a new problem, as a new concept of man. However pity, as a concept for ahe discovery of the fellowman, is no longer suspect and loses all the appearance of an ambiguous passivity; it is recognized as an ethical factor, although only as a motor of the pure will.

51. What, however, can religion initiate through pity, if it has to disregard the guilt of the one who is to be discovered as fellowman? This question is answered satisfactorily only by the social point of view. In the face of poverty it no longer makes sense to ask about guilt. No age in which poverty becomes a problem is so primitive as to connect guilt with this turbulent problem. By the early epoch of culture it is possible to trace the separation of morality from religion in the treatment of this problem.

Morality in law, in politics, and also in the beginning of ethics traces only the basic relation of these two concepts, the poor and the fellowman, not, however, their later interpenetration. Even with Socrates it is to be noted that he has no sense for the problem of poverty. He lets Solon worry about that. But Solon also rests satisfied with a temporary measure, such as the remission of debts, the *seisachtheia*. The state would have to intervene in the law, change its foundations, if it wished to assist organizationally in this case.

Socrates' teaching is preserved through his assertion of the preeminence of the intellect. This assertion is his contribution to ethics. Virtue is knowledge. But the poor man too can have knowledge. Can he actually? Socrates does not ask this question, for his world-historical spirit is directed to the creation of pure ethics. He does not let himself be diverted from his theory by premature questions about matters of practice and application. This disadvantage is connected with the advantage which the new theory establishes for the future.

52. The prophets, on the contrary, are not theoretical moralists. Therefore for them there cannot be even a temporary difference between theory and practice. Their problem is religion, monotheism, the correlation of man and God. And this correlation is intertwined with the correlation between man and man. The first, between God and man, may seem to be merely theoretical; the other, however, between man and man is immediately practical. And the fellowman belongs to this second correlation. Therefore the prophet cannot allow any doubt to divert him from the problem: how the fellowman is to originate out of pity for the poor man.

Poverty is the universal suffering of the human race. Pity must meet poverty if man is finally to arise as an I. Before this social fact of human suffering the primeval human feeling of pity has to flame up; otherwise one would have to despair about human feeling in general. Should the prophet have curbed human feeling because the religious idea of guilt restrained him? The prophet would not beget religion if he remained suspended in this dilemma.

53. The distinction between religion and mythology, between monotheism and polytheism, again clearly asserts itself here. Polytheism has its center of gravity in the myth. The spell of myth fills the spirit of primitive man much more strongly than his heart can be stirred by suffering and therefore be moved to pity. Tragedy, too, which grows out of myth, is and basically remains a product of polytheism.

Perhaps the absence of tragedy in Israel's mind can be explained through the onesidedness of its monotheism. Suffering is to be resolved in reality and not merely in the illusory feeling of the spectator. The prophet becomes the practical moralist, the politician and jurist, because he intends to end the suffering of the poor. And it is not enough for him to assume these various callings; he has to become a psychologist as well: he must make pity the primeval feeling of man; he must, as it were, discover in pity man as fellowman and *man* in general.

CHAPTER IX

The Problem of Religious Love

1. We usually consider self-evident that which is genuinely new. As with miracles, so is it also with the self-evident things in literature. *Love* in religion is considered as such a self-evident thing. However, it is neither in itself clear, nor psychologically established, what love means in the case of God, neither God's love nor the love for God. And, hence, it is as little self-evident or established in literature what the so-called love of one's neighbor demands. In experience as well as in literature love is known as sexual love. And in the example of the degeneration of the latter into homosexual love, Plato shows the comprehensive significance of *eros* for culture in general. But the love of one's fellowman, as such, is absent even in this broad ramification of eros. Nothing is more characteristic of the inner difference between the ethical morality of idealism and monotheism than love.

2. If a proof is still necessary that religion has a share in reason, the proof is given here. What reason cannot achieve in ethics, the universal human love of men for one another, this reason achieves in religion. It permits God to love man, while polytheism permits God to love only heroes. Only the latter, who at the same time are sons of gods, are called "beloved of the gods" (θεοφιλής).

Thus, polytheism does not require of man the love of God, which is an entirely new idea, and which does not occur in the entire mythology. Indeed, it is peculiar enough. It is therefore very consistent with pantheism when Spinoza says: "Who loves God cannot aspire *(conari)* that God should love him in return" (properly, counter-love him [*contra*]). However, Spinoza ignores the beginning: how is it conceivable that man should love God? According to Spinoza, man is able to do this because his love is knowledge only.

We, on the contrary, ask: is love in its religious meaning identical with knowledge, which has a theoretical meaning, and indeed a double one, one for logic, and one for ethics, so that the concept of knowledge

144

is not unambiguous? Is love in the religious sense now to be identified with this dual concept of knowledge? Love is a new concept of religion, which is not identical with sexual love, nor with eros, nor therefore with aesthetic love either. Love is not a self-evident thing. It has to be explained and established at every point in religion, as God's love, as love for God, and finally as the love of man for man.

3. The mistaken conception of love as self-evident is responsible for the failure of people to consider the relation of these three basic forms of love to one another as problematic. We must ask: which of the three basic forms of love forms the beginning and is the objective foundation?

According to polytheism the answer would fall on the side of the gods. Mythical, as well as all metaphysical, consciousness always begins with the gods, who form the primeval beginning, as chaos is the beginning of cosmos. Myth does not know the love for God; it allows only the love of individual gods for their sons, for the sons of gods. One would suppose that monotheism, which lets everything proceed from the unique God, should all the more let love originate in God, from whom it is later transferred to men and imitated by them. It seems, on the contrary, that the reverse is the case. And here again it is possible to recognize the ethically important distinction between religion and every form of polytheism.

4. From the notion of the stranger we have already learned that monotheism began with human love. The legislation for the stranger showed us the way to the historical sources of the love of one's neighbor. In the stranger the fellowman was first discovered. And pity arose first with regard to the stranger. This pity is therefore the original form of human love. "Love ye . . . the stranger" [Deut. 10:19]. The first reason given for it says: "for ye were strangers in the land of Egypt" [Lev. 19:34]. Thus the required new feeling is made vivid on the basis of historical consciousness. As little as the memory of the slavery in Egypt should be frightening, so little is it permissible to ask about the stranger's moral qualities, let alone his religious convictions. Only the fellowman is to be discovered in him. Thus here at once pity appears as love.

5. There is another reason for loving the stranger, one which refers to God: "God loves the stranger." Here one can see clearly that this reason is the later one. First, man has to learn to love the stranger, if he is to understand that God loves the stranger. First of all, love as pity must be awakened in man. This pity is not lacking here, although it seems to appear only as love. "For ye know the heart of the stranger" [Exod. 23:9]. This is an appeal to one's own heart, for one knows the

mood of the stranger. This, however, is a recourse to pity. And yet the concept of the stranger is only a preliminary step, as the political concepts generally are preliminary steps to the social concepts in which the former come to maturity.

In the case of poverty the question is even more precise, for poverty is everywhere the universal lot of man, while the stranger is only a special case. But the precision of the question entails its clarification. Does God first love the poor man, or must man first love the poor man? The precise answer to this question has to lead to the precise answer to the other question: does God first love man, or does man first love the unique God?

6. Poverty is a basic concept of economics. The suffering that comes from poverty therefore originates within the framework of human customs together with the science of economics. Consequently, the pity of man for man is also of primary origin, and in it the correlation of man to man proves its fundamental power. As soon as the insight into this correlation starts to form, it occupies the entire cultural consciousness of man so much that all other considerations with regard to man, not to mention God, recede. Pity is aroused as the new original form of humanity, as love.

When a human being begins in pity to love another human being, this implies a transition from the notion of just the next man to the fellowman. Religion achieves what morality fails to achieve. Love for man is brought forth. As a miracle, as a riddle, it emerges from the head, or rather from the heart, of men. How is the selfish man able to love another man, the same selfish man who supposedly is able to love only the woman, the flesh of his flesh? Is it not an illusion, this transference, this metaphor of sexual love? Not at all. As pity, love ceases to be suspected as a metaphor. In the face of poverty there arises, in the scientific consciousness, the problem of the fellowman. For the notion of the next man, in the case of poverty, becomes a contradiction in itself, since he is not so much a next man (*Nebenmensch*) as a subhuman man (*Untermensch*). Love, which seemed an anomaly, emerges here as a norm. As inconceivable as it seemed, it is nevertheless understandable from the connection of the different intentions of consciousness that pity originates in human consciousness as true love. This insight is disclosed through suffering. And this disclosure takes hold of the entire consciousness.

In this insight, suffering reveals itself to be the essence, as it were, of man. Not only does the body suffer and hunger in poverty, but the entire man is torn out of the equilibrium of his culture.

This kind of suffering exceeds all the suffering in a tragedy. If you wish to know what man is, then get to know his suffering. This is no longer a metaphysics of pessimism; rather, on the basis of social insight the poverty of man is personified. And therefore everything, man himself, begins with this social love, with this social pity for the poverty-stricken. Thus it is established beyond doubt that love, as religious love, begins with the love for man.[31]

This love first teaches man to love men. First it teaches man to recognize in poverty the suffering of man. First it teaches, therefore, in correspondence with this social insight into suffering, the kindling in man of the primeval feeling of pity. First it teaches, therefore, the establishment in pity of the true meaning of religious love, and the strict distinction of this true love from all the ambiguities of voluptuousness and also from the aesthetic pleasure, which is interwoven with it. First it teaches, therefore, the discovery in the next man of the fellowman.

The love for man has therefore to be the beginning, because although God created man, man must create the fellowman for himself. And religion must assist in this creation. Thus God must become the creator a second time when, through the share of reason in religion, he teaches man himself to create man as fellowman.

7. Only now, after man has learned to love man as fellowman, is his thought turned back to God, and only now does he understand that God loves man, and indeed loves the poor man with the same favor as the stranger. The stranger is rarely mentioned independently with regard to God's love, but is usually associated with the orphan and the widow. They are the types, the representatives of poverty, and their appeal is more concrete than that of the poor man simply, who is still only an economic abstraction. However, we shall see that even this abstraction becomes alive. The social conscience becomes ever clearer and stronger. The prophets become more and more insistent in combating riches and luxury, and their social compassion becomes ever more pressing politically and therefore ever deeper religiously.

The worship of God, the service, would have been to the prophets merely a spectacle, as is usual in pagan worship (tragedy originated in the Dionysiac cults), if social pity had not been their basic motivation. Even the highest holy day, on which fasting is the custom and law, is invalidated by the second Isaiah, if social pity does not govern the whole of life. "When thou seest the naked, that thou cover him, and that thou hide not thyself from thine own flesh" [Isa. 58:7]. This is the new insight that true monotheism brings about: the poor man is your own flesh. You do not consist of your own body, nor is your wife, the object of your sexual love, the only flesh that is your flesh, but the poor man also is your flesh. He reveals to you the fellowman. And the fellowman as the poor man brings God's love for man into the true light and the true understanding.

8. Of course, all men are poor in God's view. But in this argument there is still an ambiguity present which considers the love of God as self-evident. In fact, man is God's creature. And as parental love is natural and as such self-evident, so could God's love seem to be the logical consequence of the concept of the creator. Religious love, however, is more than simply a logical consequence of the creation. It ceases to be self-evident if only because it acquires its meaning only in that pity for the poor which is the primary form of human love.

God does not stop with this primary form of love, but out of it the genuine ethical meaning of God's love develops in its comprehensive universality. God loves the stranger, he loves the poor man. Thus he will also not stop with the love for Israel only, which is merely a historical point of departure, similar to that of the stranger and the poor man. He will love men as a *totality*. For he himself is not in need of man as fellowman. For him, the correlation exists in its infinity. It is here that the tendency towards Messianism originates.

9. However, precisely because Messianism has fixed the goal of the love of God in a permanent though infinite point, it is understandable that Israel is marked out, in the series of mediating points, as the recipient of God's infinite love of men. The history of Israel offers the immediate starting point for this idealization. Israel's glorious past is under the veil of saga. Its history proper is already the beginning of the end of Israel. Hence, Israel's relation to God has been conceived of by the prophet as well as the historian as a kind of suffering. God loves Israel as he loves the poor. For Israel is rejected by God, oppressed by enemies, split and divided politically, and finally even driven from its land.

It is not sufficiently considered that the idea of Israel's *election* as God's "property" is stressed mainly in Deuteronomy, thus close to the beginning of Israel's historical and political independence. Disregarding, on the one hand, the historical meaning of the idea of election as a means of inspiring enthusiasm for monotheism in the national consciousness, one should, on the other hand, not underestimate the feeling of sadness, because of the country's humiliation, as a reason in the mind of the people for God's love for Israel, his people and his property. If God loves the poor, he must also love Israel, who is exposed to all kinds and gradations of suffering, while the worshipers of idols lead their proud existence.

Was it not necessary that an idea emerge in which the notion of suffering reaches its religious climax, namely, the idea that the suffering of man might perhaps be the *vicarious* suffering of a subject who suffers?

People further connect suffering with *guilt*. If this were to be correct, it would have to be understood in the sense that the guiltless suffers for the guilty. We shall see how Messianism reaches its own peak in this climax of the idea of suffering.

10. Now, however, it is necessary to clear God's love for Israel of the suspicion that it is an anomaly in regard to God's universal love for mankind. God does not love Israel more or differently from his love for men in general, nor, needless to say, could God's love for Israel limit and impair his love for the human race. In Israel God loves nothing other than the human race. Israel is his property (סגלה); or however one may translate this Hebrew word, God loves Israel only as a model, a symbol of mankind, a mark of distinction within it, for only monotheism is able to establish the unity of the human race. This is the basic doctrine. Israel is the holy people of priests of monotheism. Israel is not a people like the other peoples.

Balaam's speech is a character sketch of Israel; this is also the case with the verse: "A people that shall dwell alone" [Num. 23:9]. This isolation is unavoidable, for all other peoples worship many gods. Also, all the other peoples have their own states. The consequence of Israel's loneliness must be the loss of the state. With this, however, its social misery begins, its existence as the social analogue of poverty. Now the idea that God loves Israel is justified, for God has to love Israel as an isolated people, as a people in misery, for this historical misery of a people without a state can truly vie with social poverty. Therefore Israel is in its history the prototype of suffering, a symbol of human suffering, of the human creature in general. God's love for Israel, no less than God's love for the poor, expresses God's love for the human race.

It is therefore a grave mistake to evaluate the election of Israel apart from its connection with the messianic election of the human race as a whole. And this mistake entails the further one of misunderstanding the messianic election of the human race as a means for Israel's glorification. At this point we can only point out, but nevertheless already now assert, that the election of Israel is in no way an exception, but is rather the symbolic confirmation of God's love for the human race.

For this purpose we may refer back to the meaning of creation, and indeed to the creation of man as a reasonable creature. This creation is necessarily a continuous one, so that it means the *preservation* of the human race for the messianic realization of morality on earth. Creation therefore is also God's providential plan for the human race, as it has been already established through God's covenant with Noah. This providential plan of world history expresses God's love for man. And so all formulations of the correlation between God and man may be said to be the expression of this, God's love. Revelation, which is as much as a result of God as it is of the holy spirit of man, may also be called a high act of God's love.

11. However, we understood love in a seemingly narrower sense as social love and therefore as pity. Therefore, also, in God we cannot be fully satisfied with intellectual love only. There must be assumed, in God also, a corresponding affect of pity that is an impulse of the will. This is the origin of the notion that satisfies the demand for love in God, namely compassion (רחמים), which means more than loving care (חסד), even more than mercy which is actualized more specifically in other respects. The Hebrew word for compassion stems from a root which means "mother-womb," and it corresponds to the metaphor of God as the father of man. The Hebrew language employs, particularly with regard to love, sensuous roots, so that in Jeremiah and the Psalms there is "burning of the intestines" as an expression for *longing*. Therefore, this term compassion (רחום), which is derived from the word "mother-womb," is particularly significant among the expressions for God's love compiled in the theophany in Exodus.

12. Several other terms in which God's love for mankind is symbolized through his love for Israel have an equally original force. God is the "bridegroom" and the "husband." He loved Israel with a "young man's love," and he attracted her with "bonds of love." He is a "shepherd who carries the lamb in his arms and in his lap." At this point social relations emerge as love. But no other term designates the origin of the correlation between God and man more profoundly than the term "compassion." And upon no other situation and with no greater propriety could the primitive strength of compassion direct itself than upon poverty, the fundamental obstacle to the brotherly equality of men.

13. There are several terms for the poor man, for the needy man, who is oppressed; Saalschütz, however, well observed that there is no expression in the Hebrew language for "beggar"; thus, the word for "alms" is lacking too. Moreover, it is significant that in the linguistic usage of Judaism until now the word for charity is expressed through the term *zedakah*, which originally meant justice and later piety in general. This identity is proven even more through the distinction that Judaism makes between charity through almsgiving and

charitable deeds of loving kindness in general, the latter being designated by a separate word. Aiding the poor is merely called justice.

We have previously shown how the legislation concerning the
stranger influenced the Judaic frame of mind toward him. In a similar
way, we will consider the *legislation for the poor*. At this point, too,
we encounter the atrocious view that opposes the peasant's indigenous
social conditions to moral universality (E. Troeltsch). It is exactly
this economic constriction that concurred in bringing about the broadening of the moral horizon.

14. It is already a distinctive mark of monotheistic ethics that strict
property rights are curtailed in favor of the immediate satisfaction
of one's hunger: "When thou comest into thy neighbour's vineyard,
then thou *mayest eat grapes* until thou have enough at thine own
pleasure; but thou shalt not put any in thy vessel. When thou comest
into thy neighbour's standing corn, then thou mayest pluck ears with
thy hand; but thou shalt not move a sickle unto thy neighbour's
standing corn" (Deut. 23:25). Thus, desire is restricted to the satisfaction of one's hunger, but property rights are similarly restricted.

15. The *tithe*, also, which must be given every three years, not only
to the Levite but to the stranger and the poor man as well, is a
measure designed to curb rigid property rights. "At the end of every
three years, even in the same year, thou shalt bring forth all the tithe
of thy increase, and shall lay it up within thy gates. And the Levite,
because he hath no portion nor inheritance with thee, and the stranger,
and the fatherless, and the widow, that are within thy gates, shall
come, and shall eat and be satisfied; that the Eternal thy God may
bless thee in all the work of thy hand which thou doest" (Deut.
14:28).

16. This tithe, moreover, is even more expressly dedicated to the
task of social education through its connection with the offering of
the *first fruits*, during which a confession has to be made, which has
the classic original form of a *prayer:* "A wandering Aramean was my
father, and he went down into Egypt and sojourned there, few in
number; and he became there a nation, great, mighty, and populous."
The verses that follow tell of their misery there and of God's help,
which freed them from Egypt and brought them into this land. "And
now, behold, I have brought the first of the fruits of the land, which
Thou, Eternal, hast given me" (Deut. 26:6-10).

This historical national reflection is not sufficient. With this personal
act of social welfare goes another confession: "When thou hast made
an end of tithing all the tithe of thine increase in the third year, which
is the year of tithing, and hast given it unto the Levite, to the stranger,

to the fatherless, and to the widow, that they may eat within thy gates and be satisfied, then thou shalt say before the Eternal thy God: 'I have put away the hallowed things out of my house, and also have given them unto the Levite, and unto the stranger, to the fatherless, and to the widow, according to all Thy commandment which Thou has commanded me; I have not transgressed any of Thy commandments, neither have I forgotten them'" (Deut. 26:12ff.). Something which clearly has the meaning of a social disposition is here declared to be holy. The author of Deuteronomy designates, in the following words, these regulations as "statutes and ordinances" to which he appeals as the wisdom of the Torah.

17. Other laws about *gleaning the corner* as well as the *cultivation* in the seventh year also attempt to curb the exclusiveness of property. "And when ye reap the harvest of your land, thou shalt not wholly reap the corner of thy field, neither shalt thou gather the gleaning of thy harvest. And thou shalt not glean thy vineyard, neither shalt thou gather the fallen fruit of thy vineyard; thou shalt leave them for the poor and for the stranger: I am the Eternal your God" [Lev. 19:9-12]. "When thou reapest thy harvest in thy field, and hast forgot a sheaf in the field, thou shalt not go back to fetch it; it shall be for the stranger, the fatherless, and for the widow; that the Eternal thy God may bless thee in all the work of thy hands . . . When thou gatherest the grapes of thy vineyard, thou shalt not glean it after thee; it shall be for the stranger, for the fatherless, and for the widow. And thou shalt remember . . ." (Deut. 24:19 ff.).

18. The laws concerning the *Sabbatical Year* are in keeping with this attempt: "When ye come into the land which I give you, then shall the land keep a sabbath unto the Eternal. Six years thou shalt sow thy field, and six years thou shalt prune thy vineyard, and gather in the produce thereof. But in the seventh year shall be a sabbath of solemn rest (שבת) for the land, a sabbath unto the Eternal; thou shalt neither sow thy field, nor prune thy vineyard. That which groweth of itself of thy harvest thou shalt not reap, and the grapes of thy undressed vine thou shalt not gather; it shall be a year of solemn rest for the land. And the sabbath-produce of the land shall be for food for you; for thee, and for thy servant and for thy maid, and for thy hired servant and for the settler by thy side that sojourn with thee" (Lev. 25:1-6).

19. The *Year of Jubilee* is joined to the Sabbatical Year: "And thou shalt number seven sabbaths of years unto thee, seven times seven years . . . then shalt thou make proclamation with the blast of the horn on the tenth day of the seventh month; in the day of atonement

shall ye make proclamation with the horn throughout all your land. And ye shall hallow the fiftieth year, and proclaim liberty throughout the land unto all the inhabitants thereof; it shall be a jubilee year unto you; and ye shall return every man unto his possession, and ye shall return every man to his family . . . And if thou sell aught unto thy neighbour, or buy of thy neighbour's hand, ye shall not wrong one another. According to the numbers of years after the jubilee thou shalt buy of thy neighbour, and according unto the number of years of the crops he shall sell unto thee. According to the multitude of years thou shalt increase the price thereof, and according to the fewness of years thou shalt diminish the price of it; for the number of crops doth he sell unto thee. And ye shall not wrong one another; but thou shalt fear thy God; for I am the Eternal your God. Wherefore ye shall do My statutes, and keep Mine ordinances and do them . . . and the land shall not be sold in perpetuity; for the land is Mine; for ye are strangers and settlers with Me. And in all the land of your possession you shall grant a redemption for the land" (Lev. 25:8-24).

20. Even today students of the Bible declare this agrarian legislation to be utopian. Against this widespread opinion, however, speaks the connection of the Jubilee Year, not only with the Sabbatical Year of the soil but with the *Year of Release:* "At the end of every seven years thou shalt make a release. And this is the manner of the release: every creditor shall release that which he hath lent unto his neighbor; he shall not exact it of his neighbor and his brother, because the Eternal's release hath been proclaimed. Of a foreigner thou mayest exact it; but whatsoever of thine is with thy brother thy hand shall release" (Deut. 15:1ff.).

Because Kautzsch opposes, in the above passages, *rea*, the brother, and the foreigner, *nokri*, his translation is proven to be wrong. It errs not with regard to the *rea*, whom he designates as neighbour, but with regard to the brother, whom he designates as "fellow countryman." For between the fellow countryman and the foreigner stands the "stranger-sojourner"; where does the latter belong, since it is impossible to think of him as of a foreigner? This passage also proves that the stranger, who is not a foreigner, is not only a *rea* but a brother. And the legal proof of this is that the commandment of the Year of Release applies equally to the stranger-sojourner and to the native. To be sure, the stranger, who remains in the land only briefly, cannot be included in this law of the land. The following verses however, contain the basis for the warding off of pauperism.

Here too Kautzsch translates incorrectly: "however there will be no needy [at all] among you" (verse 4). Rather it has to mean: "it should be impossible that needy shall be among you." This is also the way one rabbinical interpretation reads these verses after setting "lest" (פֶּן) equal to "not at all" (אֶפֶּס): "lest there be needy among you." Other rabbinical interpretations, however, do not assume that these words mean the prevention of poverty, but simply the future which is, indeed, to be a consequence of obedience to the commandment of the Year of Release. When, soon after, the verse says: "For the poor shall never cease out of the land" (verse 11), this cannot be understood as a contradiction. For immediately the verse continues: "therefore I command thee, saying: 'Thou shalt surely open thy hand unto thy brother, thy poor and needy, in thy land.'" This last verse too proves the correctness of the interpretation given to the preceding verse.

21. To this agrarian legislation is joined legislation concerning the *debtor* and the *worker*.

The humaneness of the law is shown first in the notion of the *pledge:* "When thou dost lend thy neighbor any manner of loan, thou shalt not go into his house to fetch his pledge. Thou shalt stand without, and the man to whom thou dost lend shall bring forth the pledge without unto thee. And if he be a poor man, thou shalt not sleep with his pledge; thou shalt surely restore to him the pledge when the sun goeth down, that he may sleep in his garment and bless thee; and it shall be righteousness (equal to piety) unto thee before the Eternal thy God" (Deut. 24:10). "If thou at all take thy neighbor's garment to pledge, thou shalt restore it unto him by that the sun goeth down; for that is his only covering, it is his garment for his skin; wherein shall he sleep? And it shall come to pass when he crieth unto Me, that I will hear; for I am gracious" (Exod. 22:25). "Thou shalt not pervert the justice due to the stranger, or the fatherless; nor take the widow's raiment to pledge" (Deut. 24:17). "No man shall take the mill or the upper millstone to pledge; for he taketh a man's life to pledge" (Deut. 24:6). Thus, as with private property in general, so the mortgage law is curbed.

The worker is, in his mildest form, a worker by the day. "Thou shalt not oppress a hired servant that is poor and needy, whether he be of thy brethren or of thy strangers that are in thy land within thy gates" (Deut. 24:14). Since the verb as well as the attribute for the stranger is lacking, it is at least questionable whether the stranger-sojourner is meant, or perhaps only the stranger passing by. It says further: "In the same day thou shalt give him his hire, neither shall the sun go down upon it; for he is poor and setteth his heart upon it; lest he cry against thee unto the Eternal, and it be sin in thee" (Deut. 24:15ff.). In all of these legal relationships the element of the soul is particularly considered, and this serves the purpose of mediating the connection between the law and man's relation to God.

Generally speaking, everyone who renders service is a worker. There is no special name which distinguishes the slave from the worker. The same word *"ebed"* means the alleged slave as well as the worshiper of God or God's servant; finally the Messiah, in whom the messianic message is fulfilled, is called the servant of the Eternal. Therefore, all the legislation about the slave is in accordance with the monotheistic notion of love of the neighbor. The slave can never become a thing (*mancipium*), but must always remain a person and a human being.

The law of an eye for an eye, rather of a tooth for a tooth, probably originated because of the slave. The slightest injury of his body brings him freedom. And if he runs away from his master, nobody is permitted to return him. A particular law of *piercing* the ear of a slave with a bore exists to warn him against rejecting his release because he feels comfortable in the house of his master. Biblical research should finally recognize the obvious sense of this law.

From Job we learn that complete respect for the slave and for his rights was considered a moral obligation of personal righteousness. "If I did despise the cause of my manservant or of my maidservant, when they contended with me—what then shall I do when God riseth up? And when He remembereth, what shall I answer Him? Did not He, that made me in the womb, make him? And did not One fashion us in the womb?" (Job 31:13).

The unique God is invoked by Job as the common creator of the slave and the master. And simultaneously Job appeals to the fact that the same creation fashioned both in the mother's womb. Similarly it says in the Proverbs: "He that oppresseth the poor blasphemeth his Maker: but he that is gracious unto the needy honoureth Him" (Prov. 14:31). Again, it is the equality of men, based on the fact that all have the same creator, which turns pity into a duty.

22. All these particular laws start with the poor and are extended to cover all other moral and legal relations. However, monotheism surpasses even all these particular laws in order to express God's love for man through one great law, which became the basic social law of the European people. Christian Church law opposed the Jewish law—its mother—by changing the meaning of this law. Although factually preserving the law, it not only separated itself from Judaism at the basic, social level, but also divested this law of its socio-ethical meaning. It is this law, the law of the *Sabbath*, which has to be recognized as the quintessence of the monotheistic moral teaching.

The Babylonian-Bible controversy has again merely shown that the meaning of the Sabbath law is not at all alive in the mind and spirit of modern man. And this is especially hard to grasp because all of social politics displays this meaning, and also because the tightening of the laws concerning the Sunday rest should have universally clarified this meaning. However, modern man thinks about the Sabbath only in terms of the division of the week, and one believes one can deny the originality of this Jewish institution because in Babylon the week also exists, and a holy day, though a changing one, is dedicated to it. There has been no doubt, since the research of Movers and the essay of Chr. Bauer about the Sabbath and holy days, that the institution of the calendar according to the seven planets is not a Jewish invention. But even if it were, it would not be a monotheistic invention. It becomes so only through the fact that the Babylonian arrangement of the week is used by the prophets in order to provide the keystone for their social ethics. Such a keystone is the Sabbath.

23. Already the two reasons that the Decalogue gives for this law are a telling example of the fundamental value of the Sabbath. In Exodus it says: "Remember the sabbath day, to keep it holy. Six days shalt thou labour, and do all thy work; but the seventh day is a sabbath unto the Eternal thy God, in it thou shalt not do any manner of work, thou, nor thy son, nor thy daughter, nor thy man-servant, nor thy maid-servant, nor thy cattle, nor thy stranger that is within thy gates; for in six days the Eternal made heaven and earth, the sea, and all that in them is, and rested on the seventh day; wherefore the Eternal blessed the sabbath day, and hallowed it" [Exod. 20:8-11]. Rest for the servant and for the maid-servant is already prescribed there, but it is not considered the cause of the law, for this is rather God's rest from the work of creation, as in the account of creation in Genesis (Gen. 2:3). Even according to Genesis, the Sabbath is already thought of as the completion of the creation. God's rest unquestionably means nothing else but the completion of his work.

Deuteronomy displays its entire spirit of social and ethical reform in this law. With the exception of the prohibition of coveting, nothing is changed in the Decalogue but the law of the Sabbath. For after the enumeration of the particular persons, as well as the animals to which the law relates, it says: "in order that thy man-servant and thy maid-servant may rest as well as thou. And thou shalt remember that thou wast a servant in the land of Egypt, and the Eternal thy God brought thee out thence by a mighty hand and by an outstretched arm. *Therefore* the Eternal thy God commanded thee to keep the sabbath day" (Deut. 5:14ff.). Already the introductory word is changed. Whereas it says in Exodus "remember," it says here "observe" (שמור). And whereas it says there, "therefore the Eternal blessed the sabbath day," the "therefore" (עַל כֵּן) is here changed by making it now refer back to God's commandment, the reason for which has already been set forth: "that thy man-servant and thy maid-servant may rest as well as thou." This "as well as thou" (כָּמוֹךָ) is the same phrase that is also used in the commandment to love one's neighbor.

Thus, already from this literary evidence, from this change in the wording of the Decalogue with respect to this law, and from the motivation behind this change, it is beyond doubt that the Sabbath is meant to secure the equality of men in spite of the differences in their social standing. And this indisputedly clarified meaning of the Sabbath is in turn an unsurpassed documentation of the fundamental morality of monotheism and of its moral originality.

24. How extraordinarily rare is true originality in social institutions! Here it is incontestable. The attempt to contest it failed. And this originality is due to the spirit of a people only insofar as this spirit merges with an idea of God which in its turn is historically unique. The Sabbath is the clear, the lucid affirmation of the ethical meaning of monotheism. To elucidate the latter, we arrived at a point constituted by God's *love* for man. *The embodiment of this love is to be recognized in the Sabbath.* The Sabbath is given first to Israel. But the world has accepted it, although it gave a dogmatic reason for its acceptance that differed from God's rest after creation. No matter, the institution became universal law, at least for the European peoples. In the Sabbath, however, all the different kinds of God's love are comprised and united.

Hence it is understandable that for the prophets the Sabbath becomes the expression of morality itself: "That keepeth the sabbath from profaning it, and keepeth his hand from doing any evil" (Isa. 56:2). Thus Isaiah puts the observance of the Sabbath on an equal level with the exercise of morality. And just as one is to rejoice in the good, so according to Isaiah one should "call the sabbath a delight" (Isa. 58:13). It is as if the prophet were to say: the Sabbath is to be thought of not only as a socio-political measure but as a peak of religious activity. And Jeremiah again makes the social meaning clear: "not to bear a burden" on the Sabbath day (Jer. 17:27). In the institution of the Sabbath, God's love for men shows itself as God's pity for man, whom he has driven out from Paradise to work. In principle the Sabbath annuls that distinction among men which arose through the manner of their work. The manual laborer, too, becomes master of himself. The weekly rest on a definite day makes the worker equal to his master.

25. The Sabbath became the most effective patron and protector of the Jewish people. All through the Middle Ages they led an existence almost like that of slaves. Even now not all of this has disappeared. But when the Sabbath candles were lightened, the Jew in the Ghetto threw away all the toil of his daily life. All insult was shaken off. God's love, which once more brought him the Sabbath on every seventh day, also brought back to him, in his lowly hut, his honor and his human rights.

Even today the scholars dispute—in self-mockery and ignorance—what in the last instance could have effected the continuance of the Jews. They do not want to acknowledge the truth of the unique God as the final reason for it. They prefer to make the law responsible for it. They think that they are at the same time able to despise the latter because of its legalistic formality and lack of inwardness.

However, the Sabbath is the genuine and most intimate representative of the law. And through the Sabbath the law, in accordance with the unique God who loves men, has preserved Judaism as well as the Jews, has preserved both of them in the mission of spreading monotheism over the earth, of ever deepening its meaning and spirit, and in accordance with its spirit establishing the true human love between the peoples of the world. In the Sabbath the God of love showed himself as the unique God of love for mankind.

We asked, what meaning does the love of God have? The answer is now found to be the pity for the poor, which God awoke in us through his commandments. This has become for us the intelligible explanation of the meaning of God's love. The Sabbath has removed that deplorable appearance of bondage and of inequality from men. As God originated in us compassion for men in presence of despicable poverty, so in this social insight he has revealed to us his love for men. This love of God is the guiding star of world history, of whose meaning one should not despair, for it is only of today and yesterday: "A thousand years in Thy sight are but as yesterday" (Ps. 90:4). World history has hardly begun: it is not yet three thousand years since the time of Moses and the prophets. And so the universal course of monotheism is just beginning. Monotheism is the true consolation of history.

26. Out of God's social love for men develops God's universal love as presented in Messianism. Now, however, we wish first to attempt to understand man's love for God on the basis of God's love for man. This commandment also is held to be self-evident, though pathological aberrations make it unmistakably clear that monotheism is still bound up with polytheism precisely in this concept of love. It is self-evident that gods and goddesses are just as much loved as they

are worshiped in their statues, the representations of the fine arts. The legend of Pygmalion is instructive in this respect. And at all times sensual love has sought outlets and disguises in the alleged love for God. The monotheistic love of God cannot be exposed to such ambiguities: "Thou shalt not make any image!" This prohibition is particularly directed to the image as an object of sensual love.

The commandment to love God follows immediately after the "Hear, O Israel!" It can be understood only in the closest connection with the unity, with the spiritual uniqueness of God: "And thou shalt love the Eternal thy God with all thy heart, and with all thy soul, and with all thy might" (Deut. 6:5). This sentence breathes primal power; this explains the accumulation of expressions for the inwardness in which this love is demanded. The nearest at hand is the heart; to it is added the soul, which stands for life and person, and finally there occurs the Hebrew expression, very difficult to translate, which in the adverbial form means "very," and therefore probably means excess, strength in its entire depth.

What actually may be intended by these expressions, which are intensified by the word "all," is the *unity* of the person from whom love is demanded. Therefore nothing would be more erroneous than to limit these expressions to instinctive sensual desires which could also be directed to human persons. The whole man out of his innermost self, out of all the directions of his consciousness, must bring forth the love of God. How could sensual love be intended, how could it be thought of in this connection? In no way is this love for God a duty of the heart only, but it is the duty of the unity of man, and therefore primarily of the spirit.

27. A more recent trend in Protestant theology argues again for the idea of God's *actuality*, and tries to deduce it from the actuality of moral men, whom the prophets must have experienced in their contemporaries. This tempting idea starts with a correct scholarly point of view, that the prophetic teaching has to be taken in the historical, and therefore psychological, context of its time. This point of view makes the prophets not only into men who admonish but also into imitators in the best sense of the word. Except for what it yields of interest and artistic value, it diverts one from pure monotheism. This view seems to be understandable only so far as through God's actuality the actuality of *Christ* is to be asserted beyond any doubt. With this viewpoint W. Herrmann may make understandable reverence and admiration for men, as well as a reverence only for a God thought of as a kind of man. However, the commandment to love the unique God cannot be made understandable in this manner.

The unique God can have no actuality. For actuality is a concept relating thought to sensation. This relation to sensation is, however, excluded from the concept of God. From the very beginning Jewish speculation combats the anthropomorphism of the Bible. Maimonides calls the proselyte Onkelos the leader of this movement.[32] Therefore Maimonides himself removes even all biological life from the concept of God's being. The history of Jewish monotheism thus displays the literary fact that it removes from God all corporeality and every kind of sensibility. Therefore love also has to be understood on the basis of the same tendency.

28. What the *idea* as ethical reality means positively, and as such is able to achieve for actuality, becomes most clear in man's love for God, on the basis of God's love for man. The power of the idea to realize itself is nowhere so clear as in the love for the idea. *How is is possible to love an idea?* To which one should retort: how is it possible to love anything but an idea? Does one not love, even in the case of sensual love, only the idealized person, only the idea of the person?

The idea of God is the idea of the holy God, the idea of the holy spirit, as the spirit of holiness, that is to say, the spirit of morality. Morality, however, is only a realm of actuality insofar as it is the realm of action. Action, however, just as it is distinct from motion in nature, is also distinct from the actuality of nature, from all actuality. Action establishes the realm of morality. In this realm there are no other actualities than goals, which are ever new actualities. The ideas are archetypes for actions. And the archetypes have no worth of their own unless they are models for the actions of reasonable beings.

29. The question of whether it is possible to love ideas is perhaps answered now. Pure love is directed only toward archetypes, toward models upon which pure moral action can be established. And no man is able to represent this archetype. This archetype is only an archetype of morality, and only as such could and should it become a model. One should not strive to imitate, but to emulate it. The emulation, however, must have its source in the whole *unity of consciousness*, in spirit and in feeling. It should as little remain intellectualized in the understanding, as it should remain only an affect in feeling and in the will; all the powers of the soul have to merge into one common effort in this emulation of God. Such a merging of all powers leads, in art, to a new creation of pure feeling as a new power of consciousness. And the pure *aesthetic* feeling also may be called love.

30. The *love for God* must be of another sort, a sort peculiar to it, if religion is to establish a peculiar kind of consciousness, which is different from the pure will of ethics, not to mention the feeling of

aesthetic love. The love of God, which corresponds to God's love, must have its basis in social love for the fellowman. The latter, however, is entirely different from love as expressed in art, in which man is only a type and therefore, at most, the next man, never the fellowman. And again, God's love can be interpreted as aesthetic love only in *pantheism*. In that case, however, God would love only the beautiful in man, for in pantheism he is the primary source of the beautiful only. The exceptions to the beautiful could be considered only as such. In that case, the idea of a fellowman as one's equal in dignity and worth could not arise.

Religion should have its own peculiar domain, but its independence would be a false one if it were not first of all compatible with and incorporated into ethics. The peculiarity of religion must also be compatible with logic and aesthetics, but in the main the establishment of this correct arrangement depends on its success with regard to ethics. The norm of ethical love eliminates also the collision between the objects of aesthetic love and love simply. It has brought about the discovery of the fellowman through love of man for man; on the other hand, God's love, as the ethical norm, has widened pity into the universality of humanitarianism. Guided by the ethical point of view, let us try to understand now without ambiguities man's love of God in its idealistic effectiveness.

31. The love of man for God is the love of the moral ideal. Only the ideal can I love, and I can grasp the ideal in no other way than by loving it. The ideal is the archetype of morality. I should not have any other model but the archetype. Any image of the archetype is a weakening of the unique realizing power that exists in the primary original force of the idea. However, I may cause the archetype as an object of knowledge to become the object of love. The archetype of morality is the archetype of action. *Action* is the effusion of the pure will.

It is only religion, by virtue of the correlation of man and God, which is peculiar to it alone, that has produced the concept of the fellowman. With this it has also produced, through the affect of pity, that is to say, through the affect of love, action, social action. In this action love is directed to man. But insofar as the archetype of all action is searched for, insofar as the archetype of the correlation between man and God is a problem, love is directed to God. This love comes into force as the quest for the fulfillment of the idea, as enthusiasm for the idea, as love for the idea, which is the original force of all moral efficacy and which in any action is a substitute for the problem of actuality.

32. It thus becomes understandable that in the fight of the Jewish tradition against anthropomorphism, one speaks only of "attributes of action" with regard to God. And it is in accordance with this that all expressions of affects with regard to God are explained. God is compassionate; this attribute the rabbis explain thus: as he is compassionate, so are you to be compassionate. The attribute has only the meaning of a model. But the model makes only emulation possible, and not imitation; it is only an archetype. This whole trend of thought carries into effect the idea: "Be thou holy for I am holy, the Eternal your God."

As holy, God is not so much the model that never can be reached, but rather the archetype and, therefore, the idea which, in the case of action, has the meaning of the ideal. This idealistic meaning is the clear, exact sense of the *love for God*. Love is not knowledge. And yet the Scripture demands knowledge as well as love. Although it demands love on the basis of knowledge, in accordance with knowledge, it does not hold them to be identical with one another. The Scripture demands knowledge only as love, and not merely in the form of theoretical knowledge. By correlating knowledge and love Maimonides seems to develop pure monotheism into a form of intellectualism, though not on the model of Aristotle, but in the spirit of monotheistic love. He does not recognize a knowledge without love, either on the part of God or on the part of man, nor, of course, a love without knowledge.[33] His rationalism, in its unity with the theoretical, is always ethical rationalism.

33. Love for God is the main theme of the psalms. And, as out of pity there resounds social love, so out of *yearning* resounds the love for the God of the psalms. Here love, unfolding out of lyric poetry, borders on aesthetic love. And yet exactly at this point monotheism has shown its power insofar as it was able to conjure away this greatest of perils, to which religious movements so often have succumbed. The pure love of the human heart for God actually became the original force out of which the lyricism of poetry could mature to its own purification.

This influence of pure love upon poetry could be misunderstood only because of partiality. For one is reluctant to admit that this purity, with all its naturalness and in the absence of any struggle with opposing motivations, could be achieved only through a purely spiritual comprehension of God. This comprehension did not even fight any attempt to liken God to human beings, but simply rejected it and left it behind and far beneath itself. Yearning penetrates body and soul, and its expression knows no limitations. But the psalm describes and sings only of anguished yearning and of the flight of the soul; God, however, remains outside of this description. Whereas lyrical poetry usually describes the beloved person, for whom one yearns and to whom one is attracted, the psalm describes only the heart which feels the yearning, and appeals to God not so much in his beauty, but rather exclusively in his goodness, thus only as the archetype of moral action.

34. There is an expression in the psalms that became a theme for all of Jewish religious philosophy, which thereby become variations on this theme: the nearness of God. "The nearness of God is my good" (Ps. 73:28). And this highest symbolic expression is connected with the strongest expression of yearning. "Whom have I in heaven but Thee? And beside Thee I desire none upon earth. My flesh and my heart faileth: but God is the rock of my heart and my portion forever" [Ps. 73:25ff.]. Upon this follows the verse that calls the nearness to God the good.

This psalm teaches the true meaning of monotheistic love for God, which consists in the connection of the purest expression of religiosity with the strongest expression of yearning: "My flesh and my heart faileth." All earthly goods are despised, and only God's nearness is desired. God himself is not desired. Only mythological love is directed to God himself. But monotheistic love desires only God's nearness: God's nearness to man, man's nearness to God.

35. These are the two senses of the nearness to God, and this is important for the meaning of the term. God should not stay afar from the spirit and the heart of man: "For what great nation is there that hath God so nigh unto them as the Eternal our God" (Deut. 4:7). Deuteronomy so strongly urges God's nearness that Jeremiah sees in it a limitation and intervenes against it: "Am I a God near at hand, says the Eternal, and not a God afar off?" (Jer. 23:23). The prophet stands up for the omnipresence of God: "Do not I fill heaven and earth? saith the Eternal" [Jer. 23:24].

Deuteronomy, however, prepares the way for the intention of the psalms. God's distance is necessary for God, his nearness is necessary for man. It is all the more necessary to carry through this concept since through it the shadow of corporeality is dispelled from God, and at the same time the shadow of sensuality is taken away from man's yearning. Emulation, not imitation! And just in the same manner: God's nearness and nearness to God.

This concept in its double meaning contains the teaching: a drawing near to God (התקרבות), but not a union with God. If this warning is in the first place theoretical and directed against pantheism, as well as against all mysticism, it is no less practical in respect of the love for God. It can only mean yearning for God's nearness, but not the unchaste desire for union with God, as is the case in sensuous love. Love for God is the striving for God's nearness, which is known and felt as the only good for man.

36. The double meaning in the word "nearness" contains an ambiguity, as if in accordance with the spatial symbolism, somehow a corporeal relationship should also be striven for. The philosophers of religion therefore changed this expression of location into an expression of action by introducing the verb in the *hithpael* form: התקרבות drawing near. It originated in the nearness, and this drawing near is designated as *self*-nearing. Thus, the whole center of gravity is placed in man's own action, which therefore does not seem to be only a means, but becomes the proper end.

God remains the goal. To the ideal attainment of this goal, however, the self-nearing is set as an end. And in this action, which forms the highest end, and in it only, originates the true, the unique love for God. Any other love is rejected as mysticism, which remains barren and inactive. This love, which is the self-nearing to God is therefore the only right love for God, because in it the holy God is loved, who makes us holy, who demands our holiness, which can become actual only in the self-nearing to God's holiness.

Love is considered as the impulse to action because it makes man himself the original source of action. If love arouses action, then no extraneous and foreign object is its motive force. The love for morality is the love for God. This thesis means for religion what the following thesis means for ethics: action does not result from an extraneous and foreign motive, nor from an extraneous command. It is the result of the will, to which autonomy belongs. Love has to exclude every extraneous and foreign motivation. This foreign is the distant, from which nearness liberates; not, to be sure, nearness in itself, but the drawing near, and indeed the self-nearing. This is the love to which the philosophy of monotheism has raised the notion of the near God and the nearness of God. At this culminating point it is possible to recognize the deepest cause and the indubitable consequence of the harmony between the philosophic rationalism of the Jewish Middle Ages and the Bible.

CHAPTER X

The Individual as the I

1. For the purpose of establishing the correlation of God and man, we have previously discovered man as a reasonable creature and, further, as a fellowman. The reasonable creature has been defined in the chapter on the holy spirit as a moral creature. Of course this creature must be an individual; however, in the context of morality only, this is an abstract individual. The religious context of the correlation with God is able to annul this abstraction and to transform it into a living and individual human creature. The abstract notion of man offers to the moral law, and on the religious plane, to God's ordinances and laws, the possibility of revelation. Man, as the spirit of holiness, is an individual only for God's law, just as in ethics he is an individual only for the autonomy of the will. Only the law makes him into an individual. However, in this respect he is almost only the negative condition for the law, merely a creature for the law. Likewise, he is an individual only insofar as he is a being bound in duty to the law. Other duties, which might be incumbent on the individual, are not taken into consideration.

2. Even the fellowman is not yet an individual who could be determined as an I. The fellowman, to be sure, is no longer merely the next man and the correlation between I and Thou is already established. Yet this I is only the I for a Thou. However, we have not begun to determine what the I might mean as related exclusively to itself. The I, as well as the Thou, are singular beings, but they are such only as members of a social plurality, or even totality, insofar as the latter can be established through social love. In any case, the singular being, who originates and exists only within social plurality or totality, is not yet the individual, who alone has to stand up for himself. It is questionable whether this concept of an absolute individual is legitimate, but one should not believe that the question is answered by the idea of the fellowman. In providing the solution

to this question the peculiar character of religion is actualized more clearly and precisely than in the concept of the fellowman.

3. What concern and what obligation is it, then, which assigns to man in his correlation with God an isolation and an absoluteness through which he is distinguished from the previous concepts of man? Man's eminent task, which consists in moral action, has already been imposed on him, and the means for its achievement, the social forces, seem to have been granted to him. Can there be any other tasks for him than those which can be comprised under moral action? If, however, the problem of the fellowman has to be supplemented by that of the I as individual, it follows that the tasks of moral action are not exhausted by social problems. It follows, in particular, that the correlation of man and God is not entirely fulfilled in the ethical problems of action.

The peculiar character of religion, though it remains unshakably connected to ethics, will only then be fulfilled, when the correlation of God and man assumes a more intimate significance for man as an individual and as an I.[34] Therefore, to the question of whether there are any problems of moral action that remain after those concerning the fellowman have been resolved, religion gives the following answer. Although it is permanently connected with ethics, religion elevates itself beyond ethics and designs its own method analogous to that of ethics. Religion will provide a foundation for, will prepare and secure, those problems of moral action which are beyond the problems of ethics, and with which ethics, due to the limitations of its method, cannot deal.

4. If we recall the social problem of poverty, we remember that the possibility of love, as pity, arose out of the refusal to ask any question about the guilt of man, out of the refusal to be at all interested in this question. In metaphysics, also, guilt appeared as a residue of myth. In any case, the question of human guilt had to be recognized as an obstacle to the vivification of social love. If the question of guilt arises at all, the solution from its own point of view would perhaps be that guilt is brought about through hostile opposition to poverty, never through poverty itself.

However, even this test-solution shows that the question of guilt cannot be entirely eliminated. If this is so, then wealth, no less than poverty, deserves the love that springs from pity, in order that guilt be averted from it also. However, law and justice should certainly not be annulled through social love. If in law the question of guilt must be preserved, however, it is imputed to the individual, and it is thereby established that guilt remains a problem also for ethics. And if guilt remains a problem for ethics, should the peculiarity of religion in regard to ethics perhaps consist in the fact that religion is authorized to say: the book of man's guilt is destroyed? Should the correlation of man and God have to demand such a remission from a basic ethical question for man, a question which constitutes the foundation of law?

The peculiar character of religion, in its constant connection with ethics, is directed against such a possibility.

5. In our *Ethics of Pure Will* we have given the following account of the foundation of the *criminal law:* the judge is authorized to inquire into the crime only according to the definition of the law and to punish the criminal accordingly. However, the judge, in proclaiming someone guilty, must be prevented from also pronouncing judgment on the man's guilt.

A clear distinction must be introduced between the judgment of the judge about the guilt according to the relevant paragraph of the law and the corresponding determination of facts, on the one hand, and the judgment about human guilt, on the other hand. We are not to think, however, that the latter has been set aside; rather, through this distinction man's guilt will come to a more exact declaration. *When he receives the declaration of guilt from the judge, the criminal himself has to take the guilt upon himself,* and only the loss of the soundness of his mind can exempt him from it.

The criminal would cease to be a man, if the court's declaration, like that of a physician, were to make him despair with regard to his competence of will. Ethics, however, can neither personally nor subjectively liberate him from this despair. Ethics must say here with Mephistopheles: "He is not the first." Mental illness in its different stages and gradations makes *responsibility,* and hence the competence of the will, conditional.

Hence, pure ethics is helpless when it comes to the consideration of a particular case. It does not allow its restricted applicability to prescribe to it its proper limits, but delineates these in accordance only with its own methodological and positive conception of free will. But what should ethics do with the poor man, who may not acquit himself of his guilt, insofar as his rational will, his free will, must continue to exist for his own poor consciousness?

6. Here lies the boundary of ethics. And where practical care begins, insofar as it is possible in such a case, there ethics borders on religion. When the man is declared a criminal, in accordance with the facts, and he is not able to help himself in the narrower correlation between man and man, in this deepest distress arises the problem of his I, and

the broader correlation between man and God offers at this point the only possibility of help.

Thus we see that even the administration of justice has to maintain the necessity of guilt; not, however, on the judge's part, but all the more on the part of the criminal himself. From this state of affairs it necessarily follows that free will must be maintained because of guilt, maintained in no way as an illusion, although as a fiction. But this fiction is the first principle of moral action in general, and if we have previously said that the peculiar character of religion originates in the problem of guilt, and, within this, in the problem of the individual, we now see that this peculiarity is directly connected with the foundations of ethics.

If man is not permitted to lay aside the consciousness of his guilt then it is ethics itself which refers man to religion, to the correlation with God. Ethics can only set up the first principles which determine the possibility of this correlation. To prescribe the boundary of the applicability of the correlation is in contradiction to the insight of ethics into its own limitations. Man looks into the eyes of men; only God looks into the heart. The guilt and the merit of man remains hidden from man. This is not the fault of ethics, but of science, which in turn receives its limits from logic. For ethics, man is, in the last analysis—one can see it clearly now—only a point to which it relates its problems, as for science also he is only a particular case of its general laws. In relation to the laws, however, only the particular man originates, and indeed as nothing other than a case.

The case that comes under a law is, however, not the individual, who addresses himself as I. The case addresses only the law. The individual, however, thinks himself isolated and therefore absolute. And in this isolation he is at his wits' end, as long as he cannot absolve himself from the consciousness of his guilt and, according to his subjective membership in the realm of moral creatures, may not absolve himself. If at this point the correlation to God did not come into force, he would be absolutely lost to the moral world, lost to his consciousness of it.

7. We repeat: if we claim that religion is concerned with man's guilt, and if we impart to religion the origin of the I as individual, we do not dissolve its connection with ethics, but, on the contrary, make the connection effective, so that ethics itself must demand the transition to religion, just as it will also have to demand that transition for the concept of God.

It is religion that enters into this methodological connection with ethics, religion—not myth, and not mysticism.

Myth has one of its deepest roots in the concept of guilt. It is the doom, the fate to which the gods themselves are subjected. And out of this *Ate,* out of the delusion of guilt, grew tragedy. If we, however, by means of guilt ascribe to religion the origination of the individual, we will here again lay bare the exact difference between religion and myth. In mythological guilt, man is not an individual, but rather the offspring of his ancestors. Tragedy, too, begins by accepting man's tie to his ancestry. To release man from it, to redeem him from his inherited guilt, becomes the task of tragedy.

The Bible, too, struggles with this received myth: God requites the guilt of the fathers upon the children. But the Bible frees itself from myth through the establishment of God's love. Owing to this new insight about God, a distinction appears in the Bible, which first restricts the punishment to those of the children "that hate Me," and then also opposes to the punishment "upon the third and upon the fourth generation" the showing of mercy "unto the thousandth generation of them that love Me and keep My commandment" [Deut. 5:9-10]. This supplement to the theophany (Exod. 34:7) is given by the Decalogue with the second set of tablets. Nevertheless "the third and the fourth generation," though under the condition of its own guilt, is still subject to the old point of view. Under the latter the individual has not come yet into its free development at all, not to say into its meaning as the I.

8. The mythical point of view therefore burdens the criminal even more than does the judgment of forensic medicine. The latter can still summon a remedy; mythical consciousness makes the criminal the grandchild of his ancestors, and to this there is only one reply: woe unto you that you are a grandchild. Therefore, Aeschylus' accomplishment in letting Athena depose the Erinyes and set up a new goddess in place of the old goddesses of vengeance, a new goddess, who as a genuine goddess establishes a court of justice, the Areopagus, is an act of methodological importance for philosophical consciousness. Thus, with Aeschylus too ethics leads to religion. Orestes stops being merely of Tantalus' generation and becomes an individual. But the goddess liberates him only after deposing the old law. Properly speaking, Athena liberates not so much Orestes as Athens and its law.

At this point, therefore, the connection of tragedy with ethics shows itself more than the connection of man with religion. Thus Orestes does not yet become an individual, but he remains the citizen of his city; only within the city is he liberated from his guilt. Even here, therefore, there is as yet no isolated individual, whose absoluteness in the presence of plurality, and even totality, is required by the

I. The I of Orestes receives neither enlightenment nor liberation. Clytemnestra remains his mother whom he killed. He killed her out of *Ate* and the banishment of the Erinyes is morally right. But why did he become the victim of this horrible delusion? To this question he has no other answer but the one which is given him by his descent. His individuality thus is dissolved into his ancestry, with which he remains enmeshed. The individual as I cannot originate out of myth.

In tragedy myth dies away; its beginning antedates even the exposition of guilt. In its beginning man does not yet distinguish between good and bad, but his might is his right. As models he has his gods, who likewise act only in accordance with their moods. It is already a higher stage when the feeling of unhappiness about a wrong he has committed comes into his consciousness, and an even higher stage when he learns to recognize guilt as the inheritance of his human existence. In Greece, too, polytheism anticipates religion with the rise of this feeling of unhappiness. And Plato has a close affinity and connection with Orphic theology.

9. The oldest mythical symbol, through which the correlation between man and the gods is achieved, is the sacrifice. Originally it is offered to the godhead, of whose envy and hatred (φθονερὸν τὸ θεῖον) one is afraid and whom one strives to appease with a sacrifice. When man becomes conscious of guilt, then one is in need of the sacrifice not only against the envy of the gods but also for the purpose of one's own purification from this contamination of consciousness. Through this, the gods become the guardians of morality, the violation of which makes man feel guilty. Thereby the sacrifice, too, receives a different meaning and importance.

For even if sacrifice is still offered only because of the gods and not expressly because of men themselves, it receives, through the different character of the gods, a different character itself. It must become a means of purification, if its effect is to be liberation from guilt. Though the purification may still be related to the gods, it must be transferable to man if he is to be liberated from his feeling of guilt. However, obscurity and uncertainty still surround the sacrifice, because the mere fact of sacrificing is thought capable of effecting this liberation from guilt. Thus the gods can be bribed. And consequently the correlation between man and gods exists only insofar as the gods have authoritative power over man's consciousness of guilt, and can exercise it in accordance with the gifts that man offers them.

Strictly speaking, the consciousness of guilt made only men better, while the gods remained envious, as their susceptibility to bribes proves. Or is it that the gods demand the sacrifice only as a proof of the human betterment caused by the consciousness of guilt? Within polytheism there is complete obscurity about this, and only in Plato, perhaps, does some light struggle its way out of this obscurity.

10. It seems that the solemn cult of animal sacrifice is inseparably connected with the following ambiguity: the deepest consciousness in man is replaced by an act performed in connection with an animal. This seems to be the basic error in the animal sacrifice; the most human is exchanged for the brutish. And, at that, animal sacrifice is already the continuation and abolition of human sacrifice. But even as a substitute, there remains in animal sacrifice the incorrigible defect of the intermixture of the spiritual with the material.

11. Among the wonders that are pertinent to the historical understanding of the wonder of monotheism, the fight of the prophets against the *sacrifice* occupies perhaps the first place. The entire classical world is attached to sacrifice; the idea of sacrifice is also the foundation of Christianity and, finally, one finds that this idea has also remained active in the most diverse modifications in the more free, modern consciousness. Not only every misfortune, but even every supposedly free moral action, is still understood as a sacrifice, if not to fate, then at least to duty. If one considers all this, it is almost incomprehensible how the prophets knew how to take superstition and paganism by the horns and how they recognized in sacrifice the root of idol worship.

12. This wonder should not be diminished by equating sacrifice with all cultic worship and by concluding that the rejection of sacrifice entails the rejection of all cultic worship, nor by finding this rejection either affirmed or denied in prophetic thought. Although sacrifice and cult are connected with one another, they in no way coincide. The cult in general, the ceremony of worship in the temple, insofar as it already existed, did not need fundamentally to be basically rejected by the prophets in order to carry through the rejection of sacrifice. And where there seems to be an intimation of such a consequence, it should not be considered a confirmation of the only true overcoming of sacrifice. Even Micah, in the famous passage, demands not only human morality but also "to walk humbly with thy God." In what does this consist? How does the prophet understand this? Does not the word indicate an isolated surrender to God's demands, even if they relate only to morality? And what else is this isolated surrender in the humble walking with God but the worship of God?

It is another question whether the prophets through their polemics against the sacrifice should have been induced to establish a separate service for the worship of God. This can be denied. One underestimates and, in general, misjudges the power of the prevailing habit which sacrifice, as public cult, constituted, if from the rejection of sacrifice by the prophets one draws the conclusion that the public cult was simultaneously rejected. This conclusion contradicts all historical sense. As we indicated above, if there are found in the prophets a few intimations of such a consequence, they may show the consistency of the thought of a particular prophet, but they do not prove at all that the prophet himself meant the complete abrogation of cultic worship. In order to understand the development of the prophetic ideas in their most important aspects of moral reformation, we must retain the above distinction between sacrifice and cultic worship.

The struggle against sacrifice is wonderful enough; it need not be supplemented by the struggle against the cult in its entirety. It is questionable whether this additional struggle would not be a shallow and fruitless one.

13. However, it might now appear that, just as the prophets did not fight the cult in general along with sacrifice, they did not in general fight sacrifice, but merely its connection with moral wrong and injustice. They may appear to have fought the connection of injustice and sacrifice, but not, however, sacrifice in itself; for only injustice does not admit of any connection with the devotion to God. However, in what way does sacrifice contradict the concept of devotion?

Isaiah says in the first chapter: "I cannot endure iniquity along with solemn assembly" (Isa. 1:13). But he continues: "when ye make many prayers, I will not hear: your hands are full of blood." It would seem that prayer is rejected together with the sacrifice. Is it its connection with iniquity, with murder, that makes it incompatible with worship? And thus could it be that only this connection makes the sacrifice "vain oblations . . . offering of abomination" (Isa. 1:13) and that there would still remain a possibility of true sacrifice?

Even the question is unhistorical, and psychologically erroneous as well. One should not ask such questions about unmistakably original and great ideas. One should not search into all corners and paths of the soul of the originators of great ideas; if one does, one obscures the new main direction which this soul pursues. How could Isaiah have begun his speeches with this polemic, and how could he carry it through in all its particular details, if he were not to see through the inner harmfulness of the sacrifice, which is for him the *mythological origin* of sacrifice? The sacrifice is the sacrificial meal, which has been preserved by the Israelites also. The worshipers of Baal partake of this meal together with their gods. And, as during this meal the worshipers of Baal serve their own insolence and feast in the triumph of their own power and vitality, in a similar way the idol worshipers in Israel became perhaps more fearful, so that in their jubilant feast they long for the assistance of their God. But for what do they request this support? For their moral life, perhaps, or for the continuation of their injustice?

The prophets recognized that it was only superstition that made the sacrifice ceremony more serious and gloomy. Only the desire of the idol worshipers to safeguard their immoral behavior, in which they persisted and from which they did not believe they were able to detach themselves, made them make their sacrifice more generous and more resigned. Therefore the thought of the prophets could not take any other direction but the alternative: either sacrifice—this, however, means persisting in injustice—or rejection of sacrifice and thereby liberation from injustice.

One has to read the first chapter of Isaiah from verse 10 to 20 in order to see in what detail there he rejects the sacrifice, together, of course, with all the festivity that was based on the sacrifice: "Your appointed seasons My soul hateth: they are a burden unto Me; I am weary to bear them." Preceding this verse were those which specify the sacrifices: "I am full of the burnt offerings of rams, and the fat of fed beasts; and I delight not in the blood of the bullocks, or of lambs, or of he-goats." One cannot in this way itemize that which is to be rejected and at the same time deride it, if one has not in principle outgrown the whole institution.

14. The prophet Amos goes so far as to ask the historical question: "Did ye bring unto Me sacrifices and offerings in the wilderness forty years?" (Amos 5:25). Thus he intends to make sacrifice suspect as a non-Mosaic ceremony. And this idea receives its final form in Jeremiah: "For I spoke not unto your fathers, nor commanded them in the day that I brought them out of the land of Egypt, concerning burnt offerings or sacrifices" [Jer. 7:22]. Maimonides builds upon this thought his whole criticism of the sacrifice, and, in complete agreement with Deuteronomy, he gives this idea a positive development by substituting the legislation of the "statutes and ordinances" in Mara for the sacrificial legislation.[35]

15. In the history of moral and spiritual ideas in general, rarely has an entirely revolutionary thought been expressed and carried out with such clarity and distinctness, with such strictness and precision, as the prophets achieved in expressing the purely moral character of monotheism. They did this through an unrestrained fight against sacrifice. All the differences which are elsewhere found in the style of the prophets and which are interpreted as great differences with regard to the

end of their prophecies concerning *salvation and disaster,* are insignificant in the face of this main unifying characteristic, which we may term prophetism. What seems to speak against this idea, we will have to consider soon in detail. In the problem of the relation of sacrifice to the cult, we have already recognized the difficulty raised by a motivation that had to oppose this main characteristic.

16. Is the cult of any use at all? This question cannot be answered by pointing to the isolation of the mind for the purpose of thinking of God, as this seems to be required by the demand to walk humbly before God. Or, insofar as the prophets did not attack the worship— and, as we shall see, even expressly demand it—should the worship be aimed at the solitary isolation of *pietism* and not at the service in the "assembly," which is the basic word of the Mosaic teaching, and at the service in the congregation, this basic word of Deuteronomy, which the prophet Ezra put into effect? Does the social spirit of the prophets contradict itself in the matter of worship?

If the prophets could have entered into an agreement with the cult, this agreement had to be in accord with the basic idea of the fellowman, therefore with the idea that the road to the individual leads through the fellowman, and consequently that the road to the I, who cleaves to his God in isolation, opens up only on the basis of the connection with the fellowman, and that therefore the I's absorption in God can be based only upon this connection.

17. If, by rejecting the sacrifice, we were, however, to retain the cult, we would put ourselves upon a difficult historical crossroads. And in order to anticipate the possible objection that we here invent consequences which are speculative, we at once put ourselves before the historical problem which confronted Ezekiel and his successors. He does not reject sacrifice: does he thereby fall away from the basic idea of the prophets? Is there only one way to fight sacrifice, which is to reject it entirely? Or could one conceive of a fight against sacrifice that strives to transform its inward meaning? And would this kind of criticism and reformation still preserve the prophetic spirit?

This question can be answered positively only on the basis of the ideas and institutions which such a criticism and reformation are able to discover and to establish. For it has to be a matter of the discovery of new ideas if the criticism is to have consequences which contradict the previous idea of the rejection of sacrifice. If, however, the fight of a new idea against an old, historically actualized national institution is the historical problem, then it is a matter of a controversial question which repeats itself in all regions, with all peoples and at all times. Everywhere the question arises of whether the old idea one fights in a traditional institution should be entirely rejected and eliminated or whether it is the case that a new idea seeks a reconciliation with the old institution.

In this case it is no longer exclusively the old idea that is the concern; but a new idea appears with its claims, and the question arises: which one of the two ideas has the greater worth? Or perhaps the old idea needs only the addition of the new one so that the criticism of the old institution made by the new idea may come to its maturity and completion through the new idea itself.

18. Perhaps the criticism of sacrifice was deficient, particularly because it seemed to exclude the cult along with the sacrifice. If an idea becomes necessary—perhaps for the concept of man—which demands some connection with the cult, this idea would perhaps be able to refute or to limit the arguments out of which the rejection of sacrifice arose. Everything will depend on the worth of the new idea and whether it is absolutely opposed to the old one or rather deepens the latter and brings it to its completion. It depends on the new idea, not only on the old institution. If the new idea is necessary, then its agreement with the old institution will depend upon the inner transformation of the institution through the new idea. And then the only question is whether the old institution is at all fit to be transformed prophetically. Upon the answer to this question depends not so much the objective religious meaning of sacrifice as its historic religious meaning.

The historical necessity of the ideas is decided not by the logical connection between the concepts themselves but by the historical connection between the concepts and the institutions. The philosopher cannot permit the course of history to prescribe for him either the disposition or the solution of his problems. But as little can he prescribe to history the course it should have taken.

19. With regard to the sacrifice, the history of prophecy proceeds in two ways. One takes the road of the rejection of the sacrifice; the other, however, aims at its transformation; the alteration becomes transformation. And it may be asked whether such a transformation is not the best kind of abrogation. With this kind of preservation would the old rejection remain in force? Such questions are raised by the special place of Ezekiel among the prophets. Moreover, his ways are typical of the prophets of the exile.

20. This question, in a broader sense, involves the general problem of the relation between *ideas* and institutions. This problem appears in both materialistic and idealistic historical research and historical judgment. In particular it is a problem of general history: whether a

new progressive motive, along with its necessary polemics against the old, must not nevertheless be intertwined with a residue of the old, insofar as the fertility and developmental power of the residue cannot be dispensed with. In the very mind which brings forth the new motive, the aftereffect of the institution which is to be fought lingers on. In this development the old motive preserves its right in the new one; it retains its share in the development toward the new one. Thus the new idea remains connected with the old one even then, when it does not entirely eliminate the old institution, but only transforms it.

Sacrifice is not controversial in prophetic thought alone: it is included in the *law*. In Deuteronomy a controversy raises a similar difficulty, namely, whether the law is preserved in sacrifice, although it is "put into the heart," and again whether the law is in opposition with the "new covenant," and whether the new teaching becomes unstable if it is connected with the law. It is a great historical question whether the new teaching of moral religiosity could have been brought to a spiritual, not to mention historical, actualization without entering into relationship with the law, with the provision of the transformation of the law in accordance with the new teaching.

21. Modern biblical research is very much in need of this point of view for the understanding of Deuteronomy, about which it distributes light and shadows without having a stable point of evaluation. It does not take into consideration that in actual history light and shadows belong together; it is the human things and relations upon which both light and shadows rest. All great reformers in spiritual history had to submit to this necessity. And the greatest and purest of all idealists, Plato, has even in his *Republic*, and not only in his *Laws*, paid tribute to this anomaly, to this fate in the realm of the spirit.

The *ideas* have to be developed according to their logical content. In this deduction philosophy must prescribe to history its path. But insofar as philosophy wants to understand the way of history, it has to investigate the reciprocal effect of those ideas, which is brought about by the course of history. And its value judgment must not isolate itself to the deduction of the one-sided principle, but it must take into consideration counter effect of motives and finally base its value judgment upon the resulting power of the whole effect. This is the demand of the scientific method everywhere.

And thus the judgment about the prophets in general, as well as about their particular social achievements, be it in Deuteronomy, in the law, or with regard to the sacrifice, can become a historical judgment only insofar as the investigation and evaluation is carried out without dogmatic one-sidedness, and insofar as one-sidedness in general is suspect in historical method. For history does not operate according to isolated motivations, but indeed everywhere in very entangled reciprocal effects. Progress, regress, standstill, all these moments are not an objective criterion. Only *continuity* is the methodogical signpost. For it, however, there is no standstill, no regress, but only that progress which is the true and the only one; it is progress which is based upon continuity, which itself is independent of such contingent and external matters as before and after, and even contemporaneity; continuity overcomes and permeates all these.

Continuity may become a principle of history only through the assumption that all ideas and all institutions in history, in whatever contradiction with one another they might seem to be, are considered as, and have as their goal, one community in reciprocal effect. As soon as an isolated principle, particularly a negative one, such as the fight against sacrifice, is one-sidedly established as the idea of the prophets, then it is already methodologically suspect. If prophecy is a historical problem, then an isolated one-sided principle cannot be predominant in it. However the positive counter motivation, which consists in true devotion to God through social morality, is itself in need of a supplement. Social morality itself is in need of a supplement. The fellowman has to lead to the individual and to the I. The correlation with God must not remain restricted only to the fellowman.

22. Therefore in this other correlation, the concept of God as well as the concept of man will have to become different. Consequently also the devotion to God will have to become different. And does not the consequence thereby also become necessary that even morality, which constitutes the basis for the devotion to God, will have to become different? Until now it has been only social morality. If now the problem of man becomes different in the individual and in the I, then history unveils the great question: whether perhaps the difference between Ezekiel's and the other prophets' relation to the sacrifice has its ultimate ground in the new relation of Ezekiel to the new concept of man and consequently to the new concept of God.

To shrink from this consequence would be a mistake in the methodological application of the principle of development, from which no concept of the spirit can be withdrawn. If then Ezekiel was called to accomplish a development in the concept of man, then this call at the same time refers to the development of the concept of God in itself.

CHAPTER XI

Atonement

1. In accordance with Deuteronomy, all the prophets up to Ezekiel made social morality the main point of monotheism. Social morality sees in the problem of man only the problem of the fellowman. However, the fellowman himself presupposes man simply, to whom the fellowman is attracted. This presupposition, however, is only silently implied, and the presupposed man hovers, so to speak, entirely in the obscurity of the background. Only through the "Thou" is the "I" to be generated. This is the guiding idea of all of the prophets up to Ezekiel.

But is indeed the I only the product of the Thou? Or is it not rather that the Thou constitutes the necessary precondition, but not the adequate creative force, which latter must come from the I itself, and from still different problems which the I contains, in order that the I might be successfully generated in a positive form?

2. The I is in the first place the *individual*. In the midst of the fellowman, however, the individual could not yet arise. The individual constitutes a problem in which the peculiar character of religion, in distinction from ethics, comes to the fore. And in the social love for the fellowman, religion has not yet realized its peculiar character.

Insofar as ethics is based on the *autonomy* of the will, it may seem that only it can succeed in generating the individual. However, the free individual of ethics, if he is not dissolved in the relative communities of social plurality but is directed and projected to his ideal completion in accordance with totality, is thereby dissolved in totality.

This dissolution of the individual is the highest triumph of ethics. The ethical individual, as an isolated single being having the basis of his life in metabolism, disappears, to be resurrected in the I of the state and, by means of the confederation of states, in mankind. This is the climax ethics can achieve for the human individual. The prophets of social morality, in their messianic monotheism, join in the achievement of this climax.

In the prophets' vision of mankind the individual, as a particular man, vanishes. "Cease ye from man . . . for how little is he to be accounted." This Hamlet-like statement in no way was a slip of Isaiah's (Isa. 2:22); rather, his enthusiasm for the unique God brought about this scorn for the men of his time. With such a judgment about humankind, however, one does not reach the problem which the particular man nevertheless poses, aside from the fact that he is worthy to soar up to totality. The fellowman has to become fellow-individual; only then can the fellowman originate.

What, after all, is social morality, if it is not founded upon the individual? Is not individual morality the precondition for social morality, without which the latter remains an abstraction, from which it cannot be freed even through the relation of man to the state? For the state, too, becomes concrete only in individuals, and only individuals make the personality of the state alive, although they have to be dissolved into it. The state must become an ideal person and, consequently, must become a true individual.

3. The characteristic of man which Isaiah condemns is precisely the one which designates the path upon which man becomes an individual. And precisely this characteristic of the individual is overlooked by the prophets of social morality, since they consider the human characteristic of *sin* in its social aspect only as it pertains to social plurality.

Considered from the social point of view, they are right. Sin seems to be the portion of men. Man, in his social plurality, is filled with envy and violence, falsehood and deceit, lust for power and greediness, fraud and waste, voluptuousness and tyranny. But is not plurality an abstraction? Is it able by itself to beget sin? Or does individual and social plurality constitute a "double mill" (*Zwickmühle*), so that the question can be reciprocally transferred from one member to the other? Here one already sees that the individual is presupposed only for the sake of social plurality and that he is as yet not thought of as an independent problem.

4. From this an important consequence follows for the censorious sermons of the social prophets and in general for their concept of morality; not only did they fail to clarify the problem of the individual as a separate problem, but their concept of sin does not yet have its ground in individual sin. Moreover, social sin can become a sin against God only through the sinner's having become an individual, and no longer through having merely the abstraction of social plurality as its carrier and its origin.

5. A prelude to the fundamental proceedings which repeat them-

selves in the entire history of culture down to this day is to be recognized in the deficiency we tried to detect in the prophets of social
morality. The sociological viewpoint, advisedly and with justice,
searches for the ground of moral wrong in the contradictions and fric-
tions of social conditions. Here sin is social sin. The one-sided religious
and religiously determined moral view isolates man in his moral power,
and believes it makes him an individual through this isolation. Both
points of view require unification with one another, if the moral, the
religious man is to be generated out of the fellowman, as the individual, as I.

For it is the I which is eliminated by the one-sided sociological
point of view. The self-consciousness of the individual must be re-
pressed if the power of social circumstances is to be brought into
proper focus. Thereby, however, the core that constitutes human
worth and dignity is lost. And if human dignity is to be re-established,
this cannot be done without the negative condition that the I itself,
and, consequently, the individual, is to sin and that the cause of his
sin cannot be shifted to the social plurality.[36]

6. Insofar as sin is being considered purely methodologically as
the means for the discovery of man as I, and thereby as the true
individual, it is implied that the sin on which the social prophets con-
centrate their censure has to be supplemented, deepened, and intensified by that sin which the individual commits as I, and of
which he has to be made conscious. The prophetic idea has to progress in the direction of the individual, in the direction of the I, and
therefore to go beyond the notion of sin held by the prophets of
social morality.

*The prophecy of Ezekiel constitutes the essential stage of this prog-
ress.* And if at the same time he takes a step which from the point
of view of the prophets of social morality could be judged a step backward, this step should not be considered and judged separately; for
it is to be examined in connection with the progress which it achieves
and which was necessary for the solution of the problem of man.

7. In order to understand the problem of sin, we must once more
look back to the mythological origins. And in these, too, the inner connection between these two problems of sin and the individual is unmistakable. We have seen how the prophets of social morality consider the mythological primordial question of *guilt*, out of which the
tragic idea grows. They make interest in the fellowman dominant,
and with this they repel the whole host of mythological and metaphysical questions. The prophets overcome these forces because they

excel them with the power and energy of their treatment of the problem of sin.

And yet the question of the guilt of man is not settled when one attains the insight that man is not merely the grandchild of his ancestors. What is he positively, as a creature in his own right? And how can he sin out of, and by, himself? Nor can this question be resolved by recognizing sin as a product of social plurality. For the latter, as already mentioned, remains an abstraction for sin, as well as for positive morality, if the individual does not elevate himself to the moral model and incorporate the abstract plurality into himself, and give it soul and spirit.

8. How can man sin by himself spontaneously? Can the question be settled through the answer that man has *free will?* If ethics is able to bestow this free will only on the basis of its method, then it can demand it as a *pure* will only, as the will to the good as a foundation of ethics. If, however, freedom of the will means the capacity of the human will to make a choice for evil as well as for good, then this meaning of the will would no longer belong to the realm of pure ethics but would refer to human experience. In that case the question arises: in the experience of man, how can the assumption of an indifferent will arise? Or a will that can choose the bad as well as the good? How can freedom of the will mean freedom of the will to sin? Hence, the moral teaching based on experience also fails to solve the question of the origin of sin.

9. Out of a misunderstanding of the Hebrew word יצר [*yezer*] arose the notion of *original sin.* The acknowledgment of man's weakness is doubtless the meaning of the passage in question. The earth and man himself upon it should not be punished because of man alone: "for the *yezer* of man's heart is evil from his youth" (Gen. 8:21). The pleonasm is noteworthy, and only because we are accustomed to the phrase "desire of the heart," do we fail to notice it. The heart alone should have been enough, or the desire.

The word "*yezer*," however, does not mean desire, or at least not desire only, but is, according to the explanation of Ibn Ezra, "the product, which is imitated after it." The desire of the heart is not evil; rather, the product of the heart is designated as bad. Gesenius translates the word in its first significance as action, as *fictio, formatio.* The same word occurs two chapters before in a complicated connection with "thoughts of his heart" (Gen. 6:5). Kautzsch's translation tries to lump together two ideas: "and all the musings and aspirations of his heart." In the later passage [Gen. 8:21] he mentions only "musings." Thus desire is not assumed there either. But "musings" and "aspiration" too are erroneous.

The word means only the product of thoughts of the heart, as the later passage unmistakably makes clear. In no way does the passage assert an inborn predisposition for evil in the human heart. It is, however, acknowledged that the effects of the musing and aspirations of the human heart are bad. Yet this pronouncement should not be considered an absolute truth. It is not an article of faith; as such it could not originate in connection with God's judgment and his providence for the preservation of the earth and everything living upon it. A teaching that makes evil an inborn desire of the human heart would not fit into this context. The products of man's heart are bad; this may mean that in the human heart yet other imaginary actions, other formative powers may be aroused, which are to be distinguished from these bad formative powers. The word *"yezer"* itself alludes to the maker of the human heart, who could not have put the bad into the human heart, which is God's creation.

This idea, which would solve our question by attributing the origin of evil to the predisposition to evil of the human heart, of the human will, cannot be supported by the passages in Genesis. Rather, man has the holy spirit in his heart. To it is issued the call, that is, the calling to holiness. The natural predisposition to evil would be in contradiction to the fundamental commandment of holiness. More fundamentally, it would be in contradiction to God's holiness. "God, the holy One, is sanctified through righteousness" [Isa. 5:16]. The holy God could not have put evil into the human heart.[37]

10. The question still remains: is man's bad experience only an illusion? Are the productions, the formations of mankind's activities, only good, and is the problem of sin a futile and a vain one?

We have come to know that a superficial optimism might mislead our historical judgment about the worth of previous world history. But disregarding this, the problem of the I and the individual would be untenable if we allow the problem of sin to become vain and thereby deprive ourselves of the only means which, when used with clarity, opens the possibility of dealing with and solving the above problems. For social sin has already pushed us away from the false aid we might have sought by assuming that man is simply good. Our insight into social sin has definitely liberated us from this illusion. Therefore only the question remains: how does sin come into man? And this question cannot be eliminated by the assumption that sin as such is an illusion.

The latter solution is possible only if one anticipates the judgment that there is no sin other than that against men, and that the sin against God is a religious prejudice. Our question in reply is: how do you, moral purist, explain the mere possibility of social sin? The social environment is an abstraction, which does not become concrete because you afterwards fill it with individuals. How do you suddenly come to these individuals who are only inferences, thus products of abstraction, and therefore could originate and be valid only as abstractions of your first abstraction?

The *sociological* point of view does not escape the vacillation of the balance between good and bad, a balance which exists only in and for this vacillating social plurality. It cannot account for evil, so also not for the individual, to say nothing of the I. Thus nothing remains but to seek out the religious point of view once again, in order to understand the origin of the possibility of evil in the individual, in the I of man. Thus we have to progress from the social prophets to Ezekiel.

11. Ezekiel is distinguished from the social prophets in that he establishes sin as the sin of the individual and in that he discovers in sin the individual. This distinction has as a further consequence that he does not consider sin merely as a social sin, therefore as mainly committed between man and man, but, more than his predecessors, attributes to sin the meaning of a sin against God. This point of view is in no way lacking in his predecessors, naturally; otherwise, how could Isaiah have recognized the holy God? But the social point of view made the purely religious one recede. It is the merit of these prophets that they fused religion and morality. This means, however, that they furthered the dissolution of religion into morality, and although they did not efface and suppress the peculiar character of religion with regard to morality, they did not make it shine forth sufficiently.

Thus, the prevalent social idea that makes the individual recede before the injustice of classes in human society is intrinsically connected with allowing the specifically religious problem to recede. And as the individual recedes before the social castes, in the same way sins against God recede before the great social and moral problems, as the themes of human sin. Justice is the mainstay of the moral religion of the social prophets. The holy God is sanctified through justice. This concise formulation of Isaiah is characteristic of this type of prophet. The violation of justice is the sin against God. There can be no other sin.

In introducing the distinctive characteristic of Ezekiel's teaching, we began with the twofold proposition that he established a new connec-

tion between sin, individual, and God. We must first of all repulse a
misconception about the relation of God to the sin of the individual, a
misconception which might emerge through the question we formulated above: where does sin come from? We have already warded
off the possibility that God might have planted it in our own being
as a hereditary quality. However, the newly established connection
of the three notions might again lead back to this fatal supposition.
And the mistake in general is strengthened by the ambiguity of the
meaning of the question itself.

We have recognized the question of the origin of evil as one that
has its own origin in myth. Alleged metaphysics also maintains its
interest in it. Ethics, on the contrary, teaches us that the ground of
freedom, consequently the ground of the good and that of evil, must
be inscrutable. The kind of ground that myth seeks is always only
causality. The latter, however, rules only over the realm of knowledge of nature. The realm of freedom, however, is the realm of
ethical knowledge, and it is governed by the principle of purpose
instead of causality.

12. Consequently, if the question about the wherefrom of sin cannot refer to the ground and origin of sin, then its connection with
God cannot mean that the ground can be imputed to God, for we
have disposed of the problem of ground as cause. What meaning,
then, does this question still have? The answer to this question should
be mediated by another question: what meaning has sin against God
as opposed to sin against man? And how can the former be protected
against the suspicion of being merely an illusion or a superfluous
fiction?

Until now in the connection of the three concepts, the main concern has been with sin and with God; but what meaning does the
individual have in this connection? Until now we have only considered that the individual is necessary and cannot be disposed of
by the social point of view of sin as pertaining only to plurality.
However, it is not sufficient to recognize the individual as an indispensable desideratum; in this context he would appear merely
as a negative condition. What, then, is the positive meaning of the
individual for sin? This question can now no longer be mistaken for
the opinion which puts the ground of sin into the inherited nature
of the individual, for this would again involve the blunder of making
causality the ground.

13. The individual must be established according to the methods
of ethics, *within the teleological teaching* of ethics, with which the
religion of reason must remain continuously connected. This teleo-

logical teaching is the methodologically homogeneous continuation of logic. The latter, however, teaches that all fundamental ideas are *first principles*, which have the touchstone of their correctness in their fruitfulness.

Such a first principle is the individual, as is sin, as is the sin of the individual. Such a first principle is also the idea of God, and also no different is the sin before God.

The individual first should unfold himself as I only through sin. This unfolding is not given to social sin, which knows only a sinning plurality. Let us, therefore, experiment with the first principle of the sin before God, to see whether, perhaps, it contains the fertility that can beget the individual as I. Perhaps a new fertility of such a sort will appear, namely such a one in which not only does the sinful individual change into the sinful I, but beyond this transformation another one is at work with regard to the sinful I. Through this, the deeper meaning of the connection of the basic concepts would appear; not only is the individual as I discovered, but the idea of God also attains a new meaning through which religion achieves its peculiar character with regard to ethics, upon the methods of which it remains dependent. And this peculiar character of religion would then bring about not only the discovery of a new concept of God beyond that of ethics but also the discovery of a new concept of man.

14. With regard to the notion of man also, sin must bring a new elucidation. It cannot present a metaphysical riddle that would set up a sphinx over man's being. Sin is nothing more or less than a first principle. It must therefore be a transitional concept for the first principle of man as I, a transitional concept which leads beyond the concept of a sinning plurality. And consequently, the sin before God as well is nothing more or less than a first principle, thus a transition which leads beyond the sin which is before man, because it is against man. And the connection of these two points of transition should have as a consequence a new first principle of the I.

15. Let us pause for a little while in order to consider once more the relation of the individual and plurality with regard to sin. The World War [I] is an acute occasion for it. And besides, war to the prophets meant what we today more profoundly recognize as capitalistic world trade. The actual warfare is undertaken by the peoples, but each minister of state talks about those who originated it. Thus one is not satisfied with the problem of *causes*, and one in no way turns away from the problem of the *originator*. And yet, from the social point of view, the question is put wrongly, and therefore never solved. For the individuals are in the last analysis merely un-

derlings. Economic motivations are the real originators, which therefore remain always hidden. How great is the effect of the opposing
force of the single, individual figure of Jaures?

This is one's judgment from the social point of view. However much
the economic motivations seem to be decisive, not only according to
the materialistic point of view of history, ideal ones also carry weight,
namely the *national* oppositions in the culture of a race. Are the vistas
of the moral individual opened up thereby? It is questionable whether
the latter would be determined even through religious oppositions.
In all cases, as in this one, it is the dark blind masses who are led
into the field of action, and no individual who sees steps forward into
the light of the moral day.

16. Call every single man who participates in the affairs of the
state, or in the press, or in the other countless administrative organs,
call him as an individual before the tribunal of his conscience. Only
the individual himself can be called to responsibility for the sin of the
peoples.

Thus *conscience* is the tribunal! In that case we would have found
the court before which the individual can originate and must exist
as an individual. Why then also a tribunal before God?

If conscience were a sufficiently correct concept, then at no time
would a philosophic ethics be necessary. Conscience is a daimon
which everyone has in common with Socrates. But Socrates himself
did not let himself be satisfied with it, but paved the way for ethics.
And this ethics has been improved further during the centuries, while
the conscience in its oracular majesty has made no progress. It has
therefore always been displaced by the tribunal before God. For the
religion of reason, however, the question remains of whether its share
of reason, which is based on its connection with ethics, remains preserved in the ecclesiastic view of the judgment seat of God.

However, we now have at hand a criterion with which we can
methodologically examine the correct concept of sin before God. It
consists of the connection of the concepts of sin and sin before God
with the individual as I. Only that sin of the individual which the
human individual holds up before the human I do we have to recognize as a sin before God. If now the human individual is isolated
with regard to the social plurality, he does not become lonely and
deserted, but rather is reborn to a new life. The I is this new creature,
or rather the moral rational creature. And the triumph of religion
consists in its unique success in bringing to the world this rational
creature, whereas ethics can beget it only in the projection of totality.

17. The I sinning before God should open the path to this new

problem of the religious I. If, however, the sinful I is to be only a transitional point for the begetting of the new I, not yet begotten by ethics, then it cannot remain the sinning I. *Liberation* from sin has to become the goal, and only through the attainment of this goal will the new I be begotten. Thus the sin is brought up before God, not in order that the individual should remain in it but in order that he be liberated from it, which liberation is necessary for the transformation of the individual into the I. If the moral law were the only court before which man in his autonomy had to answer for himself, then the abstraction of this tribunal would have no competence and no means to liberate man from his sin. In autonomy alone lies the power to assert human morality. It is due to the power of autonomy that the I rises to totality. There is no other goal and no other means for ethics.

However, for social morality the individuality of the fellowman has already appeared as a problem. The latter, however, is not yet the I. And the problem of the I is as little exhausted through totality as it is through plurality. Thus, we must take the risk and attempt to find the foundation which brings the sinful individual before the judgment seat of God.

The anticipated results of the liberation from sin cannot be heterogeneous, which might damage the integrity of the problem of the I. For every danger of eudaemonism and egotism of all kinds has long ago been surmounted. The I has already lifted itself above social plurality. It has long been far removed from the simple living creature. It has already absorbed all the moral strength of social culture. But out of this abundance of its content it now strives up to the true individuality of the I. The passage through sin before God is the preparation for this rise. Through the sin before God the individual is to penetrate to the I. Attainment of the goal of humanity, which the I liberated from sin represents, is mediated by sin before God.

18. If we now proceed to Ezekiel, we have to add to the first three concepts a fourth one which we have now obtained, the concept of *redemption.* The sin before God is the means to redemption before God. And if we now ask again about the relationship of Ezekiel and his successors to the first group of prophets, then we can name redemption as the goal of the latter also; but the concept of redemption is for them a political one, and thus the extension of a social one. Not the exclusively political redemption of Israel, nor the particularized redemption, limited to Israel, is the task of the holy God, but the redemption of mankind.

Again it has been and is from the perspective of totality that the

prophets idealize man. Mankind is to be redeemed; therefore, the redemption of the individual is the necessary consequence. But redemption is effected only through justice. What problem could then still
remain for man? We have already seen that in this universality the
individual did not yet emerge, to say nothing of the I. And thus also
redemption, as the liberation of the individual from sin, must become
a new problem and yield a new notion of redemption.

19. The manifold meaning of the *redeemer* and the redemption in
the biblical language may find its explanation in the above. The
redemption of Israel still clings to the idea of the redeemer as a legal
institution, which has to be responsible for the preservation of the
family. But the redeemer from sin is not known to the people, not
to say to the tribe or to the family. For Ezekiel there exists the individual only and the authorization to prepare the individual road
to the I.

A new term, which, however, cannot be a new concept, is added
here: *atonement*.

20. The origin of this concept, too, lies in myth and in polytheism.
The anger of the gods, which is based on envy, has to be appeased.
Sacrifice is supposed to be the atonement that reconciles. The sin,
which subjectively is the sacrifice, has only the objective goal of this
atonement before the gods. The holy God, on the contrary, can be
angry with men only because of their injustice. And the zeal of the
prophets against sacrifices is sufficiently explained by their opposition
to the false gods, who could accept atonement apart from human
morality. For them, therefore, no concession should be permitted
with regard to the sacrifice, which is the absolutely dangerous symptom of the worship of false gods.

And in spite of this, Ezekiel is supposed to open up a new road,
although he wants to retain the sacrifice! Is not this an insoluable
contradiction? Let us see whether antonement itself does not offer
a new mediation, in order to make sin before God fruitful for the
liberation of man from it and for his development into the I.

21. Just as the redemption does not remain the redemption of the
people, so on the other hand it does not remain the atonement before,
and reconciliation with, God; these are the more distant goals whose
attainment must first have the effect of reconciling in man the *contradictions* that hinder the individual from developing into the *unity
of the I.*

Until now we have paid attention mainly to God, in order to beget
the I through the notion of the sin before God. Now redemption as
reconciliation leads us back again to man, whose elevation to the I

makes the concepts of God, sin before God, and redemption through God merely into mediating concepts. They will again be at the summit and designate the final goal once it has been already reached, namely, through atonement, which man himself, in all the contradictions of his commissions and omissions has to strive for and to achieve.

Only in order to carry out his own independent work will he be in need of God's tribunal. The reconciliation, which man has to achieve within himself, has its final solution in the redemption through God, which at the same time is the reconciliation with God. This is the goal. This is the task of the moral I, in distinction from all social, from all universal morality.

22. With these problems in mind we now approach Ezekiel. The sin before God leads us to man as I. The sin before God leads us to the redemption by God. The redemption by God leads us to the reconciliation of man with himself. And only the latter leads us in the last instance to the reconciliation of the I with God. It is only the reconciliation with God which brings the individual to his maturity as the I.

It is a peculiar feature of biblical thinking that the object of its reflection and astonishment is not so much the guilt of the ancestors in its connection with their descendants but rather the discrepancy between the guilt of the parents and the *punishment* of the children. The mythico-tragic thinking about the inheritance of guilt seems not to have any roots there; it is as if one were in no way able to think that God is capable of burdening guiltless man in such a way. On the other hand, the religious consciousness, from the earliest times, in the case of Abraham with regard to Sodom, resists the daily experience which suggests that the guilt of the parents subsequently brings about the misfortune of the children.

This misfortune of the children appears as the aftereffect of the guilt of the parents in the punishment of the innocent children. For the children are never conscious of their own guilt, and the contemporaries, too, pay more attention to the guilt of the parents than to the possible guilt of the children. Perhaps it is already a step forward in religious consciousness if only the punishment is considered hereditary, but not the guilt itself.

23. Of the better times, which Jeremiah prophesizes, he says: "In those days they shall say no more, the fathers have eaten sour grapes, and the children's teeth are set on edge" (Jer. 31:29). And what does he say positively about those days? "But every one shall die for his own iniquity: every man that eateth the sour grapes, his teeth shall be set on edge" (Jer. 31:30). And those are the days in which God

will make a "new covenant" with Israel (Jer. 31:31). This is all Jeremiah has to say in order to appease the opinions of people; in future times everyone will die because of his own sin. Only to this extent will the children be protected from the aftereffects of punishment. The sinning fathers, however, are delivered up to the death they deserve.

However, it is only through opposition to the punishment of the children that the prophets came to express the idea that everyone has his "own sin." But this new teaching that each man has his own sin is not yet sufficiently clarified, particularly in opposition to the mythico-tragic view. This teaching is not yet proven through the cessation of the aftereffects in punishment. For punishment may not always follow immediately after sin. Punishment by itself cannot be the correct proof of the actuality of sin. At this point, therefore, sin is still understood in the general sense of social sin, to which every single man is forfeited. It is, however, not understood as the sin of the individual proper. The pronoun "his," in the phrase "his sin," cannot represent the new idea.

24. This new step Ezekiel accomplishes with the following statement: *the soul sins.* The soul is the expression for the person and for the individual.

One may think that the soul has been already anticipated by Deuteronomy in the notions of the heart and the inward. However, the heart is only a collective designation for the inwardness of man, and thus only for the inward proper. The localization of man in one of his organs and even in the totality of them does not yet comprise the entire man, who singly and as such has to be made the originator of his sin. The soul is thus to be distinguished from heart and the inward. Only through the notion of the soul can the individual mature into the I. And only the I, the soul in its entirety, may begin to do something with the knowledge of sin which may lead beyond this knowledge. For one should not rest satisfied with the knowledge of sin. It must become the incentive to free man from the burden of sin. The *Ate* of the mythical view never permits man to attain this freedom. The mythical belief enchains man, as does the belief in oracles. For it, the only way is to surrender to fate.

The unique God not only has no fate above him: he has none in him. Therefore, knowledge of sin in monotheism can only mean: to become free from sin. If, however, the prophet Jeremiah does not draw from the new insight any other conclusion but that the sinner dies because of his own sin, he rectifies with this only the unjustified punishment; the knowledge of sin, however, is not yet developed to that fruitfulness which monotheism demands.

25. It is already characteristic of Ezekiel that he does not merely mention the above saying briefly, as Jeremiah does, but that he refutes it after a thorough examination. It is a mistake to consider that this examination is long-winded; this fullness of detail is rather a proof of the novelty of the idea. "What mean ye, that ye use this proverb in the land of Israel, saying, the fathers have eaten sour grapes, and the children's teeth are set on edge? As I live, saith the Eternal God, ye shall not have occasion any more to use this proverb in Israel. Behold, *all souls are Mine;* as the soul of the father, so also the soul of the son is Mine; the soul that sinneth, it shall die" [Ezek. 18:2-4].

The last sentence may suggest that Ezekiel's concern too is only with punishment. However, the context shows that only from now on could punishment be regarded as a sign of sin, because it follows only after the sin of the person himself. And what a great progress lies in the warding off of the parable, of the proverb "concerning the land of Israel" and the "life" of the Eternal. And what positive progress lies in the concise declaration: "Behold, all souls are Mine." The soul of the father does not have an aftereffect in the soul of the son, as if the latter did not have his own soul, but God becomes the owner of the human soul, and out of God's ownership of man's soul the son now, as the father before, receives his own soul. Now, therefore, the soul cannot merely find its end in death, but other characteristics of each man's own soul are joined to it.

26. And now it is all the more remarkable that Ezekiel describes both the righteous man and the evil one only in terms of *moral* actions and transgressions, and never describes any one of them in cultic piety or sacrificial sacrilege. It is incredible that this is usually overlooked. Only the pagan sacrifice is mentioned. Otherwise, the righteous is described as he who "neither has defiled his neighbour's wife . . . and hath not wronged any, but has restored his pledge for a debt, hath taken naught by robbery, hath given his bread to the hungry, and has covered the naked with a garment; he that hath not given forth upon interest, neither hath taken any increase, that hath withdrawn his hand from iniquity, hath executed true justice between man and man, hath walked in My statutes and has kept My judgments, to deal truly, he is just." (He is the truly just, because he is in the spirit of pure morality.) "He shall surely live, saith the Lord the Eternal" (Ezek. 18:5-9). Righteous life is now demanded on the basis of the knowledge of one's soul. And if this righteous one "beget a son that is a robber, a shedder of blood . . . and defiled his neighbour's wife,

hath wronged the poor and needy, hath taken by robbery, hath not
restored the pledge, and hath lifted up his eyes to the idols, hath
committed abomination, hath given forth upon interest, and hath
taken increase . . . he shall not live . . . his blood shall be upon him"
(Ezek. 18:11-13). The positive conclusion is found here, although at
first only in reference to punishment: it is his own blood which comes
upon him. He does not die for the sin of his father.

And now the description proceeds to the good son of this bad
father. This specification is in itself important. It is in no way impossible for the bad father to have a good son. Such a one should not
die for the guilt of his father, but he should live. The proverb is wholly
defeated. The bad father now has not only a good son but also a
happy one. This intensification is now justified, because what matters
is that the consciousness of the people judge according to this criterion.

The prophet has so much regard for the opinion of the people that
he continues: "Yet say ye, Why doth not the son bear the iniquity
of the father with him? When the son hath done that which is lawful
and right, and has kept all My statutes, and has done them: he shall
surely live. *The Soul that sinneth, it shall die;* the son shall not bear
the iniquity of the father with him, neither shall the father bear the
iniquity of the son with him; the righteousness of the righteous shall
be upon him, and the wickedness of the wicked shall be upon him"
(Ezek: 18:19-20). The prophet thus turns against the opinion of the
people, who, according to the above proverb, do not find the punishment of the son astonishing nor do they take offense at the righteous
son of a bad father remaining responsible for the guilt of the father.
The saying thus remains on the level of generalities; as soon, however,
as the single case is specified with regard to morality, superstition still
clings to the idea of inherited guilt. Only through further specification
can this superstition be destroyed.

27. The saying has a skeptical tinge. Now, however, in its continuation, it reaches the proper consequence of its idea: "But if the
wicked turn from all his sins that he hath committed . . . he shall
surely live, he shall not die. None of his transgressions that he hath
committed shall be remembered against him; for his righteousness
that he hath done he shall live. Have I any pleasure at all that the
wicked should die?, saith the Lord the Eternal: and not rather that
he should return from his ways and live?" (Ezek. 18:21-23). A new moment enters in the process of sin and punishment: the *return* from the
evil way of life. With this, the above distinction between good and
evil is transcended. And the above saying is thoroughly refuted. The

father, as unqualifiedly bad, has now vanished: he might have turned
from his evil ways. Also, the exact correspondence between sin and
punishment is now broken. In its stead enters the correspondence between sin and the turning away from it.

28. God's essence, too, is changed accordingly. Punishment is not
the infallible sign of his rule, but rather the pleasure he has in the
turning away of the sinner from his ways. God, therefore, has no
pleasure in his death, but rather in his life.

And just as the character of the evil man is not unchangeable,
neither is that of the righteous man: "When the righteous turneth
away from his righteousness, and committeth iniquity . . . none of his
righteous deeds that he hath done shall be remembered . . . yet ye
say, the way of the Lord is not equal. Hear now, O house of Israel:
is it My way that is not equal? Is it not your ways that are unequal?"
[Ezek. 18:24-25]. At the end of this exposition the decisive word regarding the wicked occurs: "Again when the wicked man turneth
away from his wickedness that he committed, and does that which is
lawful and right, he shall save his soul alive" (Ezek. 18:27). "Therefore
I will judge you, O house of Israel, every one according to his ways,
says the Lord the Eternal. Return ye, and turn yourselves from all
your transgressions; *so shall they not be a stumbling block of iniquity
unto you*" [Ezek. 18:30].

Thus the new man is born, in this way the individual becomes the
I. Sin cannot prescribe one's way of life. A turning away from the
way of sin is possible. Man can become a new man.[38] *This possibility of self-transformation makes the individual an I.* Through his
own sin, man first becomes an individual. Through the possibility of
turning away from sin, however, the sinful individual becomes the
free I. And only with this newborn man can the correlation between
God and man become true. God does not want the sinner and his
death, but he has pleasure in man's turning away from his ways and
therefore in his life, in his new life.

29. This chapter [of Ezekiel], which contains one of the deepest
of all prophetical discourses, concludes with the practical application
of the proposition which comes to be articulated in it: *guilt cannot be
an offense*, it cannot be a hindrance to the liberation from sin. From
every guilt there is a turning away.

The Hebrew word for offense (מכשול), upon which the prejudice
concerning the impossibility of eradicating sin is based, is usually used
for the designation of "stumbling against God's commandment." This
prejudice about sin is from now on such a stumbling. There is a libera-

tion from sin. Man is able to begin a new mode of life, a new way of life.

And now the whole conclusion is set forth: *"Cast away from you all your transgressions, wherein ye have transgressed; and make you a new heart and a new spirit"* (Ezek. 18:31). With this passage Ezekiel excelled all his predecessors. For they have only prophesized of the new heart and the new spirit, which, according to Jeremiah, God will give when he will make a new covenant with Israel; but Ezekiel says: make yourselves a new heart and a new spirit. *Now the individual comes to full fruition in the I.* In the recognition of his own sin, man became an individual. Through the power to create for himself a new heart and a new spirit, however, he becomes the I.

Now, too, for the first time it becomes clear of what this new heart and this new spirit can and should consist: of the turning away from the previous way of life, and of the capacity to enter upon a new way of life. Only now does man become the master of himself; no longer is he subject to fate. It was fate that would not allow man to abandon the way of sin. Man becomes free from this fate through the teaching that sin does not become a permanent offense for man, a permanent reason for stumbling. Through this, man first becomes an individual who is not absolutely dependent on the relations of the social plurality in which he is enmeshed. He is an autonomous spiritual unity, because he is a moral one. The capacity to turn away from his previous way of life bestows upon him the value of this sovereign unity.

30. However, with all due acknowledgment of this new height of knowledge, we must nevertheless raise the question of whether, besides the progress in principle, there is also an actual, a practical progress beyond the moral preachings of Ezekiel's predecessors. The latter admonished men to walk in the ways of righteousness. Ezekiel, however, admonishes men to walk anew in the ways of righteousness, since the previous way was false, as he and his predecessors emphasize. What difference does the newly achieved distinction between plurality and the individual bring forth in regard to moral admonition? The individual is now supposed to be able by himself to choose a new way. What distinguishes this new way of the individual's return from the old way of the people's turning away? Does not the return remain a mere object of admonition, or in what lies the power which makes the individual effective in the return?

31. The Hebrew word for return (תשובה) changes into a new word, which, however, has been inexactly translated by the German word for *penance—"Busse."* In Germanic law the word means "ransom," and thus the word contains a meaning which does not coincide with,

is indeed entirely different from, the meaning of return. On the contrary, the new Hebrew word indicates the change which was accomplished by the return. Penance is *punishment*. And the punishment is actually the means through which the return is to be distinguished from a merely moral abstraction.

The punishment itself, however, is not the real object that makes the return concrete and practical. In legal procedure, too, it is not the judge's declaration of punishment that satisfies the law, for such a declaration must not have as its basis a declaration of guilt by the judge. Therefore, it is all the more important that the criminal himself could and should proclaim himself guilty. In this, his own declaration of guilt, lies the inner reason for punishment. Punishment is to the criminal the only consolation for the relentless consciousness of his guilt. It is for him the only support for his liberation from this almost intolerable burden.

Thus, for the return in so-called penance, the punishment also must be employed as a means of liberation. The way legal procedure shows us in the self-confession of guilt by the criminal is the right way. If the individual must have the knowledge of himself as the originator of his guilt, he also must acknowledge and confess himself to be such.[39] In this acknowledgment and confession the I comes to light. *The confession of sin is the penance, which the sinner must take upon himself.* This confession with all the agony and distress, with all the overwhelming remorse which borders on despair, is the beginning of the execution of the punishment the sinner must impose upon himself, if God is to liberate him. This self-punishment is the first step on the road of the return which is open to him.

32. Now, however, again the question arises of the practical procedure through which this confession can become a reality, so that it loses the last vestige of mere moral abstraction. Legal procedure cannot be extended to the embarrassing conflicts of the human heart. Where is there an analogy to legal procedure? The return would remain merely a word of admonition, and the confession of guilt, too, would not become an actuality if it were not joined to a public institution. Is there such a public institution for the religion of the individual?

At this point the problem of *divine worship* arises. And there dawns upon us the understanding of a fact that cannot be entirely denied, that the prophets of social morality left the problem of specialized divine worship in the balance. They understood sin primarily as social sin, which could only be atoned for by social justice. For Ezekiel, however, the individual raises himself up out of his social environment, and indeed through his own sin. But this sin is not an end-station for man, but rather an ever-repeated beginning of an ever-opening new life.

This constantly new beginning must be joined to a public institution; it cannot be actualized merely in the silence and secrecy of the human heart. It is the meaning of all moral institutions that they support the individual in his moral work. This indeed is also the meaning of legal formulations, that they formulate the idea of the will, and through this help man to achieve the actuality of action. A similar actuality is to be demanded for confession and to be sought in a public institution. This desire is satisfied by divine worship.

33. At this point historical considerations become necessary, because we are considering a turning point, at which *prayer* as divine worship hardly existed, and in any case had not yet become independent. We shall see that it could and had to originate at this point. What then was there for Ezekiel to add, if his new notion of the individual was not to hover between heaven and earth, if he was to actualize the confession in an act of penance? In what else could he find support but in the national institution of sacrifice, which was common to Israel and all nations of the earth? With what else but sacrifice could he connect the individual penance, the sacrifice, which, up to now with the exception of Israel, has been preserved in the entire moral world, even though only in the form of the symbolic usage of blood?

34. Historical consideration must also be given to the political circumstances under which Ezekiel's reformation was actualized. The *state* had been destroyed, and its reestablishment could not and was not permitted as long as Persian supremacy had to be respected. What other means could be tried out in order to uphold Israel's call to the prophecy of the unique God? Even today the belief that this means can be only the state is not eradicated.

Ezekiel and, above all, his successors were inspired by another political and religious insight. They confidently put the state out of view. We shall see later how monotheism only fulfilled itelf by breaking away from the particular state. But no community can do without an encompassing unity, even if it has a purely spiritual content as its task. And this encompassing unity, if it is to be of a great historical dimension, must become a public institution. What kind of institution is analogous to the unity of the state?

35. We think today of the *Church* as a unity analogous to the state. But such an analogy was already rejected by the original monotheism. In a theocracy the Church would have been not only an anomaly but a pleonasm. The meaning of theocracy warns against it. If, however, the state is destroyed, could then perhaps the Church be devised as a

surrogate to replace the state? Did not the Church originate rather as an institution by the side of the state, with a claim to be set over and supplement the actual state? Without the state the Church could not originate.

36. Thus the *congregation* originated as the unity exclusively suited to the unique task of religion. And as religion here reached the point at which the individual originated, it is understandable that the public institution suitable to the individual's need for a completion of confession by punishment could in no way be the state, and so also not the Church, as analogous to the state, but only the new institution of the congregation, which had its model in the *city community*. The latter, however, presupposes the individual in his precise meaning in opposition to his merely symbolic meaning as a member of the state. The Hebrew root for the word "congregation" [קהל] already shows that it is based on unification and not on lordship and dominion, as the state is.

37. How could the congregation come to be established, if it had to ward off the distrust of the Persians who might suspect that it meant the establishment of a new state? What kind of public means could be found for establishing this kind of community, without investing it with the coercive force of the state? Certainly it could be only religious means, only public means of divine worship, which could be employed in order to establish this kind of community. Since, moreover, a new concept of God had to be made in conformity with the new concept of man, therefore the sacrifice as divine worship demanded a reformation and modification. Thus it was historically natural that this original institution of the cult should not be simply eliminated, that it could not be relinquished. No other public instrument of the religious spirit was in existence.

Already in Deuteronomy it appears as a contradiction that the clear and penetrating emphasis on purely moral notions and commandments is connected with the preservation of sacrifice. Just as there, however, idol worship is counteracted by the demand that the sacrifice is to be performed *only* in Jerusalem, so also Ezekiel clings to Jerusalem in order to establish there, in the sanctuary, the center for the formation and organization of the congregation as a substitute for the state.

Already in Deuteronomy the national assembly and, for this purpose also, the distinction of the Temple in Jerusalem had been chiefly used as the means of strengthening monotheism. Now this means, which already has been refined by distinguishing a single place, in which the sacrifice is centralized, is used for the further development and deepening of monotheism.

Therefore, the question of whether it would have been better if sacrifice had been entirely suppressed is unhistorical. The true historical question must unite an interest in principle with the deeper question: whether the connection with sacrifice is in all respects damaging to monotheism or whether, in spite of all sound considerations against it, the requisite deepening of monotheism beyond the social prophets demanded the bringing into play of sacrifice, which not only failed to hinder and impair this goal but perhaps was indispensable to its execution.

One could expect to find the evidence for this historical meaning of the preservation of sacrifice in the fact that the use of the sacrificial cult itself was changed in accordance with the new reformation. And this requirement, this expectation, is fulfilled.

38. People have pointed out that it is a defect of the whole institution of sacrifice that the sacrificing man steps back in favor of the *priest*, who in his ritual functions performs the sacrifice. However, not only does the man step back behind the priest but God does so too. Only the priest acts during the sacrifice; he slaughters the animal, he sprinkles the altar with blood and performs other symbolic acts which all have the purpose of expiation. In this entire performance of expiation God has no share. Nowhere in this performance of sacrificial expiation is God mentioned as the one who expiates. God takes no part in it at all. And this is the great advantage which emerges out of the entire sacrificial rite.

For with God as well as man receding behind the priest, who is the sole actor at the sacrifice, the unmediated connection between man and God is involuntarily prepared. This is the negative advantage of the sacrifice. And because of this advantage alone one could accept the preservation of sacrifice not merely as a historical but also as a psychological tool. For if the I is in need of the community for the confession of its sins, then the I-individual must obtain that independent communication with God which may be mediated by a symbolic act, but not by the person of the priest. Through the priest the formation of the new person of the I would be definitely hindered.

The priest can and should not weaken the *self-activity* of the man who confesses his sin and who, with the use of sacrificial symbols, has to accomplish the act in and by himself. *Expiation must be distinguished from atonement proper.* The latter ensues immediately in the relation of man to God and God to man. Atonement is not achieved through expiation but depends on the self-purification for which man has to strive in his confession of sin. The declaration of the sin of one's

I means for this I the preparation of the way for the return and for so-called penance with all its effects.

39. The ritual of the sacrifice itself still permits the discernment of a distinction, with regard to purification, between priest and man. This is conveyed through the meaning of the phrase "before the Eternal." The priest expiates, and it is already questionable whether he himself purifies, as in the case of the leper, but there is no question at all that purification is always achieved only with regard to God, "before God." Everywhere purity—the symbolic expression for atonement—is clearly attributed to God, and distinguished from expiation, which is the work of the priest. Through purity, the homonymy of the Hebrew word כפרה, which may mean expiation as well as atonement, is abolished and the emphasis is put on atonement. God is to effect only the latter, and for this—his proper task—the concept of God is changed in accordance with the deepened concept of man, a concept deepened and made more inward beyond the concept of social holiness.

40. For the relative suitability of sacrifice for this inward reform, it is of no little importance that sacrifice in general became limited to that concept of sin which is designated by *unwitting* transgression (שגגה). For sins which were committed intentionally and in defiance of the law, sacrifice was not permitted, according to the rabbinical law. And we shall see, when we consider the *Day of Atonement*, that atonement [reconciliation] is proclaimed under the supposition of this character of sin, namely sin as *shegagah* [unwitting].

In this insight, monotheistic religion, at this point in its development, again makes contact with the ethics which is of *Socratic* origin. As Socrates identifies all virtue with knowledge, and therefore explains all injustice by ignorance, so the prophets in this reformation of the concept of holiness declare that sin is committed unwittingly.

If it might at first seem as if this highpoint is in contradiction with the transitional point of the self-knowledge of sin and the confession of it, then the meaning of the expression "transitional point" alone will lead to the correct orientation. The self-knowledge of sin is indeed a transitional point for the engendering of the I, but it is not the conclusion. The conclusion is the atonement, which depends on liberation from the consciousness of guilt.

Of course, this liberation has to be self-liberation. The work of penance is determined as such. However, the individual needs the congregation for his confession, and within the congregation, sacrifice. The public institution of the congregation must help the individual to mature into the I. The congregation stands for the state, and the sacrifice becomes a legal institution. The aid must come from this institution.

And its first sign is the judgment: any sin of man, insofar as it qualifies for purification because it is not entirely derailed from human tracks, may be understood as *shegagah*. This may still be evaluated as a social truth. Indeed, it arose out of the social institution which is analogous to the law. But this social truth becomes the stepping stone for the true individual, who is purified in the I.

41. Thus sacrifice as a social institution, as an institution of the congregation, becomes an important means for the origin of the I in its religious meaning, and the latter finds its fulfillment in the correlation of man and God. The priest represents symbolically the purification, which the individual has to accomplish in himself by a penance which has its peak in confession. This "in himself," however, is included in the correlation to God. And this correlation is brought about by the symbolic sacrifice. Its motto is: "before God." Thus, through the sacrifice the correlation is introduced and secured. And the fundamental condition for sacrifice, which makes it permissible, is this basic ethical idea: the sin of man, that is to say, the sin in which man is and remains man, is *shegagah*. This is the condition under which he is not considered an animal or a monster, for which latter possibilities pathological explanations have to be consulted.

All human sin is error; it is wavering and vacillation. This is the basic meaning of the Hebrew word. In one passage this concept is expressly elucidated, as if to stress that it is new: "And the priest shall make atonement for him concerning the error which he committed, though he know it not" (Lev. 5:18). The not knowing explains the erring.

But man is not permitted to give himself this explanation, this security of man against his own mistake, for then he would impair his self-knowledge. This justification can be granted to him by a public institution only. The mediation for this purpose is taken over by the sacrifice, which therefore is generally a useful instrument for the subjective consciousness of man, for his liberation. Exceptions to this are cases which belong to criminal law. For a sin which cannot be subsumed under the genus of *shegagah* remains inaccessible to sacrifice. The sacrifice is a means of purification only for sins committed unwittingly.

From this fundamental point of view the procedure that Ezekiel brings into play in sacrifice is not only excusable and to some extent understandable, but becomes at the same time connected with another point of departure used by Ezekiel for the discovery of the human I. Through sin man is to become an individual, and indeed an I conscious of itself. Is not this a contradiction? It is not; for the sin is the sin of human frailty. And this too is no contradiction. For without finding one's way through all of human frailty, man cannot find his way to God. And without the correlation with God, the final act of atonement cannot be accomplished.

42. The sacrifice of the *shegagah* turns out to be less and less heterogeneous to the formation of the I. The priest functions only in the symbolic expiation, whereas he does not collaborate in man's atonement before, and reconciliation with, God. This negative gain over the idea of sacrifice becomes a major gain, which is explained by the religious history of mankind hitherto. In this idea the most profound content of the notion of the unique God comes to fruition.

The correlation of man to God should bring atonement and reconciliation with God. This assurance is given by the unique God. He is the unique redeemer. Only he brings about the redemption which consists in the reconciliation of man with God, and, through this, also in the reconciliation of man with himself, in himself, and indeed to himself. As the uniqueness of God above all means his unity, so the reconciliation and redemption proceeds solely from him, without any kind of collaboration.

Even if it were at all conceivable that a *Logos,* a mediating power, could have collaborated in the creation, the correlation between man and God in reconciliation and atonement would exclude any such collaboration. Only the unique God in his true unity can effect redemption.

This conclusion is made evident by the sacrifice. For in it an animal is sacrificed, not a man, not to mention a godlike being. And no God either sacrifices or is sacrificed; the priest alone is the expert of the sacrificial rite. The gaze of the sacrificing Israelite is lifted above the priest and above the altar at which he officiates, upwards to God, before whom he stands. This is the meaning of the expression "before God," which is used throughout the prophetic teaching.

Man stands not before the sacrifice, not before the priest, so that he might participate in purity. Rather, "before God you should be purified." The correlation is fitted to, and concluded between, man and God, and no other link can be inserted. As man is to become an individual conscious of himself, so God proves himself in this correlation, and also in his unity, which excludes any co-redeemer. Any collaboration of anyone else destroys God's uniqueness, which is even more necessary for redemption than for creation.

43. However, we shall expound only later the attribute which, as a consequence of the unity of God, results for this problem. At present we still have to worry about the individual as I, and therefore we have

to establish more precisely the work of repentance, which is his duty. From this, his own work, God's collaboration is to be excluded. It says "before God," not through God, or even with God, but positively only before God. This determination needs to be discussed more precisely.

If our basic methodological idea is correct, the autonomy of the will must remain inviolably in power. If ethics demands that the will fulfill the moral law as the law of moral reason, then it can be only a methodological distinction when the religion of reason teaches one to think of the will of reason as a command of God. This command of God is in the heart of man and has been elucidated in the spirit of man's holiness. The origin of the moral law is not at all in question in a particular task of the moral will. And if the purpose of penance is to gain self-knowledge of sin which serves as a transition to the liberation and purification of moral consciousness, then, in crossing and wandering past this transition point, the autonomy of the work of will must be unimpaired and uninfluenced by any other force of will. What the will has to achieve for the origin of law is now no longer a question. Now only man as I is at stake, and the stake is lost if the autonomy of the will is not absolute.

Man must only look back at his own way of life, and only at the turning away from it. For the possibility of taking a new way of life, he needs first of all to confess before the congregation on the occasion of the sacrifice. But all these means of support should be to him only auxiliary means to his own independent work of looking back and looking forward. And the look forward is directed to God. Hence, in this look forward lies the entire perspective of holiness and the whole horizon that is illuminated by the correlation with God. Man must begin and achieve the projection toward this horizon entirely by himself. Any assistance, any collaboration in repentance, would make out of the return a being-turned, and would thwart the autonomous accomplishment and task of man.

For the safeguarding of this idea the sacrifice is not an unimportant means. For who would be so deeply involved in mythology as to regard the sacrifice as an adequate means to self-purification? At most it can be a symbol, but nothing more. Repentance, however, should be more than a symbol; it should be a real, a realizing action of the will, which elevates man to the I-individual. Therefore it can be only an action of proper self-achievement. It must require all the conditions of the most strict work of the conscience.

The *conscience* cannot accept that others be privy to it, and consequently can accept no assistants or accomplices. Is God, too, thereby excluded from it? This question can no longer arise. Repentance has to be effected "before God." He is the goal toward which one's own work is directed. What God, as such a goal, positively performs for the attainment of this goal is the success of redemption, with which we will have to deal later. At this point, however, it is important merely to make clear that the bringing about of redemption is man's independent action.

44. If we ask once more about the individual steps by which repentance has to proceed, then the general answer, which lies in the following basic instructions, is certainly not sufficient: "Cast away from you all your transgressions . . . and make you a new heart and a new spirit" [Ezek. 18:31], for the possibility of casting away all sin and the making of a new heart and a new spirit is exactly what is in question. However, one has only to compare this admonition with that of Jeremiah, "Let us search and try our ways, and return to Thee," (Lam. 3:40), in order to recognize the difference between the searching of the ways and the abandoning of the ways. The searching is a precondition, the indispensable one, but no more. The casting away of all sins is the new power in which the I comes to life. This new power is proof of the new I.

Repentance rises to this positive achievement in the preliminary step represented by *remorse*. The latter is only a negative precondition for the abandonment of the old way of life. If one were to abide in remorse, one would come to despair, while actually a new life is in view. The cheerfulness of the self consciousness can be produced only through the feeling of one's own independent work. Remorse is only the expression of the feeling of the affect, which involuntarily accompanies the condemnation and disdain of the old way of life; but this accompanying affect is in itself not productive. What is productive is the knowledge of sin and the confession. To have a clear consciousness in knowledge and action is what matters most, and thereby the foundation is laid for the new structure of life.

All that is signified by the term "intention" must be achieved by these two deeds of consciousness. The intention is the expression for the inwardness out of which the external deed is to come forth. Inwardness is active in these two directions: in knowledge and in confession. Confession is the first step toward action, which in turn proceeds in two steps: in the casting away and in the new creation. Intention cannot refer only to a theoretical inwardness, such as the knowledge of sin, but must be transformed into action. Thus, intention distinguishes Ezekiel's notion of penance from the notion of trial in Jeremiah, which also in Isaiah has the same direction.

45. Now, however, a new question arises. We have called the man of social plurality an abstraction. Is it not the same with the new individual as I? Is he perhaps a single empirical being? Or is the latter rather a popular illusion which mistakes the ideal moment of a development, which is only present as an intrinsic goal, for the finished concrete shape of this moment in its full development? With this question we confront one of the deepest problems of ethics, which therefore also must be of fundamental importance for the religious problem.

The new heart and the new spirit are and remain *tasks*. The I, too, can be considered as nothing other than a task. As little as it is possible to imagine that a new heart is formed in actuality, so little is it possible for the meaning of the I which is to be formed to have a definitive shape. Like ethics, religion too must always be concerned only with tasks which, as such, are infinite and therefore can require only infinite solutions.

The I, therefore, can mean nothing higher and certainly nothing other than one step, a *step* in the ascent to the goal, which is infinite.

Does the I thereby perhaps become a mere abstraction? On the contrary, it thereby first becomes a true reality. It remains an abstraction, on the contrary, both within the social plurality and as an isolated subject. If, however, it is lifted up in the moment of its ascent, it achieves true moral life. Repentance provides man with this new life, which, to be sure, can last only in the bliss of a moment. But this moment can and should repeat itself unceasingly: it should never grow old, and it must and can constantly rejuvenate and renew itself.

This constancy, which is demanded by the task of this ascent, liberates the I from the suspicion of being a mere abstraction, and it is only from the continuity of these moments of ascent that the I acquires the capacity to subsist and endure. All other alleged phenomena of subjectivity are nothing but the ghosts of materialization. The subject as I is determined by the moment and by the continuity of moments.

46. It is especially in Isaiah that we became acquainted with holiness as a religious term. God is the holy God. This is the new knowledge of God. And the holy God demands: "Ye shall be holy." This sentence too appears to contain a contradiction; for how could man be holy because God is holy? Here, too, "being holy" can only mean "becoming holy." The task itself is the goal: the infinite task is the infinite goal.

Therefore the following biblical sentence is meant to provide an explanation: "Sanctify yourselves therefore, and be ye holy" (Lev.

11:44). We must ward off the suspicion that the demand directed to man could be or should be satisfied by God, and not by man himself. For this ambiguity might seem to be contained in the two sentences: "Ye shall be holy; for I the Lord your God am holy" [Lev. 19:2]. If, however, being holy means rather *becoming* holy, then the achievement which is not final cannot be imputed to God; it can only be the lot of man. This explanation is expressed in the sentence: "Sanctify yourselves . . . and be ye holy" [Lev. 11:44]. This commandment of *self-sanctification* can have no time limit. It relates to every moment of man's life. And it has its eminent relation to the moment in which the I is steadily rejuvenated to new life. In this continuous rejuvenation the I has its only existence and permanence.

47. We have asked about the particular steps by which repentance is achieved. The most important answer has now been found. Repentance is *self-sanctification*. Everything that can be meant by remorse, turning into the depths of the self and examining the entire way of life and finally, the turning away and the returning and creating of a new way of life, all this is brought together in self-sanctification. It contains the power and the direction in which repentance must employ itself for the new creation of the true I. Sanctification is the goal; self-sanctification is the only means.

And in this means the goal is contained, as well as the goal in the means. Only man himself can actualize self-sanctification; no God can help him in this. God already effects much in giving the commandment; and he will effect more. But he may not put a spoke in the wheel of man's work, which the commandment demands of man. The task is put upon man; it is infinite because the solution is infinite. God as a collaborator would have to bring the solution to a final end. Since such an end contradicts the concept of this solution, it would also contradict the concept of the task if God should have a share in the handling of this task.

48. Before we proceed any further, one preeminent step in the achievement of repentance should be considered. It is designated by the expression "way" for sin and also for return. "Let us search our ways." As much as it is important to grasp and to designate the ascent from sin in the moment, so important is it, on the other hand, to consider sin not as an isolated unit but as something connected to the whole framework of human *life*.

It is not an erroneous metapyhsics that considers each single action of man in a causal connection with all others. One does not thereby confirm the scholastic sentence of which Schopenhauer makes use: *operari sequitur esse* [activity follows being]; but the work of repentance can become thorough and serious only when it aligns each single sin with the whole frame of life. This unified whole is designated by the word "way." Each sin is nothing but a step on the way. One should not fool oneself into thinking that each sin is isolated, so that it might appear to be an abnormality. In true repentance sin may not be looked upon in this way. Each particular sin is the embodiment of the man, a token of his essence, which in biblical language is designated, with regard to God and man, as "way." "Show me now Thy ways" (Exod. 33:13). Thus Moses implores God for the knowledge of his essence. And "the ways of man, God knows." The way is the embodiment of actions.

49. We have recognized repentance as self-sanctification, and the return as the creation as much of a new way as of a new heart and a new spirit. We have now to proceed from man to God, who, although not a collaborator, is the goal of self-sanctification.

The return contains an ambiguity, similar to that of holiness. The return should be to God. But insofar as it also means the creation of a new heart, it is at the same time a turn into this new heart. The latter has been understood by us as the unity of the infinite task with the infinite solution. However, up to now the other meaning of the return has not been made plain, namely, the return to God. What positive meaning belongs to it, insofar as we determined God, limiting ourselves strictly to the goal, as the final goal of self-sanctification? What meaning has this final goal as a support, although not as a collaborating helper? The goal belongs to the action; therefore it also must be valid as a support; therefore it belongs also to the inventory of the powers necessary for repentance. This kind of support must be exactly and clearly determined.

50. Ezekiel, with his great exhortion "Cast off all your sins," did not speak his last word. Rather, he merely used this thought to verify in a new way the old monotheistic fundamental thought: God pardons, forgives; he "bears" the sin. Man himself must cast off his sin, but whether his own deed succeeds, whether it leads to the goal, this he cannot know. His concern is only the task of casting off sin; he is deprived of the knowledge of the result and the success of his action.

However, one cannot say, one cannot be compelled to say, that the question of success is not at all one's concern. Although one should not make the action, which is an unconditional commandment, dependent upon the foreknowledge of success, one need not consider this independence from success as simply a lack of interest in success. The latter would be close—or equal—to a degradation and defeat of the commandment. Looking toward the sentence, "for I am holy, your

God," absolutely belongs to the whole process of self-sanctification. Looking toward God belongs to the process of self-sanctification.

This looking toward God can mean nothing other than looking toward the solution of the infinite task, a solution which, though it is infinite, nonetheless actualizes itself. The solution is infinite, for it is only a moment in the infinite task; but the solution as this moment signifies infinite success, the infinite result. God can assign no task that would be a labor of Sisyphus. Self-sanctification must arrive at its infinite conclusion in the *forgiveness* of sin by God.

51. Let us just clarify anew in what conceptual way forgiveness contributes to repentance. It is not an eudaemonistic result of the action of penance, but it belongs to action as a goal.

Now, however, the question might arise: if forgiveness belongs to repentance, does not heterogenous element enter the work of penance in that God represents this goal and thus has to effect forgiveness?

Does not forgiveness, which is with God, then violate the independence and purity of self-sanctification?

The question must be put more precisely: is not the entire element of forgiveness through God external to the idea of self-sanctification? And should not forgiveness be replaced by self-sanctification insofar as the latter contains in itself the infinite solution, even though it ever remains an infinite task, so that self-sanctification would be identical to forgiveness? Ezekiel says "yes": "Cast away from you all your transgression . . . and make you a new heart and a new spirit" [Ezek. 18:31]. Does he not thereby identify the task with forgiveness and does he not thereby eliminate redemption through God?

52. One has only to consider the patchwork of all human theoretical, as well as practical, endeavor; one has further only to consider the unceasing controversy of world views, as it is displayed in quietism and pessimism, in pantheism and monism, in skepticism, and finally in the resignation to the limits of knowledge in agnosticism, in order to gauge the weightiness of this question. However, the idea that the goal belongs to the work of penance cannot have the consequence that the goal is put in man himself, and not in God, for then the main scaffolding of religious knowledge, which we erected in the correlation of man and God, would collapse. If, however, our methodological framework must remain standing, then we have to recognize the new meaning of the correlation in the *meaning of God as the redeemer from sin*. Regardless of whether we would be able to achieve the solution of the task by our own independent work, and to succeed in liberating ourselves from sin, it is necessary for the notion of the correlation with God, for the concept of God himself, that he and only

he be the redeemer; it is necessary that he only accomplish this redemption by pardoning, by forgiving the sin. In the spirit of the
theodicy one could say: sin is explainable through God's forgiveness
of it. God's being could not be conceived as understandable in his
perfection, if the forgiveness of sin were not his proper achievement.

53. Up to now the highest point in the concept of God has been
his holiness. But the latter, in all the abundance and depth of its
meaning, is, properly speaking, related merely to the embodiment of
social morality. Indeed, it is the social commandments in the third
book of Moses that follow immediately after the principle of holiness.
And Isaiah evaluates his basic concept of God's holiness in the same
way. Now, however, the problem is the individual, and, moreover,
the individual as I. Even now, to be sure, holiness remains the standard, and self-sanctification the rule. But ultimately we cannot remain
with the attribute of holiness only: how are we to understand that
already Jeremiah calls God the *Good* One (טוב) and that the psalms
make the attribute of goodness almost the embodiment of God's essence? What particular meaning has *goodness* in distinction from
holiness?

The question is the more important since, when we bring goodness [instead of good] into play, the word loses its neutral significance
and is reinterpreted in reference to a *subject*. Formerly the word
"good" had been used only in the general sense of suited and ex-
pedient, and therefore also in the ambiguous sense of well-being. It
was used chiefly with regard to a thing, and if with regard to a person, then also with the above eudaemonistic ambiguity. But now the
word is related to God. With this the ambiguity has to disappear;
for with God the feeling of well-being does not make sense.

God, even in the ethical sense, is not good *(das Gute)* but the
Good One (der Gute). The object of morality is thus elevated to God's
being, and through this unavoidably elevated to the concept of a
subject.

God as the Good One must therefore accomplish a kind of personal
achievement of goodness. The scope of his task cannot be circum-
scribed by holiness only: "The holy God shall be sanctified through
righteousness" [Isa. 5:16]. In this way Isaiah elucidates his concept of
the holy God. His conception of God's holiness is directed to social justice, which at the same time is social love. If, however, the problem now
is the I, then the holiness of God still remains the general guide,
which proves itself in self-sanctification as the particular guide. But
since God must be the goal to which the guide points, the question
remains whether God's holiness is the sufficient characteristic, and

whether it is not more understandable that God's goodness is the attribute which complements God's holiness. Consequently we can understand that in the thirteen characteristics of God, which are accepted exclusively in accordance with the theophany in Exodus, holiness is not mentioned, but only goodness, albeit in various expressions. But among these expressions there already appears this: "He bears the iniquity and transgression and sin." *The forgiveness of sins becomes the special and most appropriate function of God's goodness.*[40] And thus it becomes a feature of the style of the psalms to equate the good God with the forgiving God.

The universalism of the psalms is without reservations open to God's goodness: "The Eternal is good to all; and His tender mercies are over all His works" (Ps. 145:9). Goodness and love therefore remain united. But although, according to the prophetic style, they both are identified with justice, so that justice and love are most closely connected, in the style of the psalms and related writings there appears a connection between goodness and forgiveness of sin. "Good and upright is the Eternal; therefore will He instruct sinners in the way" (Ps. 25:8). "For with Thee there is forgiveness that Thou mayest be feared" (Ps. 130:4). Thereupon, the entire monotheistic worship is based on forgiveness of sin. And in it the particular attribute of goodness makes itself manifest.

What else in general could goodness come to mean that was not already taken care of by love? *Grace* is already on the borderline between love and goodness. "And I will be gracious to whom I will be gracious, and will show mercy on whom I will show mercy" (Exod. 33:19). These words should express not so much God's discretion in dispensing love and grace, but rather the truthfulness and illusion-free reality of God's acts. But even here grace precedes. It destroys and thwarts all that in sin which threatens to oppose it. The etymological connection of the substantive חן (*gratia*) with the adverb חנם (*gratis*) could be explained through this. Grace makes everything which resists it a lost and futile cause, so that it is in vain.

54. All the dialogues that Abraham, as well as Moses, has with God are concerned with this problem of the forgiveness of sin, and in every case it is solved clearly, though without a suspension of justice. The antinomy between justice and mercy proves, to be sure, continuously vacillating, yet the point of gravity remains firmly in the forgiveness of sin. And it is Ezekiel's merit to make this point of gravity a central point of monotheism. It becomes sufficiently clear how only the concept of the human individual could make this attribute of God into the central attribute.

In the poetic image of a shepherd and his flock, it is possible to see the precise distinction. Isaiah says: "Even as a shepherd that feedeth his flock, that gathereth the lambs in his arm, and carrieth them in his bosom, and gently leadeth those that give suck" (Isa. 40:11). Similarly Jeremiah: "He that scattered Israel doth gather him, and keep him, as a shepherd does his flock" (Jer. 31:10). God is always the shepherd of his flock, and the lambs he collectively carries in his bosom. On the other hand, Ezekiel: "As a shepherd seeketh out his flock in the day that he is among his sheep that are separated, so will I seek out My sheep, and I will deliver them" (Ezek. 34:12). Although it is here merely a separation from the flock which the prophet intends, it is already an individualization. And thus he says: "Behold I judge between lamb and lamb" (Ezek. 34:17). God becomes the advocate of justice for the individual sheep. The hymn *"Unethane thokeph"* is entirely in the spirit of Ezekiel in using this simile on the New Year and on the Day of Atonement: "As a shepherd musters his sheep . . . so dost Thou pass and record, count and visit, every living soul." Here also God is thought of as the shepherd of each soul.

The psalm too carries through the simile: "The Eternal is my shepherd; I shall not want" (Ps. 23:1). God is the individual God, the shepherd of the individual, and upon this is based the main theme of the psalms, which one might designate *hope for the forgiveness of sin.*

And also upon this theme is based the hymn of the psalms, "O give thanks unto the Eternal; for He is good" (Ps. 118:1). One may perhaps translate it better: acknowledge the Eternal as the one who is good. The monotheistic acknowledgment and confession is united with this individual's confession of his sin. And the unification is achieved in God's goodness.

55. As God's goodness is now expressly understood in the redemption from sin, it becomes understandable that Ezekiel coins a new term for the concept of man accordingly. Soul is not sufficient to him. This word has too many ambiguous meanings in the language. When Micah addresses man, he turns to every man, but not expressly to every individual. But Ezekiel is concerned with the individual both in the sense that man is conscious of himself as such and also no less in the final sense, that God forgives the individual as individual and extinguishes his guilt. This is done for the individual himself, not on account of the covenant with the fathers, but for himself in his individual sin. Ezekiel was thus able to grasp the anomaly which lies in the concept of man, namely, that he is an individual and yet at the same time remains the offspring of his ancestors. This anomaly had to

remain for Ezekiel, for God is to forgive the individual sin. How could this be thought of in human terms, however, if the individual was to remain in his entirety?

The concept *"son of man"* (בן אדם) came into existence for this reason. Jeremiah had already used the term, but only Ezekiel uses it throughout. Man deserves forgiveness of his sins, for although he is an individual, yet he is at the same time only the son of man. He should become an individual; the knowledge, acknowledgment, and confession of sin should mature him to this individuality. But if he is to create for himself a new heart and a new spirit, he is yet, in his striving, dependent on God's grace. And God's goodness shows itself to him in forgiveness.

In the language of prophetic poetry the question could arise whether there could be another reason for this change than that man always is and will be only a son of man. God's goodness answers to the son of man in man.

It is a tragedy of monotheism that precisely the attribute of God's goodness, the forgiveness of sin, has endangered pure monotheism through the concept of the son of man. It endangers the concept of God as well as that of man.

56. Man must gather together all his individual powers and must prepare himself in order to have mastery of his self-sanctification. But at the same time he always feels himself to be innately infirm and defective: "In sin did my mother conceive me" (Ps. 51:7). In reality, his humanity therefore begins with his rebirth, which he attains through the confession of sin. He is a son of man; everything which belongs to man, both outside of himself and within, cannot give him the certainty that the preparations for his rebirth, which are his own, will be successful. Therefore only God can help him. God's goodness is his only refuge. Therefore he puts his confidence in it. Thus arises *trust* in God.

57. Trust in God is also an original concept, which therefore is expressed in many ways.[41] Bahya distinguishes ten words for it in the Hebrew language. He does not even count the most frequent word, which, however, is usually translated as *faith,* or belief, but etymologically means "firmness." And the word used for trust (אמונה) has the same meaning. This word too means certainty, corresponding to the abstract word "confidence," and is the Hebrew formation of the word expressing God's certainty and trustworthiness. Biblical faith allows no tinge of doubt to arise. The faith is fundamentally rooted in the firm trust in God as the Good One: who, beyond doubt, in his goodness, forgives the sins of man.

It is not doubt that creeps into the spirit of the believer. But as soon as he has recognized himself as a soul, as an individual, the soul swings its pinions. And the innermost power of the soul struggles forth out of the son of man. The spiritual evidence of the soul is furnished not by doubt in God but rather by the search for God, the *desire* for God, the desire for nothing else but God. For nothing else concerns the soul more than God's forgiveness of its sin.

58. What is generally meant by trust the psalms express as *longing*. Psalms are written in the style and form of *lyrics*. Lyric is the soul's confession of its love. In lyric poetry the main theme is the love of the sexes. The poet of the psalms could not sing lyrically about the love to God if he were not to have experienced, in body and in soul, the magic of human love of the sexes. But he transfers this love to the love to God—and who can test whether he does not want to overcome it through this transference? He transfers it to the love of God, who should liberate him from his sin, and not least from the sin of sexual love.

And now sin is entirely overshadowed by the bright light which longing for God radiates. The soul dissolves entirely in this light, in this purity of its longing. Everything of the body is thought of as in dissolution. "My bowels burn." "With my soul I long for you at night." "With my tears I wet my resting place." This all-powerful longing for God presumes to go even to the frontiers of sensuality.

59. And despite this, the border of mysticism is never touched. *Union* with God is nowhere desired. If God were not the unreachable One my longing would have to find its end. But this end would not be the end of my humanity. I remain man, and therefore I remain a sinner. I therefore am in constant need of God, as the One who forgives sin. Longing is not directed, as in lyric poetry, to the union of the lovers, but in this case merely to the forgiveness of sin. Therefore what the psalm calls *nearness* to God gets its precise meaning. "The nearness of God is my good" (Ps. 73:28). Only nearness to God, not union with God, can be the object of my longing. An this nearness I gain in God's forgiveness. Sin alienates me from God; forgiveness brings me near again. And thus is formed an unceasing two-way communication between God and the human soul: the longing and the *bliss*, consisting in trust.

60. The place elaborated for the psalms in the Canon would not be understandable without Ezekiel, although Jeremiah, and before him Isaiah, developed effective steps toward this literary style. The hymn in general was already in existence in Babylon and since it is the original form of every divine worship, it need not, therefore, be

original in monotheistic worship. But for the transformation of the hymn from the praise of God into the longing of love for God, which drives the soul to God, as this power of the soul is celebrated in the songs of the psalms, for this new creation Ezekiel was the prototype. He was the model with his notion of the soul sinning, and with forgiveness of the sin by God, who does not have pleasure in the death of the sinner, but in his life, who does not have pleasure in the punishment of the sinner, but in the forgiveness of the sinner.

61. Through this lyricism *sacrifice* is overcome more than through the polemics of the prophets. The latter always remains satire and mockery of man, who lets himself be reached by such divine irony. Irony and satire, however, can only be preparatory; the positive solution is brought about only by the redemption of the individual through the inward forgiveness of his sins. 'The sacrifices of God are a broken spirit: a broken and contrite heart, O God, Thou wilt not despise" (Ps. 51:19). The lyrical expression that describes the *humility* of the heart is in sharp opposition to the proud sacrifice of the fat bulls and lambs.

The heart, and, indeed, the humble heart, is by this time the proper object of sacrifice. Humility is the way of the soul when it is genuinely in love, genuinely longing. Longing presupposes dissatisfaction with oneself and, therefore, the striving beyond oneself. What already happens in sexual love occurs, in its highest and most intense form, in the longing for God. In the latter case it happens insofar as this longing is based on confidence in being liberated by God's goodness from human frailty, from personal sinfulness.

62. Forgiveness of sin is the simple consequence of God's goodness. In distinction from holiness, God's goodness guarantees this result. He is "good and ready to pardon" (Ps. 86:5). Therefore, just as self-sanctification constitutes the concept of man, insofar as he becomes through it the individual-I, so also must God exclude any collaboration in the forgiveness of sin. It is the essence of God to forgive the sin of man. This is the most important content of the correlation of God and man. Through goodness the result of this correlation becomes clarified and distinguished. God's goodness, connected with holiness, secures the morality of man as I. What secures the success of the self-sanctification of man is God's goodness.

Therefore no special *arrangements* in God's essence are necessary for the forgiveness of sin. Creation and revelation are the sufficient preconditions; they both create the holy spirit of man. And this holy spirit, whose self-preservation is accomplished by self-sanctification, is entirely secured against relapse into sin through God's goodness, whose particular task is forgiveness.

63. Since any collaboration and any particular arrangement are excluded from this major divine act, all mysticism is therefore also removed from it. It is a noteworthy symptom of this immanence of forgiveness in the idea of God that the Hebrew words for forgiveness and pardon (סליחהו מחילה), expressing the attribution of these qualities to God, are distinguished from the old word for atonement through sacrifice (כפרה). The latter originally meant the covering, or, as it were, the closing of the wound which sin forms in the human organism, or the covering of a gap which sin tears open in the requisite connection with God, or the covering up of a shame which sin leaves open in man. This covering is provided by the priest. And the entire sacrificial rite serves this kind of atonement of man with the offended God.

Monotheism fundamentally severs *forgiveness* (סליחה) from the wholly mythological, original form of atonement. The old word remained and was even retained for the later meaning of forgiveness, but in the sacrificial order it became limited to the priest. "The priest shall make atonement for them, and they shall be forgiven" (Lev. 4:20). "The priest shall make atonement for him as concerning his sin, and he shall be forgiven" (Lev. 4:26; 5:16). "And the priest shall make atonement for all the congregation of the children of Israel, and they shall be forgiven, for it was *shegagah*" [Num. 15:25]. "And the priest shall make atonement for the soul that erreth, when he sinneth through *shegagah*, before the Eternal . . . and he shall be forgiven" (Num. 15:28). This is how clear and exact the distinction between atonement and forgiveness is made. This is how clearly and exactly God's attribute is distinguished from the function of the priest. This is how clearly and exactly the salvation of man by God is distinguished from the sacrifice.

64. This, God's achievement for the preservation of man's dignity, is distinguished as God's goodness, and with this God's entire relation to man is assigned to the domain of *teleology*, which is different from all causality and from every metaphysics connected with causality. Therefore there cannot be any question about the mechanisms through which God effects forgiveness or through what mediation it is infused in man. The teleological meaning of this relationship is turned away from all such pseudo-theoretical interests.

It is the meaning of God, and as well of man, that God has to grant atonement to man. Man has received from God the holy spirit; nonetheless he remains fallen into sin, "for that he also is flesh" (Gen.

6:3). But it is not a diminishing of the dignity of man that his sin is forgiven him; for this forgiveness through God depends on the self-sanctification of man. And just as little is this determination an encroachment upon God; for his essence consists in the correlation with man, or, as the ancients expressed it, his attributes are those of action. He is the archetype for the actions of man.

The correlation of God and man establishes the realm of morality, the *Kingdom of God* on earth. God's goodness, in the special aspect of the forgiveness of sin, is the token of the moral world, insofar as its members are individuals, and not merely social human beings whose condition is regulated by holiness. In the world of final ends, holiness unites with goodness, as the plurality of men unites with the individual man. Humanity, in its unity, is the analogous concept to the unity of God; it unites both elements.

Thus goodness, as the fundamental concept of the moral world, reaches beyond the individual and beyond the forgiveness of sin and becomes the precondition for the further development of the Kingdom of God. But we shall see that these consequences, too, continue to presuppose the individual with his sin and his redemption from it.

First, however, we must consider the consequences which Jewish monotheism drew from the problem of atonement, and which it put into effect by establishing and developing the *congregation* to serve the purposes of the individual. Individual and congregation might appear to be opposites, if the liberation from sin, this pathfinder of the individual, had not brought about an accomodation. Atonement, therefore, becomes the cardinal point of monotheism.

And thus it becomes understandable that in Judaism the atonement becomes the center of the entire worship and that a special holy day is established for it, one day among all the holy days of the year. On this day, the individual, as well as the congregation is to reach and maintain its high point.

CHAPTER XII

The Day of Atonement

1. Polytheism dealt with the problem of purification and purgation from sin by establishing *feasts*. These were the sacrificial feasts proper, the original cults. In ancient Israel, also, purification was the main purpose of almost all the feasts. Even the feast of *Passover* need not be excepted from this.

It is significant, however, that the idea of the feasts, beginning with the New Year and ending with the feast of Tabernacles, is epitomized in one single day. Although originally the feast of *Tabernacles* constituted the main feast of purification, for which the other two were merely days of preparation, gradually the opposite arrangement came to prevail, whereby one day is assigned as the *Day of Atonement* for the purpose of purification. This day was put in the middle of the series of feasts, so that, from that time on, the New Year becomes merely a day of preparation and the feast of Tabernacles concludes the series.

We will not here become involved in an antiquarian investigation of this important fact and the particular steps in its historical development. We should note, however, the significance of the singular fact that one day of the whole year is singled out for that concern that preoccupies the whole congregation and every single member of it throughout the whole year and which ought not be neglected even for a single moment in a man's life. Even though the people adhered to and executed this insoluble task in all strictness, a day with a special significance for this general concern is set apart. The significance of the Day of Atonement could not be suppressed from the very time of its biblical institution as part of the whole sacrificial ritual.

2. In the Bible the Day of Atonement is, to be sure, properly speaking only a day of sacrifice for the high priest, who expiates first for himself, then for the priests, and finally for the whole of Israel. An old Mishnah discloses how even this day of expiation was celebrated

entirely in the pagan pattern of a festival.[42] Young men and maidens went to the outskirts of town to have a bridal show. Incidentally, this Mishnah also discloses the moral delicacy with which the ancient Israelites improved upon the moral tone of festivals intended to promote marriage: the maidens were permitted to dress only in white linen, in order not to embarrass the poorer ones among them or put them at a disadvantage; in the evening the whole crowd and the whole people went before the house of the high priest, who gave a big banquet. This was the concluding event of the expiation sacrifices that the high priest had to perform, and this in turn had its climax in the sending away of the scapegoat *(Azazel)* into the desert. This was the form of the ancient Day of Atonement within the sacrificial rite.

3. However, because *shegagah* [unwitting sin] became the primary condition for the sacrifice, and this consideration, characteristically enough, was used to draw the *stranger* into the indigenous legal community, the climax of the doctrine of atonement was implanted in the whole sacrificial rite with the sentence: "And all the congregation of the children of Israel shall be forgiven, and the stranger that sojourneth among them; for in respect of all people it was done in *shegagah*" (Num. 15:26). *This sentence as the Talmud expanded it for the history of Judaism, became the motto for the Day of Atonement.*

Thus the two main elements of atonement, its beginning and its end, were laid down for the Day of Atonement—*shegagah* and forgiveness. There is no forgiveness without satisfying the provision of *shegagah.* Frivolous violation of the law precludes the possibility of forgiveness. But also, there is no *shegagah* without forgiveness as the final result. Just as the prejudice of blood vengeance was fought through the establishment of the cities of refuge, so doubt in God's forgiveness is declared to be disbelief in God's goodness. It is not the *Azazel* that bears away sins, but God's forgiveness itself is called the bearing of sins. "He bears the sin." He takes it upon himself, he takes it away from man. Thus, the forgiveness of sin also appears simply as a consequence of the *shegagah.*

4. However, the *confession of sin* constitutes the central point of the liturgy on the Day of Atonement. To begin with, one should consider that this is not the exclusive prerogative of the Day of Atonement; in the prayer at the hour of death it is the last refuge.

But even this fundamental use does not circumscribe sufficiently the distinctive character of the confession of sin on the Day of Atonement. For all prayers on every day are pervaded by the confession of sin, although merely in the general atmosphere of the basic idea. One might believe that the distinctive character of confession on the

Day of Atonement replaces this basic element of the daily liturgy.
However, in this may perhaps be found a distinctive mark of pure
monotheism.

In order to bring out this distinctive mark we ask another question. Should confession of sin be made in the midst of the congregation at all and therefore in its *public* worship? The Talmud reports
a difference of opinion as to whether confession should be made individually and in solitude or in the chorus of the congregation. The
decision was made for the congregation, for *public* confession. And
through this decision the Talmud may well have saved the purity of
monotheism in its ritual profundity. For, in the first place, the public
nature of the confession shows trust in God's forgiveness. Moreover,
the act of confession, analogous to punishment, as we have shown
earlier, implies a demand to carry it out within the congregation.
Now, however, we are guided by the point of view of trust in God's
forgiveness, which takes away from the individual a false sense of
public shame. Confession and remorse merge into one another. Thus
remorse is already fully active when confession breaks forth. How
can one shrink from and avoid the community of the fellow guilty,
of one's fellow confessors?

Just as the collaboration of the congregation cuts off all mysticism,
all the occult arts of priests, and "soul-curing" from the innermost
workings of the individual soul, so must the confession of sin be
expressed publicly. Confession is at the same time also the public expression of trust in the good God, before whom the sin of man does
not endure. Hence the question asked above is clearly answered.
Properly speaking, the confession of sin belongs to public worship
alone, and that worship in general has its center of gravity in this
confession to the good God.

5. It is, further, a very valuable sign of the inwardness of the intention which inspired the institution of this prayer ritual that in
this confession of sins, so far as they are specified, *only purely moral
transgressions* between man and man are explicitly mentioned. To be
sure, the rabbis, and particularly the Mishnah teachers, not only
knew the distinction between purely moral and ritual commandments
but distinguished their specific values. And the rabbis or their successors introduced into the daily morning prayer one such Mishnah
concerned with this distinction. However, in spite of this they were
convinced of the unity of the Torah and, therefore, of the lack of
difference between the moral laws and the ritual. These builders of
traditional monotheism are the more to be admired and esteemed because they avoided, without exception, an express formulation of all

the ritual transgressions in the great confession of sins on the Day of Atonement, although they were convinced of the sinfulness of these transgressions.

In this choice, in this restriction to purely moral transgressions, one has to acknowledge a great act of monotheism on the part of the rabbis. And this is no light matter, for this great confession of sins is a long catalog with an exact list of specific moral transgressions. In it, an entire psychology and pathology of human passions manifest themselves. It must have been hard for these men to restrain themselves from mentioning the ritual transgressions, yet they succeeded. And they succeeded not merely through their own merit, their ethical maturity, and their inner freedom from the fetters of the ritual laws that they themselves partly put upon themselves; their success is a strict consequence of the conception of sin as *shegagah* and, at the same time, of trust in God, who, as the Good One, forgives the sin of man. What could be clearer evidence of God's goodness than that his forgiveness also should include sins that were committed against commandments not purely and exclusively concerned with the relation of man to man? For the so-called sins against God, the special so-called sins against the ritual of divine service, have their only meaning and value in the moral improvement of man. Hence, the confession of sin in this spirit of moral purity is the equally distinctive token of the *Day of Atonement* with its introductory motto of *shegagah*.

6. The final prayer of the Day, too, is of a significance as illuminating as it is overwhelming. The main prayer *(Shemoneh Esreh)* of the final prayer *(Neila)* cannot be praised enough. "Thou givest a hand to transgressors, and Thy right hand is stretched out to receive the penitent (the returning); Thou hast taught us, O Eternal our God, to make confession unto Thee of all our sins, in order that we may cease from the violence of our hands, that Thou mayest receive us into Thy presence in perfect repentance." The concluding sentence of this paragraph forms a confession that is taken into the daily morning prayer: "What are we? What is our life? What is our love? What our righteousness? What our virtue? What our strength? What our heroism? . . . The pre-eminence of man over the beast is nought, for all is vanity." But this prayer, just as little as Ecclesiastes, does not end on this skeptical note.

7. The new paragraph immediately starts with a correction. "Thou hast distinguished man from the beginning and hast recognized his privilege that he might stand before Thee." Thus man is, nevertheless, distinguished from the animal, and therefore not everything is vanity. Man is set apart, is marked out, is acknowledged to stand

before God. This *standing* before God is in fact one of the technical terms for worship. Man stands before God. Thus, man's independence in the correlation with God is proclaimed. In this standing before God the individual accomplishes his self-purification.

It is characteristic that in the confession of sins the otherwise customary expression of *prostration* is not used. The latter, as well as the bending of the knees, might be appropriate to adoration, to the solemn acknowledgment of God; but at the moment of acknowledgment and confession of man's sin, and the related acknowledgment of trust in the good God's forgiveness of sin, in such a moment prostration is much less fitting than an upright posture before God. Otherwise, man's distinction from the animal would not be complete. It consists in his upright posture, and, therefore, man's worthiness for redemption from sin is expressed in his standing upright, albeit humbly before God.

"The day thou stoodest before the Eternal thy God in Horeb" (Deut. 4:10). This is the expression for the posture in which the people received the revelation. Hence the prayer that has its climax in the confession of sin and in the plea for forgiveness, this form of standing before God that distinguishes man from the animals, is a further development of the election constituted by revelation. Thus, the actualization of monotheism is expressed throughout in the rabbinic shaping of the Day of Atonement. It is, therefore, understandable that the Day of Atonement became the distinctive mark of the pious worship of God.

8. It is to be noted that the rabbinic shaping of the Day of Atonement (*Versöhnungstag*) did not fail to make the reconciliation (*Versöhnung*) of man with God dependent upon the reconciliation between man and man. It is no mystical reconciliation that, as it were, casts a veil over the moral trespasses in transactions of everyday life; it is rather human frailties that are to be freed from the shadow of fear and melancholy. "For transgressions that are between man and God the Day of Atonement effects atonement, but for transgressions between a man and his fellow, the Day of Atonement effects atonement only if he appeased his fellow."[43] This law takes precedence. Hence atonement with God is at the same time an admonition to reconciliation with man.

However, all the moral endeavors of man remain imperfect, and unity of character is only man's ideal, which can be achieved only by approximation. The practical aspect of the worship of God, as distinguished from the archetype of morality in God, takes cognizance of human frailty. Out of this central idea the institution of the Day of

Atonement reached its mature monotheistic meaning. It was not a mythical pretext to make easier or to discard moral duties toward one's fellowman.

The Day of Atonement, in which the high point and perfection of religious consciousness is represented, is at the same time a model for the *principle of development* that guides and regulates all religious ideas and institutions. Out of the joining of primitive sacrifice with primitive folk festival, which everywhere accompanies the great sacrificial feasts, this unique day grew to its purity, which is perhaps unique in all the histories of religious communities. It grew to its purity, so that only the most intimate questions of human destiny, those between man and God, which usually come within the domain of tragedy, were treated on this day. For indeed life and death, these basic questions of tragedy, are not separated from the question of sin and its consequences. The deepest examination of the entire worth of human life is taken up on this day by the humble human heart. "Thou knowest the secrets of eternity and the most hidden mysteries of all the living." This is said in the prayer of this day. The Israelite makes destiny and the meaning of life his supreme question on this day.

In a prayer that originated in the Middle Ages and gained central importance in the *Mussaph*-liturgy, the pious poet found an original and characteristic analogy of the shepherd. "As a shepherd musters his sheep and causes them to pass beneath his staff, so Thou dost pass and record, count and visit every living soul." Just as Ezekiel entrusts the individual soul to God, and just as the shepherd carries each lamb in his bosom, in the same way the poet here selects individual souls of all creatures of the flock and lets them be examined and counted by God (cf. p. 210).

9. The Day of Atonement is connected with the *festival of the New Year*. The New Year is the first of the ten days of repentance, the tenth day of which is the Day of Atonement. Hence, both of these holidays, which are called "Days of Awe," are united by the common problem of human fate. They are, therefore, the days of divine *judgment*.

Actually, for monotheism fate does not exist. What polytheism calls fate and doom, monotheism calls judgment and redemption. There is no judgment before God without redemption, which is the final end of judgment. But there is also no redemption without the process of judgment. The connection between justice and love in God is the secret of God's essence. We have to recognize them only as his attributes. The unity of these attributes is God's essence, God's substance. We would understand God's essence if we could understand the connec-

tion between justice and love that eternally actualizes itself in God's
unity. It is, therefore, possible to designate these days as the holidays
of the idea of the unity of love and justice in God. This unity is the
unity of God.

10. On these days God's judgment is unceasingly invoked, and man's
hope is placed in God's love in judgment. However, the horrors of the
judgment are not dampened; the contrition of remorse and penance
paints the punishments of judgment in terrifying images. On the other
hand, an arrangement occurs in the liturgy that cannot be sufficiently
admired. The words of the theophany that contain the thirteen characteristics are recited almost exclusively on these days; but the rabbis
dared to make a change in the wording of the scripture [Exod. 34:7].

Whereas the concluding words of the sentence after the words "He
bears iniquity and transgression and sin" read thus, "and He will not
leave [the guilty] unpunished" (ונקה לא ינקה), the Talmud left the
negative of the verb out of this liturgy, so that now the positive word
means "and He purifies" [the guilty]. This change may, without exaggeration, be called an act of the deepest piety and of the most ardent
love of man, which did not shrink from infringing upon the letter of
the most holy words of revelation.

Apparently the rabbis said to themselves that on these days sufficient
thought is being given to divine judgment and punishment. When,
however, in the epitome of prayer, God's essence in its thirteen characteristics is invoked, then the thirteenth characteristic should not be
punishment; rather, the last characteristic should conform to the previous ones, all of which specify love: "The Eternal, the Eternal, God,
merciful and gracious, long-suffering and abundant in love and truth,
keeping love unto the thousandth generation, He bears iniquity and
transgression and sin, and He purifies."

Thus all the offshoots of love terminate in this, that God makes the
sinful man pure and guiltless again. Although in the text of the revelation justice is still the conclusion of the specifications of God's love, the
Talmud changes the holy text for the liturgy of these days and, by
making this change, brings it into inner agreement with the meaning
of these days, which is the atonement and, hence, the purification of
man.

11. This change is completely in agreement with the meaning of the
day. The watchword of the day is, according to Scripture: "You shall
be pure before the Eternal" [Lev. 16:30]. Accordingly the Eternal can
be called upon only in this way: "He purifies." The words used for
purity vary indeed, but the word used above, and made positive, means
innocence (נקי). Neither innocence nor the word referring to it is used

at all in the sacrificial ritual, although purification is achieved through the latter. Now, however, it says, "God makes innocent," and this sentence is the highest paean of triumph of these days.

Man is born anew. He receives anew the holy spirit, the spirit of holiness, which the divine spirit implants in the human spirit. Could *pantheism* achieve anything higher than this union of man with God in the spirit of holiness? This is precisely the great difference that distinguishes monotheism from this erroneous idea: in monotheism the harmony between the archetypal spirit of holiness and man remains the infinite task, whereas pantheism, imitating material nature and its laws, in which there must be identity between the law and its realization, must posit identity between the task and its actualization. On the contrary, monotheism says: God makes innocent. The spirit of holiness is thus freed from doubts about its inviolability. And man can again strive and err.

To err, to go astray, is man's lot, but therefore *shegagah* is the limit of man's fault. Whenever this limit is overstepped, only God knows what happens to man. Human wisdom is at a loss in the presence of the possibility of *evil* in man. The Day of Atonement maintains the fiction of the unshakable moral preservation of everything human: all man's sin is *shegagah*.[44] Therefore, God can forgive without relinquishing his justice. Therefore he can make man innocent. Guilt should not be a "stumbling block." Guilt can in no way establish the evil character of man. Rather it is the gateway to his perfection, to that higher elevation where his innocence can be recovered. Such a point of view is found in the Talmud (Menahoth 48a).

12. Thus it is understandable that Rabbi Akiba, the great Mishnah teacher and great martyr, could say about the Day of Atonement: "Blessed are ye, O Israel, who purifies you, and before whom do you purify yourselves? It is your Father in Heaven."[45] The Father of men, who in the archetypal language of the Bible is distinguished from all earthly existence by having his abode in the heavens, manifests himself in the purification of men. Still Akiba does not stop with God but establishes, in the latter part of the sentence—which is its climax— Israel's worthiness for atonement: "And before whom do you purify yourselves?" It is not God who purifies, as little as he expiates. The Scripture says only: "Before the Eternal you shall be pure." But since the Scripture elsewhere says, "Sanctify yourselves, and you shall be holy," so Akiba achieves the proper climax with his sentence: you shall purify yourselves, before your Father in heaven you shall purify yourselves. No man purifies you; and no man who is at the same time supposed to be a god. No son of God shall purify you, but your Father

only. And also you shall not purify yourselves before any other mediating being. Only when God, simply and solely, is the unique and single aim of your self-purification, only then can purification be achieved.

The entire idea of monotheism is contained in this watchword of Akiba's. Thus one could answer the question about the deepest meaning of the unity of God in the following manner: God is the Unique One because only before him is man able to purge himself. If one were to mingle with the Unique One some other being or some other idea, then the possibility of man's achieving self-sanctification is forfeited. It must be an unbridgeable chasm that towers before him, before which alone man's ascent can begin and succeed. Truly the Day of Atonement is the day of monotheism.

13. However, the final meaning of the Day of Atonement has not yet been set forth, even with this glorification. There is indeed no more noble glorification of humanity than the self-purgation of man. And hence the Day of Atonement is for the Jewish consciousness the symbol of one's trust in God only in conjunction with one's own power of *repentance*.

The Talmud expresses this confidence in the power of repentance in the great sentence: "If during the day a man committed a sin, he should not brood over it at night; for certainly he did repent." Hence Jewish piety considers the act of *repentance* a daily practice. "Repent one day before your death" (Pirke Aboth 2). With this cryptic remark the Mishnah makes repentance a life duty of every day.[46]

It is the most unfounded reproach in the world that Jewish piety is self-righteous or that the meticulous observance of the law promotes self-righteousness. For the most meticulous observance of the law, which extends to and governs the whole of life every day and almost every hour of the day, can never render repentance superfluous. Rather, the whole purport of all particular laws and the entire concern for legality is nothing but guidance to repentance, to the turning into the correlation with God.

14. Therefore, the notion that atonement could result in a feeling of exultation, in which man would be deprived of his main duty, namely, *humility*, is illusory. The exultation that atonement brings to man relates exclusively to God, and in no way to man. Man's exultation about his innocence, attained anew, is only a feeling of gratitude to God, as being the Good One, besides being the Holy God. This exultation is only the certainty of trust in God, the confidence in the truth, which consists in the correlation of man with God. The exultation is therefore simply nothing other than *faith in God*.

15. Regarding man himself, so far as he is the other link of the cor-

relation, his purity appears to him—not to God—in entirely different colors. The knowledge and confession of sin cannot entirely satisfy him. Even before an earthly judge, the case is not closed when he recognizes and acknowledges his guilt. He does not thereby let himself be shorn of his responsibility, but must also undergo his *punishment*. For the public confession of one's guilt is only accomplished in taking upon oneself the punishment. Thus before God, too, man must travel the way of punishment. As far as he is concerned, he cannot believe that he will be reconciled with God in any other way but through voluntarily taking upon himself, as it were, the execution of the sentence.

Or, one may explain the desirability of punishment in the following way: before God one might believe oneself acquitted of punishment; God's grace is incomprehensible. But one's own moral autonomy must not be impaired by the additional religious relation to God. Since ethics, because of its method, remains the norm to which religion has to conform and into which it must incorporate itself, the correlation with God must not infringe upon the ethical essence of man. However, it would appear to impugn the validity of ethics if God should favor grace over justice. For God this may be right; we do not understand it, although we define God's essence in this way. However, for man, insofar as he is a moral being and must be preserved entirely as such, it would be absolutely incomprehensible if he could work his way up from the deepest abysses of penance to the very heights of innocence by himself. And only because of such penance is God's forgiveness said to come into force. Therefore, for man himself there is no other keystone of repentance but punishment.

16. Punishment does not require any prison; for life itself is this prison of sin. The punishment need not be thought of as infliction of special pain; for, in the proper mood of penance, man's life as a whole is regarded as *suffering*, which is only interrupted by moments of illusory pleasure.

The suffering of man is, after all, also the suffering that comes from being a man. What more severe punishment could there be than this suffering from being a man, from the essential humanity of man. "The grand feelings, which bestow life upon us, they stiffen in the earthly tumult."* Our ideals become illusions. The rocks of our confidence are shattered by the unfathomable untrustworthiness of the human heart. And the rock, which is constituted by our own heart, melts away into vain nothingness in the transitoriness of our wishes and strivings. Can there be a greater suffering than the coming to nought of our most

*Goethe: *Faust,* p. I. [S.K.]

yearned-for hopes? Can there be a greater suffering than this suffering that comes from being man?

17. Pessimism laments the sum total of human existence. Moreover, pantheism puts on a mask of wisdom when it finds all this perfectly in order, because, in relation to the cruel necessity of natural laws, all moral as well as aesthetic distinctions are nothing but isolated individualizations (modes) of thinking. From this point of view the individual phenomenon has its value in itself: it cannot be excelled by any other. This is the wisdom of the fool lamenting the suffering of man. But monotheism must consider suffering, ordained to man by God, differently.

In the divine order of the world there is only good and bad. "Woe to them, who say to the good bad and to the light darkness." If the Second Isaiah draws the defiant conclusion that God also "creates evil" (Isa. 45:7), we have rather substituted ill (cf. p. 21) for this evil. What man calls ill because it hurts him, this is in truth not ill but happens for his own good. *Suffering is the punishment that man demands inexorably of himself for himself.*

With regard to the suffering of one's fellowman, one is not entitled to interpret his suffering as punishment that befalls him because of his sin. For one has to discover and affirm one's fellowman through compassion. For oneself, on the contrary, one cannot waive punishment. Hence, suffering is proper to oneself: one considers it a punishment that one has to demand for oneself and for which one calls and appeals.

18. It would be an immoral *confidence in God* if man were to expect forgiveness merely because of God's goodness and if he would not rather establish this confidence upon his own confession of sin along with the declaration of his readiness to accept punishment. He himself has to recognize that he deserves and is in need of punishment. Deeming oneself deserving of punishment manifests itself in the acknowledgment of suffering as a necessary step in the self-development of man.[47]

19. The morality of pantheism is based on the principle of the instinct for *self-preservation.* In pantheism the natural instinct for life becomes the foundation of morality. Life demands preservation. The preservation of the elemental power of life is the elemental right of man. The instinct for the preservation of life establishes the *identity of might and right;* but the self that this instinct tries to preserve is the natural being, the biological creature.

20. Religion does not recognize such a notion of an isolated creature who exists merely to stay alive. For religion, the self exists only in the correlation with God, within which alone the correlation of man to

man comes to be. I am not permitted to explain the suffering of my fellowman as punishment. I am in no way interested in his possible guilt. Perhaps he suffers for my guilt. One may confidently ascribe such intimate effects to the correlation of man with man. My own self, on the contrary, with all its hidden motives, becomes a necessary problem to me, and when I come so far in the solution of this problem that I have gained self-recognition of my sin and achieved confession of it, I am not even yet at the end of the road, until the confession has as its consequence the acknowledgment of suffering as the just punishment. For the affirmation of my self, for the preservation of my self, I may not be satisfied merely with my trust in God's forgiveness.

The confession of sin, despite it all, would be merely a formality if the declaration of my willingness to suffer did not confirm it. *Suffering is related not so much to sin as to its forgiveness,* and to redemption, insofar as the latter is dependent on self-sanctification. Self-sanctification culminates in the insight into the necessity of suffering and in the voluntary self-sacrifice of submission to the suffering of punishment.[48]

21. It is Maimonides' profound idea that Job also is a prophet, that suffering is a genuine form of prophecy. Through this idea he interprets the meaning of this prophetic, didactic poem, in which suffering as a form of prophecy is incorporated into the theodicy of the organization of the moral world. Suffering is not a defect, no dysteleology, but an independent link in the moral system and, thus, full of purpose.

Job's friends are not right when they wish to console him in his suffering by reminding him of his sin. His friends should have acknowledged him as a prophet who could instruct them about the value of suffering. Job is a prophet from whom his friends should have learned that suffering is a force in God's plan of salvation. This plan, however, is obscured and dissipated unless the sufferer is considered as suffering for the sake of others. It is obscured if one thinks erroneously that suffering and punishment are related as cause and effect.

On the other hand, Job himself does not lack the deeper insight that he is in need of suffering and deserves to pass through it, though not so much as a single individual but as a self in its correlation with God. Our routine thinking of sin and punishment, of punishment and suffering, as cause and effect should cease. God makes this moral of the fable known at the end of the poem. At the same time in *God's justification of Job* it is explained that Job suffers for the sake of his own justification.

What God proclaims to be the meaning of the entire poem is expressed negatively in Job's conviction, in which he rejects sin as the cause of his suffering. He is a prophet, and as such the symbol of humanity. But insofar as he is aware of his prophetic position, he needs to recognize the cause of his suffering in order to preserve his self. Job has had earthly enjoyment and possessions in abundance, and after he has lost them they are given back to him. Is there anything that could give his life more value when he has already participated in all wisdom and piety? Are prosperity and earthly self-esteem the highest things for human self-consciousness? Is not the moral economy of the world deficient precisely in that the prophet is needed for the world? Job points to this deficiency in his lamentations. And he bases his suffering on the need for his prophecy.

But that which the world is in need of, the prophet, in the first instance, is in need of for himself. However, the need of the human self seems to recede in the consciousness of the prophet. This difficulty exists for the *self-awareness of the prophet* in general, and it is indeed not lacking in Job's case. The ambiguity in Job's suffering therefore remains: as a prophet he suffers for others, but he himself remains a man and, as such, is in need of suffering for his own self.

22. The value of the biblical poem is limited to the refutation of the prejudice that there is a causal relation between sin and suffering; it rather introduces suffering, as do all the other prophetic writings, into the working of the theodicy of the moral world. However, the Day of Atonement does not pursue such a poetic solution of the riddle of the world. Its task is to affirm and preserve, in spite of sin, the self-awareness of the I of the individual in his correlation with God. The Day of Atonement therefore puts suffering into an immediate relation to the individual's own problem.

Jewish piety accordingly recognizes suffering as a step to redemption. Suffering is indeed not longed for as in ascetic mysticism, but it is validated in *prayer* by the entreaty for liberation from and protection against it in all detail. The *fast* on the Day of Atonement is the symbol of this understanding of the necessary value of suffering.

Suffering may be the common lot of men. Nevertheless, it must first of all become the *watchword* for the I. I am not merely an organism. Eudaemonism cannot become the key to my being. The blind alternation of pleasure and pain cannot regulate my moral life. Only a certain permanency of suffering gives my existence its correct meaning. My suffering is not an effect but an end for my self, or, possibly, only a means to this, my final end.

23. It is of moving significance that in the prayers of the Day of Atonement, in which the warding off of the gravest extremities of life

is spelled out, *unfounded hatred* is explicitly mentioned alongside hunger, plague, and similar calamities, and also in addition to sin.

This notion is a result of rabbinical ethics. In biblical language there is false, delusive hatred (שנאת שקר —Ps. 35:19), but this vain and empty hatred, which is generally referred to by the word "gratuitous" שנאת חנם , is the deepest word for the condemnation of hatred. "Thou shalt not hate thy brother in thy heart" (Lev. 19:17). This pronouncement destroys hatred through both words: "brother" and "heart." The one whom you desire to hate is rather your brother, and when you desire to hate you misuse your heart, which exists for loving.

So all hatred is unfounded, vain, and empty. In general, there is no reason or justification for misanthropy. Vain hatred of man has occupied the foremost place among the sufferings of men and is the tragic feature of all past *world history.*

24. This suffering within the human race has been primarily the suffering of *Israel.* This is the ancient theme that resounds through all the prophets, the psalms, and the entire literature that folows. We shall see later how the highest figure of monotheism, the Messiah himself, is transfigured through this suffering so that he suffers for mankind. And as he himself is only a symbol for Israel, so Israel suffers for the peoples who do not accept the unique God.

This is precisely the theodicy, the moral that the story of Job is meant to teach us. Is not the people of Israel itself in need of suffering and of the recognition of its obligation to suffer? If this were not the case, Israel, too, could not be redeemed. This is the highest meaning of the Day of Atonement, that repentance is in earnest only in the recognition and taking upon oneself of suffering.

Israel stands, as everywhere, simply as the symbol of the individual. Since Ezekiel, every one has become "a soul," and since that time the soul no longer means merely life and person, but the self that strengthens itself in self-responsibility. One measure of this self-responsibility is the acknowledgment of the value of suffering. It cannot be ignored, it cannot be eliminated. It is the precondition for the individual who is conscious of himself. And from the individual it is transferred to the people.

What other people, what other religious community is there whose distinctive mark in history is such martyrdom? As a Job it wanders through world history. And always and everywhere the surrounding contemporary world destroys itself through the self-righteousness with which it interprets for itself Israel's suffering as the result of Israel's unworthiness. When will the time dawn in which the peril of this self-righteousness will be recognized? This question, however, belongs to the subsequent chapter about the Messiah. At this point, it is still the redemption of the individual that is in question. The recognition of suffering is to lead to the attainment of redemption.

25. Other systems of faith made the mistake of thinking that suffering is not a means but a final end. Thus it became possible to represent the divine itself as suffering, as human suffering. Although in this idea the end of the redemption of men is seen along with and beyond suffering, yet the redeemer himself must take this suffering upon himself. And through this idea, suffering becomes and is the end. Moreover, there is a corrupting attraction in the idea that suffering is a divine end in itself.

Nonetheless, this idea is false. Only morality itself, only the correlation of God and man can be an end in itself. Everything else in morality, everything else in religion, is accessory and a means to this unique end. Therefore, suffering also can only be a means. And the end itself, which is redemption, cannot be thought of in isolation from its means; both have to cooperate in order to achieve the end. Hence, redemption and not suffering is the final meaning of life. In order to consummate redemption man and God cooperate; in this the correlation of man and God receives its highest confirmation.

26. Redemption is liberation from sin. In suffering sin became thinned out. Thus redemption is also liberation from suffering. In religious existence, so far as it is regulated and developed by the guiding thread of morality, everything is only valid for moments of ascent and transition. There is no fixed, rigid existence; rather everything is transition. Hence liberation from suffering, too, is only a moment in the course of moments, and suffering has to become again the disciplinary means for the self-discipline of man.

Moreover, the feeling of joy in being liberated from suffering has its validity only as a moment. Such a moment is redemption. Also the place upon which the self sets itself up and builds its sheltering booth is such a moment. It gives protection only for the moment. Only for the moment does the I have stability. Only for a moment can it demand and use redemption.

This difference between the moment of ascent and stabilized existence brings about the separation with regard to redemption between pure monotheism and other creeds. We are not yet discussing *immortality*. We have not even finished with the human world below. But since we have now set up, beyond the fellowman, the man as I, we need for the concept of his redemption from sin the limit determining the moment of redemption. Redemption is to be thought of only for one moment's duration. Only for one moment, which may be followed by moments of sin. No matter! They also will again be relieved by the moment of redemption.

At this point, particularly, the methodological connection in which religion is established on the norms of ethics holds true. Religious being is to be distinguished from sensible existence, though the ascent to religious being must begin from sensible existence. As with all religious being, so also redemption is only a moment of such elevation above the vicissitudes of earthly existence. "Before God": this is the watchword for the whole deed of repentance, of self-sanctification, and of redemption.

27. "Before God": this is the watchword. Monotheism has early marked out superstition as its adversary. In the biblical writings the historical sections form an enigma of their own. This early bent for historical writing has been acknowledged as ancient Israel's literary originality. But even this literary bent is still stamped with religious import.

The *heroic saga*, "the glory of men," usually forms the prehistory of nations. Antiquity is depicted as the primeval world of great examples, against which, as in a mirror, contemporary men should measure themselves. *Ancient biblical historiography* is of an entirely different objectivity. It is naive in the deepest sense, and this not solely in the area of the epic.

Here prehistory is reported not at all in the naive consciousness that makes no distinction between good and bad; this distinction is stressed clearly enough. No fascination with heroism and no piety for the heroes of their people induce the Jews to explain away those deeds that deviate from the right path. Moreover this path was not yet even delineated throughout as the way of God. Moral considerations are unmistakably manifest in the judgment immanent in the narrated events.

28. This historiography has, therefore, the mature value of a *self-characterization*, which is not possible without the thoroughness and lucidity of moral reflection. The latter is only transparent in the narrative, and therefore it does not destroy its basic naive character. Naiveté without primitive, immanent reflection is an immature and preliminary stage, not yet in itself the beginning of culture.

Balaam's speech contains such a self-characterization of Israel from the view point of its monotheism, and the whole episode seems to be a prophetic insertion into the account of the wandering in the desert. A pagan prophet appears there even before the prophets proper of Israel, with the exception of Moses, come forth.

This alien prophet blesses Israel on the basis of the characterization:

"For there is no snake-charming with Jacob, neither is there any divination with Israel" (Num. 23:23). Kautzsch translates, apparently in
accordance with the usual Christian translation: "For no enchantment
clings to Jacob and no bewitchment to Israel." This translation perhaps adapts itself to Balak's reasons for Balaam's commission, but it
is not in agreement with either what precedes or what follows, or
with the spirit of the whole speech. The Jewish interpreters understand the words in accordance with the translation we gave above.

The immediately following verse agrees with our meaning: "In due
time it will be told to Jacob and Israel what God hath wrought." Israel does not have to resort to divination, for the prophets announce
what God does and what his acts mean. Thus the next speech becomes
intelligible: "How goodly are thy tents, O Jacob, thy dwellings, O
Israel" (Num. 24:5). And, in the same way, from this interpretation
we can understand how the following sentence precedes the verses
about divination: "None hath beheld iniquity in Jacob, neither hath
one seen perverseness in Israel; the Eternal his God is with him"
(Num. 23:21). What could do greater injustice and harm to the monotheistic consciousness than idol worship, which is the hearth of all
divination? Finally, out of this reflection the historical observation
becomes understandable: "Lo, it is a people that shall dwell alone
and shall not be reckoned among the nations" (Num. 23:9).

A set of historical characteristics is brought together in this self-
characterization of the monotheistic people. Separateness leads the
way. This was already the precondition for the elevation of the people
to monotheism, not to mention the preservation of the latter. Furthermore, injustice is not to rule in Israel. This is the first imperative condition. And it, in turn, has as its consequence that magic and divination
cannot arise in Israel, because it is in communication with the Eternal
its God, and because Israel's prophets say and interpret to them what
God does. And hence Balaam tentatively concludes his speech with
the exclamation: "How goodly are thy tents, O Jacob, thy dwellings,
O Israel." They are "planted by God" [Num. 24:4,6].

29. This self-characterization of ancient monotheism is of historical,
as well as of substantive significance. The superstition of magic stands
in contradiction to monotheism. Only monotheism is to explain and
to interpret what God does. Neither the soothsayer nor the snake
charmer is permitted to assume the role of an interpreter of God's
acts. Therefore, divination as well as idol worship have to be destroyed.

If someone should arrive at the strange conclusion that the commandment, "Thou shalt not suffer a sorceress to live" (Exod. 22:17),

became the basis of witchcraft trials, one could as well say that the commandment to destroy the idol-worshipping peoples became the basis of the Inquisition and all kinds of religious fanaticism. In the same vein one could as well say that the commandment to kill the murderer is also the cause for the preservation of murder. The last example is not used for such an absurd conclusion, although in killing murderers a judicial murder may occur. Yet the destruction of a murderer is considered necessary. To consider magic as if it were a harmless delusion undeserving of punishment is therefore a residue of the superstition about magic that does not recognize the absolute necessity for its prohibition and the obligation to destroy it.

The reason for this skeptical attitude toward the destruction of magic lies deeper, namely, in an attitude of indifference with regard to the unique truth of monotheism. If, however, monotheism is the only salvation for mankind, then there is no escape from the fact that idol worship and all kinds of magic must be destroyed. Tolerance is a principle that cannot be valid for the origin, setting up, and establishment of monotheism. With regard to this question there can be no oscillating or any mutually conditioned and restrictive recognition of opposites: the being or non-being of the moral universe is at stake here. And the moral world is not handed over to the angels, as the talmudic expression has it with regard to the Torah, but is to be instituted by men in their legal maxims and in their criminal courts. Thus, the destruction of magic as well as of idol worship had to be commanded.

Basically, these errors in men's concepts of God are the greatest afflictions of man, and perhaps the cause of the greatest suffering which men bring upon themselves again and again. Moral offenses have their deepest origin in these fundamental notions of men about God. It is the greatest suffering of mankind that its ideas about God bring about schisms, perpetually thrown into relief and aggravated until they become the deepest inducements to the self-laceration of men and peoples. And yet this is the course that history has taken until now, and this is the way one has to understand it: the pride of human reason became man's greatest affliction. Zeus nailed Prometheus to the rock. Reason brought about the schism of man and his God.

In monotheism suffering is only a link in the chain of redemption. It cannot complete it. Suffering cannot be represented as the ideal image of man, as if it were itself the divine. It is only a preliminary step to redemption, to the completion of humanity in accordance with the perfecting concept of the unique God.

We are coming ever nearer to this completion of monotheism, and we have led up to the point that through suffering this completion will be achieved. But we considered redemption as the road to the human self, and we have already recognized the I of the individual in its symbolic transference to Israel. In this symbolic meaning Israel is not the people in its plurality and its social needs and obligations, but this symbolic Israel embodies, with more precision than the individual, the ideal concept of the I, which redemption is to bring about.

30. Thus it becomes understandable, even if we should not know anything about the symbolic figure of the suffering Messiah, that the people of Israel, professing pure monotheism, became the suffering people in history. If today, as in all times, one is moved to ask the question of how the monotheistic people could preserve itself in the midst of all these persecutions, and if one is not satisfied with the answer that the historical reason of its preservation lies in those truths that the Jewish community took upon itself to preserve, then perhaps one could acknowledge as a sufficient historical reason that it has been a people of suffering in its entire past history. Suffering has become its vital force.

What significance can all earthly happiness, all the power and glory of this world have in the face of this national privilege, which has its roots in faith? Israel is the historic people of suffering, of suffering for its unique God. This suffering also has bestowed uniqueness upon the people. Although other peoples have also suffered in their existence, their suffering coincided with their decline. As long as they were on the world stage, their suffering alternated abundantly with the joy of earthly splendor and power. Their suffering started to become typical of them only with the period of national decline. Properly speaking, this suffering existed only in the perspective of history. Israel, on the contrary, started its proper course in history only at the point when it broke with all the national treasures of this world and started a new existence, an entirely new kind of existence in its world mission. Its other suffering belongs to the pattern common to all political peoples. Its martyrdom, however, begins with its world mission.

Thus Israel's suffering has no tragic connotation, since it has no national particularism as its motivation, and therefore no aesthetic interpretation can give a proper account of it. Suffering is the characteristic feature of religion, and it is the task of monotheism that is symbolically expressed through the suffering of those who professed Jewish monotheism. Monotheism had to become self-consciousness in those who profess it. Therefore, just as one acknowledges the punishment meted out by an earthly judge, so those who professed monotheism had to recognize and acknowledge suffering as God's providence, ordained for the purpose of their self-sanctification, their education to the maturity of the I in its correlation with God. Israel's suffering symbolically expresses the reconciliation of man with God. Israel's suffering is its "long day," as the German vernacular calls the Day of Atonement.

31. Suffering is the precondition for redemption. The latter, however, is the liberation from all the dross of empirical humanity and the ascent to the ideal moment in which man becomes a self. We shall later have to consider this completion of man in messianic humanity, and in it the completion of redemption. At present, however, since we have interpreted the example of the history of Israel as typical for the suffering of man in general, we may perhaps see in this example also the redemption of mankind. Redemption cannot be lacking, for suffering is only a prelude, even if its lasts thousands of years.

It is a definite part of the concept of monotheism that the redemption of Israel cannot be thought of separately from the redemption of all men and peoples. But we understand redemption to be only a moment. Therefore, it need not have its only meaning as the final link in the development of mankind, but it can and does take place at each moment in the historical development. Thus, in the entire history of Israel we can detect the uninterrupted connection that exists between suffering and redemption. Redemption need not be postponed to the end of days; rather, it clings to every moment of suffering, and constitutes in each moment of suffering a moment of redemption.

Thus Israel's suffering loses its obscurity. It ceases to be a riddle in the picture gallery of the peoples. Suffering carries out and achieves Israel's self-preservation. For this suffering is not the ascetic suffering of mysticism, which has its satisfaction in itself, but has been acknowledged and has been borne as a trial, in which those who profess monotheism have to purify and harden themselves for the great calling that has been allotted to them by their unique God. Suffering does not contradict preservation but rather is its most effective foundation. Without suffering—no redemption. Without self-sanctification and indeed also in suffering, there is no ascent to the true freedom of humanity. But there is a liberation from suffering, if the goal for self-sanctification is set in the unique God. The Day of Atonement is the symbol for the redemption of mankind.

CHAPTER XIII

The Idea of the Messiah and Mankind

1. As the notion of man as a rational being emerged out of God's attributes of creation and revelation, two concepts of man have appeared up to now in the correlation of man to God: the fellowman and the I. In both of these concepts the peculiar character of religion in this correlation has been evident. Both concepts stem from religion. And to both concepts, in which the peculiarity of religion has been evident, a double concept of God corresponds: the God of social love and the God of forgiveness of sin.

The peculiar character of religion is methodologically different from the autonomy of ethics. This autonomy means that the peculiar character of religion has to be subordinated to it. The method of religion is based on the method of ethics. This is, in general, the method of scientific reason in treating all its problems.

In accordance with this basic methodological requirement, the redemption of man before God has been carried out in agreement with the autonomy of moral reason. Only with the unimpaired autonomy of ethics could the religious concept of the human individual be discovered. And compassion, too, through which the fellowman is discovered, is in methodological accord with *honor* and *respect*, the affects through which ethics engenders man.

2. Within ethics, however, and on the basis of its method, there is left for man only identity with mankind. But for this ideal concept of man, ethics itself is in need of methodological complements. It seeks to provide these complements in the doctrine of *virtues*, which is to be applied to historical experience. This demands the addition of the affect of *love*, while the basic ethical affect is merely honor, which is equivalent to respect.

Thus in ethics, under the concept of mankind, appear *relative pluralities*, of which the state, the law, and society are in need. Only for the I does ethics reject any complement which would exceed the competence of the autonomy of pure will. At this point, in particular, religion had to step in with the double notion of sin on the part of man and forgiveness of sin on the part of God.

3. Nor does ethics have need of a complement with regard to God. The problem of God is exhausted for it in God as the guarantor of morality on earth. The shortcomings in the actualization of morals on earth do not in principle concern ethics at all, since the infinite goal provides the remedy. The question of the time of actualization concerns ethics as little as the degrees of actualizations in particular periods of time or in particular representatives of mankind. At this point, the peculiar character of religion steps in with its new notion of man as individual, and with its new notion of God for the individual. But the independence of ethics is ratified and maintained in the two concepts: mankind and the God of mankind.

4. At this point the question arises: does perhaps religion, with the character peculiar to it, have a share in these two concepts and their correlation? If it were not so, if religion had nothing to contribute to mankind and to the God of mankind, then certainly the value of religion would be greatly diminished, and all the peculiarity which religion could show with regard to the two meanings of man, and correspondingly also of God, could not make up for the deficiency which religion would exhibit with regard to mankind and its God.

5. This is actually the case; religion can contribute nothing to ethics in this respect. And yet the value of religion is not only not diminished, but on the contrary increased. For although the *independence* of ethics remains inviolate, it is merely a methodological independence. And only by virtue of its method can it produce its content. Ethics knows neither man nor God; it begets these concepts through its method. Since its method is not only its norm, but also its tool and its productive power, it can, without concern, take its problems from experience, and indeed from contents and objects. The received concepts anyway have first to be passed through the crucible of its method.

And in any case, from where should ethics take its problems if not from *experience?* If experience did not offer to the mind extended bodies, even pure mathematics could not come to its problems. The same would happen to ethics, if people in their social connections, as well as in the history of law and state, did not provide the occasion for ethical problems. To be sure, experience does provide nothing more than the occasion. The occasion is used by pure understanding, which elevates it to a point where it can reshape independently and therefore actually reproduce the material provided by experience.

Thus the procedure of ethics with regard to religion also becomes understandable. Does ethics take its impulse for its concept of man exclusively from history, jurisprudence, and politics? Or does perhaps religion, too, provide it with material for the problem of man which is not to be despised? Would it endanger the autonomy of ethics if it were to put itself in the same relation with religion as it does with history in general, and with jurisprudence in particular?

We can disregard here the logical relation which might exist between ethics and jurisprudence, because we are concerned merely with the material of man. And if the concept of mankind must be understood as pertaining to the conceptual material of religion, then ethics in its methodoligical independence is as little endangered when it takes from religion the concept of mankind as it is with regard to jurisprudence. The only question that remains is whether ethics can take from religion, and from it only, the concept of mankind. But there is no longer any question that ethics takes this concept, as it does any other material content of human culture, as a problematic theme, in order autonomously to produce the concept anew with its own method.

It is indeed the highest triumph of religion that only it has produced the idea of mankind.

6. Classical Greek philosophy knows man only as the problematic individual of morality. And it is its greatest merit that, being dominated by the idea of the *state,* Greek ethics discovered in this model the microcosm of man, the soul of man. But from the methodological relation between state and soul it follows that when man is thought of there as soul, he and his soul are considered only as an individual, as an idea. Just as the multiplicity of individuals represents in every case only a repetition of the same idea, so also does the microcosm of the soul remain one and the same in however many individual exemplars it might represent itself. The Greeks do not think about the individuality of peoples at all. The barbarians are not within the horizon of the Hellenes.

How could the idea have arisen there that the correct concept of the human soul could only arise when the barbarians and the Hellenes are brought together and that only then could the true microcosm of man become a problem? It is characteristic of Plato that among the several examples he gives for the problem of the idea, the soul is missing, not to mention his failure to establish one idea about man.

7. The merit that Philo, the Jew, is said to have in the development of the Platonic doctrine of ideas has not yet been adequately estab-

lished. One thing, however, cannot be denied: he marked out the *idea of man* as a particular idea; he made man into an idea. There can be no doubt how he acquired the great merit of such an important formulation: he knew Moses and the prophets. Although his knowledge of the Bible was not based on an exact knowledge of the language, and although his understanding of the Bible was not supported and enlivened by acquaintance with the rabbinical literature which was already flourishing at that time, nevertheless, the fundamental ideas of monotheism were alive in his believing soul. And it may have been exactly the prophetic idea of mankind which gave philosophic ardor to his belief in the unique God.

However, Philo belongs to the most intimate original forces of Christianity, for which he paved the way, because he was overwhelmed by Greek philosophy and could not assert himself in purely monotheistic terms. He failed to solve the problem of the individual, particularly in its relation to God, and of the possibility of God's influence in general upon man and the world. Thus, he violated monotheism through the idea of the *Logos,* which he derived from those Platonic passages which turned away from the method of the ideas. However, the idea of *mankind* remained alive in his idea of man.

8. The Jewish religious philosophers of the Middle Ages did not becloud their historical sense with doctrinal prejudices, either with regard to Christianity or to Islam. They granted to both religions the merit of spreading monotheism among the peoples of the world. And just as the Talmud already recognized that the verdict of idolatry is not valid for peoples who are different from those of Canaan, in the same manner the Jewish philosophers of the Middle Ages did not see in the Christian Trinity the absolute negation of monotheism, but they characterized it as association, as "partnership" (שיתוף).

However, if the spreading of the idea of the unique God in history has a precise content, it may consist in this, that the unique God, as the world God, as the God of all peoples, is thought of in these religions as conveying a definite demand with regard to them. In the idea of a *world religion* Christianity made the idea of one mankind the content of religion, and on this idea it has based its claim to world conquest. Therefore, as much as the individual and his salvation is its central point, its periphery, one mankind, still remained its universal objective.

Man, who for the Greeks was the Hellene only, became to the Christian of every nation, despite the enmity among the nations, the one and the same man whose salvation is through the one Christ. Hence, with regard to this historical principle, Christ became, to be sure, the Messiah of mankind. For the particular requirements which Christ set forth for salvation, and consequently for the realization of the idea of mankind, receded before the problem itself, which is set forth in one and the same mankind, which is sinful and to be saved.

9. Throughout the entire Middle Ages the gravest antimony surges between the particular peoples and the one Christian world. And is this antimony at present overcome, or more than merely glossed over? In spite of the contradictions between the historical aspirations of the nations and the moral and religious ideas of Christianity, as soon as the central point had been declared to be the idea of one mankind, it could not be shifted.

"What is man that Thou art mindful of him!" [Ps. 8:5].

One could exclaim this together with the psalmist if man were to mean merely the next man, not to say the man of a nation, or finally the man of one's own nation; if man were not to be elevated as the man of one mankind, elevated to that honor and dignity which the psalmist attributes to him.

The sciences too, no less than the arts, achieved a kind of internationalism; hence, a community of human letters arose amongst the peoples, such as had not been remotely achieved in antiquity. And thus finally the *Renaissance*, with its humanism, was the origin of the renewal of jurisprudence and political science. This was everywhere historically connected with the classics, but always complemented by religion, and contained biblical influences. It was particularly influenced by the theory of *natural law* and the *international law of nations* which originated with the Stoics, but which took over from the Bible its cosmopolitan spirit.

Joining in this development was the new philosophy in the strict sense of the word. Modern philosophy already represented a communicaton and, as it were, a dialogue of international minds. This Republic of Sciences, as it was called at that time, emerged in the French Revolution with the doctrine of universal human rights. However, it aroused more of a political claim than a universal human one. The latter, however, was already very much alive in the cosmopolitan spirit of philosophy, and Leibniz, who inspired the *German Enlightenment,* was particularly conscious of it.

10. Modernity as such, with its general philosophy, stimulated deep reforms in all spheres of the mind. Only scholastic philosophy remained tied to the past, particularly with regard to ethical problems. In its arrangements and applications of these, it stuck fast to its connections with theology and the disciplines of law. Then Kant appeared and created for the first time a real *ethics,* namely such a one

as did not contain in itself logic and metaphysics, but presupposed them and built itself upon them; ethics, consequently, as a part of a system of philosophy.

This ethics, which was conceived as independent and pure philosophy and not as, for example, psychology, which was entirely modern in its method, and entirely independent of the ways of scholasticism, was yet in its innermost spirit related to the new religiosity of the *Reformation,* as well as to the Pietists. On the other hand, it was influenced by Rousseau, and thus animated by the social problems and the political ideas of the betterment of the general condition of the world. Thus, Kant's ethics breathes the spirit of mankind.

The exact terminological meaning of the word "mankind" in Kant is, to be sure, first of all determined by opposition to the empirical man as understood in psychological and historical experience, so that mankind is equivalent to the moral rational being. However, in his terminology the term does not refer exclusively to the rational being derived from the methodology of ethics. Mankind occupies the most important position in all his formulations so that there is no doubt that it has for Kant the universal, *cosmopolitan* meaning. "Respect mankind in your person, as in the person of every other man," reads the formulation of the categorical imperative.

11. It makes no sense to deny the tremendous influence of Rousseau on Kant, but it makes as little sense to consider it decisive. Rousseau did indeed influence Herder the theologian and the great German adherent of universal humanitarianism. And while Herder was not very teachable, and therefore also an ungrateful pupil of Kant, he was, however, of one and the same understanding with him as regards the idea of German *humanitarianism,* and thus became the author of *The Ideas for a Philosophy of the History of Mankind.*

It was, however, not an accident that he was at the same time the author of the *Spirit of Hebrew Poetry*. And he discerned the spirit of mankind already in the earliest documents of the Old Testament, not first in the Prophets only. This was an important insight which guided Herder's entire conception of the spirit of the Bible: *he discerned Messianism in the principle of monotheism.*

12. From the very beginning we have recognized the inner difficulties in the basic notions of Messianism and its conflicts with the historical conditions and concepts that had to appear as its consequence. Such was the concept of a spiritual God, from whom all corporeality had to be eliminated, and who nevertheless had to communicate himself, reveal himself to man.

First of all he was the *unique being*, but this could only mean that he was presupposed by any and every other kind of being, which could not be thought of without him. And when creation and revelation were acknowledged, a new difficulty arose within the national spirit. It had to become inflamed with monotheism, so that the latter had to be made into the nation's own deed and thus penetrate, and be accessible to, the nation.

A new impetus arose in the awakening of the national spirit, which had as its consequence the historical call to Moses. In the dim antiquity of national memories, this national spirit demanded for its founder a hero of the same spirit as the people's own spirit, and one who therefore had to become the immediate receiver of the divine revelation.

All these contradictions occurred and appeared openly and freely, and they were mastered. The *Torah* came to be; its existence was based on the harmony between God's ideas and the moral "statutes and ordinances," which this God commanded.

13. Now, however, with the *prophets* a new contradiction appeared in this, as it seemed, harmoniously closed teaching. This teaching was intended for the people and for the little state which this people established after a long preparation. Hostile and peaceful contacts with neighboring peoples were not lacking; wars were led, and alliances concluded; but the horizon was limited to the one small land.

In all of antiquity the political horizon, even the horizon of the *polis,* was at the same time the horizon of the world in the geographical and all the more in the ethical sense. Who, in the antiquity of the classical times, would have glanced in his mind, not to mention his heart, beyond his own state and beyond his own people?

The prophets arose as if they had come from a new world, and exhorted men to a kind of politics as if they were eighteenth century cosmopolitans. However, as much as they were subject to an unheard of social radicalism, they were at the same time restrained by a national patriotism, and the latter was guided by ethical monotheism.

If, therefore, the prophet threatened his own people with the most rigorous punishment, with the downfall of the state itself, this judgment of damnation affected no less the other peoples, the enemies of Israel; for the insult to the national feeling had its clearly recognizable ground in the lofty teaching of the holy God, who demands justice.

If out of this spirit came forth a general enthusiasm for all men and all peoples, the narrow-minded patriots might certainly become perplexed about this. They were nurtured in the belief that they were "God's property," and now it seemed that all peoples should get a share in the true knowledge of God and in the true worship of God. How could the narrow national consciousness elevate itself to such a broadness of heart, without experiencing doubt and perplexity about itself and about the unique God, whom previously the unique people alone had worshiped? And just as we must consider the people's disinclination for this new and great idea, so this idea in its novelty must appear to us surprising even in the prophets themselves.

14. However, from the very beginning monotheism, with all its accessories, appeared to us as a wonder. Particularly from the historical point of view, which demands evolution everywhere, monotheism is and shall remain a mystery. No people and no spirit on earth had thought of the unique God. There were indeed analogies everywhere, and if historical research into development is able to satisfy itself with them, it may be content with that; but all these analogies remain alien to the heart of this thought. The primal human thought of the unique God is present only there, where the concern is not merely with unity, but with ethical uniqueness. Nothing else touches the root of the matter. Thus the question remains: how could this thought of a unique God become manifest uniquely and alone to the spirit of this people?

Now a new wonder in the spirit of this people arises in Messianism. But perhaps one wonder might be explained through the other. Let us first clarify the new phenomenon in all its strangeness.

The unique God "should be called Lord over all the earth," and all men and all peoples should know and worship him. The plurality of gods should absolutely disappear from the earth. But if the one God is to be worshiped by all peoples, does not the suspicion arise that the peoples themselves will lose their independent unity, and that while this independence is being dissolved into a unified worship of God, they would, and perhaps should, be dissolved into a unified mankind? And if this is actually the ultimate meaning of the unique God and the unified worship of God by all peoples, does not this universalism call into question not only Israel, but every people in its particularity?

It is well known how even in our days cosmopolitanism is felt to be in lively opposition to the consciousness of one's own nationality. How incomprehensible the origin of Messianism in the midst of a national consciousness must appear to us, inasmuch as it had to think and to feel the "election" of Israel as a singling out for the worship of God.

15. Furthermore, the political circumstances under which the thought originated do not seem to have been the natural ones. No sooner were the tribes united into a national state than the state split into two kingdoms which fought one another, and each of which

drew the great neighboring peoples into the conflict against the brother kingdom. Gradually both of them were destroyed, one after the other, and both had to wander into captivity and to endure there the existence of a stateless nation. Under such confined, such sad, humiliating political conditions, such national sorrow, how could such a joyful thought arise, a thought of the most daring human and world political courage?

16. *I. The end of the world.* We proceed now to disentangle the knot of the problems that are enmeshed in the messianic idea. All the problems of man and of his fate, his dignity and worth, are intertwined in this idea.

The question of the meaning and the worth of human existence belongs to the deepest, but also to the most primitive problems of an awakening culture. With this question man outgrows the myth and the naive consciousness which dissolves in actuality and there finds its contentment. Doubt makes itself felt with regard to the highest good of life and with regard to the entire world. With this question of the meaning of human existence thought about, the *world* might first arise. Not thought about the heavens or nature, or the cosmos, but about the *Aion* as that world which particularly comprises human life.

And when doubt is first raised about the value of this world, then the thought about the *end of the world* also arises, that first critical thought which also accompanies, in Greek philosophy, the first steps of speculation about the cosmos. The world has to pay the punishment („δίκην διδόναι") for its existence.

But at the same time this thought of *punishment* contains in itself a correction of the thought about the end of the world. The punishment cannot be meant only retrospectively, but, just as in the life of society, there must be in it a foresight, a provision for the future.

17. The end of the world includes in it the *renewal of the world.* Destruction is not thought of without regeneration. The absolute end, the disappearance of existence is not a primitive thought; only a later fantasy can become so desolate. The myth always thinks in terms of an alternation of being and becoming, and therefore only in this sense of being and non-being. Out of *non-being* a higher being is to come forth.

18. The prophets have taken over into the "Day of the Eternal" this myth of the end of the world, which also appeared among their people. In the mythical belief, fear and dread are not separated from ecstatic joy. Fear should be drowned out by jubilation.

Thus, Amos warns about the double meaning of confidence in the

"Day of the Eternal." "Woe unto you that desire the day of the Eternal! . . . It is darkness, and not light" (Amos 5:18). That shortsighted thoughtlessness that intends just to get over the fear of the day is here condemned. One enjoys the expectation of the end because it brings a new beginning, hence, as if one were to expect a new God and also a new world. This cycle of coming into being and passing away, however, contradicts creation, which is based on providence, whereas the thought of a cycle presupposes fate and chance. Evolution and progress to a meaningful goal are opposed to the myth of the burning up of the world (ἐκπύρωσις). In monotheism the idea of the end of the world can be made use of only as God's *judgment*. But already God's covenant with Noah makes a complete destruction impossible.

19. The poetic power of the prophets and particularly of Isaiah (chap. 13) indulges in images. In describing the "Day of the Lord" they become the nature poets of the end of the world. They pile up images of storms, earthquakes, flood, heat, devastation, wreckage, and stoneheaps; they depict volcanic changes, the splitting of valleys, and the melting of mountains. Zephaniah makes God's judgment into a sacrifice for God. Pestilence, hailstorm, hunger, lack of burial for the dead, desecration of corpses, such are God's judgments which overcome the peoples, but no less Israel. Already this grouping together of Israel with the peoples in the universal destruction prepares the way for a transformation of the mythical thought of the end of the world.

20. Out of the notion of God's punitive judgment gradually emerges the thought of the purification of Israel and no less of the other people. As soon as this thought of purification flashes forth, the thought of God's *guidance* and *education* of the world emerges with it.

This guidance further demands a step by step *development*. Thus the "Day of the Lord" becomes the symbol of the Messiah. In Malachi, Elijah becomes the precursor of the Messiah. In Joel the pouring out of the spirit "upon all flesh" appears. This, however, is a symbol anticipating the rejuvenation of the spiritual and moral world. Thus the "Day of Judgment" inspires the thought of the renewal and re-creation of the world.

The thought of repentance, which originates in Ezekiel, is in Jonah transferred to Nineveh, apparently unconsciously and against his will, as a consistent consequence of the unique God. As no individual can be abandoned to destruction, so also can no people, insofar as it has access to and is conversant with the power of repentance. Repentance carries with it the basic meaning of return, the guarantee of restoration. "And they shall come back from the land of the enemy" (Jer. 31:16). The restoration of the people is the immediate hope during the exile and in all political affliction in the present and in the future.

This is the transfiguration that the "Day of the Lord" underwent. In its mythical origin it was a sacrificial feast at which men and gods eat together; in its origin chiefly a feast of lords and heroes, who celebrated their victory, it gradually became a national day of honor, in which joy and horror alternate one with another. The horror gradually was overcome, and hope in a new existence for one's own as well as for the alien nation was established.

21. The end of the world even in the myth means the *Last Judgment*. At first, the heroes invoke it against one another in the way that the gods of the different tribes fight one another. Always, however, the naive thought that there is a unity of force and violence with the godhead prevails.

Amos fights against this unity; one's appeal to God should be not to power but to the moral forces. The mighty of the earth oppress the poor and commit social injustices. Such proofs of power are alien to the very essence of the unique God. Therefore his priest cannot be a *haruspex* who examines the entrails of sacrificed animals or the flight of birds, or who conjures with snakes. His priest does not look at animals, he looks at man. Thus the prophet becomes the politician, a politician of social legislation. And with regard to international relations the prophet turns his thought to history, he becomes the originator of the concept of *world history*.

22. But he can become all this only because he is the creator of religion, of the revelation of the true God, admonishing to the true worship of God, which cannot be thought of separately from the true service to men, from the service between man and man and between people and people. It is in this connection that the concept of the *good*, first objectively and then as applied to God, originates.

Thus even in its mythological inception, religion is already founded on morality. The myth, however, as the natural form of worship, becomes suspect in the face of all questions concerning its cult. The myth celebrates power in gods as well as in heroes. Religion cannot be the worship of power. In the myth, only the heroes are "loved by God" (θεοφιλεῖς). The new concept of God, however, demands justice and love for all men.

This fundamental thought changes the meaning of the *Last Judgment* into the "Day of the Lord." Woe to God's own people, its princes and mighty ones, its priests and its false prophets! Thus admonishes the prophet. Agreement, even the agreement of the nation with God, cannot be assumed and celebrated in an ecstatic feast, as men have hitherto imagined. Power does not join power; rather, in true religion the Lord of morality demands submission to his commandment. The earnestness of the moral commandment frightens complacent joy and self-assurance away from the "Day of the Lord." This Day is ominous with punishment and grief.

We shall later have to derive other consequences from this transformation of the myth of the end of the world. At present we still remain in the circle of mythology.

23. *II. Death.* The most difficult question, which arises even in the primitive consciousness, is presented by *death*, the end of the individual life. It is the question mark against the value of human life in general. As soon, therefore, as the *soul* becomes the principle of life, it also becomes the principle of *afterlife*, though life in the realm of the dead might be less valued than earthly existence. Biblical antiquity too knows of the netherworld (שאול) as this realm of the dead. And the soul, which originally is in the blood, as is also the psyche, as the soul of smoke, gradually becomes the principle of the unity of the person. And so sings the psalm: "For Thou wilt not abandon my soul in *sheol* [netherworld]" (Ps. 16:10). Man is not left to perish in *sheol*, and thus arises a new kind of existence for man, for which the myth has already prepared the way.

24. But the myth prepares this even farther. The myth of the *Isles of the Blessed* is a deepening of [primitive] thought about the soul. The wretched ones deserve and find their end, but the good men, who give honor to their own souls, not only have an afterlife, but one which is also worthy of their soul. The Isles of the Blessed is a locality beyond space and time. The thought of such a utopia can therefore be grasped only by poetry, and only in folk poetry can it become a folk belief. But the notion of the immortality of the soul first comes to fruition in philosophy, in the Greek consciousness, where, however, it is definitely restricted to educated circles.

25. Since the beyond is a utopia, so it is also beyond time. Therefore, for this beyond, the concept of historical *future*, can as little arise as that of a personal future. While the fantastic connection with the past cannot be entirely discontinued, on the other hand it cannot be maintained in the actual present, except insofar as the offended *souls of the ancestors* can interfere avenging in the living actuality.

But this existence itself is spaceless and timeless. Therefore, the prophet has to erect between this utopia of mythical belief and his own world a dividing wall, as the psalmist does with regard to the

sheol: "An eye hath not seen it, O God, beside Thee only" (Isa. 64:3).
We shall later expect to see the monotheistic transformations of this
mythical notion of the beyond. Now, however, we have to evaluate
the Isles of the Blessed, in spite of its negativity, as a preparation
for Messianism. For in it human existence has nevertheless been
extended beyond the borders of sensuous actuality. This extension is
the merit of the myth. Monotheism, however, must give this extension a positive form. Thus originates the religious analogy to
the moral concept of *infinity* demanded by the concepts of God and
man. That monotheism has turned away from the myth is further
shown here inasmuch as the aspiration for infinity is for infinite
time and not for space, which still remains the finite earth, created
by God.

26. *III. The Golden Age.* Another mythical concept which precedes monotheism is that of the Golden Age. The Greeks might have
become conscious of it at the same time as of the Isles of the Blessed.
This innocent prehistorical tale is also the content of the *Paradise saga,*
which Genesis also took over. In these myths, moral criticism as well
as opposition to Promethean knowledge, distrust of its ambiguity,
is already awakened; therefore, together with the awakening of the
knowledge of good and evil came doubt of their absoluteness.

The entire moral world here emerges as a sphinx. And the relation
of God and man becomes subject to the same dualism. Why does
God give man orders and commandments and with them awaken
him from the slumber of innocence? Without the law man would be
sinless. Thus Paul carried his polemics against the law too far, stretch-
ing it even to the moral law. In primeval times there was no sin.
This is the way of mythical thought, which does not take into consideration God's orders. Classical antiquity in its entirety culminates
in the longing for peace and reconciliation in this bliss of the primeval time, of the absolute *past.*

That Messianism is directed to the *future* already distinguishes it
from the myth of the Golden Age, which, however, in itself is a
preparatory motif of the times of primeval innocence.

27. However, the monotheistic treatment of the Paradise saga already introduces the change. Innocence is abolished, and for this
God's commandment offers the first occasion. Soon, however, the
breach of the innocence of man is perpetuated in murder. The in-
trusion of murder into human life destroys all concord in nature.
Messianism is unmistakably linked with the relation to murder, insofar as *war* is its pervasive motif. Any analogy with the Golden
Age is thus inwardly banished; the presentiment of concord in it

cannot be mistaken; however, *the past is transfigured into the future.*

28. It is a deplorable feature of the modern understanding of Messianism that even in biblical research the two thoughts are assumed to be identical: the Messianic Age is even called the Golden Age. Even if motifs were taken over from one by the other, the intention and content of the thought has already been changed and transfigured by the sequence of time. Into the peaceful primeval world, murder has intruded; in the future, however, wars shall disappear. Moreover, this distinction is not the only difference; the contradictions are deeper.

Knowledge is summoned against innocence. It is to become, in the future, universal with all men.[49] Thus the Messianic Age becomes the age of *culture*, whereas the Golden Age is, at most, along the lines of Rousseau's description. The symbolic apparatus of images is taken over by the prophets from mythical poetry; so also is the decoration and the coloring. And in the description of this world peace as a *peace of nature*, the prophets become great poets, and indeed not only poets of nature. They do not describe the Messianic Age as an idyll, for in it knowledge is to be the universally governing principle. This ideal future is in opposition to the past and present and, therefore, to every previous eudaemonistic sort of historical existence.

29. The messianic future is the first conscious expression of the opposition to moral values derived only from empirical sensibility. One may therefore describe it as an *ideal* in opposition to actuality. How could it be identical with the Golden Age, which is merely an improved actuality, but by no means an ideal? The primeval past is as little the ideal as the beyond of the afterworld. The latter, too, is merely the continuation of the past and present, but not the newness of a future. This newness consists in the dawning of the ideal in contrast to all actuality. Myth is everywhere the sunrise of culture, but the sunny day of morality does not yet dawn with it.

30. The ideality of the Messiah, his significance as an idea, is shown in the overcoming of the person of the Messiah and in the dissolution of the personal image in the pure notion of time, in the concept of the *age*. Time becomes future and only future. Past and present submerge in this time of the future. This return to time is the purest idealization. All existence sinks into insignificance in the presence of the point of view of this idea, and man's existence is preserved and elevated into this being of the future. Thus, the thought of *history* comes into being for human life and for the life of the peoples.

The Greeks never had this thought of a history that has the future as its content. Their history is directed to their origins; it is the history that narrates the past of its nation. Other nations constitute a historical problem only for their travel descriptions. A history of mankind is, within this horizon, impossible. Mankind did not live in any past and did not become alive in the present; only the future can bring about its bright and beautiful form. This form is an idea, not a shadowy image of the beyond.

31. The concept of God's being, too, becomes different under the impact of this idea. The creator of heaven and earth is not sufficient for this being of the future. He must create "a new heaven and a new earth." The being of previous history is inadequate even for nature, for *development* is required for the course of things, and development presupposes a goal to which it strives. Thus progress is required in the history of the human race.

This is the meaning of the future as the establishment of true being, that is, God's being on earth; the future, this idea of existence, represents exclusively the *ideal* of history, and not the Golden Age, or Paradise. Both have already been.

The future, in opposition to all these myths about the past, makes another transformation: the "Day of the Lord" comes to be "the End of Days." With this prospect, in this perspective of an infinite plateau of mankind, the notion of man is raised to that of mankind, as the concept of God is to the "Lord of the whole Earth."

32. Even in the notion of the future a mythical element came to be idealized: that of the *Aion*. Originally the *Aion* meant a period of the cycle from the end of the world to its renewal. It is personified time, therefore, also the personified world in the eternity of its cosmic development. But the myth does not know any nature above this world and therefore no living creature who would aspire to a spiritual and moral world. *Aion* knows neither the moral man nor the holy God.

The cycle of the Dionysus myths is the origin of the profound idea of *Zagraeus*, the dismembered god, who is scattered through the world, but who strives for the reunification of his parts. We can detect in this thought, which already influenced the oldest philosophy, the first flaring-up of an absolute moral demand in the godhead. Nowhere, however, does mythical thought achieve in this respect more lucidity or clearness of penetration. Everything in the myth remains history in the sense of the past; never and nowhere does history appear as the idea of the future of mankind under the guidance of God.

33. *IV. The stories of the Flood.* Monotheistic literature as early as Genesis has taken over from the Persians not only its notion of Para-

dise but also the story of the Flood. In the adaptation of this story the purity of monotheism comes even more to the fore than in the adaptation of the story of Paradise. God makes a covenant with Noah; this fact in itself is important.

The covenants which God otherwise makes with a man are always related to the man himself and at most to his descendants, but here Noah becomes a symbolic representative of the human race, and, as the best of men, even of all living creatures. And what is the content of this covenant? Nothing else, nothing less than the *preservation*, thus the future, of the human race.

Thus Noah is, properly speaking, already the Messiah, because he is the ideal representative of eternal mankind. And the *rainbow*, the sign in heaven of this covenant with the earth, is the symbol of this horizon of the infinite development of mankind. The rainbow, too, is the image of the idea of true existence, founded by God's covenant with Noah—the ideal man.

We shall see more clearly than we have already seen that this ideal man, therefore, could be entrusted with the ideal teachings of morality. God's covenant with Noah is at the same time God's covenant with the earth against its destruction. Thus, through this covenant, earthly existence is idealized and hence protected from the appearance of nothingness, from which only the beyond may save it.

34. *V. The Jewish state.* The *political* circumstances of the Jewish state have also to be taken into consideration as preconditions. How differently were the Greeks, and even Plato, affected by the *polis*, the city-state with its tribal basis. There the idea of a world state could not arise, and only the individuality of a military genius could give rise to it and seal the decline which had already been inwardly prepared. In the people of monotheism, however, the tribes were never so isolated that they could become independent states. The unity of the kingdom, the time of the blossoming of the nation, whose cultural symbol is the poetry of David, was only a short episode. Soon it was followed by the split into two kingdoms, and finally came the ruin of both kingdoms, one after the other.

But how little the state meant to this people is manifested in the continuation and the blossoming of the people even after the destruction of the state. Greece did not achieve such a second blossoming, not even in Alexandrian literature, which could not be considered properly Greek. With this people [Israel], however, the great event occurred: without the state, even after the destruction of the state, the people flourished and grew into an inner unity.

35. Hence the split into two kingdoms may be regarded as a prelude to the world history of Judaism: David's realm is not the proper soil for the world of monotheism. Neither in this short and bygone past nor in any political present does Israel's historical calling lie. *The meaning and value of monotheism had to prove itself in this historical and political contradiction.* The future becomes the actuality of history. Therefore only a spiritual world can fulfill this national existence.

Another riddle is explained through this contradiction. The state had to perish; the people, however, had to remain. It was otherwise with Greece; with the state, the people too disappeared. How could the Greek spirit be preserved for the world, while even the people and not only the state perished?

36. The Greek spirit preserved its life for eternal fertility in its literary and artistic productions. It had to continue only in its *productions* in order to win the world through them. But this fertility, which the Greek spirit effects, was to bring about the development of the spirit of the individual peoples it has influenced. The Greek spirit needed to remain alive only in its productions in order to beget new life in the individual peoples.

The case is different with monotheism. There it says: no other Gods except the One! Homer did not create in another people a new Homer, and yet the poetry of all times is an imitation of his spirit. And it is the same with Greek plastic arts, and no less with Greek philosophy. It is an influence everywhere, but everywhere this influence means a new formation in the new individual spirit of the people. There is no unique way in art; rather, the infinity of genius is the only law.

37. The way of science is different from that of art. Mathematics is in no way dependent on the individuality of a nation. Pythagoras and Archimedes continue to remain the eternal guides just in the sense that their propositions remain eternal truths. Monotheism is, therefore, in no way a strange anomaly in light of the way all knowledge develops. Monotheism is entitled to lay claim to what is methodologically valid for all scientific truth.

Monotheism claims that not every people may have its own peculiar God, but that there is *one* God for all peoples, as there is one mathematics for all peoples. In the latter case, the immortal works of mathematics itself influence other peoples at all times, so that the preservation of the nation of its origin is not necessary.

38. Monotheism, however, did not come to a final close in the Bible, as did the Greek spirit in its various works. Monotheism required a

continuous development *beyond the Bible,* which could not be entrusted to those peoples who did not produce the ancient Bible.

The continuity of the spiritual power of one people was necessary in this case. And this power could remain alive, despite the fact that the state did not hold it together any longer; for it had already been effective before the foundation of the state and immediately after its decline.

This explains the duality of Israel's political fate. That the state declined, while the people were preserved, is a providential symbol of Messianism; it is the sign of the truth of monotheism. No state, but yet a people. But this people is less for the sake of its own nation than as a symbol of mankind. A unique symbol for the unique idea; the individual peoples have to strive to the unique unity of mankind.

Thus Israel, as a nation, is nothing other than the mere symbol for the desired unity of mankind. The Greek people could not present such a symbol; for it did not know the concept of mankind. The idea of one mankind could only arise under the one God. The one God, however, arose in the one people. Therefore this one people had to endure.

39. The endurance of the Jewish state, on the contrary, would have been an anomaly, as it already was in its origin, with regard to "the Lord over all the earth." Already the split of the kingdom gave the prophets the occasion to take sides for Judah against Israel and later on to demand the ruin of both kingdoms and their restoration under monotheistic conditions.

If this latter thought, which their natural patriotism demanded, again awakened the old anomaly, there was also a correction in the consequence they drew, namely, that along with the restoration of the Jewish state they demanded the restoration of the states of the enemy peoples, whose ruin they had also prophesied. There is no doubt that their Messianism corrects their own national particularism. And just as the national disaster is only the preparation for the messianic future of their own nation, so the restoration of the other peoples is the necessary means to win and incorporate them into the messianic future.

40. Jeremiah is, even in his own person, the tragic prophet. With a merciless fervor he inveighs against the national consciousness with all its historical traditions, against the sacrifice, against the Ark of the Covenant, even against circumcision itself. He is at the same time the gravedigger and the poet of lamentation; he is the satirist and the elegiac poet in the same breath; he is tragedy personified.

Ezekiel, on the other hand, is the national politician in the deepest, although concealed, spirit of Deutoronomy. Therefore he is able to further positively the messianic idea, whereas Jeremiah would have remained stuck fast in criticism, had not elegy freed him from it.

The Deutero-Isaiah again shows the double face of the antinomy between the people and messianic mankind which passes through the whole of Jewish history. This antinomy is the point of gravity of the development of Jewish history; every form of inner inhibition comes from it, but it also sets into continuous motion all development. For the furtherance of monotheism we must remain a national individuality, because monotheism has stamped upon us an historical singularity. And since this national existence is not inhibited by a state of one's own, it is protected against the fate of a materialization of its nationalistic idea. The national peculiarity in its stateless isolation is the symbol for the unity of the confederation of mankind, as the ultimate value of world history. It is the unity of mankind in monotheism and in the morality founded upon it. All the other productions of the human spirit are dependent on the peculiar spirit of a people, and hence depend on the preservation of the individual peculiarity of these peoples. Only the knowledge of God establishes a unified community of men. This knowledge, as a common good of all men and peoples, makes Messianism capable of unlimited expansion. Universalism connects second Isaiah with the first. "And all nations shall flow unto it" (Isa. 2:2). The universality of Messianism is the consequence of the anomaly between state and people in the history of Israel.

41. *VI. God's holiness.* This universalistic precondition becomes immanent in the concept of the unique God, as the holy God. *Holiness* is morality, and the latter is distinct not only from all knowledge of nature but also from all natural powers. All the sensuality of the empirical world, with the contradictions it contains, is surmounted.

Historically, therefore, justice and love form an almost irreconcilable antinomy. The essence of the gods is suspended in this alternative, as it is generally in the *separation* not only of powers but of affects as well.

As a consequence even the sexes receive separate deification. However, any separation of moral principles is contradictory to God's uniqueness.

Every punishment is therefore at the same time a reward, every reward almost a punishment. Morality is one, as God is one. His justice is therefore identical with his love. *The unique God means the unity of morality.* Within this unity, the God of punishment is at the same time the God of forgiveness.

42. Hence, also, the human race must be everlasting, for God's creation always means new creation and preservation. If mankind is to be eternal, its eternal value has to be based on its tendency to eternity. And this tendency is fulfilled in the striving of the people to their unification. Eternity cannot have, nor can it exhaust, its value in variety by itself.

Thus the unity of God becomes the model for the peoples of the world so that they set their unity in mankind as the goal of their historical existence. The unity of men is the eternal value of the human race. Messianism is the straightforward consequence of monotheism.

43. An important consequence follows from this. Without the strict purity of monotheism, Messianism cannot attain its clear expression. If, therefore, the Messiah, as a subject, is admitted into the unity of God himself, then monotheism is as much injured through this as the meaning of Messianism is changed.

The foregiveness of sin cannot become the act of the Messiah, for it is the exclusive act of the unique God. However, the task of the Messiah is to make the holiness of man before God the ideal concept of man. Holiness is not sinlessness, but it is ideal humanity, because it is ideal morality. This ideality of man has as its condition the unity of mankind.

The two tasks of the Messiah, the ideal morality and the unity of mankind, are united in that idea of the Messiah, who cannot be immanent in God, because he must be immanent in man. And "not a man is God." God and man do not constitute an identity, but a correlation. God's ideality is fulfilled in his uniqueness, but the ideality of man is fulfilled by the Messiah in the ideal morality of the united mankind, in which the peoples are relieved of all conflicts.

44. VII. *Israel's cultural peculiarity.* The cultural peculiarity of Israel constitutes an important predisposition for the creation of a Messiah. Israel is a people without interest or creative participation in *science.* People were therefore mistaken about the general spirituality of Israel's culture, and therefore also about the *original* peculiarity of the people.

Because of this deficiency and the psychological interpretation given to it, people also drew conclusions about the general validity of religious culture. And these considerations become more weighty because along with the deficiency in the sciences there is also lacking independent philosophy in this one-sidedly religious literature. However, this doubt about the creativity of monotheism must also be limited or even cease to be entertained. We have already recognized the share of reason in monotheism, and therefore considered it as a kind of philosophy, although not a scientific one.

45. Monotheism itself and only it is able to solve the riddle its isolated appearance in Israel poses. This *one-sidedness* was necessary for the first creation of the thought, which finds similarities everywhere, but nowhere identity. And this self-confinement of the thought seems to explain why this singular thought was considered to the exclusion of all others.

In the presence of this interest in the unique God and in man, who is determined only by the unique God, all the other interests, which usually dominate the ancient peoples, gave way. That the Jewish people was not lacking in disposition and energy for these other interests also is later proved beyond any doubt. But at first the unified double concept of God and man had to be secured before any questions of the human spirit, which lie outside the correlation of God and man, could claim the interest of the Jewish people.

46. In *poetry*, too, this one-sidedness repeats itself. There is no dramatic poetry, and also no lyric poetry in the erotic sense; there is no connection of the spiritual with the erotic—the Song of Songs, according to Graetz, is idyllic poetry and at the same time a satire on the satrapy. Everywhere poetry is checked by morality; everywhere, therefore, it involves the turning away from the egotistical, the curbing of weaknesses in order to unify men. Thus poetry itself leads to Messianism.

All poetical questions about human fate are also turned into questions of *providence*, the guidance by the unique God. "Let not the wise man glory in his wisdom, neither let the mighty man glory in his might . . . but let him that glorieth glory in . . . that he understandeth and knoweth Me" (Jer. 9:22-24). Knowledge is the knowledge of God. God, however, is the father of all men and peoples. Therefore this *knowledge* has to spread to all men, without distinction of rank, and to all peoples. "Are ye not as the children of the Ethiopians unto Me?" (Amos 9:7). Thus Amos introduces his messianic idea by putting the colored people on a par with the Israelites. This concentration upon knowledge is demanded of all men without distinction. And without this universal demand of knowledge, monotheism would remain a fragment, an illusion.

47. How justified historically this Jewish one-sidedness is can be seen in the example of Plato, the greatest idealist of all times. Plato discovered scientific idealism. Knowledge is to him scientific knowledge. Since, however, science is not accessible to all men of all classes, knowledge also is not accessible to them. In this last sentence the first

clause is already a mistake, a contradiction in Plato's mind. How could this happen? Only the absence of concentration on the knowledge of God could give a satisfactory explanation for this striking violation of Plato's idealism.

The Jewish one-sidedness becomes through this more and more understandable. Not only has the isolation from all other problems furthered Messianism, but the concentration upon the single value of the knowledge of God is the key to it. But, of course, there is a reciprocal effect here. Without this one-sided restriction the concept of God in his correlation with man would not be so exhaustively marked out.

48. *VIII.* This restriction to religion produced the holy spirit, as the spirit of holiness, as the spirit of moral knowledge. As the disciples of this spirit the prophets felt the calling to combat the priests who claimed to be the legitimate representatives of holiness. These polemics against the priests are an important means for the shaping of messianic universalism. The priest is not the treasurer of God's spirit. Joel lets the spirit be poured out over all flesh, even over male and females slaves. *The holy spirit is the human spirit.* Not even the Messiah possesses it as a special gift, but "God's spirit rests upon him," as it rests upon every man. This spirit of God, this holy spirit in every man, leads directly to messianic universalism.

The *prophet* too is nothing more than a messenger of God by virtue of God's message to his spirit. God communicates without mediation to the prophet, eliminating any oracle or any priestly activity. In this, its negative and positive determinations, the institution of prophecy is unique in Israel. This historical uniqueness, too, would not be understandable without the above-mentioned restriction of knowledge to knowledge of God.

And *theocracy* is also the political consequence of this one-sidedness, which prepares the way for Messianism. Theocracy does not mean a priestly hierarchy; from the very beginning the prophets and judges, the former without a proper office, were spiritual leaders of religion and society. Early history already symbolizes this state of affairs: Moses is above Aaron.

49. Therefore the *teaching profession,* which spread in this people as nowhere else, could develop directly from the schools of prophecy. This also explains the prophetic school itself, which takes the place of the usual academy. It is also most characteristic that Ezra, the founder of the community on the ruins of the state, is called scribe (סופר). The scholar is the founder of the religious constitution. The restriction to the knowledge of God loses more and more its one-sided-

ness as it proves itself useful in the creative organization of the continuation of religion. And the latter isolates the religious people only in appearance; for the kingdom of priests is to become the *Kingdom of God* on earth.

50. This concentration and intensification of religious self-consciousness became the driving force for the continuation of the original revelation into the literature of the *Canon* and beyond it to the Oral teaching. This extension of the revelation to the tradition is unavoidably a *dissolution of revelation into knowledge*. For the rabbinical claim of authenticity "from Sinai" can have only symbolic validity.

It was, therefore, not the pride of the rabbis which made this claim but the consequence of the share of reason in religion, which the rabbis drew in this formula in accordance with the messianic idea. For it is only an unhistoric prejudice to think that through the "fence" which they set up about the Torah the isolation of Israel became to them an end in itself. Gradually the historic insight gained ground, that without this principle of isolation—and it is only the question of a principle in such great historical problems—monotheism would not have been capable of living on and resisting the many assaults of opposing movements.

Therefore, the religious one-sidedness, which *rabbinism* carried into the whole ritual, must be also regarded, in the light of a higher historical meaning, as a preparation for Messianism. "Let all your deeds be done for the sake of the Heaven" (Pirke Aboth 2:12). This proverb became the principle of all the practical affairs of human life, in the same way as religious knowledge became the principle of all knowledge in general. And without permeating the entire life of the people in the whole of its civic existence, Messianism could not be attained.

To show this, it suffices to point to the distinction between the Church and the *laity*. The universalism of the Church is not to be equated with Messianism, because in the former the priest with his *sacraments* stands between God and the layman. If, however, the sacraments are not the Church's own work, but belong to the private inventory of the individual man, then the mighty lever of the messianic idea cannot be mistaken. It consists in the substitution of the *ritual*, as instituted by the rabbis, for the sacrificial cult.

Any judgment of the particular details of these laws is therefore unjust, if it does not take into account the historical point of view which distinguishes private ritual from the works of the Church and, furthermore, if the one-sidedness of religious knowledge is not evaluated as a principle continuously influencing this institution.

51. *IX.* The intellectual restriction brought about the maturity of *ethical rigor.* In it monotheism fulfills its opposition to *eudaemonism.* We have already recognized (cf. p. 21) that only Isaiah could have said about his God: "He makes peace and creates evil." In this brave surpassing of Zoroastrianism, evil rather means ill. God cannot be the creator of evil, yet he makes the ill, which men, in their delusion, consider evil. But God is the creator of peace, and in peace, according to the Hebrew root of the word, the creator of perfection transforms the seemingly unsuitable ill into his highest end.

Is perhaps well-being, earthly happiness, to be identified with the good? This question reverberates through the entire later literature. And are distress and suffering perhaps the recompense of evil, the punishment for sin? God's relation to these obvious contradictions in human life demanded the piercing of this riddle. In the most important biblical passages we therefore notice a correction of the idea of *God's judgment,* a correction which the Decalogue already expresses by restricting judgment to the behavior of the children with regard to hatred and love of God. Finally Ezekiel solves the problem on the basis of his own suppositions.[50]

52. We have already considered how only through the social insight which defines poverty as suffering could the separation of suffering from punishment be clarified. *The poor become the pious.* This identity is the high point of ethical monotheism. Plato's ethical idealism never reached this height.

Thus the seeming negativity of religion's one-sidedness turns out more and more to be positive. Out of it ethical *socialism* becomes explainable; it is permeated by the Mosaic idea of poverty, which has in the *Sabbath* its programmatic expression. The fight of the prophets against the Kings, the princes, and the rich is only a continuation of the basic motif that dominates the whole of biblical Judaism.

Finally the psalms, in which the identity of the poor and the pious constitutes the vital breath, make this identity into the basic chord of Messianism. The soul, the individual soul according to Ezekiel, becomes the universal human soul: "Let every soul praise the Lord" (Ps. 150:6). All the different motivations of particularism and universalism, caused by David's more or less fictitious authorship of the psalms, find their harmony in Messianism.

53. *X.* Finally it is a consequence of the ethical rigor that *national* limitations are abandoned for the sake of Messianism. Consequently, the "people of Israel" becomes "the remnant of Israel." The people with all its members is not worthy of ethical monotheism. Therefore they cannot one and all be worthy of Messianism. However, the

original worthiness, which is expressed in the election of Israel, cannot be absolutely abolished. All the prophets struggle with this antinomy. Finally, in the notion of the remnant of Israel the solution is found. In it "the holy tribe" is alive; "the holy seed," indestructable.

This "remnant of Israel," however, is the Israel of the future and not the historical Israel of the past or the present. It is the ideal Israel, which indeed, as everything ideal in the life of men and peoples, must be deeply rooted in the actual. But these depths are from the outset of ideal significance. If one disregards the fundamental historical meaning, that through the election the national consciousness was to be substituted for the religious calling, then the election of Israel has only a symbolic significance. From the very outset this higher symbolism presaged Israel's messianic call, its *elevation into one mankind.*

54. The prophets condemn the nationalistic pride that violates the universalism of monotheism. "Sodom is thy sister" (Ezek. 16:48). And Amos takes the lead of the literary prophets with his lashing sarcasm: "You only have I known of all the families of the earth: therefore I will visit upon you all your iniquities" (Amos 3:2). The election thus becomes God's prerogative to punish.

The prophets would not have foretold the ruin of the state, in which they had to see the only support for the people, if the idealization of the people in the notion of the remnant of Israel had not been firm in their minds. In principle, therefore, for the messianic idea the people means the remnant. The remnant is the ideal Israel, the future of mankind.

55. *XI.* To the idealization of the people in the remnant of Israel corresponds the idealization of the Messiah. Originally he is the offspring of David, who will again restore the royal throne of David, for the House of David shall never lack descendants. However, the entire moral image of the world has now changed. Not only is the people transformed into a remnant, which one can hardly think of as possessing the original fullness and glitter of its power, but an opposition has also been set up against the identity of piety and all previously established forms of power and glory. The poor have become the pious. And nobody has yet thought that David's throne and kingdom could be a fitting symbol of poverty. On the other hand, they could no longer remain the symbols of piety and justice.

Thus, it could not be otherwise than that the scion of David, the scion of the king, had to recede in favor of the poor man, who had now become the legitimately pious man. And thus the new image of Messiah as the "servant of the Eternal" was coined by the Deutero-Isaiah. The son of the king had to become a servant. For the poor man had become the representative of piety. No disdain could affect this servant, for he is the servant of God.

56. All Israel and finally all men should become servants of God. The Hebrew word for "to serve" and for "to be a servant" is used throughout for divine worship and divine service, along with its alternatives "knowledge" and "love of God"; a special word for slave does not exist. If the Messiah now acquires the new name of the servant of God, then this new word only confirms the old, universal meaning: Israel and all peoples are, and must become, God's servants.

Consequently the Messiah must transmit to all Israel, and no less to all peoples, a special symbolic task. Therefore he can no longer have the meaning of an individual *person;* his dynastic designation, as in general his political and particularistic limitations, must be abandoned. They are already abandoned wth regard to the social significance which the Messiah represents. More and more the image of the Messiah conveyed, through this social meaning, its religious and, therefore, its original moral value. In an entirely objective development, which was merely furthered by historic circumstances, the Messiah has become the loftiest ideal figure of religious symbolism.

Not only the identity between the poor and the pious has led up to this loftiest figure, but no less, also, the idealized dissolution of the people into the remnant of Israel. The Jewish commentators of old, like Rashi and Kimhi, had the penetration to recognize in God's servant the people of Israel. They were able to interpret the Messiah in this way because the prophets suggested it to them in their demand for the transcendance of the national limitation into the messianic remnant of Israel. This total liberation from the national patriotism, as well as from opportunism and eudaemonism, upon which the rule of social power groups is based, is to be attributed to the ethical rigor, which in turn is the consequence of the above-mentioned religious one-sidedness of monotheism.

57. *XII.* Messianism must be considered as a creation of ideas brought about by the prophetic concept of history. *The concept of history is a creation of the prophetic idea.* If one bears this in mind, then the religious one-sidedness of monotheism grows wider and turns into its opposite.

What the Greek intellect could not achieve, monotheism succeeded in carrying out. *History* is in the Greek consciousness identical with knowledge simply. Thus, history for the Greek is and remains directed only toward the past. In opposition, the prophet is the seer, not the scholar. To see, however, is to gaze. The Hebrew word חזה corresponds entirely to the Greek one for the formation of ideas. The prophets are the idealists of history. Their vision begot the concept of history, as the being of the *future*.

The literary prophets never perform *miracles*. They are exceptional only in their vision. But what they contemplate is only the *future of human history*. Their image of mankind, however, is not a creation of scientific abstraction; the idealism of the prophets is therefore to be understood only figuratively. But as far as the content is concerned, it is certainly a product of idealistic contemplation. They turn their gaze away from the actuality of their own people, as well as from the actuality of other peoples, in order to direct it only to the future. Thereby originates their new concept of history, namely, that of world history.

58. Together with this hope for the future, the prophets still adhere, to be sure, to their national consciousness. One should not blame them for this, for they are men and as such offspring of their people, and without this natural *origin* they would not be able to give a natural coloring to their historical image of the future; they would in general be unable to represent their concept of history in an image. For what distinguishes this concept from the idyllic images of the Golden Age and the images of natural peace is precisely the social and political vividness, present even in the invective, which can originate only in a natural and national surrounding.

Mythical and natural elegies, on the contrary, are withdrawn from the world; they lack the blood of political and social actuality. When, in opposition to this, the Deutero-Isaiah and Ezekiel describe the future glory of the new Jerusalem, then their very patriotism is, properly speaking, only universalism. In the remnant of Israel the people became entirely changed. And for Ezekiel it is even the *resurrected* ones who are revived from the dead bones. However, it is always the historically idealized nation that still constitutes the basic foundation of the old election to spread the true worship of God to all peoples of the earth.

59. Thus monotheism is the immediate cause of Messianism as well as of the concept of *world history*, as the history of one mankind. Without the unique God, the idea of one mankind could not arise. And without the idea of mankind, history would remain a problem of knowledge of the past of peoples, on the basis of the past of one's own people.

National history, however, is in general not yet history. It cannot even be a methodological foundation, because it cannot be the point of departure for scientific orientation. Mankind must just become first the object of *human love* in order to become the point of orientation for the problem of history.

Deuteronomy makes it clear how the national history of Israel is an idealization from the point of view of its historic task, to which it is called as its future. Therefore, history here, as the literature of *historical writing*, is so natural and truthful. Idealization, if it is guided by a true idea, is everywhere, even subjectively, the best guide to truthfulness. This historical writing blamed the ancestors of the people without pardon when they relinquished the true God, although it was concerned only indirectly with these ancestors, because the real ancestor is uniquely and exclusively the unique God.

60. The wondrous *names* which Isaiah gives the Messiah indicate his authorship of history as the history of the future. The Messiah is introduced as a *child* and as born of a *young woman*. And yet he becomes the central point of the contemporary world. "With us God" (Immanuel). Although he is a child, he is also called father, namely, "the everlasting father." This opposition to the name "child" perhaps explains the wondrous name of "the counselor of the mighty God" [Isa. 9:5]. He sits in the council of the future for the world of man. Thus "the shoot out of the stock of Jesse" [Isa. 11:1], as a child, significantly becomes the Atlas of the future.

In such images the concept of history ripens. The Darwinian theory cannot be the teleology of the human race because the ethical sense of mankind requires its own teleology. Only under this one-sidedness of morality could the thought of world history originate, as the thought of the future, of which the child is the expressive image.

61. We have previously recognized creation as providence. But the end of providence is Messianism, the historical providence. For "man doth not live by bread only" (Deut. 8:3). Bread stands here for earthly happiness in general. This saying wards off the idea of eudaemonism. The value of human life lies not in happiness but rather in suffering. The social viewpoint directs the vision as well as the creation of history. This deepest insight grew out of national politics. The messianic concept of world history is focused upon the suffering of the majority of mankind hitherto.

XIII. The historical concept of Messianism produced a concept, namely, that of the *vicarious* sufferer, which will now be elucidated. This concept seems to contradict the fundamental concept of ethical autonomy, because morality in all its stages has to be one's own deed, and does not admit of any representative. However, this autonomy means only that a representative for guilt is excluded, but not for *suffering*. Social insight and feeling have disclosed the way this distinction is to be understood, and this understanding has the value almost of a new revelation. Only through the above distinction can the identity between God's justice and love become understandable. Man's sufferings become "chastisements of love."[51]

Consequently the man, the Messiah, is conceivable as representative not of the guilt of men and peoples but of the suffering, which otherwise would have to be their punishment. Only through the Messiah's taking the earthly suffering of man upon his shoulders does he become the ideal image of the man of the future, the image of mankind, as the unity of all peoples. He becomes through this not a Tantalus or Sisyphus but the Atlas who supports the moral world of the future.

Only through this concept of the representation of human suffering could the messianic concept of history be fulfilled. For the *concept of power* in history is only naturalistic, anthropological, ethnological, or nationalistic. The ethical concept of world history must be basically free of all eudaemonism. Therefore, power cannot be the standard of ethical history.

62. The *Christological* interpretation of God's servant has, therefore, mistaken the concept of history, because it made of the representative of suffering the representative vicar of guilt. There is no such thing, and cannot be, inasmuch as ethics remains the methodological norm of religion. Only God can take guilt upon himself. This is the love of his justice. But the ideal image of man would be distorted if someone were to assume the guilt of men, which would at the same time relieve man of it. Man, however, cannot be relieved of his consciousness of guilt. The ideal image of man therefore cannot be such as to detach from man the task which he himself would not permit to be detached from him. Thus, through this representative of guilt, not only is God's essence curtailed, but man's being is also distorted. In Christology the Messiah becomes God, but disregarding this difference, he, as the representative of guilt, cannot be the ideal of man.

On the contrary, the Messiah, who is the representative of suffering, brings with his dark shadow the most shining light upon the history of mankind. Poverty is the moral defect of previous history. But the poor have become the pious. And the pious are the forerunners of the Messiah. The representative of suffering brings into the world this teaching, and with it the foundation of the ethical concept of history: that every eudaemonistic appearance is nothing but an illusion; and that the genuine value of life for the entire history of peoples lies in moral ideas and is therefore represented among men only by those who are accredited as carriers of these ideas.

It does not have to be the case, and certainly it shall be different in the future, that there should be only tragic representatives of morality. This is a conception of dramatic poetry, to which ethics in no way has to consent.

However, history, because it is directed by ethics, is also directed by its method and therefore built upon the experience of economics, law, and state. *Experience* is indeed not the methodological basis but the factual, original material with which the method has to begin. This is the path which the prophet intuitively takes by virtue of the share of reason in religion; poverty is for him the objectification of human suffering, and these poor ones, who already have been acknowledged as the pious ones, become the representatives of human suffering.

63. What is the ultimate meaning of this representation, and what does the ethical concept of history gain by it? The gain is not only in the negative value of turning away from all eudaemonistic desires; this turn from the superficiality of earthly happiness is also the first step toward the positive elevation to the dignity of man.

Why is *humility* the most sure sign of piety? Ascetic disdain of earthly things is not its true meaning, but rather opposition to the acceptance of superficial human reality as displayed in power, in splendor, in success, in dominion, in autocracy, in imperialism; as an opposition to all these signs of human arrogance, to vain pride and to presumption, humility constitutes the counterpart of the ideal man.

At this point the distinction between—and the progress from—the notion of the *pious to that of the humble* must be delineated. The pious man represents the isolated I; the humble man bears the whole of mankind in his heart. Therefore he can become the representative of suffering, because he can fulfill his moral existence only in suffering. He knows the guilt of men; how could the poor man not know it since he suffers from the injustice of the world's economy? Although he cannot unburden men from their guilt, he suffers under the weight of a consciousness of guilt that includes his fellowmen.

And while he suffers *about* them, he suffers *for* them. For his suffering is the true, the moral one, which men in their guilt would not be able to undergo, however much they were punished in their bodily pleasures. The humble man is therefore the true sufferer, he is the representative of suffering. Only he is able to undergo suffering in its moral essence. He is not only the representative of suffering but even more the only true bearer of it.

64. Only now arises out of the messianic point of view a *tragic*

concept of man. The ideal man suffers. The Messiah is seized by the distress of mankind in its entirety. But even poetry, with all its magic, indeed every form of art, distorts the pure image of this sufferer of mankind. He is, therefore, as much without beauty, without the attractions of art, as he is without any signs of heroism. He is diseased and weak and despised by men, yet he will enter the new world, even if only riding upon an ass. His symbols are the old symbols of the image of the Messiah: that "with the breath of his lips shall he slay the wicked" [Isa. 11:4]; that he will restore justice and peace on earth. Humility is the positive power which defeats all eudaemonism. Humility, which makes representative suffering the end result of the historical and social insights of monotheism, is the climax of Messianism.

The Jewish doctrine of virtue places *humility* above all the virtues.[52] It is very close to modesty, which in itself is of fundamental significance for man, but descriptions of it make it clear that humility is something more than modesty. There is a convincing example that supports this remark. Moses is called "very meek, above all the men that were upon the face of the earth" [Num. 12:3]. And certainly humility here means more than modesty, although the boundary is not exactly delineated.

However, even God's own humility is stressed. A talmudic passage that has been incorporated into the evening prayer at the conclusion of the Sabbath says: "In every passage where thou findest the greatness of God mentioned, there thou findest also His humility." This arrangement is confirmed by the Pentateuch, the Prophets, and the Writings. Now it is true that God's attributes have only the meaning of attributes of action; as such they disclose the archetypal image of morality. In fact, the passages referred to in the three groups of writings describe humility only as God's concern for the poor in their different manifestations. God's humility is his willingness to stoop to help those who suffer. The powerful effect of suffering on God has already been recognized. It is, then, only the transference of this to the Messiah which, in his vicarious suffering, signifies his humility which is the peak of humanity.

65.*XIV*. The "Servant of the Eternal" is the Messiah, and as such he has replaced the "scion of David." But the prophetic idea never became abstract and secluded from the world; how could it become so in the messianic idea? If God's servant can no longer mean the King's scion, he cannot, on the other hand, be alien to the national memory, to the national history. The Jewish commentators recognized early that this "Servant of the Eternal" can only be the servant in the sense that every Israelite ought to be. Thus God's servant became for them unambiguously the people of Israel itself.

As the national point of view has always awakened in monotheism the messianic idea, so it happened in this case. The image of the poor, as the suffering man, lights up and brightens only the social horizon. If, however, the poor sufferer is the people of Israel and its messianic perfection, the "remnant of Israel," then the historical picture evolves, and the people of Israel comes before the council of the peoples. And only at this point does suffering as historical power reach an elevation that surpasses social misery.

The misery of the Jewish history does not begin with the exile, for the loss of the national state has already been determined by the messianic idea. On this, however, is based the *tragedy of the Jewish people* in all its historical depth. How can a people continue to live and fulfill its messianic task, when it is deprived of the universal human protection the state gives to a people? And yet this is the situation of the Jewish people, and such must be the meaning of Jewish history, if the messianic idea constitutes this meaning.

He who recognizes the world-historical idea of messianic mankind as the task of the Jewish people must recognize in Jewish history the signpost of this goal. The question cannot be asked whether God could have arranged it differently, or in the future would arrange it differently; rather, the course of history itself informs us of the teaching which is contained conceptually in Messianism.

66. But Jewish history, considered as history, that is, insofar as it exhibits moral ideas, is a continuous chain of human, of national, suffering. These servants of the Lord have always been despised and pierced through, cut off from the land of life. And despite the fact that astonishment at the continuation of this oddity among the peoples never ceased, what the text so properly expresses always remains true: "And in his generation, *who was mindful of it?*" The messianic people suffers vicariously for mankind. This opinion about the mission of Israel cannot be an exaggeration, if the messianic realization of monotheism is the historical task of the religion of Judaism.

The vicarious sufferer is the solicitor who intercedes for the sin of the peoples. This is considered to be the last word in that chapter [Isa. 53]; but it is not the final word. The idealism of the future breaks through. God's servant is not dead because he has been cut off from living, but because "it pleased the Lord to crush him by disease . . . that he might see his seed prolong his days . . . and that the purpose of the Lord might prosper by his hand" [Isa. 53:10]. With this kind of living-on, tragic life and incurable death are surmounted.

67. Every injustice in world history is an accusation against mankind, and consequently the misery of the Jews has been at all times a great rebuke against the other peoples. But from the messianic point of view, a light of theodicy is cast even upon this riddle of world history. Considered from the point of view of eudaemonism, the suffering of the Jews is, to be sure, a misfortune. But the messianic calling of Israel sheds another light upon its own earthly history. As Israel suffers, according to the prophet, for the pagan worshipers, so Israel to this very day suffers vicariously for the faults and wrongs which still hinder the realization of monotheism.

And this suffering need not be limited in particular to the actual or nominal bearer of monotheism. The people of Israel, as God's servant, according to the Talmud, has already received in its bosom *"the pious of the peoples of the world."* Far from the continuing vicarious suffering of Israel offending the other religions, they also, according to the acknowledged doctrine of Judaism, have their fully entitled share in this messianic suffering.

And through this widening of the national limits of suffering, which is demanded by humanitarian ethics, the true sense of the messianic idea is satisfied and fulfilled. It belongs to the warding off of the idea of eudaemonism, that the external doctrinal and national limitations should be removed, if the symbolism of God's servant should reach its true historical significance, its pure symbolism. This purity is demanded by the ideal image of the vicarious sufferer. The people too, the remnant of Israel, is a symbolic concept for this ideal image. This idealization of the remnant is the completion of the idealization of the Messiah.

CHAPTER XIV

The Messianic References in the Prophetic Writings

1. Let us start with Hosea. First of all he stands up for the kingdom of Judah against the disloyal kingdom of Israel. However, both states are to be united again through God's help; God will make a covenant for them with the animals of the fields and the birds of the heavens, so that no bow or sword shall come again to their lands. "And I will betroth thee unto Me forever; yea, I will betroth thee unto Me in righteousness, and in justice, and in loving kindness, and in compassion. And I will betroth thee unto Me in faithfulness: and thou shalt know the Eternal" (Hos. 2:21-22). The image of the *marriage* of God with Israel dominates the entire religious imagination of the prophet.

Hosea, therefore, begins his prophecy with the simile of the unfaithful wife. The power of the religious symbolism is weakened, even destroyed, through the philistine and narrow-minded supposition that the prophet was unhappily married. God's marriage with Israel could rather appear to be unhappy. Therefore, Hosea revels in a naturalistic poetry describing the future intimate relationship between God and Israel: "I will be as the dew unto Israel: he shall blossom as the lily, and cast forth his roots as Lebanon" (Hos. 14:5). They shall return home. Nobody shall in the future further recall an idol. And they shall "seek the Eternal their God, and David their king; and shall come trembling unto the Eternal and His goodness in the end of days" (Hos. 3:5). This last is probably not yet the precise expression of Messianism, but merely means the escape from the present, pointing toward the future, pointing back to the past.

2. Amos, Hosea's contemporary, also begins, according to the common text, with an attack against the seceding kingdom: "I will not utterly destroy the house of Jacob . . . in that day I will raise up the

tabernacle of David, that is fallen, and close up the breaches thereof; and I will raise up his ruins, and I will build it as in the days of old . . . behold, the days come, saith the Eternal, that the plowman shall overtake the reaper, and the treader of grapes him that soweth seed; and the mountains shall drop sweet wine, and all the hills shall melt . . . and I will turn the captivity of My people Israel . . . and I will plant them upon their land, and they shall no more be plucked up out of their land which I have given them" (Amos 9:8-15).

The significance of Amos for the messianic idea does not lie in his reminiscence of the "tabernacle of David," which, by the way, is still different from the 'Throne of David," but rather in his zeal against the *worship of the sacrifice* and consequently in his moral and chastising preaching against the peoples, as well as against Judah and Israel. He also condemns Israel together with the peoples.

He is the first to give moral meaning to the popular belief in the "Days of Yahveh." "It shall come to pass in that day . . . that I will cause the sun to go down at noon, and will darken the earth in the clear day" (Amos 8:9). But from the threat of punishment he elevates himself to hope: "Behold, the days come, saith the Lord the Eternal, that I will send famine in the land, not a famine of bread, nor a thirst for water, but of hearing the words of the Eternal. And they shall wander from sea to sea, and from the north even to the east; they shall run to and fro to seek the word of the Eternal, and shall not find it" (Amos 8:11-12). This hunger, this search for *God's word* only, appears here as the dawn of the new meaning of the Day of Yahveh. Only after this is Amos able to prophesy the restoration of Israel.

3. Micah is akin to Amos in his moral aim. He is zealous against idol worship and demands a "House of the Lord, for all peoples." The peoples make war upon Israel, but out of the tribe of David shall rise a ruler, under whose rule all the peoples will not learn the art of war any more. The morality is the soul of Micah's Messianism. "But in the end of days it shall come to pass that the mountain of the Eternal's house shall be established in the top of the mountains, and it shall be exalted above the hills; and people shall flow unto it. And many nations shall go and say: come ye, and let us go up to the mountain of the Eternal, and to the house of the God of Jacob; and He will teach us of His ways, and we will walk in His paths; for out of Zion shall go forth the law, and the word of the Eternal from Jerusalem. And He shall judge between many people, and shall decide concerning mighty nations afar off; and they shall beat their swords into plowshares, and their spears into pruninghooks: nation shall not

lift up a sword against nation, neither shall they learn war any more. But they shall sit every man under his vine and under his fig tree; and none shall make them afraid: for the mouth of the Eternal of hosts has spoken . . . Now many nations are assembled against thee, that say: 'Let her be defiled, and let our eye gaze upon Zion.' But they know not the thoughts of the Eternal, neither understand they His counsel; for He hath gathered them as the sheaves to the threshing-floor. Arise and thresh, O daughter of Zion: for I will make thy horn iron and I will make thy hoofs brass: and thou shalt beat in pieces many peoples; and thou shalt devote their gain unto the Eternal, and their substance unto the *Lord of the whole earth*" (Mic. 4:1-4; 11-13). National reminiscences permeated thoughts of the future divine dominion of the world.

4. The fifth chapter, too, begins with a *new* David from Bethlehem and ascends to the "remnant of Jacob." "But thou, Bethlehem Ephratah, which are little to be among the thousands of Judah, out of thee shall one come forth unto Me that is to be ruler in Israel; whose going forth are from of old, from ancient days . . . and he shall stand, and shall feed his flock in the strength of the Eternal, in the majesty of the name of the Eternal his God; and they shall abide, for then shall he be great unto the ends of the earth . . . and the *remnant of Jacob* shall be in the midst of many peoples as dew from the Eternal, as showers upon the grass, that are not looked for from man, nor awaiteth at the hands of the sons of men. And the remnant of Jacob shall be among the nations, in the midst of many peoples, as a lion among the beasts of the forest, as a young lion among the flocks of sheep, who, if he go through, treadeth down, and teareth in pieces, and there is none to deliver . . . and it shall come to pass on that day . . . that I will cut off thy horses out of the midst of thee, and I will destroy thy chariots; and I will cut off the cities of thy land, and will throw down all thy strongholds; and I will cut off witchcrafts out of thy hand; and thou shalt have no more soothsayers; and I will cut off the graven images and thy pillars out of the midst of thee; and thou shalt no more worship the work of thy hands" [Mic. 5:1-12].

Very characteristic are the two similes of the dew and the lion that follow one another and signify welfare and misfortune. The Messiah must bring both. If welfare precedes, as is the case here, then the goal is put forth first, for which misfortune—the destruction of the peoples—is only a means. For this means of destruction is exercised also upon Israel, as the following verses attest.

5. The image of God's house on top of the mountain, to which all

peoples will flock and where they shall not learn war any more, is common to Isaiah and Micah (Isa. 2:1-5). However, Isaiah assumes his own style in the same chapter: "Enter into the rock, and hide thee in the dust, from before the terror of the Eternal, and from the glory of His majesty" (Isa. 2:10). "When He ariseth to shake mightily the earth" (Isa. 2:19). "The lofty looks of man shall be brought low, and the haughtiness of men shall be bowed down, and the Eternal alone shall be exalted in that day. For the Eternal of hosts hath a day upon all that is proud and lofty, and upon every one that is lifted up, and he shall be brought low . . . cease ye from man, in whose nostrils is a breath; for how little is he to be accounted!" (Isa. 2:11-22).

This is in the style of Hamlet. The following third chapter predicts heavy punishments, first for the bad administration of justice, and then for the pride and haughtiness of the women. Thereupon, the fourth chapter begins again with the message of salvation: "In that day shall the growth of the Eternal be beautiful and glorious, and the fruit of the land excellent and comely for them that are escaped of Israel. And it shall come to pass that he that is left in Zion, and he that remaineth in Jerusalem shall be called *holy*, even every one that is written unto life in Jerusalem. When the Lord shall have washed away the filth of the daughters of Zion, and shall have purged the blood of Jerusalem from the midst thereof by the spirit of judgment, and by the spirit of destruction" (Isa. 4:2-4). Already here there is a pointing to those who are left over, the later remnant.

6. The new state, after the destruction of the old, still needs for its preparation much more poetry. "The people that walked in darkness have seen a great light . . . for a child is born unto us, a son is given unto us: and the government is upon his shoulder: and his name shall be called Wonderful in counsel. God the mighty God, The everlasting Father, The Ruler of Peace. That the government may be increased, and of peace there shall be no end, upon the throne of David, and upon his kingdom, to establish it, and to uphold it through justice and through righteousness from henceforth even for ever" (Isa. 9:1,5-6; cf. p. 263). Although the throne of David is here newly established through law and justice, a new age is announced through the child with the wonderful names, of which one points to the counsel of God the wonderful and another of which at the same time makes the child into the father of eternity. Now the Day of the Lord can no longer be thought of seriously as close at hand, for the new time is to mean a new eternity.

7. The same thought is continued in chapter eleven: "And there shall come forth a shoot out of the stock of Jesse, and a twig shall

grow out of his roots: and the spirit of the Eternal shall rest upon him, the spirit of wisdom and understanding, the spirit of counsel and might, the spirit of knowledge of the fear of the Eternal; and his delight shall be in the fear of the Eternal: and he shall not judge after the sight of his eyes, neither decide after the hearing of his ears; but with righteousness shall he judge the poor, and decide with equity for the meek of the earth: and he shall smite the land with the rod of his mouth, and with the breath of his lips shall he slay the wicked. And righteousness shall be the girdle of his loins, and faithfulness the girdle of his reins" (Isa. 11:1-5). The spirit of counsel is here particularly stressed, so that the meaning of one of the wondrous appellations of the Messiah is explained. But a holy spirit, which should distinguish the Messiah from men in general, is not attributed to him, whereas his delight in the fear of the Lord is expressly acknowledged. Furthermore, the poor and the meek are the special object of his administration of justice.

8. Now, however, the poetry of the *natural peace* appears, which brought about the confusion of the Messianic with the Golden Age. "And the wolf shall dwell with the lamb, and the leopard shall lie down with the kid; and the calf and the young lion and the fatling together; and a little child shall lead them. And the cow and the bear shall feed; their young ones shall lie down together; and the lion shall eat straw like the ox. And the sucking child shall play on the hole of the asp, and the weaned child shall put his hand on the basilisk's den. They shall not hurt nor destroy in all My holy mountain; for the earth shall be full of the knowledge of the Eternal, as the waters cover the sea" (Isa. 11:6-9; cf. Hos. 2:20).

Two supplements are added here: first, the disappearance of *evil*, and, furthermore, the fullness of *knowledge* of God upon the earth. The development of the messianic ideas is based upon these conditions. "And it shall come to pass in that day, that the root of Jesse that standeth for an ensign of the peoples, unto him shall the nations seek; and his resting-place shall be glorious." Finally, a homecoming for the "remnant of Israel" is predicted, similar to its liberation from Egypt (Isa. 11:10-16).

9. The following chapters predict the decline of Babylon, Assyria, the Philistines, Moab, Damascus, and Israel, and finally Egypt also. "How can you say unto Pharaoh: 'I am the son of the wise, the son of ancient kings'? Where are they, then, thy wise men? And let them tell thee now; and let them know what the Eternal of hosts hath purposed concerning Egypt" (Isa. 19:11-12). The prophet triumphs over the wisdom of Egypt, but this triumph is acknowledged in a mes-

sianic way: "And the Eternal shall make Himself known to Egypt, and the Egyptians shall know the Eternal that day; yea, they shall worship with sacrifice and offering, and shall vow a vow unto the Eternal and shall perform it . . . in that day shall Israel be the *third* with Egypt and with Assyria, a blessing in the *midst* of the earth; for that the Eternal of hosts hath blessed him, saying: 'Blessed be Egypt My people and Assyria the work of My hands, and Israel Mine inheritance'" (Isa. 19:21-25). Here a highpoint in the messianic idea of the unification of peoples is reached. The anomaly of the election of Israel is resolved: Israel is named the third among these peoples, which previously were doomed to destruction, but to which God's blessing is now granted. God now calls even Egypt "My people," and Assyria, "the work of My hands." What meaning can there still be in God's "possession," and "inheritance" of Israel?

10. The *cosmopolitan* idea is expressed even more strongly: "And in this mountain will the Eternal of hosts make unto *all* peoples a feast of fat things, a feast of wines on the lees, of fat things full of marrow, of wines on the lees well refined. And He will destroy in this mountain the face of the *covering* that is cast over all peoples, and the *veil* that is spread over all nations. He will swallow up death for ever; and the Lord the Eternal will wipe away tears from all faces; and the reproach of His people will He take away from all of the earth" (Isa. 25:6-8).

Again, the idea of the unification of all the peoples is advanced to a new critical clarification. A cover and a veil are spread over the peoples as long as they are not united by God. The cover is a cloak of sorrow, or at least a screen, and the veil is philologically reminiscent of an idol. If, however, the peoples become parts in God's work of creation, then they will recognize their unity, and their difference, like a cover, will be removed from them.

When the antagonism of the peoples has been conquered by the messianic idea, who can doubt that then also tears will be effaced from the countenance of men? Although it remains uncertain whether the prophet was thinking about the disappearance of death mainly in connection with death caused by war, the cessation of death is nevertheless only a simile, one of the many which describe the peace of nature. What is of importance is expressed in the final clause: God will efface the tears from every countenance. God will bring true consolation for every suffering. He will not abolish suffering and let it disappear entirely, but he will give to men and *peoples* the suitable consolation. This is the meaning of the simile.

11. It is only a mitigation of the same simile, when in another

connection it further says: "And in that day shall the deaf hear the words of a book, and the eyes of the blind shall see out of obscurity and out of darkness. The humble also shall increase their joy in the Eternal, and the neediest among men shall exult in the Holy One of Israel. For the terrible one is brought to nought, and the scorner ceaseth, and all they that watch for iniquity are cut off; that make a man an offender by words, and lay a snare for him that reproveth in the gate, and turn aside the just with a thing of nought" (Isa. 29:18-21). What happens with the deaf and blind is not much less miraculous than what happens with death; all these examples are unmistakably similes. And this is also a simile: "Moreover the light of the moon shall be as the light of the sun, and the light of the sun shall be sevenfold, as the light of the seven days, in the day that the Eternal bindeth up the bruise of His people, and healeth the stroke of their wound" (Isa. 30:26). Misfortune and welfare alternate almost regularly in these predictions. It is wrong to distinguish the prophets according to these watchwords; they are almost always intertwined.

In one of the immediately following chapters, in which the destruction of Jerusalem is predicted, the annunciation of salvation is suddenly introduced. There it says in the midst of this context: "Until the spirit be poured upon us from on high, and the wilderness become a fruitful field, and the fruitful field be counted for a forest. Then justice shall dwell in the wilderness, and righteousness shall abide in the fruitful field. And the work of righteousness shall be peace; and the effect of righteousness quietness and confidence for ever" (Isa. 32:15-17). The Messiah is here called "the spirit from on high," and his effects are *peace* and quietness and confidence, as the works of righteousness. Even in those passages in which the prophet depicts the Messiah only with regard to Israel, it is not merely the prosperity of the land which is prophesied but prosperity conditioned by righteousness as well. And the prosperity itself is comprised in peace, which in turn is the general symbol for the peace of the peoples, the symbol of the Messiah for the peoples.

The song of the pslams (Ps. 67:3-6 and 68:32-33) is similar: "That Thy way may be known upon earth, Thy salvation among all nations," and "Sing unto God, ye kingdoms of the earth."

12. Zephaniah, one generation before the exile, announces God's judgment over the peoples of the world and over Judah. However, he too, in the midst of his speech full of indignation suddenly says: "For then I will turn to the people a pure language, that they may all call upon the name of the Eternal to serve Him with one shoulder . . . and I will leave in the midst of thee an afflicted and poor people,

and they shall take refuge in the name of the Eternal. The remnant of Israel shall not do iniquity, nor speak lies, neither shall a deceitful tongue be found in their mouth" [Zeph. 3:9, 12-13].

The prophet formulates important matters for the Messianic Day, the first of which is the pure lip and one shoulder for the divine worship of all peoples. Furthermore he defines the remnant of Israel as the afflicted and poor people, who are remote from injustice and deceit. But in the sentence that follows the simile of the pure lip, he also says: "From beyond the rivers of Ethiopia shall they bring My suppliants, even the daughter of My dispersed, as Mine offering" (Zeph. 3:10). This is a new motif, which we will find repeated in the Deutero-Isaiah (Isa. 66:20). The messianic idea of the conversation of the peoples is here united with the idea of Israel's restoration, which is expressed in the delicate manner that the peoples themselves will give Israel's prisoners as a *present* to God.

13. To harmonize this discord becomes the fundamental problem of Jeremiah. He, too, suddenly interrupts his speech, full of expressions of punishment, with the hopeful admonition: "Return, O backsliding children, for I am a husband unto you: and I will take you one of a city, and two of a family, and I will bring you to Zion; and I will give you shepherds according to My heart, who shall feed you with knowledge and understanding. And it shall come to pass, when ye are multiplied and increased in the land, in those days, saith the Eternal, they shall say no more: The ark of the covenant of the Eternal; neither shall it come to mind; neither shall they make mention of it; neither shall they miss it; neither shall it be made any more. At that time they shall call Jerusalem the throne of the Eternal and all the nations shall be gathered unto it, to the name of the Eternal, to Jerusalem; neither shall they walk any more after the stubborness of their evil heart" (Jer. 3:14-17). Immediately after this he promises the return of Judah and Israel to the land of their fathers.

In his speech castigating the faithless shepherds "that destroy and scatter the sheep of My pasture, saith the Eternal . . . And I will gather the remnant of my flock out of all the countries whither I have driven them, and will bring them again to their folds; and they shall be fruitful and multiply. And I will set up shepherds over them which shall feed them; and they shall fear no more, nor be dismayed, neither shall any be lacking, saith the Eternal. Behold, the days come, saith the Eternal, that I will raise unto David a righteous shoot, and he shall reign as king and prosper, and shall execute justice and righteousness in the land. In his days Judah shall be saved, and Israel shall dwell safely; and this is his name whereby he shall be called, the Eternal is our righteousness. Therefore, behold, the days come, saith the Eternal, that they shall no more say, 'As the Eternal liveth that brought up the children of Israel out of the land of Egypt'; but: 'As the Eternal liveth, that brought up and that led the seed of the house of Israel out of the north country, and from all the countries whither I had driven them'; and they shall dwell in their own land" (Jer. 23:1-8).

The polemic against national obduracy, which contradicts the messianic idea, cannot be carried out more rigorously than in this renunciation of the historical and at the same time religious origin of the nation: the liberation from Egypt. And it is not the return home again which is to excel the first liberation; rather, the excellence of the future liberation is based on the fact that justice and righteousness will rule in the land, that God himself will be acknowledged, as in Isaiah, as the Holy one of Israel, as "our Righteousness" in the words of the quotation above. The scion of David is therefore also called "the righteous scion."

14. In view of this righteousness, which is the shield of the new kingdom, the repudiation of the false shepherds means specifically that they are the representatives of the whole of the previously existing teaching. A new teaching is opposed to the old one, and what always matters to the prophet is the *new* teaching.[53] Even where the prophet speaks with the most glowing patriotic passion and with the tears of an elegiac poet, even there he does not terminate his hopes with the announcement of God's love, of consolation, of memory of past love, and he does not content himself with this saying for the new kingdom: "The Eternal bless thee, O habitation of righteousness, and mountain of holiness" (Jer. 31:23). Rather he again opens up the old wound: "Behold, the days come, saith the Eternal, that I will make a *new* covenant with the house of Israel, and with the house of Judah; not according to the covenant that I make with their fathers in the day that I took them by the hand to bring them out of the land of Egypt; forasmuch as they broke my covenant, although I was a lord over them, saith the Eternal. But this is the covenant that I will make with the house of Israel after those days, saith the Eternal, I will put My law in their inward parts, and in their heart will I write it; and I will be their God, and they shall be My people. And they shall teach no more every man his neighbor, and every man his brother saying, 'Know the Eternal,' for they shall all know Me, from the least of them unto the greatest of them, saith the Eternal; their sin I will remember no more. Thus saith the Eternal, who giveth the sun for a light by day, and the ordinances of the moon and of the

stars for a light by night, who stirreth up the sea that the waves thereof roar; the Eternal of hosts is His name: If those ordinances depart from before Me, saith the Eternal, then the seed of Israel also shall cease from being a nation before Me forever" (Jer. 31:31-36).

15. Again we see the heart of the patriot in harmony with the preaching of the new messianic teaching. God will make a new covenant with Israel, inscribing the Torah in their hearts. And this new covenant he distinguishes from the old one precisely by that determination which contains the foundation of the new age of the world: in this future age the knowledge of God will be a common good for all.[54]

In this universality of knowledge, God will prove himself to be the true savior who forgives sins. Much more important than the statement about putting the teaching into the heart of man is the following practical norm for the religion and morality of the future: the knowledge of God will become the common good of all.

16. A subsequent chapter is connected with this purification from all guilt: "Behold, the days come, saith the Eternal, that I will perform that good word which I have spoken concerning the house of Israel and concerning the house of Judah. In those days, and at that time, will I cause the shoot of righteousness to grow up unto David; and he shall execute justice and righteousness in the land" (Jer. 33:14, 15). Under this repeatedly stated presupposition of righteousness of the scion of David, the continuity of the throne of David as well as the Levitic priests is assured. But the prophet has in the same way predicted the restoration of Egypt, Moab, Ammon, and Edom. To all evil neighbors he prophesied exile and restoration. "And afterwards it [Egypt] shall be inhabited, as in the days of old, saith the Eternal" (Jer. 46:26). "Yet will I turn the captivity of Moab in the end of days, saith the Eternal. Thus far is the judgment of Moab" (Jer. 48:47). "But afterward I will bring back the captivity of the children of Ammon, saith the Eternal" (Jer. 49:6). "But it shall come to pass in the end of days, that I will bring back the captivity of Elam, saith the Eternal" (Jer. 49:39).

17. And in general, Jeremiah proclaimed this restoration for all *neighboring peoples:* "And it shall come to pass, after that I have plucked them up, I will again have compassion on them, and will bring them back, every man to his heritage, and every man to his land. And it shall come to pass, if they will diligently learn the ways of My people, to swear by My name, 'As the Eternal liveth,' even as they taught My people to swear by Baal; then shall they be built up in the midst of my people" (Jer. 12:15,16).

The apparent restriction that the evil neighbors will be spared only if they acknowledge God may seem objectionable. To overcome this we must first remember that they led the Israelites astray and then that they will be built again "in the midst of My people." This indicates that they will be received into messianic Israel.

18. Moreover, the prophet believes in the *conversion* of peoples: "O Eternal, my strength, and my stronghold, and my refuge in the day of affliction, unto Thee shall the nations come from the ends of the earth, and shall say: 'our fathers have inherited nought but lies, vanity and things wherein there is no profit.' Shall a man make unto himself gods and they are no gods?" (Jer. 16:19,20). Consequently, the conversion of the peoples is thought of by the prophet as self-conversion, as the recognition of the nothingness of the gods.

19. Ezekiel appeared during and even before the exile. We have already considered the difficulty of his historical situation. Whereas his predecessors took up the fight against the world with the moral ideas of monotheism alone, we have to recognize in him a connection between idealism and realism. At this point it is important to bear in mind that his practical sense, with which he adheres to the sacrificial order, although he transforms the sacrifice in accordance with his ethical spirit, does not distinguish him entirely from his predecessors. Isaiah and Jeremiah fight against the sacrifice, but they also do not reject it unambiguously for the future, rather, it remains with them in the nimbus of the symbolic material of the historical tradition.

With regard to attachment to the other rituals of the Pentateuch, Ezekiel also preserved his reformatory independence and in no way made himself absolutely dependent upon his predecessors. For a methodological characterization there remains, therefore, only the question of whether and how Ezekiel as a political, historical, and patriotic realist at the same time preserved and advanced the ideal meaning, which, according to the understanding of Deuteronomy, already constitutes the genuine foundation of monotheism. His position with regard to the messianic idea is best suited to the examination of this question.

Again it is characteristic of Ezekiel that his message of salvation suddenly interrupts a message of disaster. And particularly impressive is his new beginning: "Son of man, as for thy brethren, even thy brethren, the men of thy kindred, and all the house of Israel, all of them, concerning whom the inhabitants of Jerusalem have said: get you far from the Eternal! unto us is this land given for a possession. Therefore say: Thus saith the Lord the Eternal: although I have removed them far off among the nations, and although I have scattered them among the countries . . . therefore say, thus saith the Lord, the

Eternal; I will even gather you from the peoples, and assemble you out of the countries where ye have been scattered, and I will give you the land of Israel" (Ezek. 11:15-17).

Does he, however, remain at this merely political restoration? Or should one be satisfied with what the next verse demands, to take away "all the abominations"? On the contrary, the following verse says: "And I will give them *one heart*, and I will put a new spirit within you; and I will remove the stony heart out of their flesh, and will give them a heart of flesh" (Ezek. 11:19).

Ezekiel not only puts the "new spirit," already known from Isaiah and Jeremiah, into the inner man, but also the one heart is there, the new heart, which is freed from discordant opinions and passions. Inwardness is for him, too, the norm and guarantor of worship.

20. Nationalism in its arrogant shape is the most offensive antithesis to Messianism. The prophet stands up against it: "Son of man, cause Jerusalem to know her abominations, and say: thus saith the Lord the Eternal unto Jerusalem: thine *origin* and thy nativity is of the land of Canaanite; the Amorite was thy father and thy mother was a Hittite" (Ezek. 16:1-3); and he repeats and even completes this line of thought: "And thine elder sister is Samaria . . . and thy younger sister . . . Sodom" (Ezek. 16:46). And just as the prophet refutes the self-conceit of nationalism, so it is typical, not only for his poetic power but for his Messianism as well, that he terminates his tidings of disaster for the peoples with a message of salvation, in which the warm human heart of the prophet beats.

21. The second part of his message is concerned with the future of Israel. The prophet declaims with zeal against the false shepherds: "And I will set up one shepherd over them, and he shall feed them, even My servant David; he shall feed them, and he shall be their shepherd. And I the Eternal will be their God, and my servant David a prince among them" (Ezek. 34:23,24). The shepherd becomes a prince, because God alone is the proper shepherd. With this message the chapter closes, after it has proclaimed the "covenant of peace" with the animals also: "And ye My sheep, the sheep of My pasture are men, and I am your God" (Ezek. 34:31). The grouping together of flock and man is entirely in the style of the "son of man." You are my flock; for you are men, for whom I have pity. This is the way the prophet of the "son of man" lets his God speak.

22. Ezekiel also establishes an important connection between his new theory of *repentance* and the messianic idea. The purification of Israel is thought of in connection with "the sanctification of God's name" among the peoples of the world: "And I will sanctify My great

name, which hath been profaned among the nations, which ye have profaned in the midst of them; and the nations shall know that I am the Eternal" (Ezek. 36:23). Now, however, this sanctification is achieved in the purification of Israel: "Then I will sprinkle clean water upon you, and ye shall be clean; from all your uncleanliness, and from all your idols, will I cleanse you. A new heart also will I give you, and a new spirit will I put within you, and I will take away the stony heart out of your flesh, and I will give you an heart of flesh. And I will put My spirit within you" (Ezek. 36:25-27). In this passage it is God who will put a new spirit and a new heart into man, while for Ezekiel's theory of repentance the variant reading is important, according to which men themselves have to make the new heart (cf. p. 194).

In the next chapter Ezekiel repeats this thought of purification through God, but adds: "And the nations shall know that I am the Eternal that sanctify Israel" (Ezek. 37:28).

23. This chapter begins with the interpretation of the traditional myth of *resurrection*. God's question to the prophet is as follows: "Son of man can these bones live? And I answered, O Lord, Eternal, Thou knowest" (Ezek. 37:3). The prophet then receives the order to prophesy to these dried-up bones and they become alive again. "Then He said unto me: 'Son of man, these bones are the whole house of Israel. Behold they say: Our bones are dried and our hope is lost: we are clean cut off . . . Behold, I will open your graves, and cause you to come up out of your graves, O My people'" (Ezek. 37:11,12). This political and messianic utilization of the myth of resurrection is an important symptom of Ezekiel's rationalism.

The prophet is able to recognize in the notion of resurrection, which became known to him in Persia, the resurrection of the people. Therefore, the emphasis on the words "My people" is particularly significant. It is found in the following verses, and particularly repeated at the end of the sentence. At this point the magic teaching of resurrection touches the messianic idea, and it is noteworthy that Ezekiel already interprets this in terms of a philosophy of history. The people cannot die. The death of the people is only a frightened illusion of despair, an illusion which is healed and removed through messianic confidence. Just as death is not real, so the resurrection is only the rejuvenation to a new historical life.

24. It became an important means for the spiritualization of Messianism that the Persian king Cyrus was recognized as God's messenger, as the Messiah for the redemption of Israel. With this, the magic of the house of David was broken. And further, the idea of the messianic leveling of all national contrasts and inhibitions for

the sake of the uniform worship of God became immediately evident.

Deutero-Isaiah and his successor complete this tendency. Only once is David mentioned, and even this one time in an interpretative passage regarding the "mercies of David" (Isa. 55:3). After Ezekiel, no prophet of the exile speaks of an offspring of David. Deutero-Isaiah thinks of the Messiah as being mainly for the conversion of the *peoples* of the world. Therefore, he transforms the offspring of the king, who bears with him the symbol of national glory, plainly into God's servant who, significantly enough, expresses the antithesis to the offspring of the king.

25. From the very beginning *God's servant* signified most clearly the people of Israel, just as Ezekiel had already called it often "My servant Jacob" (Ezek. 28:25; 37:25). "But thou Israel, art My servant, Jacob whom I have chosen . . . and said unto thee: thou art My servant" (Isa. 41:8, 9). "Behold my servant . . . I have put my spirit upon him: he shall make the right to go forth to the nations" (Wellhausen translates: the truth). "He shall make the right to go forth according to the truth" (Isa. 42: 1, 3). "He shall not fail nor be crushed, till he have set the right in the earth; and the isles shall wait for his teaching . . . I the Eternal have called thee in righteousness, and have taken hold of thy hand, and keep thee and set thee for a covenant of the people." (Herzfeld translates: "For a covenant of men," according to vs. 5 and 40:7.) "For a light of the nations . . . I am the Eternal, that is My name; and My glory will I not give to another" (Isa. 42:4-8). "And now, saith the Eternal that formed me from the womb to be His servant . . . *'it is too light a thing* that thou shouldest be My servant to raise up the tribes of Jacob and to restore the offspring of Israel; I will also give thee for a light of the nations, that My salvation may be unto the end of the earth' . . . and give thee for a covenant of the people" (Isa. 49:5-8). The difference between the Messiah's vocation with regard to the nation and mankind is nowhere else formulated with such precision.

26. Therefore the prophet can introduce the highest idealization which was bestowed upon the people of monotheism in relation to the whole of mankind. This is brought forth at the close of the fifty-second chapter of the Deutero-Isaiah as an introduction to the fifty-third chapter in which the ideal image of the Messiah, as God's servant, is celebrated.

The reflective historical style of this chapter exhibits the messianic idealization of the people of God as the servant of God: "Behold My servant shall prosper, he shall be exalted and lifted up, and shall be very high. According as many were appalled at thee—so marred was his visage, unlike that of man, and his form unlike that of the sons of men—so shall he startle many nations, kings shall shut their mouths because of him; for that which had not been told them shall they see, and that which they had not heard shall they perceive" (Isa. 52:13-15). Thus reads the introduction to this historical reflection on the liberation of Israel from its pitiable outward appearance.

To this promising prognosis the next chapter is joined, after a sentence in which historical reflection once more has the leading word: "Who would have believed our report? And to whom hath the arm of the Eternal been revealed? . . . He had no form nor comeliness, that we should look upon him, nor beauty that we should delight in him. He was despised and forsaken of men, a man of pains, and acquainted with disease, and as one from whom men hide their face: he was despised, and we esteemed him not" (Isa. 53:1-3). Up to this point the opinion has prevailed that there is correspondence between suffering and punishment, though the punishment is here manifested as the contempt of man. Now, however, comes the decisive turn: not only does the sufferer suffer innocently, but he suffers *for* the guilty one.

One may ask how the prophet could come to such a view, which is compatible only with the idea of sacrifice, which he, however, had already overcome. How could this view arise and exist in him, in the face of his belief in God's justice? However, this consistency of thought, which has no regard for any subordinate consideration, not even those concerning God, testifies to the tremendous moral energy of the prophet.

27. The problem of *evil* which traverses the whole of biblical literature, is here transferred from the individual to the historical image of the peoples. All the peoples are slaves to idol worship and they glitter and blossom in history. Only Israel suffers from the persecutions of the idol worshipers, and Israel has the calling not only to maintain the true worship of God but also to spread it among the peoples. Such a contradiction in historical imagery between past and future history does not permit any other solution but the following: *in suffering for the peoples Israel acquires the right to convert them.*

This historical suffering of Israel gives it its historical dignity, its tragic mission, which represents its share in the divine education of mankind. What other solution is there for the discrepancy between Israel's historical mission and its historical fate? There is no other solution but the one which the following consideration offers: to suffer for the dissemination of monotheism, as the Jews do, is not a sorrowful fate; the suffering is, rather, its tragic calling, for it proves the heartfelt desire for the conversion of the other peoples, which the faithful people feels.

It is not a desire for power and not a historical instinct which spurs Israel on to this course; rather, the freely assumed suffering declares the historical dignity of the sufferer. There is no other means but suffering to bring about this dignity in its purity.

This tragic suffering has the final good as its end, and therefore despises all transitory, eudaemonistic prosperity. It is also the peak of *ethical autarchy,* which seems not even to be concerned about the problem of God's justice. The latter is to be revealed truly only in the future. At that time suffering will not only cease, but its result will have been achieved: all the peoples will worship the unique God.

28. Now we can continue with the text of the chapter. "Surely our diseases he did bear, and our pains he carried; whereas we did esteem him stricken, smitten of God, and afflicted. But he was wounded because of our transgressions, he was crushed because of our iniquities: the chastisement of our welfare was upon him, and with his stripes we were healed" (Isa. 53:4, 5).

Fundamentally this is the same theodicy which produced, in the case of the poor (*anawim*), the identification of the poor with the pious. In this identification, too, the prophets and the psalmists were not concerned with divine justice; they only thought to take away from the poor the appearance of injustice. God will bring about the right of the poor. Ethical monotheism has no doubts about this.

This identification of the suffering one with the messenger of God is transferred from the social anomaly of poverty to the historical anomaly which is represented by Israel's history. And the solution of this world-historical riddle provided by theodicy is formulated in the line "chastisement for our welfare." This is the prophetic characterization of Israel's historical course. Israel's suffering is the tragic chastisement which is to bring about peace among men.

29. The historical reflection of the prophet goes further. He lets the people speak: "All we like sheep did go astray, we turned every one to his own way; and the Eternal hath made to light on him the iniquity of us all. He was oppressed, though he humbled himself and opened not his mouth; as a lamb that is led to the slaughter, and as a sheep that before her shearers is dumb; yea, he opened not his mouth" (Isa. 53:6, 7). The repetition of "open not his mouth" is very characteristic. It may point to the missing *justification* of Israel in the course of its history. The peoples go on living in their diverse idolatries; they all oppress and torment Israel to whom justice is not done, and who

is not able to open its mouth because nobody would listen, and who, if it were to speak, would not be understood.

30. Let us follow the further exposition of this thought: "By oppression and judgment he was taken away, *and with his generation who did reason* for he was cut off out of the land of the living, for the transgression of my people" (Herzfeld: "of the peoples") "to whom the stroke was due. And they made his grave with the wicked and with the godless" (properly "with the rich," who in this connection are opposed to the poor, as the pious) "his tomb; although he had done no violence, neither was any deceit in his mouth. Yet it pleased the Eternal to crush him by disease; to see if his soul would offer itself as a *guilt offering* that he might see his seed, prolong his days, and that the purpose of the Lord might prosper by his hand" (Isa. 53:8-10).

Particularly noticeable in this verse is the address to the "generation." And the generation is reproached for its lack of consideration about Israel's being cut off from the land of the living. It is a misconception to understand this as *death;* for death is the common lot of man, and that it comes also upon Israel could not be astonishing to the generation; therefore it cannot be a reproach to the generation that it does not think about it. Therefore, the grave is just as much a symbol as is the figure of the rich beside the wicked.

The meaning is, rather, that the peoples believe Israel to be dead and died out and that they give it its grave beside the idolators. Thus God makes the *apparent death* of Israel in its suffering a guilt-offering for the peace of mankind. After this apparent death follows an unconstrainedly long and fruitful life, so that the work of God might thereby succeed.

31. The task of God's servant becomes ever more complicated. The conclusion of this chapter completes this historical vision: "Of the travail of his soul he shall see to the full, even My servant, who by his *knowledge* did justify the Righteous One to the many, and their iniquities he did bear. Therefore will I divide him a portion among the great, and he shall divide the spoil with the mighty; because he bared his soul unto death, and was numbered with the transgressors; yet he bore the sin of many, and let himself intercede for the transgressors" (Isa. 53:11, 12).

To begin at the end: Kautzsch's translation of the last phrase as "and for their misdeed was a mediator" is wholly inadmissible. The expression (הפגיע) is repeated only in verse six. What may give novelty to these verses through this expression is the declaration of the *voluntariness* with which God's servant takes upon himself the suffering, or rather exposes himself to it. This affliction of his soul reveals this tragic significance, from which one cannot remove the eye of one's mind or, rather, which one should contemplate, and from the contemplation of which one should be nourished and fulfilled.

The expression of this voluntariness is "his knowledge." Knowledge here means the intention which will make the righteous particularly righteous, because it will bring to him the acknowledgment of the "Righteous One." This also explains the division of the spoils of victory among the many and the mighty, which corresponds to his readiness to take upon himself "the sin of many."

Thus the repetition of the word for "many" in the sentence "My servant for many" (Isa. 53:11, 12) is understandable. God's servant is set in opposition to the majority of the peoples; he lets himself be stricken for "the sin of many." This tragic intention will bring to the righteous honor and historical justification. And this is the share that is assigned to him out of the spoils of history. Hence, with the messianic solution, the tale of Israel's suffering comes to an end. The voluntariness and knowledge with which the servant takes upon himself suffering completely refute the opinion that these could refer to the taking over of sin; they refer to the taking over of the guilt-offering only. God's servant with his knowledge could in no way have voluntarily assumed the sin! However, his knowledge of the divine education of mankind may lead him to the free assumption of the historical suffering. He bears the sins for many, he takes their burden upon himself. Thus, while he takes the burden of sin upon him, he makes of himself a guilt-offering. The suffering represents the burden of sin. The idolator does not recognize this burden. It is the knowledge of God's servant which unveils the meaning of this burden.

It is always only the tragic suffering of which God's servant becomes the symbolic bearer. As opposed to this, he would decline to the level of a common tragic hero if he were to take upon himself the guilt of men. The guilt remains with the guilty one; but the righteous one takes upon himself the suffering and with this brings the generations of men to a reconciliation with God.

World history with its messianic goal actualizes this reconciliation of the peoples with God. And in the vision of God's servant the people of Israel is more than a priest; it is, rather, the sacrificial victim who exposes himself to suffering because of his knowledge of the irreplaceable value of this suffering for the historical welfare of mankind.

32. One more remark should not be suppressed at this point. It is obvious how the story of Christ's passion was conceived exactly in

accordance with this highly poetic vision. However, in modern biblical research no work indicates that there is this connection between poetry and history. And yet it claims to be not merely theology but also the history of literature as well. At least one should be able to recognize the admission that biblical research no longer wants to build theology and religion upon history!

33. At this point it would be appropriate to insert earlier prophetic speeches, because they correspond to the development now attained. Perhaps nobody has pictured so powerfully the destiny of the people as related to the image of God's servant as Joel, who proclaims the Last Judgment in the valley of Jehoshaphat (the name means "God judgeth"). But, already in this early prophetic time, Joel not only connects the Last Judgment with the fact that in Jerusalem "the mountains shall drop down sweet wine, and the hills shall flow with milk" (Joel 4:18), but with this external happiness of his own land he connects inward signs of the messianic future: "And it shall come to pass afterward, that I will pour My spirit *upon all flesh,* and your sons and daughters will prophesy, your old men shall dream dreams, your young men shall see visions. And also upon the *servants* and the *handmaids* in those days will I pour out My spirit" (Joel 3:1, 2). In this social universalism the similarity between God's servant and the calling of the prophet, not to mention the Last Judgment, is evident. As the idea of God's servant generalizes the calling of the Messiah, so also the calling of the prophet is here extended to the entire people, and significantly, with the expressed inclusion of the slaves, generally humanized, although the peoples, beside Israel, are not expressly mentioned. Since, however, in accordance with the time, the peoples have already received their punishment, the expression "I will pour My spirit over all flesh" gives also to the peoples other than Israel their share in the universalized prophetic calling.

34. Furthermore, several chapters of Zechariah are attributed to an earlier time. "Rejoice greatly, O daughter of Zion, shout O daughter of Jerusalem; behold, thy king cometh unto thee, he is righteous and victorious, lowly, and riding upon an ass, even upon a colt the foal. And I will cut off the chariot from Ephraim, and the horse from Jerusalem, and the battle bow shall be cut off, and he shall speak peace unto the nations" (Zech. 9:9,10). Although the Messiah is here called king, he is at the same time humble and riding upon an ass, since the Hebrew word means not so much humility as poverty. The exact translation would be: ". . . behold, thy king cometh unto thee, righteous and victorious, poor and riding upon an ass." Thus, the king is a prelude to "God's servant."

It is in this spirit that in the midst of the description of the horrors of the "Day of the Lord" there emerges the great statement of the messianic religion: "And the Eternal shall be king over all the earth; in that day shall *the Eternal be Unique and his name unique*" (Zech. 14:9). Thus the "Day of the Lord" is transformed into the day of the Messianic Age, which brings fulfillment to monotheism through the uniform acknowledgment of the name of God. It is as if the prophet intended to say that only when his name is unique will his uniqueness be continual. Messianic idealism may ascribe to itself the merit of giving this meaning to God's name and its unified acknowledgment.

35. However, the prophet connects these joyful tidings for the "remnant of the people" not only with the "seed of peace" but also with the admonition: "Speak ye every man the truth with his neighbor; execute the judgment of truth and peace in your gate" (Zech. 8:16).

In this genuinely messianic idea, which is based on social justice, the prophet rises above the piety of the national *days of fasting*, which are to become feasts of joy under the condition: "love ye truth and peace" (Zech. 8:19). In the earnest spirit he proclaims the hope: "Yea, many peoples and mighty nations shall come to seek the Lord of hosts in Jerusalem, and to entreat the favor of the Lord. Thus saith the Lord of hosts: in those days it shall come to pass that ten men shall take hold, out of *all the languages* of the nations, shall even take hold of the skirt of him that is a Jew saying: we will go with you, for we have heard that God is with you" (Zech. 8:22,23; cf. vs. 2:15). In the last cited passage, however, one notices an intensification of the idea: "And many nations shall *join* themselves to the Eternal in that day, and *shall be My people*" [Zech. 2:15]. Thus, also those peoples who join Israel will be unified with Israel. Like Israel, they will be for God his people. Hence the nationalistic idea of the election is completely overcome. This is the height Zechariah reaches.

36. A new motivation, of which perhaps Zerubbabel might have been the cause, is introduced by Malachi; he lets Elijah precede the Messiah: "Behold, I will send you Elijah the prophet before the coming of the great and terrible day of the Lord. And he shall turn the heart of the fathers to the children, and the heart of the children to their fathers" (Mal. 3:23,24). It is as if the preliminary mission of first restoring concord among families is allotted to Elijah, before the Messiah can restore concord among the families of the earth.

He also furthers this concord through his demand that the fear of God stand against all *skepticism*. A correspondence of the poor with the pious is to be found here in the correspondence between those who fear God and those who are his own (סגלה): "And they shall be Mine, saith the Lord of hosts, in the day that I do make even Mine own treasure" (Mal. 3:17). The title, which usually (Exod. 19:5) is valid for the whole of Israel, is limited here to those who fear God. This change also is of profound messianic significance.

37. Up to now we have reviewed the modifications which the basic messianic idea underwent before and after the exile. The psalms add to it a special variation. We shall be able to go into this later, in connection with prayer. But the greatest change arose through the connection of this idea of mankind with the questions of the individual soul.

If one surveys the entire collection of the messianic references in the Bible, in which nothing indubitably messianic should be omitted, then it first of all follows that the understanding of Messianism as *eschatology* is wrong. For, if one disregards the one reference in Isaiah, in which "death shall forever be swallowed up" [Isa. 25:8], then all other instances indicate an earthly future, be it of Israel or of all the peoples.

This single reference about death could as well be understood as poetry similar to that about the peace in nature, which also extends to animals. But even if it originated under the influence of magical teachings, this influence, transferred into poetry, would prove even more how alien to Jewish thought this mythological element was. All the prophets, before and after the exile, always understand by the "end of days," even if some of them thought it close at hand, only the political future of their own people and of mankind.

In support of the predominance of the political motive we may cite the fact that the end of days is not explicitly depicted as a very remote, inconceivable future, although the exact time is left uncertain. It is simply the future, in opposition to the present actuality in which power and amorality predominate, which is important to the prophets. This opposition extends to the past, with its terrors as well as its incentives to piety. Only upon the future do they focus their gaze, and to it they want to direct the view of man to the earthly future, with its duties, cares, and hopes.

This is the great cultural and historical riddle which Messianism poses. All peoples transfer the Golden Age into the past, into the primeval time; only the Jewish people hopes to see in the future the development of mankind. Messianism alone maintains the development of the human race, while the Golden Age represents the idea of a decline. Therefore the designation of the Messianic Age as the Golden Age is a gross mistake, which entirely reverses the idea. In

Messianism past and present disappear in face of the future, which exclusively makes up the consciousness of time.

This cultural and historical riddle cannot be understood as an ethnological one; to do so is only to give another name to the riddle. It will also remain a riddle, if one considers the natural instinct of the Jewish people as the ultimate cause that explains such a cultural and historical peculiarity. Besides, from the other direction, namely from the absence of an *eschatology*, the riddle would only repeat itself and increase. How is it to be explained that of all ancient peoples only the Israelites could oppose the myth of the netherworld and its permanent connection with the world above? Would it be correct to answer this question by considering the messianic idea as a substitute for eschatology?

Clearly this answer would be rather a new question, a repetition of the old one. For how is it to be understood that an ancient people presents such an anomaly to the universal attraction of this myth, which penetrates everywhere into mature cultures? Or should this anomaly perhaps be explained through the fact that the biblical world experienced a great stimulus from the idea of immortality and assimilated it?

We shall see that, characteristically enough, the idea of immortality in no way remained alien to the biblical spirit but was invigorated and spiritualized anew by it. But this positive fact strengthens the significance of the negative one: the absence or the insignificance of statements about immortality in the eschatology. Immortality, therefore, presents an intensification of the question which the absence of an eschatology brings about.

This negative attitude can only be explained through positive motivations. However, the idea of immortality, which, as we shall see, was by all means present, was not developed in a way that could expressly abolish eschatology. And thus the question of the positive motive, which could have accomplished the removal of eschatology, still remains.

An answer that would rely on racial qualities would also in this case ruin every inquiry. From the racial point of view, one would stray into vague superficialities, such as the so-called *sense of reality* of the Jewish people. The people is supposed to be depraved to such a degree that it had sense only for the present actuality with its overwhelming power, in opposition to any interest in the supernatural world! Against such an abnormality it is already significant that this people sets up the future in the place of the present and past. And is it possible to object that this future is thought of as of this earth, which would irrefutably prove again that the desires of this people are governed by sensible actuality?

Against this testifies the almost inconceivable fact that Messianism absolutely defies the whole present political actuality of its own as well as of the other peoples. Messianism degrades and despises and destroys the present actuality, in order to put in the place of this sensible actuality a new kind of supersensible actuality, not supernatural, but of the future. This future creates a new earth and a new heaven and, consequently, a new actuality. This creation of the future, as the true political actuality, is the greatest achievement of Messianism. And this creation could only be the product of monotheism.

Another objection still has to be considered. We already know enough about the share of reason in religion, and we know that this share of reason does not absolutely depend on philosophy, but that this share in itself is a kind of philosophy. And we could acknowledge this peculiar kind of philosophy because we recognized in scientific philosophy the peculiarity of philosophy itself. Scientific philosophy is idealism. The supersensible, which is produced by philosophy, is, so to speak, its own daily bread, with which *Platonic philosophy* has provided it for all times. The good, the moral, is "beyond being," namely, beyond mathematical, physical, scientific being.

Thus, Plato created a new space for ethics, and this space does not coincide with sensible space, which discloses the realm of experience. Thus, the idealism of scientific knowledge creates space for the possibility of ethical idealism. In it, too, beyondness is not a supernatural sensibility, and yet it is the foundation and the guarantee of a moral world which is distinct from nature. Could that which scientific idealism has achieved and could achieve because of its strict method become possible and understandable in religion, possible by virtue of its share in reason, though without the technical collaboration of scientific philosophy?

A new wonder sets in. Plato founded ethics on this *transcendence of the good.* From this, passing over millenia, a straight road leads to Kant. However, during these millenia ethics did not remain fruitless, although not, undoubtedly, within philosophy proper.

If one must grant that the sciences went their independent methodological road in spite of or, rather, because of the immanence of philosophy in them, then this is definitely even more true for the *sciences of culture (Geisteswissenschaften)* in their practical applications in *law* and *state*. Practically as well as theoretically, the *Middle Ages* became dependent for the sciences of law and the state at least as much upon religion as on classical philosophy and its further development. Now the question arises, whether through this fact we can explain that the messianic idea itself, as a kind of idealism, was able to liberate itself from eschatology.

This question arises the more naturally as the opposite question must be directed to Plato: how is it to be understood that this creator of idealism who was most consistent in systematic ethics was nevertheless so wavering and inconsistent in his *political* models?

This question cannot be put aside by pointing to his *utopian* designs, which turn away from the present actuality, so that the thought of the future seems to impress itself here similarly as in Messianism. In truth, however, such a similarity does not exist at all. Plato in his ideal state does not think at all of a *development* of the people who constitute this state. And as little does he think in this ideal state of people or nations other than the Hellenic citizen-squires already admitted to it. He does not think about the future at all, unless it is the unceasing repetition of the present.

Plato's political idealism, therefore, does not recognize a future proper, insofar as it would be a new peculiar creation and development. The beyond which he grants to the good means only that the good is beyond the being of the world of the mathematical and physical sciences. It does not mean, however, a beyond with regard to the past and present of the historical experience in the development of the peoples. The latter beyond, however, in distinction from the eschatological one, is the clear meaning of the messianic future.

If we have previously asked the question, how could messianic idealism be explained by the collaboration of reason only, without the collaboration of scientific philosophy, then we have now found a surprising answer to this question. We became aware of the fact that scientific idealism, even in Plato's case, failed to create and guarantee a messianic, supersensible world. If, however, it has become clear that prophetic reason could conceive, through Messianism, such an ideal future, then religious reason, the reason of religion, and therefore, to speak more exactly, the religion of reason, has stood the test.

The creative power of the religious spirit, of religious reason, brought forth in Messianism a supersensible future as a new kind of actuality which surpasses all present and past actuality. Religious thought has secured this supersensible actuality of the future. Therefore, one is permitted to call this future supersensible, if, on the other hand, sensibility is chiefly the instrument for knowing the actual present.

That which could not be apprehended by the sense of reality of all historical politics, that which even the political imagination could not conceive, has been magically produced by the messianic idea of the future of the human race as the true actuality of mankind. It was, rather, not a magic marvel but the necessary consequence of the messianic idea of God. The supersensible, earthly future of the human race within its natural development is the creation of Messianism.

And in this creation the peculiar idealism of religion proves itself true with the most powerful evidence; it is an idealism which even Plato did not attain. In this creation the religion of reason proves itself with exactitude and perfection.

We now see how misleading is the ethnological point of view, which tries to explain Messianism exclusively by the racial origin of the Jewish people. This thought is methodologically wrong. At best, the notion of the race is itself only a question mark. It can never be an answer to questions which arise within its questionable domain.

Besides the methodological mistake, however, we now recognize the harm which this nationalistic point of view inflicts everywhere upon questions of culture, and here upon the value of religion. The highest value of religion is obscured if one does not recognize in Messianism the purest fruit of monotheism. Only the thought of the unique God can explain the spiritual marvel of Messianism, which is a creation of thought absolutely unique in the entire world of spirit. All analogies, if they intend to prove identity, therefore not only are wrong but also endanger monotheism in its uniqueness.

If, therefore, the mythical Golden Age were not in itself the reversal of the Messianic Age, the analogy would still be ominous, because it equates monotheism in its most important aspect, the moral, with polytheism and thus defeats the moral idea of monotheism. Polytheism is able to acknowledge only the primeval *innocence* of man. The unique God, however, opens up another possibility.

The Golden Age is concerned with the *guilt* and *punishment* of men. The mere fact that there is a plurality of gods precludes a definite solution to the unavoidable conflicts that arise from this concern. However, the unique God is the forgiving God for each human individual, and therefore also for all men. The liberation of men from the burden of sin is therefore provided for in the very concept of this God. It is not possible for the matter to remain at the fact that men always sin and that God always merely forgives.

If, instead, the concept of God and the proper meaning of his love and goodness is to forgive man for his sin, then this concept must include this meaning: he will bring about the complete disappearance of sin from the human race. And if this consequence did not explicitly become part of Messianism, it is still evident that the cessation of political and historical sin committed in wars and the cessation of the social injustice of pauperism clearly governs the hopes of the messianic prophet.

War is, therefore, a very instructive symbol in the messianic imagination. As much as the latter is overcome by the imagery of war in depicting the Last Judgment, so much does it liberate itself with great energy from this magic image of war when the image of the future of mankind is in question. All the instruments of war become recast into instruments of peace, into instruments of agriculture and vine growing: and the peoples "will not learn war any more" [Mic. 4:3]. The messianic imagination depicts this symbol of historical wickedness with all the power of its poetry, and the plasticity of its ethics has its greatest achievement in the description of this demonic symbol of all previous world history.

Whether God will blot out sin altogether among men—about this the prophets do not muse. For in God's forgiveness lies the ultimate power of resistance to sin. But their practical kind of ethics, their religion, the prophets test in politics, first in social politics and after that in international politics. In the latter especially the good God has to confirm himself, after he has already acted on behalf of the poor in the state. Now, however, he is to show his goodness not only to the poor, the widow, the orphan, and the stranger but to all men and, indeed, to all peoples. Hence, Messianism is the new consequence of the unique God, the God of love and goodness.

Among the biblical references with regard to Messianism, we did not refer in detail to the messianic *psalms*, which, with joyful confidence, summon all peoples and see them come to the service of the Eternal.

Of particular interest in this respect is the designation of God in the psalms as the Good One. "Give thanks unto the Eternal; for He is good" (Ps. 136:1); more exactly this may mean: acknowledge the Eternal as the Good One. The goodness of God extends over all men and all peoples. God's goodness is the main basis for the Messianism of the psalms.

This attribute of God is, at the same time, the most appropriate to the *lyric* style of the psalms. Love is the state of the soul of the lyric singer; it designates his longing, his need, his desire. Therefore, God's love for man cannot correspond to this loving desire of the human soul for God; God's goodness takes the place of love.

When man seeks God with his love, then God seeks man with his goodness.

Goodness seems to be a better substitute for the ambiguity which, as matters stand, is contained in love, than that *amor intellectualis* of which pantheism everywhere took possession, although it in no way invented it. This intellectual love can be dispensed with when love is strictly determined as goodness.

Therefore, God is good with regard to all human beings, not only in regard to social matters but, what is no less important, in regard to the messianic goodness that extends to all peoples.

The psalms seem to be aware of the newness of this thought, which explains the repeated usage of the expression "Sing unto the Eternal a new song" (Ps. 33:3). God's goodness, as the foundation of the Kingdom of God for all peoples, is the theme of this "new song," of the song of the psalms in general, as it is also the new way of describing the knowledge of God and the worship of God. Thus, the new song is the new confirmation of monotheism, as the unique and sufficient cause of Messianism.

CHAPTER XV

Immortality and Resurrection

1. The idea of the immortality of the soul originates in myth, which in turn is linked with the most primitive notions of man and his connection with the family and tribe, and their origin and development. Erwin Rhode says in his *Psyche* that immortality was never a popular belief in Greece. The thought of immortality presupposes the thought of the soul. But what a development the notion of the soul had to go through!

The soul is the soul of smoke, or, rather, the soul of blood, insofar as the warmth of the spilled blood rises as smoke; or it is the soul of breath insofar as in breathing the breath of life is perceptible. In both of these forms, the soul is the only vitality of life. For the functions of the spirit, or even for those of passions, Homer's language only has the expression used for bodily organs, the midriff; the soul is not yet thought of as the organ of a spiritual organism.

2. We are able to observe in Plato how the soul gradually becomes a spiritual principle. We observe how in Plato's dialectics the philosophical problems of *consciousness* appear one after another, and how much they intertwine with one another. Thus, the concept of the soul grows to a diversity and, with this, also to its unity.

Primarily, the soul stands for the *thinking* power and in this isolated sense for consciousness (μνημη). Soon, however, it has to be drawn upon for the solution of moral problems, and thus arises reason (νους), which is thought of originally as theoretical reason only, but, at the same time, becomes pregnant with meaning as the practical or moral reason. As soon as the soul attains this extended meaning, immortality becomes a necessary attribute of the soul.

3. In no way, however, does the origin of immortality lie in the ethical concept of the soul. This point of view is refuted by the circumstance that the concept of the soul did not originate for philosophic speculation in the problem of man, but rather in that of the *cosmos.*

The soul is the life-principle of the cosmos, insofar as the latter is based on motion. Motion, however, requires as its principle *self-motion*. And thus the soul, as *world-soul*, is the principle of self-motion.

This self-motion is then transferred from the cosmos to the microcosmos, and, consequently, the life of the human animal is also based on the principle of self-motion. About this extension of the principle of soul to the cosmos and to all life, Plato therefore says: "All soul is immortal." All that is soul, and all that the soul everywhere has to mean, is designated as immortal.

4. This is the speculative and, no less also, the methodological transformation, which the concept of the soul experiences in Plato. If, from this light, one looks back to the meaning of the soul as a hobgoblin, which intervenes maliciously into the order of the upper world, or, as in the cult of the ancestors, establishes the connection of families and arouses piety and moral obligations beyond the grave, then one becomes aware of the spiritualization and idealization which has occurred in the treatment of the problem of the soul, and which did not occur with such a variety of meanings and expressions in any other concept of culture.

Already in Plato, however, it is remarkable and characteristic that, although his high abstractions are far removed from the mythical origins of the concept of the soul, he nevertheless re-enters all the highways and hiding places of myth as soon as he passes from the methodological foundation of ethics to its consequences for religion.

We have already seen the great difference in Plato's general outlook in the transition from ethics to its application in law and the state. The political anomaly is explained by the religious one.

5. Plato's philosophical *style*, more than that of any other philosopher, is tied up with a poetic style. Consequently, it is not religious prejudice or old-fashioned piety, which does not allow him to despise the native myths, particularly as they were at that time reformed by *orphic* theology, but it is the poetic point of gravity of his personality which induced him to play with the myths.

His poetic imagination could not avoid the problem of *satire*, which is represented by the myths of Hades. Why should he have restricted his field of satire to the *Sophists*, when the entire netherworld presents a myth of the punishment of human vices and weaknesses? This poetic motivation must be thoroughly considered if one is to avoid a literal understanding and evaluation of the poetic images and interpretation of the Hades myth in Plato.

6. The painters of the Middle Ages and the Renaissance, too, may have set about their pictures of the Last Judgment not without the

collaboration of a sense of *humor*. The idyllic pictures of the blessed alone did not appeal to them, but they were more fascinated by the frightening pictures of the punishments. Were they perhaps tormentors? Or are they not in these pictures of slaughter rather genuine creators of humor?

The same question must be directed to Dante. In which of the parts of his great poem does the most original power of his poetry gush forth: in Paradise or in Hell? Or has Dante been more of a satirical than an elegiac poet? And if he was perhaps more the former, could he be anything else than a poet of the original power of pure creative humor?

7. The matter is the same with Plato. Not even with regard to the Sophists does he harden into a merely satirical writer, but pure *humor* holds sway in the stinging speeches of dialectics.

How much more offensive would it have been for Plato's artistic powers if he were, like a boring preacher of morals, to describe and to mete out with detailed precision all the *punishments* which are imposed in Hades on the evildoers of all kinds and did not, rather, allow the humor and hilarity of the great moralist to emerge out of the towering masses of punishments.

Whoever could still doubt this would have to learn the correct state of affairs from the fact that Plato did not rest satisfied with punishments in the netherworld; they are continued and regenerated at the calling back to life and the *resurrection*. After this logically consistent continuation of the theory of punishment and recompense, the netherworld apparently is not the shadow world of the world above; rather, the opposite seems to be undeniable, that the world above is the image of the world below which, as the original abode of justice, becomes the *primeval world* of justice proper.

What a perverted world the moral world of Plato, the teacher of ethics, would be if he were not to be considered in the light of his concepts and ideas, but were taken at his word in his fantasies; if his being beyond being were to have only a mythological meaning and not a methodological meaning in accordance with his doctrine of the idea of being! Only in accordance with his idea of the good could these statements about the punishment of the evil be understood— although the difference between the foundation of his ethics and its application to politics has had disturbing influence.

8. Even more noticeable than the battlefield of punishments in Plato's mythological poetry is the distortion which the ethical concept of the soul suffers from the idea of *resurrection*, and it is surprising that Plato took no offense at it. His Pythagoreanism is expressed em-

phatically enough in the idea of a *withdrawal from* the *world.* "To withdraw from here to yonder." This is the watchword for the soul in its quest for liberation from "the prison of the body." When this liberation is achieved, should this suffering perpetually start all over again?

Of course the meaning of the soul, as the life-principle, makes this continuity unavoidable; but is this compatible with the ethical concept of the soul? Clearly there is an insoluble contradiction between the two meanings of the soul, between the basic, animal principle and the principle of moral life and, therefore, of consciousness itself.

9. This contradiction extends to religion and confuses reason's concept of immortality insofar as it is connected with resurrection. However, we have to consider whether this connection is simply a confusion and an error, or whether there is an original homogeneity of thought that has to be considered independently of the expressions it found.

We have already noticed the complications in the problems of immortality and resurrection which, in different ways, all flow and cross into one another. In the share of reason in religion is to be found the criterion which would make it possible to clarify and establish a foundation for the religious meaning of the resurrection of the soul, for man as an individual, and also as a member of the human race. The share of the religion of reason in man's moral teachings must probe the problem of immortality, as well as everything else, in order to find out the exact difference between religion and mythology.

10. Resurrection seemed to us to be a degradation of immortality, for it is the resurrection of the body, while immortality is, and should be, of the soul only. In the same way also, the world below, as the place of punishment, seems to be in contradiction with the religious teaching of man, which says that his soul is capable of repentance and therefore of salvation. Should there be a limitation of the power of man to repent, or even a limitation of God's power to forgive? At this point a harmony arises between true religion and myth, insofar as the latter invents the Isles of the Blessed. However, the stories the myth has to tell about Tartarus, even Platonic philosophy, as it seems, is unable to reconcile these with religion, insofar as the latter assumes no limit to the self-purification of man, and therefore also to God's forgiveness.

11. In the last analysis, however, the *grave* is already an abuse of the soul because it is an acknowledgment of the body along with the soul, or, rather, without it. The correct evaluation of the soul as man's

only human value would therefore simply be the acknowledgment of the nothingness and the destruction of the body. In this way the institution of *cremation* is to be understood, which came down from the mythical into the civilized world. The putrefaction of the body is considered right and acknowledged through cremation.

If, however, the myth acknowledges the grave as an institution, representing the servitude of the family to the cult of the ancestors, then from the accessories of the grave one can also see the original mythological meaning of this custom, the meaning which is also preserved in the *catacombs*. There is no lack of food and drink for the dead in the grave, or of ornaments and weapons, which testify to the continuation of his earthly honors. Thus, the grave faithfully joins all the other instances which oppose sensibility to the spiritual and moral token represented by the human soul.

12. Yet, human history sets before us the task of investigating these contradictions, these anomalies in the development of those concepts of the soul which remained affected by sensibility and material existence. Our task is to investigate how these contradictions adjust and preserve themselves in the development, how the offensive impulse becomes an incitement, how the opposition becomes a stimulant. We shall examine this later in connection with the problems of punishment and resurrection; in the problem of the grave this transformation is already evident.

Abraham does not leave the land until he acquires a family grave for Sarah, and Joseph leaves no other will for his brothers and sons than the request that they take his bodily remains with them when they enter the Promised Land. There is no thought yet of resurrection; Abraham does not think of it for his Sarah, nor Joseph for himself. What does the grave mean in these conceptions, which in the case of Abraham are clearly those of piety?

One has to consider that the myth of the netherworld could not contribute to them. It would rather seem that the establishment of a grave as a family grave is in opposition to the notion of a netherworld. The latter is, in the first place, the property of no individual and also not a common property of men, but a world under the rule of the infernal gods who inhabit it. Although this myth is present in the notion of *sheol*, it could not influence the description of the original sagas.

Similarly, we shall also see how the *sheol* forms only a negative element in the religious consciousness of the Bible. The netherworld is based on the gods of the netherworld. However, such gods exist as little as those of the upper world, whereas God is unique, and would have to rule the netherworld as well as the upper world. Consequently, the netherworld would have to be only for the purpose of retaliation, and indeed, only for the purpose of punishment, if this again were not to be an insoluble contradiction to the God of forgiveness.

Therefore, if immortality is a necessary attribute of the concept of the human soul, it must gain an entirely different meaning in monotheism.

13. What is the idea in the biblical consciousness that accompanies death and, particularly, the burial of the dead?

We meet there an important expression: "He is gathered to his *people*" [Gen. 25:8]. This expression is ambiguous because the word for people is in the plural, so that it may mean the tribes or only one tribe. Also the "gathered to," the "be put in," is ambiguous, for this word points etymologically to withdrawing and finishing and terminating; and yet a new beginning seems to be made there.

14. A more definite meaning is contained in the expression: "And thou shalt go to thy fathers" (Gen. 15:15). Hence, Abraham at this point already has such fathers. The *"fathers"* is a more precise expression than the less exact "people" in the plural. The "fathers" is also a more definite expression than the "ancestors." The forefathers still remain fathers. This expression is used also for the founder of a family, but the latter is not thought of as a single generation. Therefore, the fathers differ from the ancestors, who are always the geniuses of the generation, the princely or the heroic generation. The fathers are fathers of individuals. However, the individual *is* only by virtue of his soul. Although in this context the soul plays, so to speak, the role of a silent spectator, yet it plays the main role since it is the bearer of individuality; without the soul the individual human being would be merely a transitory organism.

If man enters into the abode of his fathers, he is thereby elevated above the character of an individual being. And if the fathers in their turn do not connect the individual with his hero-ancestors, then it can be only a broader horizon which their connection opens up for the human soul; it is the *people*, it is the people's soul into which the individual soul enters. The people does not die, but has a history which continues. And *history*, the history of one's people, gives duration and continuity to the individual soul. *Immortality acquires the meaning of the historical living-on of the individual in the historical continuity of his people.*

What a perspective Messianism now opens up for the historical meaning of immortality, according to which the individual soul acquires its immortality in the historical continuation of the human race!

15. The Bible bestows this elevated, this true meaning of immortality

on the human soul. And in this meaning of immortality and, through it, also of the soul, a new point of separation between religion and mythology is to be seen. Messianism actualizes this point of separation. And hence it is understandable how Messianism and immortality, or, in the case of the connection between resurrection and immortality, also Messianism and resurrection, touch and have a reciprocal effect upon each other.

16. Since we have recognized the historical meaning of immortality, it can further be understood that *resurrection* could become a lever for the formulation of immortality. For we have already seen that Ezekiel interpreted immortality as the immortality of the people: "These bones are the whole house of Israel" [Ezek. 37:10]. Thus, the image of resurrection even more than that of immortality could make clear the idea of the continuous migration of souls, or, rather, the continuous duration of individual souls in the historical unity of the people. "Generations come and go, but the earth continues eternally." This holds true more exactly for the generations of men and their history. Much more than the earth, the history of the people and the history of the messianic people of mankind endures forever.

17. Next to the principle of *development*, which has its roots in Messianism and which has its analogy in the historical living-on of the fathers, the religious motif of *holiness* collaborates in the prophetic reformation.

Holiness for men is originally priestly holiness, and as such it is altered by being transferred from the priest to the people: "Ye shall be unto Me a kingdom of priests and a holy people" (Exod. 19:6).

The basic concept of holiness becomes also the basic concept of God, who is called "the Holy One of Israel." Originally, holiness is the separation from everything profane, and so it favors the separation from all exclusively earthly life, as if holiness had actually to mean the only real and true life.

When, however, moral holiness becomes a religious concept of holiness, and God becomes the original image of holiness—no longer for the sacrifice, but for the tasks of morality—then the concept of life must be extended beyond the boundaries of earthly *life*. Human life has also to be extended into death. *Death* cannot be regarded merely as the end of life. It has to suggest the idea that it is only a transition to another life, for holiness has become the ideal of life.

18. However, holiness has produced man as an individual. Man has the task and the power of repentance and, thus, the power of self-renewal and *rebirth*. The holy God therefore becomes the God of re-

demption and reconciliation. All these concepts grow beyond earthly boundaries and illuminate the horizon of another life.

This other life, however, should not be imagined as the continuation of earthly life. The mythology of the grave symbolism and of the cult of ancestors cannot gain admission there. For the otherness of life has already begun with holiness in the earthly life. The life of the final *task*, the life of the idea, is based on the commandment of holiness.

The difference from the earthly life is, therefore, already prepared in the idea of holiness, and it needs only a consistent continuation for the problem of life after death. The idea of holiness provides the possibility of fulfilling this demand without falling into the errors of the myths. For the myth, without exception, is concerned with the cult of ancestors, and in it the individual has only the semblance of a soul. In the myth, the soul is nothing other than the tie between the great-grandfather and the grandchild.

19. But holiness has created the individual. The self-knowledge of sin has become the individual's knowledge of himself. If man is to become holy, he should become so as an individual and not merely as a link in the chain of his generation, and not even as a member of the holy people. The chain should not make the link alive, but rather the link the chain. Thus, the concept of the individual, as the individual of sin and forgiveness, had to broaden the concept of man in its entirety and, consequently, also the concept of human life and of human death in the sense of immortality.

20. We have now recognized how the demand for holiness makes man the carrier of the spirit of holiness. The soul becomes spirit, and, indeed, not because the mind is in need of a special power but because holiness requires a special soul, which is not identical with the soul of an organism.

Thus the "soul of all the living" becomes the spirit of holiness, the spirit of humanness. This spirit of holiness is nothing but an *idea*. It denotes the task and, therefore, the motive power of holiness. It can be said to have life only in the concept of an idea. If, on the other hand, the spirit is decisively to determine the human soul, how could it be thought to have no influence upon life and death, and consequently upon the afterlife of man?

21. Already the psalm could not find the God of holiness and forgiveness compatible with death, which destroys the moral individual: "Thou wilt not abandon my soul to the netherworld, neither wilt Thou suffer Thy godly one to see the pit" (Ps. 16:10). It would contradict the concept of the pious man as the one who strives for holiness if one were to see him lose his humanity and individuality. The desire for

another life is unavoidable, for the destruction of the soul contradicts the spirit of holiness, with which the soul has been stamped.

22. However, if the question naturally arises about the kind and closer determination of the other life, the afterlife, one must in the first place bear in mind that this question belongs to the sphere of interest of myth. The myth raises the question in this way because polytheism in general asks causal questions. Monotheism, on the contrary, has determined in God's uniqueness only the *difference* and has not given a positive characterization of the existence of the other life.

Monotheism must argue in this way with regard to immortality also. Myth asks the question: where goes the soul when the body dies? And the myth has a ready answer, that the soul flies away, as if it were like a butterfly. Therefore, properly speaking, the soul does not live on; only the "shadow image" of man has an afterlife, hence, only the second man, who in the earthly life is united with the first one. The soul which flies away flies, therefore, simply into nothing; only the shadow has an afterlife.

Consequently, mythical immortality is, properly speaking, not the immortality of the soul but rather that of the shadowy image of man. But the soul remains what it originally was—a principle of life—and therefore it has done and played out its duty with life.

23. The myth does not ask from where the soul comes, from where life came. This question is answered by the general cosmology, which at the same time is a theogony. Everything has its coming-to-be and therefore its destruction, the gods as well as the cosmos. Why should not the soul be the same way? From where is the coming-to-be? From chaos. With this concept, the myth explained and arranged everything. It is, moreover, only emerging science that raises new questions, which make even the coming-to-be itself a problem.

24. Monotheism, on the contrary, sets for man another origin: God has created man, and he has created man not only as soul but also as spirit. He has put his spirit into man. And he has put his spirit of holiness into man, and therefore bestowed upon him the spirit of holiness. If the mythical question is now not silenced even within monotheism—in his primitive disposition man always remains the mythical man—then the question, *where* does the soul go and what becomes of it, can be answered only in accordance with the question of where it came from, and who gave it to man.

Since God, as spirit, established in man the soul as spirit, its destruction is first of all impossible. For what comes from God as spirit is preserved by God. We have recognized creation as an unceasing *creation anew.* Furthermore, and positively by virtue of its origin in God, the soul as spirit returns to God. The spirit is the "portion of God from above" (Job 31:2).

Ecclesiastes formulates the problem in the same sense: "The dust returneth to the earth . . . and the spirit returneth unto God who gave it" (Eccles. 12:7). With this sentence the question receives its positive answer. The soul does not go to the *sheol*, but returns to the place from which it came. The soul has become spirit, namely, the spirit of holiness that God planted in man. Death, therefore, can only be the return home to God.

However, holiness is an *infinite* task. If the former has become part of the spirit of man, he has thereby become imperishable. All the ambiguity that was still connected with the soul as long as it was the soul of breathing and the soul of smoke is removed by the spirit. And, therefore, through spirit man has become immortal in the infinite, undying task of his holiness.

25. The soul has kept man in connection with all living creatures. The spirit however, reopens a new connection of man with God; for man is determined as the spirit of holiness, of infinite morality. The immortality is not only that of the soul, but much more that of the spirit, and even more specifically of the holy spirit. The infinite task of sanctification can have no end for the human spirit.

Nor can that task be restricted to certain determined ways, steps, and means in the process of sanctification, neither for man nor for God. Therefore it cannot be restricted to the mechanism of *retribution*, neither for man nor for God. For man, self-purification remains an infinite task. And of God's justice, I may know only that it is identical with his love. The latter, however, is his forgiveness, in which his love becomes goodness.

Since self-purification remains an infinite task for the individual, it cannot have its termination in death. The requirement of holiness lights up a horizon of another kind of life, and this horizon is within the field of vision of every human individual. Immortality, to be sure, is therefore the paramount problem of the individual, but this individual, morally purifying himself, is not identical with the empirical individual creature. It is always only the viewpoint and the zenith of morality, to which the individual of sensibility must ascend, insofar as he makes himself a moral individual.

Just as the moral individual originates only in the moment of this ascent and only has existence in this moment, so can he have duration only in it. What kind of existence does this duration have? Only the mythical man can ask in this manner; for the ethical question has already separated the individual from, and elevated him above, mere existence. Such a question has already been answered: the spirit returns to God. The individual, as the carrier of the soaring force of the infinite ascent, makes this return to God sufficiently understandable: it is the return to the infinite task of holiness, which has its origin in God.[55]

26. Thus defined, the immortality of the human spirit separates religion from those dangers of mythology contained in mysticism. The return to God is not union with God. The return means nothing other than what the origin means: holiness is the command and the power of God, which are transferred to man, but which do not make man and God identical. Even with this transference, God remains the Unique One. And this is the way he must remain when the transference is reversed, namely, when he determines and makes possible man's return.

Monotheism protects immortality from the mysticism of a pantheistic *panpsychism*. It does not save the immortality of the human soul at the expense of infringing upon God's uniqueness. Such a foundation would not be the salvation of man, but rather his end. And if this end is in God, and therefore cannot be called destruction, it would still be the end of the specifically human in man, namely, of his holiness as an infinite task. The latter, however, is excluded from God's being, and that is why immortality cannot identify man with God. The individual as human would be nullified, if it could come to a union with God.

If, on the other hand, the infinite task of holiness constitutes the immortality of the human spirit, it can establish the immortality of the individual, but not because of the union of the individual with God. In order that the individual should still remain a human individual, immortality has to become a characteristic of his own problem. Union with God, however, abolishes the individuality of man, no matter what recompense it may offer instead. And, consequently, the return to God cannot mean the entrance into a union with God, but nothing else than the regaining and acknowledgment of the origin that was given to man's spirit.

27. If, however, in the fulfillment of his infinite task, the individual stands only for the moment of his ascent, then there arises again the question of the exact meaning of immortality for this moment of the individual's ascent. We could hardly abandon the mythical suspicion that the individual has no afterlife of its own if the individual has to be thought of only as the infinite impetus of ascent in the infinite task. This insight is already difficult to understand in

terms of earthly life; it must become more difficult for the required other life, although the latter is required only by the infinite task, which is its meaning.

28. This difficulty, which has its basis in the empirical prejudice, is countered by the messianic idea of the future development of the human race and consequently of the *development of the human soul* as individual soul also. For all abstraction presupposes as its consequence the preservation and continuous effect of the *original conditions*. If the soul has been tied by God to the body, which is not merely an organism but dust and matter, then the individual in his development remains tied to the conditions of matter. Dust returns to the earth. The body again becomes matter. What it performed as an organism may cease, or rather may continue in another arrangement of matter.

The individual is not tied exclusively to the organism. If this were so, the individual could be made identical with it. The individual's own identity depends, rather, on his relation to God on the basis of the spirit of holiness. This spirit returns to God. With it, the individual also returns to God; how could it in that case remain tied to the organism, to which it was only temporarily tied? The development removes the individual from its seeming identity with its former body, and turns it over to the infinite development of matter, as the negative condition for the infinite task of holiness.

29. Messianism proclaims and vouches for this infinite development of the human soul. And at this point we can positively see how fateful the confusion of Messianism with *eschatology* is. From the world beyond it is difficult to throw a bridge to matter, which is the necessary condition for the development of the dispositions of the soul, the dispositions *heredity* has to assume and nurture. Messianism, however, in opposition to eschatology, remains in the climate of human existence. And if it makes the future of mankind its problem, then it is the task of the historical future, the future of the infinite history of the human race, which becomes the task of the holy spirit of man.

30. Through this, man is elevated above the limitations of the individual biological creature, and also above the empirical creature of history. For the concept of history and of historical experience is now elevated beyond the borders of the past and present; the proper existence, the actual reality of human life and of the whole human race, is put only in the future and in the development toward the future.

The disposition to this thought is expressed in the "Gathering to the Fathers," which means the fathers of the national history. The Messiah, however, becomes in a new sense the *father* of men. Originally he was only the father of Israel, but with irresistible consistency he gradually becomes the father of mankind. And thus also the individual in the infinite task of his holiness becomes the *individual of mankind*.

Immortality, too, can have only this messianic meaning for the individual. The human soul is the soul of the messianic individual. Immortality, therefore, can be thought of only in the messianic concept of the individual soul of man. Only in the infinite development of the human race toward the ideal spirit of holiness can the individual soul actualize its immortality. The individual soul is always only the impetus of the ascent, always the sum total of ascents, which come together in the infinite development.

The infinity of the ascent is only actualized in the messianic development, and since the latter is different from eschatological existence, it can never be deprived of the connection with its material background. Already the messianic God guarantees the preservation of the natural background and its connection with the infinite task of morality. Thus, also at this point, Messianism is united with monotheism in order to establish the immortality of the human spirit in the development of the human race. Furthermore, both of them at the same time guarantee infinity for the individual.

31. The moral individual is the *individual of totality*, and therefore not only does he not vanish, but he achieves completion only in historical development, as prescribed by Messianism. The moral concept of the individual could not be realized apart from this development. *The idea of the historical development of the individual represents the total value, the high point of the concept of the moral person.*

The concept of immortality is thereby tied, on the one hand, to the sum total of moral ascents and, on the other, to physiological life and its infinitely ramified *heredity*. A harmony between material conditions and moral demands is thus made possible, while the myth remains based upon the egotistical, empirical I with all its respectable, yet ambiguous, affective and emotional claims. The hope for a reunion in the afterlife is the symptom of all those complications the notion of the empirical individual brings about.

Religion, on the contrary, makes use of the ethical concept of the I of totality, which Messianism demands. And this connection of the messianic future of the human race with its providential origin in the patriarchs of monotheism makes the Jewish teaching of immortality of unambiguous value. The patriarchs are the historical representatives of messianic mankind, and at the same time, as progenitors, they represent the biological background of propagation and heredity.

32. From these considerations it becomes more understandable how the Jewish tradition connects the concept of immortality, as the immortality of the future world (*olam habo*), with that of the Messianic Age, as the future times (*athid habo*). At this point we are again reminded of Ezekiel's understanding and interpretation of the magic teaching of resurrection. For him this means the resurrection of the people (Ezek. 37:11). Also the verbal form in *hiphil* may have occasioned the idea that the preservation of life is synonymous with resuscitation. The preservation itself is an unceasing resuscitation.

In the literal sense resuscitation would relate primarily to bodies and either through them to the souls or actually to the bodies only, while the soul would live on anyhow. In any case, the preservation of the historical individual would be questionable, for he can neither be determined by the bodies or by the soul alone. For his continuation the historical individual needs *development;* the latter, however, is not guaranteed by the resurrection of the body. Resurrection, therefore, needs the complement of immortality, and it is a question whether immortality is a complement *homogenous* with the preservation of the soul.

33. Since, however, it happened that under the Persian influence immortality and resurrection became alive in the Jewish mind and were connected with one another, it is understandable that both concepts were soon connected with the concept of the Messianic Age. In the entire rabbinic literature, in the Talmud, in the Midrash, and therefore also in the oldest prayers, they appear sometimes as if they were one and the same thing, sometimes, however, as if they were separated, as if they were not thought of as identical. This development contributed to the erroneous notion that Messianism is synonymous with eschatology, and since the latter was not thought of in the historical sense, the messianic future, too, was in danger of losing its historical character.

34. Moreover, this danger went beyond this important historical problem; it assailed the fundamental religious concept, which originated in connection with the resurrection in Daniel and Sirach, of "the Kingdom of Heaven," "the *Kingdom of God*" (מלכות שמים). "The Kingdom of God" of the messianic future was thereby confused with "the Kingdom of Heaven" beyond.

This "Kingdom of Heaven" became the messianic concept of Christianity, which is therefore eschatological. Without entering into a detailed discussion of the differences that exist in the determination of "the Kingdom of God" within the Christian faith and the messianic "Kingdom of God," it seems particularly important to stress one difference that is a consequence of the above fundamental difference. It concerns the taking on of responsibility for "the Kingdom of God," the personal moral obligation for and under "the Kingdom of God."

35. In the "Lord's Prayer" the entreaty reads: "Thy Kingdom come." Let us leave it undecided whether this entreaty extends only to the world beyond, or whether it includes the bringing about of the moral world in history. But even regardless of this question, it is characteristic that the *Kaddish-Prayer* entreats this moral world in the sanctification of God's name: "in the world which He hath created according to His will, and may He establish his kingdom during *your days* and during the days of all the house of Israel." In this prayer confidence is directed to "the Kingdom of God", the express prayer is for the earthly days, for the historical days of the people which, in the messianic sense, means the whole mankind. Every obscurity and ambiguity, every confusion with the shadowy kingdom of the beyond, is definitely banished. This prayer did not originate in a polemic but in pure messianic naiveté.

36. Another consequence follows from this. Because the messianic confidence is absolutely connected with monotheism, it is identical with the duty of worship. The latter, however, does not wait for the future, but fills my whole life and every moment of my existence. And the same must also hold for the messianic future.

This is the advantage that comes from thinking of this as the "Kingdom of God." *For my personal worship the Kingdom of God is not to be a future advent, but must be a permanent actuality.* This idea is expressed in the Jewish term "to take upon oneself the yoke of the Kingdom of God." In old prayers the expression is found: "I prepare" (הריני מתכון) (the Hebrew term for devotion [כונה] means in its root: to be established, fortifying, preparing) "to take upon myself the yoke of the Kingdom of God." I do not wait for "the Kingdom of God" to come and merely pray for its advent but bring it about through my own preparedness; through my own will I bring it about.

Thus, the Kingdom of God is present to me and is a personal actuality for my consciousness of duty. Therefore it is more than just an object of hope and confidence. This realization and actualization of the messianic future was made possible through the above-mentioned distinction between the messianic future and the beyond, which, in spite of all connection, remained alive in the Jewish consciousness, particularly because it was maintained by the idea of resurrection.

37. It is, therefore, the great merit of Maimonides to have dis-

tinguished sharply between "the future world" and "the future time."[56] This corresponds with his basic tendency to dissolve all dogmatism into ethical rationalism.

Through this distinction he first of all secured purity for Messianism and, at the same time, for immortality by severing any idea of eudaemonism from both. Thereby he liberated Messianism from *utopianism*; nevertheless, he inscribed and laid down in Messianism the main features of ethical *socialism*. The material and economic conditions should never become a hindrance to the realization of the moral and spiritual culture of *all* men without any distinction. To suspect this kind of social welfare of eudaemonism shows a lack of understanding or worse. Through this kind of ethical security, eudaemonism is rather invalidated.

38. Immortality, too, is liberated from the idea of eudaemonism. And there is one form of eudaemonism which, though not considered as such, nevertheless is the most dangerous variety of it, namely, the use of the world beyond for reward and punishment. The idea of *retribution* and punishment is particularly dangerous and even Plato did not escape this danger in his play with the world of the myth. He demands an afterlife as if its only meaning were to afford sufficient time for the punishment of the soul. At this point eudaemonism coincides with the mechanism of divine retribution.

This Platonic idea of the afterlife also includes *education* through punishment, an education that sweetens the pain of suffering a little bit, although it remains questionable whether an educational development is possible together with punishment. It is unavoidable that this development becomes a secondary aim when the pain and torment of suffering are unfolded as the main content of afterlife.

39. The ambiguity that is unavoidably connected with *rewards* hardly requires a more detailed discussion. In most cases rewards preserve the mythical connection with the sensibility of the upper world, except where they are restricted to the strictly spiritual. At this point, perhaps, Aristotle might be a good example, if he did not disclose at the same time the dangers of his one-sided intellectualism. Only the *thinking* part of the soul *(Nous)* is, according to him, immortal. Therefore only those human souls are immortal in whom pure thinking can become an organic activity.

Or perhaps it is only God himself in whose reason thinking becomes energy. This was already a matter of dispute in ancient Bible-exegetics and this dispute was reproduced in the Arabic-Jewish Middle Ages. In any case through this intellectual exclusiveness eudaemonism was excluded from the rewards in afterlife.

In the rabbinical writings some passages are found that eliminate any positive or negative eudaemonism from reward as well as from punishment: "In the other life there is no eating nor drinking, nor any sensuous enjoyment, but the pious sit with their crowns on their heads and nourish upon the divine splendor."[57] The enjoyment of thinking, of the Aristotelian *theoria,* here becomes the enjoyment of God's splendor. Thus theoretical intellectualism has been religiously purified. All of the pious can participate in this enjoyment even if they have not participated in speculative thinking.

Particularly characteristic, however, is the expression of Resh Lakish in the Talmud, according to which there will no longer be any hell in the Messianic Age.[58] The principle of self-perfection in the development of man is not compatible with the principle of retributive punishment: the latter is replaced by the former and therefore there can no longer be a hell in the Messianic Age. Moreover, hell is not to be thought of as a permanent place of retribution, for after purification the sinners are supposed to go to heaven. Therefore, a necessary consequence became valid: there are no eternal punishments of hell.[59] This consequence follows from the connection of divine forgiveness with the human work of repentance and its effect on the development of the human race. The messianic future thus has overcome and eliminated the share of punishment in immortality. For the purpose of retribution immortality is no longer necessary. Because the notion of the soul has changed and become moral, it now fulfills all the conditions of retribution. The soul has become spirit. The spirit of holiness achieved this consequence. Holiness requires development for the spirit. It is in this sense that the expression of Rabbi Tarphon in the *Sifre* to *Nezikin* is to be understood. The historical factor becomes the consequence of the spirit for the development of holiness.

All these motivations serve to explain the surprising caution of the Jewish sources with regard to all eschatological materialism, fatalism, eudaemonism, and every kind of metaphysics not determined by pure ethics. Already the talmudic simile about the enjoyment of God's splendor is subject to great doubts. Though the splendor is thought of only as reflected splendor, it almost touches God's being, and the knowledge of God can never relate to his being, but only to his archetypal image for moral actions. What new knowledge can immortality offer for the understanding of this archetypal image, which is only love for God? Only moral development is able to bring new knowledge, and with it, so to speak, new enjoyment for the individual. But here there is truth in the oft-used saying about the connection of pleasure and pain, a connection which necessarily stirs the desire for further development. As understood in this manner, enjoyment in the godhead may be permissible as self-improvement in accordance with the archetypal image.

Truly profound, and of the highest clarity, is this sentence in the Talmud which guided Maimonides: "All the prophets have prophesied for the days of the Messiah only."[60] But about the future world the following words are valid: "neither hath the eye seen a God, beside Thee, who worketh for him that waiteth for Him" (Isa. 64:3). Consequently, according to the above rabbinical statement the world beyond is generally separated from the problems of prophecy. The prophets are only concerned with the Messianic Age, with the historical development of the human race. But immortality belongs to God's secrets; it is an object of human hope. The messianic future is thus removed from the sphere of human hope, because it belongs immediately to belief in God. The messianic confidence is removed from the irresolution and uncertainty with which hope and expectation are always connected. It belongs absolutely to the knowledge of God, and this is acknowledged in the love for God. In the messianic future, God's love to men proves itself, and his forgiveness and reconciliation with man deepen.

The separation of immortaility from prophecy avoids another danger in the notion of immortality, namely, the danger of materialization by way of mysticism. The above-mentioned talmudic statement about the enjoyment of God's splendor shows that the notion of immortality is in danger of bringing the human soul into a mystical union with God. We have already mentioned the distinction which exists, according to the psalm, between union with God and the "nearness to God." The pious thinker Yehudah Halevi said: "What more can immortality bring me, if I have nearness to God?"

Here, too, Maimonides took an important step forward by disclosing in the "nearness to God" the activity of self-nearing to God (התקרבות).[61] Through this the psalm is explicated and improved. Nearness to God is by itself not yet my good; it can become so only as my task, my ideal for my own activity of self-nearing. This, however, is identical with my task of self-perfection, which Maimonides elevates to the highest principle, and through which the Aristotelian principle of happiness is refuted and eliminated. Self-nearing and self-perfection are nothing other than self-development. And, thus, the latter remains the only meaning and the only task of immortality. This, its unique task, can be fulfilled only through the messianic concept of the soul, which must remain the guiding concept for immortality and therefore cannot become identical with it.

With regard to retribution, we have already seen that it has been
drawn into the historical view, though with a higher, purely moral,
social-political meaning. The poor are the sufferers and they are the
pious. Furthermore, the servant even became, in his tragic suffering,
the vicarious sufferer for the sinners. Consequently, retribution is removed from the judgment of the dead, and instead becomes a goal
for moral culture and control. If retribution were to take place only
in the beyond, it would be of no use, either for myself or for others.
Justice is God's attribute; if it does not exhaust itself in love and there
has to be necessarily also punitive justice, then this residue of justice,
in its modifications which do not dissolve in love, remains God's
secret. It is God's secret insofar as it belongs to God's essence, the
knowledge of which I am deprived. In this sense it says: "Mine is the
revenge and retribution"(לי נקם ושלם). Revenge is merely the poetic expression for punishment. It also says:"The judgment is God's"(כי המשפט
לאלהים הוא). The archetype for human justice is God's love only; but
the punishment, the retribution, are his own secret; for with regard to
them he is not the archetype for human action. Therefore, even immortality would not be able to give a positive answer to these questions,
which, by the way, are of no concern to my own morality, and therefore
of no interest. On the other hand, immortality can be compatible with
the messianic times, insofar as it makes the motive of love in God's
justice into a principle of human morality. Through this, all the moral
motivations, which the mythical cult of ancestors brought forth, are
utilized in transfigured form. Thus immortality arouses respect, and—
in retrospective gratitude—also love for the pioneers and guarantors of
the messianic world.

Before we continue this thought with respect to Israel's ancestors,
we should like to consider a Midrash that brings to light the idea of
development in a far-reaching statement: "The King Messiah does not
come, before all souls are brought into bodies."[62] Or in another version,
"until all souls are created, who were thought to be created." This
passage is involved in manifest contradictions, for it puts the Messiah
at the actual end of the biological development of man. The Messiah
would then not signify the infinity of the development of the conception of the soul, but the termination of it. At the same time, immortality itself would come to mean only the whole development of the
concept of the soul, and would thus pass over into the idea of the
Messiah and find in it its completion. In this transition the contradiction is solved. The Messiah comes only at the end of the development
of the soul, which is synonymous with immortality. In fact his coming
is not an actual end, but means merely the infinity of his coming, which

in turn means the infinity of development. Consequently, one may consider the above Midrash as the correction of the material understanding of the beyond. This correction is accomplished by the Messiah, who represents the time of the future, that is, the infinite development of the concept of the human soul. In the principle of the development of this concept of man, of this concept of the soul, the future world and the future time are united. In the mythical concept of the individual they are separated; in the principle of historical development they are united both biologically and world-historically.

In the history of Jewish religious philosophy the two motivations of mythical-mystical immortality, namely, the union with God and the meticulous execution of retribution, are in most cases rejected. We already have remarked that Yehudah Halevi designates the nearing to God as the only good on earth.[63] According to this view the future life is to be thought of only as the continuation of the moral striving on this earth and, therefore, as it were, as an ideal of moral life.[64] Bahya conceives of nearness to God in a manner more biased in favor of traditional mysticism. Kuzari, on the other hand, mentions that resurrection is only a biblical notion, while he accepts immortality as a truth of reason, which is therefore not expressly taught by the Bible. Ibn Daud, too, does not mention resurrection. Maimonides conceives of nearness to God only intellectually, as knowledge of God, in which all morality is involved. Besides, he depreciates resurrection in assuming that after it a new life begins with a second death. From this it follows that there is no salvation for the entire soul, but following Aristotle, only for acquired reason. It alone is that substance of the soul that is separated from the body. The soul in this case is limited to thought, to the spirit, which, however, is not the spirit of holiness but is limited to theory, to the spirit of thought. Only because Maimonides assumes self-perfection (השתלמות) does he renounce Aristotle's notion of eudaemonism, which consists in the bliss of thought. In this self-perfection the myth is again overcome and the messianic principle of self-development is retained.

With regard to the other motif, namely, retribution, the above-mentioned thinkers in the same spirit partly reject it and partly introduce variations of it. Kuzari offers a theodicy which corresponds to that of the prophets and the psalms. The suffering of the single individual has to be considered in the light of the universe. Hence, the social idea becomes the idea of the universal world. For Maimonides, Paradise (*Gan Eden*) and Hell (*Gehonnim*) are only symbols. Kuzari does not mention the manner of punishment at all. Maimonides makes the principle of socialism valid for the messianic times, and does so with precise clarity. Joseph Albo, in general, identifies retribution with immortality.[65]

This survey shows the tendency of Jewish thought to connect immortality with Messianism for the purpose of the principle of development. Resurrection also has played a mediating role, insofar as it has stressed the historical meaning of development. The continuity of development could now also be connected with the patriarchs, as the ancestors and models of history. This historical point of view became connected with the basic notion of piety, which we came to know in the identification of the pious with the poor and also in the final designation of the Messiah as God's servant, and as the one who suffers vicariously for earthly sorrow. We have now to consider from the same point of view another term, connected with all these problems and giving them a new expression: "the merit of the fathers" (זכות אבות).

The old question of the relation between merit and guilt, on the one hand, and happiness and misfortune, on the other, found a social solution in the identification of the poor and the pious. And yet this identification comprises in it the question of the compatibility of God's justice with the suffering of the guiltless. God's servant was to help overcome this question through vicarious suffering, and to be sure, without vicarious guilt. The Messiah was to bring the decisive answer to the above question in particular. The age he is to bring about will make an end to these grievances. Behind this thought the idea that the vicarious suffering of the poor brings about social development is obviously at work. This whole chain of reasoning is governed by the point of view that a single individual, and particularly a certain social group which represents morality, can achieve personal and individual merit.

An entirely new question, however, arises about the possibility of individual merit in general. It is only an evasion if one already assumes merit in poverty or in social suffering as such. Can an individual have merit at all? Can salvation have this final meaning, and does it not contradict its concept insofar as that concept is merely of the possibility of unending ascent in self-purification? *Merit designates the balance of an account, its final reckoning.* The account man must give in an unending repentance does not tolerate any such balance, so that a return can never be counted and determined. The merit of man must consist exclusively in the activity of his giving an account he can never balance.

That is why immortality of the soul was bestowed upon the people and therefore also upon its originator. With the same intention the problem of merit was related to the merit of the fathers. This concept is naturally connected with the thought that pervades the entire Jewish consciousness: the life of the single individual is connected with his history, and his history is characterized by its origin in the patriarchs. This is the final expression which the basic historical idea of the people, in its national and its gradually maturing messianic calling, has found for the primeval problem of guilt and misfortune, as well as for merit and happiness, a problem that had previously found a variety of solutions. The individual has no merit at all, but the appearance of his merit is sufficiently explained through the merit of the fathers, which continuously affects history.

This concept expresses the depth of Jewish piety. This concept, too, originates in the national consciousness, which becomes an historical one, while the concept itself becomes a bastion of individual morality. Through it the individual is definitely protected against self-righteousness. The merit of the fathers thus brings to a close the problem of individual merit. Such a kind of merit cannot exist, but, then too, one is not in need of it. Whenever I become aware of human morality, there, of course, I should be permitted to recognize the temporary result of self-purification, but even in this I can and must recognize the enduring effect of the fathers.[66] To their merit I attribute all the good that I would have to recognize in the life of individuals. The latter are thus liberated from a false gleam of glory, without, however, the worth of their own action being diminished. Their action remains good, and they remain the initiators of their action, but the merit, which I, according to the usual habits of moral evaluation, would have to ascribe to them, thereby exposing them to the dangers of illusory heroism, this merit I acknowledge, with better insight, to belong to the fathers and consequently to the historical development, to which an individual of even the highest standing is indebted for his best actions.

If, then, the merit of the fathers wards off the illusion of one's own merit, it would be of little help if this illusion were to be transferred from one individual to another, if it became a means of exchange and perhaps misused for retribution. It is the fathers, not the individuals as such, to whom merit is traced back. The fathers are not such in an absolute sense; they are rather the fathers of the development, the standard-bearers of history. In no way are they to be thought of as exceptional individuals, as individual saints. As such they, too, could have no merit. It is only the fact that something begins with them, something that surpasses them, which makes them into starting points for the problem of merit.

If, on the other hand, merit is thought of as an entry in one's account which could be balanced against guilt, and even against the guilt of others, then the idea is turned in a completely different direction, which falls entirely outside the problem at hand. Already in the chapter on atonement and reconciliation the idea of a means of balancing of guilt or of any retributive measure has been excluded. The question at hand is not the question of guilt and punishment at all, but the completely different one of merit, with which a compensation is usually connected. These two concepts should be separated from individual action, to which they simply do not belong by right. In this thought the problem of atonement and redemption is developed further. The atonement the individual achieves, becomes, so to speak, only a provisional or fictitious one. The individual soul is, rather, a historical soul. The duty of repentance may not be encroached upon by this insight. Self-sanctification has to think only of the self and not of its historical connections. But with regard to redemption I need not dismiss this insight. Rather, it will lead me to a deeper understanding, and also to a deeper understanding of the proper meaning of immortality with regard to the historical development of the soul. And hence I can confidently ward off the danger that lies in the pretence that through redemption I could or might arrive at my own self's complete good. This is opposed by the notion of the merit of the fathers, which, to be sure, does not limit my personal act of repentance and self-purification but does ward off the danger of self-righteousness that lies in the notion of one's own merit. The patriarchs alone have all merit, which their grandchildren may acquire.

For the Jewish concept of virtue this concept is of fundamental significance. It is always related, however, only to the positive moral achievement, and in no way to the negative one, to the sin for which a vicarious substitute may be sought. The substitute is sought not for guilt but for merit. Merit itself appears here as sin. It would be an irredeemable sin for the individual; therefore it has to be diverted to the originators of the historical development. They are not affected by this sin. Merit is not inserted into their consciousness. Only the gratitude and humility of their descendants is transferred to them, whose personal consciousness is no longer alive, but has passed over to the historical development that starts with them.

Nothing so manifestly contradicts this notion of merit than its connection with any sort of excess. Man's merit always remains deficient: "For there is not a righteous man upon earth, that doeth good, and sinneth not" (Eccles. 7:20). All merit could be only a part of one's obligation; the measure of duty can never be fulfilled by man. If, therefore, the problem is not merit, but rather guilt and its retribution, then a complete shift in the problem has occurred. And if in this shift the impermissible idea is advanced that the merit of some individuals can be considered as excess and reckoned up in the balance against the guilt of others, for which it is used as compensation *(satisfactio)*, then we have deviated even further from the original idea. In the idea of the merit of the fathers, compensation is not in question at all. Even the patriarchs could not achieve this. They would not have been permitted to do this. There is no other compensation for sin but the one which one's own self-sanctification can achieve. The holiness of some other person cannot make amends for my own guilt. And there is no question at all about my guilt, but only about the possibility of my merit. Therefore, it is entirely inadmissible to assert an analogy between the merit of the fathers and the merit of saints, which is artificially assumed in history.

This analogy is aided by an expression which is linked with this concept, that of "the treasure." One has to assume that the root of the word occasioned the seduction. The "bundle of life" (צְרוֹר הַחַיִּים) is an expression for the afterlife: "The soul . . . shall be bound in the bundle of life" (1 Sam. 25:29). Such a "bundle" is also a "container," which becomes a "treasure." There is no danger in this image for the national consciousness. The merit of the fathers is the most secure treasure of the descendants. As it is the proper safeguard against their self-righteousness, so is it their best treasure. This image becomes dangerous only when the merits become coins, so that "treasure" comes to mean the piling-up of these coins. But it is not dangerous when it reserves all merits to the fathers so that the descendants are not in danger of ascribing them to themselves. Consequently, the analogy of the merit of the fathers with the *thesaurus meritorum* [treasury of merits] must be rejected in every respect.

In the latter concept merit is assumed to be an excess over and above an action according to duty. Such an excess cannot exist. Further, this excess is supposed to be able to make amends and as such to be reckoned in the balance. Such a reckoning is not permissible; it cannot offer amends. The notion of the merit of the fathers, however, is not concerned with amends at all since it is not concerned with guilt and sin, but only with merit. Further, the notion of an excess and an exceeded good makes the latter a quantity, and thus relative.

Finally, psychologically, too, such a surpassing of duty is impossible even if it were ethically and religiously permissible. How could it be psychologically possible? The answer to this in the above-indicated teaching is the following: through effort and mortification. These acts of martydom, however, are only relative concepts, through which the relativity of the good is intensified. Even martyrdom proper, the acceptance of death for the sanctification of God's name, is nothing but duty and plain obligation, which is shown by the numerous examples in the history of all religions, in all moral tasks, and, particularly, in political ones. The martyr, therefore, cannot have any historical claim even to the semblance of a hero. Their number is legion. If it were not for human self-conceit, which slinks even into this temple of honor, the over-large chapter of martyrdom would be sufficient evidence against the pessimistic view of radical evil in man. There is only one means of protection against the danger as well as the suspicion of selfishness and self-adoration in martyrdom. It consists in limiting the value of individual martyrdom. The martyr does his duty as he may, and he is not to be distinguished from the one who does it without risking his life in a publicly exposed position. It is possible, in a simple sampling in various fields of civic morality, to find in all strata of society men who endanger their positions in life and, with this, their own life, and suffer the loss of it.

There is an elevated historical sense in the idea that, in order to satisfy the demands of human humility, only the fathers were declared the guarantors of merit and not any saints. In the adoration of the saints on the contrary, although "the treasury of merits" is attributed to Christ and Mary, it is also transferred to the saints. And since the flock of the saints may be continuously augmented by the Church, the treasury of merits becomes a treasury of the Church. The Church refers this kind of treasuring up of saints to its doctrine of the communion of the saints in the body of Christ. But it is the Church itself that makes these saints privileged and with them the treasury, out of which it reckons up the amount of compensation. This has its ultimate reason in the idea of the *opera supererogatoria* [works of supererogation]. According to it, morality does not remain the infinite task of man, but is terminated in a norm, which can be exceeded. Through this the subject of morality is separated from its object. The objects, the works, become independent, externalized things, which therefore can be collected in a treasure. Hence, merit is entirely separated from action, as well as from its originator, to whom alone it should be related.

This brings about the new consequence that the man who is separated from his action can also have a man who substitutes for his responsibility and, hence, who also substitutes for his punishment, which is the complement of his sin. Just as the origin of this error lies in the notion of the possibility of exceeding one's duty, so it ends in the notion of redemption through a vicar. However, redemption aims at sin, while the vicar has at his disposal a surplus of merit.

The merit of the fathers is not all concerned with the question of atonement, but in God's historical providence the merit of the fathers is accepted as a bulwark against the moral arrogance of the individual. The individual has no merit at all; all merit belongs to the fathers alone. Therefore God's "remembering," which is so often, and also in this case, appealed to, is to be understood in the following way: when it says "he remembers the love of the fathers," then the fathers are there in the *genitivus objectivus*. God remembers not so much the love of the fathers for him as God's love for the fathers, which is considered the permanent foundation of the history of Israel. And this meaning of the sentence agrees with the sentence which follows: "and he brings the redeemer to their children's children." Hence, the merit of the fathers does not constitute a treasury of values, but consists merely in an historical ideality, in the idea of a theodicy in history. Confronted with history, the individual divests himself of his pride and his selfishness, but wins instead of it his courage and consolation. The fathers have nothing to do with retribution and forgiveness, which is God's act only and in which they have no share. For this there is no need of them, not to mention any other mortal men. Already the murderer Cain has said, according to a Midrash, that he does not despair of God's power to forgive: "Heaven and earth you can bear and not my sin!" At this point the double meaning in the Hebrew word for forgiveness comes to a Promethean expression: it means to bear sin and to take sin upon oneself. God must be able to take upon himself the sins of those who are made in his image.

The error of "the treasury of merits" discloses the general danger that is connected with the problem of retribution. Only that punishment is strictly moral which the confessing man adjudges for himself and takes upon himself, and which he therefore asks from God for his redemption. The punishment is therefore conditioned by his redemption. However, the positive side of retribution, the reward, belongs to the prohibited land of eudaemonism. There is only one reward that does not fall under this verdict, and this is the one which is identical with the good act itself. This identity the Mishnah expressed in a great passage: "The reward of duty is the duty."[67] Spinoza translated this passage of the Mishnah literally without mentioning the source: *praemium virtutis virtus*. There is no other reward, and there can and should be no other reward, than the infinite, unceasing task of morality itself. Any other reward is heterogeneous to morality and therefore injures its purity.

That the Torah does not tie a reward to the observance of the commandments would deserve the greatest admiration if this were not
recognized merely as a consequence of the monotheistic idea. Three
exceptions particularly confirm the rule. The commandment to honor
one's mother and father promises long life. But this long life is promised not to the single individual but to the people "in the land, which
the Eternal your God, gives you." The prohibition not to take from
the bird's nest the mother with her young ones at the same time is to
be understood in the same way. This commandment, which presupposes already in animals a sense of family, lays the historical foundation for life in the state. Of course, the state is already a concession to
pure morality. Since the latter, however, is dependent upon its application, the concession is at the same time a positive determination. So
also, to be sure, the above-mentioned reward of long life promised
for the state is a weakening of the idea that the reward consists only
in the action itself. Since the action, however, as a human and historical one is necessarily related to the state, this weakening is, nevertheless, at the same time an amplification. If the state is promised duration, this duration is thought of as a reward which is immanent in
the piety to parents, in the duty to the family. The parents are here,
as it were, the symbol of the fathers.

The merit of the fathers is therefore the precise consequence of the
fundamental biblical idea that rejects any individual reward, and relates and limits all notions connected with merit and expectation of
reward exclusively to the historical continuance of the people. Only
the fathers have merit, and only the people in its history may expect
reward. For the individual, however, the reward consists in the action
itself, to which he is called, but which never can become a merit, since
its measure can never be fulfilled, let alone exceeded. As the highest
reward for the individual there remains the goal set for him in the
"nearness" to God, in the nearing of oneself to God.

Thus the idea of the psalm prevails, that the nearness to God is
my good. And, therefore, Albo's idea, that the nearness to God accomplishes that which the beyond has to mean, also prevails.[68] For
retribution, too, is accomplished in immortality, which is that of the
spirit and its infinite self-perfection in the infinite development of the
human race. The nearness to God has to lead to this infinite development of the concept of the soul, which we could also find in the above-
mentioned Midrash.

All these notions are the consequences of monotheism and its messianic idea. In this messianic concept of the soul, we can recognize the
opposition to the pantheistic concept of God as well as to the pantheis-

tic concept of soul. In the presence of the infinite concept of the soul of the human race, the concept of the soul of the universe disappears. The human soul is not the world-soul. Its infinity does not coincide with that of the world, but it has always to remain limited to the specific concept of man and his moral infinity. The universe has no morality. Its infinity is a mathematical-physical one and is contained in it. It can be thought of as a task only with regard to mathematical insight and inquiry. The human soul, on the contrary, is always only an infinite task, which can never be contained in any finite element.

Here, too, it is possible to see that the value of human morality is only patch-work, and can never be meritorious. It always needs the reconciliation with God and, hence, God's grace. Every apparent merit is always infected with sin. But because of this the moral work of man is not defiled, for sin too occurs unwittingly *(shegagah)*. Thus, in the system of monotheism, every link is linked to the other. And, thus, this system of correlation between God and man shuts itself up, with complete inner consistency, against the monistic error of pantheism. One God and one soul, a human soul: this is the teaching of monotheism. Pantheism, on the contrary, says: one world-soul, which itself is the one God. The world, however, has only mathematical necessity. In it there is only the logic of that which occurs, but not the ethics of action. Man only is in possession of action. The latter, however, is an infinite task.

One has to recognize the great value of the idea of the merit of the fathers; through this formula all the ambiguities connected with the problem of the world beyond are eliminated. All offensiveness is mitigated, all contradictions become accessible to solution. The punishments, which in principle are already disposed of in repentance, are brought to naught in competition with the messianic times. Moreover, reward by itself deprives moral action of its own worth and damages its purity, as reward in the afterlife damages the moral independence of infinite development. It also threatens to endanger responsibility by introducing the danger of mythology into the false concept of merit. The merit of the fathers conjures away all these dangers. Only the fathers have merit, and only they are permitted to have it as that light in history which illuminates the wandering in the desert in the history of the people, as well as in the history of mankind, and should illuminate the goal of the road.

Truly, it is not an isolated saying: "Be not like slaves, that minister to the master for the sake of receiving a bounty" [Pirke Aboth 1,3]. The Talmud already pointed to the order of the words in which the reception of revelation was confirmed: "We will do and hearken."

First, the doing was assumed and only thereupon the hearing and understanding. This is no offense against the fundamental demand for knowledge of God. For this knowledge is at the same time love; it is therefore moral knowledge, knowledge of practical reason. One has to assume the moral task only; one has solely to assume God's command. This duty has precedence over knowledge, not to mention its independence of any success and any reward that might follow it. "The reward of duty is duty." This saying conveys only the idea that the receiving of a reward cannot be made into a condition of worship.

There is another saying in the Talmud, which formulates the autarchy of duty: "Better is the one who acts being commanded, than the one who is not commanded and acts."[69] Apparently, through the command the act loses its autonomy and its origin is put in God's command. But this also eliminates from the act any egotistical motive. Every thought of success, not to mention reward, is far removed from this origin. The command comes from God. He is the unique good. His command is therefore the command of goodness. With regard to this good, what meaning could a reward have? Could it be a new good, a good of its own? We may recognize in the concept of the command and its identity with duty the reason which liberated religion from eudaemonism. All reward belongs to eudaemonism. Duty, as the law of God, is the opposite of eudaemonism, is identical with the law of morality. For God is the guarantor of the autonomous morality of man, insofar as he is the guarantor of the infinite development of the human soul.

God's command is the religious expression that may not contradict, but rather must be equivalent to, the principle of autonomy, except for their methodological difference. If I act of my own will, I must first of all prove to myself that my will is not an affect,* but pure will. Therefore, pure ethics, in its application to man, cannot do without the concept of duty; it must change the moral law into duty. The analogous change is completed in religion by transforming moral law into God's command. Now, however, in the notion of the merit of the fathers, it can clearly be seen how religion is bound to the method of ethics, and into what danger it runs if it separates itself from ethics. Pure will must stand the test of submitting itself to the law of duty. This submission is not a violation of autonomy but rather its confirmation. Moral law is the law of moral reason. If it should be applicable to the psychological nature, to the soul of man, it must be formulated as the law of duty. Moral law is the autonomous law of my reason, inso-

*For the relation of affect to pure will, see p. 404. [S.K.]

far as I can certify my will as the will or reason through my submission, through taking upon myself the law as my duty.

Thus, we also recognize a further opposition to the notion of the treasury of merits. The martyr has no merit, for his action has to be simple duty, the measure of which he is unable to exceed. He would be a superman if he became a saint. His will would not remain the human will of duty if it were not based absolutely on submission to duty. Where martyrs are bred, the concept of the hero makes the concept of the soul ambiguous, and this ambiguity affects the pure morality of the afterlife. Only for three sins must a human being endure death: for idolatry, for murder, for incest.[70] In order to resist the inducement to the commission of these sins, man is permitted to disdain the earthly life. But this devaluation of the earthly world should not at the same time bring about the devaluation of the world beyond, nor should the latter through a change in meaning be made a substitute for the earthly world. This, however, happens when the world beyond is made a treasure-house through the alleged merits of this world. The strict meaning of duty overthrows any notion of merit or reward. It also liberates the beyond from the suspicion of being a penitentiary, or a Paradise with its delicacies. The spirit returns to God. This sentence expresses the soul's origin as well as its last refuge. And with this, the soul is definitively liberated from the concept of hobgoblin with its mythical origin. It is also liberated from being retroactively applied to the earthly life with its sins and its alleged merits. The soul has no retroactive connection, but its continuity consists exclusively in the future, in the infinity of development. This wisdom is contained in the saying about the merit of the fathers.

We must now anticipate a point that is important for the characteristic form of Jewish prayer. "Not because of our righteousness do we lay our supplications before Thee, but because of Thy great love." This is said in the daily morning prayer. "What are we, what is our life, what is our righteousness, what is our charity, what is our help, what is our power, what is our courage?" In such a detailed manner is one's own worth denied and all hope is directed to God. But this hope invokes the merit of the fathers, in which again God's merit, which is his care for the fathers, is included. It is invoked for the sake of historical understanding and for the continuation of striving and life on earth. For as we already found it formulated in prayer, the love of the fathers is not their own love for God, but rather God's love for them. Hence, the merit of the fathers is another expression for the final and only support of the religious consciousness, which is God. The merit of the fathers is the merit which God in his love for them, in the covenant which he concluded with them, bestowed upon them, or rather bestowed in them to their descendants. Thus the merit of the fathers becomes a standard for the vocation of the people.

We turn now to another problem connected with immortality. A great difficulty for personal human morality is presented in the problem of the application of the ethical distinction of good and evil to particular human actions and their initiators. This is even more difficult than the evaluation of good and bad with regard to well- or ill-being. If one were generally to abstain from any judgment, then the dangers of indifference and opportunism would be unavoidable. Personal judgment must be ventured; it is not to be left to the courts, or submitted in humility to God. Moral judgment is an unavoidable duty, upon the exercise of which depends the vitality of morals. However, religion must create precautions in order to prevent the encroachments of personal judgment and, in general, to circumscribe the area which may not be transgressed.

The "Sayings of the Fathers" is that part of the Mishnah which has been inserted, in its entirety, into the sequence of prayer for Sabbath afternoons during the summertime. These Sayings of the Fathers are introduced with the sentence: "All Israel has a share in eternal life (*olam haba*)." The difference between good and evil is apparently entirely ignored here. If the question of the permissibility of ignoring this difference arises, then the first valid answer is: repentance and redemption hold good for everyone. Consequently, the morality of everyone is, in principle, presumed to be unimpaired. The possibility of redemption exists beyond any doubt; therefore, it can be assumed as realized in each individual case.[71] To which concept are we indebted for assistance in the case of the difficult moral conflicts of personal judgment?

Afterlife, immortality, has rendered this assistance, not the messianic future. To be sure, the thesis holds: "There is not a righteous man upon earth, that doeth good and sinneth not" [Eccles. 7:20]. But against this stands the talmudic sentence: "On that place, on which the repentant sinners stand, the perfectly righteous could not stand."[72] The power of repentance overcomes every human sin. Therefore, it is just to ascribe to immortality at least, to eternal life, the possibility of effacing the difference between good and bad. The Mishnah does not say that all Israel is equally good, but it grants to all Israel, without individual distinction, a share in the eternal life.[73] This share is mediated and secured by repentance. It is in every man's power to repent; therefore everyone has a share in eternal life. The threat of eternal hell does not exist for anyone. This specific form of punishment does not exist at all in the Jewish notion of retribution.

The above thesis therefore is a precautionary and educational measure for the management of moral judgment. Absolute condemnation is not permitted. The individual continues to belong to the whole of Israel, and as such has a secure share in eternal life. This share is the religious expression of moral acknowledgment. The loss of moral dignity is therefore generally impossible, and the moral judgment receives from this thesis of the moral dignity of every man its precise directive, which is valid for each individual case. This directive is at first given in the spirit of religious limitation; for only within these limits can repentance, with all its conditions fulfilled, be assumed to achieve redemption as its assured goal.

However, religion, as we have observed, oversteps these narrow boundaries, which promoted and carried out a humane use of moral problems at first among one's own people. We have seen that the general love for mankind is the messianic consequence of monotheism, for which the love of the stranger paved the way. God loves the stranger. Therefore you should love the stranger. You were strangers in the land of Egypt. You know the heart of the stranger. National history offered the occasion for the monotheistic direction of social as well as general politics. Furthermore, the stranger becomes not only the "righteous stranger" but also the "stranger-sojourner." The Torah granted equal rights to a non-Jew under the Jewish law and state. However, the Jewish consciousness was not satisfied even with these precise regulations of the fundamental religious concept by the state.

Thus to the notion of the stranger (*ger*) was joined the notion of the "son of Noah." It is the complement to the "children of Israel." The notion of the son of Noah is based on the presupposition that revelation, that religion, did not begin only with the revelation on Sinai. The patriarchs already precede this revelation. Noah, however, stands in a more universal relationship to religion. For with Noah, God made a covenant with the human race and with the earth, that no destruction would come upon them any more. Thus, all men are under Noah's protection, through God's covenant with him. As a religious concept, the son of Noah requires its religious foundation, which becomes the moral complement for any specific religion. "The seven commandments of the sons of Noah" form this moral foundation. The first of these seven commandments is the establishment of juridical institutes (*Gerichtsverfassung* – דינים). Law is the foundation of human morality. Custom cannot be a sufficient substitute for it. The only sufficient basis is the formulation of laws, the establishment of a court of justice and juridical institutes. What the love of God as the sum total of all laws expresses within religion, law formulates for universal human morality.

Therefore, Maimonides could take law as the basis for his understanding of the sacrifice, which in turn is the foundation for his general understanding of the ceremonial law. Jeremiah says: "For I spake not unto your fathers, nor commanded them in the day that I brought them out of the land of Egypt, concerning burnt offerings or sacrifices" (Jer. 7:22). Maimonides then interprets this sentence, by relating it to the institution of the statutes and judgments in Mara (Exod. 15:25). Law is the true foundation of the Torah, and the Torah makes itself equally valid for the stranger and the native: "One Torah shall there be to him that is homeborn, and to the stranger that sojourneth among you" (Exod. 12:49). Only through the idea of equality before the law did the love of the stranger, and the concept of man it contains, become truly actualized. Thus the Torah itself demanded that foundation which Deuteronomy laid for it in the political-legal concept of man.

The concept of man, however, should be secured not only through this establishment of law. Messianism demanded an extension of this concept, which corresponds to its kinship with the idea of immortality. Hence, eternal life had to be granted also to the stranger. This was really a daring venture, for with this the prerogative of monotheism would have to be abolished. All Israel possesses the prophylactic means, which is repentance. Now the juridical institutes are to replace the religious court of judgment and the seven commandments of the sons of Noah are to replace the six hundred and thirteen positive and negative commandments of the Torah. Moreover, with respect to the highest goal of human hope—eternal life—the sons of Noah are considered on a par with the sons of Israel. This is exactly the way Messianism wants it to be. Only through this consequence does it achieve its truth. Thus, eternal life has to become an auxiliary means for the gigantic task of actualizing Messianism. For, truly, the sons of Noah are the giants in the struggle against a monotheistic Olympus.

The danger that lies in the concept of the son of Noah is alleviated by another concept, which has also been brought about through the medium of imortality. The stranger and the son of Noah become "the pious of the peoples of the world." The son of Noah belongs to the prehistory of religion. And as much as the latter is already shaped providentially, it still remains a primitive prehistory as against the proper, messianic history of mankind. In the latter, the actual forces are the "peoples of the world," in contrast to which

the sons of Noah are merely symbolic masks. What matters is to acknowledge literally the moral equality of the peoples of the world.
The sons of Noah still veil this equality, even though they are defined by the seven commandments. The point of gravity in the latter
is still only in the foundation of morality; but it is important to grasp
the entire problem in its full extent. What is of importance is to acknowledge the peoples of the world, and indeed to give religious
expression to this acknowledgment. In this way originated the term:
"the pious of the peoples of the world" (חסידי אומות העולם). The peoples of the world do not have the Torah, yet piety may originate
among them. This expression of moral recognition is more definite and
therefore even more daring than the acknowledgment of the share of
all peoples in eternal life. Only now is the concept of man saved, only
now is it created. The peoples of the world have pious men in their
midst.

What could be the fundamental meaning of the pious one (*chas-
sid*)? He is the one who exercises *chessed*. And what is *chessed*? It
occurs mostly in connection with grace (חן) and love (אהבה). Hence,
it might perhaps be a middle term between grace and compassion, and
as such correspond to mildness, beneficence, and also to meekness.
With respect to this term also, God is the original concept, and therefore the pious man belongs immediately to his God. About the pious
the psalm says "Thy pious." Now, however, this exclusive relation of
the pious to the unique God has to be loosened and broken. How
could this have been achieved? How could this notion of the pious
of the peoples of the world originate?

Here, too, immortality had to help out. Thus arose the sentence in
the Talmud which Maimonides in his legislative code (*Mishneh Torah*)
formulated as follows: "The pious of the peoples of the world have a
share in eternal life."[74] This removes all doubt that the non-Jew may be
acknowledged as pious: eternal life procured him this acknowledgment. The immortality of the human soul won religious equality for
him in the form of moral equality. The concept of the world also contributed toward this. The peoples of the world are elevated to citizens
of the future world. Hence, the future world is the idealization of the
present one. Now the son of Noah is surpassed by these "pious."
Now it is not only a fundamental moral-judicial concept, but it has
become a religious one. The man who takes upon himself the seven
commandments is not only a son of Noah but, by all means, a
pious one. Through this, the seven commandments, although not
put on a par with the six hundred and thirteen commandments, are
coordinated with them, and this coordination by all means corresponds

to the basic ideas of the Mishnah, as we shall see more precisely.

The moral values are turned into full-fledged religious ones. The pious of the peoples of the world are able to produce such values of pure morality. We shall see later that piety (חסידות) occupies the highest rank in the Jewish teaching of virtue, and this in accordance with the precepts of the Mishnah. At present, however, we would like particularly to consider the consequence Messianism attains from the idea of immortality. The share the peoples of the world have in eternal life has brought about complete religious equality between Israel and the other peoples. By the means of immortality the concept of the soul has elevated the concept of man above the differences of peoples and even of religions. What the concept of mankind did not succeed in achieving completely even in the messianic idea of mankind, which presupposes the positive acknowledgment of monotheism, this height, this secured position of the absolute concept of man, has been achieved by immortality. Now man stands only on the seven legs of pure morality, and nevertheless he is the absolutely complete man. Eternal bliss helped him to this and bestowed upon him this final security of his human rights. As long as eternal bliss is still bound to certain conditions of faith, not only is it itself illusory, but with it the moral equality of men, as well as true humanitarianism, are also illusory.

With the principle involved in the notion of the pious of the peoples of the world, the Talmud has achieved a fundamental distinction between Judaism, on the one hand, and Christianity in all its variations, on the other. Salvation for all of the latter means salvation through faith in Christ. In whatever manner this faith may be developed, in its entirety as in its particular determinations, it always, in all of its nuances, remains faith in Christ. Christ remains the indispensable condition of salvation. Thus, there is within this affiliation no true humanity, insofar as the latter is based on the religious equality of the right to bliss. Through the talmudic sentence, however, bliss is granted to man as such, and the conditions of humanity are determined only within pure human morality. Faith in the unique God is not demanded, but only abstinence from blaspheming God and from idolatry, which latter has its positive share in the violation of morality with respect to chastity. While, therefore, in Christianity not only faith in God but also faith in Christ is demanded, Judaism does not even make faith in God a condition for bliss. Such a height of consistency is reached through the medium of immortality.

This is how we survey the sequence of the concepts, which are at work here in their ascent. The stranger has become the son of Noah, and the latter has become the pious of the peoples of the world.

Here too, as everywhere in Jewish dogmatics, politics has rendered its salutary mediation. The stranger has not only become the ideal son of Noah, but, as the stranger-sojourner, he has remained a political concept. The latter concept is, however, in conflict with the concept of natural law, which in this case is represented by the religious concept. Should political science be satisfied with this identification of the stranger-sojourner with the pious of the peoples of the world, particularly when this still remains a living problem for the continuing legal teaching of the rabbinical literature? Could the danger which this concept of natural law, with its religious acknowledgment, carries for the state be overlooked? Should not precautionary measures be taken that would secure the state against this complete religious equality of the stranger-sojourner with the pious of the peoples of the world? These measures would guard the state against the subjective changes in the beliefs of this religious citizen, changes that are unavoidable because of the state's purely moral regulations. If now this pious one changes his subjective beliefs, what would it help if he were to deprive himself of human moral rights, since he, as stranger-sojourner has already acquired religious citizenship? The rabbinical teaching, therefore, had to make a provision against this danger that lies within its own legal concepts.

With regard to this point, Maimonides had all the more pressing reason to protect the Jewish doctrine of the state, since through his own formulations Jewish religious teaching had been brought to its highest and purest expression of humanity. This statement would be necessary on account of the religious teaching itself, but this necessity is intensified so as to become a duty because of Spinoza's polemic against Maimonides. For Spinoza's polemic has become the source of a fundamental misunderstanding of the Jewish religion. As such it has affected the most noble ages of German literature, and even today has not exhausted itself. Kant obtained from Spinoza his knowledge and his judgment of Judaism. While Leibniz, like the Middle Ages and modern times, still knew and valued Maimonides, Kant came to know Maimonides only through Spinoza. It seemed to Kant, through Spinoza, that in Maimonides Judaism is rightly condemned. It is therefore important to refute Spinoza on this point and to justify Maimonides. Just as he makes rationalism effective for the entire teaching of Judaism, so he perfects it at this crossroad.

In two passages Maimonides grants, without any limitation, eternal life to these pious of the peoples of the world (Tshuba 3,5; Eduth 11, 10). Only in one passage (Melach., sect. 8) does he attach a condition to it, which, as a competent commentator says, he does "out of his own opinion," and for which there is no basis in the Talmud.[75] This passage reads: "Everyone who takes upon himself the seven commandments and is intent to practise them, is of the pious of the peoples of the world and he has a share in the world to come, but under the condition that he takes them over and exercises them because the Holy one, praised be He, commanded them in the Torah and proclaimed them through our teacher Moses, that the sons of Noah were bound by them before. But if he has exercised them out of the judgment of understanding, such a one is not anymore a stranger." In this political tractate (about kings), Maimonides no longer discusses the rights and duties of the stranger-sojourner only from the point of view of the natural-law concept of the Noachide and, as such, of the "pious." Therefore, Maimonides attaches to the taking over of the Noachidic commandments the condition of their acknowledgment as a Mosaic law. Through this acknowledgment the sojourner in no way pledges himself to a personal belief in this origin of the commandments, but only to compliance to them in that sense. This sense is the origin of the law of the state into which he wishes to enter. Therefore, he obligates himself only to protect himself against the possibility that his reason, his understanding, might one day cause him to decide differently, for instance, with regard to his abstention from idolatry in the Jewish state or from incest. If this decision were to be left to his own understanding, as his original decision would have been, the state would not be protected against his subjectivity.

In the dispute between Rabbi Joshua and Rabbi Eliezer about the Noachide as the pious man, Maimonides decided for Rabbi Joshua. All the more he had to feel obligated in the case of the stranger-sojourner to add the above condition as his own consideration. In the text of the subsequent passage there is an admitted writing or printing error. Therefore one has to suppose that the subsequent exclusion of the "pious" could be accounted for by this error; or this exclusion of the pious one could be explained by the fact that the Noachide is not to be counted as a pious one in the sense that he thereby also has to be a stranger-sojourner. Moreover, in the passage that limits the rights of the Noachide, one should notice, beside the error, a new concept: in addition to the pious of the peoples of the world, their wise people are also distinguished and bequeathed with eternal life. In the corrected passage the Noachide who would not accept the above-mentioned condition would be counted only among the wise of the peoples of the world. It is, however, questionable whether as a wise man he does not already have a share in eternal bliss.

Spinoza's entire argument is therefore untenable. The condition Maimonides attaches is found only in one out of the three passages, and in this passage the problem is not that of the pious man, but of the stranger-sojourner, whereas in the other two passages this unauthorized condition is not advanced. The Talmud, on the contrary, does not know anything of this condition. And thus it remains that the Talmud acquired for all times the great merit of having achieved the strictly moral realization of messianic monotheism in this term "the pious of the peoples of the world." With this the Talmud has merely carried out a consistent development. The Tosefta (Sanhedrin, Sect. 13) had already stated this clear determination, so that Maimonides' decision is supported by it. The rabbinical development only carries the fundamental messianic idea to its consequence. And it is to be noted that this consequence at first makes a division between the wise and the pious, but finds its final formulation in the pious. The wise, therefore, form a cultural and historical occasion for the messianic consequence; however, only the pious, only the purely moral value, bring the idea to its terminological conclusion. How much, however, the acknowledgment of the wise contributed to the execution of tolerance and humanity can be recognized from the benediction one is obliged to make at the sight of a wise one of the peoples of the world: "Blessed be He who bestowed of his wisdom to the flesh and blood." In the case of a Jewish wise one it says: "to them that revere Thee." Thus, the share of divine wisdom is acknowledged also in the wisdom of a non-Jew and made an occasion for a benediction.

Let us now survey the whole sequence of concepts, which arose in close connection with the idea of immortality. It confirms a point that seems to us to hold good for the classical origin of the philosophic idea of immortality in Plato. The soul is not assumed for the sake of immortality, but immortality only for the sake of the soul. In his teaching on immortality, Plato intended, with all his proofs, to provide a deeper foundation for the concept of the soul and the development of all its conditions for the human consciousness as human. The soul, in the first place, had to be proven to be the sum of all the activities and capacities of pure thought. For this purpose it had to be separated from all bodily organs and their activities. And this separation had to be carried through with such a rigor that even the appearance of mysticism was not shunned. Moreover, one could always take over from mysticism an advantage from which ethics could profit.

Above all, immortality had to designate the soul as the sum total of moral ideas. No instinct, no bodily affect, no pleasure and no pain, no animal-like drive, should be permitted to be called the foundation and power of the human will. Only the soul wills; the body desires. Only the soul is capable of the good; only the soul thinks the idea of the good, and only it itself, with its will, is capable of executing the good; the soul alone is capable of action. Only it has reason and is reason, in the double sense of theoretical and practical reason.

Plato establishes immortality for the sake of this essential and systematic characterization of the soul. For the body is mortal, and everything mortal must be body, as it must in general be matter. But the soul is spirit in the logical and ethical sense. Only with Plato, therefore, is the soul essentially liberated from all the primitive, mythological meaning attached to it, although Plato himself in his poetic spirit still remains bound up with mythology. Thus, we can solve all the riddles which the arguments and the proofs of the Platonic teaching on immortality necessarily pose. The thesis proper is only hidden in immortality, but is actually related to the concept of the soul itself, which cannot be bestowed on the mortal body. Through the medium of immortality Plato carried out the intention of his teaching on the soul, which so much determines his entire doctrine of ideas that one is tempted to identify them.

We can represent the connection of these concepts in the Jewish teaching of immortality in an analogous manner. We had to start with the idea that Jewish piety does not procede to formulate the teaching of immortality in a didactic manner. This is connected with its desire to limit itself to moral teaching. It does not have to prove that the soul is spirit, but only that it is moral spirit, the spirit of holiness. With this the separation from all corporality and mortality is sharp enough. Who could believe that holiness can die! Jewish piety, therefore, had to reject the myth: "For Thou wilt not abandon my soul to the nether-world; neither wilt Thou suffer Thy godly one to see the pit" (Ps. 16:10). And since, in addition, the concept of God created the messianic future, the soul was also assured of a future. Thus, Messianism added to the concept of the soul the factor of development, and made the soul the messianic principle of development.

To the messianic development the individual's development could and had to be joined. For holiness had been secured in the reconciliation and redemption through God. Thus, man had become not only the symbol of mankind but—as the individual, as the person, as I—the appointed carrier of holiness. Thus, it is understandable that Ezekiel, though in another methodoligical connection, established the concept of man with the same word, "soul." What else the spirit has to govern is of no interest at this moment; but with the most intense energy the spirit turns to the religious concept of man, which is founded in man's morality, in his repentance, and is fulfilled in his reconciliation with God. What else immortality may mean is here represented by the share of God in the human soul. It is "the portion of God from above and the heritage of the Almighty from on high" (Job 31:2). What need is there for a statement on immortality, or even a proof of it, if the human soul is provided with a share in the divinity?

This explains the caution of Jewish religious teaching with regard to the dogma of immortality. In any case, the latter borders on mysticism at this point, and we have seen everywhere else that Jewish teaching touches this border, but does not cross it. The difference between God and man should always be preserved and exactly maintained. It is very difficult consistently to separate monotheism from mysticism, in regard to the exposition of the idea of immortality.

As in Plato the purpose of immortality is to bring out the concept of the soul as the sum total of consciousness, so also the purpose of the Jewish teaching of immortality is to develop the concept of man for the sake of the correlation between man and God. Accordingly, immortality receives a name analogous to that of the messianic future, namely, that of a future world. *olam* [world] in the Hebrew language already has the secondary meaning of eternity.

The future time carries in it this eternity of development. Moreover, the eternity of the world in itself makes the human soul a carrier of infinite development. But this development always has the uniform task of increasing, of elevating, and of penetrating more inwardly the correlation of man and God. That even the concept of piety itself is internalized into the concept of man through the medium of immortality is a corroboratory symptom. This task of internalizing the relation of man to God had to be felt as the consequence of monotheism. The concept of the Noachide had been originated. Consequently, the concept of the pious of the peoples of the world had expressly to be formulated for the future. Only in it does the messianic concept of man receive its completion.

What did even the concept of merit gain through this medium! All the mythology of retribution, particularly of retributive punishment, so far as it was not transfigured, was eliminated. And what an idealization of immortality lies in the merit of the fathers! The fathers are immortal because their merit lives on in their effects. They are, therefore, immortal in their merit.[76] And since their merit benefits their descendants, the latter also become immortal, because they participate in the merit of the fathers. It is merit that makes men immortal. It is merit that constitutes the soul. The soul, in the first place, is the historical soul, and only as such is it also the individual soul of man. Merit lies in history, not in man, and even in the fathers only through their being the fathers of the history of Israel and, through it, of the history of mankind. This is the further ferment that the notion of immortality produces.

Immortality is the immortality of merit—but what is all human merit? Even the fathers do not have it by themselves. God's love for them is their merit. Only God's merit is their merit. This is the deepest meaning of the Jewish concept of immortality. God has made his covenant with man. God's covenant with man contains the immortality of the human soul. God made the covenant already with Noah. Consequently, the son of Noah had to become the pious of the peoples of the world. Thus, the human soul had to become immortal and, indeed, without any further condition being attached to its share in eternal life. The human soul as such became capable of being saved by God. No mediation was allowed to enter; it would have broken the immediacy of this correlation. It would have called immortality into question, because it would have attached conditions. The soul is given by God. And it returns to God, who gave it.

No condition is attached to immortality. Even redemption cannot be made the condition for immortality. Redemption is rather the presupposition of immortality. And to redemption itself no other condition is attached but the self-redemption of the human soul in its correlation with God and, consequently, in its confidence in God. Therefore, just as merit is not an allowable element in the concept of immortality, neither is the possible positive proof and legitimation of sinlessness. Thus, the following thesis of the Mishnah is of fundamental importance: "All Israel has a share in the world to come." For this share no special demonstration of positive piety is necessary. The whole of Israel stands here for the concept of man in general, for the whole of Israel includes messianic mankind. Consequently, the pious of the peoples of the world arose out of the above thesis of the Mishnah. In the presence of the concept of immortality, sin disappears from the concept of the soul of man. Man is immortal, he has an equal share with all men in eternal life—this thesis effaces the moment of sin from the concept of the human soul. The latter is not thereby betrayed into indifference with regard to good and bad, but is only exempted from the indelibility of sin. This condemns as false the idea that sin is an essential part of man. Sin only presses its way to man as long as he lives. But his sin is only *shegagah* in God's eyes. And

God forgives it, because man in his confidence in God is able to achieve his self-sanctification and self-purification. Therefore, he does not die with the death of his body, but the messianic God also gives his individual soul an infinite development, an eternal existence. Thus all the fundamental concepts of religion radiate in the direction of the immortality of the soul, and from it the rays shine back to the center— God. And this radiation evolves in its entirety from the correlation of God and man.

To the eternity of God corresponds, as an anthropomorphic consequence, the eternity of man. Liberated of the anthropomorphic setting, this eternity of man means only the infinite continuation of the correlation of man and God. Without immortality God's creation, revelation, and providence could not have existence. Thus, Messianism is only an analogy of immortality, while monotheism itself in its correlation of God and man has immortality as its necessary consequence. Messianism offered the main conditions for the concept of man; all these conditions culminate in the concept of the pious of the peoples of the world. On the other hand, for the concept of God, monotheism in itself disclosed the idea of immortality; for this goal, all of its fundamental concepts culminate in the concept of reconciliation. Man does attain reconciliation with God. Sin does not possess with him an indestructible character. His soul is pure and therefore immortal. God gave it to him; therefore sin is never his inheritance; his inheritance is rather only and exclusively his soul; it is as a human soul that the soul is immortal, not as the soul of a faith, not even of the faith in the unique God. If the soul has not yet found God, it always may: it is immortal.

CHAPTER XVI

The Law

The correlation of God and man is the norm of monotheism. This basic notion has also guided the notion of immortality. Through immortality, man is to be brought to the highest, infinite development, but still as man. Polytheism, on the contrary, with the exception of Platonic philosophy, assumes immortality to mean only deification. Man desires to become God. This is the longing of classical man. Christianity, like the classical world, also took over this idea of deification. Monotheism, on the contrary, maintains the separation between God and man in all its concepts.

It is certainly also a characteristic difference between the religion of Moses and every form of polytheism that the unique God does not decree particular commands to particular people, but gives commandments that are valid as laws for all men: the worship of God is tied to obedience to these commandments; they are meant first for the chosen people, then through them for messianic mankind. Correlation requires this. God cannot remain isolated on his Olympus, but as creator of man and as Lord of the whole earth must impose his commandments upon man as laws for their life. The commandment is an isolated order; the law is intended to be valid as the foundation of the moral world.

The law, therefore, is preeminently called teaching. It is not a subjective order, but a theoretical instruction, which therefore can become a duty for man. In all its designations, the only point of reference of the law is always man himself; only the origin lies with God. However, the law never refers to God's being; it therefore never becomes a symbol of God's being and just as little does it become a symbol for the deification of nature. Man alone is the object and the goal of the law. The only goal of the law is his moral perfection, his fulfillment as man. He should not become God but ought always to become more human. He ought always to remain man.

338

The first form of the law, the sacrifice, already reveals the monotheistic character of the Mosaic law. The prophets do not leave any
doubt that the admission of the sacrifice was a concession to the times.
And the philosophers, who are at the same time dogmatists, confirm
this immediately clear circumstance. Psychologically, also, it would have
been impossible for the prophets to rail with such zeal against sacrifices if they had not supposed that the people themselves surmised
the inadequacy of sacrifice and its incongruity with the worship of
the unique God. Although they nevertheless admitted and accepted
sacrifice, they blunted the point of the mystery, in which the pagan
cult has its final goal. In pagan consecration feasts, which are the climax of the sacrificial cult, with its asceticism as well as its voluptuousness, the difference between God and man is supposed to be abolished.
In his sacrifice the Israelite never had such an immediacy: in his
sacrifice the priest always stands between him and God. The Israelite
could wish to become a priest, but never God.

This is also the reason for overcoming the tendency to human
sacrifice. The man or woman being sacrificed to God is supposed to
become of God's kind. Such a goal is considered blasphemous in the
Mosaic law, and therefore human sacrifice could become an abomination. Sacrifice was to become only a means to education and is acceptable only for the sake of man as man. Then came Ezekiel's reformation, which made sacrifice an accessory to the real education
man has to achieve in himself through repentance. Through the latter,
man attains reconciliation with God, but in no way a merging with
God or deification.

Thus, sacrifice is, on the part of man, what creation and revelation
are on the part of God. As revelation is the necessary means for this
correlation, so also is the law. Revelation and law are therefore identical. If the law were not the necessary form of the achievement of
the correlation between God and man, revelation would not be so
either. Thus, God's law is a necessary concept of monotheism.

We already have mentioned that God's law does not contradict the
autonomy of the moral will. There is a difference only in the method
of formulating the concept, which is the difference between ethics
and religion. With regard to sacrifice, however, there arises an important difference of content in the concept of law. We have already
seen how Deuteronomy distinguishes the statutes from the laws, at
least by using two terms. However, Maimonides also defines the
distinction in content between the two concepts, asserting that the
statutes (חקים) are concerned with the entire sphere of the ritual;
the laws (משפטים), however, with the purely moral and political

sphere. Consequently, within religion itself, because within God's laws, a distinction is recognized accordingly as the moral laws are concerned with human life under law and the state, or are exclusively or chiefly concerned with the sphere of worship. In the latter, sacrifices are prominent but do not stand by themselves. The divine work of education makes use of extensive means and precautions. About all of them, it is to be supposed that they belong to the moral education of man, but this education might take wide detours in its course that often may appear roundabout. From the point of view of ethics, this second meaning of the law constitutes a great difficulty for the law of religion.

From the very beginning we have observed how monotheism struggles its way out of polytheism. We have just observed this again in the case of sacrifice. It is most natural to recognize in the law also the early root of its controversy with polytheism. Maimonides, in particular, has for prophylactic purposes surveyed the entire range of this root. It is known how Scripture itself explicitly cautions against seduction by pagan customs and cults. This explains the harsh prescriptions for the destruction of idolatry and the idol worshipers. The cause for some laws, a cause we cannot find, might have lain in the warding off of idolatry. In addition, it might have been that some laws even have their basis in mythological prejudices, or are the result of concessions to them.

A further explanation is contained in the indifference Jewish antiquity displays to the distinction between religion in its narrow meaning and all other branches of worldly culture. Religion becomes the basic constitution of the state. Therefore, the rights and laws of the state become at the same time religious laws. With this, the borderline of pure moral laws is touched and their purity is endangered. For, now, political considerations of only relative value, particularly those of a social and political character, can assume the force of law. This is particularly a danger in the cases of ancient hygiene and medicine, especially since these are connected with the priesthood. This promotes the appropriation of hygienic measures by religious law; in the case of a primitive and incomplete hygienic knowledge, the sphere of the religious law is therefore immensely expanded.

Finally, the cult itself requires its own laws, besides those concerned with the sacrifice and its requirements. But here, also, the collision with the pure moral laws is inevitable. To begin with, the tithes are not merely a tribute to the priest but also tithes for the poor. Similarly, just as little are the firstlings only taxes for the priest, but are alms also. Furthermore, the general consideration of soil improvement introduces the Sabbatical Year with its untilled fields, or the prohibition of the fruits of the trees in the first three years of bearing. Finally, the Sabbath, the central point of all the holidays, is right on the borderline. According to one understanding, it is a symbol of the completion of the creation; according to another understanding, it becomes the symbol of universal human rights, the symbol of the emancipation of the slaves. The other holidays are similarly ambivalent, as already became clear with regard to the Day of Atonement, which, out of the day of sacrificial offering, became the messianic representation of monotheistic reconciliation, and in this mission transformed the New Year's Day into a day of preparation. However, the three other festivals, originally nature and harvest festivals, became at first national and historical festivals, for instance, *Pesach* and *Sukkoth* [Passover and Tabernacles], but through this mediation of history they became religious festivals proper, having their climax in the Feast of the Weeks as the feast of Revelation. Thus, the festivals are part of the legislation that forms the mediation between the religious and the moral meaning of the law. The dietary laws are the most difficult part of ritual legislation; they have developed on the foundation of the commandment concerning animal slaughter. As this foundation itself means a liberation from the otherwise exclusively sacrificial slaughter of animals, so, in the laws about the prohibited animals, with their amplifications in the rabbinical ceremonial law, we find merged all the mythological and anti-mythological considerations alluded to above, as well as manifold hygenic and medical considerations.

Finally, deep historical problems have to be considered here. As it says in Balaam's blessing concerning Israel, "It is a people that shall dwell alone, and shall not be reckoned among the nations" (Num. 23:9), so the history of Israel has worked out and so it is to be understood. Only in this way is it possible to explain to some extent how the nation and with it religion could have preserved itself. We could not understand at all how this people of faith could preserve itself if its habits of life had promoted marriages and economic community with other peoples. This historical motivation may solve in the most simple and decisive way the question regarding the reasons for the commandments which Maimonides so clearly discussed. The historical instinct of the nation established a bulwark against the leveling of its own peculiar character and guarded against its complete destruction. What is involved in this question is the deep mystery of the historical power of an idea to survive. Political considerations, as well as cultural conflicts of various kinds, are unavoidable in this connection. The development of religion itself is connected with the phases in which these cultural problems take place. But the reason of religion hides or reveals itself in these grave conflicts, which cannot change anything in the great historical task: to preserve alive the religious idea in its own peculiarity and in its historical efficacy. Extremes in the use of ways and means are inevitable in this process; the balancing-out has to be left to development. The law in its rigid strictness, as well as in its living flexibility, can only be understood in its historical significance, in which it is a model for the problem of cultural and historical influence in general; this is the problem of the extent to which ideas or customs and usages are the prevailing powers in the preservation and development of spiritual phenomena. What for history in general takes on the meaning of the opposition between spiritual and material conditions takes on a narrower meaning for the cultural history of religion. Only from this point of view it is possible to evaluate the problem of the Jewish law in a methodologically correct way.

As for the opposition between idea and usage in Jewish law, it is to be noticed that it struggles to come to the fore and unquestionably came to the fore in large areas of its application. Already the fact that the entire ritual, insofar as it is not concerned with hygienic matters but is to have an educational effect, is introduced and is retained expressly as a system of symbols with the technical name of "sign" or "memorial," imprints upon the ritual this ideal character. This ideal character is in no way changed by any of the required signs that are added to the commandment. For the commandment of the fringes does not lose its symbolic character through the fact that the action required at the putting on of the fringes is an unconditional prescription. This prescription is related to a kind of action that can be thought of only as symbolic: "Ye may look upon it, and remember all the commandments." In itself, the fact that one commandment is made the embodiment of all other deprives the action of its absolute value, and through this relation to all the other commandments it becomes an unmistakable symbol. The fringes are therefore an instructive example of the whole class of these laws, because they are associated with seeing. Thereby, seeing becomes beholding by the mind.

The *Tephillin* which were wrongly translated as "phylacteries," have the same symbolic meaning. They are never designated as a means of protection, however, but always as signs for remembering only. The four passages that are put into the cases prove the symbolism unmistakably. The "Hear, O Israel" and "Sanctify unto Me" are the main content.

In the prayers a distinction is found that is conclusive for the symbolic character of the laws. Throughout it says: "Blessed art thou O Eternal our God, King of the Universe, who has sanctified us by his commandments." This wording might seem to suggest that it is through obedience to the commandments themselves that our holiness is brought about. With this, however, the commandments would lose their symbolic character and assume that of the sacrifice. However, in another place in the prayer it says: "Sanctify us with Thy commandments and purify our heart." Here again the symbolic character is made unmistakably clear. The power of sanctification is not in the commandments themselves; instead God is asked to further our sanctification and let it be achieved through the commandments.

Bodin is right, therefore, when in answering the accusation made against the Jewish law, he lets the Jew, Salomo, say that Judaism has abolished the sacrifice, which is preserved in the Christian sacrament, and that the substitute, which is constituted by the ceremonies, consists only in symbolic reminders.

Distrust of the value of the law was aroused principally by Paul, and it has been kept alive through his criticism and polemics. However, it is precisely this criticism that shows the doubtfulness of the opposing point of view. To begin with, Paul's own example reveals how difficult it is to leave the moral law undamaged if one fights against it as a religious law of life. It is not only a personal paradox for Paul when he opposes law to innocence and therefore also to moral law—as if innocence would not be lost without law. In that case the first prohibition in Paradise brought about human sin and then the moral law would be not only superfluous but, even more, damaging.

Paul's intention is to disparage the law as moral law also, because he wants to establish faith in salvation through Christ as the only basis for human morality in its only value, eternal life. Here, therefore, the law as moral law is not opposed to ritual law, but, much more, as moral law it is opposed to faith in Christ's death and resurrection as affording the salvation of man from sin and its recompense, death. In this very polemic one may clearly recognize the value of the law. The law is moral law, or an aid to the moral law. It means nothing else except the education and sanctification of man. However, if it were to have the meaning which Paul, in opposing it, gives to faith, it would have been transferred from man's horizon to that of God. It would then come to that level of sacrifice the Jewish sacrifice abandoned. It would then intervene in God's authority and arrangements, which God causes to be fulfilled in his own being and in the depiction of his being in sacrifice. The sacrifice of Christ in the Mass cannot be called a symbol in the same sense as, say, the Fringes. For if the practice concerning the Fringes is not observed, then the calling to mind of God's comandments which arises from them may not come about, but this would be a breach in the work of human education; with respect to God's being, however, nothing would change. However, the sacrament of the Holy Communion, even if, according to Zwingli, it should be thought of merely as a symbol, still remains confined to God's being and action, to his self-sacrifice for the salvation of man. If, then, the transsubstantiation, the transformation of the material wafer into the body of Christ, is also to be thought of only as the symbolic act of the priest or the preacher, this symbolic act would nevertheless be and remain the depiction of an action in God's being. This is exactly the distinction between the sacrament, even if one were to understand it symbolically, and the symbol of the law, for which the Fringes contain the norm: "in order that ye may look upon it and remember." It never says: produce an action, which imitates God's being. For the Jewish law, God's being consists exclusively in the archetype for the morality of man, not, however, for his bliss. Immortality does not belong to the domain of the law.

As much as Kant strove to bring about an agreement between the idea of Christ and the autonomy of morality, he did not fail to mention that faith can be as statutory as the law with its works. In his unpublished manuscripts, even more than in his published writings, we can find repeated expressions of his doubts and reflections about this difference between Judaism and Christianity. Although he often takes sides with Paul against the statutory law, nevertheless he sometimes takes sides against Paul, recalling the equally grave danger of the statutory faith. According to this, however, the entire problem of the law would no longer belong to the dogmatics of religion, but to practical theology and education.

It is entirely wrong to equate the law with the work of the Church. For the latter is expressly valid as *opus operatum* [performed act]. Intention and faith need not necessarily be excluded from it. The dispute between Catholicism and Protestantism would revolve about a moot point if it were urged that their difference lies only in the matter of intention, only in faith. However, even if faith and intention are included in the works of the Church, they remain, as such, doubtful and open to objection, because the Church is made the only authority that is able to consecrate works as personal actions. While this distinction may indeed exist for Protestantism, it is all the sharper and more fundamental for Jewish Law. There is no Church, no holy shrine, no house of God, and no community from which holiness could stream out over a lawful action. Holiness lies in the lawful action itself and is achieved in it. Man originates holiness, which passes, without the mediation of any other influences, from the action back to its initiator. Therefore, the lawful action never becomes a work that has an absolute value in itself; the work is rather only action and, therefore, the welling-over and exhibition of the actor's intention: it is the offspring of its begetter, of the person who initiates the action.

The two senses of the word for law are very instructive: *Mitzvah* [commandment] means at once law and duty. The correlation of God and man becomes alive in this word. The law comes from God; the duty, from man. And the law is at the same time duty, just as duty is law. God commands man, and man in his free will takes upon himself the "yoke of the law." The law remains a yoke. Even according to Kant's teaching, man is not a volunteer of the moral law, but has to subjugate himself to duty. Thus, the Israelite also must take the yoke upon himself; but with this yoke of the laws he also takes upon himself the "Yoke of the Kingdom of God." There is but *one* yoke: that of the laws and the Kingdom of God. There is no other Kingdom of God but the kingdom of the laws. What other kingdom could there be? The kingdom of morality perhaps? But this is exactly the kingdom of law. Of course, there is a distinction among the laws; this should not be denied. But this distinction is not of the sort which introduces a contradiction into the unity of the law. For what is not moral law in itself is at least thought of and expressly characterized as a means to the promotion of, and education in, the moral law. It may well be another problem whether this identification actually holds true in all cases. This may be disputable; there may be a difference of opinion, of interpretations and judgments, but it is an absolute misunderstanding, an erroneous judgment, to contest or deny the inner relation between these two parts of the law. The authority of the Talmud speaks against this misunderstanding. Its established positive teaching in these matters is not merely a matter of apologetic defense. Therefore, it was possible for religious philosophy to complete the talmudic fortress of religious teaching, as we shall see later.

The objection that the authority of the law is extended too far is not a superficial one, since the law penetrates, with the minuteness of miniature paintings, the whole of life with all its obligations, dominating actions that seem most insignificant as well as the most intimate. One could reply to this that the value of what in itself is right is not diminished in the least, even with exaggerated application to the minute details of life. This point of view, however, does not sufficiently consider the distinctions among the cultural tasks of mankind.

The religious law may in itself be effective as a moral law, but the moral law itself must be limited for the sake of man's other cultural concerns. The moral law should be the supreme guide over all human activities but not the immediate one, not to say the unique and sufficient one. Man also has theoretical and even aesthetic interests that he must foster by concentrating on their goals. If he were to examine and to direct all his cultural tasks and his interests in life exclusively from the moral point of view, he might be lacking in the sovereign impartiality of which the approach to all other cultural activities is in need. The Jewish law, in its one-sidedness, is to be understood and judged fairly only from the viewpoint of the ethical one-sidedness which had as its consequence abstention from any independent interest in natural science, its foundations as well as its branches. The real but also the only danger of the absolute power of the law lies in this one-sidedness of the moral interest with regard to culture.

However, if one disregards this danger, then the privation due to one-sidedness becomes an advantage with regard to their dangers. The motto of the law is the device of the Mishnah, which is taken over in the liturgy: "All thy actions should be for the sake of God's name" (וכל מעשיך יהיו לשם שמים). God's name is the only goal of human action. The name of God contains the fundamental command for the sanctification of God's name. The name of the unique God is joined to the concept of the unique God: "In that day shall the Eternal be Unique and His name unique" (Zech. 14:9). This prophecy has also been taken over into the daily prayer. "Thou shalt not take the name of the Eternal thy God in vain" [Exod. 20:7]. Already the Decalogue stresses the name. This insight into the necessary connection of these concepts should not be spoiled by any cheap information about the superstitious usage of names in paganism and magic. For there, magic is in question, and God's name is taken as a charm. In Judaism, however, the name is joined to the unique God and thereby the connection with hocus-pocus is broken. All thy actions should be in the name of God! In this motto the name cannot signify a magic work, but can be thought of only as a formula that shows how the action of sanctification is made subordinate to God's name. The name of God is synonymous with the Kingdom of God.

This significance of God's name for human action leads to the already mentioned danger that arises from the extension of this guiding concept to the whole area of human action, to "all thy actions." The law embraces the whole of life, with all its actions. As no single action can be withdrawn from the unity of life, in the same way no action can be excluded from the law. If the law is not to recognize any difference between moral law and statute, it cannot allow any exception in its application to all the details of human life.

This principle has an important consequence for the law, which, like every one-sided notion, contains dangers: the distinction between holy and profane is abolished.

It has been abolished as a matter of principle in accordance with the concept of monotheism from the very beginning of Israel's history. Even the prophet is not to constitute any exception of the whole people out of which he came: "would that all the people of the Eternal were prophets" [Num. 11:29]. The priest, moreover, is to occupy an exceptional position only as a Levite and as a servant of the temple. Fundamentally this principle is valid: "And ye shall be unto Me a kingdom of priests, and a holy people" (Exod. 19:6). As the entire people is holy, and not only the priest, so should life in its entirety be holy and not only a life dedicated to a particular kind of holiness. Also, the asceticism of the Nazirite, just as the sacrifice, is merely permitted, not demanded as a holy condition with any special value of holiness. In general, no moment of life and no step in life is to be thought profane. Everything in human life is holy; every human action serves, and is therefore under, the ideal of holiness. Holiness has been already transplanted from the sacrifice to the moral law. Hence, also, the law is the substitute for the sacrifice which became all the more necessary since the sacrifice was concerned only with one single element of life. This isolated singularity, this exclusiveness of the sacrifice, has to be recognized as questionable and therefore supplemented or, rather, surpassed and replaced. A particular element in life may not be distinguished as holy and, hence, a single, solemn action should not be singled out from life in order to idealize life. Such prominence would make the idealization merely symbolic, but, in fact, it has to become real. The genuine worth of an idea must be in the actualization of the ideal. The actualization is better than any symbol. The tendency of the law is directed to this actualization. Therefore, it extends to all actions.

It is from this higher point of view that one must evaluate the objection against the absolute power of the law over all the tasks and labors of life. The objection seems to have a good point; it stresses a real danger that truly exists for the history of religion as well as for its continuation within cultural life. In spite of this, however, it is not decisive with regard to the value of the law itself. For already the absolute power of the law, which permits no difference between the holy and profane, makes it possible to recognize clearly the great cultural value of the sovereignty of the law.

Even apart from this historical significance, the intrinsic worth of
the idea is the decisive standard. Provided that the law contains
in it the moral norm, both theoretically and practically, it cannot
tolerate any exception. Furthermore, should the sphere of the opera-
tion of the law have to be limited on account of other cultural
tasks, history has to develop measures that will be able to bring
about the balancing of the different tasks of culture and consequently to limit the one-sided absoluteness of some of them. Such
modifications through inner reform, traces of which with regard to
important legal forms are already found even in the Talmud, prove
rather than disprove the correctness of the basic principle.

The fundamental norm of our method, which is the correlation
between God and man, has long ago led us to the correlation between man and man, included in the first correlation. To this more
limited correlation corresponds the relationship of sin between man and
man. The necessity of separating this group of sins between man and
man from those between man and God makes the distinction between
purely moral commandments and religious commandments in the
narrower sense unavoidable. We have already found this distinction
in the notions of atonement. Even the Day of Atonement makes the
prior reconciliation between man and man obligatory. Accordingly,
the *Shulchan Aruch* stresses the importance of the reconciliation between man and man for the meaning of *Yom Kipur*.

The Mishnah formulates this distinction in the same spirit. This
Mishnah has been taken over into the daily morning prayer. "These
are the things which have no fixed measure: the corners of the field,
the offering of firstlings, the appearance (on the three festivals), the
deed of loving kindness and the study of the Torah" [Mishnah Peah,
ch. 1]. All these commandments are unmistakably concerned with social
and moral conduct. The corner of the field designates the prescription to
leave some of the harvest behind in each corner (Lev. 19:9-10). The
offering of firstlings is concerned with the offering of the first fruits
(Exod. 23:19), a commandment which came to be restricted to the
first fruits of the soil (Deut. 26:1-14; cf. p. 151). This offering of the
firstlings is especially significant in that it becomes the substitute for
the sacrifice. Another kind of offering branches out from this point;
the consecration (נדר) becomes the substitute of the vow (ודוי).
It is such a consecration, particularly through the prescribed hymn,
that the offering of the firstlings of the fruits of the field becomes.

Not only is one's appearance required on the three feasts (Deut.
16:16), but one must also bring a gift, which develops into the tithe
for the poor (מעשר עני). Of particular significance are the so-

called "deeds of lovingkindness" *(Liebestätigkeit)* (גמילות חסד),
which are distinguished from almsgiving. The verb גמל is significant. Even if the basic meaning of the word is not "recompense,"
but apportionment in general, it is nevertheless beyong question that
the inner linguistic form of the word means predominantly recompense. Certainly, it is not unimportant that this meaning of the word
could become so significant for the deeds of lovingkindness. All
these deeds of lovingkindness are only a recompense for God's love.
This is the meaning of the fundamental term "recompense" which
supplements the proper term for compassion *(Barmherzigkeit)*.
The latter also came to be expressed in the same spirit. Justice is its
fundamental meaning, but the prevailing secondary meaning came
to be charity. This kind of charity, which is mainly actualized in
supporting the poor, is now distinguished from the charity of the
deeds of lovingkindness, which is designated by the word that
means recompense. All deeds of lovingkindness are a recompense, a
recompense for God's love to man, which man has to render to man.
This recompense designates the kind of deed of lovingkindness that
seizes man's inner life with more intimacy than all almsgiving.
The Talmud distinguishes between the charity that is concerned only
with the poor and the superior deeds of lovingkindness of which the
rich man also is in need. In this connection the Talmud does not
treat almsgiving with particular distinction, except that it mentions
it in connection with the "corners of the field," etc., but brings the
"deeds of lovingkindness" into prominence.

Finally, the above Mishnah mentions an apparently purely spiritual
virtue that is also without limit: "the study of the Teaching" [Torah].
It is just this demand that establishes the foundation of the Jewish
religion precisely and securely. The worship of God should be the
knowledge of God. No distinction is admitted between a purely
theoretical and a purely practical knowledge. Knowledge is love,
and love is knowledge. The study of the Teaching is recognized as
the foundation of social morality. If the Talmud had drawn only this
consequence from Scripture, its merit on this account alone could
not be excelled, and would be everlasting for Israel itself as well as
the standard for the entire history of man. For the study of the
Teaching there is no limit set for man, not to speak of a barrier that
would limit it to a special group of men. At this point there is an
irreconcilable difference between monotheism and Plato's philosophical idealism, which considered it a utopian dream that all men
should ever be able to participate in philosophy. Spinoza, too, discloses at this point his inner incongruity with monotheism when he

also declares that it is impossible for the multitude to be capable of morality. The Mishnah, on the contrary, lays down the study of the Teaching as the basic norm for all human beings.

The above prescriptions of the prayer formulate only general fundamental norms of human morals. The prayer, however, is continued in another Mishnah (Baraitha), which reads as follows: "These are the things, the fruits of which a man enjoys in this world, while the stock remains for him for the world to come: viz., honoring father and mother, deeds of lovingkindness, timely attendance at the house of study morning and evening, hospitality to wayfarers, visiting the sick, dowering the bride, attending the dead to the grave, devotion in prayer, and making peace between man and his fellow; but the study of the Torah excels them all."

Whereas in the first Mishnah it says that for these things there is no measure, namely, that there is no set measure established by the Torah, in the second Mishnah the distinction is made between the fruits and the stock. At the same time it is striking that in both versions no mention is made of reward. The fruits are enjoyed as such in this life; the other life preserves the stock from which, however, no deduction is made for the fruit already enjoyed. Thus, the stock is inwardly separated from all reward and, therefore, also from the earthly fruit. If, then, the stock as such consists of eternal life, the latter is acknowledged through this to be infinite life and the infinite development of the human soul.

Under the above category of commandments the commandment of the Decalogue, the honoring of father and mother, stands first. However, the Decalogue promises a reward precisely for this. It would seem therefore, that the reward, which properly speaking is not a personal one but one which secures the preservation of the state, should be more closely characterized in this Mishnah by the distinction between the fruits and the stock. Furthermore, it expressly mentions deeds of lovingkindness without explicitly mentioning the other kind of charity which is concerned with almsgiving. Whereas in the first Mishnah the study of the teaching is mentioned generally, in the second one it is supplemented by particular stipulations, namely, activity in the house of study and early attendance in the morning and evening. Further, the social duties are specified: hospitality to wayfarers, nursing of the sick, burial of the dead, and a more intimate family care in the dowry for the bride. Beside these social duties, which are deepened by the duty of making peace between men, mention is made of a duty concerned with the inner person: devotion in prayer. For this devotion a word is used here that usually means to meditate, although the general expression for devotion (כונה) means, characteristically enough, the preparation and readying of the soul, in this case for prayer. This word for devotion alone would show sufficiently that intention is the fundamental factor of Jewish worship and of all religious activity.

However, this sentence says that the study of the Teaching excels all other activities. It might seem that intellectual endeavor, asceticism, and mysticism are thereby supported. In this respect, however, the Mishnah is supported by the body of religion, which does not permit a separation between theory and practice, and therefore can assert that theory is the root of all education and development of man. There is no correct knowledge which would not bring forth a correct action. From this fundamental insight the Mishnah derives the result, that study excels all other commandments.

In making the above distinction and in rendering prominent the purely moral commandments, there is no doubt that the Talmud distinguished between the purely moral commandments and the religious commandments in the more narrow sense, but it did not separate them. As we see from the example of devotion in prayer and from the prominence given to the commandment to honor one's parents, the moral commandments are clearly thought of in connection with the religious ones. In this connection we recall the prominence given to the confession of purely moral transgressions in the prayer of the Day of Atonement. Furthermore, we recall the distinction that was already fundamental in Deuteronomy, namely, that between the ordinances (חקים) and the judgments (משפטים).

Maimonides starts with this distinction. However, he was preceded by a religious philosopher whose wise path he could follow. Ibn Daud was at the same time a historian, and as such he was able to survey the religious laws from the point of view of a religious historian. With the freedom of a scientist he dared to make the following formulation: "The parts of the Torah are not of equal value."[77] He based this distinction in value on the distinction between prescriptions and moral principles. He even distinguishes those regulations according to the distinction introduced by Saadiah between principles of reason (שכליות) and prescriptions of obedience (שמעיות).[78] This distinction was taken over by Bahya, from whom Maimonides derived it. Yehudah Halevi also has the same distinction, in a different formulation.[79]

Ibn Daud proceeds from this fundamental distinction to a more exact classification: "The Torah is a guide which consists of many parts. The first is faith and what is connected with it; the second is the virtues and their rank; the third, the management of the household; the fourth, management of the state; the fifth, concerned with commandments based on theory. And if a man truly considers this he will find, that the Torah consists of four parts . . . we would like to say first that the parts of the Torah, be they five or four or however many, are not all of equal value, even if one directs one's intention to them" (or considers them subjectively). "But the main point of the Torah and of the worship is the faith" (in God). "Therefore, you find all peoples in agreement or almost in agreement in their civil habits . . . but the rank of the commandments, the causes of which are not rational, is a very weak one in comparison with the fundamental laws. Many passages of Scripture already have shown this, as for instance the exclamation of Jeremiah: 'Heap your burnt offerings and your sacrifices more and more, and eat meat, for I did not speak to your fathers,'" etc. "And all this shows the weak standing of this part of the Torah, and that the other parts are more worthy of attention. Since, however, its rank is so weak, it cannot be denied that the causes also are weak." To such daring the philosopher rose, who is of importance not only in the fight against the Karaites, but who showed deep philosophical insight in rejecting the pantheism he detected in Ibn Gabirol's *Fountain of Life [Fons Vitae]*. Despite all the respect he expresses for that profound and warmhearted religious thinker, he nevertheless stresses the great danger that lies in his inclination to pantheism. For the history of rationalism in general, it is important historical evidence that this opponent of pantheism is the true precursor of Maimonides.

Maimonides is the rationalist of Judaism. He must, therefore, subject the laws to that rationalist criticism which is presupposed by the erection of the positive structure of the teaching. Hence, he must ask whether the cause of the law is reason alone, or whether other causes are effective in it. What Ibn Daud calls causes is called by Ibn Tibbon, in the Hebrew translation of Maimonides, reasons. From the outset the criticism becomes more subjective; it does not restrict itself to historical causes. The latter are, in the last analysis, only occasions and not conceptual foundations. The danger of speculating about the reasons of the laws, of which people from the very beginning were afraid, actually exists in the problem of reasons. People also ask for reasons for the concept of God; but here the reasons which are sought are proofs. The concept of God is the thesis, the truth of which is beyond doubt, but which ought to be proved. If, however, the question about reasons is asked with re-

gard to the laws, then the assumption of their truth is not an assertion of the same kind as in the case of the idea of God. The question, to be sure, is directed against skepticism, but it arises from it.
Moreover, only on the basis of a thesis about God that is beyond
question is it possible to answer the new question about the laws.
In the latter case, therefore, the reasons considered as proofs do not
have the same methodological power as they do in the question
about God.

However, despite this methodological distinction in the significance of the reasons, the critique of principles executed in genuine
rationalism demands reasons for the laws. This critique determines
the scientific and philosophic direction of rationalism toward idealism.

The reasons, after mature consideration, cannot be thought of as
causes at all, for causes have their validity only in the sphere of the
knowledge of nature. In the sphere of the cultural sciences(*Geisteswissenschaften*), however, causes can only be ends. Can, then, the
reasons sought be thought of as ends? This is the question that
rationalism raises in contrast to all kinds of positive laws, including
those of the administration of justice and of the state, a question
that leads it to distinguish natural law, natural religion, and so on.
For monotheistic rationalism, natural religion and, similarly, natural
law cannot be a sufficient foundation; for it, the only foundation is
the unique God. The latter, however, becomes identical with morality. For of his being we only have knowledge in the attributes of
action. His being therefore is either entirely hidden from us, or
knowable only as the moral archetype. Important consequences follow from this for the question about the reasons for the laws.

If we have just now recognized that the reasons mean ends, we
must face the difficulty of having to assert the identity of the ends
that are sought and the only two ends that have been set forth in
religion: God and morality. Only these ends are absolute ends. Only
they have their own value in themselves. This same value includes
the correlation of God with man. Morality is contained in God's
being; there cannot be, therefore, any other ends but these two,
which are united in the one end: God. Only because the concept
of God is recognizable in the concept of morality is this specification of ends permissible and useful. If now the reasons of the law
must be thought of as ends, then a conflict arises with the unique
absolute ends, and we cannot avoid the conclusion that the laws
themselves cannot be thought of as goals in which ends are actualized. Only God and his morality are such goals. If then, however,
the laws cannot have a full and proper value in themselves, in

which knowledge and action find their goals, then, also, the reasons cannot logically and subjectively be thought of as ends; they can only be thought of as means.

A faith that does not want to be guided by rationalism rightly considers this a serious danger. To degrade the law to the status of a means is to make the law relative, a consequence faith thinks it avoids when it views the law simply as God's commandment. Such an assumption, to be sure, contradicts the idea and the commandment of the knowledge of God. As the object of knowledge the commandment can only be proven to be God's commandment through the fact that God is the God of holiness or the God of morality. Hence, is must remain that the final reason of the law has to lie solely in divine morality. From this it follows that all commandments must be weighed as to whether they can be appropriate means to this unique end.

Logical coherence thus entails the unavoidable consequence that all the manifold laws have to be subsumed under the unity of the end of divine morality, as a means to this unique end.

Maimonides, in his whole treatment of teleology with regard to biology as well as ethics, showed himself a true rationalist, who paved the way for idealism. Thus, it was necessary for him to consider the entire problem of the law from the point of view of teleology. Consequently, when he asks about the reasons for the law, this question has the meaning of a question about the ends that God pursues with the laws. Hence, the question properly speaking is a question about God's ends. For God is the only end for which everything except God is only a means to knowledge, which can be attained only through these means. The reasons for the laws are therefore understood as means to the knowledge of God, and since knowledge of God is identical with worship of God, the reasons of the laws are recognizable as means of worship of God. This is the positive meaning this original criticism has attained. All true idealism only sets out with criticism; in its results it is always positive, and it alone is able to produce and to secure a positive result.

Maimonides (*Moreh* III, 31) begins his investigation of the reasons of the laws by repelling the enemies of this problem, whose view he designates as a mental illness, and also as a weak-mindedness that degrades God's wisdom. He points to Deuteronomy, which bases its truth upon the wisdom of the laws. "Everything depends on three things: knowledge, morality and civic activity."[80] Starting with this fundamental idea, Maimonides outlines his entire presentation, in which he at first returns to his biological teleology of the arrangement of the human organism. Just as an organism develops only gradually, so the wisdom of the Creator has made provision for bringing forth religious insights gradually and deemed it proper to adapt these to the primitive views of the men of the time. Hence, God did not abolish the cult of the sacrifices. If he had disregarded this habit of human nature, this would have been "as if in our time a prophet arose and would call for the worship of God and would say: God commanded you that you should not pray to Him, not fast, not seek His help in the time of trouble, but you should worship Him in thought, and not by action."[81] Maimonides views the whole apparatus of sacrificial legislation, including the altar and the sanctuary, as such a concession to the psychological nature of man. Furthermore, he raises against himself the objection that these many laws would not then have any end of their own, but he refutes this objection with his basic teleological idea about the nature of man, which God does not want to change.

The positive aspect of Maimonides' criticism shows itself in the distinction that he makes between primary and secondary ends, whereby the sacrifices are relegated to secondary, while prayer is nearer to the primary ends. According to him, God "set a great difference" between the two kinds of ends. Further, he adopts from Ibn Daud Jeremiah's polemic against sacrifice and gives it a positive confirmation which corresponds to his ethics. In interpreting the striking polemic of the prophet he expounds his ulterior reasons: at the time of the exodus from Egypt, in Mara, God instituted the Sabbath and the judicial organization, and he interprets the Sabbath as "statute" (חק) and the judicial system as "ordinance" (משפט). According to this interpretation, even the statutes should be counted under the category of moral laws, since the Sabbath represents social legislation. "This is the primary end: the knowledge of truths . . . and further, besides the knowledge of truths, the end is the removal of injustice from mankind." Therefore, the order of the sacrifices belongs to the secondary ends. This idea of Jeremiah is also confirmed by the psalms.

In the thirty-fifth chapter [of book III] of the *Guide*, Maimonides divides all the commandments into fourteen classes on the basis of the divisions of his *Code*. The first of these comprises the "fundamental principles of knowledge" (שרשיות). The question of the usefulness of these fundamental laws is meaningless as is; therefore, the question of their reasons also. The second class comprises the laws concerned with idolatry and what is connected with it. In this case, too, "the cause is known." The third class comprises laws for the "improvement of customs" (תקון המדות). This also includes laws of the state. The fourth class contains social laws. The fifth class concerns laws for the prevention of violence (והחמס מניעת העול). The sixth concerns legal punishments. The seventh class is concerned with property and all kinds of obligations concerning it. The eighth class finally turns to religious commandments in the narrower sense, to the Sabbath and the festivals, the reasons for which are stated in the Scripture: "to procure a true opinion, or rest for the body, or both of these." The ninth class is concerned with worship; with "activities which strengthen our knowledge in the love of God." The tenth and eleventh classes are concerned with the Temple and the sacrifices, the twelfth with the purity and impurity of the cult. The thirteenth puts together prohibited foods with vows and abstinences and sets as their common end the training against inordinate desires and lust. The fourteenth contains the sexual laws, under which Maimonides also includes circumcision.

Finally, he divides all the laws into two classes: laws between man and God, and laws between man and man. This, however, is done not with the intention of separating the two classes from one another and designating, perhaps, the first as the purely religious one. Rather, he says: "Every commandment, be it a positive or a negative commandment, which has the end of teaching good customs, or knowledge, or the improvement of actions, and which is intended for the perfection of man himself, is among those called laws between man and God." This new dichotomy illuminates the previous division in two respects. The sacrificial laws and those resembling them are not solely or exclusively concerned with the relation between man and God; rather, they are only subordinate ends for the unique and true end which is the knowledge of God and the true worship of God through human morality. On the other hand, the moral laws, too, do not remain isolated, but indirectly are concerned in their ultimate end, only with the relation between man and God. Hence, not only are those laws that usually are considered as belonging to the relation between man and God deemed worthy as means to the unique end of morality, but not less also those that usually are considered primarily moral laws; they too become means to the unique end, which is the knowledge and worship of God. This is the twofold power of the identity of God and morality.

In the same spirit Maimonides also wrote his *Book of the Commandments* (ספר המצות).

The expression "ceremonial law" is used for the first time by Simon Duran (1423) and afterwards by Albo (*Ikkarim* 3, 25).

The more recent development of Judaism only begins, significantly enough, in the age of the German enlightenment; it comes about in connection with changes in the attitude toward the ceremonial law. Moses Mendelssohn has only an indirect share in this inner development. His philosophy, in its best and deepest tendencies, belongs to the age of the great Leibniz. Although Mendelssohn unambiguously elucidates the relation of reason to religion in general, out of the spirit of the latter's philosophy, he obscures the concept of Judaism by limiting it to a religion of law. The reason of religion is the common property of reason in general, according to him. The specific character of the Jewish religion consists in obligation to the law.

To this understanding of Judaism, which is contrary to the history of the Jewish religion as we have surveyed it, Mendelssohn, however, joined a great—we would like to say—messianic tendency, which became important not only for the Jews but also for the teaching of Judaism. He addressed himself directly to the German Jews, but these constituted at that time, as on the whole they still do today, the cultural bond for the Jews of all lands. It would appear to be an inner contradiction that Mendelssohn could bring about a new modification of the cultural life of Jewry and of Judaism as well on the basis of the isolation of Judaism under the law. His political and cultural effect has been messianic; his inner religious teaching and practice seem to make primary that which, as long ago as the Middle Ages, was recognized as secondary. This apparent contradiction requires discussion and resolution.

The idea that religion is a personal experience seems to be at no point more convincing than in connection with the question of the law. We could account for hostile judgments about the law—disregarding the widespread lack of scientific and sound historical knowledge—in most cases by an ignorance of life under the law and a lack of comprehension of the religious experience of the law. Jülicher said that a religion could be judged only out of this intimate knowledge. Kant was therefore wrong with regard to Mendelssohn's point of view when he reproached him for "lacking friendliness for man." This view is only possible if one considers it self-evident and beyond doubt that the Jewish laws can be experienced only as a heavy yoke. Was Mendelssohn a hypocrite then, who obeyed all these laws with meticulous strictness all his life long and then wanted to burden the Jews with them? Or was he perhaps so ignorant of the world and so politically shortsighted, or even blind, that he did not see how this yoke was becoming lighter from year to year? Or was he perhaps so doctrinaire that he wanted above all to secure the religion of reason, even though Judaism might be slighted by a narrow definition? Or, biased by an enlightened in- difference with regard to Judaism, did he believe that he had done enough in bringing out the differences between Judaism and Chris- tianity and in thus bringing Judaism safely under cover? Among all these possibilities, the last one would do the greatest injustice to the historical memory of this new Moses, as his contemporaries called him, in relation to Maimonides. Mendelssohn's position with regard to the law needs, therefore, more careful elucidation.

Great changes in the history of culture are never judged correctly if they are examined narrowly in terms of their immediate effects. The historical account of the time of Mendelssohn remains narrow if it considers only the falling away from Judaism and not, at the same time, the inner impetus at work and the related acquisition of general cultural interests. On the other hand, a correct evaluation is not struck by measuring and weighing both of these historical effects one against the other and dividing them into light and dark- ness. Knowledge gained in this way remains superficial. It can be- come inward and truly historical only by answering the question of the relation between this obvious progress and that seeming regress. How could both of these ideas arise for Mendelssohn, side by side, and gain a firm hold, if one of them opened up, to the Jews and Judaism, culture and religion of reason, while the other bound them to the biblical-rabbinical yoke?

For a century and a half we have gradually advanced, and the first decades of the new century in particular, more exactly the last years of the great World War [I], have enriched us with many a dis- appointment and made us clearsighted with many a resignation. The inner reformation of the Jewish community had to do with a factor we shall have to discuss later: worship. The philosophy of Judaism did not entirely lay fallow, to be sure, and here too the historical approach of post-Kantian philosophy became prevalent and benefited the science of Judaism (*Wissenschaft des Judentums*), particularly the history of the Jews and of Jewish literature. It was the natural consequence of Mendelssohn's cultural reform that in the inner re- ligious development, too, a balance was sought between the old forms of worship and the national spirit and culture of those peoples in whose historical development the Jews had taken an increasing role. Worship was a part of the law, and as the former became assimilated, so the whole of the law was expected to undergo a cor- responding transformation.

We are still in the process of this great development, which appears to be a disintegration; but in view of the fact that Jewish worship, which, in spite of all transformation, undeniably preserved its ancient firmness and its genuine character, it would be superficial to think that in modern Judaism the power of the law is absolutely broken and destroyed. In view of the fact that the Sabbath and the holidays, in particular the messianic festivals of the New Year and the Day of Atonement, even today have their validity and affect the entire religious life of the modern Jew, it could be said that the power of the law has been weakened, but in no way destroyed or undermined.

The reformation had aimed to weaken and to depreciate all those elements that distinctly mark the Jewish national character. The reform proceeded from the nationalistic viewpoint of the civilized nations of the time and was aimed at worship, and also, more or less expressly, at the law itself. Let us first consider that idea of the reformation that attributes national meaning to the law. This idea is historically correct. The law was the product of a national ferment and has been thought of as such from the beginning, and preserved and developed as such through the whole history of Judaism. Isolation was absolutely necessary if monotheism was to come to thrive at all. Moreover, isolation remained necessary if the Jewish kind of monotheism was to preserve its undiminished value against the other two kinds. It befits the theoretical character of the problems of this book that we do not evade the question of whether the future continuation and further development of Jewish monotheism is still incumbent on the burden of isolation.

If, however, this question were to be answered in the affirmative, then we would have to attribute a permanence to the law in its essential validity, making allowance for all those limitations and transformations history has continually effected, externally and internally, upon these seemingly rigid forms.

We must give this idea thorough consideration, because otherwise it is exposed to grave misunderstandings which are difficult to avoid within the tendencies of modern culture. For us, the law should rightly be a valid means for the isolation of Judaism. At the same time we wish to recognize the quintessence of Judaism in Messianism, which, indeed, exists not only for the sake of mankind but just as much for the sake of monotheism. Here, too, the correlation remains our guidepost. However, how is isolation compatible with the messianic mission? Is it perhaps correct that both of these tasks exclude one another?

The transcendence of this seeming contradiction depends upon the correct determination of the meaning of isolation. At the time when the reformation began, this isolation was thought of exclusively as a national isolation. Any other kind of isolation would, therefore, have to be in opposition to the nationalistic. Religious isolation was not thought of as such and it was desirable not to acknowledge it as such. Therefore, the law was attacked as the seat of national isolation, from which religious isolation was distinguished and considered merely the historical first step to the messianic future of Judaism.

Meanwhile, the political concept of the nation had changed. The Teutonic aspirations of the wars of liberation (*Freiheitskriege*) were banished, and scientific endeavors in search of a national spirit (*Volksgeist*) were well-nigh blunted in Hegel's notion of a world-spirit (*Weltgeist*); more and more the "national" was changed to mean the "political." What mattered was the founding of a state, which in the Italian and German striving for national unification became the problem of the age. The cultural concept of nation, which originated in the Enlightenment and was again enlivened by the new humanism, became definitely transformed into the concept of state. The state was to be founded on a nation; the nation became the natural means to the end of a state. Hence, the Jewish community could expect a strengthening of its status in all modern civilized states. It desired everywhere to be a community of believers, and never strove for a separate state of its own or for a state within a state. But how did it now stand with their law? The isolation which the latter effected could in no way be thought of as isolation in statehood. Nevertheless, the appearance of national isolation still remained attached to the law, even though this was contrary to the inner core of the teaching or, at least, was not in accord with it. Therefore, resistance to the law continued unabated. Did the disintegration alluded to make further progress?

From the above considerations it is possible to explain the origin of the episode of Zionism in the more recent history of the Jewish people. When the Jews fought for emancipation, the objection was raised against the Jews in all lands that they prayed for the restoration of the Jewish state. The emancipation succeeded because the peoples were convinced that this idea of the prayer was only a reminiscence of religious piety. Since, however, the concepts of state and nation became gradually so intertwined that the nation became identical with the state, the paradoxical consequence ensued that the Jewish nation required a Jewish state. But besides this, the demand for a state was occasioned and provoked by severe political oppressions, persecutions, and maltreatments. The effect of both concepts was reciprocal: the nation demands the state, and the state demands the nation. But are these two concepts the only ones that are in question? Is it not rather the concept of religion that constitutes the focal point of the whole question? Is not the Jewish state in contradiction to messianic religion? And is not, therefore, the Jewish religion in contradiction to the concept of nation, insofar as the latter is the lever of the state?

All these questions are countered by the opposing question: does the concept of the nation have an exclusively political meaning, if the anthropological, the racial meaning of a nation is disregarded? Is it not possible that the concept of the nation has another meaning, which does justice to the notion of isolation insofar as the latter must be preserved for the sake of religion and can be so preserved above all through the law?

Another view of the meaning of the nation gradually dawned during the World War [I]. Originally, a nation was thought of as a naturally given fact of a people's tribe (*Volksstamm*). Politics taught and even compelled the abandoning of this meaning of the word and the adopting of the idea of the nation as an engendering and formative concept of the state. Hence, nation and state became identical. But no sooner had the nation cleansed itself of its earthly odor in the ideal concept of the state than the latter, in its ideality, was attacked by the struggle of material and economic interests. As the individual states themselves were strengthened and at the same time poisoned by the ambiguous desires for economic power, the World War [I] broke out as a recompense for, and consequence of, this materialistic antagonism of the individual states. The ideal cultural meaning of the state based on the national background and history of the people was narrowed to the concept of economic power. The idea of the state seemed in danger of decay through imperialism.

Then a new virtue arose out of necessity, namely, a broadening of the concept of the state, through which the idea of the state comes to its completion. The states cannot remain isolated, and that which they were not able to achieve for the purposes of war they will not be able to overcome in peace. The state matures before our eyes into a confederation of states. Messianism becomes a factor in world history. The state, as an individual state, based on the nation, is built up into a confederation of states. And just as the states unite, so also must the peoples unite, harmonize inwardly. This is the intrinsic logic of the development of the state, against which no opposition can arise.

That which the war is going to achieve with the states, and, indeed, no less with the neutral states than with those involved in the war, has long ago manifested itself as a historical power within the individual states. Ethnic nationality has been considered a foreign body, which, like a cancer, endangers the organism of the state; nonetheless, one has to use the foreign body as an organic factor in the life of the state, and hence to recognize it. Just as the confederation of the states, in which the idea of the state finds its completion, can find no contradiction in the manifold variety of the peoples united in it, so the individual state should not take exception to the manifold variety of the ethnic elements of the population which it has to unite.

In agreement with some views, which appear to head in the same direction, I have tried to establish a distinction between nation and nationality. Nation is a concept interchangeable with that of the state. The nation is the nation of a state, and the state is that of a nation. The unity the state has to represent is established through the nation. The nation is therefore an ideal concept, the meaning of which lies in the establishment of the state. A false or culturally impure ideality is inherent in the meaning of race. Its danger lies in the exclusiveness the race demands from the state, while the state as individual state actually requires a plurality of nationalities, just as the confederation of states requires a plurality of peoples. Or perhaps the state does not need nationalities, even in the sense in which it preserves and develops them? Or is it permitted to destroy them? On the basis of this question, one can determine the direction the ideal task of the state must take with regard to the nationalities. The state depends on the nationalities. Nationality is not in contradiction to the state, and therefore it cannot be in contradiction to the nation.

If we now return to the Jewish problem, then we recognize the backwardness of Zionism with regard to the concept of nation. If the isolation of the Jewish community remains necessary, then isolation in a separate state would be in contradiction to the messianic task of the Jews. Consequently, a Jewish nation is in contradiction to the messianic ideal.

Since isolation in a nation is, thus, not permissible and Judaism needs isolation in the law, the latter task might become illusory if the notion of the nation were not replaced by the notion of nationality. Insofar as isolation in a nationality is necessary, it is in no way hopeless, for its realization is possible without a state of one's own, and even within the individual states and cultures of other peoples. This is even demanded by the idea of the state for its own sake as well as for the sake of the confederation of states. There remains only the question of whether nationality remains a necessary task, and the further question of whether it can be actualized through isolation in the law.

As for the meaning of the question of the necessity of nationality, we have first to consider the concept of necessity. The necessity of the concept of the nation turned out to be relative to the concept of the state. Hence, it is unlikely that the necessity of nationality can be thought of as an absolute, rather than relative, concept. There can be no doubt that nationality can stand in relation only to religion. The concept of the nation has already been deprived of its anthropological, or ethnic, element, and its idealization was realized only in the state. The tribe, with its physical basis, was not thereby depreciated; although it is true that one no longer recognized ideality in the tribe itself, the possibility of its being idealized by the highest human ideal—by the state—was acknowledged. The idealization of nationality follows the same method. Nationality is in no way irrelevent or inferior, although the ideal does not lie in nationality; rather, it is elevated to the ideal insofar as it serves as a means to the establishment and continuation of religion. For the establishment of religion the people of Israel was necessary. That is what it means for Israel to be the chosen people. Furthermore, it is also beyond doubt that the continuation of monotheism was linked to nationality, once the nation, in the sense of the state, was done for. Ezra's policy of thwarting marriages with pagan women was a necessary religious policy. However, at all times the most profound Jewish thinkers did not consider nationality an end in itself; rather, they acknowledged it only as the indispensable means for the preservation of religion. The true verdict is expressed by Saadiah Gaon: "Our people is only a people through its teachings" (אומתנו אינה אומה כי אם בתורותיה). The only possibility of the idealization of nationality lies in this necessary relation to religion. Its share in ideality consists only in religion.

In accordance with the human and, particularly, the political conditions within the civilized religions, their internal and external contradictions and struggles, there can be no doubt that nationality must remain the necessary foundation of the continuation of the Jewish religion as long as it stands in opposition to other forms of monotheism. The point in question is, therefore, nothing other and nothing less than the character and value of Jewish monotheism itself. If it were devalued, replaced, or were replaceable by those other forms, then not only would its continued existence until now be a riddle, but also its future continuation would be untenable. If, on the other hand, out of the sources of Judaism, Judaism can be proved a religion of reason, then the continuation of Judaism is, conceptually, secured. It need not be a question whether Judaism is the only religion of reason, for the other forms too may have and preserve an essential share in reason. But if Judaism itself also is incontestably a religion of reason, then its continuation is made historically necessary by the principle of reason. Even if experiments about the possibility of its replacement were possible, they would in principle not be permissible. For if each of several religions had its share in reason, no one of them may be supressed. The idea of replacing one religion by another makes no sense historically since it contradicts the philosophy of history, which has to ward off the idea of the absolute and has to investigate the share of reason in the various phenomena of culture.

When religious bias claims to become scientific and methodological and Christianity is declared absolute, then the dispute cannot be finally settled in the sphere of scientific methodology, but only in the disputed problem itself. Whoever acknowledges monotheism only in its Christian form does not grasp the purity of Jewish monotheism. "He is unique and there is no second to compare to Him and to consort with Him," a poem of the Synagogue says about God. The unique God, God as the Unique One, God as the unique being, this is the meaning of Jewish monotheism. "Fill with it thy heart as large as it is."* But this is exactly the difference between Goethe's poetry and Judaism, that Judaism does not say, "Call it, then, what thou willst,"* but insists on, and persists in, the idea and its development and execution: "His name is unique." The name has to express the concept. There cannot be various names, because there cannot be various concepts of God. The human stands in correlation with God but is not identical with him. Moreover, through the mediation of the human, nature is also in relation to him; pantheism, which asserts an identity between nature and God, is the absolute contradiction of Jewish monotheism. Hence, it is fully understandable that in its strictness Jewish monotheism itself is a difficult problem for a culture that oscillates between different centers because of its many-sided interests in science and art. Judaism, however, tolerates only one focal point for all spiritual beings: the unique God, who is incomparable with anything the human spirit is able to think or imagine. For Judaism the spiritual world has a focal point that is able to emit rays into the infinite breadth of culture but which is not, in turn,

---

*Goethe, Faust, pt. I [S.K.]

displaced by any of the interests of culture. Here no skepticism is possible, not even as a beneficent impulse against dogmatism. Rather, one has to find the way from dogmatism to this highest idealism in which all existence becomes nought in comparison with God's unique being. Skepticism bars itself from the road to this idealism. Pantheism, too, must be recognized as the defeat of the monotheistic problem.

If, then, in accordance with the general method of the philosophy of history and especially in accordance with the doctrine of the unique God, the preservation of Judaism and of Jewish nationality for its sake is a necessity of the history of reason, then, after we have recognized this necessity with regard to religion, the question is to be asked about the necessity of the law.

Like a specter, there now appears to us the sentence in which that freedom of thought, which so often breathes freely in the Talmud and Midrash, expresses itself with titanic daring: "The laws are abolished in the Messianic Times." Should this apply to all laws? An exception must be made immediately: "except the Day of Atonement." This exception is very characteristic; it takes from the sentence the best of its force. For just as the main pillar of religion, the Day of Atonement, must remain eternal for this religion, so the broader question immediately arises whether yet other laws are to be included in, or added to, this exception. This question, however, must be directed backward from the messianic goal, and it is an important guide for this, properly speaking, historical consideration, that in the Messianic Age the law cannot be abolished without exception.

The question of the eternity of the Torah is a prevailing problem in the Jewish Middle Ages. Already Saadiah (*Emunoth* 3, 7-10) raised it and considered it. Even in his time, attacks of such a kind were not lacking in both Jewish and non-Jewish circles. Biblical criticism, which was used by Christianity and Islam for the purpose of verifying the predictions of their prophets, offered sufficient opportunity for these attacks. Saadiah's judgment discloses an admirable maturity and objectivity in the face of such circumstances.

Since we have already become acquainted with the rationalism of Ibn Daud, we may expect from him, particularly as historian, a methodological insight into this question also. In fact, he already uses biblical criticism's modern argument about the discovery of the Torah.

Also, a great fight was led against the articles of faith, particularly against the formulation which Maimonides gave them, and, especially, against the article regarding the revelation as a whole. Maimonides had put the Torah together with nature as God's two creations.

In opposition, Crescas distinguished between the fundamental teachings (שרשים אמתיים) and the truths of faith (פנות ויסודות התורה).[82]
Isaac Arama continues this criticism (*Akeda* 99). Finally, Joseph
Albo brings it to completion (*Ikkarim* 3, 13-22), declaring that changes
in the Mosaic law are possible according to reason and even according
to the Scripture itself.[83] Albo, too, argues from the discovery of the
Torah in the reign of King Josiah.[84]

We are, therefore, on the classical ground of Jewish thinking when
we try to answer the question of the relation between law and religion not in the dogmatic sense, but in accordance with our method.
The ancient thinkers have proved with audacious clarity how various
biblical laws were already changed in the Talmud. Moreover, they
drew attention to the distinction between the Torah as a whole
and the number of the particular commandments. The problem for
us can only be the general concept of the law. This concept of the
law means, in particular, its appropriateness for the preservation
and the development of religion. The statutes and ordinances are
comprised under the supreme concept of the Torah. The law consists
of laws. The unity of the laws, however, is the teaching, the religion.
This alone can be the methodological question of the value of the
laws: what is their relation, objective and historical, to the continuation of religion?

The continuation of the religion of the Jewish monotheism is therefore bound to the continuation of the law in accordance with its
general concept—not to the particular laws—because the law makes
possible that isolation which seems indispensable to the care for, and
continuation of, what is, at once, one's own and eternal.

Isolation in the world of culture! Does not what is required here
from the point of view of the law constitute a condemnation of
Judaism? However, one should bear in mind that, in the final analysis,
isolation is not demanded from the point of view of the law, but from
that of pure monotheism. Monotheism is at stake; in the face of this
how could the community of the world of culture be its legitimate
tribunal? With monotheism, the world of culture is at stake. Hence,
the consideration of whether the law contains hindrances to the ease
of cultural communication is opportunistic and eudaemonistic. Considerations of this kind have to step back when the question involves
the unique God. There is general consent that culture as a whole
has no fixed center in God. However, here the reason for this general
consensus is disclosed: only the unique God of Jewish monotheism
can form this firm center, which bestows on culture a steady balance
for the plurality of its interests. Therefore, isolation is indispensable

to Judaism, for its concept as well as for its cultural work. Consequently, the isolation of its believers in their nationality is also unavoidable.

The law, even if it were to be adhered to only on the holidays, and even, for some or for many, only on the Day of Atonement, is a bulwark against levelling pure monotheism, with its teaching of the reconciliation of man with God, as the salvation of man by God. In the same way, the preservation of the Sabbath for the community is a signpost of the fundamental social and ethical teaching of Judaism and a protest against the transformation of the Sabbath into a day of remembrance of Christ's resurrection. This transformation of the meaning of the Sabbath is a more weighty matter than the substitution of one day for another.

It is not our task to give more than methodological allusions to the detailed practice of Judaism. The investigation of the share of reason in religion should not pass over into a historial speculation, which would prescribe to the future development its ways. From the point of view of the philosophy of history, the lever the law constitutes for religion' is unmistakable. Previously, we have boldly taken up the common objection against the law at its word and conceded its force. However, the value of the law is in no way exhausted by the negative moment of isolation. Rather—and this cannot be grasped in its entire profundity by any outsider—inherent in the law, in its many forms and usages, is a positive force that stimulates, inspires, fortifies, and deepens religious ideas and beliefs. One may wonder whether those forms of the law are not at the same time the forms that produce the religious feelings. It is the old question of the relation between idea and actuality that is involved here. But since the question here concerns the relation between the idea and its realization, the answer is easier. As the idea has to produce the actuality, the latter cannot be heterogeneous to the idea, if it serves it as an occasion and is made subject to it. What matters is only the appropriateness of the form, or rather the degree of appropriateness, for complete adequacy cannot be achieved. The endeavor to reform the worship is, therefore, completely in agreement with the old law, which puts great stress upon the dignity of the forms of worship. The entire tendency of the reform is a truly religious one; it cannot therefore be depreciated as merely extrinsic. But here, nevertheless, the main question always remains the difficult problem of the relation between law and religion, on the basis of which each particular question concerning a particular law is to be considered. In order that a particular mistake, which is apt to be made in abolishing a particular law, be avoided, it is necessary for us to recognize the principle of the law itself in its relative necessity and to hold to it as a standard for the consideration of the particular case.

It is already an important element in the concept of the law that the law is not only valid for worship, but that it merges worship with the whole of domestic and civic activities. This indeed makes private life more difficult; a burden is imposed upon it, but this burden should be the yoke of the Kingdom of God. At this point the word "experience" has its value for religion: whoever has not experienced for himself the life under this yoke of the laws will never understand that this yoke is borne as a ladder to heaven. Therefore, it is and remains the great question of the future, which is the future of pure monotheism, not whether the yoke is to be borne—this is no longer a question—but how far the burden of the yoke of the law can be reduced if it is still to be retained and be ever more profoundly transfigured without suffering any loss in its efficacy for the entire future.

Although the plastic arts and painting were kept away from pure worship, Heine has said, in his poetic language, that Moses chiseled pyramids of men. This work of art that produced men who believe in the unique God he achieved through the means of the laws. Thus the laws themselves cannot be completely without artistic value, which above all might manifest itself in poetry. As poetry the artistic value of the laws permeates all forms, the tragic as well as the idyllic. Even the Christian neighbor participated not only in the tragic spectacle of the worship on the eve of *Yom Kipur* but no less in the idyll of the *Succah,* the airy structure and the natural poetic adornment of which he shared. And how much the law means for the solemn ennoblement of life and the tranfiguration of death and the honoring of the dead in burial! From the very beginning of each man's life, in which God's covenant with Abraham is renewed in every newborn son of Abraham, to its termination, the law penetrates all the moments of life in order to strengthen them for the true worship of God. At the same time, it connects worship with all human activities and seeks, through this connection, to transfigure all human deeds in the light of the eternal.

Isolation is not the unique end of the law, but rather the idealization of all earthy activity by the divine. Worship is not limited to the synagogue; the law fulfills and permeates the whole of life with it. Of course, through this the whole of life is directed to the unique end. However, it is only opportunistic to fear withdrawal and alienation from culture in this positing of an end. Culture is given a firm center through this, and isolation, so far as it is unavoidable, may nevertheless permit and promote dedication and familiarity with all the branches of culture; only independence with regard to one's own point of gravity remains intact. It would be a fateful prejudice if one were to consider isolation through the law equivalent to disassociation from the independent interests of culture in theoretical and practical matters. The isolation in one's own worship only establishes and strengthens the independence and sovereignty of moral judgment in its decisiveness for all the directions and aspirations of culture in general.

Out of the bonds of the law at all times came forth those Israelites who achieved important things for culture in all its branches. Out of the bonds of the law came first of all the great moral impulses, which were animated by the sons of Israel for practical life and its moral perfection. The profound connection of the law with public morality could never be mistaken. Men have preferred to see the motivation for this in subjective piety, whereas it is, rather, the objective power of the law itself that is the root of the driving force in the spirit and feeling of the Jew, in whose memory the sublimity of the law is inherent, or in whose blood the primeval power of the law is unconsciously still effective. The Jew is known for his outward appearance, but insufficiently for the continuing effect of the law on his inner life and for the hereditary foundations of the law.

Therefore, mere isolation is replaced for the fellow believer by a new, positive responsibility, both for the whole future as well as the present. It is an old proposition: "All Israelites vouch for each other." Historical continuity demands this reciprocal security of the fellows of one truth. The question of the law is, therefore, not only a theoretical question about the preservation of religion but a practical and actual question for the people who are born into this religion, in order that they may grow up in it and be preserved in it. The question of the preservation of faith is therefore the question of the people of this faith. The value of the law for the continuation of religion has therefore to be considered for the sake of these people of the future. But, of course, concern for the future is connected with piety for the past. The old idea of the merit of the fathers obtains a new meaning at this point. The fathers remain the fathers of the sons of the entire future, and the all of latter need the merit of the fathers; they are not permitted to ascribe merit to themselves. It is preeminently in the law that the merit of the fathers became alive, and in the law it must remain capable of begetting and preserving life.

The founder of the science of Jewish antiquity, the immortal Zunz, describes in the following words the blessing of the law, which binds the past with the future: "As often then as the external symbol becomes visible, long established love rises from the internal and draws all those into the consecrated circles who find edification in the common belief, and who implanted virtues in us along with religious habits, yea, all those come close to us who felt the same grief, or with whom we bear the same suffering, and a sea of glowing love engulfs and melts away the cold selfishness . . . on the contrary, when your soul has delight in the religious law you will remain attached to those who honor, in the same law, the same holiness." In this historical power lies the meaning of the law as a symbol. Of course, it has no value of its own, but this is exactly the value of a symbol, that it is able to awaken the genuine value. What is not a symbol is therefore limited to the form that it may be able to represent through action or image. The symbol, on the other hand, extends beyond the special image of its own representation and reaches out to the infinity of images and forms, which it evokes and therefore brings forth. As great as the danger of a symbol is, as great is its encompassing value. If we finally consider the law as a symbol, we exceed the expression with which the Mishnah distinguishes the law from the teaching, calling the law the "fence around the teaching." The law is not only a fence, which isolates the teaching in order to guard and protect it, but, considered as a symbol, it becomes a lever which is not only a positive support of the teaching but a means for engendering the teaching. We still have to show more clearly how the law as such is a positive source of the power of religion.

When we survey all the laws Maimonides reviewed in his characterization of them, it would seem that the proper viewpoint is still not established. The connection between the purely moral commandments and the commandments concerning worship must be clarified. Is there a law in which the connection, so to speak, between religion and morality is established? If such a law exists, then the ideal concept of the law should be recognizable in it. For this is the meaning of the law: to establish and to maintain the connection between knowledge and action, and therefore also between knowledge as religion and action as moral deed. If there is a law that is neutral with regard to theory and practice both in the worship of God and, in accordance with its meaning, in morality, then in this law we should recognize not only the connection between religious knowledge and religious action but even the connection between religion in general, including theory and practice, and pure autonomous morality, insofar as the latter, according to our presupposition, is connected with the share of reason in religion.

CHAPTER XVII

Prayer

That form of the law which establishes the double connection we demanded in the previous chapter is the prayer. It establishes, namely, the connection between religious knowledge and religious action, and at the same time between religion and morality in general. Has prayer been marked out at all as a specific commandment among the six hundred and thirteen commandments? It flows through the whole chain of commandments, so that it comprises in itself the entire content of worship. If there were no prayer, worship would consist only in sacrifice. It is therefore possible to say that sacrifice could not have ceased if prayer had not originated in sacrifice and from sacrifice. Speaking from the literary point of view, it is perhaps possible for us to say that the psalm would not have originated, that the religious style would not have advanced beyond prophetic speech, if the prayer, as a particular style, had not developed out of prophetic rhetoric. For if the prophetic ideas had not preceded, the origin of the prayer would hardly be thinkable.

Prayer is an original form of monotheism. Of course, in this case too, as in that of all monotheistic creation, the general principle of any historical religious development holds true. No people lacks, and could not lack, the general type of prayer insofar as that people expresses its relation to a godhead in language. The first stammering of man in his direct address to God can be nothing other than prayer, but just as the language does not remain wholly at stammering, so the entreaty, which is addressed to the godhead, is not yet prayer in the sense in which only monotheism developed it. Monotheism must achieve its own peculiarity in the prayer, if prayer is the language of religion and language the proper expression of reason.

This assumption, that prayer is the peculiar product of monotheism, we must now demonstrate in the example of Jewish prayer.

We first pay attention to the necessity of a complement to prayer,

371

which, for the purpose of reconciliation and atonement, is demanded
by the work of repentance. This demand is predominantly of a purely
moral character; for its work is directed to the examination and purification of the self. It is done with a view to God, which is the additional religious aspect of it. This view to God is the trust, the confidence
in the good God, who as such is the God of reconciliation and redemption. As regards this confidence, however, there is an obscurity that is
not yet illuminated. What does the view to God mean? One cannot
behold God. In what manner then does the confidence in God proceed?
It cannot be an affect. And even if this were possible, there would
still remain the question about the manner of expression of this affect.
Hence, for the trust in God, for the confidence in God's forgiveness, a
language is unavoidably necessary, and prayer constitutes this form
of language.[85]

The great extent to which prayer is considered an expression of
thought is shown by the Hebrew word that became the technical term
for the preparedness of the state of mind in prayer: *Kawanah*. The
word in general means to be firm, to be established, and signifies,
consequently, one's intention in prayer. However, its predominant
meaning is the preparation and separation of the mind for prayer. It
became the word for devotion.

To begin with, this preliminary stage for the prayer, too, is of a
purely moral character. For all spiritual, for all moral action, the mind
needs to withdraw into itself; it needs the concentration of all its inner
forces and prospects. As the solitude of the soul becomes a necessity
in opposition to the whirl of sense impressions, so the soul psychologically is in need of withdrawal into itself, into its most inner depth, if
it is to rise to the dialogue with the godhead. Prayer must be such
a dialogue when it has to express in language confidence in God.

How much prayer is a creation of monotheism is shown by another
creation of this genuine religion, the psalm, which we have already
brought into view. The psalm too has its analogy in the Greek, as well
as in the Babylonian, hymn. However, the peculiar character of monotheism causes the peculiar character of its psalm. The psalm would
lose the historically indubitable character of its monotheistic origin if
it were not different from the so-called Babylonian psalm. That which
in the psalm and in its stylistic form is not immediately clear becomes
clear from the viewpoint of prayer. Considered as prayer, the psalm
loses the appearance of being a solemn song to the godhead, or a
dithyramb to the god who helped a hero to victory, or a song for the
hero himself and for his ancestry, praising victory, songs such as Pindar
sang. The distinction between a psalm considered as prayer and a

heroic song is obvious, despite all external similarities: in the psalm the I itself, the subject, becomes object. The singer himself is not the subject, but he must first bring the subject forth out of himself. In this, it does not help the singer to invoke his ancestry and sing about its mythical deeds. The shaft of one's own inner self must be unearthed, if the I in its new, free independence and purity is to arise. For this, however, the dialogue with God is necessary, and this dialogue is constituted by the monologue of the prayer.

There is an analogy to the psalm, consisting in the original poetic form of the lyric. The lyric poem is the confession that the soul itself utters about its innermost and most intimate experience. This most intimate experience is love. Of course, it is in its first sprouting the natural drive of sexual love, but out of the Aphrodisiac cults the Greek spirit conjured forth eros. Hence, eros became in Plato the general expression for the soul, for all its most deep and tender, all its mightiest creations. What in the Greek spirit is eros is in the Jewish spirit prayer, brought forth and uttered in the psalm. Does the psalm perhaps lack the fundamental power of love, because love for God is removed from eroticism with all its secrets? It is rather that this love could not have achieved all the power and definiteness of its pure and distinctive character if monotheism had not allotted to it the power to transcend all sensuality, and to transfer to God, in chastity and innocence, that which the most ideal sexual love otherwise devises for the beloved. While, however, the lyric style of love can and may not sever this idealization of the beloved person from the original sexual desire, the latter is meaningless in monotheism. One cannot love God as a man or a woman, and yet one loves and seeks God, and confesses these longings because they are true experiences of the soul. This is indeed a riddle in the history of the soul, but so is monotheism itself. The literary expression of this riddle is the psalm, the highest achievement of monotheism, for the prophet only admonishes one to love God; the psalm, however, confesses this love as an actual experience of the soul. This confession of the experience of the soul is the psalm as prayer.

Now we recognize the complement, which the prayer has to add to the moral work of repentance in order to insure the success of the reconciliation. Now we also recognize the purely religious factor of reconciliation, which we denoted before by trust and confidence in God. We asked for a more precise expression for this religious condition, for a psychological expression for this objective condition: prayer is the psychological form of the religious factor of reconciliation.

The fundamental form of religion, the logical expression of which is the correlation of man and God, is, psychologically, the love for God. This love is the love expressed in the psalms; it is the love expressed in the prayer. The prayer is love. One would like to reverse this sentence. Is not the idealization in love basically only a modification of prayer, in which the beloved is besieged with all the powers of the mind, with all the magic of infinity?

Lyric poetry has yet another basic psychological power, which proves useful to the idealization of the beloved person, and which, in prayer, turns into a peculiar healing power. The lyric poem is the confession of an experience, but not of one out of many experiences, not of a particular and transitory experience; rather, the experience is expanded to the sum total of one's own life. The finite, the transitory, becomes infinite, eternal. It is, therefore, not quite correct to say that the actual, momentary occasion is the proper content of a love poem. In it the occasion is immortalized and hence the actual becomes infinitely distant. When love is praised in song as actual and present, then the lyric becomes epigrammatic. Lyric poetry itself needs the distant, which therefore becomes the ideal of actuality. Furthermore, what distance means spatially takes place as a psychological factor in longing. Longing is the idealistic element of affect. Although longing desires the actual presence of the beloved, it is based on the substitution for presence of the distant image, which it paints with the glow of its heart. Longing, therefore, holds fast to its distant goals without which it cannot accomplish the activity of approaching the beloved, without which it cannot maintain the balance of its pendulum-like swinging. Love is the longing for the essence, which is not present in perceptible actuality, and should not be, insofar as it is being longed for. So also is the prayer a longing for God, who should not be desired as a perceptible actuality; as such he cannot be sought for in knowledge, and therefore also not in love.

Prayer is longing.[86] The desire for God expressed in prayer is a quest for God and always wants to be quest only; for the finding cannot be actual, but can have as its goal only "the nearness to God," only the drawing near to God. This drawing near, however, is always love, always longing, always an affect, and never only an intellectual attitude. It is therefore never a vision. The latter can only be a delusion, which produces an enchantment of actuality, and which in this case must always remain false enchantment. For God can never become actuality for human love. The quest is the end in itself of the religious soul. The longing signifies and fills the entire inner life of the soul, insofar as it is focused on the correlation with God for the purpose of engendering religion. The psalm is the legitimate style of prayer, because it has become the stylistic form of religious love, of love for God.

What longing is to love, devotion is to prayer. It is the preprararation, but it can never cease, never break off as long as the prayer continues. Every new moment of the prayer is a new beginning, a new impetus of devotion. Longing, too, must always remain animated by a spontaneous, self-creating agility; otherwise it slackens and turns into melancholy, which takes from it all vigor and activity, so that the consciousness becomes engulfed in the stifling present and is deprived of the ability to anticipate the future and to make it effective. This power of anticipation is, in general, the power of the consciousness of time. In longing, this power becomes as fruitful for the soul as it is logically for the origin and all the continuity of motion, of which it constitutes the arsenal. At this point we are considering only the source of anticipation as a power of the soul.

The significance of longing in the psalm as prayer is not exhausted by the analogy to the longing of love. The love for God is, indeed, of another kind than the most intimate love in the bond of the sexes. The longing for God is the longing for redemption, for liberation from the constraining burden of the feeling of guilt. The longing here originates in dread which brings man to face the danger of running away from himself, of losing himself. The longing for God corresponds, therefore, to the natural urge of man not to despair of himself, and to clasp the anchorage of self-assurance in order not to be ruined by despair and self-abandonment. Hence, longing is the hope of rescue from the danger of the throes of death. The longing of the prayer wrests itself away from the struggle for repentance, to become hope in the deliverer, the redeemer.

One recognizes ever more clearly the origin of prayer in the psalm, and in it the dialogue which repentance conducts between the I and God. This dialogic monologue could not be aroused by prophetic rhetoric; it could be created only by lyric poetry, which is the original form of love in longing. The psalm, however, idealizes this longing, in analogy to eros, by means of the highest human end in life, which is constituted by redemption from sin; the idealization proceeds to that freedom of confidence in God, thanks to which the love for God is, at the same time, the foundation for the continuous renewal of the I.

The love for God is rooted in the belief in the good God. Good is more than goodly, an expression that dangerously weakens the meaning of God's goodness. God's goodness is simply the expression of divine teleology, of the highest end which God constitutes for nature and the human world. The human world is the world of the human individual. God's goodness means his forgiving of human sin. He is "good and forgiving" (טוב וסלח), and upon this redemption from sin is based the existence of the individual, who is destroyed by sin.

The individual is now rescued. The prayer has its conclusion in the termination of the tragedy, which here, however, brings about the true solution, the rescue of the hero. The prayer has secured the basic form of religion: the correlation of God and man. Longing has drawn God nearer to man, and redemption, which God actualizes in the prayer, has given back to the individual his worth and dignity. Now the individual is no longer rooted only in his natural feeling for life; now his moral foundation has been sanctioned. In the religious deed of repentance and reconciliation prayer has proved itself also as a moral factor. Conversely, it is possible to say that although repentance is a purely moral factor, the regard for God expressed in it through prayer makes it a religious factor proper.

The individual is now confirmed, is morally justified. It is the triumph of religion, which it celebrates in prayer, that religion itself is called upon to bestow this moral justification on the individual. Now, however, religion asserts its claims, which it bases on its assistance in the moral redemption of the individual. The individual is now not only an element of totality, the symbol of mankind, but his moral nature, as obtained in the prayer, is to himself, as it were, an absolute individual. Redemption came to exist for man, not only fictitiously, as if imposed upon man in the idea of mankind—under this idea man has no sin and does not need redemption—but man became through sin and redemption an individual with a value of his own. This value consists of those moments in which the impetus of the individual toward redemption is actualized. This still poses the problem of the individual, the religious problem, which is justified on the basis of ethics. However, the religious problem requires, for man as for God, some connection with nature. God is the creator of nature and of man, the creator of nature for man. In the last analysis, God is the creator of man. But man needs the connection with nature; he is not only the spirit of holiness. He is immortal and therefore his soul needs the eternity of nature for its infinite development. Man's body could not be heterogeneous to his soul. The conceptual distinction is here confused with the factual one. The soul of man needs the biological individual, and, on the basis of the latter, the historical individual. Thus, the religious I demands, as its negative condition, the empirical basis of the I. Longing becomes the thread which unites both natures of the I, and prayer consolidates these threads into the concern and hope for the rights of the individual. When, at last, heaven and earth are connected, then there creeps into the prayer, ever more openly, the divining rod of the personal. The individual now considers himself justified in thinking about his own self insofar as the self must be concerned for its bodily and its whole material sustenance.

Here, too, religion shows how much help it can give against the one-sidedness which is necessary within ethics and, indeed, is there a source of clarification. We have seen how it was the ethically penetrating glance of the prophets that led them to recognize the suffering of man in poverty. From this point of view streamed rays of hope for this discovery of religion. However, human suffering is in no way limited to the social problem of poverty. Death is, indeed, not merely a mythological problem. Age and disease pose justified questions for the individual. Poverty itself is the origin of other needs of the individual, which do not simply belong to the sphere of economic weaknesses. "Cast me not off in the time of old age." This request to God is made by the same psalm that breathes confidence in the preservation of the holy spirit in the sinful man (Ps. 71:9). The sphere of earthly suffering is widened in the individual's prayer for God's goodness, so that the latter might not be limited to the forgiveness of sin.

It is noteworthy that the main prayer of the *Shemoneh Esreh* unites in the first benediction earthly concern with that of the afterlife: "Thou sustainest the living with loving-kindness, quickenest the dead with a great mercy, supportest the falling, healest the sick, loosest the bound, and keepest thy faith to them that sleep in the dust." The prayer thus binds life to death, and in life it distinguishes the falling, the sick, and the bound. It is not merely economic need that brings about man's fall, that brings about sickness and bondage, and therefore God's help against all other sources of earthly suffering has to be detected in the prayer. This detection of all kinds and all sources of needs, which is the presupposition for the detection of all kinds of means for help, is the content of the prayer's devotional thoughts.

As soon as the person, in all his ethical ambiguity, is conquered by religion, the latter makes a virtue of necessity, and justifies the duty of concern for oneself. The individual now no longer needs to defend himself against the suspicion of egotism. Because the concern for one's person is a duty, this duty to oneself makes the self the object of a religious concern, which bestows worth and dignity upon the self. Dread about one's own life and its security is not egotism, but is transfigured to a duty which prayer may embrace.

With the individual the family has also grown, and becomes in its turn a new and purely moral support of the individual. Now, however, prayer obtains entirely new wings, for even if prayer for one's own self is still suspected of egotism, prayer for one's next of kin is a natural urge, which calls heaven to witness. It would seem like suicide if one were not justified in getting hold of every means when the heart beats for the need of one's next of kin. Now that religion has produced the prayer, should it be used only for one's own redemption from sin, and not also for the liberation from one's greatest dread about the life of one's next of kin?

Here again the difference between ethics and religion appears. Ethics says, and Plato is the chief witness for it, that it does not recognize any difference among men, therefore also not between parents and children. Religion, however, says: "Honor thy father and thy mother." You must know and honor your own father, as well as have him. In this respect, too, man is not only a symbol of mankind; the correlation between parents and children produces a human value of its own, which bestows upon the individual an independent value, and this value is dignity. This commandment could originate only on the basis of a national history which takes its fundamental roots from the fathers of the tribe. From them grew the tribes which made the people into the "children of Israel." Hence, out of the individual's concern to belong to the family grew the prayer that is exempt from anything individual, which is directed to God for the preservation of religion. Hence, through prayer and religious community, the individual becomes closely connected with messianic mankind.

Whosoever calls the prayer for the life and prosperity of the individual's blood kin a superstition does not want to understand the human heart, which he must understand at this critical moment. Without belief in the success of the prayer, devotion could not gain power. The concern presses more heavily upon man than all sin. The individual's concern becomes an imperative duty. Therefore, this prayer is not only a sheet anchor but simple duty. However, the prayer depends upon belief in the good God, who wants to, and can, help the individual man. Whether he will help does not concern me in the performance of duty based on my need. I should never ask about the success of my duties. If, however, belief in success is necessary for the magic power of my devotion, then no skeptical poison should assail me. My soul achieves the innocence of belief in the good God. Therefore I pray to him. My prayer becomes my belief. So intimately does the prayer connect me as an individual with my God, with the God who in this prayer more than ever becomes my God.

However, the religious individual is not only enlarged by prayer in the sphere of the empirical I but also united with the ethical self. The moral I is infringed upon by dissipations, conflicts, and contradictions, which constantly threaten to split and cleave it. Once again the psalms prove their original power in this psalm that was incorporated into the daily prayer: "Make one my heart" (Ps. 86:11). The unity of consciousness is the highest problem of systematic philosophy. Religion in its own way adopted this problem; for all the struggles and contradictions of the heart, prayer seeks unity and pleads for it as the highest grace. Sin is only the religious expression of the cleavage of the heart, and reconciliation, therefore, is the religious expression of this unification, which the heart attains again in itself. Thus, the God of redemption becomes also the redeemer of the individual in the psychological sense, the savior of his self-consciousness, and the prayer, which pervades the effort of redemption and concludes it as its song of triumph, becomes the linguistic means that continuously secures and establishes anew the unity of consciousness, the unity of heart, which is always threatened, always at stake.

However, not only is God manifested as the good God through this prayer for the unification of the heart, but the correlation proves itself also with regard to man. In this prayer for oneself the individual is not only liberated and generally renewed; it is not only the redemption from sin in which the actual success of the prayer consists, but besides this success, the force of prayer is effective for the inner worth of man. The act of atonement consists not merely in sin, repentance, and reconciliation. The prayer must bring about reconciliation even without sin and repentance. Were this condition not relevant, religion would have to be dissolved in ethics. Man's self-examination, without explicit repentance, must accompany his entire life, and only through this does life become moral life. If it were to remain solely at this, religion would be superfluous for normal life; it would be only valid as a medicine for sinful life. Prayer, however, achieves for religion a hygienic value for the life of the individual, for the safety of his moral worth. If prayer has to take care of the individual, it has not only to intercede for his redemption, not to mention his earthly safety, but also has to have a share in the moral safety of the individual. This right of prayer is fulfilled in the unification of the heart of the individual.

To unification corresponds unity, which is the concept common to God and man. However, even in the case of God the concept of unity did not suffice for religious knowledge. Knowledge becomes objective not only in the concept of unity, however much this concept is the fundamental concept of knowledge; but from the content of the object it goes back to its own reasons and prerogative. In searching for its own justification, knowledge establishes as its highest problem the concept of truth. What would knowledge be, if it were not based on truth, hence if it were not truth itself? Thus, even for God, truth becomes the highest expression. "The seal of the Holy One, blessed be He, is the truth." This is a sentence from the Talmud (Sabbath 55a). Hence, even for God, truth becomes the highest expression of himself. Unity is not his seal, but truth.

What is true for God must be even more true for man, for he is, as the man of reason, the man of truth. Truth and holiness would be identical if holiness did not limit itself to morality, while truth unites the theoretical with the ethical and hence more than holiness becomes the ideal of reason. Truth, therefore, is the binding link between science, including ethics, on the one hand, and religion, on the other. If man must ask for his highest good, he must ask for truth, and if man must direct his prayer toward the truth, he is not merely to be thought of only as the symbol of mankind; the individual, too must direct his prayer toward the truth.

Truth for the individual becomes truthfulness. We must here anticipate the next chapter. Truthfulness is a virtue. We shall see, from the concept of virtue, that religion stays within its own aims when it shows concern in prayer for the truthfulness of the individual. In truthfulness a weapon is forged, and constantly preserved and hardened, which is necessary for the atoning work of repentance. Atonement cannot begin and it cannot make steady progress if truthfulness is not the fountain of youth from which the individual is continuously rejuvenated. The dangers that threaten truthfulness are impenetrable. The individual has no concern for which prayer is more necessary or more the proper source of strength than for truthfulness. For the lie is not only an external serpent; rather, mind and heart are always entangled in new cunning in order to veil the sources of deceit, and even to make truthfulness doubtful and illusory. All human strength seems to fail in this, and prayer to be the only help.

It is very significant that the preliminary early morning prayer, which we have already mentioned and in which we have already recognized important treasures, contains in the introduction, in which the futility of all human power is expressed, the following sentence: "At all times let a man fear God as well in private as in public, confess the truth, and speak the truth in his heart." This admonition to truthfulness is, in general, the motto of the prayer. Even if all other ends of the prayer be contested, this one is beyond doubt. The concentration of the soul, of the entire consciousness, which the prayer demands, is the irreplaceable means for the achievement of truthfulness. Therefore, the prayer must profoundly connect religion and morality. The correlation of man with God is adapted in the prayer to man's turning inward to his most profound moral powers. This turning is devotion, which in Hebrew also means "to be established." The devotion of the prayer establishes the unity of consciousness. No other vice threatens this unity as much as the countless snares of untruthfulness. Against all these deceptions and excuses repentance must arm itself, and prayer prepares this armament.

Prayer is therefore the fundamental form, the fundamental religious act. For in this goal of prayer, the rooting of the consciousness of man in truthfulness, God appears as the other link of the correlation. God is the God of truth, and man is to become the man of truthfulness. Therefore, man prays to God. Man would be perfect, and he would be able to redeem himself without looking to God, if he were able to establish and accomplish his truthfulness without praying to God. This is his main prayer, as the psalm expresses it: "Create me a clean heart, O God; and renew an established spirit within me" (Ps. 51:12). The adjective "established" belongs to the same root as the word for devotion. One could therefore translate the psalm: and renew in me a spirit of devotion, a spirit capable of devotion. The power of devotion is the power of prayer. The clean heart is the highest good of man, which he can think of only as a gift from God. Were he to have it by himself, no God would be necessary. He needs a clean heart for himself and therefore must entreat God for it.

Again we must refer to the early morning prayer, which contains surprising treasures: "O my God, the soul which thou gavest me is pure; thou didst create it, thou didst form it, thou didst breathe it into me; thou preservest it within me; and thou wilt take it from me, but wilt restore it unto me hereafter." The Talmud is the author of this prayer too. Purity of the soul is the presupposition of truthfulness. If the soul were bad, the task of truthfulness would be a contradiction. How could God have given man an impure soul? In that case he could not have given the soul at all. Since, however, he gave man a pure soul, man may ask him to renew continuously this purity of the soul, this devotion of the spirit. This renewal, this continuous new creation of the soul, is the condition for man's truthfulness. It is the chief meaning, the chief content of the prayer.

In the prayer quoted above one must consider the phrase: "Let a man confess the truth." Confession is not merely a condition for true repentance; it is not merely the confession of sin, but also the confession of truth. This confession, too, is the duty of man. Prayer elevates man to the height of his task, qualifies him for the candor of this objective confession of truth. The confession of the truth should not be the final product of his truthfulness—then it would be only a theoretical result—but it should become a means to sharpen and strengthen his truthfulness. The confession of truth is, for the prayer, the confession of God. The prayer is directed to God, to the God of truth for the sake of one's own truthfulness. In this confession the prayer connects man with God. Purity of the heart distinguishes the confession of truth from the confession of sin. The soul of man is pure; it is capable of truthfulness. God gave me a pure soul: man has the task of confessing the truth.

Prayer elevated man as an individual far beyond the empirical level, but he is still in need of God's protection against the dangers of the world. The morning prayer contains an additional sentence, laid down by the Talmud: "May it be thy will, O Eternal our God and God of our fathers, to make us familiar with thy Torah, and to make us cleave to thy commandments. O lead us not into the power of sin, or of transgression or iniquity, or of temptation, or of scorn." Two main ideas are to be distinguished in this prayer. First, the idea prevails that the knowledge of, and the care for, the Torah are the fundamental conditions of religiosity. Hence, God is asked to make us famiilar with the Torah and to make us cleave to the commandments. This is not in contradiction to one's own freedom, which the Talmud expressly exempts from God's omnipotence: "Everything is in the hands of God, except the fear of God" (Berachoth 33b). This prayer asks only for "familiarity," but there are hindrances to it and the prayer asks for their removal. When the hindrances are removed or lessened, then the familiarity can proceed without inhibition.

The second danger to man's morality lies in the temptation to sin. In the "Lord's Prayer" the Hebrew word is translated incorrectly: "Lead us not into temptation." This is at least inexact, for God cannot lead into temptation. He is the good God, and not Satan. But the Hebrew verb is in the *hiphil* form and means: "Let us not come into temptation." This entreaty is permissible and is connected with the preceding one. The following word, too, is similarly connected with temptation: "scorn." It is a particularly dangerous enticement to temptation. The illusion of looking down upon men constitutes the gravest danger to our own truthfulness and autonomy. It is the gravest temptation. Man is unable to remove all these obstacles from the path of his life, but it is in no way eudaemonism when he asks his God to liberate him from these temptations.

The "Lord's Prayer" also adds the entreaty for daily bread. This too is not eudaemonism; for although it is true that "man does not live by bread only" (Deut. 8:3), it is just as true that man cannot live without bread; life with its biological conditions is the negative condition for man. In this case, too, indeed, the translation from the Hebrew original is inexact. For the civilized man it is not enough to ask for daily bread, because this might appear to contain the wrong meaning, as if the civilized man had to care only for each day separately, like the savage pulling down each evening the hut he needs again the next morning. The Greek text is better: there one asks for *seemly* bread. The original text (Prov. 30:8) is free from all ambiguity: "Give me neither poverty nor riches, nourish me with the food of my statute" (הטריפני לחם חקי). The statute designates the appointment which dispels any doubts. It is the same word that is used for God's statutes in general. The pronoun in the phrase "my statute" adds the subjective meaning to the bread; it is appointed to suffice me. One could therefore translate it: the bread which suffices me. Now all provision for the individual is taken care of. The most grave temptations are still the material ones; they exist, however, in riches as well as in poverty. This idea is expressed in the Proverbs.

Why did the morning prayer not adopt the above sentence? This question is independent of the question of why it was adopted in the "Lord's Prayer," and the answer to this question is of importance for the character of Jewish prayer.

Most of the prayers of the so-called main body of prayers, which were written partly by the men of the Great Synagogue, partly by talmudic scholars, abstain from the consideration of earthly possessions. Therefore, not only riches but also poverty are not expressly drawn into the sphere of prayer. In prayer and through prayer the individual is to be turned away from all eudaemonism. Only that which connects man with God is to be the content of prayer. Prayer is to further only the impetus to man's infinite task. Therefore, besides the moral, only the spiritual, the knowledge, and the study of the Torah were made the concern of the individual in prayer.

A more general consideration is appropriate here. The second Isaiah demands a house for prayer, entirely in the sense of the dedication speech of Solomon's temple: "My house shall be called a house of prayer for all peoples" (Isa. 56:7). This name was not retained; by talmudic times the expression "house of assembly" had already originated, probably as a translation from the Greek *"synagoge."* The Hebrew word designates a greater intimacy than is conveyed by the word assembly: ingathering, drawing in, preserving, and sheltering. All this is in the meaning of the expression "congregation of Israel," a meaning also tied to another word for assembly.

However, another name also appears for the "house of prayer":

"the house of learning" בית המדרש. Here again the basic element of knowledge manifests itself in religion. Prayer did not remain the independent content of worship in the prayer house, but received an important supplement in the reading of the Torah, readings on Sabbaths that span the year of prayer. Moreover, to the Torah section a section from the prophets (*Haftorah*) has been regularly joined. Thus, the most important content of sacred scripture, the Pentateuch, and a great part of the prophetic texts have been incorporated into worship. The reading of both of these texts has not been limited to the Sabbaths, but these sections of learning from the Bible have also been added to the prayer on all festivals and on other distinguished days. There is no prayer without this learning. This, then, is an important characteristic of Jewish prayer according to the Mishnah: "The study of the Torah outweighs all commandments." Prayer must be teaching, it must have a share in teaching.

Hence, it is understandable that the house of learning became connected with the house of prayer, that the house of learning assimilated the prayer, that the name "house of learning" could have displaced the name "house of prayer." In German-Jewish jargon the synagogue is still called "*Schule*" [school] although recently the word "*Tempel*" [temple] has come into use. Yet with all these considerations, the reasons that brought about the predominance of the name "house of assembly" have not been exhausted.

A deeper reason has not yet been considered. No image was permitted to be made of the unique God: How could a house be built for him? The temple in polytheism is a house of god's image, and it was in analogy with this that the tabernacle of the Ark of Covenant was probably conceived. When, however, the knowledge of God had matured to monotheism, Solomon had first of all to make an objection to himself: "The eternal hath said that He would dwell in the thick darkness. I have surely built Thee a house of habitation" (1 Kings 8:12,13). The dwelling of the unique God is a mystery, and the building of a house for God seems to be an insult. There remains only one alternative: the house is not built for God, not even for his image, which does not exist, but for man, who does not want to sacrifice in it, but rather to pray. This is the unquestionable consequence: if the monotheistic idea takes offense against a house for God, it must think of this house as a house of prayer. Only in connection with prayer could the sacrifice be thinkable in this house (cf. 1 Kings 8:27,28,29).

The house, however, is not only an offense against God, but, as a house of prayer, it is also an offense against man. Must not prayer originally be individual prayer? Is prayer natural in chorus, or only in solitude? Must not prayer, wherever it is uttered, in the first place be thought of as something personal which only the individual himself and for himself, can say? Does not the assembly of people contradict the inward character of prayer? Is prayer able to open up and secure the motives of the heart, if the individual has to stand in rank and file for the prayer? Not only is the house a contradiction with regard to God, but the house of assembly seems to increase the contradiction with regard to the individual man.

All these considerations are reconciled in the essence of the prayer itself, which unites all of them. We have previously related this main content of prayer to the individual man. The individual, however, is in need of the prayer in order to cleave to God. This connection of the individual with God cannot be conceived by the prayer only individually, for the prayer is the universal means for the connection with God. Hence, it is universal humanity, the human community *(Gemeinschaft)*, by virtue of which the individual is able to seek, and entreat for, his own connection with God. Hence, even the concept of God becomes in the prayer the Kingdom of God (מלכות שדי), and man if he desires to establish himself as an individual, can strive for this only within the community of the Kingdom of God. Therefore the most important prayer, the concluding prayer of the day, and of every time of the day, is *Alenu*. The establishment of the Kingdom of God constitutes the main content of this powerful prayer, and everything else is twined around it. We shall return to this topic later; for the Kingdom of God is only the pinnacle of the community, which at first had to be established for the individual as the praying individual.

The prayer establishes the congregation; therefore, the prayer belongs not so much to the individual as to the congregation. It also establishes the individual, but the extent to which it can succeed in this depends on the extent to which the individual is united with the congregation, on the extent to which individuals as a plurality are united into the unity of the congregation. The congregation is the original soil of the Kingdom of God. The congregation is the assembly of worshipers for the confession of the unique God. This assembly for the confession of God is and remains the original soil of the messianic Kingdom of God. The latter belongs to the future, but the present also is in need of prayer, and the future cannot be achieved if the present does not work for it. Therefore the yoke of the Kingdom of God must be taken upon one's own shoulders on every day and with every prayer. This is the meaning and the content of the concluding prayer *Alenu*.

This is also the meaning of the *Kaddish Prayer*, which, as the prayer during the year of mourning for one's parents, is an important constituent of Jewish prayer. "May He establish His kingdom during your life and during your days, and during the life of all the house of Israel." Thus, one prays that the messianic kingdom of God might become present: through the prayer the messianic future is made alive in the present. It is a moving sign of piety that, despite all the bitter fights against him, a dedication in memory of Maimonides was added to the above sentence by the people of his generation: "and in the life of Moses ben Maimon." This addition could, of course, not have been preserved, but it does express the deep understanding, admiration, and gratitude for this truly great spirit of Jewish religion. However, the testimony his generation tried to set up for him as a highest memorial by inserting his name into the most important prayer, that testimony is everlasting. It tried to express that the right meaning of the Messianic Age is only fulfilled through its connection with the present, and that Maimonides elucidated this meaning not only by making a distinction between the future time and the future world, but also through his entire connection of religion with ethics.

The congregation is the indispensable preliminary step to messianic fulfillment. The prayer of the individual must accordingly become the prayer of the congregation. Mysticism and pietism tread dangerous paths when they isolate the individual in prayer. Solitude can only be a transitory state of the human mind. Man is the carrier of mankind. For this purpose he must first of all assemble into a community. The totality of mankind must be his final goal, but for this totality he must first achieve the unity of plurality. Mankind is the totality., The unity of plurality is the congregation. The congregation of Israel is God's assembly. Thus the house of prayer became "the assembly house."

Hence the being of the congregation and its preservation also became an important part of prayer. In the estimate of religion, the congregation is almost substituted for the people. "Whosoever separates himself from the congregation has no share in eternal life." Deep insight into the significance of the congregation has led to these harsh words. The congregation has preserved religion and the people for religion. That variety of disbelief in the truth of monotheism which takes refuge in the materialistic theory of history cannot sufficiently express its astonishment at the riddle of the continuous preservation of the people of Israel. The congregation comprises the solution to this riddle; the congregation took the place of the state. The state had to be displaced by Messianism, and if the identity of state and people had to be destroyed, another identity, namely, that of the people and the congregation, arose. The people of Israel became "the congregation of Israel." Here the word for "assembly" also came into usage. The congregation of Israel became "the assembly of Israel."

Here again we have to consider the morning prayer that expresses the following two benedictions: "Blessed art Thou . . . who crownest Israel with glory." In the glorification of Israel the foundation for the glorification of God is entreated. Israel here means "the congregation of Israel" the foundation of religion. The wording of the other benediction is "who girdest Israel with heroic power." This benediction precedes the first one. We let it follow because glorification is the goal, the girding the means. Heroic power is not in itself the goal; it is entreated for the sake of the glorification of God, which is the only goal. These benedictions are also of talmudic origin.

The people as the congregation corresponds to the I of the psalms that are the basic form of prayer. The psalm is in the lyric style. It confesses the soul's love for God. It feels this love as longing for God. This lyrical confession has to sing a monologue in the dialogue. The soul unites both persons of the dialogue; for the soul itself is given by God, and is therefore not exclusively a human soul. Hence, it can seek God and speak to God and with God. The prophets had already connected Israel with God through love and therefore called it bride and wife.[87] According to a Midrash, Israel is called God's bride in ten passages. Israel is also called sister and friend. Parts of the early morning prayer are called "Love" (*ahabah*). And in the New Year's prayer the verse from Jeremiah is adopted: "Is Ephraim a darling son unto Me? Is he a child that is dandled?" (Jer. 31:20). In a variety of symbols of love, the prophets and the psalms sing God's covenant with Israel and Israel's covenant with God. This basic form of love has the prayer as the matrix upon which it builds.

In prayer the congregation becomes the loving one and the one beloved by God. Sulamith particularly becomes the symbol for the religious poetry of the late antiquity and the Middle Ages. Prayer fuses the love for God with the love for the congregation. The congregation is at once the people and the religion. The true meaning of the prayer does not find a contradiction to messianic mankind in this. The latter is the goal which, however, can neither be reached nor striven for without the preservation of the congregation. It is not particularism when the majority of Jewish prayers are directed to the preservation of Israel. Truly, there is no lack of prayers that are concerned with man generally, with "all flesh." The universal relations of reason, such as knowledge, are directed to man in general. It says in the main daily prayer: "Thou favorest man with knowledge, and teachest mortals understanding." Nevertheless, the concentration upon the congregation of Israel must be preserved at all times, for in it the crucial point of religion is secured. Even the Church adopted the name Israel, although it would like to extend the meaning of Israel to all the peoples of the world.

The congregation of Israel must therefore become a special obligation for the prayer of the individual. Prayer must be recognized and developed as the special means for the preservation and development of the congregation. The congregation carries and propagates religion. Therefore, all the considerations that are valid for the law must, in a higher degree, be valid for prayer. Certainly, the preservation of the congregation cannot be limited to prayer. However, the important stipulations, which are represented not only by the "house of prayer" but also by the "house of learning," and which in the prescribed readings of the Torah are also adopted by the former, all these fundamental stipulations of the teaching and of its study would remain ineffectual without the collaboration of prayer. The prayer is, as it were, the language of reason of the congregation. Through the organ of prayer all the spiritual differences among individuals become reconciled. The language of the heart becomes the uniform language of the spirit.

Thus, prayer is a prominent socializing power, which is adequately complemented by the assembly house. That all men are equal before God, a principle that exemplifies the messianic character of religion, every religious man is heartily willing to acknowledge through his own deed. This conviction unconsciously urges everybody to the synagogue. However, the common place of worship by itself does not yet secure the fulfillment of socializing striving, if a common language is not spoken in the common place. Prayer is this common language, and as such it excels all the means of knowledge. Since prayer is the language of the congregation, the act of praying must be an act of the congregation as a whole. It does not displace individual prayer, but it shows the latter its earthly goal beside the heavenly goal.

All the difficulties the demand for law must encounter are therefore repeated in the case of prayer. Insofar as the strength of the congregation and its ability to develop, and hence religion itself, depend on prayer also, prayer must take upon itself, as does law, the danger and the duty of isolation. The danger here seems to be even greater than in the case of the isolating law; for language is not only the organ of prayer but also that of culture in general. In the case of language as a form of culture, the demands of one's

own state and nationality are particularly heavy. The language of
the prayer is the language of the heart. The language of the heart,
however, is the mother tongue. Hence, the efforts in modern times,
directed at changing the language of the Hebrew prayer into the
languages of the appropriate cultures, become understandable. These
efforts have to be evaluated from the point of view of their ideal
contribution to the national state and to the unity of the appropriate
culture. This ideality distinguishes them from the translations of
old, which were made with a view to the practical consideration
that in Babylonian times the country people were no longer familiar with Hebrew. Of course, the latter consideration also has a
voice in the modern tendencies toward reformation, but the former,
ideal moment is predominant. However, it is a question whether
this all important consideration has to be the only decisive one, or
whether it has to have a voice, but not the decisive one. The great
question of the law and its power of isolation repeats itself here.
It must become an explicit question whether a special isolating significance must be attributed to the language of prayer itself, or
whether in prayer the isolation should be limited to the religious
content, in which the isolation is to exhaust itself.

A deep psychological problem is hidden in this. The difficulties involved in the problem of translation are well known to
modern scholarship. If there may be a question whether Homer is
translatable, the problem with Plato is even more difficult. The
more the reality of the universe of thought is interwoven with the
individual art of a particular language, the more difficult, the more
futile any attempt at translation seems to become. One can only
translate words and hardly the texture of a sentence, but only in
the sentence does the word receive its inner life. And without the
soul of a word, the spirit of a word also remains lifeless in a different language.

The general difficulties of translation increase when the content
is a religious one. In the case at hand the content does not merely
involve a question of a denominational creed. The latter expression
evades the difficulty that is imposed upon Jewish monotheism. As
matters stand, Jewish monotheism is in opposition to the other
forms of monotheism and, as regards the great problems of culture
in general, it has to assert itself against Christianity, which in its
various forms is predominant in culture. The difficulty is even more
entangled because Christianity not only originated from the original
treasures of Judaism but to this day rejuvenates itself through them.
Hence the language of Judaism must in part turn against its own

language in the context of Christianity if it desires to assert itself. However, its own language did not remain the original language of Christianity, but became a translation. Therefore, we should have to defend the original Hebrew not only against the German vestment, but also the Christian, with its Greek translation of the New Testament, which already carries with it a transformation of the original Hebrew thought. Moreover, the translation from this language of the New Testament into a language of a modern culture is a further transformation of the original text. Hence, one is able to measure the great psychological difficulties that possible changes involved in a translation present. These general linguistic difficulties also beset the question of prayer.

To begin with, in order to allay the justified practical objections, it has to be said that the problem in question is concerned with the principle only, and that the latter is not thought of as normative for the application to particular cases. In no way does the principle demand the exclusion of the languages of the different cultures from prayer, and, as a matter of fact, not only should the lack of understanding of the Hebrew language in the widest circles be regarded as a determining factor, but the viewpoint of the national state one lives in should be recognized as normative. The follower of Judaism should be a modern man of culture, and as such he should employ the language of his culture not only for business or for the general cultural use of the mind, with the exclusion of religion, but should also honor it and use it effectively in prayer. He should also let himself be inspired by it for his religious feeling. General culture would remain mute and soulless for him if it were not able to penetrate the most intimate life of his religious spirit. In no way, therefore, should an opposition be formulated between the language of culture and the language of the prayer. Only a distinction is to be admitted and the consequences that follow from the distinction are to be considered in principle.

The principle is the peculiar content of Jewish monotheism in the necessity of its isolation. From this principle follows irresistibly the isolation of the language of prayer, but only to that extent compatible with the other principle, that of the sense of community with one's culture. Consequently, this conflict will only be concerned with the proportionate allotment, in which both principles divide the material of prayer between the two languages. It is according to this criterion that the new order of worship has been shaped in most German congregations. This criterion is in accordance with both necessary principles. If we consider the motherland of all problems of religious culture in modern Judaism, if we consider Germany in particular, then prayer in German must be retained, but Hebrew should not be pushed back any further. Rather, the content of religion in regard to what it can teach should perhaps be the determining factor in the choice of Hebrew texts.

For prayer is the language of the congregation, the language of the religious community. Prayer itself, therefore, must be evaluated and used as a means of education to the content of faith in order to introduce and impress the most important ideas upon the religious mind. For this purpose the original text is necessary; for through translation the Jew would inhale the Christian spirit even in the original biblical idea. The general culture is also the common atmosphere for religious concepts. As compared with the entire bastion of the surrounding culture, how ineffectual is fragmentary religious instruction even in its most thorough form! Home and family can be effective only in a truly complementary manner if they nurture not only religious knowledge and law but also specifically religious feeling. The psychologically unavoidable separation between knowledge and feeling, and, regretfully enough, also between the practice of the law and feeling, can be bridged better by the language of prayer, which is the immediate language of feeling. It is characteristic of Christian translations that they do not express the uniqueness of God, but in most cases substitute the numerical word "one." What this example reveals is repeated in all words in which the Christian meaning is different from the Jewish one. It suffices to point to "redemption," to "the shepherd" and "the lamb," which is led to slaughter. In all these concepts the Christian heart beats differently from the Jewish one. In this respect there is psychologically no other way than to let the original language effect the original concept and the corresponding original feeling. It is an instructive example that in broad Jewish circles the Redeemer is not known as an original Jewish concept, because in the general understanding the Redeemer came to be known as a Christian concept. Then, too, the deepest harm that Jewish monotheism suffered from all kinds of defamation and misinterpretation because the notion of neighborly love was not attributed to it would not have occurred if the original word *rea* (רע) [fellowman] had not been wrongly translated "neighbor" [meaning fellow countryman]. What would not have become of "Torah," translated exclusively by "law," if the word were not preserved alive in the original!

Let us consider the richness of purely spiritual treasures that are stored up in the original stock of Jewish prayers. There is first the

large number of psalms, which are either taken over in their entirety
or emerge in individual sayings and turns of epression in the newly
formed prayers. The same is the case with sentences from the Pentateuch and from the prophets and other biblical expressions and
thoughts that are interwoven in the new prayers. The style did not
thereby become eclectic and imitative; a homogeneous spirit pervades this original world which is still governed by a uniform
power. For the Canon had not been completed at the time, and
before it was completed, the Midrash and the Haggadah in all their
ramifications had already assured it a new future and the connection
of that future with antiquity. The Midrash itself is active in the composition of prayers. Moreover, the Midrash presents itself not only in
its own special form but also as the common fundamental power in
the twofold expression of the Talmud: in Halachah and Haggadah. The
unity of the Midrash in these different spiritual expressions and
styles would have been an incomprehensible riddle if it were not for
the original biblical spirit that wielded the psychological scepter
there. Whoever knows the Midrash and the Talmud only super-
ficially must be amazed at how vivid the biblical verses had to be
in the consciousness of these people, if they could make use of them
in their ingenious and often far-fetched arguments. To assume that
they had the idea first and afterwards searched the Bible for its
foundation would not be a psychological explanation. This might
have been true in individual cases, but it cannot be the case with
the entire style of this kind of hermeneutic. The presupposition cannot be avoided that thesis and biblical verse emerged together in
one flash. Then, however, a new puzzle arises: how is this simultane-
ous emerging of the idea and the biblical word psychologically understandable? Only the inner vividness of the biblical word makes
it understandable. Jewish life in later times has retained enough
examples of this most inward, continuous life of the biblical word
and its volcanic, or rather organic, agility and creativity. However,
in the classical time, in which the oral tradition originated, this
vividness had a still deeper power and fruitfulness.

Out of this vividness of the biblical language and of the biblical
feeling for language the original stock of prayers arose. How could
this originality be suspected of imitativeness and eclecticism! These
prayers, rather, bear the imprint of the original Jewish spirit, which
does not die away with the establishment of the Canon, but lives
on and continues to create. And as in all cases of an inner connection
with an original idea, the continuing formation of new prayers keeps
the classical pattern. This augments the spiritual treasure, if not in

respect to the teaching itself, then with respect to the feeling for the teaching which the prayer arouses and keeps active. This power of the prayer is bound to the power of language; for the ideas grew in this language and the feelings intertwined with it. Therefore, in the treasure of prayers, the congregation must preserve a fundamental portion of prayers intact entirely in Hebrew for the purpose of producing and animating these peculiarily Jewish religious feelings.

Could the objection be raised against this principle that the other principle, that of the cultural community, is hindered and impaired by that principle of religious peculiarity? The indication that these prayers are stock prayers of classical content, of original biblical content, disposes of this objection. And now we can turn the tables. The cultural content of the modern mind is not limited when prayer in Hebrew is preserved to a certain extent. Moreover, it is not only the Jewish religious spirit that is fructified with peculiarly Jewish religious feelings by these prayers, but the classical content of these original forms of prayer—taken from the prophets and the psalms—causes a new flow of universal and religious spirituality into the modern world through the Jewish upholders of general culture. The whole of Christian culture is pervaded by the Old Testament. The highest ideas of poetry are derived from, and nourished by, this spirit. In this respect, too, Herder became Goethe's nourishing father. Generally, therefore, one should not speak of isolation or separation from the language of culture at all when the necessity of prayer in Hebrew is demanded to a limited extent. Rather, from these channels a new influx is to be expected, indeed, a new accessibility and widening of the ancient sources. It is only prejudice, which still persists against Jewry in its peculiar development and effect, which allows suspicion of prayer in Hebrew to arise. With the peculiarity of Jewish monotheism, which in principle demands the preservation of the law, adherence to prayer in Hebrew is also demanded in principle.

The stock prayers are grouped about the fundamental forms of faith. Thus, the *Shema* ["Hear, O Israel"] is first taken from Deuteronomy. It is Israel's watchword, the watchword of the unique God. One should reflect upon the regulation of the Talmud, which says that while uttering in the *Shema* the word "unique" (*Ehad*) the praying one in his thought and feeling should dedicate his entire soul and life to God. This regulation is only understandable from the inner linguistic form of the word, for in its verbal form the root took on the meaning of dedication. When, therefore, the uniqueness of God is thought of with the right feeling, man has to make himself one for the unique God, to dedicate himself to him, to surrender his entire life to him, as the next sentence demands. This surrender is love "with all thine heart, with all thy soul, and with all thy might." Hence, the Unique One and the unified heart are correlated, and the unified heart manifests itself in the surrender to the unique God.

The *Shema* is joined by the main prayer, the Eighteen Benedictions (*Shemoneh Esreh*). This consists of three introductory and three closing benedictions, but its proper content comprises the entire sphere of human concerns, to which concern about religion, about the community, along with its messianic extension is joined. It is characteristic, however, that the first supplication of this main prayer is for knowledge: "Thou favorest man with knowledge, and teachest mortals understanding." Here only man is named and not the Israelite. Man, the mortal one, is the horizon of the prayer for knowledge and reason.

The concluding prayer of the *Shemoneh Esreh* is also characteristic: "O my God! guard my tongue from evil and my lips from speaking guile; and to such as curse me let my soul be dumb, yea, let my soul be unto all as the dust. Open my heart to thy Torah, and let my soul pursue thy commandments. If any design evil against me, speedily make their counsel of no effect, and frustrate their designs. Do it for the sake of thy holiness, do it for the sake of thy Torah. In order that thy beloved ones may be delivered, O save with thy right hand, and answer me. Let the words of my mouth and the meditation of my heart be acceptable before thee, O Eternal, my ,Rock and my Redeemer." In such humility does the main prayer conclude. The soul has to be silent against curses and has to be dust unto everybody. Upon such humility the hope for God's help is based.

Humility as a virtue we shall later have to consider more precisely. It is the state of the soul which the psalm substitutes for the sacrifice: "a broken and contrite heart, O God, thou wilt not despise" (Ps. 51:19). "The sacrifices of God are a broken heart" (ibid.). The prayer is mainly directed toward reconciliation with God. The prayer is to replace sacrifice in order to achieve reconciliation. The broken heart takes the place of the slaughtered animal. Hence, humility originates in the correlation of man with God. Here is manifested the connection of the individual with the sacrificial community, which becomes the praying community; only in the latter is the individual brought to prominence. Just as the matter could not end with the individual, so it cannot end with the congregation of Israel. Even with regard to Sodom and Gomorrah, Abraham had to pray even then to his God for the forgiveness of their sins. And Moses prays: "Blot me out . . . of Thy book" (Exod. 32:32) when God does not want to forgive the people. The individual cannot and does not want to exist without the congregation, and Messianism demands that the congregation should be extended to mankind.

We have, however, to consider first the third main section of the prayer: the *Sanctus (Kedushah)*. The threefold "Holy" originated at the call of Isaiah [Isa. 6:3], and we have already considered how this threefold repetition corresponds to Isaiah's conception of God as the holy God. The uniqueness of God is joined by holiness, and holiness is not only a complement to, but a foundation for, uniqueness. Through holiness all attempts to know God through numerical determination are thwarted. His uniqueness rests in holiness, which is the religious expression of morality. This confession of holiness becomes an important part of every congregational worship, and in the *Kedushah* on the Sabbath and on all the holidays the "Hear, O Israel" is added.

The "Hear, O Israel," however, becomes with the prophets a messianic watchword: for "in that day shall the Eternal be Unique, and His name unique" (Zech. 14:9). Hence both watchwords, that of the unique God and the unique name, grow together. Had they not grown together by themselves, the prayer would have forged them into one. Prayer originated with Abraham as a prayer for sin and for an alien tribe. If the prophets, as politicians, could not yet entirely get rid of national particularism, the psalm, as the original form of prayer, broke through national limitation. "Every soul praises God": thus concludes the book of the Psalms.

We have just seen how the main prayer puts man as such ahead of the Israelite. This happens not only in the prayer for knowledge, but also in the prayer for healing, in which God is called "Physician of all Flesh." Of course Messianism is always burdened with care for the faithful people, for the "servant of God." Hence the schism always remains in the prayers: on the one hand the return to Zion, the restoration of the sanctuary along with sacrifices, pervades the entire prayer cycle; this particularism, on the other hand, is deeply connected with messianic universalism, and hence the latter had unavoidably to transfigure and broaden the confinement of the former.

We have already recognized the culminating point, constituted by the *Mussaf-prayer* of the New Year in the three sections of the *Zikronot*, the *Malkuyot*, and the *Shoferot*.

The Bible verses that are united in the *Malkuyot* proclaim the government of the world, those of the *Zikronot* the judgement of the world, and those of the *Shoferot* the redemption of the world.

The government of the world is fulfilled in the messianic Kingdom of God. Therefore the text of the third introductory benediction of the *Shemoneh Esreh* on the New Year and on the Day of Atonement, which are united under the name "the Days of Awe," is as follows: "Impose Thine awe upon all Thy works, and Thy dread upon all that Thou hast created, that all works may revere Thee and all creatures prostrate themselves before Thee that they may all form a single band." This band—this one covenant of all men—is the highest achievement of God's government of the world. In this one covenant of all mankind the Kingdom of God is realized on earth. God's covenant with Noah is completed in this covenant of God with mankind. The covenant of mankind, as the unification of all men, is the covenant of man with God. This covenant is the sign, the guarantee, of God's government of the world.

The government of the world distinguishes monotheism from pantheism. What is the difference between government and development? To development a goal must be set; it cannot set it by itself. Only government can set a goal for it. Government is providence united with omnipotence. Government is not an attribute. It is, rather, idetntical with the concept of God as the guarantor of the realization of morality on earth. The government of the world is the setting of an end for the world and the realization of that end for the world in its double meaning, as nature and as the human world.

The government of the world as the setting of an end for the world, and the realization of it, in the world, is the meaning and content of monotheism. Therefore, the prayer above closes with the "Hear, O Israel." And before it, God's eternity is expressed: "I am the first, and I am the last; and beside Me there is no God" (Isa. 44:6). In the same way the next benediction invokes God's rule over all the earth: "upon all the inhabitants of the world." All creatures will understand that they are created by God. The Kingdom of God is creation and providence; this is God's government. As the governor of the world he is "the God of truth." The government of the world is the moral order of the world. If morality and nature are different methodologically, then the order of the world, as moral order, must be the government of the world, and this establishes the difference between monotheism and pantheism.

The moral world order of the Kingdom of God, as the kingdom of the world, requires the Judgment of the World. We know by now how myth is dominated by this idea. Myth makes the end of the

world a consequence of the Judgment of the World. Out of the end
of the world may emerge, at most, a renewal of the world and an
alternation between this renewal and the end of the world. The
government of the world must eliminate the end of the world. By
the time of Noah God had made a covenant against the recurrence
of the flood, and as a sign of this covenant, as a remembrance of
this covenant, the rainbow is set upon the vault of heaven. Thus the
New Year becomes the festival of creation, the "Day of Remembrance" (יום הזכרון). The *Zikronot* describes Gods omniscience in
this remembrance: "All things are manifest and known unto thee,
O Eternal our God, who lookest and seest to the end of all generations." And the remembrance now becomes the Judgment of the
World.

Not only are the works of men judged, but also "man's . . . thoughts
and schemes, his imaginings and achievements." Now the remembrance of Noah comes forth and with it is connected the remembrance of the covenant with Abraham, Isaac, and Jacob. Finally, the
prophet speaks the more intimate words: "I remember for thee the
affection of thy youth, the love of thine espousal; how thou wentest
after Me in the wilderness" (Jer. 2:2). "And I will establish unto
thee an everlasting covenant" (Ezek. 16:60). Thus the Judgment of
the World surprisingly turns into remembrance about the world,
about the covenant with the world, which God repeatedly made with
his world. The Judge of the world becomes a party to the covenant
with man. The Judge of the world becomes an associate in the covenant with man.

The prayer that follows stresses in the history of the patriarchs
the important act of abandoning human sacrifice. That which appears as a commandment to offer Isaac actually represents the
abandonment of pagan sacrifice. The word "sacrifice" did not become the used name for this act, but rather "binding" (*akeda*): "The
binding with which Abraham our father bound his son Isaac on the
altar . . . he overbore his fatherly compassion in order to perform
Thy will with a perfect heart." The name in use is significant: not
sacrifice but binding is what this episode is called in the history
of the patriarchs, in the history of the sacrifice. This portion of the
prayer for the Judgment of the World thus concludes with the remembrance of the binding of Isaac, which manifests the reciprocal
effect of Abraham's love for God and God's love for him and his
descendants. Thus, the myth of the Judgment of the World unequivocally becomes the judgment of man through God's love.

The *shofar* is the general musical instrument for every holy day, and also for the New Moon. At the revelation on Sinai, too, the sound of the *shofar* resounded among thunder and lightning. It therefore becomes the foremost instrument in the Hallelujah of the psalms, and therefore it also becomes the "horn of the Messiah."

The New Year celebrates not only the government of the world and the Judgment of the World, but also the messianic redemption of the world. The *shofar* is the symbol of the Messiah. Therefore, the portions of the prayer which refer to the redemption of the world are called *Shoferot*.

As the trumpet of the redemption of the world the *shofar* transforms the terror of its tone into joy, into eternal joy, into the joy of eternity.

These messianic prayers are the climax of Jewish prayer. In them the prayer frees itself from all the limitations of national particularism, from all the narrowness of individualism. The individual removes himself from his natural, his empirical individuality, but the congregation, too, rises above its empirical actuality to its task, to its future in the "one covenant" of mankind. The Judgment of the World becomes the reconciliation with the world, and only in the latter is the government of the world fulfilled. The Kingdom of God is religion's highest good, and this highest good is the highest content of prayer.

Thus prayer becomes the fundamental religious means for the idealization of man. Religion, too, if it has its own peculiar character, must have, besides morality, its own share in the idealization, in the elevation of man to the idea of his task. In repentance, religion competes with ethics. Morality guides man's work of repentance, but the religious confidence in God achieves the success of redemption.

In the prayer which pervades the work of repentance, but which also concludes it in a triumphal song, we now recognize another element of the competition between religion and morality. Ethics defines its God to itself as the guarantor of morality on earth, but beyond the definition, beyond postulating this idea, its means fail. The peculiar contribution of religion to the ethical idea of God is the trust in God, the confidence in the messianic fulfillment of this idea. Thus prayer, as the language of the correlation of man with God, becomes the voice of Messianism, and therefore the universal language of humanity. In the psalms this universal language assumed its office; it began its messianic career. The messianic prayer has become the voice of humanity, the voice of man as mankind.

Mankind is the high point of the correlation of man and God. In the idea of mankind, God is implicitly thought of too. Messianism is the quintessence of monotheism. In the same way, also, the concept of man and mankind is completed. As we have recognized prayer as the voice of mankind, so it has thereby also become the voice of man for the idealization of the individual. This is the great meaning of prayer, this is the solution of the mystery, which the psalms constitute in world literature: that they, as the ideal form of prayer, reveal this idealizing human power of prayer. The man who cannot pray is unable to unburden himself of his finiteness, with all its dross and dread. On the other hand, he who can pray is not a slave to superstition or self-interest, which merely imitate the degenerate kind of prayer. Whoever has the mastery of true prayer loses earthly fears and earthly heaviness in his ascent to infinity. He forgets the suffering that occasioned the prayer, because in this capacity of his soul he rises above the finiteness of his I. His entire consciousness is transformed into yearning and elevation. The entire content of his consciousness passes into this soaring, which becomes a stronger basis than what actuality usually offers for our participation. If thought, directed to knowledge, produces the ideality of the scientific world and establishes it as the true reality, in the same manner we now recognize in prayer the fundamental power of religious idealization, which continuously brings forth and fortifies the community of God and man that is demanded by their correlation.

Thus, prayer is the proper language of religion. All the thinking of this language about God and about man, all the thinking of this correlation, would remain theoretical if prayer were not that activity of language in which the will becomes active in all the means of thought. The devotion of the prayer is the will of religion.

CHAPTER XVIII

The Virtues

There is only one morality, but ethics as well as religion has at all times set up a plurality of different virtues. The identification of virtue with morality was fatal for ethics because from the plurality and the difference of virtues people believed they could deduce the relativity of the moral law. For if there is only one morality, there could be only one virtue.

The unity of virtue is a principle of Socrates' teaching. Socrates' teaching, however, is the preparation for, rather than the actual beginning of, ethics. The beginning actualizes itself only with the idea of the good, therefore only with Plato's doctrine of ideas. The idea is prepared, however, through the "concept," which Socrates makes into a problem of knowing (*Wissen*). The good is for Socrates the concept of the good, and through the concept of the good and in it originates the knowing of the good. This knowing, however, is not yet knowledge which is based on the idea.

This explains why Socrates, as well as Plato in his preliminary dialogues, treats the good as identical with virtue, and the knowing of the good as identical with the knowing of virtue.

This also explains the connection of the following two principles in Socrates' teaching: the principle of the unity of virtue and the principle of virtue as knowing.

Virtue as knowing does not mean the same for Socrates as for Plato. With Plato it is not enough that the thought of the good is elevated to a concept. The concept itself must be established and accounted for. The account of the concept is accomplished by the idea. Consequently, if with Plato the good is considered as knowing, this means that the good is an object, a problem of knowledge, which is unfolded in his teaching of ideas.

Socrates, on the contrary, lacks the doctrine of ideas. For him the concept is not yet the concept justified by the idea. To be sure, this

principle that the good is knowledge already has a preparatory theoretical significance for Platonism in ethics, namely, that the good is not
an illusion and not a convention or an expediency, but that it is
rather a problem as worthy of study as nature, as the state and the
law, as the art of war, and as all human vocations. However, from
these contrasts, the very polemical power this principle of knowledge
implies becomes evident. This peculiar meaning of the principle,
however, becomes evident only from the other principle with which
it is intrinsically connected, namely, with the principle that virtue
is knowledge. The latter principle too is unmistakably directed
against sophistry. The Sophists not only say that virtue is an anti-
quated illusion; but they also say that it is only a matter of routine,
which at most has only practical value but with which one cannot
attract much theoretical attention. There is, therefore, no other way
to become wise but through instruction and education, of which the
Sophists consider themselves the appointed masters. Against this
denigration of the knowledge of virtue, Socrates steps forth with the
proposition that virtue is knowledge, which he bases on his own concept of the good. With this he does not invalidate the pedagogical
significance of practical education for virtue; rather, he turns the
tables and elevates and deepens the meaning of practical education
through this proposition.

For, while he makes virtue knowledge, he throws the first light
into the deep darkness of the will and its freedom as against the
compulsion of the desires. The will is not yet discovered, but, as it
is based on—and consists of—freedom, Socrates discovers freedom for
the will even before the will itself came to be defined. This freedom of the will is established through the teaching that virtue is
knowledge.

The Sophists say that everything that people call virtue is only
illusion and convention, and at most natural instinct. Socrates, on the
contrary, comes forth with the ethical enthusiasm that is revealed in
his teaching: whoever has knowledge of virtue is unable to violate
virtue. You say that habit has produced this illusion. On the contrary, the discoverer of the concept teaches: he who has mastery
of the concept and, through it, of the knowledge of virtue, is unable
to do wrong. Through knowledge, through thought, the moral will is
established. Virtue is not practice according to habit, because knowledge of virtue defeats, frustrates, and invalidates any such practice. Virtue is knowledge—this proposition means: virtue consists of
knowledge, not of practice. Practice is the inevitable consequence
of knowledge. How, then, could virtue be the creation of imagina-

tion and of habit, if it proves itself in knowledge as a force that brings to naught any practice?

Only now does the connection of both propositions become clear: that of knowledge and that of virtue. Of course, this connection has its most immediate ground in the language, which thinks of virtue as practical capability and denotes it as manliness (ἀρετή: *virtus*). This capability should not remain fragmented, as life presents it. Hence, the proposition that the unity of virtue is based on knowledge follows. This proposition puts knowledge in the place of capability, in the place of virtue as practical capability. Knowledge itself makes capability merely a consequence. This explains why virtue becomes the main problem, before which the problem of the good recedes. It also becomes understandable that the Socratic teaching about the good was unable to liberate itself from the ambiguities of utilitarianism and eudaemonism. This is only a matter of appearance, but this appearance is unavoidable. The good could not remain the chief and exclusive problem, not only because virtue had to become the great motivating problem but also because the good remained merely a concept and could not yet become an idea. Hence, it is understandable that virtue became identical with the good. When, however, with Plato the concept of the good became the idea of the good, this identity had to disappear; for the idea of the good, although as an idea it belongs to knowledge, has, considered from the point of view of science, to be differentiated from the mathematical idea. Therefore the good cannot be made identical with a natural object of scientific knowledge. The identity between the good and knowledge is abolished by the idea.

Therefore the identity between the good and virtue also cannot continue. The road that leads from knowledge to practice is securely prepared by the distinction between the idea of the good and the mathematical ideas. Virtue has to lead on this road to practice. This is not expressly said by Plato, but from several considerations this must be thought of as his tendency. First, this would explain his deviation from the Socratic principle, which teaches the unity of virtue. Plato assumes four cardinal virtues, apparently because he considers them as special roads to morality, and therefore has to distinguish them as such. Further, this tendency follows from his entire method. He outlines his ethics in his political teaching. Thus, he expounds his ethical teaching in political practice. One may, therefore, call his political teaching his teaching of virtue. Hence morality, as the doctrine of the idea of the good, is now distinguished from virtue, as theory is from practice.

Aristotle's rejection of the idea of the good entails first of all the characteristic consequence that ethics as knowledge is abolished and further that ethics dissolves into the teaching on virtue. Here too in the distinction between the intellectual virtues (ἀρεταὶ διανοητιχαί) and the ethical or moral virtues (ἀρεταὶ ἠθιχαί) there is a remnant of Platonism, which has not been overcome. Because the good as knowledge is abolished by Aristotle, ethics is dissolved into the teaching on virtue.

Yet another consequence is fateful for Aristotelianism. The idea of the good is abolished in *eudaimonia*. What with Socrates was an idea of religious reformation—*eudaimonia* is for him the moral belief in the good gods, not evil gods—becomes in Aristotle the biological foundation of ethics; and the principle of pleasure, which Plato fought in the Sophists, is again reinstated.

With *eudaimonia* Greek classical philosophy goes to its grave, and its dissolution into the dispute between the Stoics and Epicureans is introduced. Pleasure becomes negatively or positively the focal point of ethics, into which scientific philosophy is dissolved. Where scientific philosophy ends, idealism ends, and where idealism stops, the dualism between materialism and spiritualism is unavoidable. This dualism is the characteristic of Stoicism, and in the case of a favorable judgment, of Epicureanism as well.

Out of this dualism grows the spiritualism of Christianity. It intends to conquer the flesh by the spirit, but it is unable to detach the spirit from matter. All spiritualism is ambiguous. The doctrine of the Trinity also suffers from this schism.

Jewish monotheism was not exposed to the danger of making morality identical with virtue, for morality is in the first place God's problem, and only then a human problem. Morality in God is called holiness. However, God's being could be known only insofar as it is designated as the archetype for human morality. Hence it is understandable that holiness, too, as God's proper being, unfolds in a plurality of attributes, in which God's being becomes the archetype for human morality. These attributes are therefore to be spoken of as virtues. What else is justice, what else is love?

Hence, we recognize that the fundamental Jewish teaching at least encourages the distinction between morality or holiness on the one side, and the virtues on the other. God's holiness is identical with God's uniqueness. His attributes, however, become the concepts of virtue for man.

In our *Ethics of Pure Will,* we have defined the concept of virtue as the way to morality. We must distinguish as many virtues as there are ways to morality. Therefore, the principle of classification of the virtues at once becomes a problem of the types and kinds of these ways. The principle of classification is found in the double concept of man: as the individual of plurality and the individual of totality. From this double concept follows a double concept for the connection and unification of men. Plurality establishes only a relative community; totality alone establishes an absolute community.

This point of view must also become decisive for the correlation of man with God. Moreover, in distinguishing three different concepts of man in correlation with God, we have also distinguished a threefold correlation.

Yet another principle of classification is found in the *Ethics,* namely, in the relation that exists between both moments of the pure will: affect *(Affekt)* and thought *(Denken)*, both in their relation to one another and in their begetting of the will. This relation is divided in accordance with the predominance of one of these moments over the other. When thought predominates, the affect becomes honor; when the affect predominates, thought becomes love. In accordance with the variety of these affects that move the will, the virtues are distinguished as virtues of the first rank, which establish the absolute community, and virtues of the second rank, which establish relative communities.

Honor is the first pure affect. The paradox of this expression disappears, if one substitutes for honor "honoring," which is similar to esteem, and makes manifest the activity, which is similar to love, the other kind of affect. However, honor itself is to be maintained as an affect. It is the watchword, the pillar of fire that shows the way through the desert of moral wandering.

Honor is also one of the main expressions for God's being. In Scripture itself one can recognize in the honor of God, which is badly translated as the glory of God, the trace of the way upon which monotheism seeks to break off from anthropomorphism. By the glory of God one still indicates the appearance of brightness that accompanies God's revelation. God's honor, however, represents the archetype of morality, of which alone God's being consists. Thus, honor does not remain a veil in front of God's mystery, which is rent apart all the same by the fact that God's honor fills the whole earth (Isa. 6:3), but honor becomes the proper connecting link in the correlation of God and man. God's honor cannot mean God's glory in the mystical sense, because it passes over to human honor. Honor becomes a synonym for soul. In his blessing Jacob says against Simon and Levi: "Let my soul not come into their council; unto their assembly let

my honor not be united" (Gen. 49:6). And in the psalms the entire
lyrical consciousness of man is built equally upon the concepts of
soul and honor. "Therefore my heart is glad, and my honor rejoiceth"
(Ps. 16:9). "Let the saints exult in honor" (Ps. 149:5). Just as the
psalm makes God the "king of honor" (Ps. 24:7), and just as "the
heavens declare the honor of God" (Ps. 19:2), so the soul of man becomes his honor. In his honor the personality of man is established,
even more precisely than in his soul. Honor is the fundamental power
of his will, the means of safeguarding his personality.

The will of man is armed with this power of honor in order to
arrange and to affirm the virtues of the first rank, which demand the
totality of man. Man's honor is absolute; it makes man into mankind;
only as a carrier of mankind can honor make man into the carrier of
the will. The virtues of honor must therefore become the virtues
of totality. Through these virtues man has to mature to mankind.
The triumph religion achieves in Messianism secures for religion in
these virtues of totality, too, its peculiarity with regard to ethics.

The other affect of the will is love. We have considered it extensively in the reciprocal action between man and God, and we
have recognized a four-fold division of reciprocal action. God loves
man. And man loves God. However, that man loves God is practically
and psychologically not merely the reversal of God's love for man. A
double mediation must be added, in order to mediate the love of man
for God. Man must love his fellowmen first of all. In this love, which
produces social politics, lies the true foundation of human love. Only
on this foundation can the idea arise that man can also elevate himself to the love for God. And how would he be able to do this, if
God by means of the holy spirit, by means of the spirit of holiness,
had not put the spirit of love into his heart?

From this a fourth kind of love follows. If God loves not only the
totality and plurality of men, and if man, too, is to be loved not only
as the carrier of the idea of mankind but also as a symbol of plurality, as a fellowman, then man's own self—man as an individuality
on his own—is no less a member of this plurality, a fellowman for
the other man, as the other man is for himself. The commandment
of neighborly love, which appeals to the love of oneself, is only now
justified. I may love myself; I may consider myself as an object of
love, because I must consider myself an individual who is subject
to God's love, which extends also to myself. We know this reciprocal
activity of love. It is the idea of reconciliation. The love of myself as
an individual is the concern for my reconciliation with God. My
trust in God is fulfilled in the reconciliation, which God promises

me on the basis of my own work of repentance. Redemption from sin
is God's love for the individual. Hence the four-fold love between
God and man. God loves man as totality and as plurality. My
own individuality is contained in the plurality. And man loves God
first insofar as he is the representative of the idea of mankind, but
then also as a member of a plurality, through which man at the same
time assumes the character of an absolutely isolated unit, for the
purpose of redemption.

The Mishnah has in two tractates established a ten-fold classification
of the virtues. The two arrangements differ only in respect to the
order of succession in which the particular virtues are placed. The
one (Abodah Zarah 20b) begins with the Torah and in connection with
it distinguishes caution (זהירות) . In the other arrangement (Sotah,
last Mishnah [9,15]) the following order of succession is found: 1. Eager-
ness [zeal] (זריזות) ; 2. Purity and innocence (נקיות) ; 3. Purification
(טהרה) ; 4. Abstinence in separation (פרישת) ; 5. Holiness (קדושה) ;
6. Humility (ענוה) ; 7. Fear of sin (יראת חטא) ; 8. Pious lovingkindness (*liebestätige Frömmigkeit*) (חסידות) ; 9. Spirit of holiness (רוח הקודש) ; 10. Resurrection (תחיית המתים). Besides the
difference already mentioned, the other tractate differs only in the
order of succession of the virtues. What is there [Sotah] in the first
place, is here [Abodah Zarah] in the third; what is there in the second, is here in the fourth; what is there in the third, is here in the
fifth, while in the fourth place there is no difference. But what is
there in the fifth, is here in the ninth; what is there in the sixth, is
here in the seventh; what is there in the eighth, is here in the sixth;
what is there in the seventh, is here in the eighth; what is there in
the ninth, is here in the tenth; what is there in the tenth, is here
by itself, with the additional sentence: "But pious lovingkindness
(חסידות) is greater than all of them." Hence this kind of piety
exceeds not only the holy spirit but also the resurrection. This piety
that consists in deeds of lovingkindness, the last of which transcends
even almsgiving (צדקה), becomes therefore the highpoint of all
virtues, although it is ranked here in the sixth place. We have already
mentioned that the word for piety becomes the term for interconfes-
sional piety, which consists of virtue on the basis of the Noachide
commandments. Hence, piety becomes a virtue.

When we now continue to survey the entire classification, we notice
the special position of humility. All other virtues, namely zeal, innocence, purification, abstinence, holiness, the fear of sin, and even the
holy spirit and the resurrection, the last of which brings with it a
peculiar difficulty, are preeminently concerned with the relation of

man to God. But humility is concerned not only with this relation but preeminently with the double relation toward man: to the fellow-man and to one's own self. Humility thus becomes a privileged virtue, along with lovingkindness and the Teaching, which means the study of the Torah. Whereas piety is the preeminently ethical virtue, the study of the Torah is the preeminently theoretical virtue, which nevertheless is set at the head of all the virtues, and is thus their foundation. An analogous special position, however, is due humility, which indeed is also humility before God. This, however, in the form of modesty, is the human virtue proper, the guide and educator of the human individual.

Disregarding these three virtues, all the others mentioned are more religious virtues than moral ones. They are therefore concerned not so much with the man of totality, not even with the man of plurality, but rather with the individual in his correlation with God. Purity, purification, abstinence, sanctification—they all establish the spirit of holiness, and, in it, man as a religious individual. If the three other virtues were not specifically marked out, one would have to consider the entire list of virtues insufficient.

In fact, if we think of God's attributes, the opinion must be maintained that in them God is to be thought of as expressing the archetype of moral action for men; hence he is to be thought of as the model of virtue. In accordance with this opinion, it is therefore appropriate that we try another selection and another order of the virtues, and, following the main idea of this opinion, try to follow the order of virtues of our *Ethics*.

Before we turn to our own arrangement of the virtues, let us once more consider the main worth of the arrangement in the Abodah Zarah, which starts with the Torah. This beginning is fundamentally in agreement with the main idea of the Jewish worship of God, which is based on knowledge. The knowledge of God is equated with the love for God. And although love is in a reciprocal relation with its complement fear (יראה), it is knowledge that makes this reciprocal effect possible. The fear of God is always sustained by love. To be sure, its root is in the fear of sin, but the latter is subdued and purified by trust in the reconciliation with God, which in itself is the effect and the cause of the love for God. The entire correlation has its deepest ground in the fact that it is dependent on knowledge. We shall soon have to consider the still more profound consequences of this principle.

Our understanding of the virtues as the ways to morality, is in accordance with the terminology of the teaching of virtues in Jewish religious philosophy. The term for moral practice, measure (מדה) has a variety of meanings. It is also the term for the rules of hermeneutics, of which Rabbi Ishmael assumed there to be thirteen in accordance with the thirteen characteristics of God. The word therefore means also the attributes of God. However, these "measures," in the sense of virtues, are at the same time yardsticks for the evaluation of the degree of moral achievement, and hence of the stage reached in the "drawing near" to the ideal of morality. As such measuring stages the virtues are not thought of as already fixed psychological quantities, but indeed as stages of development. Hence, they, too, are to be understood as ways to morality, which, as such, are the ways to the knowledge and love of God, as the center of all piety, of all religious morality (מעלות). The teaching of virtue is therefore able to show that there may be collisions and difficulties between religion and morality, but never contradictions. The "measures" of the virtues correspond to the attributes of God, which in turn have only the meaning of ideals for human action.

However, the Jewish dogmatists were not afraid to formulate certain limitations even for God's being, which the principle of knowledge of God made necessary. God's omnipotence is limited by the general axiom of theoretical reason, the law of contradiction. Even God's omnipotence is not able to think in contradictions. God's omnipotence also finds its limit in the moral reason of man, because it is based on the knowledge of God. The relation of man's knowledge to man's will is the relation of the theoretical to the moral reason of man. As the theoretical reason has its independence and self-determination in the laws of thought, which even God cannot violate, so also does moral reason have its independence and autonomy in the freedom of the will.

Deuteronomy has formulated the freedom of the will in this sentence: "See, I have set before thee this day life and good, and death and evil" (Deut. 30:15) . . . "therefore choose life" (Deut. 30:19). The choice of the good is man's task. The freedom of this choice is the fundamental condition of moral reason. For it, for the freedom of the human will, as moral will, there cannot be any limitation in God. God's will, God's being, demands this freedom of the human will. Without this correspondence, God could not be the archetype of morality.

The Talmud has coined the sentence: "Everything is in God's hand, except the fear of God" (Berachoth 33b). We have already recognized this freedom as man's responsibility, and we will soon have to consider it in a new exposition with regard to virtue. Now we consider only the meaning of the way of virtue as it concerns human freedom and God's omnipotence with respect to the concept of virtue.

Freedom of the will makes recognizable the ways of virtue as the stages (מעלות) of "drawing near" to God. We have understood this drawing near as man's self-perfection. If the necessary distance from God were based only on the dependence upon God, then the fear of God would be the only guiding principle. However, in spite of the necessary distance, the drawing near to God is also imperative; hence, steps in this ascent and gradations and progress in the ascent are assumed. In this ascent, the principle of love manifests its positive power, and in this positive love for God which effects the progress in the ascent to God, the freedom of the will of human reason is manifested. God remains the guide to virtue, but human reason, which establishes God's will in its own freedom of the will, purifies this will into the will of the love for God. The positive power of this will of knowledge and love sets up the stages of drawing near to the goal, which is constituted by God as the redeemer.

The ascent of virtue is described even more exactly than by the "measures" by the other term, "steps" (מעלות). The word is known from the psalms, from the "Song of Steps" (שיר המעלות). As the Levites ascended the steps of the Temple to the altar while singing these songs, so is all virtue an ascent to the heights. If fear were the only guiding principle, then the way of virtue would not be secured as an ascent to the heights; it would hardly be protected from the sloping plane, and at most the same level would remain in view. The concept of virtue, however, is connected with the development toward higher degrees of approximation to the divine archetype of morality. Hence the "step" acquired the meaning of advantage, which also designates the positive progress in the development. It is the positive result as well as the positive achievement that matters in the genuine concept of virtue.

It is almost exclusively such positive tasks that are mentioned in the above specifications of the Mishnah; the only exception is "abstention." However, the fear of sin is not to be understood as a merely negative virtue, since in it the knowledge of sin collaborates as a positive factor. One may be tempted to evaluate abstention, which is the root of the word for Pharisee, in this exclusively negative way. We shall have to consider later whether this evaluation is fully correct, but now we may point to the connection of abstention with the other virtues in order to be able to assume that abstention is the source of strength for martyrdom. That the knowledge of God, as the love for God, unconditionally demands martyrdom, we have already recognized. The root for this highest ascent to God, for this highest step of human virtue, lies in abstention. "Life is not the highest of all goods." The Pharisees made this thesis of the German poet true in teaching and life. Therefore we can understand abstention not only as a negative source of asceticism and the mystical love of God, but here, too, we can presuppose the connection with the guiding idea of knowledge as the love for God.

And now, according to our classification in the *Ethics of Pure Will,* we may try to arrange the virtues as they are to be derived from the sources of Judaism.

In the *Ethics of Pure Will* we have set up the concept of truth as a special term for God. Truth exists neither in natural knowledge only, nor in ethical knowledge. Theoretical knowledge has exactness insofar as it is determined by its first principles. Ethical knowledge, besides its own first principles, is also determined by the accord and analogy of the latter with the first principles of theoretical knowledge. Nowhere, in either of the two ways of the mind taken separately, does there govern a certainty and independence that might be called truth. Theoretical knowledge remains imperfect without the complement of ethical knowledge, and ethical knowledge is unable to erect its own foundation if it is deprived of the ground theoretical reason constructs. This reciprocal connection of both kinds of reason is a problem in itself. It cannot be considered accidental that they point to one another, but this reciprocal pointing to one another is a problem in itself; it establishes a necessity of its own, a fundamental law of the highest kind.

The highest fundamental law is the law of truth. Truth alone is the law of the necessary connection of the knowledge of nature and the knowledge of morality. This truth is more than exactness, more than finality. Truth is the accord of theoretical causality with ethical teleology. This accord of both kinds of lawfulness had been from of old the philosopher's stone. It is the original problem of systematic philosophy, but it is also the fundamental meaning of the idea of God. On this share which the idea of God has in the original problem of philosophy, in its fundamental problems, and in the continuously increasing difficulties of scientific knowledge equally in the natural and the cultural sciences (*Geisteswissenschaften*)—on this the share of religion in reason is based.

Through this concept of truth we mark out the concept of God. God means that peculiar lawfulness which demands, as well as brings to completion, the harmony between the two kinds of knowledge.

In the peculiarity of this concept the uniqueness of God is proved again. Only God represents the peculiarity of this concept: no other concept can share this competence with him; every other concept has to deal only with itself. There must be, however, a concept whose task it is to deal with all other concepts and not only to control each one separately but to examine its harmony with all others. This harmony of the great species of knowledge, which also must be extended to the third part of the system—aesthetics—is the proper content of the concept of God, the proper content of the concept of truth.

Truth also belongs to those fundamental concepts of knowledge that are not yet unambiguously established in scientific usage, and this ambiguity is a bad sign for the scientific method, particularly in philosophy. However, the absence of an unequivocal determination of the notion of truth is particularly harmful for religion because the method of religion is as much an object of dispute as the concept of God and the content of religion in general. If a kind of knowledge, a share in reason is denied to faith, and if precisely in this denial one attempts to establish the peculiar characteristic of religion, then the concept of truth is untenable. For what would truth be without the foundation of scientific knowledge! Then the truth is supported only by feeling or even experience, and these supports are subjective. This logical subjectivity is unable to establish the foundation of the ethical subjectivity of a personality. Religion must be truth. Since, however, it is not identical with scientific logic, or with systematic ethics, the important conclusion follows that its truth must be its own peculiar characteristic, whereas the other kinds of knowledge must set up another methodological means in place of the truth. To this peculiar characteristic of truth in religion also corresponds the peculiar concept of God and, consequently, also the peculiar concept of man in and through religion. Since religion establishes a concept of God and man of its own, it is understandable that only to it belongs that concept of truth that signifies the kind of knowledge that is directed to the correlation of God and man.

Scripture therefore makes continual use of the connection between God and truth. To be sure, the word "truth" does not have a philosophical connotation in the biblical religion. The word אמת belongs to the root that is concerned with firmness. To it corresponds, therefore, the word that means faith and faithfulness (*Glauben and Treue*) (אמונה). To the same root belongs the word "amen"' which as a formula for the expression of confirmation, particularly for the benediction in the congregation attained universal usage. The word for truth is therefore also used continuously in connection with loving-

kindness (חסד), and in part with peace (שלום). How could the
truth be better established for the moral consciousness than through
the connection with God? And how could God be better established
in the religious consciousness than through the connection with
truth? We are acquainted with some other connections, such as holiness, love, justice; what distinguishes the connection with truth from
those other connections? It is obvious that the mind of the prophets
felt impelled to oppose to the allurement and the illusion of idolatry—
God as a being of an entirely different kind. Even the attribute of
living did not seem sufficient to distinguish the unique God from the
idols. In Jeremiah it becomes clear how he opposed the falsehood of
the "plastic" of idolatry to the reality of the God of truth. "Who
would not fear thee, O King of the nations?" The name of God,
"King of the nations," is very significant. "For it befitteth Thee; for
as much as among all the wise men of the nations, and among all
their royalty, there is none like unto Thee. But they are altogether
brutish and foolish: the vanities by which they are instructed are but
a stock; silver beaten into plates which is brought from Tarshish, and
gold from Uphaz, the work of the craftsman, and of the hands of
the goldsmith; blue and purple is their clothing: they are all the work
of skilful men. But the Eternal is the God of truth, He is the living
God, and an everlasting King" (Jer. 10:7-10). Kautzsch translates:
"But Yahveh, however, truly is God." Not only does the position of the
words make this translation wrong, but it does not do justice to the
powerful meaning of this sentence. Not only does it distinguish the
truth of the everlasting God from the trifling nothingness of the artificial pagan images, but on the basis of this truth, on the basis of
this true reality, it establishes the connection between God and
life, as well as between God and the King of all nations, who is the
eternal King, the King of the universe and eternity. In all these connections the God of truth is manifest.

The Talmud coined the sentence: "The seal of the Holy One, be He
praised, is the truth" (Sabbath 55a). Why is it not holiness? Why not
love and justice? Why not, in general, the sum total of the thirteen
attributes? How is it possible that a property that is not contained
in all of these, the only legitimate attributes of God, is termed God's
seal?

The sense of the language decided the matter. In the thirteen characteristics truth (אמת) is of course also contained, but only in connection with love (חסד), in which it is understood mainly as being true to.
However, the Hebrew sense of language implies truth also in the
word in which the meaning of faithfulness (אמונה) predominates.

Whereas love is elucidated more fully in what follows, this is not accomplished through the word that in the thirteen attributes is understood as true to, although it appears there in its basic meaning of truth (אמת), which at this point cannot be explained any further. Hence in the legitimate thirteen attributes, truth is also acknowledged.

If we recall again how Deuteronomy confirms the unique God through the wisdom of his laws, then the connection between God and the truth, which the prophets had to try to establish, becomes clear and familiar. God, as the revealer of wise laws, upon the adoption of which shall be based the wisdom and rationality of the people, could be thought of only as truth. His wise laws are true laws. The prophet Malachi characterizes God's covenant with Levi against the priests thus: "The teaching of truth was in his mouth . . . for the priests lips should keep knowledge, and they should seek the teaching of his mouth: for he is the messenger of the Eternal of hosts" (Mal. 2:6,7). The teaching of the truth is here connected with knowledge and with the Torah as knowledge. Through this connection the priest is to become God's messenger.

Also, the blessing after the reading of the Torah section by those who are called to it contains the following wording: "Blessed are Thou . . . who has given us the teaching of truth and hast planted everlasting life in our midst." Significant too in this blessing is the connection it establishes between the teaching of the truth and life. The eternal life is based only upon the truth of the teaching. If one were not to think that the article of faith in eternal life is contained in the teaching itself, this connection between truth and eternal life would be unthinkable. However, as this connection is established, the eternal life can have no other meaning, no other surety, than in this truth of the teaching. Therefore, it is characteristic that according to the above blessing eternal life is not promised to us, but that it is planted in us, into our inner life. The planting of our inner life, of our soul, is the planting of eternal life. The God of truth could not have given us a soul which is perishable together with our body and is like our body. Truth here always means the genuine as opposed to appearance, as opposed to the images of fantasy. But the truth is also more than all actuality, which is imitated by fantasy. As God is the unique being, so is he also the unique truth. For truth is the unique being which therefore cannot be designated through anything else. God is not actual, nor is he living in the sense of living creatures.[88] In this regard Maimonides has vigorously put an end to analogies. Truth is the only valid designation which corresponds to God's being.

Truth is God's being. This at least has to be verified through one of the attributes, and this attribute cannot be a bodily or a sensible one. As an attribute of action it must have its basis in an attribute of knowledge, although this knowledge has to relate to action. But truth, as the truth of knowledge, excludes any kind of sensibility, even the kind of sensibility that exceeds itself, namely, intuition and mysticism. Truth is the truth of knowledge, although the latter is not exhausted in scientific knowledge, but is the basis of moral knowledge and also religion. Intuition, as all mysticism, is in contradiction with logical reason. We have to inquire whether the *Cabbala*, with its dialectical many-sidedness, is resigned to the truth, or intends to surpass and to displace it. God is truth; this means for us: only the connection of theoretical and ethical knowledge, only the connection of both sources of the scientific consciousness, is able to fulfill the idea of God.

This makes it understandable why the idea could arise and be upheld that the attributes, which are only moral attributes, do not give any knowledge of God's being. Because they are only ethical, and not at the same time logical attributes, they cannot be adequate to God's being. Truth is the only adequate attribute; it, however, already stands within the correlation to man, and therefore cannot be explicitly named as an attribute of God alone.

Unity, too, is not explicitly an attribute; it is God's being. So also is the truth nothing other than God's being. In reference to the verse in Jeremiah [10:10] in which the God of truth is connected with the God of life, an ancient exegete makes a remark which is close to pantheism: "He is the life of all creatures" (מצודת דוד). In the same way Rashi explains the connection of God's word with the truth: "The beginning of Thy word is truth" (Ps. 119:160). Kautzsch translates wrongly "The essence of Thy teaching is faithfulness," and he bases "faithfulness" on the truth in the moral commandments of the Decalogue. The first three commandments could be related by the people to God's honor only. "But when they heard, honor thy father and thy mother, thou shalt not murder, thou shalt not commit adultery, then they acknowledged from this closing of thy word also the beginning (head) that it is truth." Ibn Ezra too says that the beginning [head] of the commandments is truth. Hence, according to these classical exegetes, revelation is characterized by truth, the truth of reason, the ethical truth, which is based upon logical knowledge.

Analogous to the truth of the Teaching is the truth of God's commandments: "All Thy commandments are *emunah*" (Ps. 119:86). So also Kautzsch translates it [as truth], although emunah is not the same word as *emeth* [truth]. In the commandment the root is not the command, but the truth, if not love, as in Psalm 111:8. Hence, the simile the religious philosophers always use becomes understandable: "For the commandment is a lamp; and the Torah is light" (Prov. 6:23). "And all Thy commandments are truth" (Ps. 119: 151). The light is the light of reason and is therefore equal to truth. The philosophers therefore distinguished between the lamp as the religious law and the light as the moral commandment of the Torah. Also Psalm 19:9, "The commandment of God is pure, enlightening the eyes," expresses this relation to knowledge, to truth.

The connection between God and truth becomes clearly and securely established through the connection of the truth with the teaching and with all the laws of God. The enthusiasm of the monotheistic consciousness not only has its climax in this connection with the truth but also receives in it its most profound foundation. God is the truth. Therefore the unique God is the highest content human consciousness can transfer to a highest being. The unique being is the true being. The true goal of knowledge is found, made certain.

In his attributes of action God becomes the archetype of human morality. Therefore one of the virtues must correspond to God's truth; this virtue must be the first of the virtues, for the truth, as the epitome of all the attributes, is the first of the attributes. But how is it possible for man to have a virtue corresponding to God's truth? To be sure, virtue is merely a way of virtue, which is to lead to its goal in a straight line. But is even a drawing near to this highest goal to God's being possible? The answer must be clear and simple. The duty to draw near to God would be untenable if it could not be directed to the highest goal. There are no grades of distinctions in God's attributes. Only subjectively, in our own evaluation, are such distinctions possible. Which virtue then corresponds to God's truth, to the ideal of truth?

The German language with its philosophical power of expression distinguished truthfulness as a virtue. The Hebrew language does not have such a term. Instead it has "pure heart" and "holy spirit." But what is lacking as a noun seems to have been designated in a verbal form, as an inward speech, even if, at the same time it means a prophecy. Thus, the psalm says about the ideal of pious man: "He wortketh righteousness, and speaketh the truth in his heart" (Ps. 15:2). He who speaks the truth in his heart possesses truthfulness.

The virtue of truthfulness follows not only as a consequence from God as the God of truth, but also from the whole prophetic preaching about the true worship. The latter consists not only in an opposition to pagan worship but also in the most profound tendency against the sacrificial cult. As much as we have in all previous discussions sought to explain the rejection of sacrifice by the prophets, conspicious to the whole world, another motive still seems not to be superfluous in the explanation of this: this motive is to be recognized in the strict sense for truth.

Sacrifice is not an immediate action of the one who offers it, but needs the mediation of the priest. Through this indirect relation the sacrifice becomes a symbol, and the indirect symbolism is an impediment to the truth; it diverts from it. The symbolism of the sacrifice intensifies the offenses which the symbol of the pagan image arouses. The latter is a fabrication, although an artistic one, but the material for it is also used for heating and for roasting. All these symbols are distortions of the truth.

What about the intervention of the priest? Is not the priest also a man? Through the sacrifice of the priest not only the concept of the one who offers sacrifice but also that of man in general becomes ambiguous. Because of the mediation of the priest, man's immediate relation to God is put into question.

Now about the offering. The proper, direct objects of the sacrifice are not the animals, neither their blood nor their fat, but rather the heart of man. "The sacrifices of God are a broken spirit: a broken and a contrite heart, O God, Thou wilt not despise" (Ps. 51:19). Heart and spirit are the proper organs for the relation between God and man; but are the bodies of animals the proper symbols?

Slaughtering, that is, putting to death, is a kind of activity that constitutes a difficulty for the symbol. Not death but life designates the relation of God and man. "He shall live by them" (Lev. 18:5). Hence putting to death, just as death in general, is an untrue symbol of this primeval relation.

Finally, a new difficulty arises in regard to the sacrifice, from the attempt to transform it. The latter consists of the new idea: "the soul that sinneth" (Ezek. 18:4). The intervention of the priest veils the unveiled soul of the subject. If it is the soul that sins, it also has to effect reconciliation, which cannot be mediated by the priest. The reconciliation between God and man must be effected in person, with one's own soul. The latter does not admit of any mediation by another person. The concept of soul makes this symbolism entirely unbearable, because it defeats the new truth of the soul. Wherever a principle is at stake, truth puts the symbol in question.

Therefore the prophets determine the true worship through the connection of the truth not with the spirit—what is the spirit if not heart?—but indeed with the heart and its moral power. "Serve him in wholeness and in truth" (Josh. 24:14). Wholeness (תמימות) is simplicity. To translate it as perfection is misleading. "Thou shalt be whole-hearted with the Eternal thy God" (Deut. 18:13). Man should not and could not be perfect alongside God, but he ought to be whole, that is, unified and simple. Hence, this simplicity, this freedom from discord, becomes the expression for truthfulness in human life. In the same way: "Serve Him in truth with all your heart" (1 Sam. 12: 24; cf. Jer. 32:41). By connecting truth with the whole heart and the whole soul, the prophets warded off the sacrifice as an external symbolic action.

The true worship is "the worship of the heart" (עבודה שבלב). God is close to the heart: "The Eternal is nigh unto all them that call upon Him, to all that call upon Him in truth" (Ps. 145:18). This truth is the truthfulness that is the prerequisite of prayer. Truthfulness makes the soul objective in prayer. Thus lyricism could become the style of the psalms.

The polytheistic prayer is strictly speaking not a prayer but a hymn into which phrases of prayer are intertwined. The object of this entreaty makes necessary a particular personification and localization of that divinity to whose sphere the object belongs. In Jewish prayer, on the contrary, it is a question not of the object of the entreaty, which as the occasion becomes insignificant and remote, but always of the subject, of the I in the plight of its soul.

Therefore longing is the fitting lyrical affect. Dependence even upon the infinite is insufficient, and is, in addition, confusing, because it arouses fear instead of longing; yet the latter is much more joined to hope and confidence. The helper and redeemer, for whom the prayer longs, is in an immediate relation to the soul. This immediacy is clearly expressed by the word: "haste to help me" (חושה לעזרתי), Ps. 38:23). Longing is unable to wait and it feels so immediately connected with its beloved God that his speedy coming is expected. All this is not symbolism; this is truthfulness, because it is the immediacy of thought and feeling. Even the classical prayer was unable to imitate this immediacy, and it therefore adopted the psalms into its own cycle. It was somewhat easier to strive to imitate the prophetic prayer, which serves the preservation of Israel, the preservation of monotheism, but in the psalms it is the God of truth himself whom the soul celebrates.

The profound inner connection that exists between God's truth and the truthfulness of worship explains anew the prohibition of idol worship. However, for this we may refer back to the development we found to exist between the first and the second of the Ten Commandments. Now it is also from the point of view of the truth that one must consider the difference between Jewish worship and Christian symbolism. The man who is God can be thought of only as a symbol, and the finest idealization is able only to make the Trinity, the divinity of Christ, understood as a symbol. Every symbolism, however, that concerns the concept of God himself is an obstruction to the truth. The concept of truth loses its univocal meaning through any symbolism. There can be no doubt about this.

Nor ought one to conceal that when the truth is made ambiguous, truthfulness too is unavoidably impaired. Jewish religiosity is based upon unlimited truthfulness, insofar as it is related to monotheism itself. The concept of the unique God is an exact and univocal concept of religious knowledge. Even for the common religious consciousness it is of univocal content, excluding everything related to sensibility. Only with the intention of thinking of the unity and uniqueness of God can one become familiar with the "Hear, O Israel." No symbolism can creep into this uniqueness. To the exactness of the concept of God there can and must correspond the univocal, clear, and certain profession of God. To the truth of the unique God corresponds the truthfulness of the Jewish profession of God.

Truth establishes truthfulness, and truthfulness is the backbone of the moral man. Thanks to the power of religious truthfulness the moral man is the religious man. And the religious man is the historical man. How could this unique people of faith preserve itself among all the peoples of the world? This singular question does not take notice of the vital strength that is rooted in religious truthfulness. The Jew does not practice any symbolism with his unique God. His God of truth is "the rock of wholeness" (צור תמים). From this rock springs Jewish truthfulness.

There is much skepticism in Jewish religious philosophy with regard to fundamental ethical concepts, and even with regard to God's attributes and prerogatives. But God's being itself, the uniqueness of this being, its incomparability with any kind of being, and therefore the impossibility of its mingling with any other kind of being, indeed not with man, is never and nowhere doubted. Atheism is absolutely no match for pure monotheism. And also pantheism, to use a well-known simile, is only the tribute which faithlessness pays to faith. But pantheism too is symbolism. Therefore it was never and nowhere able to establish truthfulness.

The truthfulness of the Jewish consciousness of God is the very reason for the warding off of the plastic arts. The scorn of the prophets and the psalms for the empty trifles of the pagan images, which have

no spirit and no soul, makes this reason evident. But in poetry monotheism nevertheless established its alliance with art. Is this a contradiction against the unity of the arts in the unity of the aesthetic consciousness? There is no such contradiction. One merely should not
assume the unity of the human consciousness in the aesthetic consciousness itself, while the latter merely represents one link of the
former. However, the aesthetic consciousness itself is determined by
the constant collaboration of the ethical consciousness, and the religious consciousness with its own peculiar character is linked to the
latter. The religious peculiarity creates its own notion of God and its
own notion of man. Furthermore, because both of these religious
concepts are violated by the irony of plastic art, religious consciousness looks for refuge in another direction of the aesthetic consciousness in order not to miss an important link in the unity of human consciousness as shaped by culture. Moreover, the religious consciousness
is richly recompensed by lyric poetry for what it loses in plastic art.
Here, too, the religious truthfulness holds good. Monotheism makes
no concessions to plastic art, for thereby the idea of the unique God
would be endangered; no symbolism may threaten it. It is significant
that the scorn of the prophets and the psalms for the pagan images is
expressed through the idea that the idol worshiper will be ashamed.
One misrepresents the thought by translating it: "They shall be confounded." The Hebrew word יבושו means the inner shame that
overcomes a man. This shame is the symptom of truthfulness that will
arise in the pagan worshiper. Pagan worship has suppressed it. Truthfulness is as much the effect as the presupposition of true worship.

Truthfulness, in turn, is also the cause of the uniqueness of the
psalms. Only truthfulness could create this original power of lyricism.
It could achieve, free from any eroticism, a purity of longing for a
spiritual being, such as the Greek eros could not achieve completely
even in Plato. This love for God, which has all the strength of a passion, laments and wails and rejoices and feels jubliation; it moistens
with its tears the resting place, and it makes the intestines burn. Yet
this love is never beset by an enticement that would mar its chastity
and invalidate its innocense. Such a complex problem, which is surrounded by all sorts of demonic difficulties, could only be solved by
the plain truthfulness of a faith for which there can be neither any
doubt nor any possible change in the meaning of God. "For God is not
a man" (1 Sam. 15:29). It is instructive that the verse continues:
"that he should lie." If he were man he could not be the God of
truth, and, hence, man can only become truthful through the truth of
his God, who is not man.

Monotheism is absolutely opposed only to plastic art; but lyric poetry achieved through it such heights that without the psalms great heights would not seem to be attainable even in German lyric poetry. This historical riddle is solved by the mediation of history. Since the German spirit did not despise the influence of the psalms, they have to be understood as the historical cause for that truthfulness that singles out the German song among the lyrics of the world.

One could take offense at the uniqueness of the people to whom revelation was granted with regard to the truth of the unique God. One could surmise a defect in the truth of Israel's election, and therefore also a defect in Jewish truthfulness. However, even from this point of view one has to admire the development monotheism achieved in Messianism. The chosen people becomes the chosen mankind. The unique God restores his truth, and Israel maintains its truthfulness. For Israel itself now becomes a symbol. Man, a people, may become a symbol; only the unique God may not, and with the people of Israel, its entire national history becomes symbolic. The Temple becomes a symbol, as do Zion and Jerusalem. Finally the people becomes symbolic in the "servant of the Eternal," this last form of the symbolism of the Messiah. For the Messiah, too, is a symbol of the uniform realization of the idea of the unique God, and Jewish truthfulness attains its deepest and most secure support from this faith in the Messiah, from this confident, earthly expectation. All confidence in the power of the good is expressed in the symbolic prayer, "Speedily cause the offspring of David to flourish," or in the other prayer, "Blessed art thou, O Eternal, who causest the horn of redemption to flourish." The throne of David has passed over into the other symbol, which is "the horn of redemption."

Without this self-transformation of the chosen people into messianic mankind, Jewish truthfulness could hardly have been maintained. From the very beginning, however, the logical power of the truth of the unique God continuously held open the perspective of a messianic mankind. Nationalistic narrowness could not thereby be entirely uprooted, but religious truthfulness could not be infringed upon. It always remained strongly rooted in the connection of the unique God with the unique mankind.

This messianic connection also preserves the correlation between God and man. Therefore, any intermingling between God and man is made as superfluous as it is impossible for each of these concepts. The truthfulness of man, not only the truth of God, is at stake, if the thesis is violated: "To whom then will ye liken God?" (Isa. 40:18). With this question Isaiah excludes not only any symbolization of God through things but also the comparison of God to the human person.

Religious truthfulness also guards against false determination of the relation between religion and philosophy. The thesis *"credo quia absurdum"* becomes entirely impossible. Equally, the separation between faith and reason is only permissible for the purpose of the methodological distinction. The distinction may not be strained to the point of contradiction. Only a distinction is to be assumed, not a separation. Our point of view prevails here. Religion has its peculiarity, but in no way does it have autonomy with regard to ethics. The share religion has in reason binds it to ethics. The methodological connection with ethics has always been the compass of Jewish religious philosophy. This is the meaning of the title which Saadiah gave to his book, and which one could actually translate *Faith and Reason:* אמונות ודעות . This unifying tendency attains its classical maturity in Maimonides, but his predecessors are not inferior in their frank rationalism on this principal point. Bahya says (*Duties of the Heart* 1,2): "It is true, when the philosopher says that the final cause and the final principle could be honored according to their nature only by the prophet of the time or by the competent philosopher." Futhermore Joseph Albo makes a valid distinction between theory and practice with regard to the concept of heresy. Theory he sets free. In no way should this permit a double truth, but only freedom of thought; the autonomy of philosophy is protected against the revealed faith with its laws. No religious truthfulness can be established exclusively on authoritarian faith; for through this the authority of reason would be renounced, which, together with the truthfulness of knowledge, cannot be denied. For the prophetic consciousness also, God's truth is established upon the knowledge of God's holiness, hence upon his moral legislation. The collision with the laws whose moral reason is not evident was not considered as a decisive instance. Truthfulness offers new strength to this pervasive rationalism.

The cohesion of religion and rational knowledge is the secure ground for the virtue of truthfulness in all human concerns, particularly in all questions of science and in all problems of inquiry. Truthfulness presupposes a foundation of truth upon which it rests. For the systematic connection of all the questions of knowledge, God is the principle of truth. For the particular kinds of knowledge this root of truth has as its offshoots the particular principles of method. Thus, for ethics the general principle of the moral law becomes this offshoot of the truth. Without this principle, ethics deteriorates to skepticism and sophistry, which abolish the objective foundation of truthfulness. For politics as well as for private life, morality then becomes an illusion or a matter of expediency. The condition of the truth, which ethics claims on the basis of its method, saves for it the privilege of truthfulness. If in religion God is elevated to the absolute foundation of truth, then accordingly its fundamental meaning for the security of human truthfulness is also increased.

We have already considered, in connection with prayer, the Mishnah sentence which uses the words of the psalm about thinking the truth in one's heart.

The duty of truthfulness is enjoined in the Pentateuch by the prohibition of lying. Moreover, the lie (שקר) is also called falsehood (שוא) and fraud (מרמה). "Keep thee far from a false word" (Exod. 23:7). This sentence is preceded by the prohibition of refusing assistance to the enemy when his ass succumbs under its burden and, further, the prohibition of favoring a poor man in his cause. The prohibition of lying is followed by other prescriptions concerning the administration of justice, and in this negative form the prohibition is also connected with the other words for lying (Lev. 19:11). However, it is also said positively: "Speak the truth one to another" (Zech. 7:9). The psalms are more than full of aversion to lying: "Let the lying lips be dumb" (Ps. 31:19). "Deliver my soul from lying lips" (Ps. 120:2). "Every false way I hate" (Ps. 119:128). "He that speaketh falsehood shall not be established before Mine eyes" (Ps. 101:7). Finally the wonderful word to the hero: "Ride on, in behalf of truth" (Ps. 45:5). Proverbs also enjoin truthfulness: "The lip of truth shall be established forever" (Prov. 12:19). "Buy the truth and sell it not" (Prov. 23:23). "Lying lips are an abomination to the Eternal" (Prov. 12:22). The following are also wonderful: "Truth springeth out of the earth" (Ps. 85:12); and "Thou desireth truth in the inward" (Ps. 51:8). The prophets lament injustice in the land in their lamentation about falsehood and deceit. Truth is thereby connected with justice, and negatively, also with love. "No truth and no justice" (Hos. 4:1). Everywhere in the Scripture truthfulness is considered the foundation of piety.

The regard for law, which requires the testimony of a witness and an oath, was connected with religious awe for God. The oath was administered with the invocation of his name, in order to strengthen the duty of truthfulness through this judicial form of declaration. "Ye shall not swear by My name falsely" (Lev. 19:12). According to the rabbinic understanding, this prohibition is made by the third of the Ten Commandments. Here, however, the other word for falsehood (שוא) is used. The oath itself, however, is only an intensification of the testimony, and is therefore based on truthfulness, which

in turn is founded on God's truth. However, truthfulness is also based
on the personality of man himself, which is represented by the soul,
which in turn is represented by honor. Honor itself, however, is only
the expression of the worth, the dignity of man. The lie falsifies the
honor of the speaker, of the man who in his speech testifies to his
soul. Honor is the affect, which transfers the truth from God to man,
to the fellowman and to the self of man.

The Talmud strove to sharpen the conscience for strict truthfulness
through a prohibition that even in its wording has educational significance: the theft of opinion (גניבת דעת).[89] "It is prohibited to steal
the opinion of creatures, even that of an idolator" (Chullin 94a). Jona
Gerondi explains: "This sin weighs heavier with the wise of Israel
than the robbery of an idolator. And we are bound to make a fence
about the truth (truthfulness) for it is one of the foundations of the
soul" (היראה 'ס). The most innocent things are considered to be
theft, if a false opinion is aroused with regard to them. It is possible
to be guilty of theft with regard to an opinion or an indifferent point
of view. Every deception is theft. With regard to truthfulness, there
is no indifferent expression. Truthfulness is the foundation of the soul,
and the soul is shaken even when deceit is introduced into any opinion. This is the great value of this rabbinical intensification of the
biblical commandment of truthfulness: that no indifference (ἀδιάφορον)
is permitted in this strict ethics.

Yet another sentence of the Talmud says: "Whosoever equivocates
in his speech, it is, as if he were practicing pagan worship" (Sanhedrin 92a). And another sentence, occurring frequently, says: "He who
punished the man of the generation of the Flood and of the Builders
of the Tower, he will punish the one who does not stand by his word"
(Baba Metzia 48a). Untruthfulness is here made equal to idolatry, and
the recompense for it is compared to the punishment that reached
the wicked in prehistoric times. No casuistry and no "plausibility" here
protect the absolute sin of untruthfulness, which is attributed partly
to idolatry, partly to the pre-religious stage of culture.

Honor is the moving affect of pure will, which has to establish all
the steps of the concept of man up to the unity of mankind, but within and beneath these great divisions in the concept of man more narrow structures of human community are actualized. The ways of
virtue must also be directed to these relative communities; they cannot only pave great highways for the individual and for mankind.
From the point of view of the fellowman there emerge the various
relative communities such as the family, the tribe and the people,
corporations of one's trade, and associations of more or less binding

character, all needing the care of virtue. The affect which guides the will in these virtues of the second rank is love, which is assumed by the Bible for all virtues. We have noticed the dangers that are unavoidable in this absolute sovereignty of love. On the other hand, love becomes a driving force of eminent significance, if its range of dominion is limited.

Truthfulness is an absolute virtue. It can never be violated. Nevertheless, it puts on man demands that seem to exceed the measure of man. It is not the casuistry of the necessary lie that is the difficulty; rather it is the inner dangers that oppose the unconditional application of truthfulness. Truthfulness is based on truth. Who, however, can have certainty about the truth? Can the conditions be fulfilled that are required in each case for the determination of the truth? Truthfulness commands one to intercede in behalf of truth without dismay and to come forward against falsehood without error. Who, however, is able to assert the certainty of his knowledge, which establishes, positively as well as negatively, the objective ground of truthfulness? The imperfection of human knowledge, the narrowness and the dissipation of human consciousness, seems to make untenable the condition on which truthfulness depends.

Nonetheless, exemption from this virtue is impossible. Truthfulness is unconditionally and unlimitedly valid. Since, however, its objective determination is a continuous problem, it itself demands, not as an exception but rather as its confirmation and for its own safety, a complement, which by itself must be a kind of truthfulness, although not in the absolute sense, but in the subjective and, therefore, relative sense. Through the imperfection of human knowledge, through a permanent defect of human consciousness, truthfulness seems to be shaken. This defect, therefore, has to be remedied. To make a virtue out of necessity, in this case, has to be made literally true. Only one virtue can rescue truthfulness from the necessity which it suffers, the virtue which truthfully acknowledges the subjective weakness that besets the attainment of truth. This virtue is modesty.

Modesty may not and cannot release me from the virtuous duty of truthfulness, but it opens a way out which is not an escape that serves to avoid or to veil my subjective inadequacy with regard to the objective truth. Modesty does not curtail my honor, but in forbearance to my weakness, as well as to the weakness of my fellowman, lets love prevail over strict honor. Love causes forbearance to be exercised in judging my weakness and inadequacy as well as in judging the corresponding deficiencies of the fellowman. Hence, modesty becomes a support for my love of my fellowman, as well as for my own moral self-esteem, which I need in various ways for the various stages of my moral self-consciousness, before the great road of repentance finds its conclusion in the reconciliation with God. Upon this great road I must in various ways try to come to terms with myself, and for this I need the self-knowledge of modesty, which, in the presence of great questions, leads me to humility. Modesty and humility thus become supports of truthfulness. In them exists the virtue which is relative in comparison with the absolute virtue of truthfulness.

With regard to the connection between truth and love, upon which the supplementation of truthfulness by modesty rests, we have already called attention to the various connections of these two concepts in God's attributes. In the psalms it says, "Love and Truth meet together" (Ps. 85:11), or "Kiss each other" (ibid.). Humility cannot be uttered of God directly; all the more characteristically is it ascribed to Moses. "Now the man Moses was very humble, above all the men which were upon the face of the earth" (Num. 12:3). No other spiritual or psychological quality of Moses does the Pentateuch praise except his relation as a prophet to God; but among all his human qualities, his humility is asserted. No higher testimony to the significance of humility in the judgment of the Scripture can be conceived. Humility alone guards man from the danger of pride about his worth as man, a worth that is based only on his fear of God, on his submission to God's truth.

From this viewpoint, the often quoted saying of the prophet Micah gains a new significance. The Eternal requires of man not only "to do justly and to love lovingkindness." This seeming pleonasm is also significant. In the case of justice it is enough to do it; with lovingkindness the deed is not enough, not even the intention to perform the duty: love is required for it. Lovingkindness may not be exercised merely out of duty; it must blossom out of love. Duty is here transformed into love; or honor is transformed into love.

However, the prophet is not satisfied with these requirements, but adds: "and to walk humbly with thy God" (Mic. 6:8). The prophet does not rest satisfied with the requirements of loving and reverencing God, but as he turns to human nature, he grasps it in humility, as if he were grasping in it the most profound foundation of man. Moreover, the prophet does not say merely humility; this perhaps explains that his expression does not read "before God," but "with God." In every relation with God humility is the presupposition for man. This condition justifies the correlation between man and God;

pantheism, however, contradicts this humility. Humility therefore also negates the association of man in the concept of God.

It is, therefore, not a contradiction of the foregoing, but rather a confirmation, that the Talmud associates scriptural references to God's greatness with his humility, to which statement we already have referred (cf. p. 266). Humility thus becomes, even as love, a complement to the truth of God. If, however, we consider the examples the Talmud cites in the passage in question, which is adopted in the prayer at the termination of the Sabbath, we find there only those moral attributes by virtue of which God protects the lowly and the oppressed ones, by virtue of which he "revives the spirit of the humble" [Isa. 57:15], loves the stranger, is the father of the orphans, the counsel of the widows. God loves the humbled ones: in this consists his humility.

This invention of a new divine characteristic proves with particularly persuasive power that the attributes in general are models for human morality.[90] In the literal sense, it is as impossible to think of humility as a characteristic of God as it is of his justice and his love; but what is called a characteristic of God is not a characteristic in the the logical, but only in the ethical sense. The attribute is not in a logical relation to the substance of God, but rather in an ethical relation to the substance of man. Only in this relation to man, is the Mishnah able to think of God's humility. Actually it is only in this way that one can think of God's justice. This lesson is to be taken from this Mishnah about God's humility. Thus, it is also understandable that the Mishnah in Abodah Zarah attributes to humility the same preeminence that the Mishnah in Sotah attributes to the study of the Torah or to pious deeds of lovingkindness. Maimonides agrees entirely with the Mishnah when he makes humility a cardinal virtue; in a moving account of the journey of a passenger on a ship, he illustrates the duty of humility even in the face of the gravest humiliations and insults. This characteristic of humility distinguishes Jewish ethics from classical, as well as post-classical, Greek ethics.

Here the prophets have shown the way which the Psalms and the Proverbs followed. "Seek justice, seek humility" (Zeph. 2:3). In the above-mentioned psalm, "Gird thy sword upon thy thigh, O mighty one, thy glory and thy majesty. And in thy majesty proper, ride on, in behalf of truth," there is added, "and humility and righteousness" (Ps. 45:5). "And before honor goeth humility" (Prov. 15:33; 18:12). So high is humility esteemed in the morals of the people.

The most important testimony, however, for this high esteem of humility lies in the change Messianism underwent in its final formulation. The Messiah is equated with the pious man. This is what we have previously said. However, the exact translation has to replace "pious" by "humble." Just as the poor man, the original social image of the humble, became the ideal image of the pious, so the humble undergoes this change in meaning. Not only do the poor become the pious, but only through the mediation of humility, which is expressed in the poor, is piety manifested in them. Hence, humility becomes the foundation of messianic mankind. The vocation of man, the future of mankind, cannot be fulfilled unless every man for himself and every people for itself strives for humility. All human heroism comes to nothing, all the wisdom and all the virtue of man remain without the last test, if they are not tested by humility. There is no exception to his, neither for any man, nor for any people, nor for any age. Culture can progress as high as it may, yet the human heart and the human spirit itself in its highest striving and achievement will never be able to do without the virtue of humility. Maimonides is right, as a psychologist as well as a moralist, in following the Mishnah, which makes humility a cardinal virtue. Disregarding the identification of the Messiah with the humble, disregarding the social medium of poverty, humility is equivalent to moral duty in its application to human psychology.

Deutero-Isaiah is right in his self-consciousness: "Because the Eternal hath annointed me to bring good tidings unto the humble" (Isa. 61:1). All the psalms constitute not only the cry of distress of the humble ones but also their hope: "He adorneth the humble with salvation" (Ps. 149:4). Humility becomes simply piety and therefore the soul's foundation for messianic consciousness.

What humility is before God, modesty is at the same time before man. The Jewish consciousness does not feel that there is any difference between humility and modesty. Whoever has humility before God has modesty before man, and it is not possible to have modesty before men except on the ground of humility before God. Human consciousness is surrounded by so many ensnaring dangers of self-esteem that it would not be able to assert and preserve its modesty if the latter were not directed by humility before God. Before God all men are equal. There is no high or low. Before God "all heroes are nothing and all wise without understanding, and the men of glory as if they did not exist." These are the words of the early-morning prayer, from which we already have taken many a pious piece of wisdom. Therefore, it is not an exaggeration when the concluding prayer of the *Shemoneh Esreh* reads as follows: "Let my soul be unto all as dust." Dust reminds one of the end of all human happiness. "From dust you came and dust you shall be." The soul should be reminded of the dust of its origin and of the dust of the end of man. On this wisdom of the origin and end of human life, humility bases itself as one of the foundations of the soul, and therefore as one of the foundations of piety, as virtue's first way in the drawing near to God.

CHAPTER XIX

Justice

Justice is the second virtue of the first rank. It is first among God's characteristics: "The Eternal is just in all His ways and gracious in all His works . . . Thy justice is everlasting justice" (Ps. 145:17; 119:137, 142). Justice is equal to holiness: "And God the Holy One is sanctified through justice" [righteousness] (Isa. 5:16). Justice is the attribute of the Messiah: "And justice shall be the girdle of his loins" (Isa. 11:5). The cessation of wars is the negative sign of the Messianic Age; the positive sign, however, is one's learning of, and habituation to, justice. "Neither shall they learn war any more" (Mic. 4:3). It says positively: "The inhabitants of the world learn justice" (Isa. 26:9). Thus, justice becomes the sign of the Messianic Age.

However, the Pentateuch had already made justice an absolute commandment: "Justice, justice shalt thou follow" (Deut. 16:20). There, too, justice becomes the *fundamentum regni*.

To be sure, the Hebrew word for justice [righteousness] (צדקה) is the same as the word for piety in general, but precisely this alteration of meaning proves the basic power of justice. It is not diminished to the level of charity, but by means of that social virtue is universalized and becomes piety in general. The same process we observed with regard to poverty and humility we also see with regard to justice and charity, and just as humility becomes piety, so does justice, through the social mediation of charity.

There is no doubt that humility is a real virtue, for the poor man exhibits it. But what about justice? "There is not a just man upon earth" (Eccles. 7:20). As justice, piety in general becomes the ideal of man. This maxim is formulated in Proverbs: "The just one is an everlasting foundation of the world" (Prov. 10:25). Deutero-Isaiah, finally, concludes with the ideal image of piety, which is to be a substitute for fasting: "And thy justice shall go before thee, the glory of the Eternal shall be thy reward" (Isa. 58:8). Here justice becomes the testimony, the legitimation for admission to the covenant of eternal life.

Just as justice is the foundation of the state and the center of gravity of social ethics, so it also becomes the principle and norm for the laws of civil uprightness. Justice becomes the fundamental yardsick for measures and weights (Lev. 19:36).

Justice is the principle of juridical institutes that are the cornerstone of the Noachide legislation: "Judge justly between a man and his fellow" (Deut. 1:16). The prophets complain about nothing more than about false courts of justice. Therefore, they make God the advocate of the stranger, the orphan, and the widow. The feasibility of Jewish theocracy is based upon justice, because otherwise religion could not be identical with the state constitution, because otherwise God could not be King of Israel, and could not be King of mankind upon the whole earth. All the ambiguities that are connected with the concept of theocracy are invalidated through the equality of the principle of justice for both religion and the state. Worship requires justice inasmuch as it is the fundamental norm for any constitution. Through justice every state becomes a theocracy, through it the concept of religion is actualized in the state.

It is characteristic that Samuel, who was at the same time judge and prophet, and in whom, as it were, theocracy was therefore personified, had to abdicate in favor of the kingdom in which the judge was separated from the prophet, whereby the personification of the theocracy was abolished. It is also characteristic that Samuel, in his farewell address to the people, appealed to nothing so much as to the justice and uprightness of his administration: "Whose ox have I taken, or whose ass have I taken? . . . whom have I oppressed? Or of whose hand have I taken a ransom?" (1 Sam. 12:3).

The principle of justice had as its consequence the relativity of the principle of property—this bulwark of egotism, of eudaemonism, of opportunism and everything else that is opposed to religious morality. It brought forth the law of the Sabbath along with its symbolic extension of the number seven to the fields, to the Year of Release from debts, the Year of Jubilee for landownership, as well as to all other privileges of property with regard to the harvest and the second growth. The religious significance of this social legislation was fortified by the proclamation of the Year of Jubilee on the Day of Atonement. Hence, the atonement became a sign of social freedom.

The principle of justice was pushed to its extreme in the legislation concerning slaves, for whom the motto was said to be: "a tooth for a tooth!" This legislation pulled the teeth from the misconception and the defamation, which were ineradicably practiced as a result of the catchword "an eye for an eye." The Sabbath is not only for the sake of man, as is said in the Talmud (Mechilta) and the Gospel (Mark 2:27), but above all for the sake of the slave, for the sake of the worker. This Sabbath signifies at the same time the completion of God's creation of the world. It is the embodiment of all commandments. And all commandments and all festive celebrations are a sign of "remembrance of the exodus from Egypt." Hence, the entire Torah is a remembrance of the liberation from Egyptian slavery, which, as the cradle of the Jewish people, is not deplored, let alone condemned, but celebrated in gratitude.

This truly ethical justice substantiates and renders intelligible the connection of the two concepts "Justice and Love" (צדקה וחסד). It is especially weighty in criminal law, for example, in the position of the Talmud regarding capital punishment. Respect is due even to the corpse of a hanged man.

With regard to punishment by stripes it says: "Forty stripes he may give him, he shall not exceed" (Deut. 25:3). Therefore the Talmud determines thirty-nine stripes as the maximum.

Blood vengeance, as the primitive form of the notion of law, was an impediment and contradiction to the more developed stages of culture, in which there was a judicial organization. The three Cities of Refuge were established to maintain justice against blood vengeance. However, the heathen principle of the altar's protection of the murderer was abolished.

Another break with ancient law is constituted by the repeal of the ransom for murder, which was also extended to the slave and to his bodily injury, so that release was substituted for ransom (Exod. 21:26). The usually valid extension of the responsibility for the crime to the family of the criminal was also abolished (Deut. 24:16). Abraham interceded for Sodom, and Moses for the people against the band of Korah. "Shall one man sin, and wilt Thou be wroth with all the congregation?" (Num. 16:22). Abraham bases his hopes against such an act of God with the appeal: "Judge of all the earth" (Gen. 18:25). The violation of strict justice contradicts the concept of God as judge of the world.

Unlimited justice too, in the form of punitive justice, is in contradiction to the concept of man. Therefore, the body of the hanged had to be taken down, and after the decomposition of the flesh had taken place, the remains were buried in the family grave (2 Sam. 21:12-14). Also after having suffered punishment by stripes, the punished one is restored as a brother (Makkoth 23a).[91] Before execution the criminal was offered a cup of wine and incense for anaesthesia.

It is difficult to understand, not only linguistically but also with regard to the entire inner development of biblical and rabbinical Judaism, that *zedakah*—justice [righteousness]—is, on the one hand, connected with love and thereby becomes the universal expression for piety, and, on the other hand, is narrowed down and made identical to the charitable activity of almsgiving, so that the other, properly speaking, charitable activity of lovingkindness (גמילות חסד) is ranked above it.

Likewise it is striking that the Talmud lets the legal procedure of equity (לפנים משורת הדין) surpass the justice of the legislated law. The Talmud goes so far with this idea as to attribute the destruction of Jerusalem to the violation of this self-correction of justice (Baba Metzia 30b).[92]

All these seeming anomalies make manifest our idea that the absolute virtue of justice must be supplemented by a relative one, which is not enlivened or spurned by the affect of honor, as is absolute justice, but by the affect of love. This also explains the connection of the concepts of love and justice in God as well as in man. "I the Eternal speak justice, I declare equity" (Isa. 45:19). "Who exercises lovingkindness, judgment and justice, for in these things I delight, saith the Eternal" (Jer. 9:23).

We must also consider here the connection of justice with peace, particularly because the Talmud in the phrase "because of the ways of peace" (מפני דרכי שלום) formulates a limitation of justice analogous to the principle of equity mentioned just above.

However, justice, along with the juridical institutes, remains the absolute foundation, the supreme principle of the state and of every community. It is therefore characteristic of the prophets that they do not base the rights of the poor on love and pity, but on justice. For the criminal himself, too, justice is true love. Justice rescues the criminal's responsibility and with it his human dignity. On the other hand, justice examines the state of man's soul and the influences of contemporaries and environment upon it, discovers in the *shegagah* [unwitting sin] the controlling idea that makes possible atonement for all injustice, and which is more effective and more true even than all the sacrifices and also all repentance. The principle of *shegagah* also includes the share of the environment in influencing the sin of the individual.

Here, too, we must come back to the wondrous idea through which Messianism receives its crown: the idea of God's servant.

The latter becomes the vicarious sufferer, and thereby the symbol of the reformation of punishment in general.

Originally, vicarious suffering of punishment was already prohibited in Mosaic teaching. And Ezekiel transfers this rejection of vicarious suffering from punishment to sin. However, the sentence, "He visits the iniquity of the fathers upon the children," remains a correct principle of experience, which the original form of the Mosaic teaching retains in this primitive form. But the children are innocent. And their guilt is, for them as children, rather smaller than greater even "when they hate Me" (Exod. 20:5).

As against this statement, how much can it help when, in a kind of anticlimax, the next verse stresses what love brings to the "thousands." But even to this statement is attached the limiting condition: to "them that love Me."

This entire mythology of inherited guilt and of suffering as punishment could have been uprooted only by the bold blow of an axe on which social insight has bestowed courage. God's punishment would befall the innocent, if suffering were only punishment. The real bearers of human suffering are the poor (עניים). Therefore God's punishment must have another meaning than that it imposes only suffering. Therefore also, suffering must have another meaning than that it is to be considered only as punishment. Suffering is not punishment. The suffering of men, which is to be considered mainly as the social suffering of the poor, is in God's hands. And God, as the God of justice, is at the same time the God of love. Justice and love are reciprocal concepts of God's being. The suffering of the poor is based on the justice of God that is united with love. Justice is love, hence it is in no way exclusively punitive justice. Thus justice, counterpointed by love, becomes the principle of theodicy. Justice becomes the lever for vicarious suffering, which is separated from punishment.

Suffering becomes the "suffering of love" (ייסורין של אהבה). This is the theodicy which dawns upon the prophet in view of the history of his people: the suffering of the exile is transfigured by this theodicy. The prophet's patriotism becomes for him, in Messianism, a philosophy of history. Here too religion testifies to its prominent share in reason. Not only individuals suffer for their era but peoples are elected; the people of Israel is elected in order to suffer for mankind. That Israel's election means its punishment, this insight was already expressed by Amos. But that this seeming punishment is rather the vicarious suffering, this is the insight of the Deutero-Isaiah. Now all presumption and all suspicion about Israel's election vanish. The election to the teaching of the unique God is at the same time the election to vicarious suffering for the idolatrous peoples, as for all peoples who have not yet matured to the knowledge of the unique God. This meaning of Israel's election too does not violate God's justice, which from now on has to prove itself in universal theodicy of the development of mankind. Polytheism too has its cultural value. But in spite of its historical value, it remains sin, for which polytheism cannot only suffer, while it is in need of vigorous life for its historical calling. The punishment of suffering would diminish its life energy, which it needs for its creative historical life.

And again, is it not Israel's greatest happiness, which radiates through the entire history of its suffering, that it "dwelleth in the covert of the Most High . . . in the shadow of the Almighty?" (Ps. 91:1). All balancing of accounts of pessimism with optimism, of shadows with sunshine, of unhappiness with happiness, are theoretically, as well as morally, vain and trivial. The personal as well as the historical dignity of man, and of the people under whose horizon he matures, is absolutely superior to earthly suffering. If, however, the reciprocal effects of men, generations, and entire peoples on each other are determined by the historical alternation of the vital signs of joy and suffering, then the prophet was left with no deeper insight about the historical balance of the fate of his own people than that which transfigured the people's great suffering into vicarious suffering, which is the highest peak of justice. Israel's greatest happiness, its historical calling for the unique God, the people's privileged position—and as such the historical calling must be thought and felt if it is to be effective—is now balanced by vicarious suffering. Israel suffers the martyrdom of monotheism. Truly, this martyrdom is not punishment; if it is suffering, it does not affect, properly speaking, the sufferer himself; for his calling puts him beyond any earthly happiness. If, however, human weakness feels shadows even in the bright sunlight, they could have migrated only from polytheism, from the horrors of which the monotheistic consciousness has been liberated. Hence vicarious suffering is no exception to justice, neither with God nor with man. Vicarious suffering merely brings the deepest confirmation of the idea that suffering is in no way only God's punishment. Justice is not fulfilled in punishment, but indeed in the kind of suffering that man recognizes as inflicted upon him by the yoke of the Kingdom of God. Man acknowledges this suffering as a call to world history by the unique God of mankind.

The relative virtues are ties and restrictions on the self of man in its autarchy and absoluteness. We have already observed such self-restrictions in the case of justice. Before we continue to expand upon these restrictions in order to comprise them into one special virtue of the second rank, it is more appropriate at first to unfold that absolute virtue which already came into prominence in the case of justice, insofar as justice emboldens itself to martyrdom.

CHAPTER XX

Courage

Since all the virtues must be contained in God's characteristics, one can ask what courage could mean in the case of God. Literally, of course, God's courage is a matter of record. In Scripture God is repeatedly called the hero and the man of war.

The benedictions of the *Shemoneh Esreh* also address God as "the great, the hero (the mighty one) and the awe inspiring." Also it says in the Proverbs: "He that is long-suffering is better than the mighty" (Prov. 16:32). In the thirteen attributes the attribute of long-suffering (ארך אפים) is placed before the attributes of love and faithfulness. Hence, it is contained in the thirteen attributes. In the attribute of long-suffering, heroic courage is acknowledged in a higher degree. The psalms overflow with the praise of God's heroic acts: "Who can express the mighty acts of God?" (Ps. 106:2). This suffices for the scriptural formulations of courage. However, the question of how heroism could be thought of as an attribute of God still remains, if all these attributes were to be thought valid only as archetypes for human action.

In the Hebrew language the word "hero" originates out of the same idea of virtue as in the Greek (αρετη) and in the Latin (*virtus*), which both originate from "man" and originally mean manliness. In the same way the Hebrew "hero" (גבור) and "heroism" (גבורה) originate from "man" (גבר). However, man does not remain the sole possessor of heroic virtue. Just as the hero did not remain preeminently the hunter hero (גבור ציד) but became the war hero (גבור מלחמה), so also did the woman become the woman of the army (אשת חיל), as the war hero became the hero of the army (גבור חיל). However, this appellation of woman, which is found in the significant hymn at the conclusion of the Proverbs of Solomon, does not designate her ability as a warrior; the army also is rather thought of as the administrative area of courage and faithfulness to

436

duty in general. This change in the meaning of the concept of heroism affected the transference of the heroic title from the woman of the army to the upright housewife. How was this lowering in meaning accomplished?

In the Sayings of the Fathers [4,1] it says: "Who is a hero?" And the answer is: "He who conquers his desire" (הכובש את יצרו). Now the hero has even become an ascetic. However, he who subdues his passion is not thereby an ascetic but a true hero, who does not permit the senses to rule him, does not become their slave, but their master. He therefore uses their powers, whereas the ascetic by not using the power of the senses, makes himself negatively the slave of passion. He who conquers sensual desires rules them and accepts their slave services.

Here Jewish and Greek ethics touch and attest their kinship, which is based on their common relation to reason. Here one can recognize the common denominator of reason, which makes possible the analogy between Socrates and Plato, on the one hand, and the prophets, on the other. Here are the sources that unite Orient and Occident; they are, on the one hand, the streams which were considered by the Jews of Alexandria the original sources of monotheism, and, on the other, similarly fruitful streams within Stoicism. The fight against the sovereignty of the senses constitutes the original spirit of Platonism, and also constitutes the vital energy of Neoplatonism, from which Stoicism took its war cry. Upon this original soil of reason, the differences between polytheism and monotheism seem to disappear, as if they were of secondary importance in face of the main alternative: sensuality or reason.

However, even at this crossroad of reason, monotheism must prove its special strength, and it is, perhaps, the greatest triumph of Judaism that it derived its moral superiority, even with regard to Platonism, from its theology. This superiority over Platonic ethics shows itself in all the fundamental as well as particular problems of political science, and no less also in the great controversial questions of so-called metaphysics, insofar as it deals with the fate of the soul. Here, even Plato succumbs to the eschatological myth, while monotheism matured to the practical idealism of the messianic teaching. Platonic courage here becomes withdrawal from the world and escape from this earth into the beyond. This happens because the body is absolutely the prison of the soul, and also because, on this earth, there must always be people who are evil, since wisdom cannot take root in the multitude. Messianism positively opposes all these prejudices, which are only erroneous consequences drawn from correct methodological principles, while negatively, it refrains from all the fantasies about punishment in Tartarus, yet retains hope for eternal life. For Platonism has an exaggerated notion of justice, which considers God's recompense only as punitive justice and therefore as a painful, crucifying suffering of the body. This is so because here repentance did not find its homogenous fulfillment in reconciliation.

Therefore, Platonic courage has only an ending, similar to that of tragedy, in which the hero must go to ruin in order to be victorious in the consciousness of the spectator. In Judaism, on the other hand, the hero does not live only for the sake of his own heroism, but, insofar as he is man, he is in correlation with God. He is therefore able to live and to defend his life only as God's confederate, as God's servant, and hence as God's hero. He does not stand alone, but always in the covenant with God. If he were to fall, God's cause would fall. However, "the cause of our God shall stand forever" (Isa. 40:8), and from this point of view the earthly life is of no consequence for the hero. There is here no end to the spectacle, no end of the tragedy. There is no tragedy at all for the life of religious heroism. Martyrdom turned out to be vicarious justice in the form of vicarious suffering. Hence, justice and courage flow together. The martyrdom of justice is at the same time the heroism of courage. Courage is the triumph of humanity, just as justice coupled with love is the embodiment of God's attributes.

Only three commandments require a man to endure death instead of violating them: the commandments against blasphemy in idol worship, against murder, and against incest (Sanhedrin 74a). All the other commandments of the Torah may be violated, if worldly assault imposes death for obeying them. If, however, idol worship, or murder, or incest is demanded under threat of death, the Talmud orders martyrdom. Thus, courage becomes a virtue which accompanies the life of the Jew. For the sword of Damocles has hung over the Jew throughout his history, in order to seduce him to idol worship or to the denial of his pure monotheism. Therefore, one may in all sobriety call the historical life of the Jew the life of courage. It is of no consequence that the private life of individuals may contain many a blemish; this does not change anything in the historical character of this virtue of this religious community. There had everywhere been much suffering among men, and many martyrs of different kinds. Even the wise men, even Socrates, had to drink the cup of hemlock. He, however, had to suffer only for his philosophic teaching and for the practical meaning which his fellow citizens attributed to it. Though the indictment read that he wanted to introduce new gods, these were merely conceptions of his theory and of no historical validity. He himself sacrifices a cock to Aesculapius. Hence, he acknowledges the historical validity of the native divinity. Therefore his martyrdom is not so much religious as theoretical: the self-sacrifice of the philosopher.

The Jewish martyr, on the other hand, is a hero of the unique God of Israel, who is not only his God, the God of his theory and, it may be, even of his faith, but he is at the same time the God of his fathers, the God of his history, who therefore can also be thought of as the God of mankind. Jewish courage is, therefore, simply an historical virtue, the virtue of the historical, not the individual, man. Furthermore, Messianism breaks the backbone of nationalism, so that the courage of the Jew cannot be degraded to a merely national virtue. The human courage of the Jew is, as an historical virtue, humanitarian courage, the courage for the truth of the religious ideal of mankind. The mainspring of this courage is that mankind, which gradually became an ethical idea in accordance with its origin in Messianism, is a religious idea, is the highest but inevitable consequence of messianic monotheism. The pride of this, his religious consciousness, is the balm of humility of the Jewish hero, of the martyr in behalf of God's uniqueness.

"The sanctification of God's name" is that term under which all the religious duties in life are comprised. Just as self-sanctification is the embodiment of all religious morality, so this self-sanctification is objectively designated by the sanctification of God's name. While I sanctify myself, I sanctify God, I acquire for my consciousness God's holiness, and while I take possession of the idea of God's holiness, I actualize my self-sanctification, which is nothing other than the infinite drawing near to God's holiness.

Accordingly, martyrdom is called "giving one's life for the sanctification of God's name." God's name is here substituted for God, for the simple reason that the problem concerns not God's sanctity itself but the sanctification of his name through the recognition of, and testimony to, his teaching, and thus the kind of acknowledgment which actualizes the sanctification. Thus, martyrdom is an historical act, which the individual does not take upon himself for his own sake, or for the sake of his soul, but in the service of history. As God is unique, so in days to come will his name be unique. So hopes, so prays the Jew. And as the individual Jew suffers for the sake of this messianic goal, just so he becomes a martyr for this historical faith, if he is told to renounce it under the threat of death.

It is truly an unparalleled irony of history that the story of Jesus

Christ's life, sealed by his death, should have become the source of the main difference between Christianity and Judaism. The history of this passion is an imitation of the messianic imagination of Deutero-Isaiah, while the latter, as is now commonly agreed, anticipated the history of the "remnant of Israel." And hence, according to this original poetic image, the history of Christ is actually the history of Israel. The philosophy of history of future generations will have to consider and fathom this riddle of the most intimate history of the spirit, as far as it has unfolded up to this time.

For the present, the mystery of the unique God may perhaps offer us a sufficient solution. To the clarification of this mystery, the whole of the culture of all peoples, in all its spiritual branches, must contribute. However, for thousands of years, as also at present, each Jew has been contributing to it by taking the virtue of courage upon himself as his historical lot. Surmounting the worldly life of actual history, the Jew took upon himself the courage to live and, if necessary, to die in joyous resolution for the deepest and most holy idea of the human spirit, the idea of the unique God. Vicarious justice is the Jewish virtue of courage.

CHAPTER XXI

Faithfulness

The word for faithfulness is, as we must note, the same as the word for truth (אמת). Faithfulness is based objectively on truth and subjectively on truthfulness. However, it separated itself as a virtue of its own in a word which at the same time also means faith (אמונה). Both words originate from a root which means steadfastness. Through faithfulness any relation, whether between man and man or between God and man, is strengthened. The covenant (ברית) is the instrument of faithfulness. Therefore God concludes a covenant with Noah, with Abraham, with Israel. And God sets up signs of the covenant, the rainbow in the heavens for the preservation of nature, and the social sign of the covenant, the Sabbath, for the labor relations among men.

Remembering is therefore the psychological function of faithfulness. Thus, God remembers the covenant with the fathers, and Israel has to remember the benefits God bestowed on it. However, while it should remember the liberation from Egypt, this remembering is changed to an active duty: thou shalt remember that thou hast been a slave in the land of Egypt. Through this the memory changes into the social virtue of loving the stranger, as well as into the gentle treatment of the slave and the promotion of his liberation.

Hence, remembering leads to gratitude, which is a specific form of faithfulness. Gratitude, to be sure, cannot be demanded, but this limitation is valid only for the one to whom gratitude is due, not for the one who owes it. Gratitude is a form of faithfulness, which in the first place is to be exercised upon one's own consciousness, upon the coherence of the thoughts, strivings, and feelings that move the human heart, and which stand in connection and opposition to the actions and feelings of others. If, in this reciprocal process, an interruption occurs, then a disharmony of the consciousness is unavoidable. Therefore, the faithfulness of gratitude is already necessary as the psychological basis of the harmony of consciousness. The psalm expresses this strikingly: "If I forget thee O Jerusalem, let my right hand forget her cunning" (Ps. 137:5). The right hand here stands for the organ of the whole man. Oblivion of the I is invoked as recompense if faithfulness to Jerusalem should be relinquished. And what holds for religion, religion itself demands no less from all covenants and associations among men.

Hence, the Bible agrees with the Greek antiquity in thinking highly of friendship. David and Jonathan are the high points of this youthful love, which is at the same time hero worship. It is characteristic of this friendship, in which Jewish and heathen consciousness mix, that it is the legitimate son of the king who dedicates his enthusiastic friendship to an alien pretender to the throne. This love is reciprocated by David, as is shown by his lamentation, which puts this love higher than love for women. Hence, friendship, without any disturbing eroticism, appears here in the light of a spiritual eros of gratitude and faithfulness in David's heart.

There is no distinct word for friendship in classical Hebrew. Friendship is, rather, the original form of love. Therefore it is also possible to say that there is no distinct word for love. Love is, rather, love of one's fellowman, which can only be friendship. To this are added now man's love for God and even God's love for men. This reciprocal relation, too, is based on friendship, on the brotherhood of the covenant. In the last analysis everything is nothing other than faithfulness, which now becomes friendship, now love in its different forms, but never becomes any other thing; rather, it remains faithfulness.

Love, in the specific form of sexual love, leads to marriage, to the marriage bond. This bond is not a fetter. Therefore marriage, according to Jewish law, can be dissolved when moral requirements invalidate the assumptions of the marriage. Precisely the legal possibility of divorce shows faithfulness to be the meaning and foundation of the marriage bond.

The purpose of marriage is to establish a unity of consciousness above and beyond the changing impulse of sexual love, even on this borderline of sensual passion. Education and habituation to faithfulness is the meaning of marriage. Without this meaning, marriage would merely be an institution for child bearing, and any other purpose would be a vain illusion. For any such purpose, faithfulness is indeed a physiological hindrance since change heightens desire. If, however, for the consorts themselves marriage has its validity in their mutual spiritual well-being, then this mutual relationship is based exclusively on the ideal of faithfulness, which is the task of marriage. This spiritual relationship also protects the desire for child bearing from turning into an animal-like gratification.

Jewish marriage law has confirmed this meaning by making the consecration of the marriage an act of divine worship. Moreover, rabbinical legislation has sought to protect in various ways the honor of the wife against the legal authority of the husband, so that the monogamous character of marriage is beyond question, although, because of the original oriental conditions, a certain indulgence in this case also could not be avoided. Nonetheless, among all the historical documents of Jewish morality, the Jewish marriage is foremost in testifying that faithfulness is a characteristic trait of the Jewish mind. Here, too, the last chapter of the Proverbs, with its hymn to the courageous woman, serves as a poetic testimony to faithfulness.

The family also, in accordance with its concept, is an institution of human faithfulness. With the establishment of the community of children, Plato, in his *Republic,* destroyed, even more than by the community of women, the psychological foundation of faithfulness in the souls of the human beings, who are citizens of his state. If children no longer recognize their own father and own mother, it is much worse for them than when parents are not permitted to recognize their own children. In the gratitude of the child's mind, faithfulness establishes the hearth of the family, and in it the hearth of every human community.

It is characteristic of Jewish family law that the father has the duty to teach his son the Torah (Succah 42a). This instruction prepares the foundation of education. The duty of instruction is incumbent upon the father even before it is assumed by the state. Only on the basis of the father's obligation does the communal or state obligation arise: "Teachers of children should be established in every city" (Baba Bathra 21a). Hence, marriage culminates in instruction, and this high point in turn is connected with the root which knowledge in general constitutes for religion.

This establishment of instruction in the native soil of the family has made a considerable contribution to the general inspiration and animation of the study of the Torah, which therefore in itself became a major object of faithfulness. In any case, the fundamental biblical commandment emphatically enjoined one's own continuous study as well as instruction of the children, by day and at night, at home and on the journey. In addition, religious dignity and dedication surrounded the Torah and its study. Hence Torah study in its extended range became actually a scientific study which took hold of the entire people. In the life of the entire people study became an activity, an act of faithfulness to the Torah, so that poverty and riches could arise but never a proletariat proper, because a learned proletariat is a contradiction in terms. Knowledge always establishes an aristocracy that is only a semblance when it is not an aristocracy of the spirit. The Israelites, according to a saying of the Talmud, always considered themselves children of the king. Faithfulness in the study of the Torah prevented the people from losing its noble character during the thousands of years of persecution.

Justice brought forth the social legislation of religion, but it is conscious of the limitations of its own effectiveness. The virtue of the first rank had to call for help from a virtue of the second rank. The latter is almsgiving, which brought about the identity of the word for almsgiving with the Hebrew word for justice [righteousness] (צדקה). Almsgiving, too, is a form of faithfulness of which man is in need for the consistency of his consciousness. The individual consciousness cannot rest satisfied with the legislation of social justice. Too often it is convinced that social justice is only an ideal norm, the actualization of which is very often obstructed and frustrated. If almsgiving were not to assist, the chasm between the social ideal and the political actuality would become a flagrant provocation in the face of which the harmony of human consciousness could not be restored. Consciousness would have to tear off all the threads that give it its cohesion to be able to abstain from the personal duty of charity. The latter, therefore, becomes the virtue of faithfulness in the first place in regard to one's own I, and through it to the fellowman. All charity expresses faithfulness to the human community. When the Talmud says about the laws generally that their meaning is to purify men (Tanchuma Shemini, ed. Lemberg, 149b), then this holds true principally for almsgiving and its character of faithfulness. Faithfulness is the means of purification of the human heart.

Therefore, the feeding of the poor on festival days has been at the same time considered the purpose of the festival itself. Maimonides describes this purpose of the festival in wonderful words: "When we eat and drink on a festivity, it is our duty to feed and to share our meal also with the stranger, the orphans, the widows, and other poor and needy. Who, however, while surrounded by one's wife and children holds a festive meal and locks the gate of his court before the poor and the needy, and does not offer them anything, his meal is not a commanded meal of joyous festivity, but merely an animal-like meal, about which the prophet says: the sacrifices of your feasts are like meals of a mourner" (*Yad Hachazakah*, Section Yom Tow, Chap.

6, 18-21; cf. M. Bloch, *Die Ethik in der Halachah*, p. 25). Important also is the prescription that almsgiving has to be accompanied by words of sympathy to the receiver. "Who offers support to the poor is provided by the prophet with a sixfold blessing, but who adds to the alms sympathetic words, him he provides with an elevenfold blessing" (Baba Bathra, 9b; cf. Bacher, A. d. T. *[Die Agada der Tannaiten]* II, p. 55). Sympathy is satisfied with the gift itself; but faithfulness demands the expression of human community, and this is done through the addition of words of sympathy to the receiver of the gift.

Faithfulness, as the basis of the soul's gratitude, is also the ultimate and deepest foundation of the benedictions, which form the framework of all prayers. They are all variations of the one motif of gratitude. However, what else does gratitude toward God mean but man's self-education toward gratitude? And although one may doubt the value of gratitude when one considers it as an isolated virtue, if one considers it as a mode of faithfulness, every doubt disappears. Although faithfulness is only a relative virtue in relation to justice and courage, it is as such of everlasting value. What unity means for the psychological consciousness, faithfulness means for moral consciousness. The benedictions of the various prayers should give guidance in the preservation, strengthening, purification, ennoblement, and elevation of faithfulness. The eulogies are thanksgivings which man needs in order to educate himself to faithfulness, in order to secure through it the unity of consciousness in every respect.

What, in the final analysis, would be all the success of justice, and no less of all courage, if both these absolute virtues were not able to rely upon this virtue of the second rank? Even more than truthfulness is supported by modesty, justice and courage are directly accompanied by faithfulness. It is therefore not only a source of temporary assistance or even a substitute but a continuously collaborating supplement. It therefore also reaches out to truthfulness, and modesty itself can be understood as a kind of faithfulness, namely as a self-examination of the self-consciousness.

CHAPTER XXII

Peace

Among the expressions used in the Talmud to limit absolute justice, we find "on account of the ways of peace" (מפני דרכי שלום). Thus, peace is thought of as a virtue of the second rank next to absolute justice, and, among other expressions, peace stands for the legal principle of equity. However, peace is also a complement to courage and appears as an analogy to faithfulness in the expressions: "peace and faithfulness" (2 Kings 20:19; Jer. 33:6; Zech. 8:19). It is characteristic that the order of the words is not reversed: for the word for faithfulness (*emeth*) also means truth and faithfulness, which are virtues of the first rank.

Courage too, no less than justice, is in need of a correction. It cannot pass for a passion which in the heroic life of man would be an end in itself. The goal of the true virtue of courage in no way lies in the animalistic strength of heroism, but rather in measure and self-restraint, which the courageous one puts upon himself as a bridle. Self-restraint, the taming of the passions, is true courage. Courage is equivalent to the rational knowledge of God. These corrections are still within courage, but they prepare the way for the corresponding virtue of the second rank.

The Greeks have a word, hard to translate, for that harmony of the powers of the soul which they established as the highest virtue: σωφροσύνη. Here, too, there is a difference between Plato and Aristotle. In the *Ethics of the Pure Will* we have called this virtue, which concludes the ways of virtue, humanity. The entire harmony of humanity in its ascension to the heights and also in its condescension to human frailty depends upon the inner adjustment which the whole spiritual nature of man seeks for itself. The Bible calls this harmonization of the whole of morality peace.

Among God's attributes peace seems to be missing. However, it is sufficiently represented there. Long suffering (ארך אפים) is a power

446

of peace, as is forgiveness of sin, "bearing the sin." Sin is in opposition to the vocation of the soul. When God bears sin, when he takes sin upon himself, he restores the peace of the soul. Hence among God's attributes this archetype for the conclusion of the ways of virtue is in no way missing.

Thus, it is possible to account for the fact that peace is with constant emphasis called the work of God. Originally the word means perfection, then it is weakened to mean well-being of various kinds, then again it increases to the meaning of a greeting, which characteristically enough is expressed as a call to peace, "peace be with you." Bildad says, "he maketh peace in His high places" (Job 25:2). This verse has been taken over by the prayer, as the concluding sentence of the *Shemoneh Esreh*. Moreover, the Deutero-Isaiah puts peace in place of the good. One becomes aware that peace becomes the quintessence of the divine attributes. Therefore it becomes the symbol of human perfection, the harmony of the individual, and the perfection of the human race. For peace is the token of the Messianic Age, and indeed not only as the opposite of war, which will disappear, but also positively as the embodiment of all morality. The Messiah is therefore called the "Prince of Peace" (שׂר שׁלום). The unity of human consciousness is here expressed by the peace of the soul.

It is therefore as an apt expression: "Justice and peace have kissed each other" (Ps. 85:11). The kiss seals this agreement of justice with peace.

The "priestly blessing" concludes with peace, with the institution of peace. The verb "to give" is a blunting of the Hebrew word which means "institute," for example, the institution of a king. In this institution of peace God turns his countenance to the children of men. Thus, this latter sentence could be considered a reply to Moses' demand to know God's face. Peace is this face, God's "frontside," and all "backsides," all his effects and consequences, are those of peace. The meaning of perfection becomes unmistakable in this extension of the meaning of peace. God's peace is God's perfection, the highest archetype of human morality.

Therefore it is possible to consider peace the principle of finality. God makes peace, this means that he is the highest end of all existence and of all moral actions. God, as the originator of peace, is equal to the principle of finality. The latter, in turn, is identical with the principle of truth, insofar as it unites both finalities, that of nature and that of morality, in a new finality. God as finality is equivalent to God as peace.

From this point of view, too, one may recognize the inner oppo-

sition of monotheism to the principle of all sophistry, which lies in
the Heraclitean saying that war is the father of all things. War is
not the original cause of the moral universe; the end of peace becomes
the cause. Peace, which is the goal of the moral world, must also be
valid as its originating power. God is peace. God stands for the harmony between the moral powers of the universe and their natural
conditions.

God's peace is a deeper expression than God's covenant. Covenant still has a one-sided legal character, and the Latin word for
peace, which passed over to the modern languages, also stems from
the root of covenant. Even the German word corresponds to "en-
closure" *(Gehege)*, to "fencing-in" *(Einfriedigung)*, which is accomplished by legal protection. The Hebrew root meaning perfection
imparts to peace unequivocally the value of finality. Hence, peace
becomes equivalent to the principle of finality, of the end.

This teleology is now planted into the essence of the human soul.
As it says usually, "seek justice" (Zeph. 2:3), so also it says, "seek
peace, and pursue it" (Ps. 34:15). Concerning the Messiah in his
final form it says: "The chastisement of our peace was upon him"
(Isa. 53:5). Thus the suffering of the Messiah becomes a chastisement
of peace, it becomes a means to the end of peace. Peace is the ideal
of the messianic man. Only in peace is the spiritual welfare of man
completed. "The wild desires no longer win us, the deeds of passion
cease to chain."* In keeping with the way in which Goethe describes
God's love, it is only the peace of the soul into which God's love
radiates. There are no longer any passions when peace enters the
soul of man and establishes its unity and simplicity.

Only through peace, as the unifying force of human consciousness,
is love, in all its directions, liberated from the ambiguities which
are connected with it. Man ought to love his fellowman. Is he actually able to do this, selfish man? Is human love able to exceed the
few solemn moments of compassion? And does not all human love
remain affected by an earthly remnant of a grudge? And this frail
man, should he be able to love God as the archetype of his morality
and of his self-perfection? Is he supposed not merely to honor and
follow his ideal but also to be able to love it? Is this not simply a
contradiction? And, finally, God is supposed to love the children
of men, in spite of their weaknesses and their sins, or rather because
of them, since he becomes the redeemer of their guilt of sin. How are

---

*Goethe, Faust, pt. I. [S.K.]

all these meanings of love possible in themselves and reconcilable
one with another?

God's peace, insofar as it constitutes God's being, and the peace
of soul, insofar as it is the ideal of the human being, this end of peace
which designates man's virtuous path to God, the path of man's
drawing near to God, explains and solves all these seeming difficulties. Peace, as the highest goal of man, is at the same time the
highest strength of man. Peace as a way of virtue is the final step in the
development of man. Peace is perfection. Self-perfection is on the
track of the final goal when it reaches the peace of the soul.

Peace of the soul manifests itself in contentment, which is preeminently a religious virtue, for it is concerned with the acknowledgment
of God's providence and rule over the world. In face of contentment
all the assaults of eudaemonism are shattered, as are also all the
doubts that the deepest suffering of the soul might stir up. "As one
praises God for the good, so also for the bad."[93] This is the general
talmudic instruction with regard to benedictions. Contentment disregards all the differences in economic existence. The greatest teachers of the Talmud, the so-called Pharisees, these great teachers of
Israel—they were partly poor artisans and day laborers; nevertheless,
they were high-spirited in their piety and in their study of the divine
Teaching. It remained a general custom in Israel, even in the darkest
times of the Middle Ages, that the distinction of poor and rich disappeared in the face of the common duty and share in the Teaching.
The Teaching preserved in all, in spite of persecution and oppression,
a contentment with their calling as Israelites. "How goodly is our
portion, and how pleasant is our lot, and how beautiful our heritage."
Thus reads the sentence in the daily early-morning prayer, which
introduces the profession of faith.

Contentment with the material conditions is the instrument that
prepares the way for that practical idealism which does not despise
and abandon earthly material possessions, but which nevertheless
does not regard and strive for them as if they were the highest or
even the only good that constitutes the value of human life. If,
however, such a mood of the soul is not to give rise to quietism,
which favors mysticism and asceticism, and also to the withdrawal
from life and abstention from the civic duties of life in a state, then
this contentment must be armed with that cultural power which only
knowledge constitutes.

Peace of soul and earthly contentment with the actual conditions of
life are therefore dependent on knowledge and its conditions and ac-
complishments. In religious terms this means the study of the Teach-

ing. Not merely by faith may man content himself. Reverence of God is knowledge of God. Worship is rooted in, and culminates in, the study of the Teaching which, according to the saying of the Mishnah, is the embodiment of all commandments. Hence, peace of soul is based on the peace of reason. Faith, which in itself is not independent, misuses the contentment of the soul by subjugating reason to it, so that for faith no contradictions in the religious tradition exist. It is not then faith without knowledge that establishes the true peace of the soul, which is the true religious contentment with one's destiny, but rather reason, the knowledge that is the root that nourishes and strengthens all the branches and boughs of contentment.

This connection of plain living with industrious study, with a study that is not exaggeratedly called titanic, gave and preserved for Jewish life that peace, firmness, superiority, and sublimity without which it could not have withstood misery and persecution for thousands of years. Piety alone, resignation to God's will alone, not to speak of the strict tending of the laws, would not have been able to arouse and preserve alive that enthusiasm, which yields the contentment that is superior to one's worldly lot. Wisdom is based on scholarliness. The Jew, in spite of all his most base daily occupations, has, as a rule, at the same time been a scholar. As a scholar he could become a wise man, and as a wise man the basic mood of the Jew could become contentment with his earthly lot. For it is not in his earthly days that the true Jew finds fulfillment of his historical world mission. His contentment is rooted in his messianic vocation, which presupposes the knowledge of the Torah and the duty of disseminating it over the historical world. What is all martyrdom in comparison with this historical mission, what is all material suffering and even all the suffering of the soul in comparison with the pure joy of knowledge and inquiry! This joy in the Torah is the peace of the soul, the fortress of contentment.

Messianism is the strong tie that unites the man of the present with the ideal future, but which also unites the man of the future with the man of the present actuality. Peace of soul is to establish the unity of the heart. It should correspond to the unity of God. Bahya defines this analogy more precisely; he establishes a correspondence between the profession of the unity of God and the unity of heart as well as the unity of worship. The heart, the soul, is to be liberated from the schism of passions and, in unification, in the unity of the heart, it is to establish the contentment, the peace of the soul.

Is it perhaps the above-mentioned quietism which should be de-

sired because the passions have been subjugated? Quietism resists
not only the passions, but also the affect. Previously, however, we
were in need of the affect for the ways of virtue; we would not like
to eliminate it from the way of peace. The distinction between affect
and passion is important and recognizable in the peace of the soul.

The passions have their common foundation in that mystery of
the soul which is constituted by hatred. Neither psychology nor
ethics has determined whether hatred is an original direction of
consciousness, or merely a transformation of some other instinctual
force. It is above all a question of whether hatred does not rather
belong to the pathological sphere, and, growing out of it, masquerades
as a kind of psychological normality. As pain and pleasure have
grown into one another, so could love and hatred be alternating
links of the same instinctual force. Here we shall not pursue this
fundamental question any further than it concerns the definition of
hatred.

However, the religious teaching of virtue has, almost as its first
task, to combat hatred. For religion is based upon love with its
threefold ramification of God's love and human love. Peace constitutes the way of virtue, which must not only evade hatred but expel
it and bring it to naught.

What means does the peace of soul secure in order to root out
hatred from the human heart? It is not enough to oppose human
love to hatred. For the chapter on the teaching of virtue has to indicate practical means, which will smooth the path for the ways of
virtue; it cannot be satisfied merely with theory; it must offer practical solutions for moral theory. Therefore, it would also be insufficient if another designation were attempted, if hatred were perhaps interpreted as envy. For in that case there would be no less
difficulty involved in combating and destroying envy.

At this point, even without being guided by polemics, we are led
by our own considerations to the problem of love of the enemy.
The Old Testament does not contain this command, but it contains, in
fundamental expressions, the prohibition of enmity, of hatred for
men. In the first instance this prohibition is expressed in the prohibition of vengeance and resentment (לא תקום ולא תטר). Further,
it is expressed in the prohibition of forbearing assistance to the
enemy with regard to the preservation of his property (Exod. 23:5).
Finally, it results from the fundamental regulation in the prohibition:
"Thou shalt not hate thy brother in thy heart" (Lev. 19:17). In this
verse hatred is determined as opposition to the brother and to the
heart, hence as opposition to the fellowman and to man's own foun-

dation, which lies in his heart. The only question remains: through
what practical means of virtue can this fundamental regulation be
realized and hatred rooted out of the human heart?

The wisdom of the Talmud has progressed beyond the Bible. The
Bible, in the psalms, knows only the false, the wrong hatred and the
false enemies (Ps. 38:20; 35:19; 69:5). In all these verses the cause
of hatred is called false; it remains possible that there could be a
true cause of hatred. The prohibition of idolatry and the commandment to destroy idolatry lend support to this idea, as do also the
psalms which in this line of thought seem to breathe vehement hatred
and insatiable vengeance. Justice and courage may demand such dispositions of the mind, but peace has nothing in common with them,
and, in spite of its relative value as a virtue, peace has the task and
the authority to check these absolute virtues. But how can and how
will peace be capable of this?

The Talmud has discovered the concept of "wanton hatred"
(שנאת חנם) and introduced it into the prayers.[94] Not only should
hatred not have a false cause, but it has no cause at all. Any cause
for hatred is empty and vain. Hatred is always wanton hatred. This
is the deep wisdom which excels all love of the enemy and which
first secures and psychologically strengthens human love. It is not
enough that I recognize that I ought to love my enemy—apart from
the fundamental question of whether both concepts are compatible. I
can remove hatred from the human heart only insofar as I do not
know any enemy at all; the information and the knowledge that a
man is my enemy, that he hates me, must be as incomprehensible to
me as that I myself could hate a man, and therefore it must drop
out of my consciousness. The one must become as unintelligible to
me as the other. People persuade themselves that they hate one another, but this is their delusion, the fateful outcome of their ignorance about their own soul and their consciousness. The vanity which
Koheleth ascribes to everything is in this case related to hatred, and
this vanity is expressed by a word which means futile, and that which
is in vain. All hatred is in vain. I deny hatred to the human heart.
Therefore I deny that I have an enemy, that a man could hate me. I
deny this with the same clarity of my consciousness with which I
deny that I have an enemy, that I could hate a man. What is hatred?
I deny its possibility. The word, which intends to describe such a
concept, is altogether empty.

With this overcoming of hatred, with this exclusion of it from the
inventory of the powers of the soul, the way opens up for the peace
of soul. Only now can I achieve repose of my mind; only now can I

achieve true and permanent contentment. As long as hatred threatens me, my own or another man's, I cannot hope for peace and for genuine contentment. If the misery of war did not rage about us, then even the specter of war, the mere danger of war, would constitute a contradiction to the peace of the world, as well as to the peace of the soul. We do not have it, no people has it, mankind does not have it, as long as the phantom of hatred among peoples, this actual angel of death, traverses the world with his scythe. Nor can the individual man attain peace of soul without securing the peace of the world. Messianism unites humanity with every individual man. For my own peace I need the confidence that hatred among peoples will be destroyed from the consciousness of mankind. Peoples do not hate one another, but greed awakens envy, and greed and envy delude man with an illusory image, which one passes off as a power of the soul, and which one presumes to confirm as such. All hatred is vain and wanton. All hatred is nothing but illusion, nothing but the interpretation and embellishment of human baseness, which is constituted by greed and selfishness and their effect, envy. If one recognizes the illusion of a false national psychology, which in all peoples is constituted by hatred; if one recognizes in a more fundamental psychology, which is enlightened by ethics, that hatred is an illusory factor in the soul, then the greater part of the burden of sin falls from the human heart. There is no hatred when peace has pitched its tent in the heart of man. "The tent of peace" (סכת שלום) is therefore used in prayer. The tent is the tabernacle that has acquired such a deep symbolic meaning that a holy day has been dedicated to it. The Feast of Tabernacles is the true feast of peace during the wandering through the dessert of earthly existence. Peace makes all of life into a feast. Peace brings the peace of nature into the human world, it brings the mood of naiveté into the reflection upon the world. We no longer believe in the experience of history which passes itself off as the wisdom of history, according to which everything has been and always will be the same: individuals and peoples hate each other, and hatred is an instinctual power of human consciousness. We do not trust pessimism; we despise its wisdom, because we have understood the meaning of the world more profoundly and correctly. Pessimism is rooted in the psychological error that hatred is an ordering power in the economy of nature, as is the struggle for existence which destroys countless germs in order to eliminate them from the contest. Although we do not deny the tendency to destruction, as little as we deny the elimination of the inferior germs, we distinguish the animate

from everything material, even in the organic, and we reject the analogy between the two spheres, between that of nature and that of
the moral world, as a will-o'-the-wisp. The germs which fight one
another do not hate each other. When men and peoples fight one
another, they fight one another as organisms, and as animate beings
they seem to hate each other. But as surely as God's breath breathes
in man's nostrils, as surely does the spirit live in the human animal.
And as surely as spirit, God's spirit, lives in the heart of man, it is
not hatred which animates the man's deeds. Even if it were hatred,
which is rather the twin-headed envy and greed, even then this way
of the human heart would not be its right way. Just as man is able
to conceive of virtue, just as he is able to conceive of peace, so he is
also able to unmask the deadly image of hatred. Only let him seek
peace. Only let him be, as the Mishnah says, "The disciple of Aaron,
loving peace and pursuing peace" (Pirke Aboth 1,12), and the ghost
of hatred will disappear into nothingness before his sight. Peace is
that power of the soul which scares away and annihilates all the
ghosts that threaten morality and the purity of the soul. Pessimism
is such a ghost of rationalism and idealism. If, however, peace of soul
is based on the foundation of knowledge, then pessimism cannot
be frightening; for it is not the result of rational knowledge, but an
inspiration of mysticism. It contradicts God's goodness and providence, and this is precisely the deep power of Messianism, that it
could transform itself into an optimistic power of the soul. Again
we have to point to the important saying of the Talmud, that the
soul, when it is led before the heavenly judge, has to give an
answer to the question: "Did you hope for redemption?" Redemption, however, is world peace. The Jew is to nourish and carry this
hope in his heart. It has become an article of faith. Monotheism and
Messianism have grown into each other. If world peace is the innermost belief of the religious consciousness, then peace must be an
unfailing power, a reliable guide of the mind. In the testimony of
religion, peace is the characteristic of the historical world. Therefore
peace must also be the power of soul of the individual consciousness. All the disturbances and doubts of peace are impediments to
the life of the soul; they are misinterpretations and pathological
aberrations. The fundamental power of the human soul is as certainly
peace, as peace is the goal of human history.

There are two physiological signs of this life of peace in man: the
feeling of being moved and joy.

In the *Aesthetics of Pure Feeling* I have tried to show that the
feeling of being moved furnishes a proof of the aesthetic conscious-

ness. However, this view does not contradict our attempt at this time also to claim the feeling of being moved for the religious consciousness in its virtuous way of peace. For the religious consciousness uses the aesthetic consciousness as amply as the ethical consciousness, and there is no reason for the religious consciousness to claim its own originality in the feeling of being moved. This feeling is the love for the nature of man which, expressed in its pureness, shines forth in the countenance of man, where it reflects the splendor of the pureness of this feeling of being moved. The religious consciousness takes possession of this aesthetic power in order to establish the virtue of peace in the mind. Thereby the feeling of being moved originates, as a witness of the mood of peace, which animates man and which becomes a power of his soul.

Although the feeling of being moved may express itself in weeping, it is in no way the same as the feeling of pain which at other times arouses weeping. The feeling of being moved therefore does not entirely dissolve in a reflex motion, but holds itself above the threshold of the reflex sensation and remains within the realm of the pure activity of consciousness. Therefore, it is a valid symptom of the moving power of peace in the soul. In no way is it indifferent as weeping is, but is, as it were, a homogenous expression of the internal. And if a tear accompanies the feeling of being moved, it is, as a single pearl, positively to be distinguished from the reflexive chain of weeping. Therefore, poets have at all times praised it as the dew, and distinguished it from the rain.

The feeling of being moved is the physiological proof of the natural power of peace, and it is related to an appearance of the good in the human world, without this good being actually embodied in any individual man. In the example used by Kant, it is the common man, before whose morality I must bow. With the feeling of being moved, however, it is not the presence of man which compels me to have respect; rather a mere abstraction, which may be a story, an invention, brings a tear into my eyes. Such a psychological fact is a sure proof of the power of peace in my consciousness. Peace comes over me and animates me, even if I only hear of an invented action of goodness, which a man allegedly achieved. If peace were not this kind of motivating force, then the feeling of being moved would not overcome me; for the latter is the radiation of peace. Why would I be concerned with a fairy tale about a good deed, if my consciousness were not to enjoy it, and long for it? Hence, peace, as the feeling of being moved proves, is a natural power of my consciousness. Hence, I follow a natural way of human consciousness, when I add peace, as a way of virtue, to courage and justice, in order that peace may fill in the lacunae which those absolute virtues must leave behind them.

Peace also makes its appearance as a corrective for justice. "Judge every man according to the scale of his merits."[95] Here we recognize in peace a new and strong cause for the predominance of the scale of merits. Peace is put into the scale, and sees to it that the merit of fellowman predominates. Strict justice very often cannot acknowledge this, but peace is the grace which outshines justice. In private life, too, peace is effective as the fundamental norm for the reconciliation among men. It takes no notice of the dark sides of life and displays the bright sides, which are present in every man, although they are overcast by shadows. The conciliatory element in the virtue of peace forms the mediating link between this virtue and the essence of religion, which is constituted by the reconciliation between man and God, which in turn presupposes the reconciliation of man with himself. Without the peace which I establish with my fellowman, I cannot have any hope of reconciliation with God, and as little can I hope for inner peace in myself. But the feeling of being moved, of which I become capable, discloses to me the hope that the power of peace is not yet extinguished in my soul.

The other sign of peace is joy. Kant already said that joy is a more complicated sign of friendship than compassion. Furthermore, one could see in the feeling of being moved a further proof that even a mild form of pain expresses feeling more directly than a flash of shared joy. However, this opinion does not take into consideration the contribution which joy makes to the feeling of being moved. It is in no way suffering only, but also, and just as strongly, joy which reverberates in the feeling of being moved. Moreover, in fact, it is still only an abstraction which stirs the flash of joy. A good deed occurred which only interests me, but in no way because it is related to me as being advantageous for me, and yet I am moved by this alleged fact as if it concerned my own life. I must feel jubilant about this deed of human strength, which elevates the value of my own life, which increases my consciousness of the value of this life, so that I am filled with joy about it. This joy is a proof of the living power of peace.

To think that shared joy is not as immediate a vital power of the human mind as is compassion or shared suffering is a psychologically false view, a mistake of pessimism and of the common view of the radical evil in men which Kant, to be sure, idealized both correctly and profoundly. If this were true, then peace would not be genuine peace or an unambiguous way of virtue. In that case peace would merely be a sentimental bias and not the naive vigor of the spirit. Peace is as effective in joy as in compassion. The feeling of being moved has this double power, and its unity consists only in this duality, in distinction to the one-sidedness of a bias. The feeling of being moved by the experience of a good deed proves this positive power of joy and in it the reality of peace. On the occasion of hearing an account of a good deed, I do not weep about the loss of noble customs—that would not be a positive feeling of being moved—but joy shines in my eyes at the image of a good deed. This joy of being moved proves that the cold powers of courage and justice do not reign alone in my mind, but that peace too constitutes a paved highway, and is by no means only a byway or a back lane. Consciousness prefers to attach itself to that tendency which would like to detect only the good in the actions of men, because one's own peace of mind, one's own unity of consciousness, always demands and longs for this experience. Peace in man is the longing for the good in man.

In Jewish religiosity it is profoundly meaningful that the holidays that are not directly dedicated to reconciliation have joy as their watchword: "Thou shalt rejoice in thy feast, thou . . . and the stranger, and the fatherless, and the widow, that are within thy gates" (Deut. 16:14). Joy is set as the goal and end of the feast. The joy is not Dionysian, and not a Bacchanalian delight in lust. It is defined by the shared joy of the stranger and the poor man. The joy of the feast, however, should be distinguished from pity for the poor man. Joy should unite the poor man with yourself. You should take joy in the poor man, and the poor man should also take joy in you. Hence, joy should elevate one beyond all social necessity, not, to be sure, in order that one be deluded about it, but rather that one overcome it, at least in the feast. The feast would lose its meaning and value if it were not able to implant joy, at least for these few days, into the heart of the feasting man.

Hence, the joy of the feast, too, the proper meaning and reason of the feast, as a feast of joy, is a token of peace. If it is not an illusion or a deception that the feasts make joy an actuality among men, then peace as a way of virtue is established as a way of life. Must it be an illusion that the feasts are feasts of joy? Is it an illusory joy, which establishes the feast of freedom, of the liberation from the yoke of slavery and the call to become God's people, the kingdom of priests? Or is it not a true historical joy which celebrates the revelation on Sinai, the legislation of the moral world? Or is it not likewise a true joy, which unites the harvest feast with the wandering in the

desert, in order finally to complete it in the "joy of the law," the joy
for the Torah in the entirety of its content?

Joy is the confirmed legal tilte for these feasts. Hence, the "joy of
feasts," the "feasts of joy," prove in this joy that peace is a fundamental power of the soul, and with it also a way of virtue full of
promise. Among the feasts, the Sabbath is also the sign of peace, the
establishment of the true joy of life, a social institution of human joy.
If Judaism had given only the Sabbath to the world, it would by
this alone be identified as the messenger of joy and as the founder of
peace among mankind. The Sabbath took the first step which led to
the abolition of slavery, and the Sabbath also took the first step in
showing the way to the abolition of the division of labor into manual
and intellectual labor. The Sabbath is the sign of joy which will rise
over men when all men are equally free and liable to service, and
have an equal share in the teaching, in science, its inquiry and its
knowledge, as well as in the labor for their daily bread. The conquest of the world which has been achieved by the Sabbath, does
not permit one to abandon the hope, the confidence, that this joy is
no empty illusion, and that the peace which radiates in this joy is,
and will remain, a fundamental power of the human race. Among
all the ways of virtue, peace is perhaps the most forceful, magical
power. This view is not contradicted by the fact that the power of
peace is very much doubted and contested. This is so because peace
is the most inward, the most hidden, and therefore the least revealed
power of human, of historical consciousness. The "priestly blessing"
is the embodiment of God's blessing, and its conclusion is peace.
There is no blessing that surpasses peace, and there would be no
divine blessing for man, if God had not put peace into the heart of
man.[96] All virtue would proceed insecurely and erringly, if peace
were not the stick and the staff which leads to all the ways of virtue.
The Hebrew root of the word "peace" means perfection, and the latter
is the end and goal of man. Peace, too, is the end of man. It makes
all other ends of nature and spirit into its means. Peace is, properly
speaking, the spirit of holiness. Peace, as the end of man, is the
Messiah, who liberates men and peoples from all conflicts, who con-
ciliates the conflicts, and who finally effects the reconciliation of man
with God.

Peace in the joy of the feast is a characteristic of the Jewish mentality. Considering the suffering that pervades the whole historical
life of the Jew, it is surely a wonder that he could continually maintain such equanimity, such a genuine humor, without which he would
never have been able to lift himself again and again from the deep-

est humiliations to proud heights. The Jewish holidays have brought about this wonder for him. On the Sabbath and on the feasts, joy governed the Ghetto no matter how much suffering had embittered the days of the week. Joy on a holiday was a religious duty, and hence it became an inviolable and vital power in the Jewish consciousness. But it could not have been established and preserved as such a power if peace had not been, and remained, such a strong magic power in the Jewish spirit. "Peace, peace to him that is far off, and to him that is near, saith the Eternal . . . and I will heal him" (Isa. 57:19). Peace was the healing power of the prophets, peace first of all in opposition to war, but then also in opposition to human passion. Peace has the same significance as reconciliation and redemption, and it was and has remained based on knowledge, on the Torah. Therefore, the joy of the feast was always connected with the study of the Torah. Joy was therefore based in the mind, as an intellectual joy, so that it remained distinct from sensual frenzy, but also from aesthetic delusions and their enchantments. The Jew could never remain a man of mourning; his feasts and his scholarly character always elevated him into the heaven of joy. This elevation was effected by peace, as a power of the soul, which became for the Jew as natural a way of life as justice and faithfulness, and as the courage for martyrdom. His martyrdom gave him tragic dignity; his peace, however, always maintained his aesthetic humor.

This aesthetic power, which already emerges in the prophets, streams forth, although not with equal strength, yet in considerable productivity, in some works of the later Occidental literature of the Jews, as well as, up to this day, in some serious works of Jewish folk poetry. As once Isaiah called, "Comfort ye, comfort ye My people" [Isa. 40:1], so the peace of humor spread its wings over the people of the Ghetto. And as in other cases, humor and sublimity are united in beauty, so in this case humor is intertwined with tragedy, in order to bestow support and unity to the Jewish spirit. If one were to describe in one word the essence of the Jewish mentality, then the word would have to be "peace." This unity of the Jewish mentality can be grasped only by those who are able to seek it in the Jew's religious depth. Viewed from the outside, it would seem that hatred and desire for retaliation must rule the Jew, especially since he is hated and oppressed by the whole world. Would it not be a wonder if resentment were not alive in his soul? Indeed, it would be a wonder, if it were not to be set aside by the greater wonder of the Jewish teaching and the religious life in accordance with it. The life of religious duty, the life under the yoke of the law, has implanted this freedom and this peace into the heart of the Jew, so that hatred and the desire for vengeance could not settle there. The yoke of the law was to the Jew the yoke of the Kingdom of God, and the Kingdom of God is the kingdom of peace for all the peoples of united mankind. How could hatred have settled in such a consciousness, which believes in peace among men, with the entire power and duty of its faith. Messianism is, and remains, the fundamental power of Jewish consciousness, and the Messiah is the "Prince of Peace." "The Song of Songs" praises the heroine of love, the maiden of peace, even in her name, Sulamith. In the same way, the poetry of the psalms is not shepherd poetry but the heroic poetry of peace for man, and in man. What is the epitome of human life in the spirit of the Bible? It is peace. All the meaning, all the value of life is in peace. Peace is the unity of all vital powers, their equilibrium and the reconciliation of all their contradictions. Peace is the crown of life.

Human life has its conclusion in death. Death is not the end but a conclusion, a new beginning. It is significant for the Jewish consciousness that it also thinks of death as, and calls it, peace. "Peace be upon him": this is the phrase by which Jewish usage designates the deceased. Peace takes away from death its sting. It also gives a solution to the riddle of death. The man who is torn from life is not removed from peace, but rather brought nearer to it. He is now directly under the reign of God's peace. The commemoration, which is dedicated to the dead, is therefore not the expression of concern for his salvation, let alone an entreaty for his liberation from the horrors of the punishments of hell. The man died with the confession of sins on his lips; his repentance he accomplished in his self-purification; his redemption is therefore commended to the grace of the forgiving God. "Peace be upon him": this is the only and the best thing I can say about his present existence. For the survivors, therefore, his memory is manifested in the everlasting feeling of gratitude and, flowing from it, in the admonition to lovingkindness and to continued obedience, such as the ancestors have practiced.

If it were possible to doubt that peace is the main power of Jewish virtue, then this doubt would be refuted by the Jewish understanding of death, even if by nothing else. Death is the world of peace. One cannot praise death better and more blissfully than by distinguishing it from the world of struggle, from the life of error and conflict. Life ought to seek peace; it finds it in death. Death is therefore not the actual end of human life but rather its goal, the trophy of life and all its striving. Whosoever loves peace cannot fear death.

"The Eternal is my shepherd; I shall not want . . . though I walk through the valley of the shadow of death I will fear no evil: for Thou art with me" (Ps. 23:4). The unique God is with me even in death. This is the climax of the idea of, the conviction of, peace. No humor can superside this climax. It is characteristic of the Jewish consciousness that it does not fear death. This singularity can only be explained by its absolute freedom from any fear of punishment of hell. This is the power of peace, of God's peace in the Jewish mentality, that it does not permit the emergence of the idea of God as a judge in hell. God is for the Jew only the God of reconciliation, and even as a judge he is only the judge for the sake of reconciliation. Hence, there is no fear of death in the Jewish mentality. Therefore, the commemoration of the soul does not have to be concerned with the salvation of the soul of the deceased in the sense that entreaties could protect it from the torments of hell in the afterlife.

We celebrate the memory of our dead in the pious hope that their souls are being gathered to the souls of our Patriarchs and our First Mothers. This union with the history of our religious people is our only concern in the commemoration of the dead. As the patriarchs themselves, when they died, were gathered to their fathers and to their people, so even today every Jew dies in the hope of his historical survival in this union with his ancestors. Hence, death is an historical survival, and this survival is ruled and governed by peace, which is triumphant over all earthly struggle.

Peace is therefore a way of virtue also in a higher sense, in that it leads the way to eternal life. On the path of peace there can be no fear of death; peace, as the peace of eternal life, becomes itself eternal peace; it is the peace of eternity. Eternity, however, is the meaning, the goal, the end of the whole of human life. Everything temporal leads to eternity, if it goes on the right road. And this right road is peace. Peace is the virtue of eternity.

It is significant for the Hebrew linguistic consciousness that the Hebrew word for world, *olam* (עוֹלָם) , at the same time means eternity: "He hath set the world [*olam*] in their heart" (Eccl. 3:11). "The world" also means eternity, so that one could translate this sentence to mean that God set eternity into man's heart. Peace explains the contradiction which would otherwise have to be recognized in these two meanings. The present world can, of course, not mean eternity; it is perishable. Furthermore, the myth of the end and renewal of the world could not be accepted by a religious consciousness which had to make God the creator of the world, if only because this God was to be the creator of man and of his holy spirit.

But for this religious consciousness for which the world is God's creation and revelation, neither the world nor man could be simply perishable. The presentiment of the immortality of man and the eternity of the world manifests itself in this deep word *"olam."* The later language, too, still retained this presentiment in that it called the cemetery (or "God's field" *[Gottesacker]* as the beautiful German word has it) "the House of Eternity" (בית עולם). Death is peace. The grave is "the House of Eternity." This eternity is the true end of the world, the goal of earthly existence. It is to this eternity that peace as a way of virtue leads. But this eternity is only the continuation of the earthly life—the same root of the word comprises both sides of existence; hence, peace, as it leads to eternity, is also the guide to earthly life, to the beginning of all historical survival, which lies in it. Peace is the sign of eternity and also the watchword for human life, in its individual conduct as well as in the eternity of its historical calling. In this historical eternity the mission of peace of messianic mankind is completed.

ANNOTATIONS FROM HEBREW SOURCES

Compiled and supplemented by Dr. Leo Rosenzweig
in accordance with the author's notes

[1] Page 17   Midrash Tanchuma, ed. Buber, p. 265

אמר דוד לפני הקב״ה וכו . . . תיישר עולמך בשוה העשירים והעניים א״ל א״כ
חסד ואמת מן ינצרוהו.

[2] Page 23   Midrash Tanchuma, p. 265

עניים עמו של הקב״ה.

[3] Page 28   Chagiga 3b

דברי חכמים כדרבונות וכמסמרות נטועים וכו׳ ת״ל נטועים מה נטיעה זו פרה ורבה
אף דברי תורה פרין ורבין.

cf. Midrash Tanchuma, p. 635

דבר אחר האזינה עטי תורתי וש״ה לב חכם ישכיל פיהו וגו׳ וכשוונכין טן טוב
מוסיפין תורה.

[4] Page 29   Berachoth 9

מקרא משנה וגמרא כלם נתנו למשה מסיני.

cf. Midrash Shemoth Rabba 28

ולא כל הנביאים בלבד קבלו מסיני נבואתן אלא אף החכמים העומדים בכל דור
ודור כל אחד ואחד קבל את שלו מסיני.

[5] Page 33   Midrash Shemoth Rabba 30

תורה לא נתנה אלא ע׳ם שתעשו את הדינין.

[6] Page 41   Emunah Rama, ed. Weil, p. 58

וענין שהוא אחד הוא ענין שאין כמוהו דבר והוא שב אל ענין שולל, ואין אחדותו
כאחדות דבר ממה שקרא אחד אבל הוא ית׳ וית׳ יותר אמתי מכל אחד בשם האחד
וענין היותו ית׳ אחד אחדותו היא עצמותו.

[7] Page 48   Succah 45

כל המשתתף שם שמים ודבר אחר נעקר מן העולם.

463

[8] Page 64   Moreh I, chap. 58, Munk I, p. 243

ואמרנו בו מפני אלו העניניים שהוא יכול וחכם ורוצה והכונה באלו התארים שאינו
לואה ולא סכל ולא נבהל או עוזב וענין אמרנו לא לואה שמציאותו יש בה די
להמצאת דברים אחרים זולתו וענין אמרנו ולא סכל שהוא משיג כלומר חי כי כל משיג
חי וענין אמרנו ולא נבהל לא עוזב כי כל אלה הנמצאות הולכות על סדר והנהגה
לא נעזבות והוות כאשר יקרה וכו'.

[9] Page 65   Beresh. Rabba 5

בראשית ברא אלהים אין ראשית אלא תורה.

[10] Page 78   Sanhedrin 91

תורה צוה לנו משה מורשה קהלת יעקב מורשה היא לכל ישראל מששת ימי בראשית.
cf. Tosefta Pesachim 163

[11] Page 79   Midrash Tanchuma, p. 250

ויאמר ה' מסיני בא וכו' מלמד שהחזירה על כל האומות ולא רצו לקבלה.

[12] Page 81   Midrash Tanchuma, p. 188

ויאבד את לב מתנה מן התורה שנתנה מתנה בלבו של אדם.

[13] Page 90   Moreh III, chap. 51

והיה כאשר תשיג השם ומעשיו כפי מה שישכלהו השכל, אחר כן תתחיל להמסר
אליו ותשתדל לחתקרב לו ותחזק הדבוק אשר בינך ובינו והוא השכל.

[14] Page 90   Berachoth 33

גדולה דעה שנתנה בין שתי אותיות שנא' כי אל דעות ה'.
cf. (Bahya) Chovoth, ed. Stern, p. 36

ואמת אמר הפילוסוף באמרו לא יוכל לעבוד עילת העילות ותחלת ההתחלות אלא
נביא הדור במבעו או הפילוסוף חמובהק במה שקנאו מן החכמה.

[15] Page 91   Sabbath 31a

אמר רבא בשעה שמכניסין אדם לדין אומרים לו נשאת ונתת באמונה קבעת עתים
לתורה עסקת בפריה ורביה צפית לישועה פלפלת בחכמה הבנת דבר מתוך דבר וכו'.

[16] Page 95   Moreh I, chap. 54

הנה כבר התבאר כי הדרכים אשר בקש ידיעתם והודיעו אותם הם הם הפעולות
הבאות ממנו יתעלה והחכמים יקראום מדות ויאמרו שלש עשרה מדות וזה השם נופל
בשמוש על מדות האדם ארבע מדות בהולכי לבית המדרש, ארבע מדות בנותני צדקה
וזה הרבה. והענין הנה הנה אינו שהוא בעל מדות אבל פועל פעולות הדומות לפעולות
הבאות מאתנו ממדות רצוני לאמר מתכונות נפשיות לא שהוא יתעלה בעל תכונות
נפשיות וכו' הנה כבר התבאר לך כי הדרכים והמדות אחד.

[17] Page 95   Midrash Shemoth Rabba 11

אהיה אשר אהיה אני נקרא לפי מעשי.

[18] Page 96   Sifra 91b

קדושים תהיו זו קדושת מצות.

[19] Page 101   Rashi to Isa. 63, 11

איה הוא אשר שם בקרב ישראל את רוח קדשו של הקב״ה.

[20] Page 101   Rashi to Isa. 42,5

נותן נשמה לעם עליה ורוח להולכים בה ורוח קדושה להולכים בה.

[21] Page 103   Emunah Rama, p. 58

אכן רוח היא באנוש ונשמת שדי תבינם וכו׳ רוח היא באנוש השכל האנושי
ונשמת שדי תבינם רוח הקודש.

[22] Page 107   Tana Eliyahu, p. 88

מעיד אני עלי שמים וארץ בין ישראל בין עכו״ם בין איש בין אשה בין עבד
בין שפחה הכל לפי המעשה שעושה כך רוח הקדש שורה עליו.

[23] Page 108   Abodah Zarah 20

א״ר פנחס בן יאיר תורה מביאה לידי זהירות זהירות מביאה לידי זריזות וכו׳ קדושה
מביאה לידי רוח הקודש.

[24] Page 119   Jerus. Nedarim 9

תניא א״ר עקיבא ואהבת לרעך כמך זה כלל גדול בתורה בן עזאי אומר זה ספר
תולדות אדם זה כלל גדול מזה.

[25] Page 119   Chullin 100a

מבני יעקב נאסר גיד הנשה וכו׳ שהיו בני נח קודם מתן תורה.

[26] Page 121   Abodah Zarah 3b

עכו״ם נטי מקרו בני אדם שר״ל בני אדם הראשון.

[27] Page 121   Sanhedrin 63b

יודעין היו ישראל בעבודה זרה שאין בה ממש, ולא עבדו עבודה זרה אלא להתיר
להם עריות בפרהסיא.

[28] Page 122   Sanhedrin 59

אפילו עכו״ם ועוסק בתורה (בשבע מצות דידהו) הרי הוא ככהן גדול.

[29] Page 123   Tosefta Sanhedrin, p. 234

עכשיו שא׳ הכתוב כל גוים שכחי אלהים, הא יש צדיקים באומות שיש להם חלק
לעולם הבא.

cf. Maimonides Hilch. Teshubah 3,5

חסידי אומות העולם יש להם חלק לעולם הבא.

[30] Page 124   Sanhedrin 56b

י׳ מצות נצטוו ישראל במרה, ז׳ שקבלו עליהן בני נח והוסיפו עליהן דינין ושבת
וכבוד אב ואם וכו׳.

[31] Page 147   Sifra 73a

ואהבת את ד' אהבהו על הבריות.

cf. Yoma 86a

ואהבת את ד' שיהא שם שמים מתאהב על ידיך ויהא משאו ומתנו באמונה
ודבורו בנחת עם הבריות.

[32] Page 160   Moreh I, chap. 27

אונקולוס הגר שלם מאד בלשון העברית והארמית וכבר שם השתדלותו בסלוק ההגשמה.

[33] Page 162   Maimonides Hilch. Teshubah 10

בכל לבבך ובכל נפשך אינו אוהב הקב"ה אלא בדעת שידעהו ועל פי הדעה תהיה
האהבה אם מעט מעט ואם הרבה הרבה וכו'.

[34] Page 166   Sanhedrin 37a

אדם נברא יחידי.

[35] Page 173   Moreh III, chap. 32

ולזה התנה בזה הפסוק ואמר ביום הוציאי אותם מארץ מצרים כי תחלת צווי שבא
אחר יציאת מצרים הוא מה שנצטוינו בו במרה וכו' ובאה הקבלה האמתית שבת
ודינין במרה איפקוד וג' וזאת היא הכונה הראשונה כמו שבארנו וג' הנה כבר
התבאר לך שהמצוה הראשונה לא היו בה דברי עולה וזבח אחר שהם על צד
הכונה השנית כמו שזכרנו.

[36] Page 180   Tosefta to Sanhedrin 7

אדם נברא יחידי ולמה נברא יחידי בעולם שלא יהו צדיקים אומרים אנו בניו של
צדיק ושלא יהו חרשעים אומרים אנו בניו של רשע.

[37] Page 182   Midrash Tanchuma, ed. Buber, p. 19

ראה זה מצאתי אשר עשה האלהים את האדם ישר וכו' ואם תאמר למה ברא יצר
הרע וכו' אמר הקב"ה אתה עושה אותו רע.

[38] Page 193   Maimonides Hilch. Teshubah 2

ומשנה שמו כלומר אני אחר ואינו אותו האיש שעשה אותן המעשין.

[39] Page 195   (Bahya) Chovoth, ed. Stern, p. 323

הראשון שידע גנות מעשהו ידיעה ברורה וכו' והשני שידע בחיוב רוע מעשהו
וגנותו וכו' והשלישי שידע בחיוב הגמול על מעשהו.

[40] Page 209   Pesikta d. R. Kahana 158, 6

א"ר פנחס למה הוא טוב שהוא ישר למה הוא ישר שהוא טוב על כן יורה חטאים
בדרך שהוא מורה להן דרך שיעשו תשובה.

[41] Page 211   (Bahya) Chovoth, ed. Stern, p. 252

ומצאנו ענין הבטחון בלשון הקדש מליצים בעדו בעשר מלות כנגד עשר המדרגות
האלה הם מבטח ומשען ותקוה ומחסה, ותוחלת וחכוי וסמיכה וסבר ומסעד וכסל.

[42] Page 217   Tanith 26b

אמר רבן שמעון בן גמליאל לא היו ימים טובים לישראל כחמשה עשר באב
וכיום הכפורים שבהן בנות ירושלים יוצאות בכלי לבן שאולין וכו׳.

[43] Page 220   Yoma 85b

עבירות שבין אדם למקום יה״כ מכפר עבירות שבין אדם לחברו אין יוה״כ מכפר
עד שירצה את חברו.

[44] Page 223   Yoma 86b

גדולה תשובה שזדונות נעשות לו כשגגות.

[45] Page 223   Yoma 85b

אשריכם ישראל לפני מי אתם מטהרים ומי מטהר אתכם אביכם שבשמים.

[46] Page 224   Berachoth 19a

אם ראית ת״ח שעבר עבירה בלילה אל תהרהר אחריו ביום וכו׳ אלא ודאי עשה תשובה.

[47] Page 226   Berachoth 5

אם רואה אדם שיסורין באין עליו יפשפש במעשיו וכו׳.

[48] Page 227   Sabbath 88a

ת״ר עלובין ואינן עולבין וכו׳ עושין מאהבה ושמחין ביסורין עליהן הכתוב אומר
ואוהביו וכו׳.

[49] Page 249   Maimonides Hilch. Teshubah 9,2

לפי שבאותן הימים תרבה הדעת והחכמה והאמת שנאמר כי מלאה הארץ דעה את ה׳.

[50] Page 259   Makkoth 24a

א״ר יוסי ד׳ גזרות גזר משה רבנו על ישראל באו ד׳ נביאים וביטלום וכ׳ משה
אמר פוקד עון אבות על בנים בא יחזקאל וביטלה.

[51] Page 264   Berachoth 5

יסורין של אהבה.

[52] Page 266   Abodah Zarah 20

א״ר יהושע בן לוי ענוה גדולה מכלן.

[53] Page 277   Midrash Waikra Rabba, sec. 13, p. 36

אמר רבי אבין בר כהנא אמר הקב״ה תורה חדשה מאתי תצא חדוש תורה מאתי תצא.

[54] Page 278   Midrash Tanchuma, p. 126

נבואה לעתיד לבוא על כל אדם.

[55] Page 306   Ikkarim, sec. 4, 40

ולזה סיים כי עם קדוש אתה לה׳ אלהיך כלומר אחר שהוא יתברך קדוש ומשרתין
קדושים ואתה עם קדוש כל דבר יקרב לדומהו ובלי ספק הנפש ההיא תדבק עם
השכלים הנבדלים כי קדושה היא והמלאכים קדושים משרתי עליון וע״כ אין ראוי
להתגודד על המת ולהצטער עליו יותר מדאי וזה יורה שיש השארות לנפש אחר המות.

[56] Page 311   Maimonides Hilch. Teshubah 8,8

זה שקראו אותו חכמים העוה״ב לא מפני שאינו מצוי עתה וזה העולם אובד ואח״כ
יבא אותו העולם אין הדבר כן אלא הרי הוא מצוי ועומד.

Ibid. 9,2

אבל ימות המשיח הוא העולם הזה ועולם כמנהגו הולך.

[57] Page 312   Berachoth 17a

העוה״ב אין בו לא אכילה ולא שתיה וכו׳ אלא צדיקים יושבים ועטרותיהם בראשיהם
ונהנים מזיו השכינה.

[58] Page 312   Nedarim 8b

אין גיהנם לעולם הבא אלא הקב״ה מוציא חמה מנרתיקה וכו׳.

[59] Page 312   Ikkarım, sec. 4, 38

וכן בתחלת המזמור רמז לשני מיני החסד הללו ואמר הסולח לכל עוניכי לרמוז על
החסד שישוב העונש הנצחיי זמניי תרומפא לכל תחלואיכי לרמוז על החסד שישוב השכר
זמניי נצחיי, וחוזר לבאר זה ואמר הגואל משחת חייכי שזה ודאי מדבר על הגאולה
מעונשי גיהנם הנצחיים כי מן המות הגופיי הטבעי אין שום אדם ניצול היומנה

[60] Page 313   Berachoth 34b

כל הנביאים כולן לא נתנבאו אלא לימות המשיח אבל לעוה״ב עין לא ראתה
אלהים זולתך.

[61] Page 313   Maimonides Sh'mone Perakim, sec. 4

כי כשהיה אדם שוקל פעולותיו תמיד ומכוון אמצעותם יהיה במדרגה עליונה
ממדרגת בני אדם ובזה יתקרב אל ה׳ ית׳ וישיג אל טובו וכו׳.

[62] Page 314   Yebamoth 62a

אין בן דוד בא עד שיכלו כל נשמות שבגוף.

or Midrash Koheleth 3

אין מלך המשיח בא עד שיעמדו כל הנשמות שעלו במחשבה להבראות.

[63] Page 315   Kuzari, ed. Cassel, p. 64

ועל כן איננו אומר בתורה כי אם תעשו המצוה הזאת חזאת אביאכם אחרי המות אל
גנות והנאות אבל הוא אומר: ואתם תהיו לי לעם ואני אהיה לכם לאלהים מנהיג
אתכם וכו׳ . . . ויעודיה כולם כולל אותם שרש אחד והוא יחול קורבת אלהים
ומלאכיו ומי שיגיע אל המעלה הזאת לא יירא מן המות.

[64] Page 315   (Bahya) Chovoth, ed. Stern, p. 234

אבל גמול העוה״ב ועונשו לא פירש מהם חנביא מאומה בספרו וג׳ ומהם שגמול
העוה״ב אין תכליתו אלא להדבק באלהים ולהתקרב אל אורו העליון וכו׳.

[65] Page 316   Ikkarim, sec. 4, 40

וכדי להעיר על ההבדל שבין השכר הרוחני לשכר הגשמי אמר על הרוחני כי לא
דבר רק הוא מכם כלומר אל תחשבו שהוא דבר אחר זולתכם אבל הוא בעצמו חייכם
ר"ל הנפש שהיא מהות החיות הנשאר אחר המות וכו'.

[66] Page 317   Midrash Rabba I, 61a

אני ישנה מן המצות אבל זכות אבותי עומדת לי ולבי ער.

[67] Page 321   Midrash Rabba I, 67a

א"ר חייא בר אבא מהו הן יראת ה' היא אוצרו אמר האלהים אם היו לך מעשים
טובים אני נותן לך שכר ומה שכר תורה.

cf. Maimonides Hilch. Teshubah 10,2

ולא כדי לירש הטובה אלא עושה האמת מפני שהוא אמת וסוף הטובה לבא בכללה וכו'.

[68] Page 322   Ikkarim, sec. 4, 15

וחלקי במציאות הוא היות נדבק באלהים לעולם שהוא דבר נצחי ולא אפחד מן
ההפסד אחר שאני דבק בדבר נצחי וכו'. ואני קרבת אלהים לי טוב ר"ל כל טובי
הוא היותי מתדבק אל השם.

[69] Page 324   Baba Kamma 38

גדול המצווה ועושה יותר ממי שאינו מצווה ועושה.

[70] Page 325   Sanhedrin 74a

כל עבירות שבתורה אם אומרים לאדם עבור ואל תהרג יעבור ואל יהרג חוץ
מעכו"ם וגלוי עריות ושפיכת דמים.

[71] Page 326   Kiddushin 49b

האומר לאשה הרי את מקודשת לי על מנת שאני צדיק אפילו רשע גמור הרי זו
מקודשת שמא הרהר תשובה בלבו.

[72] Page 326   Berachoth 34b

מקום שבעלי תשובה עומדים צדיקים גמורים אינם עומדין.

[73] Page 326   Maimonides Hilch. Teshubah 3

וכן כל הרשעים שעוונותיהם מרבים דנין אותן כפי חטאיהם ויש להן חלק לעולם
הבא שכל ישראל יש להם חלק לעולם הבא אף על פי שחטאו שנאמר ועמך כולם
צדיקים לעולם יירשו ארץ.

[74] Page 329   Maimonides Hilch. Teshubah 3,5

וכן חסידי אומות העולם יש להם חלק לעולם הבא.

[75] Page 332   Khesef Mishne to Hilch. Melachim 8

ומה שכתב והוא שיקבל וגו' נראה לי שרבנו אומר כך מסברא דנפשיה.

[76] Page 335   Midrash Rabba II, 54

לעולם זכות אבות קיימת לעולם לעולם מזכירין ואומרין כי אל רחום ה׳ אלהיך וגו׳ ולא
ישכח את ברית אבותיך.

[77] Page 351   Emunah Rama, p. 102

ונאמר תחלה שחלקי התורה בין שיהיו חמשה או ארבעה או כמה שיהיו אינם
כולם שוים במעלה.

[78] Page 351   Emunah Rama, p. 75

ומדתות מהם מפורסמות בלשון בעלי ההגיון ואצל בעלי חכמת הדבור דתות שכליות
מפני שהם מתיחסות אל המושכלות התריחסות מה וזה כמו שהיושר טוב והעול רע
וג׳ ומהם מקובלות בלשון בעלי ההגיון והם בלשון חכמת הדבור דתות שמעיות
כמו שמירת השבת וכו׳.

[79] Page 351   Kuzari, p. 148

אמר החבר: אלה והדומה להם הם החקים השכליים והם הקדמות והצעות לתורה
האלהית קודמות לו בטבע ובזמן וכו׳ וזולתם מן התורה האלהית השמעיות.

[80] Page 354   Moreh III, chap, 31

הכל נתלה בשלשה דברים בדעות ובמדות ובמעשה הנהגה המדינית.

[81] Page 355   Moreh III, chap. 31

והיה דומה או כאילו יבא נביא בזמננו זה שיקרא לעבודת השם ויאמר השם צוה
אתכם שלא תתפללו אליו ולא תצומו ולא תבקשו תשועתו בעת צרה אבל תהיה
עבודתכם מחשבה מבלתי מעשה.

[82] Page 366   Or Adonai, Introduction (end)

הנה ראינו לחלק החלק הזה לארבעה מאמרים הא׳ בשרש שהוא התחלת לכל
האמונות התוריות (ר״ל מציאות השם) הב׳ באמונות שהם פינות ויסודות לכל המצות וכו׳

[83] Page 366   Ikkarim, sec. 3, 13

וזה, כי אף אם לא ישתנו הדעות בעצמן ולא חנותן כבר אפשר שיפול בו שנוי
מצד המקבל, לפי שמשלמות כל פועל שיפעל פעולתו כפי הכנת המקבלים ולפי
השתנות הכנת המקבל תשתנה פעולת הפועל בלי ספק, וזה לא יחייב שנוי בחק
הפועל, כי כמו שהרופא יתן הנהגה אל החולה עד זמן משוער אצלו שלא יגלתו
אל החולה וכשיגיע הזמן ההוא שנתחזק כבר החולה מחליו ישנה הרופא הנהגתו
ויתיר מה שאסר ויאסר מה שהתיר ואין לתולה להפלא מזה כי אין זה ממה שיחייב
שנוי בחק חרופא לומר שלא נתן לו בתחלה הנהגה מספקת לכל חזמנים כי הרופא
כשנתן ההנהגה הראשונה כבר ידע הזמן שראוי שיתנהג החולה על פיה ואע״פ שלא גלהו אל
החולה ידע הזמן הראוי שתשתנה ההנהגה ההיא כפי מה ששער מטבע החולה הזמן שצריך
לו כדי שישתנה מן החולי אל הבריאות וכו׳ וכן על זה הדרך איננו חסרון בחק הש״י אם
לא נתן בתחלה תורה והנהגה מספקת לכל הזמנים וזה כי הוא כשנתן-התורה ידע
שההנהגה ההיא תספיק עד הזמן ששערה חכמתו שיספיק להכין המקבלים ולתקן

טבעם אל שיקבלו ההנהגה השנית אע״פ שלא גלהו לאדם וכשיגיע הזמן יצוה בהנהגה השנית ואף אם ישנה דברים הפך ההנהגה הראשונה כך היה מסודר אצלו בתחלת, וכמו שיהיה חסרון בחק הרופא שיצוה לתת המזונות החזקים כלהם והבשר והיין אל הקטם מהחולי והילדים ויונקי שדים עד אשר יגדלו או יתחזק טבעם לסבול המזונות החזקים, כן יהיה חסרון בחק נותן התורה שיתן הנהגה שוה בכל הזמנים למתחילים ולמורגלים אבל ראוי שישנה אותה כפי השתנות הכנת המקבלים.

[84] Page 366   cf. Ikkarim 3, 22

[85] Page 372   Taanith 2

איזו היא עבודה שהיא בלב הוי אומר זו תפלה.

[86] Page 374   (Bahya) Chovoth, p. 361

וראוי לך אחי שתדע כי כוונתנו בתפלה אינה כי אם כלות הנפש אל האלהים וכניעתה לפניו עם רוממותה לבוראה ושבחה הודאתה לשמו והשלכת כל יהביה עליו.

[87] Page 387   Midrash Shir Hashirim Rabba, p. 54

בעשרה מקומות נקראו ישראל כלה.

[88] Page 413   Sefer Hamada, sec. 2, 10

ולפיכך אמר חי פרעה וחי נפשך ואין אומר חי ה' אלא חי ה' שאין הבורא וחיין שניים כמו חיי הגופים החיים או כחיי המלאכים וכו'.

cf. Moreh I, chap. 53 and 68

[89] Page 423   Mechilta to Mishpatim

ראשון שבגנבים גונב דעת הבריות.

[90] Page 426   Sotah 5a

אמר רב יוסף לעולם ילמד אדם מדעת קונו שהרי הקב״ה חניח כל חרים וגבעות והשרה שכינתו על הר סיני והניח כל אילנות טובות והשרה שכינתו בסנה.

[91] Page 432   Makkoth 23a

ונקלה אחיך לעיניך כשלקה הרי הוא כאחיך.

[92] Page 432   Baba Metzia 30b

לא חרבה ירושלים אלא שהעמידו דיניהם על דין תורה ולא עבדו לפנים משורת הדין.

[93] Page 449   Berachoth 54a

חייב אדם לברך על הרעה כשם שמברך על הטובה.

[94] Page 452   cf. Yoma 9b

[95] Page 456   Shebuoth 30a

בצדק תשפוט עמיתך הוה דן את חבירך לכף זכות.

[96] Page 458   Megillah 18a

ברכה דהקב״ה שלום.

INDEXES

References in the Text
to Biblical Passages

Chap. and Verse	Page	Chap. and Verse	Page
GENESIS		25:8	301
1:26-27	85	49:6	405
2:3	156		
2:5-7	85	EXODUS	
2:22	86	3:6	42
2:24	80	3:10-14	42
3:5	86	3:13	43
4:15	130	3:14	43
5:1	119	3:15	43
6:3	215	6:3	39
6:5	181	12:49	121, 328
6:13	117	15:25	328
6:17	117	19:5	289
7:1	117	19:6	302, 347
8:21	117, 181	20:3-4	54
9:5, 6	118	20:5	433
9:11	118	20:7	346
9:12, 16	118	20:8-11	156
15:15	301	21:26	431
18:18	118	25:35ff	125
18:19	118	21:26, 27	126
18:23	118	22:17	232
18:25	118, 431	22:20	127

473

References in the Text to Rabbinical Works

Index of Proper Names

*See also index of Biblical Passages.

°See also index of Biblical Passages.

°See also index of Biblical Passages.

Index of Hebrew Words

DATE DUE